LONGMAN

AMERICAN

Idioms

DICTIONARY

LONGMAN

AMERICAN

Idioms

DICTIONARY

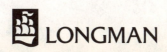
LONGMAN

Pearson Education Limited
Edinburgh Gate
Harlow
Essex CM20 2JE
England
and Associated Companies around the world

Longman American Idioms Dictionary

First published in 1999

The examples in the **Longman American Idioms Dictionary** are based on the original texts in the Longman Corpus Network. All types of information given in the examples are intended as examples of use and do not represent the opinions of the publishers and editors of this dictionary.

The British National Corpus is a collaborative initiative carried out by Oxford University Press, Longman, Chambers Harrap, Oxford University Computing Services, Lancaster University's Unit for Computer Research in the English Language, and the British Library. The project received funding from the UK Department of Trade and Industry and the Science and Engineering Research Council and was supported by additional research grants from the British Academy and the British Library.

ISBN
0 582 30576 4 (Cased edition)
0 582 30575 6 (Paperback edition)

British Library Cataloguing-in-Publication Data
A catalogue record for this book is available from the British Library

Typeset in Triplex and Optima and produced by Pen & Ink, Huntingdon, Cambridgeshire

Printed in Spain by Cayfosa Industria Grafica, Barcelona

Contents

Guide to using the dictionary

break

⇒ **GO for broke**
⇒ **if it AIN'T broke, don't fix it**

a clean break
a clear and definite ending to a bad relationship or situation so that you can start something new without any troubles from the past: *I heard that his wife left him and he wanted to make a clean break – anyway, that's the reason he gave for quitting the job.*

make a break for it
(also **make a break for** *something*)
to suddenly start running in order to escape from a place: *While police were surrounding the building, one hostage made a break for the door.*

bug

be bitten by the ___ bug
to become excited about a particular activity and very eager to start doing it yourself: *After spending two months in Africa and a great Christmas in New York, I have been bitten by the travel bug.*

snug as a bug (in a rug)
SPOKEN used to say that someone is very warm and comfortable ◆ OFTEN USED BY ADULTS TALKING TO CHILDREN: *You just curl up under the blanket – there, you're snug as a bug in a rug.*

idioms are listed under keywords, usually nouns, in alphabetical order

capitalized words in references point you to the right keyword for the idiom you want

the idioms have examples based on real sentences from the Longman Corpus Network

variant forms are shown under the main idiom in parentheses

the 2000-word defining vocabulary makes definitions clear and easy to understand

an underlined space in the idiom means that you can put in any word, usually a noun or adjective

words in parentheses can be left out without changing the meaning of the idiom

information in small capitals before and after the definition tells you when the idiom is used or who uses it

Guide to using the dictionary

cat

⇨ there's more than one **WAY** to skin a cat

let the cat out of the bag
to let people know something that is a secret, or that they are not supposed to know until later, especially without intending to do this: *Don't let the cat out of the bag – Mom doesn't know about the party yet.*
the cat is out of the bag: *Now that the cat is out of the bag, it's probably okay to talk about the merger.*

● different forms of the idiom, opposites, and noun or adjective forms are shown at the end of the entry with their own examples

devil

⇨ play/be devil's **ADVOCATE**

between the devil and the deep blue sea
in a difficult situation in which any choice that you make will have bad results: *We were between the devil and the deep blue sea. We were told we could either continue on low pay, or get more money for very difficult working conditions.*
—see also **(caught) between a ROCK and a hard place** ●

● "see also" references give you idioms that are similar in meaning

give the devil his due
used to say that although you do not like or approve of someone, they have done something good or have some good quality: *Giving the devil his due, I have to admit that my grandmother was sometimes extremely generous to us.*
—compare **give** *someone* **his/her DUE** ●

● "compare" references give you idioms that could be easily confused

dog

⇨ it's a dog's **LIFE**
⇨ you lie like a big dog (on a rug)
—see *someone* **lies like a RUG**

every dog has its day
used to say that even the most unimportant person has a time in their life when they are successful and noticed: *When asked about the winning goal, Orrell commented that every dog had its day.*

● "used to say" shows idioms that are used to give a comment or opinion about something

Acknowledgements

Director
Della Summers

Editorial Director
Adam Gadsby

Publisher
Laurence Delacroix

Associate Lexicographer
Karen Stern

Senior Editor
Ruth Urbom

Lexicographers
Korey Egge
Tammy Gales
Leslie Redick

Exercises
Susan Iannuzzi

Project Manager
Alan Savill

Senior Production Editors
Alison Steadman
Peter Braaksma

Production Managers
Jacqui Bingham
Clive McKeough

Design
Eddi Edwards
Jenny Fleet

Illustrator
Shaun Williams

Corpus Development
Steve Crowdy
Denise Denney

Keyboarder
Pauline Savill

Administrative Assistants
Liz Wrighton
Susan Braund

Introduction

 What is an idiom?

An idiom is a sequence of words which has a different meaning as a group from the meaning it would have if you understood each word separately. Idioms add color to the language, helping us to emphasize meaning and to make our observations, judgments, and explanations lively and interesting. They are also very useful tools for communicating a great deal of meaning in just a few words.

 What is included and what is not?

Our aim in writing the Longman Dictionary of American Idioms was to reflect the wide range of idioms that are being used in American English today. Using the Longman Corpus Network (see below), the Internet, and keeping our ears tuned to the media and language on the street, the editorial team has gathered information about the newest idioms being used, as well as giving complete coverage of idioms at the core of the language. In addition to the many new idioms, such as **push the envelope**, **go postal**, and **be on the same page**, the dictionary includes a range of the most frequently used idioms in the language. It covers idioms with metaphorical meanings that are fairly easy to understand, such as **put your heads together** and **can't hear yourself think**, as well as those that are less obvious, like **face the music** and **not cut the mustard**. Many two-word phrases, like **wild card** and **acid test**, are included, as are phrases with pragmatic uses, such as **just like that** and **of all things**. The book also includes many frequently used similes, such as **like two peas in a pod**.

We have not included common collocates, like **as usual**, or nouns with their operating verbs, such as **make a point**. These are defined in other dictionaries such as the *Longman Dictionary of Contemporary English* or the *Longman Language Activator*. Likewise, phrasal verbs, such as **break down** or **make up**, are not covered here, but can be found in the *Longman Phrasal Verbs Dictionary* and the *Longman Dictionary of Contemporary English*.

 **How do I find idioms in this dictionary?**

Keywords

This book is organized by keywords listed in alphabetical order, a large number of which are nouns. If the idiom you are looking for contains one or more nouns, it will be found under the first noun in the idiom. This means that **bite the bullet** is at **BULLET**, **have a heart** is at **HEART**, and **be a piece of cake** is at **PIECE**. Compound nouns (nouns made up of more than one word) are also found at the first noun. For example, **the acid test** is located at **ACID**.

If there is no noun in the idiom, the idiom is listed at the first significant word. For example, **thick and fast** is at **THICK**, and **where it's at** is at **WHERE**. Generally determiners, prepositions, and pronouns are not used as keywords.

Cross-references

We have included cross-references for idioms that do not have easily identifiable keywords and for those that are to be found as variants at other idioms.

Cross-references look like the ones shown below from the keyword **PATH**:

path
⇨lead *someone* **down the GARDEN path**
⇨**off the beaten TRACK/path**
⇨**take the LINE/path of least resistance**

The word in capital letters in the idiom is the keyword under which the idiom will be found. So, for example, **lead** *someone* **down the garden path** will be found under the keyword **GARDEN**.

Sometimes a less frequent idiom is given as a variant of a more frequent one. In this case, a cross-reference will direct you to the appropriate keyword. For example, under the keyword **ACE** you will find a cross-reference that looks like this:

ace
⇨**have an ace up your sleeve** —see
have/keep *something* **up your SLEEVE**

This tells you that the idiom **have an ace up your sleeve** can be found at the keyword SLEEVE as a variant of the idiom **have/keep** *something* **up your sleeve**.

 ## When are idioms used?

Idioms are used in a wide variety of registers and situations. They are often used in spoken language, in situations that range from friendly conversations to business meetings. Idioms are used in written English as well, especially in journalism where writers frequently use them to bring their stories to life. This dictionary gives the user information about the contexts and situations in which they are most likely to encounter a particular idiom. We have tried to include as much of this type of information as possible in the definition, for example by noting that an idiom is insulting or impolite, or by explaining that a particular idiom is used when you are annoyed, angry, pleased, etc.

Other information about register and context is shown in the following ways:

Labels such as the spoken label in the following idiom are given directly before the definition:

lamppost

between you, me, and the lamppost/fencepost
SPOKEN said before you tell someone something that you do not want them to tell anyone else: *Between you, me, and the lamppost, she's been seeing another guy.*

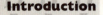

The labels used in this book are:

SPOKEN	the idiom is only used when you are speaking, but not used in writing
OLD-FASHIONED	the idiom was used in the past, but is not used frequently now
SLANG	the idiom is used by a particular group of people, but is not used by most people
TABOO	the idiom should not be used because it is extremely impolite or offensive

If an idiom is most frequently used in a particular context or by a particular group of people, this is shown after the definition:

gain ground
to make progress or gain advantages or importance in a situation ♦ OFTEN USED IN BUSINESS AND POLITICS: *It was feared that the fascists might be gaining considerable ground in southern parts of the country.* —compare **lose GROUND**

hop

hop/jump to it
used to tell someone to do something immediately ♦ OFTEN USED BY ADULTS SPEAKING TO CHILDREN: *If you finish your homework quickly you can watch TV tonight, so you'd better hop to it.*

 What does the dictionary tell me about how idioms behave?

Forms of the idioms and variants
Very few idioms are fixed in form. We have used a number of devices in order to show the ways that these phrases can vary. If part of the phrase can be left out, it is shown in parentheses. For example, the idiom *someone* **has been around the block (a few times)** can be said with or without the words "a few times," although the meaning remains the same. This technique is also used for idioms which have become cliché and are therefore often shortened, such as **you can lead a horse to water (but you can't make it drink).** Some idioms can have any word inserted, depending on what the speaker is describing. In idioms such as **the _____ of** *someone's* **dreams**, the underlined space indicates that the range of nouns, adjectives, etc. which could be inserted is unlimited.

Variants of the main idiom are shown in parentheses underneath the idiom.

hotcakes

sell like hotcakes
(also **go like hotcakes**)
if something sells like hotcakes, a lot of people buy it in a short time: *The CD sold like hotcakes, and three weeks later it was the biggest-selling album of all time.*

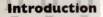

Idioms that cannot be defined together but are very closely related in meaning are shown after the main entry and are followed only by an example, as in the case of **give** *someone* **a clean bill of health** and **get a clean bill of health**:

> **give** *someone* **a clean bill of health**
> if a doctor gives someone a clean bill of health, he or she tells them they are completely healthy: *The doctors said they wouldn't give him a clean bill of health until he quit drinking.*
> **get a clean bill of health:** *If Balanger gets a clean bill of health, she has said she will run for office in the May 16th election.*

One-word adjective or noun forms of the idiom are treated in a similar way after the main entry:

> **sit on the fence**
> used to show disapproval for someone who does not decide quickly about something, or who refuses to give a definite opinion about something: *You know how things are – too many people are sitting on the fence these days. We need action.*
> **fence-sitting:** *Many economists who had been fence-sitting are now predicting a recession.*

Idioms that are directly opposite in meaning are labeled "opposite" and placed at the end of the entry as well.

Notes and features

After some entries there are tinted boxes that give you more information about the idiom. These notes may contain further explanations of how the idiom is used or varied, interesting facts about where it comes from, or, in cases where the idiom is impolite or insulting, suggestions for other idioms that may be used instead.

The Idiom Activator (pp. 183-192) puts idioms into meaning groups, allowing you to choose exactly the right idiom in a particular situation.

What is a corpus?

A corpus is a large database consisting of texts in electronic form that lexicographers use to find out how a word or phrase behaves and how frequent it is. We have used a variety of different corpora to help in the compilation of this book. The *Longman American Corpus Network* consists of:

■ the *Longman Written American Corpus*: This is a collection of extracts from different books, magazines, newspapers, and other written sources, totaling 140 million words.

- the *Longman Spoken American Corpus*: over 5 million words of everyday conversation recorded across the U.S. to provide a representative sample of the U.S. population by age, gender, region, etc.

- the *Longman Learners' Corpus*: over 10 million words of writing in English by learners of the language from over 125 different countries. The scripts are coded to show student nationality, level, task type, etc. and are keyed exactly as they were written, so that the lexicographers can see where students have difficulties.

These corpora have been used to identify idioms and all their variations, to see the contexts in which they are typically used, and to determine how frequent they are. They also provide the users of this book with access to real language, through example sentences based on material taken directly from the corpora.

Karen Stern
Managing Editor

 Your comments

If you have any comments or questions about this book, we would be happy to hear from you. You can e-mail us at **dict.edit@pearsoned-ema.com** or write to us at the address below:

Editor: Longman Dictionary of American Idioms
Pearson Education Limited
Edinburgh Gate
Harlow
Essex CM20 2JE
England

A

A

the A to Z of *something*
(also **from A to Z)**
used to say that something describes or deals with every part of a subject ◆ OFTEN USED IN THE TITLES OF BOOKS, ARTICLES, ETC.: *His new article is called "The A to Z of Fishing," and it covers more than you could ever want to know about it.*

about

⇨HOW about that

above

someone **is getting above himself/ herself**
SPOKEN used in order to say that someone has begun to think that they are better or more important than they really are: *You'll have to watch Amanda – she's getting above herself these days.*

absence

absence makes the heart grow fonder
used to say that being away from someone you love makes you love them more, because you only remember the good things about them: *They say that absence makes the heart grow fonder, but sometimes it can be very difficult to get back into a relationship with someone you haven't seen for a long time.*

accident

an accident waiting to happen
used about a person or situation that you think is very likely to cause serious trouble, damage, or harm: *Bottles of acid were mixed in among the bottles of medicine, a fatal accident waiting to happen.*

ace

⇨have an ace up your sleeve —see have/keep *something* up your SLEEVE

an ace in the hole
someone or something important that you are able to use when you need to gain an advantage: *The Democrats have an ace in the hole with a candidate like Wilson. This year they are sure to win the election.*

hold all the aces
to have all the advantages in a situation, so that you are sure to be more successful than other people: *Other countries are starting to explore for oil under the oceans, so Middle Eastern countries no longer hold all the aces.*

play your ace
to do something that other people do not expect you to do, in order to gain an advantage: *Nilsen decided to play his ace, and told them he had been offered another job.*

Achilles

the Achilles' heel (of)
a weakness in someone's character that causes them problems, or the weak part of a place, system, argument, etc., which can easily be attacked or criticized: *When it comes to diets, my Achilles' heel has always been chocolate. I just can't say no to it.*

acid

the acid test
something that shows you whether an idea, or plan works well or correctly, or shows you whether something is true: *A learning program whose results can be easily measured is a good acid test for the effectiveness of any training program.*
—compare **LITMUS test**

> NOTE▶ Acid is used to test the quality of metals such as gold.

acquaintance

have a passing/nodding acquaintance with
1 to know a person or place slightly: *The witness said that she had only a passing acquaintance with the man.*
2 to have only a little knowledge about a subject, or only a slight connection with

A

something: *McIntosh makes a lot of claims that only have a passing acquaintance with the truth.*

act

⇨a **CLASS** act
⇨read (*someone*) the **RIOT** act

a balancing act
a situation in which someone is trying to do a lot of different things at the same time, especially when this is difficult: *Dealing with American culture and capitalism while trying to stay in touch with their Russian roots can be a tricky balancing act for these immigrants.*

catch *someone* in the act
1 to see someone doing something that is wrong: *The police warned that anyone caught in the act of vandalism would be arrested.*
2 SPOKEN to walk into a place suddenly and find two people having sex: *Kim is asking her husband for a divorce after catching him in the act with another woman.*

clean up your act
to start behaving in a more acceptable way after you have been behaving badly: *If Stephen doesn't clean up his act soon, he's going to end up in jail.*

do a vanishing/disappearing act
used to say that someone has made it impossible for other people to find them, especially when it has happened without warning: *Dan doesn't really know how to talk. He asks a few questions, then does a disappearing act.*

get in on the act
to take part in an activity, business, etc. that someone else has started, in order to get some of the advantages for yourself: *Even the smaller supermarkets are getting in on the act and providing exotic fruits and vegetables for their customers.*

get your act together
SPOKEN to do something in a more organized way than before, or to use your abilities more effectively than before: *Shauna, you're going to have to get your act together and study harder if you want to get into college.*

be a hard/tough act to follow
(spoken **be an impossible act to follow**)
used to say that the way someone has done something is so successful or impressive that it will be difficult for the next person, team, etc. who does it to be as good: *The department owes a lot to Amanda for her years of leadership – she's a hard act to follow.*

action

⇨fight a **REARGUARD** action

actions speak louder than words
used to say that what you do is more important than what you say, and that people will judge you by the things you do: *Since actions speak louder than words, Dr. Salk decided to inject himself with the vaccine to show that it was safe.*

Adam

not know *someone* from Adam
SPOKEN used to say that you do not know someone at all, or have never seen them before: *"What does Kimbell look like?" "I wouldn't know him from Adam – we've just talked on the phone."*

admiration

a mutual admiration society
a humorous expression used about two people, groups, or organizations that are praising each other a lot: *Movie industry executives have identified themselves with White House officials, and vice versa. It's a mutual admiration society that could hardly be any cozier.*

advocate

play/be devil's advocate
(also **act as devil's advocate**)
to pretend to disagree about something so that there will be a discussion about it: *I'm just being the devil's advocate here, but what would you do if our suppliers don't deliver on time?*

again

⇨**THEN** again
⇨**YET** again

age

in a coon's age
SPOKEN in a very long time: *Ted! How are you? I haven't seen you in a coon's age.*

agenda

a hidden agenda
the things that you secretly intend to achieve from a plan or action, although you pretend that you are doing it for another reason: *Marge had a hidden agenda in inviting us all to the party. She wanted to see who had the best skills in dealing with people.*

agreement

a gentleman's agreement
an agreement that is not written down, but is made between people who trust each other to be honest: *The Showtime Cinema had a gentleman's agreement with the town not to show X-rated movies.*

ain't

if it ain't broke, don't fix it
(also **if it ain't broke, why fix it?**)
SPOKEN said in order to disagree with someone who wants to change the way something works or is done because you believe it works well the way it is: *Why do they need a new management structure? I keep saying if it ain't broke, don't fix it.*

it ain't all that
(also *someone* **ain't all that**)
SLANG said when you do not think something or someone is as good or special as someone else does: *Next time Julie tries to make you feel bad, you just tell her she ain't all that.*

air

⇨you could (have) cut the
   ATMOSPHERE/air with a knife

clear the air
to discuss a problem, often a personal problem in order to try to solve it or get rid of bad feelings between the people involved: *Mel finally tried to clear the air by asking Carla what was bothering her.*

hot air
used about statements that sound very impressive or threatening but really have no meaning: *Most people believe Paul when he tells them he's met all those movie stars. I think he's full of hot air.*

be in the air
1 if a feeling or idea is in the air, everyone seems to be feeling it or thinking about it: *There was a hint of panic in the air yesterday as the markets fell to their lowest point this month.*
2 if an event or change is in the air, people think that it is very likely to happen: *Rumors are in the air that the company may relocate to San Francisco.*
—compare **be up in the AIR**

out of thin air
(also **from thin air**)
used to emphasize that an idea, object, person, etc. seems to have come from nowhere in particular: *My grandfather was one of those people who could make money out of thin air.*

put on airs
used to show that you disapprove because someone is behaving as if they were more important than other people: *Even though Linda is a famous model she is not one to put on airs.*

be up in the air
used to say that something is not yet decided: *"When are you going on vacation?" "It's still up in the air."*
—compare **be in the AIR**

vanish/disappear into thin air
to disappear suddenly in a way that is surprising or difficult to understand: *I know I saw the keys on the couch this morning, but they seem to have vanished into thin air.*

be walking/floating on air
to feel extremely happy, often so that you do not notice anything else: *When I got the job and then fell in love, I was walking on air.*

aisles

be rolling in the aisles
used to say that people watching a movie, play, etc. are laughing a lot and cannot

stop: *Kavner's jokes still keep audiences rolling in the aisles.*

alarm

a false alarm
something that makes you think that something bad or difficult is going to happen, when it does not happen: *I thought I was pregnant last month, but it was a false alarm.*

albatross

an albatross (around someone's neck)
a problem that prevents you from succeeding: *Robert's financial problems were an albatross around his neck and he eventually went bankrupt.*

> **NOTE** An albatross is a very large white seabird that sailors (=people who work on ships) think it is very unlucky to kill. In Coleridge's poem, "*The Rime of the Ancient Mariner,*" a sailor kills an albatross and has to wear it around his neck as a punishment.

aleck

a smart aleck
(also a smart-aleck)
used about someone who is annoying because they think they are very intelligent, or because they always have a funny reply to what people say: *"What are you going to wear tonight?" "Clothes." "Don't be such a smart aleck."*

alert

be (put) on red alert
if a group of people such as soldiers or doctors are on red alert, they have been warned about an enemy attack, an accident, or some other dangerous situation and they are ready to deal with it: *Thousands of soldiers and police were put on red alert last night as violent gangs roamed the streets of the capital.*

alive

be alive and kicking
used to say that someone is still healthy and active, or that a business, activity, etc.

still exists and is still successful: *News of a long-awaited tour provides evidence that the band is still alive and kicking.*

all

⇒**all over the PLACE**
⇒**not be the BE-ALL and end-all (of something)**
⇒**GO all out**
⇒**be ___ in all but NAME**
⇒**it AIN'T all that**
⇒**ONCE and for all**
⇒**THAT's someone all over**
⇒**THAT's all she wrote**
⇒**to TOP it all (off)**
⇒**WHEN all is said and done**

be all about something
SLANG used to say that you are completely involved in or excited about an activity or situation, and are putting all your energy into it: *Right now, I'm all about partying. I've never played so hard in my life.*

be all dressed up and/with nowhere to go
(also be all dressed up with no place to go)
used to say that someone is completely prepared for something that they want to do, but they are not able to do it: *NASA and the crew of the delayed space flight were all dressed up with nowhere to go today, but repairs should only take another day.*

be all over someone
SPOKEN to be kissing and touching another person in a sexual way: *Julie and Pete were all over each other at the party – it was embarrassing to watch.*

be all over something
SLANG used to say that you feel happy, excited, or confident about doing something: *Man, I was all over that history test today.*

all's well that ends well
used to say that a situation has ended with a good result even though there were many problems or difficulties: *This season has been an unpredictable one for the Saints. But all's well that ends well, and they won the NFC championship over the Cardinals on Sunday.*

do *something* **for all you are worth**
to do something using all your energy:
*She saw the bus leaving, so she started
running for all she was worth to catch it.*

someone **is not all there**
SPOKEN used to say that someone does not
think clearly or seems slightly crazy: *That
woman in the store kept giving me the
wrong change – she just wasn't all there
as far as I could tell.*
opposite **be all there:** *Grandma is 86 years
old, but she's still all there and lives on her
own.*

alley

a blind alley
a situation in which you realize that a
particular method you have been using to
achieve something is not working, or
something you try that makes you realize
this: *I tried and tried to call and make
hotel reservations, but it was a real blind
alley. Nobody would answer the phone.*

be right up *someone's* **alley**
used to say that something is exactly what
someone likes or is good at doing: *I think
this multimedia course will be right up
your alley.*

alliance

an unholy alliance
used about an agreement between two
people or organizations who would not
usually work together, when you think
they have joined together in order to do
something bad ◆ OFTEN USED IN POLITICS:
*The parties in Washington have formed
an unholy alliance between the powers of
greed and special interests to run giant
political campaigns.*

altar

be sacrificed on the altar of ___
used to say that you disapprove because a
person, group, idea, etc. is being
destroyed so that something else can be
achieved, especially something you do
not approve of: *Good medical care is
being sacrificed on the altar of cost
effectiveness.* | *Schools should not
sacrifice the preparation of responsible
citizens on the altar of work.*

amok

⇨**RUN amok**

amount

⇨**X amount of** —see **X NUMBER of**

angel

a fallen angel
used about someone who people used to
think was successful or morally good, but
who is no longer thought of in this way:
*Looking back at the 1990s, history will
show us many fallen angels, and at the
top of the list, rightly or wrongly, will be
Mikhail Gorbachev.*

animal

⇨**PARTY animal**

a different animal
used to say that someone or something is
very different from another person or
thing that you have just mentioned: *This
slow post-season game was an entirely
different animal from the high energy,
high stakes games at the beginning of the
season.*

answer

someone's **answer to ___**
someone or something from one group,
country, organization, etc. which is
supposed to be equal to or as good as a
famous person or thing from another
group, country, etc., especially when
there is competition between the two
groups: *Americans have always been
fascinated by the Kennedy family, who
are regarded by many as America's
answer to Britain's royal family.*

Good answer!
SPOKEN said when you approve of or agree
with someone: *"I don't know what the
problem is with this computer. I guess I'll
just turn it off so we can go." "Good
answer!"*

someone **won't take no for an
answer**
(also *someone* **refuses to take no for an
answer)**
used to say that someone keeps trying to
get or do what they want even though

A

other people will not agree to it: *You're coming with me, and I won't take no for an answer.*

ante

up/raise the ante
to increase your demands, the risks that you take, or the amount that you spend, with the aim of gaining more from the situation that you are involved in: *The airline has raised the ante on its competitors by offering two flights for the price of one.*

> NOTE▶ The ante is the amount of money that each player gives before starting a game of cards that is being played for money. If the ante is increased or "upped", there is more risk.

ants

have ants in your pants
SPOKEN to feel excited or have a lot of energy, so that it is difficult to keep still or stay in one place ◆ USED ESPECIALLY TO OR ABOUT CHILDREN: *Can't you wait until I make coffee to open your presents? You really have ants in your pants this Christmas.*
—see also *someone* **must have had WORMs for breakfast**

anybody

⇨**be anybody's GUESS**

anything

⇨**as easy as anything** —see **as easy as PIE**
⇨**... LIKE anything**

anything goes
used to say that even unusual behavior, events, etc. are acceptable: *Who knows? In these modern times when anything goes and individuality is prized, Wender's quirky play may be a huge hit.*

ape

go ape
(also **go apeshit**)
SPOKEN to suddenly become very angry or excited: *If we suggest draining the marsh, the environmentalists will go apeshit.*

—see also **go BALLISTIC/nuclear**

> NOTE▶ Many people find the word "shit" offensive. It is less offensive to say "go ape".

appetite

whet *someone's* appetite (for *something*)
to make you want to do something, or have more of something: *To whet your appetite for shopping in Sante Fe, I am enclosing some brochures from our favorite galleries.*

apple

⇨**be in apple pie ORDER**

be the apple of *someone's* eye
to be loved very much by someone, especially an older member of your family: *My new granddaughter Sarah is the apple of my eye.*

a rotten/bad apple
used about someone who is dishonest or immoral and who has a bad effect on others in a group: *All it takes is one bad apple to ruin the oil industry with something like a major spill.*

you can't compare apples and oranges
(also **it's (like comparing) apples and oranges**)
used to say that two things are completely different and should not be compared: *Saying that women basketball players are not as good as men is like comparing apples and oranges.*

applecart

upset the applecart
to do something that spoils someone's plans, or spoils a situation that was working well: *If you're afraid that you'll upset the applecart by saying what you think, then maybe the relationship isn't as stable as you think.*

apron strings

be tied to *someone's* apron strings
1 used about someone who depends too much on their parents, especially their

mother, for support, money, and advice about how to live life: *It's ridiculous that a 35-year-old man like Rob is still tied to his mother's apron strings.*
2 used about a person, organization, company, etc. who depends too much on another person, organization, or company for money or support in their work: *U.S. airlines had been tied tightly to the government's apron strings so that when deregulation happened, only the strongest companies survived.*
cut/untie the apron strings: *Your problem isn't your mother-in-law, it's your husband – he needs to cut the apron strings and start thinking about you.*

are
⇨**THERE you go/are**

area
a gray area
used about an area of law, behavior, etc. which is not easy to understand or deal with because it does not have clear rules or limits: *Margaret always knew what was right and wrong in her life – there were no gray areas.*

arm
cost an arm and a leg
SPOKEN used to say that something is very expensive: *That new carpet must have cost an arm and a leg.*
pay/spend an arm and a leg: *Two years ago we paid an arm and a leg for this printer, and now it's obsolete!*

the long arm of the law
(also **the long arm of the state, government, etc.**)
used to say that the police and the laws are so powerful that people who do something wrong in any activity or part of society can be caught and punished: *Now the long arm of the law is catching up with criminals who operate across the border.*

twist *someone's* **arm**
to persuade someone to do something that they have said they do not want to do: *I'll call her and twist her arm a little – I think she'll give us the money.*
have your arm twisted: *Many clients of the*

investment firm had their arms twisted into buying bonds that they didn't really want.
arm-twisting: *The bill was saved from a major defeat in the Assembly's Ways and Means Committee only after intense last-minute arm-twisting.*

be up in arms (about *something***)**
if a group of people are up in arms about something they are protesting angrily about it: *As soon as Morris suggested the changes, the whole committee was up in arms.*

welcome/greet *someone* **with open arms**
to show that you are very happy to see or meet someone, or to have him, her, etc. as part of your group, organization, etc.: *If Judy ever decides to study here again, she'll be welcomed back with open arms.*

someone **would give his/her right arm to do** *something*
(also *someone* **would give his/her right arm for** *something*)
used to say that you want something very much, especially something that is difficult or impossible to get: *I'd give my right arm to be able to sing like that.*

armpit
the armpit of ___
SPOKEN used about a place that is the ugliest or worst place in a particular area: *Bob says Des Moines is the armpit of Iowa, but I have a friend who loves it there.*

arrow
a straight arrow
used about someone who you can trust because they never do anything wrong, illegal, or unusual, but who is often considered slightly boring because of this: *Vaquero is a tough, straight arrow at the Federal Reserve, where he is responsible for overseeing the nation's biggest banks.*

art
have/get *something* **down to a fine art**
to do something very well, especially because you have done it a lot: *I've been*

on so many business trips lately, I've got packing down to a fine art.

article

the genuine article
used to say that something is real, and not a copy: *A lot of places claim to serve authentic Italian coffee, but Bar Italia offers the genuine article.*
—see also **the real McCOY**

as

...as if
SPOKEN said when you think something someone has just said is very stupid or very unlikely to be true: *"Maybe if you told Janine you didn't mean what you said, she'd forgive you." "Yeah, as if!"*

as per usual
SPOKEN said when something bad happens, in order to show that it often happens: *As per usual, the bus was 20 minutes late.*

ask

don't ask me (why, how, etc.)
SPOKEN said when you do not know the answer to something: *"We figured we could spend twenty hours a month working on it – is that what we figured?" "Don't ask me. I don't know what you guys talked about."*

someone **is asking for it**
SPOKEN used to say that someone is behaving in a way that they know will make people angry or cause problems: *He's the kind of man who thinks that a woman who's been abused was probably asking for it.*

ass

> NOTE▶ Although you may hear people use "ass", some people think it is offensive. It is usually better not to use it.

⇨**nail** someone's **ass to the wall** —see **nail** someone **to the WALL**
⇨**be a PAIN in the ass**

ass backwards
SLANG used to say that someone has done things in the wrong order: *The whole system's been set up ass backwards – I have no idea what's going on!*

someone's **ass/butt is in a sling**
SPOKEN a rude expression said when someone is in trouble: *Have that report in by five o'clock – or all your asses are in a sling!*

be ass out
SLANG to be in trouble: *I'm ass out with Kate for not calling her last night.*

bust your ass/butt
SPOKEN to work very hard in order to finish or achieve something: *I've been busting my ass at work, but they still haven't given me a raise.*
—see also **bust a GUT**

cover your ass/butt
SLANG to do something now in order to protect yourself from criticism or blame if something goes wrong in the future: *I knew I'd get blamed if things went wrong, so I tried to cover my ass by lying.*

> NOTE▶ Because using "ass" is rude, it is better to use "cover your back", which is not rude at all.

get your ass/butt in gear
SPOKEN a rude expression used in order to tell someone to hurry or try harder: *Get your ass in gear, Rudy! I'm leaving in five minutes.*

someone **goes around his/her ass to get to his/her elbow**
SPOKEN an impolite expression used in order to say that someone does something in the most difficult way, when it should be very easy to do: *You can be sure that if Jordan has something important to do, he'll go around his ass to get to his elbow and we'll all be stuck waiting for him.*

haul ass/butt
SLANG to go fast in a vehicle, or do something very quickly: *You should've seen us yesterday. We were hauling ass – we had the whole thing done by 4 o'clock.*

someone **is on** someone's **ass/butt**
SLANG used when someone is criticizing someone or complaining about the way

they do something: *Kyle's always on my butt about something. I can't even just sit there and watch TV without him saying something.*

> NOTE▶ Because using "ass" is rude, it is better to use "someone is on someone's back", which is not rude at all.

someone **is talking out of their ass**
SPOKEN a rude expression used in order to say that someone is talking as if they know something when they do not: *"Pat says the account reports will be ready by tomorrow." "He's talking out his ass – he hasn't even started them yet."*

something **kicks ass/butt**
(also *someone* **kicks ass/butt at (doing)** *something***)**
SLANG used to say that you think something is very good, or that someone is very good at doing something: *Jamie's new board really kicks ass. I want one of those.*
kick-ass: *This band we heard last night really played some kick-ass music.*

kick/whip *someone's* **ass/butt**
(also **kick/whip some ass)**
SLANG a very rude expression, meaning to beat someone easily in a fight, game, competition, etc.: *Wait until I get my brother over here – he'll kick you guys' asses! | I mean, how many times do we have to whip some butt before he admits we're the best team in the conference?*

kiss my ass/butt!
a very rude expression used in order to tell someone to stop annoying you or to show that you do not respect them: *Kiss my ass, Matt. You're a pain.*

kiss *someone's* **ass**
to try very hard to please or seem impressive to someone, especially someone who is more powerful than you, in a way that other people find very annoying: *You know she gets good grades because she kisses the teacher's ass.*

not know your ass from a hole in the ground
(also **not know your ass from your elbow)**
SPOKEN a rude expression used in order to say that someone does not understand what is happening, or cannot do their job well: *If you'll excuse the expression, I don't think the company knows its ass from a hole in the ground.*

make an ass of yourself
SPOKEN to fail to do something or do it wrong, so that people think you are stupid: *The first time I tried playing the game, I made a complete ass of myself.*

my ass!
SPOKEN a rude expression said after you repeat what someone else has just said, in order to show that you do not believe it: *"He told me he runs ten miles every morning." "Ten miles, my ass – he couldn't run one mile if you pushed him!"*

> NOTE▶ Note "my foot!" means the same as this idiom, but is not as rude.

at
⇨**WHERE it's at**

atmosphere

you could (have) cut the atmosphere/air with a knife
used to say that you felt or knew very clearly that the people in a room were very angry or upset, although no one was saying anything: *The moment I walked into the room, I knew something was wrong. You could have cut the air with a knife.*

atom
⇨**make like a BANANA/atom and split**

attempt
⇨**last-DITCH effort/attempt**

attitude

have an attitude (problem)
to behave in an angry way that shows you have no respect for other people: *Ben has an attitude problem at school that needs to change. | Tillman's a tough player with an attitude on the basketball court.*

with attitude
showing the confidence to do exactly what you want, especially if it annoys or

worries other people: *I like how Liz talks to her boss, courtesy with attitude.*

authority

have (it) on good authority that

SPOKEN used to tell someone that the information you have comes from someone who knows the truth or the latest information about a situation, often when you do not want to mention their name: *We have it on good authority that First Northwestern is buying Farmers' Mutual.*

awakening

a rude awakening

used about an occasion when you realize that something that you expect to be true or good is not true or good: *Anyone who gets married expecting romance for the rest of their life is in for a very rude awakening.*

away

⇨**FAR and away**
⇨**GET away from it all**

ax

"Ax" is the usual spelling; however, it can also be spelled "axe".

an ax is hanging over *someone/ something*

(also *someone/something* **faces the ax**)
used to say that someone is likely to lose their job, or that an organization, system, etc. is likely to be ended, usually because there is not enough money: *The new recycling plan faces the ax in the city's latest budget.*

NOTE▶ You may also hear "ax" used in other phrases with related meanings.: *Policies, programs, and benefits designed to support working parents not only escaped the ax, they have been expanded.* | *People with skill and experience and ability aren't waiting for the ax to fall. They're leaving now.*

get the ax
(also **be given the ax**)

1 to be dismissed from your job: *Over 15,000 employees could be given the ax, according to one source who is close to the company.*

2 if a plan, service, system, etc. gets the ax, it is ended suddenly: *There are rumors that our healthcare plan is going to get the ax.*

someone **has an ax to grind**

used to say that a person or group has an aim that they want to achieve, or a strong opinion about what should happen, and that you think this may stop them from being fair and reasonable ◆ OFTEN USED IN THE NEGATIVE: *"I'm not a member of any party," said Meeks. "I have no political ax to grind."*

Aztec

⇨**the Aztec TWO-STEP**

B

B.A.

hang a B.A.
SLANG to pull your clothes away from your body and show your bare buttocks (=the part of your body you sit on) as a joke or to insult someone: *Ernie hung a B.A. out of my car window at some girls on the street.*

> NOTE▶ "B.A." in this idiom means "bare ass," which some people may think is offensive.

babe

a babe in the woods
used about someone who does not have much experience, and can easily be deceived: *He was just a babe in the woods when he first came to New York.*

baby

⇨sleep like a LOG/baby

be *someone's* baby
used about a plan, idea, or activity that someone has started or developed and is very interested in: *I don't think you've met Don, the program director – this volunteer project is his baby.*

throw the baby out with the bath (water)
to get rid of good, useful parts of a system, organization, etc. because one part is bad: *Some people felt that the legal actions taken to end certain research being done at the university were like throwing out the baby with the bathwater since many other projects would be affected.*

back

⇨back *someone* into a CORNER
⇨go back to the drawing BOARD

at/in the back of your mind
if a thought, problem, or idea is at the back of your mind, you are thinking about it even though you are not giving it all of your attention: *A nagging voice in the back of her mind told her she had made a mistake.*

put/push something to the back of your mind: *When I was at the wedding, I tried to put all my worries to the back of my mind so I could just enjoy the day.*

the back of beyond
OLD-FASHIONED used about a place that is far away and difficult to get to, especially one where few people live: *My parents live up in the back of beyond – you never see a soul.*

break the back of *something*
to defeat an attempt to oppose you: *Government troops have broken the back of the armed resistance in the north.*

break your back
to work very hard when you are trying to do something: *She's been breaking her back working overtime every day this month to save money for her trip.*

back-breaking: *Our CEO has the most back-breaking job in the company.*

cover your back
to do something now to protect yourself from criticism or blame if something goes wrong in the future: *The business culture today tells us never to take chances, always cover your back, and always put it in writing.*

do *something* behind *someone's* back
1 to say bad things about someone to other people, when that person is not there: *He suspected that the older girls were laughing at him behind his back.*
2 (also **go behind** *someone's* **back**) to do something without telling someone who will be affected by it, especially a member of your family or someone who you work with: *I can't believe that my own sister was seeing my boyfriend behind my back.* | *They went behind my back and appointed someone with no experience.*

get/keep *someone* off your back
to make someone stop annoying you, especially someone who is criticizing you, or asking you to do something: *He paid the newspaper a lot of money to keep their reporters off his back.*
—see also **get off my back!**

get off my back!

an impolite expression used in order to tell someone who keeps criticizing you to stop: *Maybe I'd get more work done if you'd just get off my back.*
—see also **get/keep** *someone* **off your back,** *someone* **is on** *someone's* **back**

have your back to/against the wall

(also **do** *something* **with your back to/against the wall**)
to be in a difficult situation that is very difficult to change or get out of: *After numerous demonstrations for democracy, Chun's back was against the wall. He went on television and agreed to arrange local democratic elections.*

someone is on *someone's* back

used to say that someone is criticizing or complaining about the way another person is behaving: *I had no money left, and my parents were on my back for spending too much.*
—see also **get/keep** *someone* **off your back**

know *something* like the back of your hand

to know a place extremely well: *He's lived in New York all his life. He must know it like the back of his hand.*

on the back of *something*

if something becomes better or changes on the back of another thing, it becomes better or changes because of it: *The company's consumer electronics side, which grew on the back of making headphones, is going to be kept.*

pat *someone* on the back

(also **give** *someone* **a pat on the back**)
to praise someone or show your approval of something they have done: *I think we should give Mark a big pat on the back for all his hard work.*
get/receive/deserve a pat on the back: *Students at local schools have received an official pat on the back for achieving a high academic standard.*

pat yourself on the back

(also **give yourself a pat on the back**)
to feel pleased with yourself because of something you have done: *If you answered "yes" to all these questions, give yourself a pat on the back for being a friend of the environment.*

(don't) piss on my back and tell me it's raining

(also **(don't) piss in my ear and tell me it's raining**)
SPOKEN an impolite expression used in order to tell someone that you do not believe them: *"I'll pay you back, I promise." "Right, now piss on my back and tell me it's raining."*

stab *someone* in the back

to do something that harms someone who you are working with, especially in a way that is secret or not direct ♦ OFTEN USED IN BUSINESS AND POLITICS: *I can't believe one of my own co-workers could have stabbed me in the back like that. Did you know what was going on?*
a stab in the back: *Lang's decision to leave the company was interpreted by his colleagues as a treacherous stab in the back.*
back-stabbing: *People work together in local politics; it's not like the back-stabbing that goes on in Washington.*

turn your back on *somebody/something*

1 to stop noticing or paying attention to someone, or to refuse to help them: *We can't afford to turn our back on our competitors for a second.*
2 to refuse to be involved in something: *Buchanan turned his back on religion after his baby daughter died.*

watch your back

used to tell someone to be careful because someone may be trying to cause trouble for them or harm them: *A word of warning: watch your back with Jim – I don't trust him.*

you scratch my back, I'll scratch yours

used about a situation in which people are helping each other, especially by doing things for each other that they are not supposed to do: *I realized how the army worked: you scratch my back, I'll scratch yours. A lot of trading went on between the officers.*
back-scratching: *In small towns, there's a lot of political back-scratching that goes on, which serves to expand people's incomes as well.*

backyard

not in my backyard
(also **NIMBY**)
used to say that someone does not want something useful that may be bad or dangerous to be built or developed close to where they live: *When the program for drug users was set up, the neighborhood's response was "Not in my back yard."* | *They call us NIMBYs, but we feel that this beautiful landscape is not the place for a freeway.*

in *someone's* **own backyard**
used to talk about something that happens near to you: *The new administration, which sees itself as a champion of human rights, should take a look at the injustices that are happening in their own backyard.*

bacon

bring home the bacon
to provide enough money to support your family: *The "ideal family," in which Dad brings home the bacon and Mom takes care of the family, describes only 7% of American families.*

> NOTE▶ An old English story says that any man who could say truthfully at the door of a particular church in England that he had not been angry with his wife for twelve months and a day, could take home a large piece of bacon (=pig meat). This only happened eight times in 500 years.

save *someone's* **bacon**
SPOKEN to stop someone from failing or having trouble, when they are in a difficult situation: *We had a very dry summer, but the heavy fall rains really saved our bacon.*

bad

someone's **got it bad**
SPOKEN used to say that someone is very much in love with someone else: *I think Kendra's got it bad for you.*

my bad
SLANG used to say that something is your fault and that you are sorry: *My bad, man. I didn't see you.*

> NOTE▶ This idiom is only used by young people in very informal situations. It is more common to say "my fault" or "my mistake."

bag

⇨**catch/bag some RAYS**
⇨*someone* **couldn't ___ his/her way out of a (wet) PAPER bag**

be *someone's* **bag**
SPOKEN to be the kind of thing that someone is interested in or is good at
♦ OFTEN USED IN THE NEGATIVE: *Caroline said that computers weren't really her bag, but she seemed to know a lot about them.*

a bag lady
a woman who has no home and carries all her possessions around with her in bags: *The only other person in the park was an old bag lady who was feeding the pigeons.*

someone's **bag of tricks**
used about the special methods someone uses in their work: *The Toledo offense dipped into its bag of tricks to pull out a 3–1 victory over Montreal.*

something **is in the bag**
used to say that it is definite that someone will get what they are trying to achieve or obtain: *Most Hollywood insiders bet that Foster will have the best actress Oscar in the bag.*

be left holding the bag
to become responsible for something that someone else has started, even though you do not want to be: *The city wants to be assured it won't be left holding the bag if anything should happen to Birk's development plans.*

be a mixed bag
used to say that a group of things or people are all very different from each other: *The performers were sort of a mixed bag – one or two were outstanding but a few were terrible.*

pack your bags
to leave a place or situation where you do not want to stay, or to tell someone to leave a place or situation: *Katie was so mad at Mike; she was ready to tell him to pack his bags.*

pull *something* **out of the bag**

to do something unexpected and surprising that helps you to solve a problem or defeat an opponent: *We've got other options we can pull out of the bag if the weather turns bad.*

bait

fish or cut bait

SPOKEN used to tell someone to do what they say they will, or stop talking about it: *Senior military officials said that a decision should be made by October 15th. "Then it will be time to either fish or cut bait," said Creasy.*

someone is fishing without bait

SPOKEN used to say that you think someone is slightly crazy: *The guy's obviously fishing without bait. I mean, how can he think we'd believe him?*

rise to the bait

to react to what someone is saying or doing in exactly the way that they want you to, especially when you are arguing: *McGraw began to argue, but Gupta did not rise to the bait.*

take the bait

1 to do what someone wants, and accept something that they are offering to you if you do it: *The newspapers took the bait and published the story, giving Billings the publicity she wanted.*
2 to react to what someone is saying in exactly the way that they want you to: *Some customers tried to provoke me, but I never took the bait.*

balance

hang/be/remain in the balance

if a situation hangs in the balance, no one knows yet what will happen, because this depends on events that are still happening, or on a decision that has not yet been made: *I waited for the meeting to end, knowing that my career hung in the balance.*

throw *someone* off balance

to make someone confused or less confident by surprising them: *Don't let unexpected questions throw you off balance in the interview.*

tip/swing the balance

to have an effect on a decision that is being made, or on the final result of a situation: *The new law has swung the balance in favor of home buyers, and away from renters.*

ball

a ball and chain

used about someone or something who limits your freedom to do what you want to do: *"Hi Dave, where's Cathy?" "Oh, I left the old ball and chain at home tonight."*

the ball is in *someone's* court

SPOKEN used to say that someone who you are dealing with must reply to you or take some action before progress can be made in a situation: *You've called her twice and left a message. Now the ball's in her court.*
put the ball in someone's court: *We need to write a letter that puts the ball very firmly in their court.*

bust/break *someone's* balls

SPOKEN an offensive expression meaning to angrily criticize someone ♦ USED MOSTLY BY MEN: *I'm not going back in there if all he's gonna do is bust my balls.*

> NOTE▶ Because "balls" is an informal word for testicles (=male sexual organs), it is better to use "give someone a hard time", which is not considered offensive.

carry the ball

to do all the work, or be responsible for everything, when other people should be sharing the work ♦ OFTEN USED IN BUSINESS AND POLITICS: *I've been doing all I can for years now – it's time for someone else to carry the ball.*

drop the ball

to make a mistake or fail to do something that you are responsible for ♦ OFTEN USED IN BUSINESS AND POLITICS: *This is important. We can't drop the ball where employee safety is concerned.*

have a ball

to enjoy yourself very much: *What an experience! We really had a ball on our trip.*

have *someone* **by the balls**
a rude expression meaning that someone is forced to do or accept what you want: *Maguire had him by the balls, leaving him no option but to sign the contract.*

be on the ball
to be quick to notice and understand things that are happening around you: *She's over eighty, but she's really on the ball.*

pick up the ball and run (with it)
(also **take the ball and run with it**)
to take an idea or opportunity that you have been given and make it successful: *The director seems to have let the actors pick up the ball and run with it, and the result is an enjoyable evening at the theater.*

play ball
to behave in the way that people want or expect you to behave ♦ OFTEN USED IN BUSINESS AND POLITICS: *If his lawyers don't want to play ball, we can't make them.*

start/get the ball rolling
to start a discussion or an activity, especially by being the first person to say or do something ♦ OFTEN USED IN BUSINESS AND POLITICS: *There are several points we need to discuss. Ann, would you like to get the ball rolling?*

the whole ball of wax
used to emphasize that you are talking about everything in a group of similar things, or everything that is involved in a particular activity: *The police told me the whole story – how they treated him, how he survived, who helped him, the whole ball of wax.*
—see also **the whole SHEBANG**

ball game

it's a (whole) new ball game
(also **it's a (whole) different ball game**)
used to say that a situation has changed, or that a new situation is very different from what you are used to: *I'd like to go back to work, but it's a whole new ball game now, with computers and all the new technology.*

ballistic

go ballistic/nuclear
SPOKEN to suddenly become very angry: *When Craig read her e-mail, he went ballistic.*
—see also **go APE**

balloon

a trial balloon
something you say or do in order to try to find out what people's opinions are about a new idea ♦ OFTEN USED IN BUSINESS AND POLITICS: *Reports of the chairman's resignation could just be a trial balloon to see how shareholders react.*

> NOTE▶ A trial balloon is used in order to test weather conditions.

something **went down like a lead balloon**
used to say that people did not like a remark, idea, joke, etc. that was supposed to be interesting or funny, or that they did not react at all: *You get a long silence on the phone and you think, "Well, that idea went down like a lead balloon."*

ballpark

be in the ballpark
(also **be in the same/right ballpark**)
if an amount that you have guessed or calculated is in the right ballpark, it is close to the correct amount, or close to the amount that you want: *We really don't know how many cars are on the road, but 1,200 a day seems to be in the ballpark.*
ballpark: *They think $5,000 would be a good ballpark figure for a used car.*

banana

go bananas
1 SPOKEN to become very angry or excited: *Sheila will go bananas if she finds out you bought her present from a secondhand store.*
2 SPOKEN to start behaving in a crazy or strange way, or to stop working correctly: *Take him out of New York and he goes bananas.*

B

B

make like a banana/atom and split
SLANG a humorous way of telling someone to leave, or saying that you are leaving: *Well, folks, I'm going to have to make like an atom and split.*

band

a one-man band
used about someone who does every part of an activity themselves, without any help from anyone ♦ OFTEN USED IN BUSINESS: *I'm essentially a one-man band, so my costs are very low.*

bandit

make out like a bandit
SPOKEN to receive a lot of presents or money: *Connie's kids make out like bandits every Christmas.*

bandwagon

jump/climb on the bandwagon
to start doing something because a lot of other people are doing it: *Other leading computer manufacturers have jumped on the low-price bandwagon, with many models under $800.*

bane

be the bane of *someone's* life/existence
to be something that causes continuous trouble or sadness for someone: *Slow play is the bane of a golfer's existence.*

> NOTE▶ "Bane" is an old word meaning poison.

bang

get more bang for your buck
(also **get a bigger bang for your buck**)
SPOKEN if you get more bang for your buck from a product, you get a better quality of product for the same price as other similar products: *They said I should get a Japanese car – you get a reliable car and more bang for your buck.*
give/offer/provide more bang for your buck: *In terms of giving your store more character, music gives you the biggest bang for your buck.*

go out with a bang
to end with a lot of excitement: *The season ended with a bang on Sunday, with the Giants taking the pennant easily.*

not with a bang but a whimper
(also **with a whimper not a bang**)
if something does not end with a bang but a whimper, it ends in a way that is not as effective or as exciting as you want or expect it to be: *The play closed not with a bang but a whimper, with the theater only half full and an audience only half interested.*

> NOTE▶ This comes from a line in one of T.S. Eliot's poems called "*The Hollow Men.*"

bank

⇨**be laughing all the WAY to the bank**

don't bank on it/that/*something*
SPOKEN used to tell someone that what they are hoping for or depending on probably will not happen: "*Maybe Murray has some great job for me.*" "*Don't bank on it.*"

something won't break the bank
used to say that something is not very expensive and that you can afford it: *It'll be a nice Christmas treat for her, and it won't break the bank.*

banner

do *something* under the banner of ___
to give a particular principle or idea as the reason why you are doing something: *Soon it will become legal in Arizona, under the banner of free enterprise, to advertise different brands of electricity the same way phone companies are hyped today.* | *Feminism marched under the banner of equality, while the sexual revolution marched under that of freedom.*

baptism

baptism by fire
a difficult or frightening first experience, especially in a new job or activity: "*Your first film is always a baptism by fire,*" Riker said, "*and I'm trying to prepare myself.*"

bargain

drive a hard bargain
to demand a lot and refuse to give much when you are making an agreement with someone so that you gain an advantage ◆ OFTEN USED IN BUSINESS AND POLITICS: *"I'll give you $45 for it, and that's my final offer." "You drive a hard bargain, Kelly."*

get more than you bargained for
to have more problems or difficulties while you are doing something than you had expected or were prepared for: *Bad weather on the mountain has been known to give climbers more than they bargained for.*

bark

someone's bark is worse than his/her bite
used about someone in authority who seems to be more angry, severe, or unfriendly than he or she really is: *Don't worry about Linda. Her bark is much worse than her bite.*

barrel

not be (exactly) a barrel of laughs
SPOKEN a humorous expression used in order to emphasize that something or someone is not very funny or enjoyable: *"What did you think of Segal's wife?" "Well, she's not exactly a barrel of laughs, is she?"*

have/get someone over a barrel
to put someone in a position in which they are forced to do or accept what you want: *Stein must be working for a pretty powerful organization to have the editor of "The New York Times" over a barrel.*
be over a barrel: *Some cities have sold their own equipment, then found themselves over a barrel when their contractors raised their prices.*

let someone have (it with) both barrels
(also **give** someone **both barrels**)
to criticize someone strongly and angrily: *Book critics let Jackson have it with both barrels when they reviewed her new biography.*

NOTE▶ The barrel is the part of a gun that bullets are shot through.

scrape the bottom of the barrel
to be forced to use or choose something that is not very good because there is nothing else: *That last joke was really scraping the bottom of the barrel!*

NOTE▶ You may hear people use "the bottom of the barrel" with other verbs: *The editor obviously feels these trashy stories are worthy of the newspaper's tradition of quality. In my opinion he has come right down to the bottom of the barrel.*

base

cover all the bases
to prepare for or deal with a situation thoroughly: *We have twenty detectives working on this case – we want to make sure we cover all the bases.*

NOTE▶ There are many idioms that use the word "base," which come from the sport of baseball. In this game, there are bases (=special places with a hard surface in a diamond shape (◆) on the field). A player who has hit the ball must run around all four bases, touching each of them, in order to get a point called a run.

get to first base
1 SPOKEN to achieve the first part of something, but no more ◆ OFTEN USED IN THE NEGATIVE: *Too often, producers don't even get to first base because they can't find a good scriptwriter.*
2 SLANG used to say that two people in a romantic relationship have kissed, but have not done anything more sexual than that: *Did you get to first base with Tricia last night?*
—see note at **cover all the BASEs**

be (way) off base
SPOKEN to be completely wrong about something you have made a judgment about or given your opinion of: *Barney's criticism of the performance is way off base, in my opinion. I thought it was one of the most exciting performances I've seen in a long time.*
—see note at **cover all the BASEs**

B

touch base

SPOKEN to talk to someone for a short time to find out what has happened since the last time you spoke to them ♦ OFTEN USED IN BUSINESS AND POLITICS: *Hi, Tom, I just wanted to touch base with you about the Nordberg project.*

—see note at **cover all the BASEs**

basics

go/get back to basics

1 to try using ideas or methods that have worked in the past to help you succeed at something: *Employers are going back to basics and starting to impose dress codes for employees.*

back-to-basics: *He is one of a new generation of back-to-basics country and western stars, influenced by singers like the great Hank Williams.*

2 (also **get down to basics**) to use or think about only the most important or necessary things when you are trying to succeed at something: *We played well but lost. Now we just have to get back to basics and practice hard.*

basket

a basket case

SPOKEN used about someone who is too nervous, worried, or anxious to deal with simple situations: *"I was a basket case on the field,"* Chastain said. *"I was so nervous that I didn't even want to touch the ball."*

bat

⇨**not (even) bat an EYE/eyelash**
as blind as a bat

unable to see very well or unable to see at all: *Maude shouldn't be driving at her age. She's as blind as a bat.*

do *something* **right off the bat**

SPOKEN to do something immediately: *I'd just met my mother-in-law and right off the bat she started asking when she would give her a grandchild.*

go to bat for

to support someone who is having problems, usually by trying to persuade people who have authority to help them: *I haven't always agreed with Victor or his*

politics, but I have to admit he's gone to bat for the people that work for him.

> NOTE▶ In the game of baseball, if one player goes to bat for another one, he hits the ball instead of the other player hitting the ball.

someone **has bats in his/her belfry**

OLD-FASHIONED used about someone who you think is slightly crazy or strange: *You're going out without a jacket in this weather? You must have bats in your belfry.*

... like a bat out of hell

SPOKEN if you leave a place like a bat out of hell, you leave it very fast, often because you are frightened or worried: *She suddenly realized that she was late and started driving like a bat out of hell.*

bath

take a bath

to lose a lot of money in business, or lose a lot of money that you have invested (=given to a company or a bank, in order to try to make a profit): *The companies were badly managed, and investors have taken a bath.*

baton

take/pick up the baton

to start doing something that someone else has begun, after they stop doing it: *The industry needs a strong leader who can pick up the baton that Mr. Phelan is passing.*

hand/pass on the baton: *It is the process of socialization of children that allows us to hand on the baton to the next generation.*

> NOTE▶ A baton is a short stick that is passed from one runner to the next in a relay race (=a race in which a team of runners run one at a time).

batteries

recharge your batteries

to spend some time resting and relaxing so that later you will have more strength and energy to deal with your work or your problems: *The trip to Australia gave us a chance to recharge our batteries and think about what we should do next.*

battle

⇨**FIGHT/battle it out**
⇨**a WAR/battle of nerves**

the battle lines are drawn
used to say that people involved in an argument, competition, election, etc. are ready to start and have decided on the best plan to achieve their aims: *The battle lines are being drawn for the next election, and I want to make it clear that I am still a Democrat.*

a battle of wills
a situation or argument in which the people involved are very determined, and each person or group refuses to do what the other wants: *Refusing to eat can become the child's way of winning a battle of wills with her parents.*

a battle of wits
a situation in which two people, teams, etc. use all their intelligence in order to defeat each other or get what they want: *Trying to get the burglars to stop stealing from the warehouse was becoming a battle of wits.*
—see also **a WAR/battle of nerves**

do battle (with)
to argue with someone or fight against someone: *Hertzog and his sister are preparing to do battle in the courts over their inheritance.*

fight a losing battle
to keep trying to do something that you cannot succeed in doing: *The police force is fighting a losing battle against crime.*
be a losing battle: *We try to teach our kids to respect our traditions, but with all this TV and new kinds of music it's a losing battle.*

something is half the battle
used to say that once you have done the most important or difficult part of a job, plan, etc. you will have fewer troubles doing the rest of it: *Well, you've already chosen a topic for your paper, and that's half the battle.*

a running battle
a series of related arguments or problems between two people or groups, that have

continued for a long time: *I've been fighting a running battle with the insurance company over my claim these past few months.*

win a battle but lose the war
to get one of many results you want, or win one part of an argument, but still fail to achieve the larger and more important aim: *They had won the battle to keep their jobs, but they lost the war, and the factory closed in a year.*

bay

keep/hold *something* at bay
to prevent someone or something from attacking or harming you in some way: *Moss kept police at bay for two hours and threatened suicide before finally surrendering.*

be-all

not be the be-all and end-all (of *something*)
SPOKEN used to say that something is not the most important part of your life or of a situation: *In spite of what our society believes, passionate sex is not the be-all and end-all of a relationship.*

beam

broad in the beam
SPOKEN a polite expression used in order to say that someone has large hips (=two parts of your body below your waist where your legs begin): *It's a pretty dress, but I'm a little too broad in the beam for it to look nice on me.*

bean

not amount to a hill of beans
to be worth very little or be of very little importance: *I feel like I've been working for nothing – it isn't going to amount to a hill of beans after taxes.*

cool beans
SLANG used to say that you think something is good, interesting, exciting, etc.: *"Todd says he'll take us in his car." "Cool beans."*

be full of beans
1 OLD-FASHIONED to feel eager to do things

and have a lot of energy: *I was exhausted last night, but I feel full of beans again this morning.*

2 OLD-FASHIONED a slightly rude expression used in order to tell someone that you think their opinion is wrong: *Paul went away to business school and came back with his head full of beans.*

not have a bean
OLD-FASHIONED to have no money: *It's always the same; when you're successful, people give you everything. When you don't have a bean, they won't give you anything.*

spill the beans (about)
SPOKEN to tell someone something that is supposed to be a secret: *"We're having a surprise party for Karen on Monday, so don't tell." "Don't worry, I won't spill the beans."*

bear

⇨**GRIN and bear it**

be like a bear with a sore head
to be rude to people because you are feeling unhappy or angry: *Morrison was like a bear with a sore head when I asked him if I could take an early lunch today.*

be loaded for bear
to be ready, eager, and completely prepared to do something: *Three hours before the game started, the Cardinals fans were loaded for bear.*

bearer

⇨**the STANDARD bearer of**

beast

make the beast with two backs
SLANG to have sex: *I walked in on some people making the beast with two backs in Neil's room, but we never found out who they were.*

> NOTE▶ This idiom comes from Shakespeare's play *"Othello"*.

beat

⇨**beat a (hasty) RETREAT**

beat it!
SPOKEN an impolite expression used in

order to tell someone to leave immediately because they are annoying you or should not be there: *Beat it, Tony! Can't you see I'm on the phone?*

(it) beats me
(also **(it) beats the hell out of me**)
SPOKEN said when you do not know the answer to something or cannot understand the reasons for something: *It beats me why they want a big old car like that, but that's their business.*

if you can't beat 'em, join 'em
used to say that because you cannot stop other people from doing something that you do not like, you are going to start doing it yourself, often used humorously: *"If you can't beat 'em, join 'em," I thought, and poured myself another drink.*

without missing a beat
if you react to a sudden change, or to something surprising, without missing a beat, you react as if it were normal, without showing any surprise, shock, or difficulty in dealing with it: *"And this must be your mother." "No, we're sisters," replied Meg. "I can see the resemblance now," said Joe, without missing a beat.*

you can't beat ___
SPOKEN used to say that you think that something is the best, most suitable, most enjoyable, etc. thing of its kind: *You can't beat our color printers for superb quality output. | You just can't beat Mama's fried chicken. That sure is good!*

beating

take a beating/hammering
1 to be severely criticized, badly damaged, or completely defeated ♦ OFTEN USED IN NEWSPAPERS, ON TELEVISION NEWS, ETC.: *Several million-dollar beach homes took a hammering during the recent tropical storms.*
2 to lose money or become less in value: *Carson admits that small businesses have taken a beating during the recent recession.*

beauty

beauty is in the eye of the beholder

used to say that different people have different opinions about what is beautiful: *Many orchids give off a smell that most people wouldn't go near, but beauty is in the eye of the beholder since a variety of insects are attracted to these flowers.*

beaver

an eager beaver

used about someone who is annoying or seems silly because they are too excited about doing something: *Tammy was such an eager beaver to get the invitations in the mailbox that she forgot to put stamps on them.*

beck

be at *someone's* beck and call
(also **be at the beck and call of** *someone*)

to be ready to do whatever someone else wants any time they want it, especially when this means they can take advantage of you: *He thinks his son-in-law should be at his beck and call all day.*

bed

someone **got up on the wrong side of the bed**

used to say that someone seems to be angry or annoyed without any reason: *Boy, Diane's really cranky today. She must have gotten up on the wrong side of the bed.*

> **NOTE▶** This expression probably started as "get out of bed the wrong way," which comes from the old belief that if you put your left foot on the floor first in the morning, you would have bad luck all day.

someone **has made their bed (and they must lie on it)**

used to say that someone has chosen to be in a particular situation, and they must accept it, although it is not good: *Outside the prison, the convicted man's father said, "He's made his bed, and now he's got to lie on it."*

be in bed with *someone*

to join or start working with another business company or political group, in order to get a business or political advantage, used especially when you disapprove of this arrangement ◆ OFTEN USED IN NEWSPAPERS, ON TELEVISION NEWS, ETC.: *It's a union town – which means that the politicians are in bed with the unions.*

something **is no bed of roses**
(also *something* **is not a bed of roses**)

used to say that a situation is sometimes difficult or unpleasant: *They agree that their marriage has not been a bed of roses.*

put *something* to bed

1 to finish making a decision, agreement, or plan, or to succeed in dealing with a problem ◆ OFTEN USED IN BUSINESS AND POLITICS: *I'm hoping that we can put this matter to bed because we have other, more important, things to discuss.*

2 to show that something is not true: *Halford's analysis puts several badly thought-out economic theories to bed.*

bedfellows

strange bedfellows
(also **odd, uneasy, etc. bedfellows**)

used to say that you are surprised that two very different people or groups are working together, or that two very different ideas are being used together: *A coalition of strange political bedfellows gathered to discuss the future of commerce on the Internet.*

something **makes/creates/produces strange bedfellows:** *We already know that lobbying makes strange bedfellows, but in 1937, milk producers helped lead the campaign for Philippine independence.*

bee

⇨**be the bee's KNEEs**

a busy bee

OLD-FASHIONED used about someone who works hard and is always cheerful: *Look at her run around the yard! What a busy little bee!*

B

someone has a bee in his/her bonnet (about something)
SPOKEN used to say that someone thinks something is more important than it really is, and keeps thinking or talking about it: *He's got a big bee in his bonnet about his neighbor who he is sure is taking his mail.*

beeline

make a beeline for something/someone
to go quickly and directly toward someone or something: *I'm so shy at a party that I make a beeline for someone I know, so I won't have to talk to a stranger.*

make a beeline for *something/someone*

been

been there, done that (seen the movie, bought the T-shirt)
SPOKEN used to say that you are no longer interested in doing something because you already have a lot of experience with it: *"I'd like to live in the country." "Not me. I grew up in the middle of nowhere – been there, done that, don't ever want to go back."*

beer

make someone cry into their beer
to upset someone who is not very easy to upset: *The defeat must have made American generals want to weep into their beer.*

be small beer (to/for someone)
to seem unimportant to someone, usually because they have other more important or impressive things to deal with: *Even with $10,000 to invest, you are still small beer for most stockbrokers, who usually require a minimum portfolio of $100,000.*

beet

go/turn beet-red
SPOKEN to become red in the face because you are embarrassed: *When my mom asked me if I had kissed my boyfriend yet, I went beet-red.*

beg

beg, borrow, or steal
to do everything possible in order to obtain something: *People will beg, borrow, or steal to get their hands on one of these antiques.*

be going begging
if something is going begging, it is available for anyone who wants it, because no one else has taken it: *Even low-skill, minimum-wage jobs are going begging. There just aren't enough people in the area.*

beggars

beggars can't be choosers
SPOKEN used to say that in a bad situation in which you are limited to only one or two choices of things to do, you have to accept that you cannot have what you would like most: *"I'm starving, but I don't feel like eating leftovers." "That's all there is. Beggars can't be choosers."*

beginning

the beginning of the end
used about the time when something that has been good starts to be less good or to end: *In this generation, the children understand Navajo but don't speak it, and that's the beginning of the end.*

belfry

⇨*someone* **has BATS in his/her belfry**

bell

⇨hear WEDDING bells

alarm/warning bells ring

used to say that people are starting to realize that there is a problem with something: *Alarm bells started ringing when he asked me to pay two thousand dollars in cash before he started the work.* something **rings alarm/warning bells:** *Anderson's attitude on defense is ringing warning bells in the Pentagon.*

bells and whistles

additional features added to a product that are not necessary but will make people think that it is special: *A new Corvette with all the bells and whistles would cost about $50,000.*

someone **has had his/her bell rung**

SPOKEN used to say that someone has been hit hard in the head: *He reminds me of a big old football player who's had his bell rung once too often.*

hell's bells

OLD-FASHIONED said when you are annoyed or surprised: *Oh hell's bells, didn't anything get done while I was on vacation?*

something **rings a bell (with someone)**

SPOKEN used to say that you think you remember something, although you are not certain about it: *No – the name Norman doesn't ring a bell.* | *Someone said the next meeting is Thursday – does that ring a bell with you?*

saved by the bell

SPOKEN said when you realize that you will not have to do something difficult because there will not be time or something unexpected has happened: *"It looks like we'll have to end this meeting early so we won't have time for the last speaker until next week." "Saved by the bell, Jim."*

with bells on

1 (also **with bells on it**) used to emphasize that you do something in the most complete, thorough, or best way: *"Eating is a celebration," he said. "Enjoy yourself with bells on, but don't overdo it."*

2 (also **be waiting with bells on**) if you are somewhere with bells on, you are excited about what you are going to do and expect to have a good time: *"So, you'll be here at 9 o'clock?" "With bells on."*

> NOTE▶ This idiom probably comes from a time in the past when people put bells on their horses when they were going to parties, dances, or other kinds of celebrations.

belle

be the belle of the ball

to be the most beautiful girl in a place, usually a social event: *Caroline will be the belle of the ball in that dress.*

belly-up

go belly-up

if a company goes belly-up, it fails: *With the casinos going belly-up, and with other states expanding into gambling, what does Nevada have left?*

belt

be (hitting) below the belt

to do or say something that is unfair or very unkind in an argument, fight, competition, etc.: *He showed her the ring and told her it was for someone else. I'd say that was just a bit below the belt.*

> NOTE▶ This idiom comes from boxing (=the sport of fighting by hitting with your hands). Boxers are not allowed to hit each other below the belt.

have/get something **under your belt**

to have done or achieved something useful or important: *Swenson, who had a variety of downtown projects under his belt, is looking at a new development site now.*

tighten your belt

to spend less money because you have less than you used to have: *We're going to have to tighten our belts now that we have all those credit card bills to pay off.*

B

bend

bend over backward/backwards
to do as much as you possibly can in order to help someone or do what they want: *I bent over backward, trying to be fair to her – I don't know what else I can do.*

benefit

⇨with the benefit of hindsight —see with/in **HINDSIGHT**

give *someone* the benefit of the doubt
to accept what someone says as true, even though you think it's possible that it might not be true: *"Do you think she's lying?" "I'm not sure, but I'm prepared to give her the benefit of the doubt for now."*

bent

someone is bent on (doing) *something*
(also *someone* is hell-bent on (doing) *something*)
used to say that someone is completely determined to do something, especially when you do not think they should: *I tried to interrupt, but Paul was obviously hell-bent on confessing everything.*

berth

give *someone/something* a wide berth
to avoid someone or something: *Doyle's team gave Frances a wide berth when she arrived in Phoenix for discussions.*

best

⇨(have/get) the best of both **WORLD**s

the best/better part of *something*
nearly all of an amount, especially of time or money: *They have been living together for the best part of 30 years.*

do your level best
to try as hard as you can to do something that is important: *We are doing our level best to get information out to the public.*

it's (all) for the best
SPOKEN used to say that a bad situation may have some good results: *I was really upset when Chad left, but maybe it's for the best.*

make the best of *something*
(also make the best of it)
to accept an unsatisfactory situation, and do what you can to make it less bad: *Even though we couldn't get the hotel we wanted, we decided to go ahead with the trip anyway and make the best of it.*

bet

all bets are off
used to say that if something happens, it will change a situation so that people will not know what to expect ♦ OFTEN USED IN NEWSPAPERS, ON TELEVISION NEWS, ETC.: *The Governor looks safe to win again, but if the press gets hold of a scandal, all bets are off.*

hedge your bets
to reduce your chances of failure or loss by being sure that you have several choices or possibilities available to you: *Most art dealers are hedging their bets by trading with more than one auction house.*

something is your/the best bet
SPOKEN used to give someone advice about the best thing to do or use: *If you are looking for something low in calories and animal fat, grilled or steamed fish is the best bet.*

be a safe/good bet
1 used to say that something is likely to happen, or someone is likely to be successful: *It's probably a safe bet that the world's population will double or even triple.*
2 used to say that something is a sensible thing to choose or do, and will probably bring success: *Higher interest rates would make U.S. Treasury bonds a good bet this year.*

better

⇨ **GO** one better than

better late than never
SPOKEN used to say that you are glad that something is finally being done, although it should have been done a long time ago: *"Better late than never," said Jordan when she heard about the proposal to allow women into the club.*

better safe than sorry
SPOKEN used to say that it is better to be

careful now so that nothing bad will happen later: *We knew the back road would be flooded in some places, so we thought, better safe than sorry, and stayed on the highway.*

better you than me
SPOKEN used in order to say that you are pleased you do not have to do something that you think will be difficult or unpleasant: *"I'm going to paint the outside of the house next weekend." "Better you than me – that's a big job!"*

get the better of *someone/ something/you*
1 to win a fight, argument, or competition, or deal more successfully with something than someone else: *Stewart finally got the better of his opponent, after being almost defeated in the second round.*
2 if your emotions get the better of you, they make you behave in a way that you would not normally behave: *A driver let his bad temper get the better of him when he was stopped by police. After tearing up the ticket, he smashed the windows of the police car.*
3 if a problem gets the better of you, it becomes too difficult to deal with: *Finally the hectic schedule got the better of us, and we both got sick.*

you'd better believe *something*
(also **you'd better believe it!**)
SPOKEN used to emphasize that something is definitely true or that something will definitely happen: *"It's just a piece of cardboard with a picture on it. Do they really make money out of it?" "You'd better believe it!"*

big

⇨MAKE it big

be big/hot on *something*
SPOKEN to like something very much: *You know how big I am on garage sales. There are two I want to go to this Saturday. | Don't ask me to play – I'm not too hot on sports.*

bill

fit the bill
to be exactly what you need: *If you're*

looking for a good collection of bedtime stories, *"A Child's Book of Favorite Tales"* fits the bill.

foot the bill
to pay for something, especially something expensive that you do not want to pay for: *Of course, it's the taxpayers who will have to foot the bill for all these military operations.*

give *someone* a clean bill of health
if a doctor gives someone a clean bill of health, he or she tells them they are completely healthy: *The doctors said they wouldn't give him a clean bill of health until he quit drinking.*
get a clean bill of health: *If Balanger gets a clean bill of health, she has said she will run for office in the May 16th election.*

someone has been sold a bill of goods
used to say that someone has been given an untrue description of a situation, by someone who is trying to gain an advantage: *Independent politicians like Ross Perot have tried in the past to convince the American people that they have been sold a bill of goods by the government.*
sell *someone* a bill of goods: *He is not an objective witness – he's trying to sell the jury a bill of goods!*

bin

a/the loony bin
an unkind or offensive expression meaning a hospital for people who are mentally ill, which is sometimes used humorously: *Somebody said that Kara's mom was in the loony bin. She never talks about her.*

bind

a double bind
a difficult situation in which anything you do to try to solve the problems will cause more problems: *Traditional ways of thinking put women in a double bind: if they didn't protest, nothing changed, but if they did say something, they were criticized.*

B

bird

⇨a bird's-eye VIEW (of something)

a bird brain
SPOKEN used about someone who you think is stupid: *You know who he is, he's that bird-brain sportscaster on CNN who's always screaming the scores.*

a bird in the hand (is worth two in the bush)
used to say that it is better to accept something that you have, than to try to get something better that you may not succeed in getting: *It's not the greatest job, but a bird in the hand is worth two in the bush.*

the birds and the bees
the things you tell children in order to explain sex to them, often used humorously when you do not want to mention sex directly when talking to an adult: *Didn't your mother ever tell you about the birds and the bees?*

birds of a feather (flock together)
used to say that people who have similar interests like to be with each other: *The group of them are birds of a feather. You can't expect any of them to try anything new.*

an early bird
used about someone who wakes up early, or goes somewhere or does something earlier than other people: *Our dad is such an early bird. He's already out digging in the garden by six a.m.*
early-bird: *We went for the early-bird dinner special, which ends at 6:00.*

the early bird catches/gets the worm
used to say that if you do something early or before other people, you will gain an advantage: *The early bird catches the worm, so send for your tickets now before they're gone.*

> NOTE▶ You may hear people use other words instead of "worm" in order to make it fit a particular situation more exactly: *The election is still eighteen months away, but both the Republicans and the Democrats seem convinced that the early bird catches the voter.*

eat like a bird
to eat very little: *Sheila eats like a bird – she needs to put on more weight.*

be (strictly) for the birds
SPOKEN used to say that you think an idea or suggestion is silly, useless, or not practical: *This is for the birds. I have no social life, and I never sleep – all I do is work and study.*

give/flip *someone* the bird
to make a very offensive sign by putting your middle finger up and keeping your other fingers down, when someone has done something that makes you angry: *The guy in the blue Mustang just gave me the bird. What's his problem?*

kill two birds with one stone
to achieve two things with one action: *She was hoping to kill two birds with one stone, and get the material for an article on Turkey during her vacation.*

a little bird told me
SPOKEN used to say that you know something but you are not going to say who told you: *"How did you know it's my birthday?" "A little bird told me."*

a rare bird
used about someone or something that is unusual: *The piano maker Weldon is a rare bird, a man who still takes pride in his product.*

birthday suit

in your birthday suit
not wearing any clothes: *The kids were running around in their birthday suits, and Martina had collapsed in a chair.*

bit

be chomping at the bit
to be impatient because you want to do something but someone or something is preventing you from doing it: *Tim's doing fine. In fact, he's chomping at the bit and wants to know when he can leave the hospital.*

bite

bite me!
SLANG a rude expression used when you

are very annoyed or angry because someone has just said something rude or insulting to you: *"Hey Mike, is that your girlfriend or your mother?" "Just bite me, Wiggins!"*

bite off more than you can chew
to try to do more than you are able to do or something that is too difficult: *Of course they're worried about their new business – they bit off more than they can chew.*

put the bite on *someone*
to do something that forces a person, company, organization, etc. to spend more money in order to live normally or work in the way that they normally do ◆ OFTEN USED IN NEWSPAPERS, ON TELEVISION NEWS, ETC.: *The last time Congress raised taxes, they put the bite on banks and corporations.*

take a bite out of *something*
to take away a fairly large part of an amount of money: *The heating bill always takes a pretty big bite out of my paycheck.*

that bites (the big one)
SLANG said when you are angry, annoyed, or disappointed because something that you wanted to happen did not happen: *"We'll have to pay fifty bucks more each if we want rooms on the beach side." "That bites! I can't afford that."*

someone won't bite
SPOKEN used to say that there is no reason to be afraid of someone, especially someone in authority: *Go ahead and ask him if he'll help you – he won't bite.*

bitten

once bitten, twice shy
used to say that if you have failed or been hurt once, you will be very careful next time: *From now on we're going to listen to the hurricane warnings – after all, once bitten, twice shy.*

black

in black and white
1 if a fact, agreement, or promise is in black and white, it is written down so that everyone can see exactly what it is: *I looked at the lease and it's there in black and white – we are not allowed to keep pets.*
2 if you see, judge, or describe a situation in black and white, you think about it in a way that seems too simple, as if everything or everyone in it was either completely good or completely bad: *Everything's black and white with her. You can't ask her to see the subtleties of the situation.*

be in the black
to have money in your bank account: *Peters said that the company was still in the black, but it would probably have to make job cuts.*
—compare **be in the RED**

blank

draw a blank
to be unable to answer a question, or unwilling to give information: *If you'd asked me who Bill Clinton was before the '92 election campaign, I'm sure I would've drawn a complete blank.*

blanket

⇨a SECURITY blanket
a wet blanket
used about someone who spoils other people's fun: *"It's an interesting idea, but I don't think it'll work." "Oh, don't be such a wet blanket."*

blast

a blast from the past
SPOKEN used about someone or something from the past that you suddenly remember, see, or hear about, that reminds you of that time in your life: *"He used to eat Yodels all the time." "Wow! Yodels, that's a blast from the past. I haven't had one in years."*

blaze

go out in a blaze of glory
to finish your job, your life, or your time of performing in public or playing a sport, by doing something very successful that everyone admires: *The congressman from Texas didn't exactly go out in a blaze of glory after being kicked off several committees and then resigning.*

B

bleed

bleed someone dry
to make the financial situation of a person, country, organization, etc. weaker by making it use all its money, strength, and energy: *Six years of legal battles have bled the Kentucky company dry.*

blessing

be a blessing in disguise
used to say that something that seemed to be completely bad when it happened has had good results, or may have good results: *The riots may be a blessing in disguise, if they make the community come together and work on its problems.*

count your blessings
used to tell someone to think about the good things in their situation, and be happy that it is not worse: *If you're feeling stress, take a look at the things that don't stress you out and count your blessings.*

be a mixed blessing
used to say that a good situation, or something nice or useful, is not completely good but has some bad things about it: *Owning your home is a mixed blessing, as it means that you are responsible for repairs and maintenance.*

blind

⇨be FLYING blind
the blind (are) leading the blind
used to say that people who do not know much about what they are doing are helping or advising those who know nothing at all: *The first job was the blind leading the blind – they thought we were the experts, but we'd had very little experience.*

blindfolded

someone can do something blindfolded
used to say that it is very easy for someone to do something, because they have done it often: *Morrill was an alcoholic, but he could sail a boat blindfolded.*

blink

before you could blink
(also **before you could blink/bat an eye**)
used to say that something happened very quickly, and surprised you: *When the kids are at home I spend a lot more – I go through fifty dollars before I can blink an eye.*

be/go on the blink
SPOKEN if an electric or electronic piece of equipment goes on the blink, it stops working correctly: *The VCR's on the blink again.*
—see also **be on the FRITZ**

in the blink of an eye
if something happens or a situation changes in the blink of an eye, it happens or changes very quickly: *Her mood could change from despair to excitement in the blink of an eye, and change back again just as quickly.*

block

someone's **been around the block (a few times)**
SPOKEN used to say that someone has a lot of experience of life in general or of a particular kind of situation: *I was mainly angry at myself. I've been around the block a few times, and I should have known what to expect.*

be/come/get off the (starting) blocks
(also **be/come/get out of the blocks**)
to start happening, or to start doing something ◆ OFTEN USED IN NEWSPAPERS, ON TELEVISION NEWS, ETC.: *The election campaign is now well and truly off the starting blocks.*

> NOTE▶ The place where runners begin a race is called the starting blocks.

knock someone's **block off**
SPOKEN to hit someone very hard: *If you touch my stuff, I'll knock your block off.*

a stumbling block
used about a problem or difficulty that is likely to stop people from achieving something ◆ OFTEN USED IN NEWSPAPERS, ON TELEVISION NEWS, ETC.: *A major stumbling*

block to starting peace talks is the difficulty of finding a chairman whom both sides will accept.

blood

bad blood (between)

anger or unfriendly feelings between people who have had an argument or annoyed each other: *Young felt it was time to reunite the group. Any bad blood that had been between them was forgotten.*

blood is thicker than water

used to say that family relationships are stronger and more important than any other kind: *There's this common belief that blood is thicker than water, that children belong with their natural parents.*

someone's **blood runs cold**

used to say that someone feels very frightened or shocked: *When she heard his voice again on the phone, it made her blood run cold.*

blood, sweat, and tears

a very large amount of effort that you use to try to achieve something: *Excellent progress is being made, but there are still many problems to solve and a great deal of blood, sweat, and tears ahead.*

have (someone's) blood on your hands

to be responsible for someone's death: *He has my son's blood on his hands, and I hope it haunts him for the rest of his life.*

in cold blood

if someone is killed in cold blood, they are killed deliberately, not in a fight or by someone who is frightened or angry: *He had killed two policemen in cold blood, and he knew that they would never stop looking for him.*

something **is in your/the blood**

used to say that you are naturally good at doing something, and always want to do it, especially when it is something that your parents or other people in your family did: *"Marty, you've just won top honors at the car show. Any chance you'll be here next year with a new car?" "Yeah, sure, it's in my blood now. I can't stop."*
have *something* **in your blood:** *Jen has*

running in her blood – her mother is the former state cross-country champion.

be like getting blood out of a stone
(also **be like getting blood out of a turnip**)

used to say that it is very difficult to make someone give you something or tell you something: *Getting Texans to vote for tax increases is like getting blood out of a turnip.*
—see also *something* **is like pulling teeth (TOOTH)**

something **makes my/your blood boil**

SPOKEN used to say that something makes you very angry: *He had no right to conceal this information – the whole thing makes my blood boil.*

new/fresh/young blood

new people who join a group or organization, and bring new ideas and energy ♦ OFTEN USED IN BUSINESS AND POLITICS: *It's time to get some new blood in the department.*

be out for blood

to be very determined to defeat someone, punish them, or show them how angry you are: *These two are old political enemies, and they're out for blood.*

smell blood

to realize that you have a chance to defeat or harm an opponent, and to be eager to try to do this ♦ OFTEN USED IN NEWSPAPERS, ON TELEVISION NEWS, ETC.: *The worst thing you can do when you're making a deal is to seem desperate to do it. That makes the other guy smell blood, and then you're dead.*
—see also **taste BLOOD**

sweat blood

to work extremely hard in order to achieve something: *People have sweated blood to build up their businesses, and now they feel threatened.*

taste blood

to gain enough of an advantage, or be able to do enough harm to an opponent that you want to try to do more ♦ OFTEN USED IN NEWSPAPERS, ON TELEVISION NEWS, ETC.: *The Democrats tasted blood that day and began to fight.*

B

—see also **smell BLOOD**

be too rich for your blood

used to say that something is too expensive for you: *"This one is priced at $359.95." "Good price, but a little too rich for my blood."*

bloodied/bloody

bloodied/bloody but unbowed

used to say that although an argument or criticism has affected someone badly, it will not prevent them from continuing with what they were doing or thinking: *Cranston declared, "I come before you bloodied but unbowed," and vowed to continue with his campaign.*

blood vessel

(almost/nearly) burst a blood vessel

SPOKEN used to say that someone is very angry or upset: *When I told Dad where we had been, he almost burst a blood vessel.*

blow

⇨lose/blow your **COOL**

blow hot and cold

to keep changing your attitude about someone or something, especially when you sometimes seem to like them or be excited about them, and sometimes seem the opposite: *It's hard to know exactly what Tony thinks of people. He blows hot and cold a lot.*

blow *something* sky-high

to destroy a plan, especially by telling everyone about a secret, which you think everyone ought to know about ♦ OFTEN USED ABOUT POLITICS AND BUSINESS: *It will blow the Presidential campaign sky-high if this information becomes public.*

blow *something* wide open

1 to provide new information that changes a situation completely and makes the result much more uncertain: *The case blew wide open once the military advisors found out who had been involved in the incident.*
2 to tell people about something such as a plan that has been kept secret: *We could go down to Miami, call the papers,*

and blow the whole thing wide open.

a body blow

something that makes someone extremely upset or disappointed, or that causes something to be badly damaged or destroyed ♦ OFTEN USED IN NEWSPAPERS, ON TELEVISION NEWS, ETC.: *The photos were a body blow to Mary, who never thought that her husband was the type to have affairs.*

—see also **deal a BLOW to, a death BLOW**

come to blows

if two people who are angry with each other come to blows, they begin to fight: *The two actors almost came to blows on several occasions, and by the end of the filming they would not speak to each other.*

deal a blow to

to have a bad effect on someone or something, and make people's plans or efforts less likely to succeed ♦ OFTEN USED IN NEWSPAPERS, ON TELEVISION NEWS, ETC.: *Hopes of economic recovery were dealt a severe blow yesterday when unemployment rose again.*

—see also **a body BLOW, a death BLOW**

a death blow

an action or event that makes something fail or end ♦ OFTEN USED IN NEWSPAPERS, ON TELEVISION NEWS, ETC.: *The fighting that erupted on Friday was a death blow to the latest attempts at a cease-fire.*

—see also **a body BLOW, deal a BLOW to**

soften/cushion the blow

to make the results of a decision or event less bad, or to make it easier for someone to accept them: *Divorce is traumatic for a child, but counseling could help soften the blow.*

strike a blow for

to do something that helps an idea, a belief, or a group of people: *Striking a blow for consumers, Congress voted to limit the amount of interest credit card companies could charge.*
opposite **strike a blow against:** *They sincerely believed that they were striking a blow against racism.*

blue

out of the blue

if something happens or someone does something out of the blue, you have no reason to expect it and it surprises you: *This man I was interviewing asked me out of the blue if I'd go out to dinner with him.*

bluff

call *someone's* bluff

to tell someone to do what they are threatening to do, because you do not believe that they can do it: *You can tell your boss that you've been offered another job, but he may call your bluff.*

board

above board

used to say that an arrangement, organization, or activity is completely honest and legal, and is exactly what it seems to be: *I'm sure that everything is above board, but the I.R.S. wants to check the records.*

across the board

in a way that affects everyone or everything in a particular group, place, or situation ♦ OFTEN USED IN BUSINESS AND POLITICS: *Many industries, except the health care field, are cutting jobs across the board.*

come on board

to begin working for a company, political organization, team, etc. ♦ OFTEN USED IN BUSINESS OR POLITICS: *Linda Perez came on board as the city's new police auditor.*

---

go back to the drawing board

bring *someone* **on board:** *The agency plans to bring 91 new inspectors on board by the end of the summer.*

go back to the drawing board

to start with a completely new plan or idea after other things have failed: *We had to go back to the drawing board several times to revise our software.*

go by the boards

used to say that an activity is no longer being done, or an idea is no longer being used: *Plans for a skating rink at Sarasota's Civic Center went by the boards due to lack of local funding.*

take *something* on board

1 to listen to, understand, and accept something that you are told ♦ OFTEN USED IN FORMAL DISCUSSIONS: *We'll try to take as many of your comments on board as we can.*
2 to accept new work or a new duty ♦ OFTEN USED IN BUSINESS: *If we see any new business, we take it on board, so we always have too much work and not enough people.*

tread the boards

OLD-FASHIONED to work as an actor or actress: *There are not many comics left worthy of the old vaudevillians who once trod the boards.*

boat

be in the same boat

SPOKEN used to say that people are in the same situation, and have the same problems: *During the Depression everyone was in the same boat. We all had to do without a lot.*

miss the boat

to fail to take an opportunity that would give you an advantage, especially in business or a competition: *Investors may be missing the boat if they are still waiting for prices to fall.*

rock the boat

to avoid doing something that makes a situation more difficult, such as criticizing it or trying to change it ♦ USED ESPECIALLY IN THE NEGATIVE: *They just wanted to ignore the problems in their community. It was as if they were saying, "We have a pretty good life here. Let's not rock the boat."*

what/whatever floats your boat
SPOKEN used to talk about something that someone likes or is very interested in: *You just go on and do whatever floats your boat. It doesn't bother me.*

body
⇨a body BLOW

body and soul
used to say that all your energy, thoughts, and attention are being used to do something: *This was war, and we belonged to the U.S. Army, body and soul.*

keep body and soul together
to earn enough money to buy the food and other things that you need to live, but no more: *Young adults are struggling to keep body and soul together at a time which is becoming almost a full-blown depression.*

over my dead body
SPOKEN used to say that you disagree very strongly with something that has been suggested or planned, and that you will not let it happen: *"Is Matt going to move in with us?" "Over my dead body."*

a warm body
1 SPOKEN used about someone who you do not name in order to say that they are not interesting or special in any way, or in order to say that they lack a particular good quality such as intelligence, kindness, etc.: *I have met an abundance of lonely women who are in search of a companion or just a warm body.*
2 SPOKEN used to emphasize that you are talking about a person and not a machine, especially because you think too many machines are being used instead of people: *There are so many machines answering the phone these days that a person should consider himself lucky to find a warm body at the other end of the line.*

boil
⇨it (all) COMEs/boils down to

bolt

a bolt from the blue
(also **a bolt out of the blue**)
used about something that happens suddenly and surprises everyone: *The storm in the Bay Area hit like a bolt from the blue.*

bomb

be the bomb
SLANG used to say that something is extremely good or exciting: *Some skinny girls just think they're the bomb, but I like it when girls have more shape.*

bombshell

drop a bombshell
to shock and surprise people by telling them about an important decision, or something unexpected that has happened
♦ OFTEN USED IN NEWSPAPERS, ON TELEVISION NEWS, ETC.: *Just before Christmas the company dropped a bombshell: they would be cutting 400 jobs in the new year.*
be a bombshell: *News of the experiment in low-temperature fusion came as a bombshell to the scientific community.*

bone

as dry as a bone
very dry, or completely dry: *We haven't had any rain for weeks. The land is as dry as a bone.*

the bare bones (of)
the most basic and important parts of something, especially a story, description, system, or plan: *Concentrate on the bare bones of the story – a news report shouldn't have too much detail.*
bare-bones: *Even this bare-bones program of maintenance will cost us $12 million a year.*

a bone of contention
a subject that people disagree about, especially for a long time: *The only real bone of contention in our marriage has been Cathy's smoking. I can't stand it.*

close to the bone
used about a remark or story that people do not like to talk about because it

embarrasses or upsets them: *Their conversation seemed to be getting close to the bone, and the woman tried to change the subject.*

cut/pare *something* to the bone
to reduce the amount or number of something as much as possible in order to save money ♦ OFTEN USED IN BUSINESS: *Companies have cut costs to the bone, in order to remain competitive.*

> NOTE▶ You may hear people use stronger verbs such as "strip" and "shave" with this idiom: *We've stripped the budget to the bone – we don't have the money for any luxuries.*

feel/know *something* in your bones
to feel sure that something is true or has happened, although you do not have any proof of it: *I could feel in my bones that something was very wrong.*

have a bone to pick with *someone*
SPOKEN used to tell someone that you are annoyed with them about something and want to talk to them about it: *Okay, I have a bone to pick with you – where'd you put all my computer stuff?*

> NOTE▶ This idiom comes from the idea that two dogs with only one bone will fight over it.

jump *someone's* bones
SLANG a rude expression meaning to have sex with someone: *Luke isn't interested in a relationship – he just wants to jump your bones.*

make no bones about *something*
(also **no bones about it**)
to be willing to tell everyone what you think or what you are doing, without feeling nervous or ashamed about it: *We offer a very expensive service, and we make no bones about it.*

(down) to the bone
to the most basic or central part of your character, or affecting your most basic feelings: *He was a large cheerful man – good-hearted to the bone.* | *The blues that she sings go right down to the bone.*

bonkers
⇨**DRIVE** *someone* **crazy/bonkers**

book

can't/don't/shouldn't judge a book by its cover
used to say that someone may be different from what they seem to be: *I know you want to trust him, but you can't judge a book by its cover.*

close the book on *something*
1 to accept that a difficult or unpleasant situation is over, and to stop thinking or worrying about it: *We are closing the book on the painful past and looking to the future.*
2 to stop working on something, especially a legal case, because you have done all that you need to do or all that you can do: *It's time to close the book on the Merton case.*

cook the books
to dishonestly change financial records and figures in order to steal money, or change official records in order to make an organization seem more successful than it is: *Anderson was accused of cooking the software company's books in order to avoid paying taxes.*

do *something* by the book
(also **go/play by the book**)
to be careful to follow all the rules or laws, or use the accepted methods when you do something: *Most managers will tell you that going by the book is the most effective way to get things done.*

be/get in *someone's* good books
if you are in someone's good books, you have done things that please them, especially when it is someone who is not easy to please: *I started attending every meeting, hoping to get back into Jeff's good books.*
opposite **be in** *someone's* **bad books**: *Gray's in our bad books at the moment because he lost a really important account for us.*

hit/crack the books
to study very hard: *If you want a scholarship to college, you'd better start hitting the books now.*

in my book
SPOKEN said when you are telling someone your own opinion about something, especially in order to emphasize that it is different from other people's opinions: *In my book, the Bulls' defense makes them the best team in the league.*

be one for the books
SPOKEN used to say that something is unusual and surprising: *Williams' first-inning home run is his 34th this year – that's one for the books.*

an open book
used about someone who does not hide what they are feeling, or who does not have any secrets about their life: *Helen's an open book. She won't be able to keep any secrets from her father.*

read *someone* like a book
to be able to understand exactly what someone is thinking or feeling: *I know Bob was upset – I can read him like a book.*

throw the book at *someone*
to give someone the worst possible punishment for a crime or for something they have done wrong: *The Federal Court judge threw the book at Mason, and recommended no parole.*

someone wrote the book on *something*
used to say that someone knows a lot about a subject or is very good at an activity, especially because they developed it or did it first: *Sam's great, I mean he wrote the book on how to be a supportive husband.*

boom

a baby boom
a period of years during which a greater number of babies are born than normal: *The number of people aged 45 to 54 will double over the next 15 years because of the baby boom of the late 1950s.*
baby boomer: *Bill Clinton is a baby boomer, and it is his generation, born after World War II, who are making policies now.*

lower the boom on
to become more strict in dealing with a problem and punishing the people involved: *The government outlined tough measures to lower the boom on tax evaders.*

boot

die with your boots on
to keep working hard at your job until you die or until you are unable to work anymore: *The thought of retirement scares the hell out of me. I'm one of those people who'll probably die with his boots on.*

give *someone* the boot
SPOKEN to dismiss someone from their job, or to end a relationship with someone: *It was not entirely her fault, but they gave her the boot anyway.*
get the boot: *People are afraid to complain, in case they get the boot.*

give *something* a boot
SPOKEN to kick something: *The door's stuck – give it a good boot.*

lick *someone's* boots
to obey someone in authority completely and treat them as though they are very important and special because you want to please them, especially when this makes you seem weak and silly: *We all know you used to lick his boots when he was your boss – so don't start criticizing him now.*

quake/shake in your boots
SPOKEN to feel very afraid: *It's obvious we're scared about the game. We're quaking in our boots.*

... to boot
used at the end of a series of remarks, to emphasize that the last is true in addition to the rest: *The bride was young, pretty, and from a wealthy family to boot.*

bootstraps

pull yourself up by your (own) bootstraps
to improve your situation by your own efforts without help from anyone else: *It was a mistake to think that a nation in economic decline can pull itself up by its own bootstraps.*

booty

shake your booty
OLD-FASHIONED SLANG to dance to popular music, especially in a way that is meant to be sexually attractive: *All right! It's time to shake your booty to some of the smoothest sounds around!*

bored

be bored stiff
(also **be bored to tears**)
SPOKEN to feel extremely bored: *The weather was terrible on Sunday, and the kids were bored stiff.* | *I get bored to tears doing the same thing all day, every day.*
—see also **be bored out of your MIND/skull**

boss

show *someone* who's boss
to make another person realize that you have control over them, or that you have more power and authority than they do: *It was clear in the second half of the game that the Badgers had let the other team know who was boss.*

bottle

hit the bottle
to start drinking too much alcohol, often because you are very unhappy or upset about something: *He went back east and drifted around, hit the bottle and got picked up a few times by the cops.*

bottom

⇨the bottom of the heap/pile —see the **TOP of the heap/pile**
⇨you can bet your bottom **DOLLAR**

the bottom drops out of your world/life
used to say that you are very disappointed or unhappy, and feel that there is no reason for your life to continue: *The bottom dropped out of our lives when our son died.*

the bottom falls/drops out (of the market)
used to say that people stop buying something, so that the people who sell it cannot make any money: *On Thursday October 24th, 1929, the bottom fell out of the New York stock market.*

from the bottom of your heart
SPOKEN used to say that you mean something very sincerely, especially when you are thanking someone: *I would like to say, from the bottom of my heart, how much we all admire you for what you have done.*

get to the bottom of *something*
to find the real cause of a problem or situation, when this is difficult and takes time: *The police never did get to the bottom of Dick's involvement in the land sale.*

hit/reach rock bottom
(also **be at rock bottom**)
1 to be in a very bad situation that you think could not possibly be worse: *I was at rock bottom, and I decided I had to try to give up heroin.*
2 to be at a very low level: *After six months of working without visible results, our morale and sense of purpose had hit rock bottom.*
rock-bottom: *All CDs are at rock-bottom prices, for this week only.*

knock the bottom out of *something*
to make it impossible for a business activity to continue or be successful: *The food poisoning scare had knocked the bottom out of the restaurant business.*

be/lie at the bottom of *something*
to be the basic cause of a problem or situation: *I think that lack of money is at the bottom of many family problems.*

bought

someone (has) bought it
OLD-FASHIONED used to say that someone has been killed: *The Major yelled "Lang's bought it. Get him out of the jeep."*

bounds

something knows no bounds
used to say that something is much greater than usual or seems to have no limit: *Abigail wanted her sixth-graders' imaginations to know no bounds.*

be out of bounds
if a place is out of bounds, you are not allowed to go there: *After the bomb scare,*

the town was declared out of bounds to soldiers and their families.

overstep the bounds/limits

to offend people by doing or saying things that you should not do or say: *"In my opinion, the government is overstepping its bounds,"* Thomas said. *"Wearing seatbelts should be a choice, not a law."*

bow

bow and scrape

to show too much respect and politeness to someone in authority, or someone who is famous, especially when this makes you seem weak or silly: *Why do you bow and scrape to her so much? You need to stand up for yourself.*

bowl

⇨ live in a FISH bowl

box

⇨ box someone **into a corner** —see **back** someone **into a CORNER**

⇨ **FEEL boxed in**

open (a) Pandora's box

if a new development, action, or decision opens a Pandora's box, it causes a lot of problems that did not exist before: *In questions of authors' and publishers' rights, the Internet has opened Pandora's box.*

right out of the box

as soon as you start an activity: *He was our first choice for the job right out of the box.*

think outside the box

SPOKEN to think in a way that shows imagination and an ability to solve difficult problems in new or unusual ways: *His marketing strategies are looking tired. We need someone who can think outside the box a little more.*

boy

⇨ MAMA's boy

the boy/girl next door

used about someone who is just like the average person, not rich, not famous, not extremely beautiful, etc.: *Doris Day was* dressed by the studios to look like the girl next door.

boy-next-door: *Howard still projects that boy-next-door wholesomeness on screen.*

boys and/with toys

used to say that men like to own fast cars, the most modern electronic equipment, etc.: *We stood watching the guys with their model airplanes. Bonnie shook her head. "Boys with their toys,"* she said.

the boys in blue

OLD-FASHIONED the police: *The TV show "Cops" follows the boys in blue on their daily patrol.*

boys will be boys

SPOKEN used to say that it is natural for boys to be noisy and messy, or to behave badly and do things that are not sensible: *Darren, don't knock over the bird feeder! Watch where you're going! Oh, well, boys will be boys, I suppose.*

someone's **fair-haired boy**

OLD-FASHIONED used about a boy or man who is treated better than anyone else by his teacher, employer, or parent because they think he does everything right and do not notice his faults: *My brother was always the fair-haired boy of the family; I never could compete.*

the old boy/boys' network

when men from rich families who went to the same school, belong to the same club, etc. use their influence to help each other: *A bunch of disk jockeys formed the core of an old boys' network that was capable of making or breaking new hit records.*

be one of the boys

to be part of a group of men who are friendly and spend time together, doing the ordinary things that men are expected to do: *Steve was one of the boys – basketball on Saturday afternoon and a few beers at the local bar in the evening.*

> NOTE▶ You may hear people describe a woman as being "one of the boys" if she is friends with a group of men and likes doing the things they do.

a whipping boy

used about someone or something that is blamed when things go wrong in order to take attention away from the real person or thing that is to blame: *When something goes wrong in a county, the local supervisors use the state as their whipping boy.*

brain

⇨a **BIRD** brain
⇨bored out of your **MIND/skull**
⇨be a **NO-BRAINER**

beat *someone's* **brains out**
to hit someone very hard because you are extremely angry with them: *A crowd had formed around Mike and Randy, who were in the process of beating each other's brains out.*

blow *someone's* **brains out**
to kill someone by shooting them in the head: *He expected the cops to open the door any minute and blow his brains out.*

the brain drain
a situation in which people in a particular profession or business go abroad or to another business or industry to work because they will be paid more for their work there: *The company suffered from brain drain as top brokers left to form their own companies or make higher commissions elsewhere.*

be the brains behind *something*
to be the person or people who thought of and developed a successful and often complicated plan, system, or organization: *Even though Stronti's in jail, he will continue to be the brains behind the operation.*

have a brain fart
SPOKEN a humorous expression used to say that you cannot remember something for a short period of time: *I can't answer your question right now – I'm having a brain fart.*

> NOTE▶ Many people think the word "fart" is rude and may be offended if you use it.

have *something* on the brain
to keep thinking about something all the time so that it annoys you: *Man, you have surfing on the brain. Can't you think about anything else?*

pick *someone's* **brain/brains**
SPOKEN to ask someone a lot of questions, and find out everything that they know about something: *I need to pick your brain to get a few ideas for a good present for Rob.*

rack your brain/brains
to try very hard to think of an idea or remember something: *I racked my brain trying to remember the name of that restaurant.*

brainstorm

have a brainstorm
to suddenly have a very good idea that solves a problem or helps you make progress: *I was two miles into my run when I suddenly had a brainstorm about starting up this new business.*

brakes

put the brakes on (*something*)
(also **put on the brakes**)
to make a process or activity stop happening, or happen more slowly, especially by making less money available ◆ OFTEN USED IN BUSINESS: *We have managed to put the brakes on inflation, but healthcare costs are still rising.*

brass

⇨get down to brass **TACKs**
⇨go/reach/grab for the brass **RING**

breach

step into the breach
to help by doing someone else's work when they are unable to do it: *"Who'll step into the breach when Armstrong resigns?" "My guess is it'll be Wilson."*

bread

someone's **bread and butter**
1 the way that someone earns most of their money: *Nina sells paintings once in awhile, but working in the lab is her bread and butter.*
2 (also **the bread and butter of** *something*) the most basic and usual parts of a job, profession, or situation: *Boring technical analysis seems to be the bread and butter of sports writing these days.*

B

bread-and-butter: *Their bread-and-butter product is a database program for small businesses.*
—compare **the MEAT and potatoes of** *something*

break bread with *someone*
OLD-FASHIONED to show that you are friendly with a person or group by eating a meal with them: *The homeless shelter is urging everyone to come down to join the meal and break bread with different parts of the community.*

cast your bread upon the waters
to take a risk without expecting to get any advantage from it: *Meeting Brooke here was a surprise; he'd cast his bread upon the waters, and now it was coming back to him.*

> NOTE▶ This idiom comes from a line in the book of *Ecclesiastes* in the Bible.

earn your bread
to earn the money that you need in order to live: *Myra earns her bread giving tours of the island to visitors.*

someone knows which side his/her bread is buttered on
used to say that someone knows they must help, obey, or support another person in order to get an advantage: *Wendy won't do anything to upset Phil. She knows which side her bread's buttered on.*

someone thinks *something* is the best/greatest thing since sliced bread
used when someone else thinks that something is extremely good, useful, or important, often when you do not agree: *Dan keeps talking about his new cell phone like it's the greatest thing since sliced bread.*

breadth

be/come within a hair's breadth of doing *something*
to nearly do something that could have bad results: *I came within a hair's breadth of losing both my wife and daughter in the crash.*

break

⇨**GO for broke**
⇨**if it AIN'T broke, don't fix it**

a clean break
a clear and definite ending to a bad relationship or situation so that you can start something new without any troubles from the past: *I heard that his wife left him and he wanted to make a clean break – anyway, that's the reason he gave for quitting the job.*

get an even break
to be as likely to get something that you want as everyone else ◆ OFTEN USED IN THE NEGATIVE: *When will women get an even break in the workplace? Statistics show that they still have to work twice as hard for less money.*

give *someone* **an even break:** *All I'm asking is for you to give me an even break, so I can show you that I can do the job.*

give me a break!
1 SPOKEN said when you do not believe what someone has just said: *"It took me almost an hour to finish." "Oh, give me a break, there's no way it took that long."*
2 SPOKEN (also **give** *someone* **a break**) used to tell someone to stop trying to make you or someone else do something, or to stop criticizing someone: *Come on, give him a break. It's only his second day on the job.*

make a break for it
(also **make a break for** *something*)
to suddenly start running in order to escape from a place: *While police were surrounding the building, one hostage made a break for the door.*

breakfast

eat *someone* for breakfast
to defeat someone easily in business, a fight, an argument, etc.: *Guys like Jordan could eat you for breakfast.*

breast

make a clean breast of *something*
to admit that you have done something wrong so that you can deal with the problem or stop feeling guilty: *Mrs. Abberly made a clean breast of it and returned the money.*

breath

be a breath of fresh air
used in order to say that someone has made a situation more interesting and exciting with their new ideas or new ways of doing things: *It's a breath of fresh air to see a movie that uses young, unknown actors so well.*

catch your breath
to have time to think or rest in the middle of a busy or difficult situation: *The city didn't even have time to catch its breath before the next storm hit.*

> NOTE▶ If you "catch your breath" when you have been running or doing exercise, you stop for a minute to try to breathe more normally.

don't hold your breath
(also **I wouldn't hold my breath**)
SPOKEN used in order to tell someone not to wait for something to happen because you think that it will not happen: *"When do you think I'll get the money?" "Don't hold your breath."* | *I hope that the economy is picking up again, but I wouldn't hold my breath.*

don't waste your breath
(also **save your breath**)
SPOKEN used in order to tell someone not to say anything because there is nothing they can say that will change the situation: *Don't waste your breath making excuses – I can see you're drunk.*

in the same breath
used in order to emphasize that it is strange that someone has said two things at the same time that are very different from each other: *First he said that the incident had damaged the police force's reputation, and in the same breath he said he thought there was a lot of respect for the police in the city.*

say *something* under your breath
to say something, usually something unpleasant, in a quiet voice so that no one can hear you: *Reynolds said something under his breath and stomped angrily back into his office.*

take your breath away
if something that you see or hear takes your breath away, it is so beautiful, exciting, or surprising that you stop and look and think: *The statue of Venus, the most beautiful piece in the museum, takes your breath away.*

take your breath away

with bated breath
feeling very worried, excited, or anxious: *So now I have to wait with bated breath to find out if I've been accepted into law school.*

breathe

breathe easier/easy
to feel safe or relaxed again after you have been afraid or worried: *At about 6:20 a.m., we were sure that the reactor was being shut down safely. "We all breathed easier at that point," Slocum said.*

breeze

be a breeze
SPOKEN used to say that something is very easy to do: *"I don't think I've studied enough for this test." "You'll do great. It'll be a breeze!"*

shoot the breeze/bull
to talk in an informal and friendly way about lots of different things, usually things that are not very important: *We thought the meetings were too relaxed – boys sitting around shooting the breeze instead of discussing the critical issues.*

brick

⇨**built like a brick SHITHOUSE**
⇨**drop** *someone/something* **like a hot**

brick —see **drop** someone/something like a hot **POTATO**
⇨hit a brick **WALL**
⇨hit someone like a **TON** of bricks
⇨like talking to a (brick) **WALL**

shit a brick
(also **be shitting bricks**)
SLANG an impolite way of saying that someone is extremely frightened or worried about something: *I almost shit a brick the first time I had to speak in front of everyone.*

> NOTE▶ Some people may think "shit" is offensive. It is better not to use it.

bridge

⇨**bridge the GAP**
build bridges
to try to establish a better relationship between people or groups who do not agree or do not like each other: *The local police have been trying to build bridges between the two neighborhoods.*

burn your bridges
to do something that destroys your chances of being part of a situation or relationship that you were involved in before: *She couldn't go back to Boston now. She'd burned all her bridges by cutting her ties with Tammy and her family.*

cross that bridge when you come to it
SPOKEN used to say that you will think about or deal with a problem when it happens rather than worry about it now: *When Weiss was asked how they were going to finance the project next July she responded, "We'll cross that bridge when we come to it."*

bright-eyed

bright-eyed and bushy-tailed
SPOKEN full of energy and ready to start doing something: *Two hours after her operation, Bea was sitting up in bed, bright-eyed and bushy-tailed as ever.*

bring

bring someone up short
to surprise or confuse someone so that

they stop what they are saying or doing in order to think for a moment: *A translator is often brought up short by very simple words and expressions that have no exact equivalent in another language.*

britches

someone is/gets too big for their britches
used about someone who is becoming too proud and confident, and who treats other people as if they are not as important: *Jason's been acting a little too big for his britches ever since he made the football team.*

broom

a new broom
(also **a new broom sweeps (something) clean**)
used about a new person in a position of authority who deals with problems and makes a lot of changes in a company, organization, etc. in order to make it better: *Everyone was hoping that the new police chief would be the new broom who would sweep the city clean.*

brownie

get brownie points
(also **score, win, earn, etc. brownie points**)
to do something that makes you seem impressive and makes people like you: *My husband definitely scored some brownie points last night after cooking me a fantastic gourmet dinner.*

> NOTE▶ A "Brownie" is a young girl who is in the lowest level of an international social organization called the Girl Scouts which trains girls in practical skills and helps them to develop their character. Brownies get special rewards for doing nice things, which is where the idea of "Brownie points" comes from.

bruising

someone is cruising for a bruising
SLANG used to say that someone is being so annoying or stupid that they are very likely to get into trouble, a fight, an

argument, etc.: *I'm ready to kill Todd – he's been cruising for a bruising all week.*

brunt

bear/take the brunt of *something*
to receive or feel the worst effects of an attack, criticism, or a bad situation: *It is always the small businesses that take the brunt of a recession.*

brush

paint *something* with a broad brush
to describe or explain something in a very general way, without giving details: *Scott's biography paints details with a broad brush, making the account overly simplistic.*
broad-brush: *You can take a broad-brush approach in your first few paragraphs, but then you must start treating the main questions in detail.*

tar *someone* with the same brush
to unfairly blame someone for the faults or crimes of other people who are similar or from the same group: *Paul, you can't tar every woman with the same brush just because things didn't go well for you and Claire.*

brush-off

give *someone* the brush-off
to tell or show someone in an impolite way that you do not want to be friendly with them or be involved with them: *Most of the doctors she has seen about her problem have just given her the brush-off. They say she should see a psychiatrist.*
get the brush-off: *The movie centers around a young hot-shot sales executive who gets the brush-off from his female boss.*

bubble

burst *someone's* bubble
to do something that destroys someone's happiness or hopes: *Well I hate to burst your bubble, but the trip just isn't going to work out.*

burst the bubble
to do something that ends a happy or successful situation: *The Sharks went into the game with confidence, but the Penguins burst the bubble by beating them 5–3.*

be on the bubble
used about the person who is most likely to lose their job, or the part of a business that is most likely to lose financial support, if there is not enough money for everyone ◆ USED ESPECIALLY IN NEWSPAPERS, ON TELEVISION NEWS, ETC.: *Evans and Getz are on the bubble as the coaching staff tries to reduce the number of players from 37 to 23.*

buck

⇨look like a million **DOLLARs/bucks**

the buck stops here
used to say that you are the person who is responsible for something that needs to be dealt with: *I think the captain knows that the buck stops with him and that he'll have to take responsibility.*

pass the buck
to blame someone else or try to make them responsible for a problem that you should deal with: *Burton criticized his colleagues in the state legislature for failing in their duties and passing the buck to the counties.*
buck-passing: *After two months of buck-passing by the embassy, I made a phone call and found an answer for myself.*

bucket

⇨a **DROP** in the bucket

kick the bucket
SPOKEN a humorous expression meaning to die: *When I finally kick the bucket, I want to be buried on top of a mountain or somewhere wild.*

bud

nip *something* in the bud
to stop a bad situation before it can develop and become worse: *We've tried to nip the rumor in the bud so that people don't start thinking an earthquake is about to hit.*

buff

⇨in the buff —see in the **RAW**

bug

be bitten by the ___ bug

to become excited about a particular activity and very eager to start doing it yourself: *After spending two months in Africa and a great Christmas in New York, I have been bitten by the travel bug.*

snug as a bug (in a rug)

SPOKEN used to say that someone is very warm and comfortable ♦ OFTEN USED BY ADULTS TALKING TO CHILDREN: *You just curl up under the blanket – there, you're snug as a bug in a rug.*

bull

⇨shoot the bull —see shoot the **BREEZE**

⇨strong as a bull —see strong as a **HORSE**

(like) a bull in a china shop

used about someone who speaks or behaves in a very impolite or direct way without noticing or caring that if offends or upsets people: *You're not going to go storming in there like a bull in a china shop and ruin it all, are you?*

take the bull by the horns

to deal with a difficult situation or problem in a quick, confident, and determined way: *Sarah realized that the negotiations would get nowhere unless she took the bull by the horns.*

bullet

bite the bullet

to bravely accept something that is bad or difficult to deal with: *It looks like we're going to have to bite the bullet and buy a new computer system soon.*

be sweating bullets

SPOKEN to be very worried, anxious, or afraid about something that is happening now or could happen very soon: *I'd never had a computer just go blank on me like that. I just sat there sweating bullets until the repairman came.*

bum

⇨get a bum **STEER**

⇨get the bum's **RUSH**

bummer

that's/it's a (real) bummer
(also **what a bummer!**)

SLANG said when a situation is bad, annoying, or disappointing: *It's a real bummer. Jake's going to be on jury duty, so that means I'll be even busier than I am already.*

bun

have a bun in the oven

OLD-FASHIONED to be going to have a baby: *I heard that Stacie has a bun in the oven again.*

burn

do a slow burn

to become more and more angry over a period of time: *The coach had been doing a slow burn throughout the game, as his team lost 52–0 against the Oilers.*

burner

put *something* on the back burner

to delay dealing with something until later because there are more important things that need to be done first: *A lot of tired, stressed-out people end up putting their marriages on the back burner, forgetting to give them priority over their jobs and social lives.*

be/stay on the back burner: *Maher says the plans to lengthen the news broadcast from a half hour to one hour are on the back burner for a while.*

opposite **be on the front burner:** *The movie is once again on the front burner, with Johnny Depp picked to play the lead and filming due to start next week.*

bus

drive the porcelain bus
(also **drive the big white bus**)

SLANG to bring food up from your stomach through your mouth especially because you have drunk too much alcohol: *I walked into the bathroom and saw Paula driving the porcelain bus.*

bush

beat around the bush
to talk about something without saying what you mean clearly and directly, even though the person you are talking to may not like it: *Let's not beat around the bush anymore. Sharon, we're just not happy with your performance.*

beat the bushes
to try very hard to get or achieve something ◆ OFTEN USED IN BUSINESS: *Rousten's been beating the bushes to try and get money, mostly from people in the sports and entertainment fields.*

business

the business end of a ___
the part of a tool or weapon that does the work: *The chillies were good, and hotter than the business end of a blowtorch.*

business is business
used to say that profit is the most important thing to consider in business: *"I like to have fun," said Moira, "but business is business, and I'll tear you apart in the boardroom if I have to."*

do a land-office business
if a business, store, etc. does a land-office business, it makes a lot of money: *Simmons said her travel agency had been doing a land-office business all winter.*

do *something* like nobody's business
used to emphasize that something is happening very fast, or is being done in the most complete way: *Tickets to his concerts have been selling like nobody's business. Two shows at Shoreline were sold out in a day.*

funny/monkey business
illegal activity, or behavior that is not allowed or that people do not approve of: *When they examined Nelson's tax returns they realized that there was some funny business going on.*

get down to business
to immediately start doing the most important things or talking about the most important subjects, without wasting time: *We have a lot to talk about today, so let's get down to business.*

—see also **get down to brass TACKS**

go about your business
to do the things that you normally do: *Residents in the area put on their boots and went about their business despite heavy rains.*

someone **has no business doing** *something*
SPOKEN used to say that you think someone was wrong to do something: *Mandy has no business going through my mail like that.*

someone **is not in the business of doing** *something*
used to say that someone is not doing what they are being criticized for: *We are not in the business of becoming rock stars. We just want to play the music and let people enjoy themselves.*

it is business as usual
used to say that a business, organization, etc. is working normally even though something has happened that might have stopped it from doing this: *It was business as usual today at the August Moon despite last night's bombing.*
business-as-usual: *The President tried to emphasize a business-as-usual atmosphere by answering reporters' questions.*

someone **means business**
used to say that someone is determined to do something and will not let anyone prevent them from doing it: *If you're strict and enforce the rules, everyone'll know you mean business.*

mind your own business
SPOKEN a rude expression said when you do not want to tell someone something that is private: *"Mind your own business,"* the old man warned him. *"We don't need any more trouble."*

none of your business
SPOKEN a rude expression used in order to tell someone that they do not have a right to know something private: *"What did you and Andy do last night?" "None of your business!"*

someone **was minding his/her own business**
SPOKEN used to say that someone was not doing anything unusual or wrong at the

time something bad or unfair happened to them: *I was walking along, just minding my own business, when this crazy guy just grabbed my arm and started yelling at me.*

we're in business
(also **we'll be in business**)
SPOKEN used to say that you are ready to start an activity, job, etc.: *You've got the paint – I'll get the brushes. OK, now we're in business.*

busman
⇨a busman's **HOLIDAY**

bust
⇨**GO bust**

buts

no buts (about it)
(also **no ifs, ands, or buts (about it)**)
SPOKEN said when you want to emphasize that you really mean what you are saying or that what you are saying is definitely true: *We can't change anything now – no buts about it. So just keep doing what you've been doing.*

butt
⇨someone's **ASS/butt is in a sling**
⇨**bust your ASS/butt**
⇨**cover your ASS/butt**
⇨**get your ASS/butt in gear**
⇨**haul ASS/butt**
⇨someone **is on** someone's **ASS/butt**
⇨something **kicks ASS/butt**
⇨**kick/whip** someone's **ASS/butt**
⇨**kiss my ASS/butt**

butterflies

have/get butterflies (in your stomach)
to feel very nervous before doing something: *Bates says he always has butterflies before he gets on the court, but it makes him play better.*

button

(right) on the button
1 if you arrive somewhere on the button,

you arrive exactly on time: *She's been staying out too late recently, but last night she came home right on the button.*
2 if something you say is right on the button, it is exactly the right answer or the best description of something: *Sheraton's answers were right on the button as usual, leaving the rest of us feeling a little stupid.*

push (someone's) buttons
1 (also **push/press the right buttons**) to know exactly what to do or say in order to get the reaction or result that you want: *He knows how to push his dad's buttons. All he has to do is look at Jim that way and Jim says "yes."*
2 (also **push all** someone's **buttons**) to annoy someone, sometimes when you do not intend to, by doing a lot of things that they do not like: *Man, Jamie really pushed all my buttons today. I felt like smacking him!*

buzz

get a buzz (from)
1 SPOKEN (also **catch a buzz (from)**) to get a strong feeling of physical pleasure or excitement from drinking alcohol, taking drugs, etc.: *The whole point of drinking is to get a buzz, and once you do that, it's hard to make a good decision about whether you should stop or not.* | *You catch a nice buzz, smoking one of these.*
2 SPOKEN to feel happy or excited by doing something you enjoy: *She said she gets a real buzz out of creating food and trying it out on other people.*

by

by and by
OLD-FASHIONED fairly soon: *We're improving already, and we're hoping to do better by and by.*

by the by
OLD-FASHIONED used to mention something that may be interesting but not very important: *By the by, I got a letter from Peggy last week.*

NOTE▶ "By the way" is a more modern idiom that means the same thing.

by and large
used to say that something is generally true in a particular situation: *By and large,*

the more questions you ask in a survey, the less polite people tend to be.

bygones

let bygones be bygones

used to say that you should try to forget something bad that someone has done to you and forgive them: *I was willing to let bygones be bygones, but my sister won't drop the subject.*

bypass

someone **has had a ___ bypass**

a humorous expression used in order to say that someone lacks a particular good quality completely: *It just isn't true that you need a personality bypass in order to work as an accountant.*

B

C

caboodle

⇨the whole KIT and caboodle

cage

rattle someone's **cage**
SPOKEN to do something that annoys or frightens someone: *Lamb is the sort of lawyer who likes to rattle the authorities' cages and delights in going against traditions.*

cahoots

be in cahoots (with)
SPOKEN to be working secretly with another person or group, especially doing something dishonest: *Roger was in cahoots with a group of criminals who were blackmailing the company.*

Cain

⇨raise HELL/Cain

cake

⇨be a PIECE of cake

something **takes the cake**
used to say that something is the most surprising or annoying thing you have heard: *Of all the crazy questions you've ever asked me, that one takes the cake.*

> NOTE▶ This idiom comes from a custom used in some cultures, such as the Irish-American and African-American, of giving a cake as a prize for a competition.

you can't have your cake and eat it too
used to say that you cannot have the advantages of a particular situation without experiencing the bad effects of it also: *I wish I could enjoy the kids' company without having to clean up after them, but you can't have your cake and eat it too.*
someone **wants/tries to have their cake and eat it too:** *This plan provides the advantages of a standardized system with the capacity to respond to change – a way to have your cake and eat it too.*

call

the call of nature
used to say politely that someone has to use the toilet: *Terry was answering the call of nature when a forklift driver tried to take the portable toilet away.*

a close call
1 (also **a close shave**) a situation in which you were nearly hurt or killed, or in which something bad nearly happened to you: *Residents in Southern California had a close call Thursday when a train derailed and just missed hitting several homes.*
2 a situation in which it is difficult to know which of two choices to make, or which of two things is likely to happen: *Deciding between the two applicants will be a close call. They both seem highly qualified for the job.*

there is no call to do *something*
(also *someone* **has no call to do** *something*)
SPOKEN said when you are angry because you feel that someone's criticism is unfair or unnecessary: *She needs to stop being so rude to her mother. There's just no call for that.*

a wake-up call
an event that makes people finally realize that a situation is very bad or dangerous, and that they must do something to change it, stop it, get away from it, etc.: *The Oregon game was our wake-up call. We knew we'd never get to the playoffs if we kept losing like that.*

calm

the calm/lull before the storm
a short time when things are calm before a time when there is a lot of trouble, noise, or activity: *Dave knew when his wife was angry. When she got quiet like this, it was the calm before the storm.*

camp

camp followers
people who spend their time with a particular person or group because they admire or support them or hope to gain advantages from them: *Players, caddies, referees, and camp followers made their way up to the 6th green.*

camper

someone is not a happy camper
SPOKEN used about someone who is not happy about a situation: *Dana's not a happy camper. Her car has been in the shop for two weeks now.*

can

a can of worms
when one situation or problem causes or makes you think of many other related situations or problems, especially when they will be difficult or complicated to deal with: *Ever since the casinos were opened on Indian reservations, there has been a whole can of worms opened up about the problems of gambling.*

carry the can
to say that you are responsible for something that has gone wrong ♦ OFTEN USED IN BUSINESS AND POLITICS: *When the company makes an unpopular decision, it's always the middle managers who are left to carry the can.*

in the can
if a job, an arrangement, or piece of work, especially a movie, is in the can, it is finished or made: *When this third show is finished, 26 programs will be in the can, ready for final editing.*

candle

burn the candle at both ends
to be extremely busy both at work and in your social life, often with the result that you are very tired or sick: *Carrie, you don't look very well. You've got to stop burning the candle at both ends like this.*

someone/something can't hold a candle to
(also no ___ can hold a candle to)
used to say that one thing is not nearly as good, bad, big, etc. as another: *None of the other athletes in the 400 meter hurdles final could hold a candle to Gonzalez's superb technique.*

candy

like taking candy from a baby
SPOKEN used to say that something is very easy to do: *"I've never even sat on a motorcycle before, let alone driven one." "It's easy – like taking candy from a baby."*

cannon

cannon fodder
1 ordinary people, especially soldiers with a low rank in the army, navy, etc., who are allowed to be killed or hurt during a war because the military needs to achieve its aims: *We're the cannon fodder, my friend. They're sending us in to make sure the area's cleared.*
2 used about people in any situation who are allowed to suffer in order for something else to succeed: *The problem is that police officers are society's cannon fodder. They are the ones dealing every day with the dangerous problems that society chooses to ignore.*

a loose cannon
used about someone who is likely to say or do something that will harm the group or organization they belong to, and who the organization cannot control: *Mitch was described as a loose cannon – volatile and potentially violent.*

cap

put your thinking cap on
OLD-FASHIONED to think very hard about a question or problem in order to try to find the answer: *Put your thinking cap on, Joey – we need to figure out a way to organize these files.*

capital

___ with a capital ___
(trouble with a capital T, fast with a capital F, etc.)
used with any word in order to emphasize that you are talking about an extreme type of something, for example trouble, or that something is done in an extreme way: *I was in trouble, big trouble with a capital T. | A little exercise is good for you, but it doesn't have to be exercise with a capital E.*

carbon

be a carbon copy
to be very similar to or exactly the same as someone or something else: *Judd's*

second touchdown was a carbon copy of his first.

card

⇨**have a card up your sleeve** —see **have/keep** *something* **up your SLEEVE**
⇨**the ODDS/cards are stacked against** *someone*

hold all the cards
(also **hold most of the cards**)
to have all or most of the advantages in a particular situation so that you can control what happens: *The government holds most of the cards when it comes to land conservation.*

if *someone* plays his/her cards right
used to say that if someone deals with a situation in an intelligent way, they will be successful in getting what they want: *If Susan plays her cards right, she could go to Hawaii through work and not have to take any vacation days.*

something is in the cards
used to say that something will probably happen: *The closure of the elementary school had been in the cards for years, but we didn't expect it to happen this year.*

play/keep your cards close to your chest
(also **play/keep your cards close to your vest**)
to keep your plans, thoughts, or feelings secret: *Party leaders are keeping their cards close to their chests, not wanting to reveal their opinions until the next round of voting.*

play your last card
to make a final effort to do or achieve something, after trying other methods that were not successful: *Kathy played her last card to quit smoking by going to a hypnotist.*

put/lay (all) your cards on the table
to tell people what your plans or feelings are in an honest way without keeping anything secret: *We decided that we would ask them what they could offer us first before we put our cards on the table.*

a wild card
used about someone or something that makes you worry or feel uncertain, because you do not know how they will behave, whether they will be successful, etc.: *Another wild card in the dollar-yen exchange rate is the changing political situation in Japan.*

carpet

⇨**sweep** *something* **under the carpet** —see **sweep** *something* **under the RUG**

call *someone* on the carpet
if someone in authority calls you on the carpet, they criticize or blame you for doing something wrong: *Every time one of the players does something wrong, the coach is the one who gets called on the carpet for it.*

roll out the red carpet (for *someone*)
(also **lay out the red carpet**)
to give a lot of special attention to someone who is visiting you, usually someone important or famous, in order to show that you honor and respect them: *Douglas didn't win, but we're his hometown and we're going to roll out the red carpet to welcome him home.*
red-carpet: *The French prime minister received the red-carpet treatment while he was visiting Washington, D.C. last week.*

carried

get carried away
to be so excited, angry, interested, etc. that you do or say something that is not sensible, or you forget everything else: *Mom got carried away and put half a bottle of brandy in the sauce.*

carrot

(the) carrot and (the) stick
a way of making people do what you want by giving them something good if they do it, and making something bad happen to them if they do not do it: *Most managers use both the carrot and the stick to make sure that the work gets done.*
carrot-and-stick: *We favor a carrot-and-stick approach to get unemployed people back to work.*

cart

put the cart before the horse
to do things in the wrong order, especially when this means you are doing something without the necessary preparation, or giving unimportant things more attention than important ones: *I feel we're putting the cart before the horse by planning a major advertising campaign before we have anything really good to sell.*

carte blanche

give *someone* carte blanche
to give someone complete power to do whatever they want in a particular situation: *Lisa's boss gave her carte blanche to spend any amount for the company's annual party.*

case

⇨a BASKET case
⇨case the JOINT

be a case in point
used to say that a thing, person, or situation is a good example of what you are talking about: *Package tours have changed in recent years to fit customers' needs. The cruise industry is a case in point: more and more young people are going on cruises than before.*

get off my case!
SPOKEN an impolite expression, used to tell someone who keeps criticizing you to stop: *Why don't you get off my case and think about your own problems for a while?*
—see also get/be on *someone's* CASE

get/be on *someone's* case
to keep criticizing someone or complaining about them: *My boss is always on my case about some little thing or other.*
—see also get off my CASE!

I rest my case
SPOKEN used to say that something proves what you have just been saying: *He lied about the money just like he lied when he said he'd be here today. He's not here, is he? ...I rest my case.*

NOTE▶ In the U.S., when lawyers have finished trying to prove their case in a court of law, they often say "the defense rests" or "the prosecution rests."

make a federal case out of *something*
SPOKEN to make a problem seem much more important than it really is, especially by talking about it too much: *There's no need to make a federal case out of it, Paige – I believe you!*
—see also make a MOUNTAIN out of a molehill

an open-and-shut case
used about a legal case that is easy to prove, and will not take long in a court of law: *We thought it was an open-and-shut case, but the jury took several days to decide.*

cash

cash cow
the part of a business that always produces a lot of money over a long period of time: *The shopping center just built on campus has become a real cash cow for the university.*
cash-cow: *The company faces a price war in its cash-cow personal computer business in Japan.*

(cold) hard cash
money that is available immediately, usually in the form of coins and bills: *The club has had to sell some of its prized assets to raise some hard cash.*

castles

castles in the air
used about attractive plans or hopes that are not likely to become real: *Sarah is always building castles in the air about being a movie star, but she's never even auditioned for a part.*

cat

⇨there's more than one WAY to skin a cat

(has the) cat got your tongue?
SPOKEN said when someone will not answer you or talk to you ◆ OFTEN USED BY

ADULTS TALKING TO CHILDREN: *"Did she like it?" "I dunno." "Did you talk to her?" "I dunno." "Cat got your tongue?" "No."*

copy cat
1 (also **copycat**) used about a crime, attack, etc. that is done in order to be similar to a recent and famous crime or attack: *Police are not releasing many details about the murder in order to prevent any copycat killings.*
2 SPOKEN said by children when they are annoyed because someone tries to be the same, or do the same things, as they do: *"I drew a boat." "Copy cat, so did I!"*

fat cat
used about someone who is rich and powerful and uses their position and their wealth in a way that seems unfair to you: *Fat cats in Hollywood are pushing out many of the independent filmmakers.*
fat-cat: *Every year, millions of dollars are given by fat-cat contributors to media campaigns that appeal to fear and racism.*

fight like cats and dogs
if people who know each other well fight like cats and dogs, they keep arguing, and get very angry with each other: *My sister and I used to fight like cats and dogs.*

grin/smile like a Cheshire cat
(also **smile a Cheshire cat smile**)
to have a big smile on your face so that you look stupid or too pleased with yourself: *Glover's career is doing well, but he knows better than to say anything too cocky. He just smiles that Cheshire cat smile and looks away.*

it's raining cats and dogs
used to say that it is raining hard: *The whole time we were camping it was raining cats and dogs.*

let the cat out of the bag
to let people know something that is a secret, or that they are not supposed to know until later, especially without intending to do this: *Don't let the cat out of the bag – Mom doesn't know about the party yet.*
the cat is out of the bag: *Now that the cat is out of the bag, it's probably okay to talk about the merger.*

like a cat on a hot tin roof
behaving in a way that shows you are very nervous or anxious: *Anna was pacing the floor like a cat on a hot tin roof.*

like the cat that ate the canary
used about someone who is very pleased about something that they have done or something that has happened to them: *Coop grinned like the cat that ate the canary as he told us about the game.*

look like *something* the cat dragged in
SPOKEN used to say that someone looks very unattractive, for example because they are sick or not clean: *I can't believe how wet it is outside. I must look like something the cat dragged in.*

---

look like *something* **the cat dragged in**

play cat and mouse (with *someone*)
(also **play a cat and mouse game**)
1 if two people or groups are playing cat and mouse, one person or group is trying to find the other one, and the other one is trying not to be found: *For six long months, police have been playing cat and mouse with hackers who have been stealing data from the state's computer systems.*
2 to pretend that you will let someone get or do what they want, and then prevent them from getting it or doing it: *So far, offers to release the hostages are only part of an elaborate game of cat and mouse.*

when the cat's away (the mice will play)
used to say that when someone in authority is not there, people can enjoy themselves or do what they want: *"Isn't anybody doing any work around here?" "Mrs. Pinkerton isn't here today." "Oh, I see. When the cat's away, huh?"*

you could not swing a cat
(also **not enough room to swing a cat**)
SPOKEN used to say that a room is very small, or has too many things in it: *Mike's new office is so tiny – it's like a closet. There isn't enough room to swing a cat in there.*

catbird

be (sitting) in the catbird seat
SPOKEN to be in a situation where you have an advantage: *Coleman is smiling about his new role as head of the council. "I'm sitting in the catbird seat at least for a while," he said.*

catch

⇨catch some **Z'S**

catch *someone* red-handed
to see someone at the moment when they are doing something wrong: *Police had caught them red-handed trying to break into the pawn shop.*

a Catch-22 (situation)
used about a situation in which any choice you make or action you choose leads to failure or trouble: *We're really in a Catch-22 situation; if we ask politely for what we want, they'll ignore us, but if we make a fuss, they'll call us troublemakers, and say that we shouldn't be encouraged.*

> NOTE▶ This idiom comes from the title of a book about World War II by Joseph Heller. The main character is very afraid of being killed, and wishes he could persuade military officials that he is crazy so that he would not have to fly in raids (=attacks) against the enemy. However, the officials know that anyone who is so frightened cannot be crazy, and therefore he is forced to fly again and again. This is the Catch-22 situation.

catch you later
SPOKEN used when you have to end a conversation with someone suddenly in order to say that you will have a chance to talk more when you see them again: *"I'm sorry, I've got to run to class." "All right, we'll catch you later, Matt. Bye."*

be caught napping
to not be ready to deal with something when it happens, although you should be ready for it: *Experts on Eastern Europe admit that they were caught napping by the changes of 1989.*

be caught short
to not have enough of something when you really need it, especially money: *Manufacturers were caught short when the fat-free cookies were more popular than expected with consumers.*

what's the catch?
SPOKEN used when someone has told you about a very good opportunity, in order to say that there must be some problem or difficulty with it, because it seems too good to be true: *When Debbie told her husband that she bought a cell phone and the air time was free, the first thing he said was, "What's the catch?"*

someone wouldn't be caught/seen dead
used to say that someone would never do something, spend time in a place, etc. because it would make them ashamed or embarrassed: *Many fashion-conscious people wouldn't be caught dead wearing white after Labor Day.*

you wouldn't/won't catch me doing *something*
SPOKEN used to say that you would never do something: *I'm not going unless we get a car. You won't catch me walking back to the house alone at night.*

cause

a lost cause
used about something or someone that has no chance of succeeding: *Brando, who believed Cliff was a lost cause, left him to deal with his drinking problems himself.*

caution

err on the side of caution
to always choose the safe way of doing something, in order to be completely sure that you avoid any danger or problems: *Because the law is unclear, doctors tend to err on the side of caution when treating terminally ill patients.*

throw caution to the wind/winds
to stop being careful and do something that might involve a risk: *Even if you throw caution to the wind and order ice cream, you're still getting 200 grams of calcium – an important nutrient.*

ceiling

⇨**GLASS ceiling**
⇨**go through the ROOF/ceiling**

cent

not have two cents to rub together
to not have any money: *One of us has to find a job. We don't have two cents to rub together right now.*

not a/one red cent
used to emphasize that you mean no money at all: *The magazine published my article, but I never got one red cent for it.*

put/get your two cents' worth in
(also **throw in your two cents' worth**)
to give your opinion about something, even if no one has asked you for it or no one wants you to give it: *Well, if I can just put my two cents' worth in here, I don't think Kelly is the right person for the job.*

center

be the center of *someone's* universe
to be the most important person or thing in someone's life: *I was the center of my parents' universe – we did everything together.*

ceremony

not stand on ceremony
used to tell someone not to worry about the formal rules of polite behavior: *This is not the time for our leaders to stand on ceremony. Instead we must unite and fight for what we believe in.*

chain

yank *someone's* chain
SPOKEN to deliberately tell someone something that is untrue, as a joke or in order to annoy them: *Every time I see Justin, he tells me a different version of what happened. Is he yanking my chain, or what?*

challenged

vertically challenged
(also **socially, chronologically, etc. challenged**)
a humorous expression used about someone who is not very tall, not very good at talking to people in social situations, getting old, etc.: *I'm pleading for all of us out there who are vertically challenged – and by that I mean people under five foot three inches.* | *Some of the candidates for governor seemed extremely charismatically challenged. They bored voters to death in their speeches.*

chance

blow your chance
to miss an important opportunity to do something, by making a mistake or behaving stupidly: *Wayne keeps calling and saying he wants to get back together, but I told him he's already blown his chance.*

(the) chances are (that)
SPOKEN said when you think that something is likely to happen: *If you like the house, chances are that other people will like it too, so you have to act quickly.*

fat chance
SPOKEN used when someone has suggested that something might happen, in order to say that you are sure it will not: *"Maybe they'll give you some more money." "Yeah, fat chance."*
—see also **a fat LOT of good it does** *someone*

given half a chance
(also **if you give** *someone* **half a chance**)
used to say that someone is very likely to

do something if they have an opportunity: *Given half a chance, I bet Ron would spend our whole savings on cars and bikes.*

not have a chance/hope in hell (of)
(also **not have a snowball's chance in hell**)
SPOKEN used to say that it is impossible for someone to succeed in doing something: *Frankly, you didn't have a snowball's chance in hell against him.*

have/stand a fighting chance
to be able to stay alive or succeed, but only by trying or working very hard: *If tuition keeps rising, kids from poorer families won't stand a fighting chance at a college education.*
give *someone/something* **a fighting chance:** *Teaching the public about the dangers of drinking while pregnant will give future babies a fighting chance at a healthy life.*

jump at the chance
to eagerly accept an opportunity to do something: *When a local store asked Dave to fix a TV in exchange for flying lessons, he jumped at the chance.*

on the off chance (that)
if you decide to do something on the off chance that something will happen, you hope that it will happen although you know it is not likely: *We took the first two tickets on the off chance that we could get two more later for Kirstin and Bill.*

a sporting chance
a fair chance to win or succeed at doing something: *I let Rhonda start a few seconds before me, just to give her a sporting chance at winning.*

change
⇨a **SEA change**

a change of heart
a complete change in the way you feel about something or someone: *Eleanor suddenly had a change of heart and let her daughter get married.*

that/it makes a change
SPOKEN used to say that something that is happening is better than what usually happens: *"Okay, now Jan is going to*

speak, and I'll sit down and keep quiet." "That makes a change."

chapter

chapter and verse
used to say that someone gives you all of the information available, in exact detail: *Warner told us the whole story of the breakup, chapter and verse.*

charge

get a charge out of *something*
SPOKEN to think something is funny, or that something is fun to do: *The kids always get a charge out of making homemade pizza.*
—see also **get a KICK out of (doing)** *something*

charm

work like a charm
if an idea or something that you use works like a charm, it has exactly the effect that you wanted it to have: *I used to give the kids hot milk at bedtime when they couldn't sleep – it worked like a charm.*

chase
⇨a wild **GOOSE chase**

cut to the chase
to start talking about or dealing with the most important part of something instead of wasting time with other things: *Let's just cut to the chase, Mary. How much is this going to cost us?*

check
⇨take a **RAIN check (on** *something***)**

give someone a blank check
to give someone permission to do whatever they think is right or necessary in a situation ◆ OFTEN USED IN NEWSPAPERS, ON TELEVISION NEWS, ETC.: *The senators said that they could not give the President a blank check to go to war.*
blank-check: *The general is seeking blank-check authority to launch an attack.*

cheek

turn the other cheek
to deliberately avoid reacting in an angry

or violent way when someone has hurt or upset you: *Don't fight back. It's best to turn the other cheek in a situation like that.*

cheer

a Bronx cheer
a rude sound that you make by putting your tongue between your lips and blowing: *The referee got a Bronx cheer from one of the unhappy fans.*
—see also **blow a RASPBERRY**

cheese

a big cheese/wheel
someone who has an important or powerful position in an organization: *One of the big cheeses from Accounting is going to be at the meeting, so we'd better have our numbers ready.*

cut the cheese
SPOKEN to let gas escape from the body, making a bad smell and usually a noise ◆ USUALLY USED BY CHILDREN: *Yuck! Who cut the cheese in here?*

cherry

the cherry on the cake
(also **the cherry on top**)
used about something that you get in addition to what you expected: *The Honda Civic is an excellent little car; the cherry on the cake, though, is the price.*

life is (just) a bowl of cherries
used to say that only good things happen in life ◆ OFTEN USED IN THE NEGATIVE: *Life is not a bowl of cherries for young offenders on the Community Service Program.*

chest

get *something* off your chest
to tell someone about something that has been worrying you for a long time so that you feel better afterward: *Miguel knew he'd have to tell her soon. It would be a relief to get it all off his chest.*

chicken

a chicken and egg situation
(also **a chicken and egg problem, dilemma, etc.**)

when two things happen together and it is hard to see which of them caused the other: *Shy people like to study, or else people who like to study are shy – maybe it's a chicken and egg situation.*

chicken feed
used about an amount of something, especially money, that seems very small, especially in comparison with something else: *The 14 million dollar divorce settlement given to Ivana Trump seems like chicken feed compared to her ex-husband's worth.*

the chickens (have) come home to roost
used to say that someone is having to deal with the results of a mistake that they made or something bad that they did in the past: *You lived like you were in some Hollywood movie, spending money, taking trips, but now the chickens have come home to roost.*

don't count your chickens (before they're hatched)
used to tell someone not to be too sure that what they are hoping for will happen: *"We can buy a new car if I get the raise." "Don't count your chickens."*

be no spring chicken
SPOKEN used about someone who is no longer young: *My sister still wears miniskirts, and she's no spring chicken.*

play chicken
if children or young people play chicken, they do something that is dangerous in order to see who gets frightened first: *Yet another teenager has died playing chicken on the railroad tracks.*

chiefs

too many chiefs and not enough Indians
used about a business or situation in which there are too many people saying what should be done, and not enough people doing the work: *After Paul was promoted, we had a huge number of chiefs, but we were short of Indians.*

child

⇨*something* is child's **PLAY**

childhood

second childhood
when an adult behaves like a child, especially because he or she is getting old and often forgets things: *"Look at Jamie's dad, driving around in that yellow sportscar." "He must be going through his second childhood."*

chill

send a chill down your spine
(also **send chills down your spine**)
if something that you see, hear, or read sends a chill down your spine, it makes you feel frightened and upset: *Just saying the word "imprisonment" sent a chill down his spine.*
a chill runs down your spine: *A cold chill ran down Mary's spine when she saw the place where the children were last seen alive.*
—see also **send a SHIVER up/down your spine**

chin

(keep your) chin up
SPOKEN used to tell someone to try to stay cheerful when they are in a bad or difficult situation: *Keep your chin up, Vicky – I'm sure you'll find a job soon.*

take *something* on the chin
to accept criticism or a difficult situation without becoming upset: *Lewis took the news on the chin, insisting he was capable of doing better work.*

chink

a chink in *someone's* armor
a weakness in someone's character, plans, or ideas that makes it easier for an opponent to attack them: *Their product looked good, but during the demonstration the chinks in their technological armor began to show.*

chip

cash in your chips
SPOKEN an expression meaning to die, used when you do not want to say this directly: *When my old man cashed in his chips, my mother sold the house.*

be a chip off the old block
used to say that someone is very much like one of their parents, especially their father: *Mark is a chip off the old block, an adventurer and poet just like his father.*

have a chip on your shoulder
to be easily offended or angry because you think you have been treated unfairly in the past, or because you are not as rich or well-educated as most of the people around you: *In those days, Dennis still had a huge chip on his shoulder, and never let me forget that I had had a college education.*

when the chips are down
used to talk about a serious situation, when you realize what is really true or important: *Dooley liked to complain a lot, but he knew how to be tough when the chips were down.*

choice

Hobson's choice
a situation in which there is only one thing you can possibly do, unless you do nothing: *It's Hobson's choice – either we have a private toll bridge to the island, or no bridge at all.*

choir

⇨**be preaching to the choir** —see **be preaching to the CONVERTED**

chop

chop chop
OLD-FASHIONED used to tell someone to hurry: *Come on, chop chop, we've got a lot to do this morning.*

someone is licking his/her chops
(also *someone* is licking his/her lips)
used to say that someone is very excited about something that is going to happen, because it will give them something they want or need: *The victory-starved Warriors are licking their chops in anticipation of playing the Denver Nuggets.*

chord

strike a chord (with *someone*)
(also **touch a chord (with *someone*)**)

if an idea or something someone says strikes a chord with someone, they understand or like it because it reminds them of their own lives or experiences: *Although set in 1914, the play carries a message that still touches a chord today.*

Christmas

a white Christmas

when it is snowing or there is snow on the ground on December 25th: *While many children are hoping for a white Christmas, more than 500,000 families are packing their bags and heading for the sun.*

chunk

a chunk of change
(also **big, large, significant, etc. chunk of change**)

SPOKEN a lot of money: *Sylvia and I figured out that if we put Gus in a kennel for the four weeks, it comes out to be a chunk of change. Something like 300 bucks.*

cigar

close, but no cigar

SPOKEN said when the answer to a question is almost correct, but is not exactly right, or when you almost achieve what you wanted but did not exactly do it: *"I'd guess there are about 300." "Close, but no cigar. The actual number is 349."*

circle

come/go/turn full circle

used to say that something such as an idea, fashion, or way of living has changed many times and has finally come back to the state that it was in at first: *Roberta studied art in Tucson and then traveled all over the country. Now her career has come full circle, and she's teaching art at the University of Arizona.*

be going/running around in circles

used to say that you are not achieving an aim or solving a problem because you keep trying to do it in a way that produces no result: *I felt I was going around in circles, writing letters to different people at the bank and getting no answers.*

run circles/rings around *someone*

to be able to do something faster or better than someone else because you are more intelligent or skillful than they are: *Flannery has been running circles around his competitor in this year's campaign for governor.*

NOTE▶ You may also use other verbs with this idiom to be specific about what the person is doing: *She can talk circles around everyone else in the office.* | *Mr. Young plays circles around all the other musicians.*

a vicious circle/cycle

when one problem causes another, which makes the first problem worse, so that the whole process is repeated again and again: *When more water is supplied in Silicon Valley, there is more growth, when there is more growth there is more demand for water – it's a vicious circle.*

circus

a three-ring circus

used about a place or situation in which there is so much happening that it seems confusing or does not seem sensible: *Photographers surrounded his gate, and he realized that his attempt at a dignified resignation had turned into a three-ring circus.*

city

___ city

SPOKEN used to say that there is a lot or too much of a particular thing in a particular place or situation, or that a situation or place makes you feel something strongly: *I can't believe it. It's been sun city all week, and now it rains on our wedding day.* | *It was heartbreak city – I cried all night.*

a city slicker

used when you disapprove of someone because they are from a city and do not know anything about life outside the city, especially when they think they do: *With the mayor came a bunch of city-slicker LA types – the kind of people who smile and say "thank you" while they rudely interrupt you.*

claim

a claim to fame
used about something that makes a person or place special, especially something that is not really very important or very good: *Chan's personal claim to fame is that he does his own stunts.*

clam

happy as a clam/lark
very happy about a situation or what you are doing: *Mom's been as happy as a clam ever since Katie announced her engagement.*

class

a class act
used about someone who is very good at their job, or who is a very good person: *Tom Watson, in addition to being a great golfer, is known by all for being a class act.*

clay

⇨feet of clay —see **FOOT**

clean

⇨**COME** clean

cleaners

take *someone* to the cleaners
to take all of someone's money, especially by cheating them: *If Jane doesn't agree to the settlement, the lawyers will take her to the cleaners.*

cloak

cloak-and-dagger
used about activities that are done in secret, especially when this seems unnecessary or when it is done in a way that seems stupid: *With so many lies and half-truths swirling around, the award selection process is a real cloak-and-dagger operation.*

clock

clean *someone's* clock
SPOKEN to defeat someone badly in a fight or competition: *How can someone who's in such good shape let Foreman clean his clock so often?*

clock *someone* one
OLD-FASHIONED to hit someone: *Jason was annoying me, so I clocked him one!*

do *something* against the clock
1 to work as fast as possible because you do not have very much time: *Fryer is working against the clock to get his accounts balanced before the end of the year.*
2 to try to finish what you are doing within a particular time, using a clock to check the time: *We each had to give a talk, speaking for five minutes against the clock.*

do *something* around the clock
to do something for a full 24 hours, day and night: *Scientists are working around the clock to unlock the mystery of this terrible disease.*
around-the-clock: *We kept an around-the-clock watch on the airport.*

clockwork

go like clockwork
if a complicated system or plan goes like clockwork, everything happens as it is supposed to, without any problems: *We had everything well planned, and the restaurant's first three days went like clockwork.*

closet

⇨a **SKELETON** in the closet

come/be out of the closet
1 (also **come/be out**) if a person comes or is out of the closet, they tell people they are homosexual (=are sexually attracted to people of their own sex) instead of keeping it a secret: *Mary finally came out of the closet when she was 60, after having lived a secret life for so long.*
opposite **be in the closet:** *Gay people work at all levels of broadcasting, but most are still very much in the closet.*
2 to admit to people that you have beliefs, feelings, or habits that you have been keeping secret: *In the 60s and 70s, movie stars started to come out of the political closet and openly voice their support for one candidate or another.*

3 (also **be brought out of the closet**) if a subject comes out of the closet, people start to discuss it openly or publicly for the first time: *I think it's time that this discussion was brought out of the closet, so that the public can say what it thinks.*

cloth

be cut from the same cloth
used to say that two or more people are very similar: *Don't assume that all women are cut from the same cloth. Jill won't necessarily react the same way I did.*

cut your cloth
to spend only as much money as you can afford: *We can never close the business, so we must cut our cloth to suit our income.*

make *something* out of whole cloth
if a story, explanation, etc. is made out of whole cloth, it is not true: *Julia insists that the rumors about her new boyfriend are made out of whole cloth.*

clothes

the emperor's (new) clothes
used about a situation when everyone pretends to understand or admire something that is not really sensible or special because they think they will seem stupid if they do not: *You do not need this software, so don't be seduced by the emperor's new clothes.*

NOTE▶ This idiom comes from the title of a story by Hans Christian Andersen in which an emperor (=king) is tricked into buying an expensive set of clothes. He is told that the clothes cannot be seen by stupid people, but really the clothes do not exist at all. He goes out in public wearing nothing, and everyone pretends to admire his clothes so that they do not seem stupid, until a child shouts, "But he doesn't have any clothes on!"

cloud

a cloud on the/your horizon
something bad that is likely to happen, that could spoil your happiness: *The dark clouds on the horizon were not about to*

clear as the car plant got ready to lay off two hundred more workers.

be on cloud nine
to be extremely happy because something good has happened to you recently: *After Rachel called and asked me out, I was on cloud nine.*

(every cloud has) a silver lining
used to say that a difficult or unpleasant situation has some good things about it, or may have a good result: *Don had much more time to spend with his kids after he lost his job, which made him realize that every cloud has a silver lining.*

be under a cloud
used about someone who people disapprove of or do not trust because they think they have done something wrong: *Webster left the law firm under a cloud in 1995.*

club

join the club
(also **welcome to the club**)
SPOKEN used after someone has described how bad their situation is in order to say that you are or have been in the same situation: *You think you'll never be out of debt? Join the club.*

clue

not have a clue
(also **have no clue**)
SPOKEN used to say that someone does not know anything about a particular subject or about things in general: *I wouldn't have a clue how to get to the restaurant. | I have no clue how we made it home last night.*

clued in

be clued in (about/on *something*)
to know all the facts that you need to know about a subject: *Voters are much more clued in about tax issues than they were ten years ago.*

clutch

in the clutch
(also **in a clutch situation**)
in a difficult situation ◆ OFTEN USED IN

SPORTS: *We played badly in the first half, but we came through in the clutch.*

in the clutches of
(also **in** *someone's* **clutches**)
to be controlled or strongly influenced by someone or something: *We were in the clutches of one of the coldest winters ever recorded. | Once a loan shark has you in his clutches, you'll never get away.*

> NOTE▶ You may also hear people use "the clutches" in other expressions such as "escape from the clutches of someone/something" or "be free from the clutches of someone/something" in order to show that a situation in which someone was being controlled or influenced has ended: *His parents were very relieved that he had escaped from the clutches of "that woman," as they called her.*

coals

rake *someone* over the coals
to criticize someone severely for something wrong that they have done
♦ OFTEN USED IN BUSINESS AND POLITICS: *The Democratic candidate was raked over the coals by women's groups for failing to deal with the issue of equal pay.*

coast

the coast is clear
used to say that it is safe for someone to do something without risking being seen or caught: *As soon as the coast was clear, I ran across the street and jumped in the car.*

coattails

on *someone's* coattails
(also **ride (on)** *someone's* **coattails**)
used to say that someone or something is able to be successful only because of the success of another person or thing: *My dad is a sports columnist, and I didn't want to ride his coattails into newspaper journalism.*

cobwebs

brush/clear away the cobwebs
(also **shake off the cobwebs**)
to make you have more energy again after

feeling tired: *I love to exercise in the morning – it helps clear away the cobwebs and get me thinking.*

cockles

warm the cockles of your heart
OLD-FASHIONED to make you feel happy and full of good feelings toward other people: *Every time I hear that song, it warms the cockles of my heart.*

coffee

wake up and smell the coffee
SPOKEN used to tell someone that they have to deal with a situation instead of not thinking about it, even though it may be unpleasant or difficult: *I think the people who fight sex education in our schools need to wake up and smell the coffee. Safe sex is not just about not getting pregnant – now it's a matter of life and death.*

cog

a cog in the wheel
used about someone whose job is only one of many jobs in a large business, organization, or system: *I love this business, but I'm only a cog in the wheel. One guy doesn't make a staff.*

coin

⇨**to coin a PHRASE**

cold

⇨**be OUT cold**

collar

be/get hot under the collar
to be or become angry about something: *Mr. Davis was a little hot under the collar when he found out so many employees were on vacation at the same time.*

college

give *something* the old college try
to use your best effort to try to do something, even if you know you may not be successful: *We may not be able to reach an agreement today, but we're going to give it the old college try.*

color

do *something* with flying colors
if someone completes an examination or test with flying colors, they are very successful in it: *Sheila took her final exams this summer, and passed with flying colors.*

local color
all the traditional features of a place that give it its own character and make it special: *Haight Street in San Francisco is a great place to walk and take in the local color.*

see the color of *someone's* money
to make sure that someone, especially someone who you do not trust, has enough money to pay you for what they want: *Nowadays most small businesses want to see the color of their clients' money before they provide services.*

show your true colors
to let people see your true feelings or opinions about a subject, after you have been hiding them: *By refusing even to discuss race relations, the chairman has shown us his true colors.*
see *someone* in their true colors: *Once again we see the government in its true colors – telling other people how to run their lives.*

comb

go through/over *something* with a fine-tooth comb
to examine or search through something very carefully: *I searched through my desk with a fine-tooth comb, but I still couldn't find that phone number.*

come

⇨EASY come, easy go
⇨GET what's coming to you
⇨be HARD to come by
⇨*someone* has it coming (to him/her)
 —see HAVE
⇨not KNOW whether you're coming or going
⇨THAT's where *someone/something* comes in
⇨THAT's where we came in
⇨WHERE *someone* is coming from

come clean
to finally tell the truth or admit that you have done something wrong, especially after lying for a long time: *Rogers finally came clean and told investigators where to find the bodies after months of keeping the location a secret.*
—compare make a clean BREAST of *something*

come down hard on *someone*
to criticize or punish someone very severely for something that they have done: *I think the teacher came down too hard on him. I mean, he's only six years old.*

come in handy
to be useful, often in a way or in a situation in which you would not expect it to be: *Don't throw the camping stove away – it might come in handy one day.*

come off it!
SPOKEN used when you are annoyed with someone because you think what they are saying is stupid or untrue: *Come off it, Lynn – you're not fat.*

come on strong
to rudely say things that show that you think someone is attractive in a sexual way: *I always come on too strong with men and send the message that I'm desperate to get a husband.*

come to pass
OLD-FASHIONED to happen, especially after being promised, planned, or expected: *Digging a tunnel to connect San Diego's bays is a lot harder than it looks. That's why it hasn't been done and probably won't come to pass anytime soon.*

come to think of/about it
SPOKEN said when you want to add something that you have just realized or just remembered: *Come to think of it, my meeting isn't until two o'clock, so I can meet you for lunch after all.*

come unglued
1 to become extremely angry or upset about something, often in a way that makes you seem crazy: *I got so caught up in the new-product craze and spent so much money that my wife came a little unglued.*

2 if a situation, plan, etc. comes un-glued, it fails or does not happen or work in the way that it is supposed to: *The plot, which is bad enough anyway, comes completely unglued around page 300 and never quite pulls itself together again.*

it (all) comes/boils down to
used to say what you think the most important point of a conversation is: *In the end, winning the championship all boils down to who's playing better on the day of the game.*

when it comes (right) down to it
(also **when you get (right) down to it**)
SPOKEN used to say that when you think carefully about what is important in a situation, you get a particular answer or decision: *They're both nice cars, but when it comes right down to it, we have to buy the one we can afford.*

comeuppance

someone gets his/her come-uppance
used to say that a punishment someone receives is what they deserve: *I'm glad Merton finally got his comeuppance for all his lies. I've been waiting for this for a long time.*

comfort

⇨**CREATURE comforts**

something is cold comfort
used to say that a statement or piece of news does not make a difficult situation seem any better: *Knowing that there are millions of dollars available in food aid is cold comfort for people in countries that will never see the money.*

commando

go commando
SLANG to wear no underwear: *Most backpackers take one pair of boxers to sleep in, but go commando otherwise.*

company

keep bad company
(also **get/fall into bad company**)
to spend time with people who do dishonest or illegal things: *He's basically*

a good guy who fell into some bad company.

someone is in good company
used to say that someone should not be embarrassed by something they have done because there are important or respected people who have done something similar: *Webster was ashamed to admit that heading the CIA was so difficult. But he was in good company. The job had been hard for the fourteen men before him as well.*

present company excepted (of course)
SPOKEN used to tell the people you are talking to that an impolite or bad remark you have just made does not include them: *What husband do you know who listens to his wife's opinions? Present company excepted, of course.*

present company excepted (of course)

I DON'T TRUST MECHANICS, PRESENT COMPANY EXCEPTED

two's company (three's a crowd)
SPOKEN used to say that two people would rather be alone than have other people with them: *"Why don't you stay for supper, Jill?" "No, I'll leave you and Joe alone – two's company, three's a crowd."*

compliment

a left-handed compliment
(also **a back-handed compliment**)
something that someone says to you that is both nice and not nice at the same time: *They paid me a left-handed compliment by saying I'm the only person who could live with him.*

concrete

⇨**concrete JUNGLE**

condition

in mint condition
if something old or used is in mint condition, it is in very good condition
♦ OFTEN USED IN ADVERTISEMENTS, WHEN SOMEONE IS SELLING THINGS THAT THEY OWN: *He has some pre-1969 baseball cards for sale in mint condition.*

conspiracy

a conspiracy of silence
an agreement to keep important information secret, when it should not be a secret: *The government was charged with a conspiracy of silence when it refused to release details about the deadly new virus.*

content

do *something* to your heart's content/desire
to do something as much as you want: *These cookies are really low in cholesterol, so eat to your heart's content.*

conversation

a conversation piece
used about a strange or unusual thing that gives people a subject they can talk about: *Sally says her new ring with a watch in it is a great conversation piece.*

converted

be preaching to the converted
(also **be preaching to the choir**)
to be wasting time or effort criticizing or trying to persuade people who already have the same opinions as you do, especially when it would be more useful talking to people who do not agree with you: *Mosbacher was preaching to the converted when he spoke to software experts in Silicon Valley about how to improve their exports.*

cook

⇨WHAT's cooking?
too many cooks (spoil the broth)
used to say that there are too many people trying to do the same job at the same time, so that the job is not done well: *The managers demanded that meetings be limited to 10 people, claiming, "There were too many cooks."*

cookie

⇨that's the WAY the cookie crumbles

someone is a tough/smart cookie
(also *someone* is one tough/smart cookie)
used about someone who is intelligent, confident, and determined to succeed: *Barney's one smart cookie – he knows how to play politics.*

toss your cookies
SLANG to bring food up from your stomach through your mouth: *Andy had some fish that wasn't too good last night and ended up tossing his cookies all over the restaurant floor.*

cool

⇨PLAY it cool

cool, calm, and collected
not nervous, or not easily upset or embarrassed: *Madsen said that the captain was in control of the ship during the accident and was cool, calm, and collected, as a captain should be.*

keep your cool
to remain calm in a difficult or frightening situation: *On the night of the big game between the two rival teams, city leaders asked the fans in the streets to keep their cool and avoid trouble.*

lose/blow your cool
to suddenly become angry or upset: *Wilson started getting confused and contradicting himself, until eventually he blew his cool.*
—compare blow your TOP/stack

coon

⇨in a coon's AGE

coop

fly the coop
to leave the place where you have been living or working, often to get away from a bad situation: *Most of the students had flown the coop before the end of final exam week.*

cop

⇨cop a FEEL

copy

⇨be a CARBON copy

cord

cut the (umbilical) cord
to start being independent and stop depending on your parents for help or money: *Jeff keeps saying he wants to cut the cord, but he's still asking his father for the plane fare home.*

> NOTE▷ The umbilical cord is the tube that attaches a baby to its mother before it is born.

cork

⇨put a cork in it! —see put a SOCK in it!

corn

⇨the SEED corn (of something)

corner

back *someone* into a corner
(also **force, box, paint, etc.** *someone* **into a corner**)
to put someone into a difficult situation in which they do not have any choices about what to do ◆ OFTEN USED IN BUSINESS AND POLITICS: *Backing them into a corner and trying to make them accept the deal isn't going to work.*
back/paint/box yourself into a corner: *It looks like the writers of the hot new drama series have painted themselves into a corner by killing off their most popular character in the third show.*

cut corners
to save time, money, or energy by doing things quickly and not as carefully as you should: *Some laboratories are starting to cut corners to save money, but the test results may not be as reliable.*

from/to the four corners of the earth
(also **from/to the four corners of the world/globe**)
from or to all the parts of the world: *Healthcare workers from the four corners*

of the earth have come to Ontario for the conference.

get/have a corner on the market
to control the whole supply of a particular type of goods: *The company admitted lowering prices to get a corner on the bread market.*

turn the corner
1 to start to feel better or happier after being very sick or unhappy: *We knew Dad had turned the corner when he started complaining about the hospital food.*
2 if a business, the economy, etc. turns the corner, it begins to make a profit or be more successful after a bad or difficult time: *The airline will probably need another 10 million dollars by the end of the year to turn the corner and make a profit.*

corridors

the corridors of power
the places where important government decisions are made ◆ OFTEN USED IN NEWSPAPERS: *Philips was a spy who penetrated more corridors of power and provided more important intelligence than any other spy during the war.*

couch potato

couch potato
someone who spends a lot of time sitting and doing things that do not use much mental or physical energy, such as watching television: *After dropping out of school, I was a complete couch potato – I didn't even feel like walking to the store.*

counsel

keep your own counsel
to keep your plans, opinions, etc. secret: *Even with those she loves most, Mrs. Brown tends to keep her own counsel.*

count

be down for the count
to be in an unfavorable situation and likely to fail: *When times are bad, short-sighted borrowers become convinced they are down for the count and start considering bankruptcy.*

be out for the count

to sleep deeply: *After all that food and wine at dinner, I was out for the count, and I didn't hear the doorbell.*

counter

under the counter

if you buy or sell something under the counter, you do it secretly because it is illegal: *Shop owners were buying illegal alcohol for $1.50 under the counter and reselling it for $2.75.*
under-the-counter: *New political measures have been taken against under-the-counter drug sales in California.*
—compare **under the table**

courage

Dutch/liquid courage

courage or confidence that you get by drinking alcohol: *After a few nights, I managed to get on stage without the help of Dutch courage.*

have the courage of your convictions

to be brave enough to say or do what you think is right, even though other people may not agree or approve: *Jackson praised the President for her belief in the country's ability to succeed. "She had the courage of her convictions," he said.*

course

⇒**something is PAR for the course**

in due course

at some time in the future when it is the right time ♦ OFTEN USED IN OFFICIAL SITUATIONS, BUSINESS LETTERS, MEETINGS, SPEECHES, ETC.: *Thank you, Mr. Rodriguez. I'll let you know my decision in due course.*

be on course

to be doing the things that will make you likely to achieve what you are trying to do: *Our economic recovery is on course and we're making real progress toward reducing poverty.*

over the course of time

after time has passed: *Over the course of time, we may know more about the origins of the universe.*

stay the course

(also **stay the course of** *something*)
to continue to try to achieve something even though it is very difficult: *We must help the nations of Eastern Europe to stay the course of democracy.*

steer a middle course

to find a way of dealing with something that is between two opposite and often extreme ways: *The government is attempting to steer a middle course between inflation and economic growth.*

court

⇒**a full-court PRESS**

someone holds court

used to say that someone has a lot of people around them when they talk, to make them feel important, especially when you think they do not deserve the attention: *Dressed in a fur coat, Cindy held court in Molly's Bar, where most people wear jeans and baggy sweaters.*

be laughed out of court

if an idea or story is laughed out of court, people think it is so stupid or difficult to believe that they ignore it or think it is funny: *If we tell them that we think we saw a space ship, we'll be laughed out of court.*

> NOTE▶ You may hear people use other words instead of "court" in order to make this idiom fit a particular situation more exactly: *Styles may be similar today, but if we produced clothing made from the same materials as we did thirty years ago, we'd be laughed out of the market.*

pay court to *someone*

to treat an important person, a company, etc. with respect and try to please them in order to gain an advantage: *It's sickening to see the politicians paying court to voters when they won't keep a single one of their promises.*

> NOTE▶ In the past if a man paid court to a woman, he showed that he loved her or wanted to marry her by visiting her often, giving her lots of attention, praising her good qualities, etc.

cousin

a country cousin
used about someone who is considered to be less fashionable or not as well educated because they live in the country or small town and not in a large city: *She was wearing a long black dress and looking extremely elegant, and there was I, feeling like a country cousin.*

cover

blow *someone's* cover
(also **blow the cover on** *someone/ something*)
to tell people what someone's real name is, or what the real purpose of their work is, when it is supposed to be a secret: *A police spokeswoman blamed a television station for blowing the cover on a raid.*

cow

have a cow
SLANG to become very angry and upset about something someone has done, especially someone you know well: *"I can't believe you haven't sent the rent check yet!" "Don't have a cow, I called the landlord and everything is okay."*
—see also **have/throw a FIT**

a sacred cow
used about a belief or an institution that people think is so important that they will not allow anyone to criticize it or change it ♦ OFTEN USED IN BUSINESS AND POLITICS: *Defense spending is no longer a sacred cow, and it may be the best place to make cuts.*

till/until the cows come home
SPOKEN for a very long time: *You can argue until the cows come home. I won't change my mind.*

crack

fall through the cracks
if a particular group of people fall through the cracks, a system or arrangement fails to deal with them or include them: *However good our schools are, many children will simply fall through the cracks if they don't have home environments that are stable and secure.*

get cracking
SPOKEN used to tell someone to start doing something quickly: *Time to wake up! Let's get cracking – we have a lot to do today.*

have/get a crack at *something*
(also **take a crack at** *something*)
to take or get an opportunity to achieve something: *The Venezuelan boxer will get a crack at the world title in New York on October 31st.*

> **NOTE▶** You may also hear people using "crack" in other phrases, for example "want a crack at something": *Barry wanted another crack at becoming the city's first black mayor.* People also talk about having or getting the "first crack at something" when they are the first ones to try to do something: *People who have been out of work for that long should be getting first crack at the new government jobs.*

something is not all/everything it's cracked up to be
used to say that something is not as good as people say it is: *The message in the movie is that being rich isn't all it's cracked up to be.*

cradle

from the cradle to the grave
used to emphasize that something happens from the beginning to the end of someone's life: *The leader of the religious commune stated that all its members were taken care of from the cradle to the grave.*
cradle-to-grave: *The European idea of the cradle-to-grave welfare state seems alien to Americans, brought up in an atmosphere of individual initiative.*

someone is robbing the cradle
used when you disapprove because someone is having a romantic relationship with someone who is much younger than they are: *People joked that Bill had robbed the cradle when he married Ruth when she was only 17.*
cradle robber: *At the dance, they called Lee Ann a cradle robber.*

crap

> NOTE▶ Many people think the words "crap" and "shit" are offensive. It is better not to use them.

cut the crap/shit!
SPOKEN a rude way of telling someone to stop lying or trying to trick or confuse someone: *Okay, cut the crap, Tony. Just tell me why you got home so late last night.*

don't pull that crap/shit
SPOKEN a rude way of telling someone not to try to do or say something that is wrong or dishonest: *Come on, Jerry, don't pull that shit with me. We saw you with her in the restaurant.*

someone *is full of crap/shit*
SPOKEN a rude expression used in order to say that someone lies or says stupid things: *There's no way you can expect me to believe you, Erica. You're full of crap.*

crash

crash and burn
to fail completely: *Her movie career crashed and burned in the 1970s, but she came back in the early nineties with "Stepping Out."*

craw

⇨*something* sticks in *someone's* craw — see *something* sticks in *someone's* THROAT

crazy

⇨DRIVE *someone* crazy/bonkers

be crazy about *someone/something*
to like someone or something very much, or to be very interested in something: *When I was 15, I was crazy about a boy in my class named Tom McMillan. | I like the way this suit fits, but I'm not crazy about the color.*

do *something* like crazy
SPOKEN to do something a lot or with a lot of energy: *The boy was kicking like crazy to get free, but Phil held on to him. | I've been eating like crazy the last couple of days.*

cream

the cream of the crop
someone or something that is the best of its kind: *School districts cannot just choose the cream of the crop and ignore students with special needs.*

creature

creature comforts
all the things that make life more comfortable, such as good food, a warm house, modern equipment, etc.: *The hotel is perfect for people who want good service and all the creature comforts, and are willing to pay for them.*

a creature of habit
used about someone who always does the same things in the same way or at the same time: *When it comes to clothes, men are creatures of habit.*

credit

do *someone/something* credit
to be a reason why someone or something should be praised and admired: *They sent Manuel because he was the kind of player who would do his country credit overseas.*

give *someone* credit (for *something*)
(also **give credit where credit's due**)
to admit that someone does something well, especially in a situation when they have done other things badly or you do not like them for other reasons: *Darla does a lot more around the office than she's given credit for.*

creek

be up the creek (without a paddle)
(also **be up shit creek (without a paddle)**)
SPOKEN an impolite expression used in order to say that someone is in a very difficult situation: *The developers sunk millions of dollars into the new stadium, but didn't leave enough room for parking. Now they're up the creek without a paddle, and are likely to lose a lot of money.*

> NOTE▶ Many people think the word "shit" is offensive. It is better not to use it.

creeps

give *someone* the creeps

to make you feel nervous or afraid: *Don't leave me alone with Harvey. That guy gives me the creeps.*

crème

the crème de la crème

the very best of a kind of thing or group of people: *The crème de la crème of America's science students were invited to the conference.*

crest

be riding (on) the crest of a wave

used to say that a person or organization is being very successful because they are good at an activity that is very popular, or in which conditions are good at the time: *Yan's cooking show rode the crest of the wave of people's interest in Asian cooking.*

crime

⇨**FASHION crime**

crock

what a crock (of shit)
(also **that's a crock (of shit)**)

SPOKEN a rude expression used in order to say that something is untrue, wrong, unfair, etc.: *"So now I'm being blamed for it, and he's letting people believe it's actually my fault." "What a crock of shit!"*

> NOTE▶ Many people think the word "shit" is offensive. It is better not to use it.

crocodile

shed crocodile tears
(often **weep/cry crocodile tears**)

to pretend that you feel sad, sorry, or upset: *It's time the government stopped shedding crocodile tears over child poverty, and got to the cause of the problem.*

Croesus

rich as Croesus

OLD-FASHIONED very rich: *My dad thinks that politicians won't do anything to help you unless you're rich as Croesus.*

cross

a heavy cross to bear

used about a problem that makes someone very unhappy or worried for a long time: *Joyce's husband's illness has been a heavy cross for her to bear.*

> NOTE▶ The cross in this idiom is two pieces of wood in the shape of a "T" which were used as a structure on which to crucify someone (=kill someone by nailing them to a cross as a punishment) in past times. The person being crucified often had to carry or "bear" their own cross to the place where they would die.

crossfire

get caught in the crossfire

to become involved in an argument between two other people or groups, or to have problems as a result of someone else's arguments: *The team's management is caught in the crossfire of a bitter battle between Rampling, their star player, and his agent.*

crossroads

come to a crossroads
(also **be at a crossroads**)

to reach a time in your life when you have to make an important decision that will affect your future: *Black filmmakers are now finding themselves at a crossroads. There is a large potential audience for their work, but they worry about having to compromise their message.*

crow

as the crow flies

used to explain how far away a place is if you travel in a straight line, especially when the distance by road is much longer: *It's about ten miles away as the crow flies, but the road goes around the edge of the lake.*

eat crow

to be forced to admit that you are wrong or say that you are sorry, especially when this is embarrassing: *Critics who laughingly called CNN the "Chicken Noodle News" when it began in 1980 were forced to eat crow as the network spread around the world.*

crowd

follow the crowd

to do the same thing as other people, often because you are afraid to be different or take risks: *In advertising, it doesn't pay to follow the crowd. You've got to be more daring and come up with bold new ideas.*

stand out in a crowd

to be easily noticed because of some special quality: *She dresses and moves with an elegance that makes her stand out in a crowd.*

cruel

be cruel to be kind

to do or say something that will make someone unhappy but will help them in another way: *Unfortunately you may have to be cruel to be kind, or your daughter will never learn to be independent.*

crunch

when/if it comes to the crunch

used to say what you will do when a difficult or important decision has to be made, or in a difficult situation when you may succeed or fail: *I respect many politicians but, when it comes to the crunch, they all do what is best for their own career.*

—see also **when/if PUSH comes to shove**

NOTE▶ You may also hear people use expressions like "the crunch comes" or talk about it being "crunch time": *It's crunch time now on the Seifert project – the deadline is Friday, and there's still a lot to do.*

crust

the upper crust

people who belong to the highest social class: *Michelle is on the yacht, doing research for her article on how the upper crust amuses itself.*

upper-crust: *Late night parties in the hotel led to complaints from upper-crust visitors about the noise.*

cry

⇨**cry FOUL**

be a far cry from

used to say that something is very different from something else: *The atmosphere at Ray's Bar and Grill was a far cry from the quiet elegance of the Ivy Hotel.*

for crying out loud

SPOKEN used to emphasize how annoyed or impatient you feel about what you are saying: *For crying out loud, can't you turn that music down? Don't you realize people are trying to sleep?*

cucumber

as cool as a cucumber

used about someone who stays very calm in a situation where you expect them to be nervous, upset, or embarrassed: *Ted looked as cool as a cucumber, even when the judge told him he was sentenced to life in prison.*

cudgels

take up the cudgels

OLD-FASHIONED to argue or take action in support of an idea, person, or group: *One critic took up the moral cudgels, criticizing the songs as being "filthy garbage."*

cue

take your cue from *someone*

to copy what someone does: *Taking its cue from the airline industry, the company announced that it would ban smoking on its buses.*

cuff

off the cuff

if you speak, answer, or perform off the cuff you do it without preparing for what you are going to say: *It's difficult to give you an answer off the cuff – I'd have to look at the statistics.*

off-the-cuff: *Mahoney's off-the-cuff remarks about drugs have gotten her into trouble on many occasions.*

cup

not be *someone's* cup of tea
SPOKEN used to say politely that you do not like or enjoy something: *Working underground with minimal light and electricity may not be everybody's cup of tea, but subway engineer Cindy Crow loves it.*

curiosity

curiosity killed the cat
used to tell someone not to try to find out about something, often because they might get into trouble: *I wouldn't go in there if I were you. You know curiosity killed the cat.*

current

go/swim against the current
to have an opinion that is not popular, or do something different from what other people are doing: *As a politician, it is difficult to win an election when most of your ideas go against the current.*

curtain

the curtain falls on *someone/ something*
used to say that an activity or event ends, often before you expect it to ♦ OFTEN USED IN NEWSPAPERS: *Too many public figures have seen the curtain fall on their careers because of gossip that is reported as news.*

it is/means curtains for *someone/ something*
used to say that someone will die, or that something will end: *Unless profits rise dramatically in the next quarter, it's going to be curtains for the Wordsworth bookstore.*

curve

throw *someone* a curve
to surprise someone by doing something that they do not expect so that they are confused for a while: *When my boss showed up at the party with that younger woman, it really threw me a curve. Turns out it was his niece.*

NOTE▶ This idiom comes from the game of baseball. A curve ball is a way of throwing the ball so that it suddenly and unexpectedly curves away from the batter (=person hitting the ball) just as it gets to him or her.

customer

a cool customer
used about someone who is always calm and confident, but is often not very friendly: *He's one cool customer – he had the guts to ask for a 25 percent raise.*

a slippery customer
used about someone who you do not trust: *"That new boyfriend of Rita's seems like a slippery customer." "Yeah, I agree. I wouldn't want to do business with him."*

cut

⇨cut *someone* down to SIZE

someone can't/couldn't cut it
to not have the ability, strength, character, etc. to succeed in a particular job or activity: *Some of the kids on the team decided they just couldn't cut it. The schedule was too tough.*
opposite *someone* can/could cut it: *Even though people told me I would have a tough time at Yale, I knew I could cut it.*

be a cut above (the rest)
to be better than other people or things of the same kind: *His newest movie is a cut above the recent thrillers, but not as good as some of his earlier work.*

be cut and dried
if a situation, a subject, or problem is cut and dried, there is nothing complicated or uncertain about it, and it is easy to know what will happen: *The case was basically cut and dried – we knew Robertson would win because he had the best witnesses.*
cut-and-dried: *This may be more than a cut-and-dried case of discrimination.*

cut and run
to leave a situation suddenly when it becomes too difficult, especially when you should have stayed: *The brothers face a long lawsuit, but they are not the type of men to cut and run.*

cut *something* **close**
to leave yourself very little time to arrive somewhere or finish something: *The Black Hawks won but they cut it close, scoring the winning goal only a minute from the end of the period.*

cut it out!
SPOKEN used to tell someone to stop doing something that is annoying you: *"Jeff and Chris, cut it out. That's enough. If you keep playing like that somebody is going to get hurt."*

not be cut out for *something*
to not have the qualities you need for a job or activity: *It only took me half a day to decide that I wasn't cut out for a career in sales.*

something doesn't/won't cut it (with *someone*)
used to say that a particular way of doing something or reason for doing something is not good enough: *Starting in September, "satisfactory" performance by a teacher simply won't cut it. To receive*

tenure, instructors must now show "outstanding" work.

cute

don't get cute/smart with me
SPOKEN said when you think that someone is trying to deceive you, or is not talking to you in a direct and serious way: *"Don't get cute with me young man. You tell your mother right now what you did to her garden."*

cycle
⇨ a vicious **CIRCLE/cycle**

cylinders

be firing on all cylinders
(also **be operating, running, etc. on all cylinders**)
to be thinking, working, performing, etc. well, using all your mental abilities and energy ◆ OFTEN USED IN THE NEGATIVE: *In the first half, the Falcons weren't firing on all cylinders.*

D

daddy

⇨a SUGAR daddy

daggers

look/shoot daggers (at *someone***)**
to look at someone very angrily: *We were talking about what Julie had done, and she was at the next table looking daggers at us.*

daisy

fresh as a daisy
used to say that someone is not tired, but is full of energy, and ready to do things: *Get some sleep now, and in the morning you'll be fresh as a daisy.*

oops-a-daisy
(also **whoops-a-daisy**)
SPOKEN said when someone has fallen down or dropped something ♦ USED BY CHILDREN, OR BY ADULTS TALKING TO CHILDREN: *Put your socks on now – oops-a-daisy, don't fall off the bed.*

be pushing up the daisies
a humorous expression meaning to be dead: *Just because I'm your mother, you talk as if all my old boyfriends were pushing up the daisies.*

damage

the damage is done
used to say that something has happened that makes a situation worse, and it is impossible to go back to the way things were before: *It doesn't matter at this point if she apologizes or not – the damage is done.*

what's the damage?
SPOKEN used to ask someone how much money you should pay them: *"What's the damage?" "Fifty-six dollars and eighty cents, please."*

damn

damned if you do, damned if you don't
used to say that whatever you say or do, people will think that you are wrong: *People want law and order, but they complain about police harassment, so you're damned if you do and damned if you don't.*

damn straight!
SPOKEN a slightly rude expression used in order to emphasize that what someone has just said or asked about is true: *You're asking if I don't trust you? Damn straight! I have never trusted you!*

I'll be damned!
(also **I'll be darned**)
SPOKEN said when you are very surprised: *He married Julie's sister? Well, I'll be damned.*
(I'll be) damned if *someone/something* **didn't do** *something*: *Well, I'll be damned if you didn't drink my last beer!*

> NOTE▶ Some people use "darn" instead of "damn," because they think "damn" is offensive.

damper

put a damper on *something*
to spoil an activity by making people feel less happy or confident: *This week's weather put a damper on everyone's holiday spirits.*

dander

get *someone's* **dander up**
to annoy someone or make them angry: *What gets my dander up is intellectuals telling us what we should watch on television.*

dark

be (kept/left) in the dark
to be given no information about something that is important to you: *For fifty years, the American people have been kept in the dark about the dangers of nuclear waste.*

be whistling in the dark
to be trying to show that you are more confident about a situation than you really are, or that you know more about it than you really do: *We say that the bad times are over for business, but that's just whistling in the dark.*

dawn

it dawned on *someone*
(also **the light, truth, realization, etc. dawned (on** *someone***)**)
used to say that someone suddenly realizes or understands something, especially when they feel stupid because they did not realize or understand it earlier: *Amanda was out shopping when it dawned on her that she was supposed to be picking up her kids from school.* | *I waited for a moment and then tried explaining again, until finally the light dawned on the other woman's face.*

day

⇨**(it's) all in a day's WORK**
⇨**don't quit your day JOB**
⇨**have a FIELD day**
⇨**be like NIGHT and day**
⇨*someone's* **SALAD days**

as plain/clear as day
if you can see, imagine, or understand something as plain as day, it is very easy for you to see, imagine, etc.: *When I read the names of my old friends who died in the war, I can see their faces as plain as day.*

a/the big day
(also *someone's* **big day**)
a day on which someone is going to do something very important, for example getting married or taking a test: *Get some rest tonight – you don't want to be too tired for the big day!*

call it a day
to decide to stop working or doing an activity, especially because you have done enough or are tired: *By the time they gave a concert at Candlestick Park, the Beatles had already decided to call it a day as a performing group.*
—see also **call it a NIGHT**

day in, day out
(often **week in, week out; month in, month out; year in, year out**)
every day, week, etc., for a long time: *Ambulance drivers have to stay calm when everyone else is upset; this is the emotional strain they face day in, day out.*

day of reckoning
used about a time when you are judged or made to suffer for the things that you have done wrong: *I hadn't done any work for months, and the day of reckoning was getting closer.*

> NOTE▶ According to many religions the "day of reckoning" is the day you die, when you are judged by God.

someone's/something's **days are numbered**
used to say that someone will not stay alive or be successful for very long, or that something will not continue to exist for very long: *The latest opinion polls indicate that Morrison's days in power may be numbered.*

from day one
SPOKEN from the beginning: *It was clear to me from day one that the police never had any interest in solving the case of my son's murder.*

give me (a) ___ any day
SPOKEN used to say that you like something more than you like another thing: *It's too quiet in the country – give me a noisy, dirty city any day.*

someone's **glory days**
used about a period of time in which someone is very successful ♦ OFTEN USED IN NEWSPAPERS, ON TELEVISION NEWS, ETC.: *I gave up playing professional baseball years ago, when I realized my glory days were behind me.*

the good old days
used about a time in the past that you think was better than the present time: *Tom Jones sang a few songs, introduced some contemporary guests, and talked a lot about the good old days.*

halcyon days
used about a pleasant time of happiness or success without problems or worries, especially a time in the past that was better than the present: *The late 1980s were halcyon days for investors, when it seemed that stock prices would stay high forever.*

NOTE▶ The word "halcyon" comes from the Greek word for a bird called a kingfisher. In ancient times, it was believed that the kingfisher sat on its eggs on the surface of the ocean for fourteen days in the middle of winter, during which time the ocean was always calm.

someone has had his/her day
something has had its day
used to say that the time when someone or something was successful is now over: *Silvero and Allen have both had their day, and it's time for the new manager to take over.*

something has seen better days
used to say that something is old and in bad condition: *Even though the old Jose Theater had seen better days, the public still didn't want it demolished.*

have/get your day in court
to have an opportunity to say or explain something, or to give your opinion: *For years, most historians assumed that there was no difference between Kennedy's and Johnson's Vietnam policies, but now people like Professor Newman are having their day in court.*

honest as the day is long
OLD-FASHIONED used to emphasize that someone is completely honest: *Everyone assured me they were honest as the day was long, but they never repaid the loan.*

in all my born days
OLD-FASHIONED used to emphasize that you have never experienced something before: *They kept shouting at each other – I'd never seen such fights in all my born days.*

it'll be a cold day in hell before...
SPOKEN used to emphasize that you will never do something, or that something will never happen: *It'll be a cold day in hell before Bryant spends that amount of money on any of his employees. | Justin knew it'd be a cold day in hell before he would try snowboarding.*

it's early in the day
SPOKEN used to say that it is too soon to make a judgment about a person or a situation: *I wouldn't like to get too excited about our chances of winning this early in the day.*

it's one of those days
SPOKEN used about a day when everything seems to be going wrong: *I can't get Jennifer on the phone again. I knew this would happen – it's going to be one of those days.*

it's not your day
(also **it's not your week, year, decade, etc.**)
SPOKEN said when several problems or unpleasant things have happened to you in one day: *I missed my bus, I left my lunch at home – it just hasn't been my day.*

it's not your day

live to fight another day
to be able to try again after a failure or difficult time: *This isn't the first time we've been defeated in an election, but we always live to fight another day.*

make a day of it
SPOKEN to make a trip or event continue all day instead of part of a day, in order to do things that will make it enjoyable: *Instead of just driving there and back, we could make a nice day of it in the mountains and come home a little later.*

make *someone's* day
SPOKEN to make someone very happy: *John was completely surprised when we threw him a birthday party – he said it just made his day.*

a red-letter day
used about a very special day, when something exciting or important happens: *When man landed on the moon, it was a true red-letter day for humankind.*

D

rue the day
to wish that you had not done something: *We may rue the day that we appointed an outsider to such an important post.*

save the day
to do something that makes a situation end in success, when it seemed likely to end in failure or defeat: *Talmadge, who hadn't been playing well up until then, finally saved the day with an incredible goal.*

save *something* for a rainy day
(also **put** *something* **away for a rainy day**)
to save something, especially money, for a time when you will need it: *If you won the lottery, would you spend all the money or save it for a rainy day?*
rainy-day: *Having a rainy-day fund is a good idea to protect yourself against an uncertain future.*

seize the day
used to tell someone to do what they want to do and not worry about the future: *My parents always encouraged me to do the things I want – to seize the day.*

> NOTE▶ You may also hear people use "Carpe diem," which is the Latin phrase for "seize the day": *Mark's personal philosophy of Carpe diem has given him a full and meaningful life.*

that'll be the day!
SPOKEN said when you think that something is very unlikely to happen: *"I heard you're going to get a raise at work." "That'll be the day!"*

win/carry the day
if a person, idea, or thing wins the day, they win an argument or competition, or have the most influence on a situation or decision: *Biko spoke little, but his suggestions always won the day.*

daylight

beat the (living) daylights out of *someone*
to hit someone a lot and seriously hurt them: *All I know is that after the game, Otis beat the living daylights out of him.*

in broad daylight
if something, especially a crime, happens in broad daylight, it happens in the daytime when people can easily see it: *Johnson was arrested on Saturday for grabbing a teacher's purse in broad daylight.*

scare/frighten the living daylights out of *someone*
to frighten someone very much: *The first time I met Matt, he scared the living daylights out of me – well, you know he's kind of weird-looking.*

see daylight
1 to begin to understand something: *After listening for several minutes, I suddenly saw daylight.*
2 to be discovered or noticed: *Henderson recorded three albums last year, but none of those projects ever saw daylight.*

dead

⇨*someone* **wouldn't be caught/seen dead** —see CATCH

be dead set on (doing) *something*
used to say that someone is very determined that something should be done or happen: *The board is dead set on relocating the company, even though it will cost in the millions.*
opposite **be dead set against (doing)** *something*: *The Chief Justice was dead set against the idea of televising Supreme Court proceedings.*

deal

big deal!
SPOKEN said when you do not think something is as important, impressive, or special as another person thinks it is: *I know you failed the test. Big deal! Remember, we still have two more.*

get a raw deal
to be treated unfairly: *This new legislation is good for federal employees but a raw deal for the taxpayers.*

something is a done deal
used to say that an arrangement, business deal, etc. has been completed and cannot

be changed: *It's a done deal – the merger is going ahead.*

no big deal
SPOKEN used to say that something is not as important to you, or is not as much of a problem for you as other people think it is: *Look, it's no big deal to me if we don't go. I said I'd take your dad to the game because I knew how much he wanted to go.*

what's someone's deal?
SPOKEN used to ask what is wrong with someone: *What's your deal? You haven't spoken to me all week.*

what's the deal (with)?
SPOKEN used to ask what is happening or why something is happening: *"I talked to Carter." "Oh yeah? What's the deal? Are we going out or not?"* | *What's the deal with the new highway? I thought it was supposed to be done by now.*

death

⇨ **at death's DOOR**
⇨ **be tickled to death** —see **be TICKLED pink**
⇨ **to sound/be the death KNELL**

catch your death (of cold)
OLD-FASHIONED used to warn someone that they will get very cold and sick: *Don't go outside without a hat, you'll catch your death.*

done to death
if a subject or an idea is done to death, it is talked about or used so much that people become bored with it: *Those jokes about changing lightbulbs have been done to death. We need something new.*
—see also **to DEATH**

someone is signing his/her own death warrant
used to say that someone is doing something that will cause them very serious problems ♦ USED ESPECIALLY IN BUSINESS OR POLITICS: *As the owner of a business, if you discriminate against women, you could be signing your own death warrant.*

look/feel like death warmed over
SPOKEN used to say that someone looks or

feels very sick or tired: *She looked like death warmed over. I don't know why she didn't stay at home.*

to death
1 used after an adjective in order to emphasize how strongly you feel an emotion: *The first time Billy took me for a ride on his motorcycle, I was scared to death. I bet Margot was thrilled to death when she got the money.*
2 used to emphasize how much or to what a great degree someone does something, especially when it is being done too much: *Sarah used to worry me to death when she stayed out too late. | Golding's novels have been analyzed to death by critics trying to extract every scrap of meaning.*
—see also **done to DEATH**

someone will be the death of me
OLD-FASHIONED used to say that someone is causing you a lot of worry or problems: *With all his crazy tricks, Samuel will be the death of me.*

deck

⇨ **the deck is stacked against** *someone* —see **the ODDS/cards are stacked against** *someone*

clear the decks
to get ready to start doing something new, by finishing work, dealing with problems, or clearing things away: *We've decided to clear the decks of any old projects for the new year, which should open up more time for new ones.*

hit the deck/dirt
to fall to the ground suddenly, especially in order to avoid being shot or to escape from some other danger: *The gun fired, and everyone hit the deck.*

not play with a full deck
a humorous expression used about someone who is very stupid or slightly crazy: *Any time you want to strap yourself into a race car and go 290 miles per hour, you can't be playing with a full deck.*

deed

do the dirty deed
1 a humorous expression meaning to

have sex: *Nobody believes that we didn't do the dirty deed until after we were married.*
2 a humorous expression meaning to do something wrong or unpleasant: *They did the dirty deed in the middle of the night, when the other members couldn't be consulted.*

deer

like a deer caught in the headlights
used to say that someone is very confused and does not know what to do: *I could hear the baby wailing as Jake answered the door, looking like a deer caught in the headlights.*

degree

give *someone* the third degree
to ask someone a lot of questions, in a serious or threatening way in order to get information from them: *Whenever one of my boyfriends came to the house, Dad would give him the third degree.*

...to the nth degree
as much as possible, or to the greatest degree: *Jacob has violated every law to the nth degree.*

den

a den of iniquity
used about a place where people behave in a way that is immoral or bad, often used humorously when you only disapprove slightly of what someone is doing: *Zero's Bar is one of those dens of iniquity that your mother used to warn you about.*

in/into the lion's den
among people who are your enemies or who will criticize you: *Morris went into the lion's den at the press conference, and insisted he'd done nothing wrong.*

dent

make a dent in *something*
1 to reduce the size or amount of something, especially a supply of money, a debt, or a problem: *We have tried all the solutions for homelessness in the last*

10 years, but it doesn't seem to make a dent in the problem.
2 (also **make a dent on** *something*) to have an effect on a situation and change it: *The band made a dent on the charts two years ago with "Nothing to Lose," but haven't had any great success since then.*

department

something is someone's department
SPOKEN to be part of the work that you are supposed to do, or one of the things that you are interested in: *I'm not really into modern art. That's Donald's department.*

depth

be out of your depth
to be unable to deal with a situation that you do not understand, or a subject that you do not know enough about: *I was soon totally out of my depth, as the conversation turned from politics to economics.*

plumb the depths (of)
1 to do something in the worst or most extreme way possible: *Friday television continues to plumb the depths of extremely bad taste.*
2 to find out things about a person, society, or subject that are secret or not known: *Shusaku Endo has plumbed the depths of the Japanese heart in his study of society and religion.*
3 to feel an unpleasant emotion, such as shame or sadness, in the strongest possible way: *I sat with tears on my cheeks, plumbing the depths of humiliation.*

sink to the depths
to lose all your moral judgment and do things that are extremely bad: *I can't believe he could sink to those depths. I mean, it must be pretty bad to be stealing from your own family.*

deserts

get your just deserts
to suffer or have problems that you deserve because you have done bad, stupid, or illegal things: *I guess I got my just deserts; my marriage was not happy, but then I got married for all the wrong reasons.*

designs

have designs on
1 to want something for yourself and try to get it, especially in a secret or dishonest way: *Simon always had designs on my job, and now he finally got it.*
2 to want to have a sexual relationship with someone, and try to persuade or trick them into doing what you want: *Listen, I have no designs on Tom, he's your boyfriend.*

desire

⇨do *something* **to your heart's CONTENT/desire**

someone's **heart's desire**
used about the thing or person that someone wants more than anything else: *My mother's heart's desire was a handsome, dark-eyed son, but she got me instead.*

devices

be left to your own devices
to be allowed to do what you want to do, and not be given any help or advice about it: *Children under a particular age should never be left to their own devices.*

devil

⇨play/be devil's **ADVOCATE**

better the devil you know (than the devil you don't)
used to say that although the person or situation you are dealing with now is difficult, it is safer to continue dealing with that situation than to try something new which may be worse: *The board may decide to stay with the devil they know, rather than risk a change of management.*

between the devil and the deep blue sea
in a difficult situation in which any choice that you make will have bad results: *We were between the devil and the deep blue sea. We were told we could either continue on low pay, or get more money for very difficult working conditions.*
—see also **(caught) between a ROCK and a hard place**

the devil incarnate
used about someone who you think is extremely bad or immoral: *Some people think Karl Marx was the devil incarnate; others think he was a great social critic.*

the devil makes/finds work for idle hands
OLD-FASHIONED used to say that people, especially children, should always have work to do so that they do not start to do things that are wrong or stupid: *My aunt, who believes that the devil makes work for idle hands, was trying to teach me to knit.*

do *something* **like the devil**
to do something very fast or using a lot of force: *They must have fought like the devil to get out of there alive.*

give the devil his due
used to say that although you do not like or approve of someone, they have done something good or have some good quality: *Giving the devil his due, I have to admit that my grandmother was sometimes extremely generous to us.*
—compare **give** *someone* **his/her DUE**

speak of the devil
SPOKEN said when a person who you are talking about comes into the room: *Well, speak of the devil! How did you know we were talking about you?*

diamond

a diamond in the rough
used about someone who is not very polite or well educated but has good qualities: *The team thought Rhodes was a diamond in the rough who could lead them back into first place.*

diarrhea

have verbal diarrhea
(also have diarrhea of the mouth)
SPOKEN to talk a lot without stopping, usually in a way that annoys people: *The only thing that bothers me about flying is having to sit next to someone who has verbal diarrhea.*

NOTE▶ Diarrhea is a condition in which someone has to use the toilet very frequently, so it is better not to use this idiom in situations where you want to be polite.

dibs

have dibs on *something*
SPOKEN to claim something for yourself before anyone else can claim it: *I have dibs on the leftover pie!*

dice

the dice are loaded (against *someone*)
used to say that a situation is unfair, because someone has a disadvantage and cannot succeed: *The dice were loaded against us from the start, so nothing we said could convince the court that we were innocent.*

no dice
SPOKEN used when refusing to do something you have been asked to do, or in order to say that something is not possible: *I tried to get someone to cover your shift this weekend, but no dice.*

diddly

not ___ (jack) diddly
(also **not ___ diddly-squat** or **not ___ diddly-shit**)
SPOKEN to not do, have, know, etc. anything at all: *The financial aid department was no help at all. They didn't do jack diddly for me.* | *A few months ago, a situation like this wouldn't have meant diddly-squat because the stock market was doing so well. But now it's a problem.*

NOTE▶ The verbs that are most commonly used with this idiom are "do," "have," "know," "mean," "get," and "earn." You may hear people use this expression without "not" to mean the same thing.

die

⇨**DO or die**
the die is cast
used to say that an important decision has been made, or something important has happened, and the situation cannot be changed: *The book is written, the die is cast, and I must accept the judgment of my readers.*

I almost died
(also **I just (about) died**)
SPOKEN used to say that you felt very surprised, amused, or embarrassed by something that happened: *I almost died when Selina told everyone how old I am.*

someone/something **is to die for**
SPOKEN used about someone you think is very attractive, or something that you think is beautiful or extremely good, especially clothing and food: *Huston, with a body and wardrobe to die for, is starring in the new blockbuster.* | *Their triple chocolate mousse is to die for.*

never say die
SPOKEN used to encourage someone to continue doing something that is difficult: *Come on, never say die! You'll be finished in a week if you keep working hard.*
never-say-die: *The never-say-die attitude of the Minnesota Vikings has led them through a great season.*

someone **would rather die (than do** *something***)**
SPOKEN used to emphasize that someone really does not want to do something: *I'd rather die than go back to work at that place!*

difference

same difference
SPOKEN used to say that two things are the same, or have the same result or effect: *Well, if you're already in trouble and you haven't even done anything, then you might as well do something. It's the same difference.*

a ___ with a difference
used to say that you approve because something is different and better: *These are children's book reviews with a difference, because the children themselves tell you what they've read and how they like it.*

difficult

⇨*something* is **HARD/difficult to swallow**

dime

⇨**NICKEL and dime** (*someone*/*something*)

be a dime a dozen

SPOKEN used to say that something is very common, often when this makes it less interesting or valuable: *Don't worry about being fired – jobs like that are a dime a dozen!*

on a dime

1 if a car or someone driving a car turns, stops, or parks on a dime, they do it easily in a small space: *My dad could park on a dime, but I never learned to do it.*
2 if a person, organization, system, etc. stops, changes, or turns on a dime, they are able to stop what they are doing and quickly do something different when it is necessary: *Advertisers can turn on a dime and produce new commercials in a couple of hours.*

dint

by dint of

by using a particular method: *Simon Schwartz mastered the financial markets by dint of his brilliant mind and boundless energy.*

direction

point *someone* in the right direction

to advise someone on what they should do, or tell them who can help them: *The agency may give straight advice on projects or simply point applicants in the right direction for funding.*

dirt

⇨**hit the DECK/dirt**

dig up/for dirt

to try and discover something that may harm another person: *The TV series starred Rogers as a journalist who drinks a lot and digs up dirt on famous people to print in his newspaper.*

dish the dirt (on *someone*)

to spend time talking about other people's private lives, and saying unkind or shocking things about them: *Even though Peter is in his thirties, he still dishes the dirt like he was sixteen.*

hit pay dirt

to find something valuable, or find what you have been looking for: *This week's big Lotto winner can hit pay dirt in the form of a cool $2 million.*

> NOTE▶ "Pay dirt" was what miners (=people who look for gold, silver, etc.) called the earth or rock in which they found valuable metals, especially gold.

treat *someone* like dirt

to treat someone in an unkind way and without respect: *Stinson treated his secretary like dirt for 15 years until she finally got up the courage to find another job.*

disaster

⇨*something* spells **TROUBLE/disaster**

discretion

discretion is the better part of valor

used to say that it is better to be careful than to take unnecessary risks: *Discretion is the better part of valor now, and you would be wiser to keep your thoughts to yourself rather than risk a confrontation at work.*

dish

⇨**dish the DIRT (on *someone*)**

someone can dish it out but they can't take it

SPOKEN used to say that someone likes to criticize, attack, or make jokes about other people, but they do not like it when other people do the same to them: *On the field, Pollock can dish it out but he can't take it. If anyone comes within a foot of him, he crashes to the turf.*

NOTE▶ You may hear people change the words of this idiom slightly to fit a particular situation: *After the fight Sherman told us, "I showed tonight that I can dish it out and I can take it too."*

distance

go the (full) distance
to finish what you have to do, especially to continue to the end in a competition or sport: *The boxing world seemed surprised that George Foreman could go the full distance against a much younger man.*

within spitting distance (of *something*)
very close to something: *My new apartment is within spitting distance of school.*
—see also **a stone's THROW away**

within striking distance (of *something*)
used to emphasize that you have nearly achieved what you want to do: *Supporters of the bill said they were within striking distance of getting enough signatures for a veto.*

distraction

drive *someone* to distraction
to annoy someone so much that they become angry, upset, and unable to think clearly: *The sound of my high-pitched voice drives my friends to distraction.*

ditch

last-ditch effort/attempt
(also **last-ditch appeal, negotiations, measures, etc.**)
when someone tries to prevent or change something just before it is going to happen, especially when this attempt fails or is likely to fail: *The club has voted to accept women, in spite of last-ditch efforts by some of the older members to keep them out.*

dither

in a dither
not knowing what to say or do because something unexpected or confusing has happened: *Everyone was in a dither yesterday when it suddenly started to snow.*

dividends

pay dividends
used to say that the time or effort that you used to do something is bringing advantages: *As a union official, you'll sit on various committees, and all that work pays dividends in terms of experience.*

Dixie

be whistling Dixie
1 SPOKEN to be saying something that is untrue ◆ OFTEN USED IN THE NEGATIVE: *I think he could become a national politician, and I'm not just whistling Dixie.*
2 SPOKEN used to say that someone is very happy with their situation, even though other people in the same situation or in a similar situation are not: *Our crops failed because of rain, but 30 miles away they're whistling Dixie.*

do

⇨**done to DEATH**
⇨**THAT does it!**

can/could do without *something*
SPOKEN used to say that you do not want something, especially because it may give you more problems: *I don't mind being reminded of my brother; it's the comparisons I can do without.*

could/can do with *something*
SPOKEN used to say that someone needs or would like something: *Looks like you could do with some help.*

do a ___ (on *someone*)
SPOKEN used with someone's name in order to say that someone is behaving like someone you know or like a famous person, especially in a way that is bad or annoying: *You're not going to do a Bonnie on me and cancel at the last minute, are you?*

be done for
SPOKEN to be very likely to fail or have something bad happen to you: *I knew I was done for when both my parents were waiting up late for me.*

be done in

1 SPOKEN to fail or be stopped, usually for reasons you cannot control: *Public schools have gradually been done in by a lack of quality teachers.*

2 OLD-FASHIONED to be killed: *They say he was done in by his mistress or his wife, but no one knows which.*

do or die
(also **do-or-die**)

used to say that you must try very hard to avoid failure in a difficult or dangerous situation: *Tonight's game was do-or-die for us. We did it, and now we have to look at what comes next.*

do *someone* proud

1 to make someone feel proud by doing something well: *The Marr Ranch is a wonderful place to spend the weekend, and the owners do themselves proud with a wonderful menu.*

2 to treat someone very well and make them feel special: *You've done this company proud with all your hard work.*

do *someone* wrong

SPOKEN to do something that is disloyal to someone who loves you, especially having sex with someone else when you are already married or in a relationship: *I think she's crazy. I'd never stay with someone who had done me wrong like that.*

doctor

just what the doctor ordered

used to say that something is exactly what you need: *I'm hoping that this year's vacation to Florida will be just what the doctor ordered.*

does

⇨**EASY does it**

dog

⇨**it's a dog's LIFE**
⇨**you lie like a big dog (on a rug)**
   —see *someone* **lies like a RUG**

call off the dogs

to tell someone to stop criticizing, attacking, or causing trouble for someone else, especially in a legal case: *Before I*

agree to give you the dealer's name, you have to promise to call off the dogs.

a dog-and-pony show

used when you disapprove of an event because you think it has only been organized in order to seem impressive to people: *The rock concert Valence is planning to raise money for earthquake victims promises to be a real dog-and-pony show.*

dog days

1 a period of time during which something is not very successful: *These are truly the dog days for the Broncos. They haven't won a game in five weeks.*

2 (also **the dog days of summer**) the hottest days of the summer in July and August: *Labor Day is the traditional end of the dog days of summer.*

> NOTE▶ The ancient Romans called these hot days "dog days" because a star called the "Dog Star" rises and goes down at the same time as the sun during the hottest weeks of the year.

dog eat dog

used to describe a situation, especially in business, in which people who want to succeed are willing to do anything to get what they want: *In the world of producing computer hardware, it's always a case of dog eat dog.*
dog-eat-dog: *I needed a change from the weather, the city, and the dog-eat-dog way of life.*

(be) a dog in the manger

used about someone who will not let other people use or have something that they cannot use or have themselves: *What I want to know is if she's really interested in Dave, or is she just a dog in the manger?*
dog-in-the-manger: *They seem to have a dog-in-the manger attitude and won't let us have any input in the project.*

be dog tired
(also **be dog-tired**)

to be very tired: *Jesse was dog-tired after taking the kids to the zoo all day.*

every dog has its day

used to say that even the most unimportant person has a time in their life when they are successful and noticed: *When asked about the winning goal, Orrell commented that every dog had its day.*

something **is going to the dogs**

SPOKEN used to say that a country, organization, etc. is not as successful, organized, or safe as it was and is getting worse all the time: *This city has been going to the dogs ever since Jefferson became mayor.*

let sleeping dogs lie

to deliberately avoid mentioning a subject or problem, because you know it will cause trouble if you do: *He wanted to ask about the letter, but he decided to let sleeping dogs lie.*

a shaggy dog story

a story told as a joke that often ends in a very silly or unexpected way: *I can make a shaggy dog story last forever, and when people laugh at the end, it's the ultimate compliment.*

(as) sick as a dog

SPOKEN very sick, especially so that you bring food up from your stomach: *I have to be as sick as a dog before mom will let me stay home from school.*

throw *someone* **to the dogs**

to allow someone to be criticized or treated badly because you do not need them anymore, or because you want to protect yourself from criticism: *"When it got difficult, Admiral Blair abandoned me and threw me to the dogs," Miller told the judge.*

top dog

used about the person who has the highest or most important position, especially after a struggle: *After a season of tough games, Purdue has finally come out as top dog.*

you can't teach an old dog new tricks

used to say that it is often difficult to make people try new ways of doing things: *"Who says you can't teach an old dog new tricks?" Sanchez said. "This has motivated me to work harder."*

doghouse

be in the doghouse

used to say that someone is annoyed with you because of something you have done: *I have to be home on time tonight, or else I'll be in the doghouse again.*

dollar

(I'll bet you) dollars to doughnuts
(also (I'll bet you) dollars to donuts)

OLD-FASHIONED used to say that you are very sure that something is true or will happen: *I'll bet you dollars to doughnuts she'll quit college before the end of the year.*

look like a million dollars/bucks
(feel like a million dollars/bucks)

used to say that someone looks or feels very well or very attractive: *I felt like a million dollars in the designer gown I wore to the premiere.*

the 64,000 dollar question
(also the million dollar question)

used to say that a question is very important but difficult to answer: *Whether Wyman quit or was fired is the 64,000 dollar question.*

NOTE▶ This idiom comes from the name of a game show on television in the U.S. in the 1950s called *The $64,000 Question* in which the amount of money offered for the final question was $64,000.

you can bet your bottom dollar

SPOKEN said when you are sure that you know what someone will do or what will happen: *You can bet your bottom dollar Jackie and Matt will get married!*

dollar signs

see dollar signs
(also have dollar signs in your eyes)

used about someone who sees a way of making a lot of money: *People were leaving the meeting with dollar signs in their eyes, but I knew that they didn't understand how much hard work would be involved in the project.*

see dollar signs

domino

a/the domino effect

a situation in which one event or action causes several other events or actions, one after the other: *The initial layoff caused a domino effect that resulted in as many as twenty-two additional people losing their jobs.*

> NOTE▶ A domino is a small block of wood with white dots on it, used in the game of dominoes. This idiom comes from the idea that if you stand many of these blocks up on their ends in a line and push the first one, the rest of the dominoes in the line will fall down, one after the other.

done

—see DO

don'ts

⇨the DOS and don'ts

doo-doo

be in deep doo-doo

SPOKEN a humorous way of saying that someone is in a bad or dangerous situation or that someone is angry with them: *Caroline told Dad what you said, and now you're in deep doo-doo at home.*

> NOTE▶ "Doo-doo" is a children's word that people use when they do not want to say "shit."

doom

⇨*something* **spells doom** —see
  something **spells TROUBLE/disaster**

be all doom and gloom

to have no feelings of hope for the future: *Sure, we've lost a couple of games, but it's not all doom and gloom.*

door

at death's door

very sick and likely to die, often used humorously: *Carmine, who had been at death's door a month before, was there laughing and talking as if she'd never been sick.*

behind closed doors

if something, especially a meeting, happens behind closed doors, it happens in a place where no one can see you or find out what you are doing: *Because of the recent media attention, the case will be argued behind closed doors for the rest of the week.*

do *something* **by/through the back door**

to achieve something secretly, or in an unusual or indirect way ◆ OFTEN USED IN NEWSPAPERS, ON TELEVISION NEWS, ETC.: *They're breaking their promises and trying to introduce new taxation by the back door.*
back-door: *The tobacco companies claim that the FDA rules are the beginning of the back-door prohibition of cigarettes.*

lay *something* **at** *someone's* **door**

to blame someone for something: *I'm not sure how much of our current problem we can lay at Carson's door.*

never darken *someone's* **door**

OLD-FASHIONED used to say that you do not want to see someone any longer because they have done something to make you angry or upset: *He pointed his finger at me and shouted, "You'll never darken our door again, I promise you!"*

open (the) doors for
(also **open the door for**)

to give someone opportunities that they did not have before: *Our album has opened doors for us all over the world –*

D

it's amazing how many people know us now.

the/a revolving door

1 a situation in which people in a company, organization, or system do not stay there for very long: *Since the council chairman left in December, the position has become a revolving door.*
revolving-door: *The revolving-door casting at the studio has made both actors and producers very nervous.*
2 the situation in which government officials frequently accept important positions with private companies, and people in these companies frequently go to work for the government: *Congress must act to end the revolving door between U.S. trade officials and foreign companies.*
revolving-door: *Jacobs isn't a member of the revolving-door society between government and the private sector.*

show *someone* the door

to say clearly and in an unfriendly way that you want someone to leave: *I expected him to show me the door when I told him I was from the local paper, but he agreed to talk.*

doornail

(as) dead as a doornail

SPOKEN a humorous expression used to emphasize that someone is dead with no signs of life, or that something has failed: *When we found the mouse, it was as dead as a doornail.*

dos

the dos and don'ts

the things you should and should not do in a particular situation: *Let's talk about some of the dos and don'ts before the interview.*

doses

in small doses

SPOKEN used to say that you only like something or someone if you do not have to do it or be with them for very long: *I can only stand horror movies in very small doses.*

dot

dot (all) the i's and cross (all) the t's

to look carefully at all the details before you finish something ♦ OFTEN USED IN BUSINESS AND POLITICS: *There is a very good chance that the product will be out on the market next month. We just have to dot our i's and cross our t's first.*

on the dot

exactly at a particular time: *The bus is supposed to leave at eight o'clock on the dot.*

double

⇨do a double TAKE

on the double

very quickly and without any delay ♦ OFTEN USED BY PEOPLE GIVING ORDERS: *Matthew, come downstairs on the double. I want to talk to you!*

down

down-and-dirty

1 SLANG used about a competition, argument, fight, etc. in which people say or do nasty, unfair, or dishonest things in order to defeat someone or get an advantage over them: *The down-and-dirty Texas governor's race has occupied the media's attention for the last six months.*
2 used about a way of behaving, performing, working, etc. that people admire because it is full of energy, confidence, and strong basic emotions: *The first track on the album is a down-and-dirty country-blues treatment of "That's All Right Mama," a song that was a hit for Elvis in 1956.*

be down and out

1 used about someone who has nowhere to live, no job, and often uses drugs or drinks too much alcohol: *Wright has spent a lot of his own money setting up a program to help those who are down and out.*
down-and-out: *Wallace Beery won an Oscar in the 1931 movie about a down-and-out boxer and his son.*
2 to be beaten in a competition: *The 49ers are not in the playoffs, but nobody*

could say that the team is down and out. "They're still one of the best teams in football," said Meyers.

> **NOTE▶** People often say that a person, group, team, etc. is "down but not out" when they are doing badly or in a bad situation, but there is a chance that things will improve: *The Bulls were down but not out. They struggled on, and finally overcame the Rockets in the final quarter to win 103–99.*

down under
in or to Australia or New Zealand: *I have always wanted to take a trip down under, but I can't seem to find the time or money.*

have *something* down pat
to know something very well so that you can say it or do it without having to think about it: *I shouldn't have been nervous during the play, because I had my lines down pat.*

downhill

be downhill (all the way) from here (also be downhill (all the way) from now on)
to be easy to do because you have already done the hard part: *We've been practicing for this game all season, and if we win it, it's all downhill from here.*

go downhill
if a situation goes downhill, it becomes worse: *I stopped listening to Capitol City FM months ago – I thought it really went downhill with the new management.*

dozen

six of one, half a dozen of the other
SPOKEN used to say that there is not much difference between two possible choices, situations, etc.: *In terms of time, it doesn't matter whether we take the bus or drive. It's six of one, half a dozen of the other.*

drag

be a drag
used about a situation that is boring or difficult: *That class is such a drag – do we have to go today?*

drag *someone* kicking and screaming
to persuade or force someone to do something that they do not want to do: *The new, organic methods of farming are not welcomed by everyone. Some parts of the agriculture industry are being dragged along kicking and screaming.*

be a drag on *something*
to make progress difficult for something
♦ OFTEN USED IN BUSINESS AND POLITICS: *Hogan said he's resigning because he didn't want to be a drag on the governor's success in the next election.*

dragon

chase the dragon
SLANG to smoke heroin (=an illegal drug) by heating it and breathing in the smoke: *I learned how to chase the dragon from my big brother when I was too young.*

drain

go down the drain/tubes/toilet
1 if an organization, country, system, etc. goes down the drain, it becomes worse or fails: *Industry in the U.S. is going down the drain. We need more investment and more help from Washington.*
2 if time, effort, money, etc. goes down the drain, it is wasted or produces no results: *Three billion dollars in defense money went down the drain, and we have essentially nothing to show for it.*

draw

be quick on the draw
to understand a situation and react to it quickly: *Town officials have been quick on the draw, and made sure that they themselves will have two seats on the new committee.*
—see also **be quick off the MARK**

drawing
⇨go back to the drawing **BOARD**

dream
⇨be a **PIPE** dream

the American dream
the belief that everyone in the U.S. can be rich and successful if they work hard enough: *A good education has always been a major part of the American dream.*

dream on!
SPOKEN said when you think something that someone is hoping for is not likely to happen: *"The computers should be back up by tomorrow, right?" "Dream on! We don't even have the part yet."*

dream ticket
used about a combination of people who you think are very likely to win an election or succeed in something: *Amundson and Castino are a real dream ticket compared to the other candidates.*

not in my wildest dreams
(also **never in my wildest dreams**)
SPOKEN used to emphasize that you never imagined something could happen or be possible, especially when it is happening now: *Not in my wildest dreams did I think I'd be cheering for the Raiders.*

in your dreams
SPOKEN said when you think something that someone is hoping for is not likely to happen: *"I know I'm going to get into Yale." "Yeah, in your dreams!"*

live/be in a dream world
used to say that someone has no idea of what a situation is really like and has plans or ideas that they are not likely to achieve: *Kids today are living in a dream world; they think that everything should come to them, but they don't want to work for it.*

the ___ of someone's dreams
the type of person or thing someone imagines when they think about who or what they like most: *The movie is a romantic comedy about an architect who builds a house for the woman of his dreams.*

run/work/go like a dream
if a machine or system runs, works, etc. like a dream, it works perfectly: *Except for the odd isolated problem, our old Chevrolet is still running like a dream.*

someone wouldn't dream of doing something
SPOKEN used to say that someone would never do something because they know it is wrong or stupid: *T.V. comedy writers wouldn't dream of writing a show with an unhappy ending – the audience wouldn't like it.*

dress
⇨be ALL dressed up and/with nowhere to go

dressed to kill
wearing very beautiful or expensive clothes so that people notice you: *Shanda was two hours late, but she was dressed to kill.*

dribs

in dribs and drabs
if someone or something comes or goes somewhere in dribs and drabs, they come or go a few at a time, not all at once: *News from the war zone has been coming in dribs and drabs.*

drift

get/catch someone's drift
(also **get/catch the drift of** *something*)
SPOKEN to understand the general meaning of what someone is saying: *You didn't finish what you were saying, but I got the drift.*

drink

someone is a tall drink of water
OLD-FASHIONED used about someone who is very tall: *You've gotten to be a tall drink of water just like your father.*

drive
⇨drive *someone* up the WALL

drive someone crazy/bonkers
to annoy someone a lot: *Santa Fe is a great city, but all the tourists drive me crazy!*

driver
⇨back SEAT driver
⇨SUNDAY driver

drop

do *something* at the drop of a hat
1 to do something every time there is an opportunity to do it, even though it is not suitable or necessary to do this: *Len and Debra will bring out those pictures of their kids at the drop of a hat.*
2 to do something very quickly: *When Thomas asked me to go to Mexico, I was ready to go at the drop of a hat.*

NOTE▶ You may hear people use other words instead of "hat" in order to make this idiom fit a particular situation and to be funny: *In these days of political correctness, you can be sued at the drop of an inappropriate adjective.*

a drop in the bucket
a very small amount of something compared with the amount that you need or want: *A lot of progress has been made in the war against illiteracy, but it's really just a drop in the bucket if we're trying to change the whole system.*

drummer

march to (the beat of) a different drummer
(also **march to a different tune**)
to have ideas that are different from those of most other people in your group, organization, or society: *We need good, respected alternative courses for students who march to a different drummer.*

dry

⇨**HANG** *someone* **out to dry**

duck

a dead duck
a plan, idea, etc. that is not useful or is likely to fail: *Everyone agrees that something has to be done before the next meeting, but recruiting outsiders to take over the leadership is a dead duck.*

be a duck shoot
to be a very easy job or piece of work: *Learning to drive a motorcycle should be a duck shoot for you.*

get (all) your ducks in a row
to organize things so that you are in control of a situation: *Carla was chosen to lead the project because she has no trouble getting her ducks in a row.*

be a lame duck
used about an elected official, political group, etc. who does not have much power because their time in office will soon end: *Phillipson has been a lame duck since May, when he was defeated in the Republican Primary.*
lame-duck: *The public meeting on the development project may mean that lame-duck council members could approve the controversial building.*

be a sitting duck
used about someone who cannot defend themselves against people who might harm them or try to get an advantage over them: *You're like a sitting duck when you insist on walking home alone at night.*

take to *something* like a duck to water
to learn how to do something very easily because you are naturally good at it: *Jack took to baseball like a duck to water before he was even five.*

duckling

an ugly duckling
someone who is not as attractive, skillful, etc. as other people when they are young, but who becomes beautiful and successful later: *He may be rich and famous now, but Nelson was always considered the ugly duckling of his family.*

dudgeon

in high dudgeon
used to say that someone is very angry because someone has treated them badly, especially when you think they are being stupid: *She left in high dudgeon, without speaking to anyone.*

due

give *someone* his/her due
if you give someone their due when you are criticizing them or when they have done something wrong, you say that not

all the things they did were bad or wrong: *We have to give Hoffman his due. He was a good leader and improved the quality of education at our college.*
—compare **give the DEVIL his due**

pay your dues
to work very hard or experience difficult times before becoming successful, especially when other people respect you for this: *My dad always told me I had to pay my dues as a paperboy before I could get a good job in the city.*

duh
⇨**NO duh**

dump

take a dump
SPOKEN a rude expression meaning to go to the toilet and pass solid waste out of your body: *Sorry I couldn't come to the phone – I was taking a dump downstairs.*

dumps

be down in the dumps
1 to feel very sad and have no interest in life: *I've been down in the dumps ever since Jane left me.*
2 if a business or the economy is down in the dumps, it is not working successfully: *The market is down in the dumps at the moment; you'd be crazy to sell your shares today.*

dunk
⇨**be a SLAM dunk**

dust

bite the dust
(also **bite it**)
1 to die or fail: *Hundreds of small*

businesses are biting the dust every day.
2 to fall down or fall off something suddenly: *I totally bit it when my bike hit that patch of sand!*

the dust settles
if the dust settles after a difficult, confusing, or exciting situation, people gradually stop being angry, upset, confused or excited: *The guilty members of the company quit even before the dust settled.*

be eating *someone's* dust
to be much less successful in a competition, sport, or business than someone you are competing against: *Yet again, the Cowboys have ended the season eating the Packers' dust.*

> NOTE▶ This idiom comes from the idea that when one car is beating another in a race, the second driver is forced to drive in the clouds of dust that are pushed into the air by the first car.

gather dust
used to say that something is not being used or thought about: *I won't buy you another bike when your old one is just sitting around gathering dust.*

be like gold dust
used to say that something is very valuable and very difficult to find: *This is only the second time in 35 years the team has made it to the finals, so tickets are like gold dust.*

Dutch

go Dutch (with *someone*)
to share the cost of a meal, movie, etc. with someone: *You don't have to buy my ticket – I thought we were going Dutch.*

E

eagle

⇨keep an eagle EYE on

a legal eagle
used about a lawyer who is famous for being good at his or her job: *Corbin was the team's legal eagle for eight years before his big promotion to president.*

ear

⇨(don't) piss in my ear and tell me it's raining —see (don't) piss on my BACK and tell me it's raining

be all ears
to be eager to hear what is being said: *"Are you listening to me?" "Yes, go on, I'm all ears."*

bend *someone's* **ear**
to talk to someone for a long time, especially when this is annoying or boring for them: *Munro bent Ziegler's ear for an hour about how delightful it would be to live near his children in San Jose.*

an ear (for *something***)**
the ability to easily understand everything about music, language, etc. and the way it sounds, and to sing, play, write, or speak it well: *Janowitz's recent novel proves she has a sense of humor and a great ear for dialogue.*

someone's **ears are burning**
(also **are your ears burning?**)
used to say that people have been talking about someone when they were not there, or to ask the person who is being talked about if they realize this: *Your ears must have been burning this morning – Helen's been telling us how wonderful you are.*

fall on deaf ears
if something such as a warning or complaint falls on deaf ears, no one pays attention to it, or it is ignored completely: *Many religious leaders fear the Pope's message fell on deaf ears.*
—compare **turn a deaf EAR (to** *something***),** **turn a blind EYE (to)**

something **goes in one ear and out the other**
SPOKEN used to say that when you tell someone something, they pay no attention or do not remember it: *A lot of the stuff we were supposed to learn in high school went in one ear and out the other.*

someone **has nothing between the ears**
used to say that someone is stupid: *Please stop treating your readers as if we have nothing between the ears, and give us some intelligent reporting.*
opposite *someone* **has something between the ears**: *She's obviously got something between the ears to have passed all those exams.*

> NOTE▶ "Between the ears" is a phrase that is often used to talk about what happens in your brain or your mind: *Max, my best friend and golfing partner, says that my problem is not in my hands, it's between my ears.*

have *something* **coming out of your ears**
SPOKEN used to emphasize how much of something you have: *If you eat any more, you'll have lasagne coming out of your ears.*

have *someone's* **ear**
to be listened to by someone in a powerful position, so that they are willing to support you and pay attention to your advice, opinions, etc.: *Paral said that minority groups had to get the ear of the President if they wanted to be taken seriously.*

keep/have an ear out (for *something***)**
(also **keep/have an ear cocked (for** *something***))**
to listen carefully so that you do not miss something that you are expecting to happen: *I'm just going out for a few minutes – can you keep an ear out for the mailman? | She had an ear cocked for the sound of Joe's key in the front door.*

keep your/an ear to the ground
to be sure that you find out what people are saying and thinking about a situation

that you are involved in, especially so that no one gains an advantage over you: *I want everyone to keep their ears to the ground – we can't afford to have Benson's attorneys producing any surprises at the trial.*

lend an ear

to give someone the opportunity to tell you their ideas, feelings, etc., especially if no one else will listen to them: *Every month, Mayor Dudley opens his office doors to lend an ear to ordinary citizens for an hour or so.*

listen with half an ear

to listen to someone while thinking about something else: *Victor lit a cigarette and listened with half an ear, amused by the girls' chatter.*

be out on your ear

to be forced to leave a job, an organization, or your home, especially because you have done something wrong: *Bazoft knew he would be out on his ear the moment the company learned about his criminal record.*

play *something* by ear

SPOKEN to react to a situation as it happens, because you do not know how it is going to change or develop: *"We'll just play it by ear," Zeilstra's coach said. "If she feels good, she'll play. If she doesn't, she won't."*

prick up your ears

to start to be interested in what someone is saying: *Unemployed workers across the country are pricking up their ears, wanting to hear more about the proposed retraining plan.*
someone's **ears pricked up**: *Helen's ears pricked up at Jamie's name. "I didn't know you knew him," she said rather hastily.*

set *something* on its ear

if a person or their achievement sets a place, organization, or group of people on its ear, what they have done gets lots of excited attention and interest: *This computer will not set the industry on its ear, but it does have some new features that should interest our customers.*

be smiling/grinning from ear to ear

to have a big smile on your face because you are very pleased or amused: *Maggie held her new baby daughter and grinned from ear to ear.*

a tin ear (for *something*)

when you are unable to judge what music, poetry, etc. is good, and what is bad: *Only listeners with a tin ear could dislike this CD.*

turn a deaf ear (to *something*)

to refuse to listen to what someone is asking or telling you: *Over fifty percent of office workers felt that their employers would turn a deaf ear if they complained of sexual harassment.*
—compare **fall on deaf EARs, turn a blind EYE (to)**

be up to your ears/neck/eyeballs in *something*

SPOKEN to have more of something, especially work, than you want or can deal with: *I can't come this weekend – I'm up to my ears in work.* | *He must be up to his eyeballs in debt.*

wet behind the ears

young and without much experience in life: *Glen seems nice enough, but he's a little wet behind the ears.*

earful

get an earful

to have to listen to something, usually something you do not want to hear such as complaints, bad news, etc.: *I agreed to have lunch with him, and promptly got an earful about all sorts of things, including all the problems on the K.L.S. deal.*
give *someone* **an earful**: *Dad called the phone company and gave them an earful about long-distance rates going up again.*

earth

⇨ **go to the ENDs of the earth**
⇨ **vanish/disappear/drop off the FACE of the earth**

bring *someone* (back) down to earth (with a bump)

to force someone to think about unpleasant or ordinary things in your life, after a period when you were very happy and enjoying yourself: *I had been madly in love with Dave until common sense brought me back down to earth, and I realized that marriage to him would be a total disaster.*

come (back) down to earth (with a bump): *We had an unbelievable time in Toronto, and it took us a few weeks to come back down to earth.*

did the earth move (for you)?

a humorous expression used in order to ask if an experience, especially sex, was enjoyable and special: *What did it feel like to win the election – did the earth move for you?*

someone is down to earth

used to say that someone is practical, direct, and sensible: *Recent polls indicate that most Ohio residents believe their governor is down to earth, an honest and genuine person.*
down-to-earth: *I think people trust Chris because he's one of those down-to-earth, all-American guys.*

promise *someone* the earth/moon

to promise to give someone something that is impossible for you to give: *I hope Swanson hasn't promised them the earth in the way of commission.*

ease

⇨**ILL at ease**

easier

that's/it's easier said than done

SPOKEN used to say that it would be difficult to do what someone has suggested: *"Try to forget him, Fiona." "Yeah, well that's easier said than done."*

that's/it's easier said than done

easy

⇨**GO easy on** *someone*
⇨**GO easy on** *something*
⇨*something* **isn't easy to swallow** —see *something* **is HARD/difficult to swallow**
⇨**OVER easy**

easy come, easy go

SPOKEN used to say that something, especially money, was easily obtained and is quickly used or spent: *My attitude to money is easy come, easy go – the more I make, the more I spend.*

easy does it

SPOKEN used to tell someone to do something slowly or gently, especially so that they do not get hurt: *Pull the table over this way – easy does it.*

I'm easy

SPOKEN used to say that you do not mind what choice is made: *"Should we leave the stuff here and then come back for it?" "I'm easy, I can do whatever you want to do."*

eat

⇨**WHAT's eating him/her?**

eat *someone* alive

1 to defeat someone easily in business, a fight, an argument, etc., especially in a way that completely destroys them or makes them suffer: *"Health insurance is a major financial issue. It is eating us alive,"* said spokesman Robert W. Stevens.
2 to be very angry with someone: *I'd better take you home now, or your mother will eat me alive.*
3 if insects eat you alive, lots of them bite you in a short period: *We sat outside after dinner, and got eaten alive by the mosquitoes.*

ebb

be at a low ebb

to be in a bad condition or at a level that is too low: *Recent public opinion surveys show that the President's popularity is at a low ebb.*

NOTE▸ When the tide is at low ebb, the water in the ocean is at its lowest level of the day.

economy

a false economy
something that seems to be saving you money now but will cost more later: *Tools are expensive, but it is often a false economy to get the cheapest brand.*

edge

be at/on the cutting edge of *something*
to be the most advanced form of an activity in which the newest methods, systems, and equipment are being developed and used: *The scientific and engineering skills we have developed are on the cutting edge of nuclear technology.*
cutting-edge: *Maintaining cutting-edge science and technology and an unrivaled information base is a critical element in keeping America competitive.*

fray at/around the edges
to become weaker or less effective or to gradually be destroyed: *The Sonics were beginning to fray around the edges without Shawn Kemp in Saturday's game.*

go over the edge
1 to become so worried, afraid, or unhappy that you stop behaving in a normal and reasonable way: *Our goal is to reach people and help them before they go over the edge.*
push *someone* **over the edge:** *It was the pressure of exams that finally pushed him over the edge.*
2 if a business or organization goes over the edge, it fails because it does not have enough money: *Many small businesses are now going over the edge.*

have the edge (over/on)
(also **gain, hold, keep, etc. an edge over/on**)
to have or get an advantage over someone who you are competing with
♦ OFTEN USED IN BUSINESS, POLITICS, AND SPORTS: *The Vikings have a 14–13 edge on the Packers in this season's regular games, but the Packers are looking better all the time.* | *McDermott's swift action gained the company an edge over its rivals.*

have rough edges
1 if a person has rough edges, they are sometimes rude or unkind, or do not always know what to do in social situations: *I know I have a few rough edges, but I'm hoping she'll see past those.*
2 if a performance or piece of work has rough edges, it is not perfect: *The band still has some rough edges, but it shows a lot of promise.*

lose your edge
to become less good at what you do: *I haven't lost my edge, and I'm definitely not ready to quit boxing now.*

be on edge
to be nervous, especially because you are expecting something bad to happen: *Investors have been on edge since a report showed only a slight improvement in the economy.*

be on the edge (of *something*)
(also **be close to the edge**)
1 to be in a situation in which something bad or dangerous could easily happen: *At the time, we all believed we were on the edge of a global nuclear war.*
2 to be in a situation in which you are so upset, tired, etc. that it would be easy to have mental problems: *She was obviously on the edge of despair, and there was nothing we could say that seemed to help.*

on the edge of your seat/chair
interested and eager to know what will happen, especially while watching a movie or play, or reading a book: *Star Trek fans were waiting on the edge of their seats for the next movie.*

be on a razor's/razor edge
to be in a difficult situation where a mistake or wrong decision could be very dangerous: *Politically, we are on a razor's edge, and our future may depend on the decision that we make today.*

take the edge off *something*
to make something less strong, unpleasant, good, etc.: *Advertisements claimed a new pill would take the edge off hunger.*

eel

(as) slippery as an eel
used about someone who you cannot trust because they do not give clear, direct

answers, or do not do what they have promised: *Make sure he agrees to finish the work by the weekend – he's as slippery as an eel.*

effect
⇨a/the DOMINO effect

effort
⇨last-DITCH effort/attempt

egg
⇨walk on EGGSHELLS/eggs

be a good egg
OLD-FASHIONED to be a kind and helpful person: *I like your mom – she's a good egg.*

have egg on your face
(also **have egg all over your face**)
to be embarrassed or seem stupid because of something that you said or did: *The President has egg all over his face from an incident at the press conference yesterday.*

lay an egg
OLD-FASHIONED to fail at what you are trying to do: *After laying an egg in Phoenix with a 7–3 loss, the Warriors came back with a victory.*

put all your eggs in one basket
to depend completely on one thing or action in order to be successful: *Don't put all your eggs in one basket – it's better to invest in several companies and spread the risk.*

eggshells

walk on eggshells/eggs
to be very careful to try not to say or do the wrong thing because someone gets upset easily or because a situation could easily become worse: *"We are walking on eggshells," said Helen Bell, whose house is directly in the path of the hurricane.*

eight ball

behind the eight ball
SPOKEN to be in a situation in which you lack advantages, especially because you were too slow in taking opportunities: *"Our management is behind the eight*

ball, with no credibility," Zamora said. "We've got to do a better job communicating policies to people."

> NOTE▶ The eight ball is the black ball in the game of pool (=game played with colored balls and a stick on a table), which must not be hit into any of the holes at the side of the table until you have hit all your other balls in. You are in a bad situation if the ball you want to hit is behind the eight ball, because it is likely to push the eight ball in with it.

elbow
⇨rub elbows with *someone* —see rub SHOULDERs with *someone*

elbow grease
the hard work and physical effort needed to achieve something: *Thanks to a lot of elbow grease and a few coats of paint, the church is looking as good as new.*

element

brave the elements
to go out when the weather is bad: *Officials offered free tickets to fans in Orlando who braved the elements.*

be in your element
to be in a situation that you are familiar with and are good at dealing with: *Throughout the attempted coup, Jansons appeared to be in his element – contacting world leaders and responding to developments.*
opposite **be out of your element:** *She's out of her element in this role, and even her voice seems too light for the character.*

elephant

a white elephant
something that is completely useless, even though it cost a lot of money: *For years, the county's recycling center has been considered a wasteful white elephant that taxpayers constantly complained about.*
white-elephant: *What this town needs is more parks, not another white-elephant business complex.*

E

elephants

see pink elephants

a humorous expression meaning to see things that are not really there because you are drunk: *You shouldn't have had that last beer – you'll be seeing those pink elephants again.*

elevator

someone's **elevator doesn't go all the way to the top (floor)**

SPOKEN a humorous expression used in order to say that someone is very stupid or slightly crazy: *You know how Lisa is. The elevator doesn't go all the way to the top sometimes.*

Elvis

50 million Elvis fans can't be wrong

SPOKEN used to say that something must be true because so many people think so: *"I just don't understand what's so great about those shoes." "I don't either, but 50 million Elvis fans can't be wrong."*

embarrassment

an embarrassment of riches

a situation in which there are so many good things that it is hard to decide which one to choose, or how to use them all: *The museum is fascinating – its only problem is an embarrassment of riches.*

emperor

⇨the emperor's (new) **CLOTHES**

enchilada

⇨the whole enchilada —see **the whole SHEBANG**

the big enchilada

the biggest or most important thing, which people want more than any other thing of its type: *Thomas served as a federal judge for 18 months before he thought he was ready for the big enchilada – the Supreme Court.*

encyclopedia

someone **is a walking encyclopedia** (also **a walking dictionary, timetable, history book, etc.**)

used about someone who knows a lot and always has the information you need: *Lieutenant Colonel John Hounsell was a walking encyclopedia of army rules and regulations.*

end

⇨**ALL's well that ends well**
⇨not be the **BE-ALL** and end-all (of *something*)
⇨the **BEGINNING** of the end
⇨the **BUSINESS** end of a ___
⇨*someone* will **GET** there

at the end of the day

used to say that when you consider everything in a situation, you get a particular answer or decision or realize that something is true: *We give advice but, at the end of the day, people must make their own decisions.*

be at the end of your rope (also **reach the end of your rope**)

to feel that you cannot deal with a difficult situation any longer because you are too tired, sick, upset, annoyed, etc.: *Darlene reached the end of her rope with her own children and decided she desperately needed a weekend away.*

be at loose ends

to have nothing to do or not know what you want to do: *We believe one of the reasons so many young people are at loose ends today is because they have no sense of family life.*

at your wits' end

very worried because you have tried everything you can think of to solve a problem: *I'm at my wits' end. No matter how many times I tell the post office, they never get my address right.*

come to a bad end

to die in a unpleasant way, or end your life sadly, especially because of something bad that you have done: *In Victorian novels, a passionate woman must always suffer and come to a bad end.*

a dead end

a situation in which progress is not possible: *Peace talks came to a dead end yesterday when leaders refused to compromise.*
dead-end: *Lam's parents told him pursuing martial arts was a dead-end dream.*

> NOTE▶ A "dead end" is a road which is closed at one end.

(the pot of gold at) the end of the rainbow

used about something that someone hopes to get or achieve after trying very hard, but that may be impossible to get: *Introducing a new product is difficult – but there's a tremendous pot of gold at the end of the rainbow if you get it right.*

> NOTE▶ According to an old story, you can find a pot of gold where a rainbow (=a curve of many colors seen in the sky when there is rain and sun at the same time) touches the earth.

the end of the road/line

the point at which a process or activity cannot continue: *Even if the show isn't successful, it won't be the end of the line financially for us.*

get the short end (of the stick)

(also **be on the short end of** *something*)
to be unfairly treated, or have fewer advantages than other people have: *Opponents of the proposal say it is an outrageous attempt at giving newcomers the short end of the stick.* | *Many studies show rural America to be on the short end of the social and economic scale.*

be/get thrown in(to) the deep end

(also **be plunged in(to) the deep end**)
to have to start doing a difficult job without being prepared for it: *The course in tourism helped, but we got thrown into the deep end and had to develop skills quickly.*
jump/dive/plunge in(to) the deep end: *It is possible to jump in the deep end, buy a small farm, and teach yourself. But mistakes can be costly.*

go off the deep end

to suddenly start behaving in an extreme or crazy way: *I was afraid he'd go off the deep end and kill himself.*

go to the ends of the earth

to do everything you can do, even if it is difficult, in order to have or achieve something: *I can't believe you don't like the Cowboy Junkies! I'd go to the ends of the earth to hear them play.*

I'll never hear the end of it

SPOKEN used to say that people will continue to criticize or make jokes about something you have done: *I knew that if I left the bar early, I'd never hear the end of it.*

someone/something is the (absolute) end

(also *someone* **is the (living) end**)
OLD-FASHIONED said when you are very annoyed with a person or a situation: *You are the living end! I've never met anyone who makes the kind of mess you do.*

it's not the end of the world

SPOKEN used to say that although a situation or event causes a problem, it is not a very serious one: *It won't be the end of the world if I don't get this job – I've got two other interviews lined up.*

make ends meet

to have only enough money to buy what you need to live: *At the young age of 22, Anna was divorced, caring for two children, and struggling to make ends meet.*

be on the receiving end (of *something*)

to be the person something is said about, or the person something is done or given to, often something bad or unpleasant: *You didn't have to be a client or friend to be on the receiving end of his generosity.*

play both ends/sides against the middle

to be friendly with both of two people, countries, etc. that are arguing in order to gain an advantage for yourself, especially when each of them thinks that helping you will annoy the other: *Some smaller countries managed to play both ends against the middle, and received aid from the Americans and the Russians.*

E

tie up loose ends

to complete a piece of work or finish dealing with a situation by paying attention to the less important details that you did not consider before: *The final chapter in the "Star Wars" trilogy neatly ties up loose ends from "The Empire Strikes Back."*

loose ends: *Unlike real life, the classic mystery novel has no loose ends.*

the ___ to end all ___s

used to say that something is the biggest, best, worst, most extreme, etc. of its kind: *We've decided we're going to rent a big room in a hotel and throw the party to end all parties on Tony's birthday.*

> NOTE▶ This idiom comes from the phrase "the war to end all wars", which was used to describe World War I.

enemy

be your own worst enemy

to behave in a way that causes problems for yourself: *Lazar is his own worst enemy. He continues to take steroids even though doctors have warned him of the dangers to his health.*

enfant terrible

enfant terrible

used about a person or organization whose new ideas and lack of respect shock or embarrass older or more traditional people: *Polk, once described as "the enfant terrible of western architecture," later gained much respect for his unique styles.*

> NOTE▶ Because this is a French expression, people use the French pronunciation (ˌɑːnfɑːn teˈriːblə) when they say it.

envelope

push the envelope

to do something in an extreme or very unusual way, usually because you are trying to be different from other people: *Malich promised that the new multimedia center would have technology that really pushes the envelope, things the general public has never seen before.*

envy

green with envy

used to say that someone is very upset or annoyed because they wish they had someone's possessions, abilities, success, etc.: *Before you turn green with envy, remember that fashion models often have grueling 16-hour work days and cut-throat competition.*

err

to err is human (to forgive, divine)

used to say that everyone makes mistakes, and that we should not blame someone or be angry with them for these mistakes: *To err is human, but President Kim was very quick to seek a remedy to his mistake.*

escape

a narrow escape

a situation in which you avoid something unpleasant or dangerous, although it very nearly happens: *A family of five managed a narrow escape Sunday as fire destroyed their apartment complex.*

event

the happy event

OLD-FASHIONED the birth of a baby: *"When's the happy event?" "The baby's due in the first week of August."*

everyone

⇨everyone has their **PRICE**

evils

the lesser of two evils

used about the less unpleasant or harmful of two unpleasant choices or possibilities: *Having to choose the lesser of two evils has become an increasingly familiar complaint among voters in this country.*

excuse

excuse me for living/breathing!
(also **pardon me for living/breathing)**

SPOKEN said when you think someone is blaming you or getting angry at you without a good reason: *She started yelling at me, and I was just thinking, well, excuse me for living!* | *"Could you be quiet – I'm trying to read." "Well, pardon me for breathing!"*

a poor/sorry excuse for *something*
(also **a rotten, miserable, feeble, etc. excuse for** *something*)
used to say that someone or something is much worse than they should be: *Milken's plea bargain and the limited hearing are a poor excuse for justice.*

existence

⇨**be the BANE of** *someone's* **life/existence**

expedition

⇨**a FISHING expedition**

expense

do *something* **at** *someone's* **expense**
(also **at the expense of** *someone/something*)
1 if an advantage is gained at the expense of someone or something, it causes harm or disadvantage to that person or thing: *Employers are cutting production costs at the expense of their workers' safety.*
2 if you make a joke at someone's expense, it is about them and makes other people laugh at them: *The best man's speech is traditionally full of jokes at the bridegroom's expense.*

experience

put it/*something* **down to experience**
to try to learn something useful from a failure or mistake, instead of being upset by it: *"My book proposal was rejected by the publisher today" "Oh well, put it down to experience."*

eye

⇨**before you could blink/bat an eye**
—see **before you could BLINK**
⇨**a bird's-eye VIEW (of** *something***)**
⇨**in the PUBLIC eye**
⇨**in the TWINKLING of an eye**
⇨**keep a WEATHER eye on**
⇨**a worm's-eye VIEW (of** *something***)**

⇨**someone would give his/her EYE TEETH to do** *something*

all eyes are on *someone*
used to say that people are giving someone or something a lot of attention: *All eyes are on Feinstein, who has taken a leadership role in the recent economic crisis.*

not (even) bat an eye/eyelash
to not seem at all shocked, surprised, or embarrassed, although you are in a situation where you might easily be: *When we told him what it would cost, he didn't bat an eye.*

cast an eye over/on *something*
1 (also **cast/run your eye over** *something***)**
to read or look at something quickly: *Would you mind casting an eye over this paper before I hand it in?*
2 (also **cast a critical, professional, etc. eye over**) to look at something, or consider something, in a particular way: *While you are raking leaves, cast an eye on your trees for broken branches and dead limbs.*

catch *someone's* **eye**
1 to notice someone or something, because they seem interesting, surprising, or attractive: *A karate class caught Harrison's eye in 1979, and he's been hooked ever since.*
2 to do something so that someone looks at you because you want to speak to them: *If you want to meet a man you find attractive, try subtly catching his eye from across the room.*
3 to look at someone at the same time as they are looking at you: *I caught Luke's eye in the mirror, and he winked at me.*

cry your eyes out
to cry a lot and for a long time: *Poor little Kayla cried her eyes out when her hamster died.*

do *something* **with your eyes closed/shut**
to be able to do something very easily and well because you have done it very often: *I can design these dresses with my eyes closed.*

the evil eye
the power, that some people believe exists, to harm people just by looking at

them: *Some mothers protect their children from the evil eye by hanging strings of peony seeds around their necks.*

someone's **eyes are bigger than his/her stomach**

used to say that someone has taken more food than they can eat ♦ OFTEN USED WHEN SPEAKING TO CHILDREN: *I can't eat the rest, really – my eyes are bigger than my stomach.*

someone's **eyes are popping (out of his/her head)**

used to say that someone is very surprised, excited, or shocked by what they are looking at: *Peter's eyes were popping out of his head when he saw Bethany lying on the beach in her bikini.*

an eye for an eye (a tooth for a tooth)

a system of punishment in which you punish someone by hurting them in the same way as they hurt someone else: *Angry protesters in the square demanded justice be done to their dead friends and family members. Several people held signs that read "An eye for an eye."*
eye-for-an-eye: *The mayor condemned eye-for-an-eye violence after a gang attacked three Vietnamese men.*

feast your eyes on *someone/ something*

to look at someone or something for a long time, with a lot of enjoyment and pleasure: *Alison held the necklace in her hands, feasting her eyes on the sparkling rubies and diamonds.*

four eyes
(also **four-eyes**)

SPOKEN an impolite expression used about someone who wears glasses (=things you wear on your face to help you see better) ♦ USED ESPECIALLY BY CHILDREN: *What child doesn't want to wear contact lenses after being called "four eyes" at school?*

give *someone* a black eye

OLD-FASHIONED to do something that harms someone who you do not like, by making them seem weak or stupid: *The spokesman said the settlement was offered only to resolve the matter quickly before the company got a black eye with consumers.*

give *someone* **the eye**

1 to look at someone in a way that shows that you think they are sexually attractive: *When I see someone I really like I give her the eye that inquires, "What do you think?"*
2 to look at someone in a way that shows that you are angry with them: *Sampras is giving the young Spaniard the eye. I think he's beginning to get annoyed.*

go into *something* **with your eyes open**

used to say that when you made a choice or began a new activity, you knew what the problems or difficulties might be: *I went into this job with my eyes open – I knew it would be difficult.*

opposite **to go into** *something* **with your eyes closed/shut:** *See what you can find out – you don't want to go into this with your eyes closed.*

have an eye for *something*
(also **have a good eye for** *something*)

to be naturally good at noticing things of a particular kind, and recognizing what is attractive, valuable, etc.: *Victoria always looks great. She has a good eye for fashion.*

have eyes in the back of your head

to be able to notice everything that is happening around you: *You need to have eyes in the back of your head when you're teaching a class of ten-year-olds.*

have your eye on *somebody/ something*

1 to want something and hope that you will be able to get it: *Hashimoto is a popular politician who is believed to have his eye on becoming prime minister.*
2 to notice someone who you are attracted to in a sexual way, and hope to become friendly with: *"I had my eye on Bonnie Fuller for years," Brown confessed nostalgically at the high school reunion.*

in/at the eye of the storm

involved in a situation that many people are shocked, angry, or arguing about ♦ OFTEN USED IN NEWSPAPERS, TELEVISION NEWS, ETC.: *Serrano's photograph "Piss Christ" put him in the eye of the storm surrounding the National Endowment for the Arts in 1989.*

in a pig's eye!

OLD-FASHIONED said when you do not believe something that someone has said: *"Dan got the highest mark on the math test." "In a pig's eye!"*

in your mind's eye

in your imagination or memory: *I could see in my mind's eye the exact dress that I wanted.*

keep an eagle eye on

to watch someone or something very carefully, especially so that you will notice anything that is wrong: *Rebecca's children sat near the front of the church, where she could keep her eagle eye on them from the choir.*

keep an eye out for

(also **keep your eyes open for**)
to keep looking for something or someone that you expect to see or want to find: *The teachers were warned to keep an eye out for fights and bullying.*

keep your eyes glued to *something*

to watch something very carefully, and not look away from it: *He was sitting on the sofa with his eyes glued to the T.V. screen.*

keep your eyes open

to notice what is happening around you: *Carlos developed his acting skills by keeping his eyes open and learning from experience.*

keep your eyes peeled

SPOKEN to watch carefully for something: *These guys are used to keeping their eyes peeled for cops, but I don't think they'll recognize you as a cop.*

lay/set eyes on

to see someone or something, especially for the first time ♦ OFTEN USED IN THE NEGATIVE: *She hasn't seen her daughter for years, and she's got a grandson she's never laid eyes on. | The first time I set eyes on Laura, I knew that she was the girl for me.*

only have eyes for *someone*

to only be interested in or only love one person: *Joe only had eyes for Sherry. He didn't ever even say "hello" to me.*

E

open your eyes to *something*

to realize something about your situation that you did not know before or that you do not want to know about: *Stop hesitating, and open your eyes to the possibilities for new careers that are all around you.*
open *someone***'s eyes (to** *something***):** *What first opened our eyes to the realities of war was the return home of wounded soldiers.*
opposite **close/shut your eyes to** *something*: *The world is endangered by pollution, but people shut their eyes to it.*

a roving eye

used to say that someone, usually a man, is always trying to start sexual relationships with other people even though they already have a wife, husband, partner, etc.: *Murphy's roving eye was the cause of many arguments between him and his wife.*

not see eye to eye

to disagree with someone about a particular subject, or about everything: *For some reason my father-in-law and I never saw eye to eye.*

spit in *someone's* eye

to insult or annoy someone, especially without a good reason: *"The mayor is spitting in the eye of public employees by proposing to lay off 15,000 city workers,"* declared Barry Feinstein.

there's more to *someone/ something* than meets the eye

used to say that someone is more intelligent or interesting than they seem to be, or that a situation is more complicated than it seems: *Although he has been called football's most boring player, there is more to Smith than meets the eye.*

opposite **there's less to** *someone*/**something than meets the eye**: *His rivals claim that in spite of Hanson's political success there is considerably less to him than meets the eye.*

there wasn't a dry eye in the house

used to say that an event or statement made everyone feel very sad or sympathetic, often when you think that they were stupid to be so strongly affected by it: *We don't expect there to be a dry eye in the house tonight during the "Celebration of Courage" awards program.*

turn a blind eye (to)

if someone, especially a person in authority, turns a blind eye to something that is not supposed to happen, they ignore it and do not do anything about it: *Many landlords turn a blind eye rather than send families into the streets.*
—compare **turn a deaf EAR (to** *something***)**

with an eye to *something*

1 with the hope of doing or obtaining something: *The town is holding a music festival, with an eye to making more money from tourism.*
2 if you make a plan or decision with an eye to something, you consider that thing to be important: *Choose your assistants with care, and with an eye to the particular skills that are required.*

with a jaundiced eye

if you look at a situation or activity with a jaundiced eye, you know that it is not as good as you first thought it was: *Madonna's new CD may surprise those who view her with a jaundiced eye.*

eyeball

⇨**be up to your EARs/neck/eyeballs in** *something*

eyeball to eyeball

if two people or groups are eyeball to eyeball, they are having an angry argument or discussion ◆ OFTEN USED IN NEWSPAPERS, ON TELEVISION NEWS, ETC.: *For nine hours, the illegally-parked motorist went eyeball to eyeball with a highly determined tow-truck driver.*

give *someone* the hairy eyeball

OLD-FASHIONED to look at someone severely because you do not approve of what they are doing: *We'd better stop, the teacher's giving us the hairy eyeball.*

eyebrows

raise eyebrows

to surprise or shock people ◆ OFTEN USED IN NEWSPAPERS, ON TELEVISION NEWS, ETC.: *Kasparov's outspoken behavior, global lifestyle, and Western income have raised eyebrows in Russia.*

eyelash

⇨**not (even) bat an EYE/eyelash**

eye teeth

someone would give his/her eye teeth to do *something*

used to emphasize how much you want to do something: *Wouldn't most women give their eye teeth to be married to a movie-star?*

F

face

⇨face the MUSIC
⇨someone **will be laughing out of the other SIDE of his/her mouth/face**

blow up in your face

if a situation blows up in your face, it suddenly causes you lots of trouble or embarrassment or becomes very difficult to control: *We knew the peace negotiations were a very delicate matter and could easily blow up in our face.*

come face to face with

1 to meet someone suddenly, especially when you are frightened of them: *I turned the corner and came face to face with a large, fierce-looking cop.*
2 (also **meet face to face**) to have a meeting with someone: *When I finally came face to face with the Governor, I was unable to make him understand how serious I felt the situation was.*
3 to be in a situation where you are forced to admit and deal with something unpleasant: *When people come face to face with the unpleasant aspects of the society in which they grew up, they are often distressed.*
face-to-face: *Davidovich felt that the remaining financial issues should be dealt with in face-to-face discussion.*

couldn't/wouldn't show your face

SPOKEN to feel too ashamed or embarrassed to go somewhere: *Krista wouldn't dare show her face around here after what she said to you.*

fall flat on your face

to fail at something, often in a way that is embarrassing: *You've got to recognize where the opportunities are and go for it. You can't be afraid to fall flat on your face.*

fly in the face of

if a plan, opinion, or way of behaving flies in the face of ideas that people think are acceptable, sensible, or true, it seems to ignore those ideas and is very different from them: *The idea of keeping young*

criminals out of prison flies in the face of existing government policy.
—see also **in the FACE of** something

get out of my face

SPOKEN an impolite expression used in order to tell someone who is annoying you to stop talking to you or to go away: *I wish Ms. Piper would get out of my face – it's like I'm the only one in the class who ever does anything wrong.*

in the face of something

if you do something or react in a particular way in the face of a problem, difficulty, or danger, you do it even though the situation is difficult or dangerous: *Rescue teams are doing magnificent work in the face of the chaos and destruction caused by the floods.*
—see also **fly in the FACE of**

in your face
(also **in-your-face**)

used about a way of talking, behaving, dressing, etc. that expresses ideas that are not the socially accepted ones, and does this in a very direct way that is often shocking or surprising: *Opposition leaders planned new in-your-face tactics aimed at pressing their demands for justice.*

someone is not just a pretty face

SPOKEN a humorous expression used in order to say that someone is intelligent or is good at their job: *Colin Firth proved conclusively that he was not just a pretty face, but could act extremely well.*

something is written all over someone's face
(also someone **has** something **written all over his/her face**)

used to say that someone's expression shows very clearly what they are thinking or feeling: *Harlan spoke of his hopes for the future, but disappointment was written all over his face.* | *My cheeks burned, and I knew I had guilt written all over my face.*

keep a straight face

to be able to continue to look serious even though you want to laugh: *Ladd said her lively co-stars make it difficult to keep a straight face during the filming.*

a long face

the expression on your face when you are very sad or disappointed: *I can't stand seeing you put on that long face. Come on, act cheerful at least.*

long-faced: *After the session was adjourned, Boyd shared a few minutes of disappointment with long-faced Dale Dixon.*

lose face

to do something or have something done to you that embarrasses you and makes people lose respect for you: *South Africa's African National Congress risks losing face if it is seen as compromising with Buthelezi.*

loss of face: *The Congressman cannot withdraw from the negotiations without a serious loss of face.*

—compare **save FACE**

on the face of it

used to say that when you first think about a situation it seems to be simple or the truth about it seems clear, especially when it is really more complicated or difficult when you examine it further: *On the face of it, this month's sales figures are encouraging, however there is still a lot of improvement to be made.*

put on a brave face
(also **put a brave face on it**)

to try not to show that you are afraid, worried, disappointed, or upset about something: *Attorney Stephen Jones put on a brave face after the verdict against his client was read.*

put your face on

SPOKEN to put make-up on your face: *Jenna will be out in a minute – she's just putting her face on.*

save face

to do something that makes people continue to respect you, when something has happened that might have made them stop respecting you: *We make it easy for people to save face by accepting their explanations of their conduct, no matter how unlikely.*

face-saving: *Senior officials said they hoped Baker would offer a face-saving compromise.*

—compare **lose FACE**

show your face

to go to a place where you are supposed to be, usually for a short time, even though you may not want to go: *I thought I'd better show my face at the meeting, just to make it clear that I know what's going on.*

shut your face/trap

SPOKEN an impolite expression used in order to tell someone to stop talking
♦ USED ESPECIALLY BY CHILDREN: *"What have you done to your hair?" "Oh, shut your face!"*

be staring *someone/something* in the face

1 if a bad or difficult situation is staring you in the face, or you are staring it in the face, it is very likely to happen: *We had very little food left, and starvation was staring us in the face.*
2 if a fact or idea is staring you in the face, it is very clear and easy to recognize, but you do not recognize it immediately: *We spent two days worrying about the problem of transport, when all the time the answer was staring us in the face.*

stuff your face

SPOKEN to eat a lot in a short time: *We stuffed our faces with tons of hot dogs and cotton candy.*

take *something* at face value

to accept what someone has said or written, without thinking that it may not be completely true or may have some hidden meaning: *Taken at face value, The Cardigans seem to be just a pleasant pop-rock group with little talent.*

> NOTE▶ The face value of a note (=piece of paper money) or a coin is the amount that is printed on it. However, its value may actually be more or less than that amount.

throw *something* back in *someone's* face

1 to upset or harm someone by using something positive they have said or done against them: *When you're elected, you can be sure that your opponents will throw your election promises back in your face.*

2 to angrily refuse to take advice or help that someone is trying to give you, especially because you want to be rude: *If he gives Dina money, she throws it back in his face and says it's not enough.*

vanish/disappear/drop off the face of the earth

to suddenly disappear so that no one can find or see you: *Alice was so embarrassed, she wanted to drop off the face of the earth.*

you can do *something* until/till you're blue in the face

SPOKEN used to say that although someone spends a lot of time and effort doing something, they will not achieve anything: *You can argue till you're blue in the face, I'm not going to change my mind.*

fact

the facts of life

1 the details about sex and how babies are born, especially as they are explained to children: *How to tell their children about the facts of life is something that many parents struggle with.*
2 the way that life really is, with all its problems and difficulties: *When we say that people over sixty-five have an increased risk of dying, we are simply stating the facts of life.*

something is a fact of life

used in order to say that a situation exists and people have to accept it: *My mother had been in and out of jail several times by the time I was eight years old, but I just accepted it as a fact of life, as children do.*

factor

the feelgood factor

a feeling that everything is good and people are happy: *In most Hollywood movies the feelgood factor is all-important. However, a few independent movie-makers have begun to change that.*

fair

⇨get a fair **SHAKE**

fair and square

SPOKEN used to say that a competition was won or lost in a fair and honest way: *The numbers are now in, and Lambert has won the election fair and square.*

fair to middling

not very good, but not very bad either: *My brother has a great singing voice, but mine's only fair to middling.*

fair's fair

SPOKEN used to say that a decision, idea, or situation is fair, and people should agree with it and behave fairly: *If Antony is getting time off, we should have time off too. Fair's fair.*

fairy

someone's **fairy godmother**

used about a person or organization that helps someone who has a problem, especially when they were not expected to: *Beatrix was our fairy godmother, finding us an apartment and staying with us until Mom was well enough to take over.*

> NOTE▶ In fairy tales (=children's stories about magical events), a fairy godmother often uses magic to help the main character in the story with their problems.

fait accompli

a fait accompli

used about something that has already happened or been done in order to say that it cannot be changed: *The factory closure is probably a fait accompli, but workers are still making every attempt to stop it.*

faith

⇨pin your faith on —see pin your **HOPES on**

fall

fall flat

if a remark, plan, or joke falls flat, people do not react to it, and so it fails: *Golding's proposal to postpone several future city building projects fell flat with City Council members.*

be falling over yourself to do *something*
to try very hard and very eagerly to do something, especially because you want to please someone or to gain something for yourself: *In the 1980s, banks were falling over themselves to lend people money.*

fall short (of *something*)
to be less than what you need or expect, or to fail to reach a satisfactory or expected standard: *Due to drought and civil war, this year's wheat harvest could fall short by one million tons.*

be heading/headed/riding for a fall
used to say that someone is likely to fail, especially because they are not being careful, or are trying to do something that they are not able to do: *The business is heading for a fall – they've got far too much stock and a lot of debt.* | *I was young and ambitious, and I didn't know it, but I was riding for a fall.*

familiarity

familiarity breeds contempt
used to say that as you begin to know someone or something better, you begin to have less interest in them or less respect for them: *I can't believe they're getting a divorce. They seemed to get along so well, but I guess familiarity breeds contempt.*

family

be in the family way
OLD-FASHIONED to be going to have a baby: *Winters plays a young girl from the Bronx whose one night of love has left her in the family way.*

run in the/*someone's* family
to be a common feature among many people in a particular family: *Gaining weight didn't help matters for Carolyn, not to mention the high blood pressure that ran in her family.* | *"Can you paint?" "I've never tried, but painting runs in the family. My uncle specialized in water-colors."*

fancy

a passing fancy
when you like someone or believe that something is true or good, but only for a short time: *"We want to send the message to product manufacturers that environmental concern is more than a passing fancy," said spokesman Rob Boley.*

strike/catch/tickle your fancy
used about something that seems attractive, interesting, or amusing when you see or hear it: *With over 65 performers, the music festival is bound to have something that tickles your fancy.*

fans

⇨**50 million ELVIS fans can't be wrong**

far

⇨**SO far, so good**

as far as *something* goes
SPOKEN used to give more specific details about a subject that has already been mentioned: *"Right now we need to talk about money and schedules. Ryan, do you want to start?" "Well, as far as money goes, we have very little in the budget for anything."*

far and away
used to emphasize that something or someone is definitely the best, most important, etc. of a group of similar things or people: *Carolina is far and away the most talented team in the country.*

far from it
used after a statement or question to emphasize that it is not true, especially when you want to give a reason why: *"Reservoir Dogs" offended many people, but the movie is not all bad taste and violence. Far from it. It has a point to make, and it makes it beautifully.*

farm

buy the farm
SPOKEN a humorous expression meaning to die: *When our plane flew through the thunderstorm, I thought we had all bought the farm for sure.*

a/the funny farm
an unkind or offensive expression meaning a hospital for people who are mentally ill, which is sometimes used humorously: *If you don't start acting like a normal person in public, someone's going to send you to the funny farm.*

fart
⇨have a **BRAIN** fart

fashion

after a fashion
1 used to say that you think someone does not do something very well, or that something is not happening in the best or most complete way: *She keeps the house clean, and she cooks after a fashion.*
2 used after a statement to say that it is not exactly true or completely honest: *I told everyone that Carl was my boyfriend, which he was, after a fashion.*

do *something* like it's going out of fashion/style
(also **do** *something* **as if it's going out of fashion/style**)
used to say that someone is using, buying, eating, etc. a lot or too much of something: *Dave and his friends were out by the barbecue, drinking Bud like it was going out of style.* | *In the 1950s, doctors were giving out tranquilizers as if they were going out of fashion.*
—see also **do** *something* **like there's no TOMORROW**

fashion crime
a humorous expression used about clothes that are not fashionable, or that someone thinks are unattractive: *Members of the studio audience are frequently pulled out in front of the TV cameras and ridiculed for their fashion crimes.*

a fashion victim
used about someone who always wears clothes that are fashionable, even if they do not look good, and always uses the most fashionable restaurants, designs, etc.: *My sister is such a fashion victim that she won't be seen in public unless she's wearing the perfect outfit with all the matching accessories.*

fast

be/come fast and furious
to be done quickly and with a lot of energy, or to happen quickly and in large amounts: *News of the scandal came fast and furious in the small community, and everyone delighted in talking about it for weeks.*

fat
⇨fat **CHANCE**

chew the fat
to talk to someone in a relaxed friendly way, especially about personal things, friends, family, etc.: *Jessie called me last night to chew the fat and catch up on the latest gossip.*

the fat is in the fire
used to say that someone has serious troubles or problems, or that a situation is very bad: *If your father hears of this latest development, Carrie, the fat will be in the fire.*

live off/on the fat of the land
to have a comfortable life, especially without having to work hard: *What do company directors who live off the fat of the land know about the problems of ordinary workers?*

fate

a fate worse than death
a humorous expression used to say that a situation or event is the worst kind you can imagine: *Staying there in that small town all his life seemed a fate worse than death.*

seal *someone's* fate
to make it certain that something will happen to a person, usually something bad: *Terrible script-writing and unsexy voices sealed the fate of many silent movie stars who sounded foolish in the new talking pictures.*

tempt fate/providence
1 to do something that is dangerous and involves unnecessary risks: *Hilary likes to tempt providence by skiing off cliffs.*
2 to say or do something that may bring you bad luck, for example, saying that you believe you will get something that you want: *We've got a good team, but I'm*

F

not going to tempt fate by saying that we can definitely win.

father

like father, like son
like mother, like daughter
used to say that a child looks and behaves like their parents: *Like father, like son. George Bush, Jr. has become governor of Texas, and says he wants to someday run for president.*

fault

___ to a fault
used to say that someone has so much of a good quality, such as honesty, kindness, etc. that it sometimes causes problems: *Diane has always been nice to a fault. I can never tell if she really likes something or is just being polite.*

favors

curry favor (with *someone***)**
to try to make someone like you or notice you by saying nice things about them or doing something for them: *Direct government efforts to curry favor with the trial lawyers failed today as the judge passed a guilty verdict.*

don't do me any favors
SPOKEN said when you are annoyed because what someone is doing for you is not helpful, even though they think it is: *"I could talk to Ron and explain that it wasn't really your fault." "Thanks, but don't do me any favors."*

fear

put the fear of God into *someone*
to make someone feel frightened of doing something wrong by making them realize the bad things that could happen if they do: *Border police attempt to put the fear of God into people who are thinking about crossing over illegally.*

feast

a feast for the eyes/ears/senses
something that is good to look at, to hear, to touch, etc.: *The paintings weave together a multimedia canvas of color and texture that reaches out to everyone. It's a feast for the eyes*

it's feast or famine
used about a situation in which there always seems to be too much of something or very little of it: *Last week I had three dates, but now my phone doesn't even ring. It's always feast or famine for me.*

a movable feast
(also **a moveable feast**)
used to say something can be changed depending on what happens in a situation or according to what people want to do: *"When will the fair be held?" "Whenever the weather's good. It's a moveable feast."*

> NOTE ▶ A "movable feast" is one of several religious holidays in the Church which happen about the same time every year, although the date changes from year to year.

feat

something **is no mean feat**
used to say that something is very difficult to do: *They've managed to remain partners for 15 years – no mean feat in any business*

feather

⇨**feather your NEST**

a feather in your cap
something that you have achieved that you should be proud of: *Winning the golf tournament at such a young age was a huge feather in her cap.*

ruffle *someone's* **feathers**
to upset or annoy someone slightly: *Gates' sometimes aggressive style has ruffled some feathers in political circles.*

smooth ruffled feathers
to stop people from feeling upset or annoyed after a difficult situation or argument: *Tabeka's job on the movie set often included smoothing ruffled feathers when actors got upset.*

you could've knocked me down/ over with a feather
used to emphasize that you were extremely surprised by something: *When*

I heard that Joe Calder had gotten married, you could've knocked me down with a feather!

fed up

be/get fed up (with *something*)
SPOKEN to feel annoyed, especially because you are bored or you think something happens too often: *I'm fed up with being told I'm too lazy.* | *I bet she's fed up, having to travel so far to work every day.*

feed

⇨CHICKEN feed

put *someone* off his/her feed
SPOKEN if something unpleasant that you see or hear puts you off your feed, it upsets you enough to make you feel a little sick, often used in a joking way: *The CD features some unlikely pop stars slaughtering your favorite tunes, and I can tell you, hearing Captain Kirk barking out "Mr. Tambourine Man" really puts you off your feed.*

feel

cop a feel
SLANG to touch someone in a sexual way when they do not want you to: *I'd only been talking to the guy for about 15 minutes, and he was trying to cop a feel!*

feel boxed in
to feel that a person or a situation is preventing you from having the freedom to do what you want to do: *The book claims that Hendrix felt boxed in by his fans' expectations of him as a guitar player.*

be/feel yourself (again)
(also **be/feel your old self** or **be/feel more like yourself**)
to feel healthy or happy in the way that you normally do: *Jamie hasn't been herself lately, has she?* | *It was a happy moment; I felt I was my old self again for the first time in years.*

feelers

put out feelers
to start asking people for their opinion of

your plan, idea, etc. in order to find out whether it will work if you use it: *We have put out our feelers, but nobody really expects to find a good replacement for Diana.*

feeling

no hard feelings
SPOKEN used to tell someone that you have been arguing with that you are no longer angry with them and that you hope they are not angry with you: *No hard feelings, Pat – I was the one who was wrong.*

a/the sinking feeling (that)
(also **that sinking feeling**)
the feeling that you get when you realize suddenly that something unpleasant has happened or is going to happen to you: *As we sailed closer to the place where the lighthouse should have been, I had a sinking feeling that the storm had destroyed the landmarks we were looking for.*

feet

—see FOOT

fence

mend (your) fences
to do something in order to try to improve a relationship with someone that you have had an argument with: *In order to mend fences with my boss, I offered to put in 10 hours of unpaid overtime.*

sit on the fence
used to show disapproval for someone who does not decide quickly about something, or who refuses to give a definite opinion about something: *You know how things are – too many people are sitting on the fence these days. We need action.*
fence-sitting: *Many economists who had been fence-sitting are now predicting a recession.*

fencepost

⇨**between you, me, and the LAMPPOST/fencepost**

fettle

in fine/good fettle

OLD-FASHIONED healthy or working properly: *This morning, Elise was in fine fettle – laughing, joking, and clowning around, almost as if she'd never been sick.*

fever

be at (a) fever pitch

if people's feeling are at fever pitch, there is a lot of excitement: *The football crowd was at fever pitch, and extra guards were needed around the barricades.*

few

be few and far between

used to say that there are not many of something, or that something does not happen very often, especially a good thing: *Honest politicians are few and far between these days.*

fiddle

⇨fiddle while ROME burns

fit as a fiddle

OLD-FASHIONED to be completely healthy: *I've been feeling as fit as a fiddle since I took up line-dancing.*

play second fiddle (to *someone*)

used about someone who is less important or powerful than someone else, especially when they think that they are just as important, skillful, etc. as the other person: *Bracken turned down the part in the movie because he didn't like playing second fiddle to Hutton again.*

field

⇨a level PLAYING FIELD

have a field day

to have a chance to do what you want to do, especially to criticize someone ♦ OFTEN USED IN NEWSPAPERS, ON TELEVISION NEWS, ETC.: *If the tabloids ever find out about that conversation, they'll have a field day.*

lead the field

to be the best or most successful person, group, company, etc. in an activity or competition: *The French industry easily led the field with the hundred or so movies made during last year.*

be (way) out in left field
(also **be/come out of left field**)

used about ideas, methods, etc. that are strange, unusual, or surprising: *We're surprised the ad has been so successful, but sometimes things that are way out in left field work best.* | *The Mayor's office says that stories of his drug use have "come out of left field" and are "typical of the newspaper's irresponsible reporting."*

play the field

to have many different romantic relationships: *Morton only admitted that he was done playing the field on the day of his wedding.*

fig

a fig leaf

something someone says or does to try to hide an embarrassing situation: *This is a very small fig leaf to cover a very big tax increase.*

> NOTE▶ The leaf of a fig tree was used by Adam and Eve (=the first man and woman, according to the Bible) to cover themselves after they disobeyed God. Before that time, they were not embarrassed about having no clothes on.

not give a fig about/for

OLD-FASHIONED to not be concerned about, or interested in something at all: *I don't give a fig about your health problems – I've got problems of my own!*

fight

fight/battle it out

if two teams, organizations, or people fight it out, they keep fighting, competing, or arguing about something until one of them wins: *The three final contestants will be battling it out for an all-expense paid trip to Hawaii.*

fight shy of doing *something*

OLD-FASHIONED to avoid doing something, or be unwilling to do something: *Many of the clinics fought shy of treating patients who had no permanent address, although they were the most in need of treatment.*

fill

have had your fill (of)
to no longer be able to accept an unpleasant situation or person: *I have only been teaching public school for two years, but I have already had my fill of disrespectful children.*

finders

finders keepers (losers weepers)
SPOKEN used to say that if you find something, you have a right to keep it ♦ OFTEN USED BY CHILDREN: *"That's mine!" "Too bad – finders keepers, losers weepers."*
finders-keepers: *Hughes claimed the meteorite belonged to him using a sort of finders-keepers argument, but the courts disagreed.*

find out

⇨ **find out what** *someone* **is (really) made of** —see SEE what *someone* is (really) made of

finger

⇨ **be all fingers and thumbs** —see be all THUMBs

cross your fingers
(also **keep your fingers crossed (that)**)
SPOKEN used to say that you hope something good will happen in a situation which could have a bad result: *We're hoping, and I'm crossing my fingers here, that we'll get about 5,000 people out to the Fun Day on Saturday.*

get/have your fingers burned
(also **burn your fingers**)
to suffer the unpleasant results of something that you have done so that you never want to do it again: *I'd had my fingers burned by Jackie too many times to start up a relationship with her again.*

have a finger in every pie
(also **have a finger in many, several, etc. pies**)
to be involved in many different activities and have influence over many people, often in order to get an advantage for yourself: *A good politician has a finger in several pies in order to keep the public happy.*

have/keep a finger on the pulse
to always know about the most recent and important changes and developments in a particular situation or activity: *Keillor has his finger on the pulse of working-class America. That's where his comedy comes from.*

let *something* slip through your fingers
to fail to take an opportunity, offer, etc. that is good: *We can't let the opportunity of having better public transit in the area slip through our fingers again.*

not lift/raise a finger
to be too lazy to help someone with their work, or to not care enough to help someone who is in danger: *We cleaned the garage out this weekend, and Gary didn't even lift a finger to help us!*

---

not lift/raise a finger

point the finger (of blame)
(also **point an/the accusing finger**)
often used in law, business, and politics to blame someone or say that they have done something wrong: *Conklin was afraid that if he didn't point the finger at Justin, the police would get him for murder.*
finger-pointing: *After months of name-calling and finger-pointing, leaders from both countries have promised to try and stop the violence.*

put your finger on *something*
to know or be able to explain exactly what is wrong, different, or unusual about

F

a situation ◆ OFTEN USED IN THE NEGATIVE: *You look different somehow, but I can't quite put my finger on it.*

someone's **sticky fingers**
used to say that someone steals things: *Some of the tourists with sticky fingers try to break off pieces from the castle wall.*

work your fingers to the bone
to work extremely hard: *Don't you realize that your mother has worked her fingers to the bone for you?*

wrap/twist *someone* **around your little finger**
to be able to make someone do what you want them to do: *Sheila has always been Dad's favorite kid – he is wrapped around her little finger!*

fingernails

hang (on) by your fingernails
to continue to manage in a difficult situation, although you are very close to failure: *This is our third straight loss, but we're hanging on by our fingernails.*

fingerprints

someone's **fingerprints are on** *something*
(also someone's **fingerprints are all over** *something*)
used to say that an action, piece of work, etc. is typical of a particular person, and that they must have been involved in it: *The President signed the bills to raise taxes, but the Vice President's fingerprints weren't on them. That leaves him safe to claim he has a good record on taxes in the next election.*

fingertips

have *something* at your fingertips
to have knowledge, information, etc. available and ready to be used: *Because of the Internet, we have all the information we could ever want right at our fingertips.*

fire

⇨add **FUEL** to the fire/flames

breathe fire
to behave or talk in a way that shows you are very angry and determined to get what you want: *I admit that when an angry editor is breathing fire down the phone, I make excuses I am later too embarrassed to think about.*

be/come under fire
to be severely criticized for something you have done ◆ OFTEN USED IN NEWSPAPERS, ON TELEVISION NEWS, ETC.: *The transportation secretary was under fire for increasing train fares for the second time this year.*

fight fire with fire
to use the same methods as your opponent in an argument, fight, or competition: *This kind of violent police behavior is like fighting fire with fire, and it will never earn them the public's respect.*

hang fire
to wait and not do anything about a problem, or not complete something: *He has been hanging fire for months, waiting for his trial date to be set.*

have a fire in your belly
to be excited and have the energy you need to do something very well: *Three years later, Ali returned to boxing with a new fire in his belly.*

light a fire under *someone*
to make someone work harder or do something with more energy or excitement than before: *Champions of the new Civil Rights bill hope to light a fire under voters in other states.*

be playing with fire
to be taking unnecessary risks in a situation you know is dangerous: *Since she had started secretly meeting Larry, she had known she was playing with fire, but she couldn't stop herself.*

firing line

be on the firing line
(also **be in the line of fire**)
to be in a position or situation in which you are likely to be criticized or attacked: *Once again, Keating's farm is in the line of fire as the family tries to protect the area from developers.*

be out of the firing line
(also **be out of the line of fire**)
to be away from a position or situation in which you are likely to be criticized or attacked: *Things at work have been tense – I've been trying to keep myself out of the firing line by keeping busy and keeping quiet.*

first

first come, first served
(also **first-come, first-served**)
used to say that something is being offered or sold to the people who arrive earliest or those who ask first: *Beginning at 7 p.m., the tickets will be distributed on a first-come, first-served basis.*

fish

⇒fish or cut **BAIT**

a big fish in a little/small pond
(also **a big fish in a little/small pool**)
someone who is important or has a lot of influence only in a small organization, place, company, etc.: *I don't want to be a big fish in a little pond – I'd rather run against the world champion and finish fifth or sixth in the race.*

> **NOTE**▶ You may also hear people described as "big fish" or "small fish" according to how important they are compared with other people in the same group: *The skills that made Scholfield a big fish in retailing helped him succeed as the club's manager.*

a cold fish
SPOKEN used about someone who does not show their feelings and seems unfriendly: *Everyone sees George as a bit of a cold fish, but he was very supportive when I was having problems at work.*

drink like a fish
SPOKEN to frequently drink a lot of beer, wine, etc.: *My roommate Billy drinks like a fish, but then again, so do I.*

be/feel like a fish out of water
to feel embarrassed, or nervous, or uncomfortable because you are in a place or situation that you are not familiar with or used to: *I hate going to important interviews; I always feel like a fish out of water.*

have other/bigger fish to fry
to have other things to do, usually more important things: *Roberts isn't concerned about his neighbors' complaints – he has other fish to fry.*

live in a fish bowl
to be in a situation where a lot of people know about your life and your personal affairs: *I was trying to keep some dignity while living in a fish bowl – that's what happens after divorce in a small town.*

someone **needs** something **like a fish needs a bicycle**
SPOKEN used to say that someone does not need something at all: *You men all assume that a woman can't feel complete without a man, but, as someone once said, a woman needs a man like a fish needs a bicycle.*

—compare **need** something **like a HOLE in the head**

(like) shooting fish in a barrel
used to say that one side in a competition is much weaker than the other side, and has no chance of winning: *According to the lawyers, putting this man with no money on trial is a little like shooting fish in a barrel.*

there are plenty more fish in the sea
(also **there are other fish in the sea**)
SPOKEN used to tell someone not to be upset that the person they love does not love them because they will soon find someone else: *Whenever I broke up with a boyfriend, my dad was always there to give me a big hug and tell me there were plenty more fish in the sea.*

fishing

⇒someone is fishing without **BAIT**

a fishing expedition
an attempt by the police, government officials, or people who report the news to find out information when they think someone may have done something wrong, but they are not certain: *We were on a fishing expedition, looking for signs of drug dealing.*

F

fist

an iron fist in a velvet glove

used about an organization or person who seems to be kind at first but who is actually very determined to get what they want, even if people do not like it: *Coronet Inc., a company well known for its jobs-for-life policy, has revealed an iron fist in the velvet glove with its plan to "weed out poor performers."*

rule/control *someone* with an iron fist

to have strict control over everything that a group of people does, usually so that they hate you or are frightened of you: *Our ninth grade teacher ruled us with an iron fist and would scream at us if we disobeyed him.*
iron-fist: *Arrests, torture, and executions are all part of the government's iron-fist policy.*

fit

fit to be tied

used about someone who is so angry, anxious, or upset about something that they might not behave in a sensible manner: *Ralph was fit to be tied when Gloria got the promotion instead of him.*

have/throw a fit

SPOKEN to get very angry and upset: *My mother'll have a fit if she finds you here – you'd better leave.*
—see also **have a COW**

in/by fits and starts

if a process or condition changes or develops in fits and starts, it happens for a while, then stops for a while, and then starts again: *Research into the site at Pompeii continues in fits and starts whenever the archaeologists can find the money.*

five

give me five

SLANG said when you want to hit someone's hand with your hand in order to show that you are very pleased about something you have achieved together, or that you are pleased to see them: *We did it – give me five!*

take five

SPOKEN to stop what you are doing in order to rest: *OK, everyone, let's take five. We'll continue the meeting at 2:15.*

fix

get/have a fix on
(also also get a real, firm, clear, etc. fix on)

1 to find out all about a situation or subject so that you understand it and know what is likely to happen next, or to find out about a person so you understand how they are likely to behave: *Fletcher spent hundreds of hours interviewing police to get a fix on exactly what it's like to be on the streets.*
2 to find out exactly where a plane, ship, star, etc. is by using special equipment: *The first thing the captain was asked to do was to get a firm fix on the ship's position.*

in a fix

having problems that are difficult to find a solution to: *The new bill will put the Ohio State Legislature in a fix since they have promised to back it but don't have the funds to do so.*

a quick fix

an easy and fast way of solving a problem or fixing something, used especially when you disapprove because it is not a good solution ♦ OFTEN USED IN THE NEGATIVE: *The Superintendent warned that there could be no quick fixes for the ailing school system.*
quick-fix: *Environmentalists have warned that quick-fix schemes to deal with global warming may be risky.*

flag

something is like waving/holding a red flag in front of a bull

used to say that doing or saying a particular thing will definitely make someone angry or upset: *As soon as I say "don't do it," it's like holding a red flag in front of a bull. She just does the exact opposite.*

keep the flag flying

to continue to support an idea, follow a plan, etc., especially when things become more difficult, or the idea or plan is not as popular as it once was: *Although the number of training programs has declined in the last few decades, one Alabama textile factory has kept the flag flying.*

a red flag

SPOKEN something that makes you realize that a system is not working correctly, or that something illegal is happening: *This case represents the largest bank fraud in history, and we see it as a red flag for the future. It cannot be allowed to happen again.*

wave/raise the white flag

to show that you accept that you have been defeated: *The Republican leadership finally decided to wave the white flag, to give up the search for a balanced budget agreement.*

wrap/drape yourself in the flag

to do something that seems to show great loyalty for your country but which is actually done to gain an advantage for yourself: *Political advisers know how easy it is to get votes by wrapping their candidates in the flag.*

flagpole

run *something* up the flagpole (and see who salutes)

SPOKEN to try an idea or suggest something in order to find out whether people like it or not: *Various proposals for a memorial garden have been run up the flagpole, mostly to generals, who did not salute.*

flak

catch/take/get (a lot of) flak

to be criticized, usually publicly, for something you have said or done: *The company caught a lot of flak over the $554,000 "early retirement package" it gave to its co-founder when he left in June. | I can't let you take all the flak for something that was my mistake!*

> NOTE▶ "Flak" is the word for shells (=special bullets) fired from guns on the ground at aircraft in a war. The letters of the word come from the German word "Fliegenabwehrkanonen" which is the word for the guns these shells were fired from.

flame

⇨add **FUEL** to the fire/flames
⇨go up in **SMOKE**/flames

fan the flames

to do or say something that makes a bad situation worse, especially by making people's negative feelings become stronger: *Civil Rights leaders accused the President of fanning the flames of racial intolerance with his remarks on illegal immigrants.*

an old flame

a person that someone used to have a romantic relationship with: *Jill's husband left her after 17 years of marriage for an old flame he met at his high school reunion.*

be shot down in flames

to be told that what you are saying is completely wrong, often by someone with more power than you: *My proposal was shot down in flames before I even mentioned the cost.*

flash

a/the flash in the pan

used about a fashion, song, an idea, etc. that is only popular for a short time, or about a person who is only successful for a short time: *The band's only hit was the flash in the pan "Kiss you all over," which sold five million copies.*
flash-in-the-pan: *Sheriffs have refused to cooperate in the drug sting, describing it as a "flash-in-the-pan political exercise."*

flat

⇨**FALL** flat
⇨**TELL** *someone* flat out

flavor

be flavor of the month/week

used about an idea, style, person, etc. that is very popular now, but that you think will be replaced by someone or something else very soon: *Castino, Hollywood's new flavor of the month, has been a big hit with the teenage fans.*
flavor-of-the-month/week: *Chapman's ready to lend his support to any flavor-of-the-month political causes.*

F

flesh

⇨have/take/want your **POUND** of flesh

be flesh and blood

used to emphasize that although someone seems different or is treated differently from other people, they have the same qualities and problems that all people have: *I couldn't work in one of those big companies where they treat you like numbers instead of flesh and blood!*
flesh-and-blood: *I liked the film because it presented Jesus as a real flesh-and-blood, emotional kind of guy.*

in the flesh

used to emphasize that someone who would not normally be in the same place as you is actually there with you, for example someone famous or someone you have not seen for a long time: *Thousands of U2 fans flocked to The Coliseum to see their heroes in the flesh.*

press the flesh

if a politician presses the flesh he or she shakes hands with people (=says "hello" to them by holding and shaking their hands) and talks to them in order to try to become more popular: *Yeltsin enjoyed his New York visit, attending parties, pressing the flesh in the garment district, and joking with students.*

put flesh on (the bones of) *something*

to add more details so that an opinion becomes clearer or a description becomes more interesting, or to make more decisions so that a plan becomes more definite: *Lawmakers approved a 22-item agenda designed to put flesh on the economic and social policies.*

your (own) flesh and blood

used to say that someone is part of your family, especially when you want to emphasize that they must be treated kindly because of this relationship: *It doesn't matter how much trouble he causes – he is still my own flesh and blood, and I love him.*

flies

—see **FLY**

flight

a flight of fancy

an idea that is full of imagination but is not practical or sensible: *At the time, everyone thought the movie "2001" was just a flight of fancy. Now we know it was based on reality.*

floodgates

something **opens the floodgates** (also **the floodgates open**)

used to say that someone does something that had been very difficult to do before, with the result that lots of other people want to do it too: *The floodgates have opened, and now thousands of claims are being made, suing tobacco companies for damages.*

floor

floor it

SPOKEN to suddenly make a car go very fast: *Just put it in really low gear and floor it – let's see what happens.*

wipe the floor with *someone*

to defeat someone completely or easily in a competition or argument: *We had a couple of chances to score, but in the end they wiped the floor with us, 4–0.*

flotsam

flotsam and jetsam

1 used about people who other people think are useless and unimportant, especially people without homes or jobs: *The street artist shares his stretch of sidewalk with a juggler, a dancer, and various other human flotsam and jetsam.*
2 things that have been thrown away, or seem to have no use or purpose: *With the development of modern drugs, traditional remedies were discarded by the West as medical flotsam and jetsam on the tide of progress.*

NOTE▶ The word "flotsam" is used for the parts of a ship that are found floating on the ocean when it has been destroyed. "Jetsam" is used for the things that people throw from a ship which are found floating on the ocean.

flow

go with the flow
to accept a new or different situation, without worrying about it or trying too hard to change or control it: *I know this party isn't what you expected, but just relax and go with the flow.*

be in full flow/flood
if a process or activity is in full flow, it is happening in a way that involves great energy or large numbers of things or people: *His family had come to Oklahoma in 1817, when the wave of migration from the east was in full flow.*

fly
⇨**LET fly**

be dropping like flies
SPOKEN used to say that a lot of people are becoming sick or dying, especially with the same illness or disease: *Smithers got the flu last week, and since then everyone has been dropping like flies.*

a/the fly in the ointment
something difficult or unpleasant that spoils a good situation so that it is not as good or enjoyable as it could be: *Henry had plenty of invitations to play golf at the club. The only small fly in the ointment was that the manager there didn't like him.*

I'd like to be a fly on the wall...
SPOKEN used to say that you are very interested in what people will say to each other at a private meeting, and that you wish you could see and hear what happens: *I wish I'd been a fly on the wall and heard exactly what Sam said to Evan.*

someone **wouldn't hurt a fly**
SPOKEN used to say that someone is very gentle, and no one should be afraid of them: *I know you don't like dogs, but Sam is gentle and wouldn't hurt a fly.*

flying
⇨**get/be off to a flying START**

be flying blind
used to say that you are trying to do something without enough information so that you often have to guess how to do it right: *Often we're flying blind because we*

don't have any really reliable data on which to base unemployment figures.

foam
⇨**foam at the MOUTH**

fodder
⇨**CANNON fodder**

fog

in a fog (of)
in a situation where you feel very confused and cannot think clearly: *Since our son's death, we've been living in a fog. It's very hard even to cope with ordinary life.*

foggiest

not have the foggiest (idea)
SPOKEN used to say that you do not know anything at all about something: *"I want to ring Jason – where does he work?" "I haven't the foggiest."* | *Mark didn't have the foggiest idea what he was supposed to be doing, but he was trying hard to look efficient.*

followers
⇨**CAMP followers**

food

give food for thought
(also **be, provide, offer, etc. food for thought**)
if something that you hear or read gives you food for thought, it makes you think carefully, either because it includes new information or because it shows that you have a problem: *The chapters on lesson planning will give you plenty of food for thought, and help you to structure your own lessons.*

fool
⇨**be living in a fool's PARADISE**

a fool and his money (are soon/ easily parted)
OLD-FASHIONED used to say that someone is buying unnecessary things or things that are worth less than they cost: *It's Christmas time again, and I'm busy*

buying presents that no one needs. *A fool and his money are soon parted.*

fools rush in (where angels fear to tread)
used to say that someone has done something difficult or brave, that they may not have tried to do if they had known about the problems of the situation: *There was no one to organize the conference, and so I volunteered to do it. You know what they say about fools rushing in...*

someone is nobody's fool
used to say that someone cannot easily be deceived or tricked: *Katherine was young and inexperienced in the ways of Hollywood, but she was nobody's fool. She knew enough to find a good agent.*

more fool you, him, her, etc.
SPOKEN used to say that you think someone is being stupid: *If Joel wants to spend that much money on an evening out, then more fool him.*

play the fool
to behave in a silly or irresponsible way: *Josh was playing the fool as usual, until the teacher saw him and kicked him out.*

not suffer fools (gladly)
to not be patient or polite with people who you think are stupid: *Mr. Fallon has been described as a man who does not suffer fools gladly, and who defines a fool as anyone who does not agree with him.*

foot
⇨foot the BILL

catch someone on the wrong foot
if a question, action, or event catches someone on the wrong foot, they are not expecting it and are not ready to deal with it: *The question about ethics caught the committee on the wrong foot, and they looked stupid when they didn't have a quick answer.*

dead on your feet
1 to be extremely tired: *Why don't you get some sleep? You must be dead on your feet.*
2 if a plan, idea, job, etc. is dead on its feet, it cannot continue: *In spite of what U.S. officials say, the peace plan's probably dead on its feet again.*

drag your feet/heels
to take too much time doing something, especially because you do not want to do it: *The government has been dragging its heels over the latest abortion bill.*

feet of clay
(also **clay feet**)
used to say that someone who people admire very much does things that are wrong or stupid, like everyone else: *The book builds Kennedy up to be a hero, and ignores his feet of clay.*

find your feet
to become more confident or more successful in a situation which was new to you or had been difficult for you: *Susie said she would let me stay with her for awhile – just until I found my feet again.*

be/get back on your feet
to feel better again after being sick or in a difficult situation: *Only two months after the accident, Crowther was back on his feet and working.* | *The idea was to get Vietnam's economy back on its feet so that fewer people would want to leave.*

get/have cold feet
to suddenly be afraid to do something that you were going to do or had agreed to do: *Don't worry, everyone gets cold feet before their wedding!*

get/start off on the wrong foot
to begin a new job, activity, or relationship badly, especially by annoying or offending people: *I think we got off on the wrong foot yesterday. Let me introduce myself again.*
opposite **get/start off on the right foot**: *I was trying so hard to start my new job on the right foot, but everything I said to my boss seemed to be the wrong thing.*

get/be under your feet
if a person or animal is under your feet, they annoy you because they interrupt you and keep you from doing work well or enjoying yourself: *Dad always yells at us if we get under his feet when he comes home from work.*

get your feet wet
to gain experience of a job, activity, subject, etc. that you have never tried before: *This book is an excellent guide for students who are just getting their feet wet in physics.*

get your foot in the door

to get your first opportunity to work in a particular organization or industry, or be involved in a particular activity: *I had to be a substitute teacher for four years just to get my foot in the door at that school.*
keep your foot in the door: *The French auction house has obviously decided to keep its foot in the door of this growing market.*

have a foot in both camps
(also **have a foot in each/either/every camp**)

to be friendly with, or connected to, two different groups of people, especially when they are opposed to each other or have different ideas: *As a Republican married to a staunch Democrat, you might say Schwarzenegger has a foot in both camps.* | *Relations between the Orthodox and Reform groups were strained, but as moderates we were anxious to keep a foot in each camp.*

have/keep your feet (firmly) on the ground
(also **have/keep both feet on the ground**)

to think or behave in a sensible way, even though you have a strong imagination, or have an advantage or power over other people: *We have to keep our feet firmly on the ground if we want to beat the Hornets this weekend.* | *People who work in television should keep both feet on the ground, and forget what a glamorous job it is supposed to be.*

have a lead foot

SPOKEN used about someone who often drives very fast: *Man, you have such a lead foot! If you don't slow down, we're going to get into an accident.*
lead-footed: *I'd advise you not to ride with my lead-footed son. Come in my car instead.*

have one foot in the grave

used about someone who seems to be very old or sick: *I always try to remind people that writing your will doesn't mean you have one foot in the grave.*

have two left feet

to move in a very awkward way when you dance: *Our date was going great, until he found out I have two left feet!*

land on your feet

to get out of a bad situation as a result of luck and not your own efforts: *We've been through three years of financial troubles, but this is a company that always tends to land on its feet.*

> NOTE▶ This idiom comes from the idea that when cats fall from something, they always land on their feet.

be light on your feet

to move quickly and gracefully: *The best basketball players know how to be light on their feet.*

my foot!

SPOKEN said after you repeat what someone else has just said, in order to show that you do not believe it: *"I'm sure he didn't mean to get you into trouble." "Didn't mean it, my foot. I bet he's laughing about it right now!"*

put your best foot forward

to start doing something in an excited and determined way because you want to improve or succeed: *The city is putting its best foot forward by cleaning up the downtown area and inviting conventions to make use of the Thalian Center.*

put your foot down

to refuse to allow something to happen, especially by saying something in a forceful way: *If Pierce would just put his foot down and say "no" once in awhile, people would give him more respect.*

put your foot in your mouth
(also **put your foot in it**)

SPOKEN to say something that upsets or embarrasses someone because you did not think before you said it, or because you do not understand the situation: *The Senator is an honest and likeable man, with an amazing talent for putting his foot in his mouth.*

shoot yourself in the foot

to make a mistake or stupid decision that spoils something that could have easily succeeded: *I can't insult the people that call in to my program – that would be shooting myself in the foot, wouldn't it?*
—see also *someone* **is cutting his/her own THROAT**

F

be six feet under

a humorous expression used about someone who is dead: *Well, your 40th birthday party won't be my problem – I'll be six feet under by then.*

stand on your own two feet

to be independent, and be able to take care of yourself, operate a business, govern a country, etc. without money or other support: *I want to leave home and stand on my own two feet without my parents telling me what to do.*

sweep *someone* off his/her feet

to do or say things that make someone begin to love you very quickly: *Jack swept me off my feet when I was only seventeen.*

think on your feet

to make effective decisions quickly: *Part of a doctor's training requires that they learn to think on their feet in emergency situations.*

vote with your feet

to show that you do not like a situation by leaving it or taking away your support: *If people didn't like our services, they would be voting with their feet and putting their money in other banks.*

footloose

be footloose and fancy-free

OLD-FASHIONED to be able to do what you like without worrying about your duties because you are not married or involved in a relationship with anyone: *He had spent many evenings in the Starlight Ballroom, in the days when he was footloose and fancy-free.*

follow in *someone's* **footsteps**

THIS IS MY SON, THE OTHER DR. SILVO

footsteps

follow in *someone's* footsteps

to do what someone else has done, especially to do the same job that your father or mother did: *Dad wants me to follow in his footsteps, but I hate the catering business!*

for

⇒**be for it** —see **be IN for it**
⇒**be ON for** *something*
⇒**be UP for** *something*

force

the driving force (behind *something*)

the person or thing that makes something happen: *Hillary Clinton is a shrewd, ambitious lawyer who was the driving force behind her husband Bill's pitch for the presidency.*

the forces of darkness

used about people or ideas that you think have a bad effect on the social or political situation, often used humorously ◆ OFTEN USED IN NEWSPAPERS: *Kennedy was seen as a young knight on a white charger who was setting out to overcome the forces of darkness and prejudice.*

a force to be reckoned with

used about a person or group that has enough power to be important: *The strike had not achieved all its aims, but it showed that the unions were still a force to be reckoned with.*

forest

can't see the forest for the trees

used to say that someone does not notice what is important about a situation because they are paying too much attention to its small details: *Even the best history students sometimes can't see the forest for the trees without a tutor's help.*

forewarned

forewarned is forearmed

used to say that if you are expecting something to happen, it is easier to deal with it when it happens: *Management is talking about operating with a smaller, more efficient department. I shouldn't be telling you this, but forewarned is forearmed.*

forget

forget it
1 SPOKEN used to tell someone that something is impossible and that you are not willing to do what they want: *I got home late and I was so tired I just said: "If you think I'm going out tonight you can just forget it!"*
2 used to tell someone that something is not important and they should not worry about it: *"I'm really sorry about that." "Oh, forget it, it was no problem for me to take you home."*

fort

hold the fort
(also **hold down the fort**)
to be responsible for looking after a business, department, class, etc. when the person who usually does this is away: *I need you to be here to hold down the fort while I'm at the conference in Tucson.*

fortune

a small fortune
a lot of money: *That ring cost me a small fortune, but when I saw her face, I knew it was worth it.*

foul

cry foul
to show publicly that you are angry or upset because something is being done in an unacceptable way or someone is being treated unfairly ♦ OFTEN USED IN NEWS-PAPERS, ON TELEVISION NEWS, ETC.: *A black man was arrested in Florida for calling a police officer a "white cracker". Civil libertarians are crying foul, saying police abused the law.*

fox

crazy like a fox
said about someone who seems to be crazy but is really very intelligent: *Gigante's lawyers said he was mentally unfit for trial, but the FBI said he was crazy like a fox. We'll never know.*

frame

be in a ___ frame of mind
to have a particular attitude at a particular time so that it affects the way you behave: *I wasn't in the right frame of mind to deal with any problems at that point.* | *Melissa kept herself in a good frame of mind by writing down a positive factor about her job every time she became upset.*

freefall

go into freefall
if the value of a country's money or the price of things in a particular type of business goes into freefall, it suddenly starts falling very quickly ♦ OFTEN USED IN NEWSPAPERS, ON TELEVISION NEWS, ETC.: *We bought this house about a week before the housing market went into freefall – we'll never be able to sell it for what we paid.*

freight

pay the freight
SPOKEN to pay for something that costs a lot of money: *If you can pay the freight, our clinic provides first-class drug rehabilitation service.*

French

excuse/pardon my French
SPOKEN used to say you are sorry when you have used a swear word or impolite word, and think that someone might be offended: *His jeans were hanging down so low you could see half his ass – pardon my French.*

frenzy

a feeding frenzy
used about a situation in which a lot of people are trying in an excited and eager manner to get or do something that you do not approve of: *Immigration lawyers went into a feeding frenzy at the prospect of working for wealthy Asian clients.*

fresh

get/be fresh with *someone*
SPOKEN to talk to someone who is older than you in a way that does not show respect ♦ OFTEN USED BY ADULTS TALKING TO

F

OR ABOUT CHILDREN: *Don't get fresh with me, young man!*

friend

a fair-weather friend
someone who only wants to be your friend when you are successful, and leaves you when you have problems or need help: *Richard called me a fair-weather friend, but I can't possibly loan him anymore money.*

have friends in high places
to know important people who are willing to help you: *He kept his job, in spite of the scandal, so he must have friends in high places.*

man's best friend
an expression meaning a dog ◆ OFTEN USED IN NEWSPAPERS, ON TELEVISION NEWS, ETC.: *The video "Puppy Training" gives new owners some hints on teaching man's best friend how to behave.*

fringe

the/a lunatic fringe
used about the people in a political group or organization who have the most extreme opinions or ideas: *Ogilvy, the legendary creative force of modern advertising, lashed out at the lunatic fringe he said had damaged his industry and its ability to sell products.*

fritz

be on the fritz
SPOKEN if a piece of electrical equipment is on the fritz, it is not working properly: *It was a long, boring trip, and the car radio was on the fritz.*
—see also **be/go on the BLINK**

frog

have a frog in your throat
SPOKEN to have difficulty in speaking clearly because your throat feels dry or blocked for a moment: *Right in the middle of the speech, he got this terrible frog in his throat.*

NOTE▶ This idiom comes from an old belief that if you drank water containing the eggs of a frog (=small green animal that lives in or near water), the frogs would grow inside your body. The difficulty in speaking was supposed to be caused by the frog trying to escape.

front

on the ___ front
used to talk about what is happening in a particular situation: *On the political front, developments were rapidly pointing toward war.* | *"What's going on on the Jason front?" "Oh, I don't know, I haven't talked to him in a couple of days."*

fruit

bear fruit
if a plan or activity bears fruit, it produces the good results that you wanted: *Our economic policies are bearing fruit, and the economy is stronger than it has been for years.*

forbidden fruit
used about something or someone that seems attractive because you are not allowed to have them: *I don't think we should ban kids from drinking alcohol because forbidden fruit is always more attractive.*

fruitcake

nutty as a fruitcake
SPOKEN used to say that someone is behaving in a way that is slightly crazy: *You'd have to be nuttier than a fruitcake to live in that old house.*

NOTE▶ "Fruitcake" is a cake with nuts and dried fruit in it, often eaten at Christmas. "Nutty" is slang for "crazy."

frying pan

out of the frying pan (and) into the fire
used to say that someone has gone from a bad situation to a worse or more difficult one: *If this country elects a socialist government, we'll be jumping out of the frying pan and into the fire.*

fuck

NOTE▶ The word "fuck" is very offensive to many people. It is better not to use it.

fuck you, him, it, etc.
TABOO an extremely offensive expression said when you are very angry at someone or about something: "I didn't ask for your help, so just get out." "Well, fuck you then." | Fuck it. I give up.

not give a (flying) fuck
TABOO an offensive expression used to emphasize that you really do not care about something: I don't give a flying fuck if you go or not. I'm staying here.

what the fuck?
TABOO an offensive expression used in order to emphasize that you are angry or annoyed about something: Chris, what the fuck are you talking about?

fudge
⇨fudge the ISSUE

fuel

add fuel to the fire/flames
(also add fuel to the debate, argument, controversy, etc.)
to say or do something that makes a bad situation much worse than it is, or makes people more angry than they already are: Let me talk to him alone – things are bad enough without you adding fuel to the fire. | Reports of the accident added fuel to the debate about safety regulations.

full

be full of yourself
to think only about yourself because you think you are more important than other people: As a Hollywood reporter, you soon learn which actors are too full of themselves to talk to you.

someone is full of it
SPOKEN said when you think that what someone says is wrong or stupid: He's so full of it – he kept saying he couldn't find a place to stay and that he just needed to stay with me for a week or two.

fun

fun and games
1 used about a situation that is boring, unpleasant, or difficult: "Don't forget we have a chemistry test." "Oh yeah, more fun and games."
2 used about an enjoyable experience or activities that you enjoy doing: When you're in college, life is all fun and games, even though you don't realize it at the time.

poke fun at
to make a joke about someone in an unkind way: Don't poke fun at him, Skeeter – he didn't do anything to you.

funeral

it's/that's your funeral (not mine)
SPOKEN used to tell someone that they must deal with the results of their own actions, and that you will not help them: I think you're heading for trouble, but if you don't want my help, that's your funeral.

funny

so ___ it's not even funny
SPOKEN used to emphasize how much of a particular quality someone or something has, how much or little of something there is, etc.: I really need another job – I have so much time on my hands it's not even funny.

fur

the fur flies
used to say that an angry argument or fight is happening: The fur really began to fly when Jake started insulting Peter's new car.

furniture

be part of the furniture
used about someone or something that people hardly notice because they are so used to seeing them in a place: Everybody knows me. I've been doorman here for twenty years – I'm part of the furniture.

fuse

blow a fuse/gasket

to suddenly become very angry and upset: *Nita nearly blew a gasket when she realized she had to pay 21% interest on her credit card.*

—see also **blow your TOP/stack**

someone has a short fuse

used to say that someone becomes angry very easily: *Coach Mike Ditka has always been known for having a short fuse, and it has certainly gotten him into trouble.*

fuss

⇨make a **STINK/fuss**

future

there is no future in *something*

used to say that something is not likely to continue or succeed: *I got a job moving furniture – it paid the rent but there was no future in it.* | *I just can't see that there's any future in our relationship.*

is there any future in *something*?: *Do you think there is any future in this type of research?*

G

game

⇨it's a (whole) new **BALL GAME**
⇨be a **SHELL GAME**

beat/play *someone* at their own game

to do something or try to do something more successfully than someone else does, even though they are very good at it: *Fleischer, a brilliant financial mind, prides himself on beating Wall Street at its own game.*

be fair game

if a subject or person is fair game, it is considered acceptable to ask questions about them or to criticize them: *It's not just at election time that politicians' private lives are fair game for newspapers.*

the game is up

used to say that something wrong or dishonest that someone has done has been discovered: *Just then, I heard police sirens coming, and I knew the game was up.*

game plan

the things you plan to do in order to achieve something ◆ USED ESPECIALLY IN BUSINESS OR SPORTS: *"Should we discuss this at the conference, when there are more people?" "That's a good idea, but I think we need to have a firmer game plan first."*

give the game away

to let people know about something that is supposed to be secret: *Luther stared at Eddie with a panicked look in his eyes, obviously afraid that he would do something that would give the game away.*

I'm game

SPOKEN used to say that you are willing to try something new or different: *"I want Mustafa to turn up at Rahmi's lunch party as a surprise – but I need someone to help me." "I'm game," Shirin said.* | *"Come on then, if he wants to fight, let's do it." "OK, I'm game if you are."*

new to the game

used to say that someone has no experience of an activity or a business: *They're new to the software game, so they're spending a lot on advertising.* | *Being new to the game, Susan was anxious to avoid making any unwelcome comments.*

play the game

to do things exactly as you are expected to do them, especially in order to be successful: *She felt ridiculous wearing make-up and high heels, but she was willing to play the game to please her mother.*

play games (with)

1 to talk or behave to people in a way that is not direct and honest because you are trying to make them do or believe what you want: *Just stop playing games and tell us what you want.*
2 to deal with something in a way that is not direct and honest, or is not serious enough: *Finance committee members have indicated publicly that they are not going to play games with the debt issue.*

play a waiting game

to deliberately not make any decision or do anything, because you want to see what other people do or how a situation develops: *"We may have to evacuate some more people," Van Rossum said. "But right now, we're playing a waiting game to see if the storm strengthens."*

be/stay ahead of the game

to be successful in dealing with changes in the business or activity that you are involved in: *The company has invested a lot of money in research to try to stay ahead of the game.*

gamut

run the gamut

to include every one of a particular type of thing: *Her feelings during that weekend ran the gamut from happiness to despair.*

gander

take a gander at

INFORMAL to look at something: *Out of curiosity, I glanced up to take a gander at the newcomers.*

gangbusters

like gangbusters
in a way that shows you are eager and full of energy: *He started out like gangbusters, earning a huge profit in the first month of operation.*

NOTE▶ In 1930's stories about crime, "gangbusters" were policemen who fought against large and powerful organizations of criminals.

gangplank

⇨**walk the PLANK/gangplank**

gap

bridge the gap
to reduce the amount of difference between two things, ideas, groups of people, etc., or to make the difference seem less important: *Bridging the gap between rural entrepreneurs and the larger economy means introducing them to potential investors.*

garbage

garbage in, garbage out
(also **GIGO**)
used to say that if you give a computer incorrect information, or wrong ideas to work with, what the computer produces will be of poor quality: *It's still the old principle of garbage in, garbage out. The software can only help users think through a story – it can't write it for them.*

garden

garden variety
used about something that is ordinary and not special in any way: *Military officials said the explosives could cause wide-spread destruction. "They're not your garden variety weapon," they warned.*

lead *someone* **down the garden path**
to tell someone things that are not true, and persuade them to do something that they should not do: *"No one led me down the garden path," Levine said. "I broke the law and now I'll be punished."*

gas

run out of gas
to no longer have the energy or desire to continue doing something: *The economy looks like it may be running out of gas after expanding since April 1995.*

gasket

⇨**blow a FUSE/gasket**

gasp

the last gasp
the end of a long process or period of time: *Swenson says that the budget cutbacks don't mean that this is the show's last gasp. It's too popular to cut.*
last-gasp: *The administration claimed that the attack was a last-gasp attempt by the enemy to gain ground, and that the war would soon be over.*

gates

the pearly gates
a humorous expression meaning the entrance to heaven (=the place where many people believe you go when you die): *For a second, I thought I was dead and had just walked through the pearly gates.*

gauntlet

run the gauntlet
to be in a place or situation where you are criticized, attacked, or annoyed by a lot of people: *Players have to run the gauntlet of reporters and fans after the game in order to reach their cars.*

NOTE▶ "Running the gauntlet" was a form of punishment in the military in which soldiers with weapons stood in two lines facing each other and beat the person who was being punished as he ran between them.

take/pick up the gauntlet
to accept an invitation to argue or compete with someone: *Erlich took up the gauntlet and set out to prove his claims.*

throw down the gauntlet

to invite someone to argue or compete with you: *Clarke threw down the gauntlet to his colleagues who were demanding more spending cuts instead of higher taxes.*

> NOTE▶ This idiom comes from an old tradition of throwing a gauntlet (=glove) onto the ground in order to show that you wanted to fight someone. If someone agreed to fight you, they would take/pick up the gauntlet.

gear

get in/into gear
(also **shift into gear**)

to start to happen or work in the usual or correct way, especially after having problems or doing nothing: *It wasn't until Jordan and Pippen entered the game that the Bulls' offense finally got in gear.* | *When the redevelopment agency shifts into gear next year, any property tax increases will go into the downtown development fund.*

in high gear

doing something successfully and with a lot of energy: *The program is in high gear, and we feel it is helping a lot of children in the area.*
opposite **in low gear**: *My life seemed to be grinding along in low gear.*

genie

let the genie out of the bottle

used in order to say that an event happens which makes a big change in people's lives: *We're keeping an eye on inflation to make sure we don't let the genie out of the bottle, but I think most of the danger is already past.*

put the genie back in the bottle

to try to make a situation like it was before, when it has been changed by one important event and made worse or more difficult: *Both sides can discuss arms control, but can they put the genie back in the bottle?*

gentleman

⇨a gentleman's **AGREEMENT**

get

⇨don't get **CUTE/smart** with me
⇨don't get me **WRONG**
⇨get the **BETTER** of
⇨get **CARRIED** away
⇨get cracking —see **CRACK**
⇨get/give the **SKINNY** on
⇨be/get **HET UP**
⇨get **HITCHED**
⇨get a **LOAD** of
⇨get **LOST!**
⇨get off lightly —see be **LET** off lightly
⇨get *something* **STRAIGHT**
⇨*someone's* got it **BAD**
⇨*someone's* got it going on —see **GO**
⇨*someone's* is getting **ABOVE** himself/ herself
⇨**WHAT** got into *someone*?
⇨when you get (right) down to it —see when it **COMEs** (right) down to it
⇨**WHERE** does *someone* get off (doing *something*)
⇨you're getting **WARM**
⇨you've got me **THERE**

get away from it all

to have a relaxing time in a place that is very different from where you work and live so that you can forget your problems, work, etc.: *When we want to relax and get away from it all, we go to the mountains.*

get it on

SLANG to have sex: *Do you think Linda's getting it on with Mr. Ellis?*

get it together

to be in control of a situation and do things in an organized and confident way: *Leland's been so upset over his wife's death, he just can't get it together.*

get it up

SLANG to have an erection (=when a man's sex organ grows larger and is ready for sex): *I can't even get it up with my wife – why would I want a lover?*

get real!

SPOKEN used to tell someone not to be stupid, when you think that what they are saying or doing is not sensible or practical: *"Let's go over to Phillip's house." "Phillip? Get real! I don't want to see him after what he said to me last week."*

get this!

SPOKEN said when you want someone to listen to something that you find interesting or amusing: *Brad asked if I was doing anything on Saturday because – get this – he has an extra ticket to the Knicks game!*

be getting there

SPOKEN used to say that you are feeling hopeful because you know that a piece of work or long process is almost complete: *We have a lot to do before Friday, but we're getting there.*
—compare *someone* will GET there

get what's coming to you

to get what you deserve for something bad that you have done: *Anybody who throws stones at policemen should know that he's going to get what's coming to him.*

someone will get there

SPOKEN used to say that you think someone will finish or achieve something, even though there are problems now: *Don't worry, we'll figure it out. It may take six months or a year, but we'll get there.*
—compare be getting there (GET)

get-go

from the get-go

SPOKEN from the beginning of a period of time: *Right from the get-go, I knew he would cause trouble. He just had that look.*

ghost

⇨as white as a SHEET/ghost

give up the ghost

1 to stop trying to do something because you think you will not succeed: *Even when audience figures dropped, the show's organizers refused to give up the ghost.*
2 OLD-FASHIONED to die: *Many of those who were stricken by cholera gave up the ghost within a few hours.*

not have/stand a ghost of a chance (of doing *something*)

used to say that you think it is impossible for someone or something to succeed or happen: *Our team got through to the finals, but we don't stand a ghost of a chance of winning.*

gift

gift of (the) gab

the ability to talk in a way that entertains or persuades other people: *Ratliff is a big man with a ready smile and an engaging gift of gab.*

God's gift to

1 if someone thinks they are God's gift to a group of people or an activity, they behave in an annoying way that shows they think they are more important to that group or activity than they really are: *The way Caleb walks around, he obviously thinks he's God's gift to women.* | *By the age of 29, he'd won two Oscars and could be forgiven for thinking he was God's gift to acting.*
2 something that makes a situation much easier for a particular group of people: *The drug, which was welcomed at first as God's gift to pregnant women, produced serious birth defects in children.*

gills

green around the gills

OLD-FASHIONED looking sick or pale because you are shocked, afraid, or sick: *Nervous grooms have been known to get a little green around the gills as their wedding day approaches.*

girl

⇨the BOY/girl next door

give

⇨get/give the SKINNY on
⇨give *someone* a dirty LOOK
⇨give the LIE to
⇨give *someone* the (old) HEAVE-HO
⇨give *someone/something* the ONCE-OVER
⇨WHAT gives?

give and take
when two people or groups are each willing to let the other have or do some of the things they want: *Successful negotiations involve a complex process of give and take.*

give as good as you get
to say something in an argument or do something in a competition or fight that is as effective as what your opponent has said or done to you: *If you work for Barnes, you have to be able to give as good as you get in a meeting.*

give it to me straight
SPOKEN said when you want someone to tell you something unpleasant in a direct and honest way: *Give it to me straight, Lee – are we still getting married?*

give or take
used to say that an amount or number is not exact, and often used humorously in order to say that it is far from exact: *He lived 2,000 years ago, give or take a few centuries.* | *The virus is a hundred thousand times smaller, give or take, than a human cell.*

I'll give you, him, etc. that
SPOKEN said when you accept that an idea, fact, etc. is true, even though you do not like it or do not agree with parts of it: *Even if he's not a great actor, he's a good dancer – I'll give you that.* | *Clayton's now a successful fighter – we have to give him that, but he still has to train hard if he wants to continue.*

glass

glass ceiling
a limit, caused by people's attitudes and traditional practices, that prevents women from being successful and reaching the top levels of their profession: *Long ago, Goodhue shattered the glass ceiling to become the first female publisher at Time Inc.*

people who live in glass houses (shouldn't throw stones)
used to say that you should not criticize other people when you have the same faults that they do: *Jenkins' company does business with the multinational that he criticizes. People who live in glass houses should avoid throwing stones.*

glasses

see *something* through rose-colored glasses
to think of only the good parts of a situation and pretend that the bad parts do not exist so that you always think things are better than they are: *A lot of people are looking at the stock market through rose-colored glasses, ignoring higher interest rates.*

gleam

a gleam in *someone's* eye
used about a plan or project that is being planned or considered but has not started: *At that time, CD-ROMs were just a gleam in some young engineer's eye.*

glory

bask in *someone's* reflected glory
used to say that someone is enjoying the praise, fame, excitement, etc. that a friend or family member is experiencing, although they are not experiencing it themselves: *Golfer Kenny Perry basked happily in the reflected glory of his partner, actor Don Johnson, who attracted hundreds of fans to the tournament.*

> NOTE▶ People often just use "reflected glory" on its own: *What is it that makes people start fan clubs to their favorite stars; is it addiction, or the chance of reflected glory?*

go to glory
OLD-FASHIONED to die: *You'll be telling your children tales about me long after I'm gone to glory.*

gloss

put a gloss on *something*
to talk or write about something in a way that makes it seem better than it is: *It doesn't matter what kind of gloss you put on it – the claims you're making are simply not true.*

glove

fit *someone* like a glove
to be exactly right or appropriate for someone, or exactly the right size and

shape to fit them: *I hadn't wanted a part in a T.V. series, but this one seemed to fit me like a glove.*

the gloves are off

used to say that a person or group has decided to begin fighting or competing in a more determined way than before, and is more willing to harm an opponent ♦ OFTEN USED IN BUSINESS AND POLITICS: *Pawlaski had been keeping his comments under control, but this week the gloves are off.*

treat *someone* with kid gloves
(also **handle** *someone* **with kid gloves**)

to treat someone very carefully because they easily become upset, or because you do not want to offend them: *Some people thought that students who were children of rich alumni were being treated with kid gloves.*

kid-gloves: *The administration's kid-gloves treatment of former dictators has come under heavy criticism recently.*

glutton

a glutton for punishment

used about someone who seems to enjoy working hard or doing something unpleasant: *I was the only one who came in on Saturday – I guess I'm a real glutton for punishment.*

a glutton for punishment

I'M WRITING AN EXTRA RESEARCH PAPER

LIBRARY

NOTE▶ A glutton is someone who eats too much.

go

—see GOING
⇨go APE
⇨be GOOD to go
⇨go/turn SOUR

⇨RUN/go deep
⇨THERE you go/are
⇨WHAT goes around comes around
⇨you can't go WRONG (with)

go all out

to try, using a lot of energy and determination, to get or achieve something: *The other gas stations aren't able to compete with Arco's prices, so they go all out to compete with their service.*

go bust

if a business goes bust, it cannot continue to operate because it does not have enough money: *What rights do consumers have if an airline company goes bust? Are their tickets worthless?*

go easy on *someone*

to deal with a person or situation in a way that is nicer or more pleasant than is usual or expected: *I know you don't approve of what Rachel did, but go easy on her – she's just a kid.*

go easy on *something*

to not take, use, or eat too much of something: *You can enjoy all your favorite foods this holiday season, but remember to go easy on the butter and mayonnaise.*

go for broke

to take big risks and use all your energy in order to try to achieve something: *Knowing that this was the last good chance he would have to impress the judges, Charlie decided to go for broke and attempt his most difficult performance.*

go for it

SPOKEN used to encourage someone to try to do something that they have decided to do: *I know what you're saying. Let's just go for it and see what happens.*

go off half cocked

to speak or do something without thinking about it carefully first, often with the result that you make a mistake or are unsuccessful at something: *Corso was a respected military man. So why would he go off half-cocked and publish a book that would leave him open to ridicule?*

go one better (than)
to do something better than someone else has done it, better than you have done it before, or better than you are expected to do it: *When I asked my grandfather if he'd help me get the letters typed, he went one better and bought me a computer.*

go postal (on *someone*)
SPOKEN to become extremely angry, especially in a crazy or violent way: *Kirstin went postal when she found out her luggage had been lost.*

go swimmingly
OLD-FASHIONED if something you have planned goes swimmingly, it happens without any problems: *Clarice couldn't understand why he left so suddenly – everything had been going swimmingly.*

someone's got it going on
SLANG to be very attractive: *If you ask me, Nik's got it going on. I've never seen anything so fine!*

I'm not (even) gonna go there
(also **Let's not even go there**)
SPOKEN said when you do not want someone to ask or talk about a subject because it annoys or embarrasses you: *"You like her, don't you?" "Look, just don't ask me about that. I'm not even gonna go there." | Why did he take his clothes off, anyway? No, forget I asked. Let's not even go there.*

it/that goes without saying
used to say that something is so clear that it does not really need to be mentioned: *Of course, it goes without saying that I miss my family and my daily interactions with them. | Your colleagues look at your performance; that goes without saying. But they will also consider your personality and the way you deal with personal issues.*

make a go of *something*
to manage to be successful at something, such as a job or relationship, after working hard at it: *Floyd has two failed marriages behind him, but he's determined to make a go of his third.*

be no go
SPOKEN used to say that something will not happen, or that someone cannot do something: *Finally, we tried to find work downtown, but even there it was no go.*

be on the go
to be very busy or working all the time: *Katie is constantly on the go, arranging business breakfasts and rushing from one appointment to the next.*

goalposts
move the goalposts
used to say that someone in authority has suddenly changed their aims or the decisions they made earlier so that people who are affected are confused about what to do: *Our end objectives have always been the same, but obviously we've had to change our tactics, so I don't think the goalposts are being moved.*

> NOTE▶ Goalposts are the two posts that you kick a ball through in sports such as soccer to score points. Moving the goalposts would make this difficult.

goat
get *someone's* goat
SPOKEN to annoy you very much: *They were just making things up, trying to get your goat.*

god
⇨**God's GIFT to**
⇨**SO help me (God)**

God willing and the creek don't rise
SPOKEN a humorous expression used in order to say that you hope you will not have problems doing something: *God willing and the creek don't rise, we'll be able to get through the next few months.*

pray to the porcelain god
SLANG to vomit (=bring up food from your stomach because you are sick), especially because you have drunk too much alcohol: *I was so sick. I was praying to the porcelain god all night.*

ye gods!
SPOKEN said when you are surprised or shocked at something, often used humorously: *Ye gods, Nicole, that dress is short!*

godmother

⇨someone's **FAIRY** godmother

going

⇨**be going begging** —see **BEG**

do *something* **while the going's good**

to do something while there is an opportunity and while there is no one or nothing to stop you: *Many financial advisers are urging people to invest while the going is good and guarantee themselves an income.*

be heavy going

used to say that something is difficult to understand or deal with, or that someone is difficult to talk to: *Most of the book was pretty heavy going.*

when the going gets tough

when a situation becomes difficult: *When the going gets tough with your studies, having a definite goal will help to see you through.*

when the going gets tough, the tough get going

used in order to say that people with strong characters do not have problems dealing with difficult situations: *My dad taught me that when the going gets tough, the tough get going, and that gave me the courage to continue pursuing my goal.*

> NOTE▶ You may hear people change the words in this expression to humorously suggest other ways of dealing with difficult situations: *When the going gets tough, the tough go shopping, and Fifth Avenue is the place to do it.* | *The only lesson I've learned from this experience is, when the going gets tough, the tough eat more dessert.*

gold

⇨**(the pot of gold at) the END of the rainbow**
⇨**be like gold DUST**

as good as gold

used to emphasize that someone behaves very well ◆ USED ESPECIALLY ABOUT CHILDREN: *He sat there waiting, as good as gold, until it was his turn.*

strike gold

to find or do something that makes you successful or rich: *I started looking for an apartment on Monday, and struck gold almost immediately.*

there's gold in them there/ thar ___

a humorous expression used in order to say that someone is making a lot of money from a situation ◆ OFTEN USED IN NEWSPAPERS, ON TELEVISION NEWS, ETC.: *Not only is the sale of the drug legal, it's also very lucrative – there's gold in them there pills.*

> NOTE▶ This idiom comes from the time in the late 19th and early 20th centuries when people were looking for gold in the western U.S. When gold was found, people were supposed to have said, "there's gold in them thar hills." Now people use other words instead of "hills" to make the phrase fit any situation.

goldmine

be sitting on a goldmine

to own something very valuable, especially without realizing this: *You should fix this house up a little. With this location, you could be sitting on a goldmine.*

good

⇨**GIVE as good as you get**
⇨*someone* **is up to no good** —see *someone* **is up to SOMETHING**
⇨**MAKE good**

as good as ___

1 used with an adjective such as dead, done, over, etc. in order to say that someone or something is almost dead, done, etc. and soon will be: *The war's as good as over – the boys will be home soon.* | *I haven't written the final chapter, but the book's as good as finished.*
2 used with the past participle in order to say that although someone did not really do something, it seems as if they had really done it: *I as good as stopped smoking when I got married – I just have one when I go out with the boys.*

be good to go
SPOKEN to have everything that you need, or to be in the right condition to do something: *We've sent off the form and the money's all there, so I guess we're good to go.* | *The guys really needed this day off – they'll be good to go for another couple of weeks after this.*

goodbye

(it's) goodbye ___ hello ___
a humorous expression used in order to say that one person, idea, method, etc. is not interesting or does not exist anymore because another one has replaced it
♦ OFTEN USED IN NEWSPAPERS AND MAGAZINES: *When Weber started his own business, it was goodbye suit and tie, hello T-shirt and baseball cap.*

kiss *something* goodbye
(also **say goodbye to** *something*)
to accept the fact that you will lose something or not be able to have it: *Well, if you decide to work part-time, you can kiss your health insurance goodbye.* | *At that point, Edwards knew she would have to say goodbye to her hopes of winning an Olympic medal.*

goods

deliver the goods
(also **come up with the goods**)
to do something as well as you are expected to do it: *Motta's a good player who consistently delivers the goods.*

get/have the goods on *someone*
to find out or know things about someone that they do not want other people to know about, especially about something illegal they have done: *Kim said that she had the goods on Lawrence and she was going to confront him.*

goose

cook *someone's* goose
to get someone into trouble or prevent them from succeeding at something they are trying to do: *When Bush broke his promise not to raise taxes, his political goose was cooked.*

kill the goose that lays the golden egg/eggs
(also **kill the golden goose**)
to destroy or spoil something that brings you a lot of money: *Vinney's made a lot of money playing football; I don't know why he wants to quit now and kill the goose that lays the golden egg.* | *The high-rises were built before authorities realized that they were killing the golden goose of tourism.*

a wild goose chase
when you spend a long time searching for something without finding it, especially because it does not exist: *An anonymous phone call had led the detectives on a wild goose chase.*

wouldn't say boo to a goose
used about someone who is shy and quiet: *I don't know Marty, but he looks like he wouldn't say boo to a goose.*

gorge

make *someone's* gorge rise
to make someone feel sick or very angry about something: *All the admiration surrounding sports figures can really make your gorge rise.*

gospel

take/accept *something* as gospel
(also **take/accept** *something* **as the gospel truth**)
to believe that something is true, especially when it is likely that it is not completely true: *I was naive and took almost everything people said as gospel, but now I know I should have asked more questions.*

> NOTE▶ The gospel is another word for the stories and ideas in the New Testament in the Bible. You may also hear people say that something "is the gospel truth" when they want to emphasize that it is true: *I tell you, and it's the gospel truth, I never trusted Steve.*

grab

⇨ **HOW does** *something* **grab you?**

up for grabs
if a prize, job, opportunity, etc. is up for

grabs, it is available to anyone who wants to try to get it: *Five city council seats are up for grabs in the coming election.*

grace

fall from grace
when someone stops being liked, admired, or trusted, especially by people who employ them: *Publication of the secret tapes led to a spectacular fall from grace for Chapa, previously one of the nation's most respected lawmen.*
someone **falls from grace:** *Grominsky was a movie executive who had fallen from grace at one of the big studios a few years before.*

in someone's **good graces**
used to say that someone likes you, especially because you have done things that make them like you: *People came from all over to praise Eikman and try to get into his good graces.*

someone's/something's **saving grace**
a good quality that prevents someone or something from being completely bad or disappointing: *The prison's saving grace is its educational program that gives inmates a chance to stay out of jail in the future.*

grade

make the grade
to succeed in what you are trying to do, or to reach the necessary standard: *Making the grade as a dealer sometimes means working 10–12 hours a day.*

grain

go against the grain
if an idea or way of behaving goes against the grain, it is difficult for you to accept because you would not naturally believe it or behave that way: *Making cars lighter and more fuel-efficient goes against the grain of what U.S. consumers want.*

take something with a grain of salt
to not believe all of what someone tells you, because there are good reasons to think that it might not be true: *I've learned that when Kevin talks, sometimes you have to take what he says with a grain of salt.*

grapes

sour grapes
a bad attitude that makes someone criticize something because they want it but cannot have it: *Some people regard the complaints against Ms. Meara as sour grapes from old-fashioned policemen who are unwilling to work under a female chief.*

grapevine

hear something through/on the grapevine
to know something because the information has been passed from one person to another in conversation: *I'd heard on the grapevine that the studios were looking for a recording engineer, so I called and pestered them for an interview.*

grass

the grass is (always) greener (on the other side of the fence)
used to say that what someone else has always seems better than what you have: *I think it's a case of the grass being greener on the other side of the fence – you look at someone and you wish you had her figure, or her hair.*

the grass roots
the ordinary people in an organization, rather than the leaders ◆ OFTEN USED IN POLITICS: *We ought to be listening to the grass roots and asking them what to do about this problem.*
grass-roots: *Deciding how to revitalize the community and get the most for their money was a grass-roots effort.*

not let the grass grow under your feet
to not waste time, or to start doing something without any delay: *Matthew's not someone who lets the grass grow under his feet. I would imagine he has started already.*

grasshopper

knee-high to a grasshopper
OLD-FASHIONED used when you are talking about a time in the past to say that someone was very young then: *I*

remember when we were snowed in for a week – your mom was knee-high to a grasshopper then.

grave

dig your own grave
to do something that will cause serious problems for you later: *Anybody who writes anything controversial in this paper is digging his own grave.*

someone **would turn/roll over in their grave**
used to say that someone who is dead would be very angry or upset about something that is happening now: *They looked up at a portrait of their uncle Willard, who must have been rolling over in his grave at the thought of selling the house.*

> NOTE▶ You may hear people change this idiom slightly and say that someone is "spinning in his/her grave" in order to emphasize how angry or upset they would be: *If he knew that one of his songs was being used in a beer commercial, Bob Marley would be spinning in his grave.*

gravy

a/the gravy train
used about an organization, activity, or business from which many people can make money or profit without much effort: *Some European investors know that privatization is not always the gravy train that governments promise.*

grease
⇨ELBOW grease

Greek

it's (all) Greek to me
used to say that you cannot understand something: *I tried to read an article about thermodynamics once, but it was Greek to me.*

green
⇨green around the GILLS
⇨green with ENVY

grief

give *someone* grief
to criticize or complain to someone: *Even McNeil's father was giving him grief about dropping the pass that could have won them the game.*

grin

grin and bear it
used to say that you should accept a difficult situation because there is nothing you can do about it: *This stuff smells like rotten eggs, but when you work here every day you just learn to grin and bear it.*

wipe the grin/smile off *someone's* face
SPOKEN to do something that makes someone less pleased or satisfied, especially because they are annoying you: *"I'd like to slap you and wipe that grin off your face!" he told the astonished customer.*

grip

get/come to grips with *something*
to start to deal with a problem, especially by trying to understand it: *Counselors can help students come to grips with issues ranging from homesickness to sports injuries.*

get a grip (on yourself)
to start controlling your emotions and dealing with your problems: *Stella tried to get a grip on herself as she washed the cut under some cold water.*

get a grip on *something*
to manage to deal with a situation or understand something: *As the nation struggles to get a grip on medical costs, insurance companies have started limiting people's access to care.*

be in the grip of *something*
to be in an unpleasant situation that you cannot control, especially when you cannot live or behave normally because of it: *The Northeast is in the grip of the worst winter storm for 50 years.*

lose your grip
to become less confident and less able to

G

deal with a situation: *At that time, the Democrats had been in control of Congress since 1954 and did not seem in any danger of losing their grip.*

grist

be (all) grist for the mill

used to say that an experience or problem can be used for your advantage in another situation, in an argument, etc.: *Writers of all ages see details of their lives as grist for the mill.*

> NOTE▶ "Grist" is a quantity of grain that is to be ground (=crushed into small pieces) at one time.

groove

in/into the groove

doing an activity, job, etc. easily and well, without problems: *It takes a while to get back into the groove after three weeks of vacation.*

ground

break new ground

to do or discover something completely new: *Ms. Elliot broke new ground 15 years ago when she became the first woman lawyer in the firm.*

common ground

ideas or aims that two or more people or groups share, that help them to work together easily: *The decision nearly split the Presbyterian Church apart, but we've tried very hard to find as much common ground as we can in order to prevent that.*

cover a lot of ground
(also **cover plenty/lots of ground**)

to discuss or deal with many different parts of a subject or situation: *The institute covers a lot of ground in its research, including insect biology, ecology, and animal behavior. | Ritz covered plenty of ground during his speech, but I kept thinking that there was so much more to be said.*

—see also **go over the same GROUND**

> NOTE▶ You may also hear people use "cover ground" in other expressions such as "cover new ground," "not cover much ground," "cover too much ground," etc.: *Kolnikov's movie is boring at the start and then tries to cover too much ground in too little time.*

gain ground

to make progress or gain advantages or importance in a situation ◆ OFTEN USED IN BUSINESS AND POLITICS: *It was feared that the fascists might be gaining considerable ground in southern parts of the country.*
—compare **lose GROUND**

get off the ground

if a new plan, business, or organization gets off the ground, or you get it off the ground, it starts to operate successfully: *Laura's keeping her teaching job until her husband's restaurant gets off the ground.*

go over the same ground
(also **cover the same ground**)

to consider or talk about something again when you have already considered or talked about it before: *I was hoping the discussion would end soon, but they just sat there, going over the same ground again for half an hour.*
—see also **cover a lot of GROUND**

hit the ground running

to start an activity, business, etc. with a lot of energy and with all the information, money, equipment, etc. that you need to make it work well: *Business travelers often have to hit the ground running, even after flying across multiple time zones.*

hold/stand your ground

to refuse to change your opinion when other people disagree with you: *Bates held his ground Friday, arguing that the report should not be made public.*

lose ground

to stop making as much progress or stop having as much power or importance as before: *The stock market lost more ground today, extending the decline of the last two sessions.*

regain/recover lost ground: *He said sales of the "Morning Star" fell slightly after the price increase, but the paper's circulation has regained all lost ground since then.*
—compare **gain GROUND**

someone's **old stomping ground/ grounds**

the place where someone used to live or work, or where they often went: *Mendel returned to her old stomping grounds in Austin for a series of shows.*

be on dangerous ground

to be behaving in a way that involves risk, for example risk of disapproval or failure: *Smith is clearly on dangerous ground with his latest film about AIDS.*

on home turf/ground

in a place or situation that is familiar to you: *UCLA celebrated their victory over Washington on the Bears' home turf.* | *This was Polson's first big political contest on home ground, and he was excited about it.*

be on safe/firm ground

to be doing something that you are certain does not involve risk, or talk about a subject you understand: *Taken by surprise, all the candidates scrambled for safe ground by saying they supported current policies.*

prepare the ground

to do things which will make it easier for an event or particular type of situation to happen in the future: *The book explains the role which Lenin played in preparing the ground for Stalin's regime.*

run *someone* into the ground

to make someone work very hard so that they become very tired: *Railroad workers in the early days were often run into the ground, dying from cold and exhaustion.*

run *something* into the ground

to discuss a subject until people are bored with it or there is nothing more to say about it: *Make your main points and then move on – you don't have to run your topic into the ground.*

run/work/drive yourself into the ground

to work so hard that you become very tired or sick: *Too many people work out like elite athletes but end up running themselves into the ground.*

shift/change your ground

to begin to give different reasons for what you are doing, or change your aims or opinions: *In the 1990s, China began to shift its ground in its relations with South Korea.*

take/claim/occupy the moral high ground

to feel confident because you think your decision or opinion is morally better than other people's ◆ OFTEN USED IN BUSINESS AND POLITICS: *In voting against efforts by the state legislature to adopt the death penalty, Mr. Arroyo is taking the moral high ground.* | *The administration is attempting to occupy the moral high ground by shipping supplies to refugees.*

worship the ground *someone* walks on
(also **worship the ground under** *someone's* **feet**)

to admire or love someone so much that you think that everything they do is right: *A lot of professional-type people have clients who worship the ground they walk on.* | *Dad worshipped the ground under your feet, and you left him – how can you expect me to forgive you?*

ground floor

be/get in on the ground floor

to become involved in a plan, business, etc. from the beginning: *Robinson's company was interested in getting in on the ground floor of the new laptop market.*

guard

catch *someone* off guard

to do something at a time when someone is not prepared for it to happen so that they are not able to deal with the situation well: *Mrs. Maynard's invitation had caught me off guard. I didn't want to go to the party, but I had no good excuse.*

lower your guard
(also **let your guard down**)

to stop being careful about what you do or say, or stop paying attention to what is happening so that you may be tricked or get into danger: *Hadley finally lowered his guard and agreed to give us an interview.* | *Summer is here, and it's important not to let your guard down with the kids in the swimming pool.*

the old guard
used about a group of people within an organization or group who do not like changes or new ideas: *It is common for the children of immigrants to disagree with the old guard about the direction their community should take in a new culture.*

old-guard: *Hillary's choice of an old-guard designer known for his classic styles indicated that she was taking a sophisticated but safe route.*

be on your guard
to pay careful attention to what is happening so that you avoid being tricked or getting into danger: *The police have warned us to be on our guard against bogus salesmen.*

guess

be anybody's guess
used to say that no one knows something: *I kept my passport in the drawer, but where it is now is anybody's guess.*

(I'll give you) three guesses
SPOKEN said when you think the answer to something is very easy to guess: *"I know how we can check it's really him – he's got a birthmark." "Where?" "I'll give you three guesses."* | *Hi Kirstin – three guesses as to whose birthday it is today.*

your guess is as good as mine
SPOKEN said when someone asks you a question and you do not know the answer: *"What time will Bill be home?" "God knows – your guess is as good as mine."*

guest

be my guest
SPOKEN used to politely give someone permission to do something: *If any of you want to come and ask questions afterward, be my guest.*

guinea pig

a guinea pig
someone on whom new ideas, methods, etc. are tested: *Herman's health was rapidly getting worse until he volunteered to be a guinea pig for a radical new treatment.*

gums

flap your gums
to talk a lot without saying anything that is important or interesting: *What makes me angry is people just flapping their gums and telling me to calm down instead of trying to help.*

gun

⇨**son of a gun** —see **SON of a bitch**

the big guns
the most important and powerful people in an organization, activity, company, etc.: *Novels by all of the big guns of American pop fiction were competing for attention at the booksellers' convention.*

do *something* with (all) guns blazing
(also **come out with your guns blazing**)
to use all your energy and skill against an opponent ◆ OFTEN USED IN NEWSPAPERS, ON TELEVISION NEWS, ETC.: *Committee members came out with all guns blazing Tuesday, determined to get the resolution passed.*

be going great guns
SPOKEN used to say that someone is doing something with a lot of energy, and is very successful, or that something is working very well: *We're going great guns, and we hope to do even better with sales next year.*

hold/put a gun to *someone's* head
to force someone to do something by using threats, or making it impossible for them to refuse: *What we find particularly insulting is for other nations to hold a gun to our head and tell us what to do with our economy.*

jump the gun
to do something too early before you are ready, or before the conditions are right: *I was not aware that the school board had already made a decision; that seems to be jumping the gun.*

a smoking gun
used about something that proves that someone has done something bad ◆ OFTEN USED IN POLITICS: *There are a lot of people who think that the memo is a smoking gun, proving that the Vice President was aware of what was going on.*

stick to your guns

to refuse to change your opinion about something, when other people are trying to persuade you that you are wrong: *We received plenty or criticism about the play, but we were also congratulated for sticking to our guns and doing it the way we wanted to.*

be under the gun

to be in a difficult situation because people want you to succeed and will blame you if you fail: *Coaching has become a tough job – running a team means always being under the gun.*

gunning

be gunning for *someone*

1 to try to find an opportunity to criticize, harm, or defeat someone: *"They'll be gunning for us, and they will be tough to beat," Treggs said about Saturday's game.*
2 to be trying to achieve something such as a position or job in a situation in which you are competing with others: *The Kentucky team is gunning for its third straight NCAA championship.*

gut

at gut level

if you feel or know something at gut level, you feel or know it through your emotions, as opposed to your intelligence: *At gut level, most people know that the space program is important for our nation's image in the world, even if it does cost a lot of tax dollars.*
gut-level: *People's gut-level responses to the abortion issue get more coverage on TV than anything else.*

bust a gut
(also **bust your gut**)

1 SPOKEN to work very hard in order to finish or achieve something: *We can be proud of ourselves because we didn't give up. We busted our guts and got the repairs done!*
—see also **bust your ASS**
2 to laugh a lot: *We were all busting a gut, watching him try to explain it to the cops.*

someone's **gut reaction**

used about someone's first and immediate feelings or opinions about something: *Bill, what's your gut reaction to Crowther's idea?*

hate *someone's* **guts**

SPOKEN to hate someone very much: *How could she say we're friends? She knows I hate her guts!*

spill your guts

to tell someone everything you feel, or a lot of personal or secret facts: *I hate those talk shows where the guests spill their guts for the entertainment of the audience.*

guy

the/a bad guy

used about someone who people blame or dislike for what is wrong in a situation: *I refuse to be the bad guy. You have to tell me if you're not happy and why.*

fall guy

someone who is blamed or punished for something bad or illegal that someone else did: *Biondi's defenders say he was the fall guy for troubles at two businesses that were largely out of his control.*

fall guy

NOTE▸ A "fall guy" is another name for a stunt man. Stunt men are used instead of actors to do the dangerous things in movies so that the actors are not hurt.

the/a good guy

used about someone who people like or trust because they are not doing bad or illegal things in a situation when other people are, or because they are trying to stop these things from happening: *Asner is the good guy whom Moore turns to when she needs help.*

no more Mr. Nice Guy!

SPOKEN used to say that you will stop trying to behave honestly and fairly, because people are not behaving honestly and fairly to you: *The new policy is no more Mr. Nice Guy, no more giving people money whenever they tell us they have problems.*

H

habits

old habits die hard
used to say that it is difficult to make people change their attitudes and behavior: *Manville returned the salute; he was officially a civilian, but old habits died hard.*

hack

someone **can/could hack it**
to have the ability, character, strength, etc. needed to succeed in a particular job or activity ◆ OFTEN USED IN THE NEGATIVE: *Jen's father left home and disappeared when she was young. He just couldn't hack family life.*

hackles

raise *someone's* **hackles**
(also *someone's* **hackles rise**)
to make someone angry or annoyed by doing or saying something that offends them: *Banderas says he doesn't understand why his movie raised feminist hackles.*

> NOTE▶ "Hackles" are the feathers on the back of a male bird's neck. When he is ready to fight, they stand up.

hair

⇨be/come within a hair's BREADTH of doing *something*

a bad hair day
SPOKEN used about a day when you cannot make your hair look attractive and you therefore feel annoyed and ugly, and often about a day when everything seems to go wrong for you: *Today is definitely a bad hair day. Can't I just stay home?*

get/keep *someone* **out of your hair**
SPOKEN to stop someone from annoying you, especially someone who is always near you or always trying to get involved with what you are doing: *I enjoy fishing. It gets me out of my wife's hair now that I'm retired.*

be/keep/get out of someone's hair: *The quicker you answer our questions, the quicker we'll be out of your hair.*

get/have a wild hair
(also **get/have a wild hair up your ass**)
SLANG to have a strong wish or need to do something that seems strange to other people: *"You drove all the way to Tampa, for one night with him?" "Yeah, you know, I just got a wild hair and did it."*

> NOTE▶ Although you may hear people use "get/have a wild hair up your ass," it is better not to use it because some people find it offensive.

a/the hair of the dog (that bit you)
used about an alcoholic drink that you have in order to feel better after drinking too much alcohol the night before: *The day after the carnival, the bar opened at 8 a.m. for those who needed a little hair of the dog.*

a hair shirt
used about a difficult or bad situation that someone chooses or accepts, especially if they do this because they are sorry for something that they have done: *The company will probably wear its hair shirt for a few weeks, and then go back to its old ways of ignoring employees' complaints.*

> NOTE▶ A hair shirt was a rough, uncomfortable shirt worn by some very religious Christian people to punish themselves for something or to show that they did not care about comfort.

let your hair down
to enjoy yourself and relax, especially after working hard: *Come on and dance, Carl! Let your hair down a little – it's Friday night.*

something **makes your hair curl**
used to say that a story, experience, etc. is surprising or shocking: *I could tell you a few things about Jake that would make your hair curl.*

pull/tear your hair out
used to say that someone is very angry, upset, or worried about something: *"You wait and see," said Carol. "When Cathy*

*leaves, Pat will be tearing his hair out –
but it'll be too late then."*

split hairs
to talk about small, unimportant differences between things as if they were
important: *Lawyers on the case have been
accussed of splitting legal hairs.*
hair-splitting: *In an impressive display of
hair-splitting, the diet drink claims to have
more fiber than its main competitor.*

something will put hair on your chest
SPOKEN used humorously to tell someone
to eat or drink something because it will
be good for them, especially when you
are giving them a strong alcoholic drink:
*Dennis poured her a large gin and tonic
and said, "Drink this – it'll put hair on
your chest."*

hale

hale and hearty
used to say that someone is very healthy
and active, especially an older person:
*Dirkson, looking hale and hearty at 74,
still works five days a week.*

half

⇨**GO off half cocked**
⇨**half a LOAF (is better than none)**

someone's better/other half
used humorously to talk about someone's
husband, wife, or partner: *I've got to go.
My better half is waiting outside.*

someone doesn't (even) know the half of it
SPOKEN used to emphasize that a situation
is much worse, more difficult, etc. than
people realize: *"Her husband seems like
such a jerk!" "Yeah, and I'm sure we don't
even know the half of it."*

see how the other half lives
OLD-FASHIONED to find out what life is like
for people who are very different from
you, especially much richer or much
poorer: *Just for a week, I'd like to see how
the other half lives – stay in fancy hotels
and fly around in my private jet.*

halfway

meet *someone* halfway
to accept some of someone's opinions, in
order to reach an agreement or to have a
better relationship with them: *Tell Wilson
we're prepared to meet him halfway and
offer him a pay raise if he'll take on more
responsibilities.*

halt

grind to a halt
if a system, process, or organization
grinds to a halt, it gradually stops working
◆ OFTEN USED IN NEWSPAPERS, ON TELEVISION
NEWS, ETC.: *The negotiations with the
teachers' union have ground to a halt over
the issue of tenure.*

NOTE▶ You may also hear people say
that something "screeches to a halt" if it
happens quickly: *I would call upon
Americans to conserve energy, but that
doesn't mean that life has to screech to a
halt.*

ham

ham it up
to behave or perform in a silly or funny
way or with a lot of false emotion in order
to get people's attention or entertain
them: *Jim put on a Santa suit and started
hamming it up for the kids.*

hammer

come/go under the hammer
to be offered for sale at an auction (=a
public meeting where land, buildings,
paintings, etc. are sold to the person who
offers the most money for them): *Forty
modern Russian paintings are set to go
under the hammer next week.*

hammer *something* home
to repeat something until people
understand it or agree with it: *The
candidates must get their message down
to a few simple phrases and then hammer
it home to the public.*

hammering

⇨**take a BEATING/hammering**

hand

⇨**put/stick your hand into your pocket** —see **dig/dip into your POCKET**

at the hands of *someone* (or *something*)

if something bad happens to you at the hands of someone, they make it happen: *The population of arctic seals suffered a great decline at the hands of the fur trade in the last century.*
—compare **in the HANDs of** *someone*

bite the hand that feeds you

to criticize or behave as if you are not grateful to a person or organization that has helped or supported you: *Biting the hand that feeds her, Cherie Diez sued the radio station for a share in the profits of the show that made her famous.*

someone can do *something* with one hand tied behind his/her back

used to emphasize that someone can do something very easily: *She could beat you at tennis with one hand tied behind her back any day.*
—see also **do** *something* **with one HAND tied behind your back**

be caught with your hand in the cookie jar

to be caught doing something wrong or illegal, usually something involving money: *The University was suspected of illegally luring athletes to their basketball team with cars and money. This year we finally caught them with their hand in the cookie jar.*

change hands

1 if a building, object, business, etc. changes hands, it is sold to someone: *About 162.4 million shares changed hands on the New York Stock Exchange today.*
2 if money changes hands, it is used to buy something: *I don't know how much Dad paid, but I can tell you a lot of money changed hands.*

the dead hand of *something*

used about an idea or system that has prevented progress and development in a country, organization, business, etc.: *Many teachers claim that the dead hand of bureaucracy is hindering their work.*

dirty your hands

to get involved in an activity that is dishonest or that you think is bad: *I would not want to dirty my hands with research on chemical weapons.*
—compare **get your HANDs dirty**

dismiss/reject *something* out of hand

to decide at once, not to accept an idea, argument, plan, etc., and spend no time thinking about it: *Even though Republican senators disliked some parts of the bill, they did not dismiss it out of hand.*

do *something* with one hand tied behind your back

(also **do** *something* **with your hands tied behind your back**)
to try to do something in spite of a disadvantage that makes it difficult for you to succeed: *Police are fighting car crime with few officers and one hand tied behind their backs.*
—see also *someone* **can do** *something* **with one HAND tied behind his/her back**

everything you can lay/get your hands on

(also **anything, whatever, etc. you can get/lay your hands on**)
SPOKEN used to say that you take or use everything, anything, etc. of a particular type that you can find: *The authorities had confiscated whatever they could get their hands on, and Lamar was left without even a bed.*

fall/get into the wrong hands

if something secret or dangerous falls into the wrong hands, it is discovered by people who may use it in a way that harms people: *The agreement helps to ensure that nuclear weapons don't fall into the wrong hands.*

a firm hand

strict control of someone or something: *Those kids of his just run wild – what they need is a firm hand.*

(at) first hand

(also **first-hand**)
if you see, experience, or learn about

something at first hand, you find out about it by direct personal experience: *I learned first-hand what a difference a good nurse can make when I was in the hospital for a back operation.*

first-hand: *Friedman's book is based on first-hand accounts given by witnesses to the plane crash.*

force someone's hand
to make someone do something when they are unwilling, or sooner than they wanted to do it: *Many countries were trying to force the President's hand into giving humanitarian aid.*

get/gain/have the upper hand
to get or have more power than someone or something else, and be able to control a situation: *If the government restricts our trading, this will enable our competitors to gain the upper hand.*

get/lay your hands on *something*
SPOKEN to be able to find or get something, especially something that is difficult to find or get: *The rocket is without a doubt the most popular toy this Christmas, so if you want to get your hands on one, you'd better move fast.*

get out of hand
to become difficult or impossible to control: *Police knew that if the Bulls won, the post-game celebrations would get out of hand.*

get your hands dirty
to be willing to work hard and be involved in the practical parts of a business or activity: *The new governor should be willing to get his hands dirty and start working on the environmental issues that are troubling the state.*
—compare **dirty your HANDs**

give *someone* a big hand
SPOKEN used to ask the people watching a program, play, etc. to show their approval of someone by clapping (=hitting their hands together again and again): *Tonight we have a new young singer, Stephen Pirelli – give him a big hand, ladies and gentlemen.*

give *someone* a free hand
to allow someone to do something in the way that they choose, without telling them what to do: *The board gave me a*

free hand with recruitment, and promised to support any decision I made.

someone **has a free hand:** *Wakerly has a free hand in producing the magazine's pictures, stories, and page designs.*

give/lend *someone* a hand
(also **lend a hand**)
to help someone who is trying to do something: *Sue said she could come over today and lend a hand with the yard work.*

someone **needs a hand:** *I think Mom needs a hand getting the turkey into the oven.*

go hand in hand (with)
used to say that two things are closely related and must be considered together: *For 20 years, inflation and housing prices have gone hand in hand.*
—see also **work hand in hand (with)**

hand in glove
(also **hand-in-glove**)
used to say that two things are very suitable for each other, or work very well together: *U.S. stock markets are working hand-in-glove with governments to improve their financial structures.*

someone's hands are tied
used to say that someone is not allowed or does not have the power to help someone achieve something, even though they may want to: *I wish I could help you with the test, but as your teacher my hands are tied.*

have *someone* eating out of (the palm of) your hand
used to emphasize that someone is willing to do whatever you want them to do: *Jerry is such a good salesman that after a few sentences, he has customers eating out of his hand.*

have a hand in (doing) *something*
to be involved in doing or making something: *The community owes a big thank you to all the people who had a hand in creating the new museum.*

have/keep *something* on hand
to be sure that something is near you or available to be used: *It's a good idea to have some bottled water and food on hand in case of an earthquake.*

have *something* on your hands
to have to be experiencing or dealing with a particular type of situation now, usually a difficult one: *If we don't do something to calm things down, we'll have a revolt on our hands.*
—see also **have (*someone's*) BLOOD on your hands, have TIME on your hands**

have your hands full
to have so much to do that you do not have time to do anything else: *Kim really has her hands full with three kids under four years old and a full time job.*

the heavy hand (of)
(also **a heavy hand**)
used about great power someone has over people which is used in a severe or unfair way: *Political opposition struggled to survive under the heavy hand of the secret police.*

hold *someone's* hand
to help someone in an unfamiliar or frightening situation: *I can give you a basic explanation over the phone, but I can't be there to hold your hand every time something goes wrong with the computer.*
hand-holding: *Software customers have to choose whether they want high performance and hand-holding, or basic goods at a low price.*

in the hands of *someone*
(also **in *someone's* hands**)
used to say that a particular person or organization has control over something and makes decisions about what will happen: *Nancy, these two court cases will be in your hands until I get back from vacation.*
opposite **out of *someone's* hands:** *I'm sorry, it's out of my hands. I've passed on your complaint to the manager, and there is nothing more I can do.*
—compare **at the HANDs of** *someone*

someone/*something* is in safe hands
used to say that you trust the person or organization who is responsible for dealing with something: *Don't worry, Kara's in safe hands. Dr. Peters is the best surgeon I know.*

it's all hands on deck
used to say that everyone has to work together because they have a lot of work to do in a small amount of time: *After the party, it'll be all hands on deck to get the place cleaned up.*

keep your hand in
to practice a skill so that you do not lose it: *Peterson files a few news reports just to keep his hand in, but his real purpose is to collect material for a book.*

live (from) hand to mouth
used to emphasize that someone has very little money, and can only afford to buy the basic things that they need: *Don't tell me not to worry – I'm 28 years old and I'm still living from hand to mouth.*
hand-to-mouth: *I could hardly ask Helen to marry me and share my hand-to-mouth existence.*

someone needs a hand
—see **give/lend** *someone* **a HAND**

be an old hand (at *something*)
to be very good at something because you have been doing it for a long time: *Carole, the leader, was the first to arrive at base camp, and it was obvious from the way she talked that she was an old hand at climbing.*

be on hand
to be in a place at a particular time, often when something special or unusual is happening, in order to watch or help if you are needed ♦ OFTEN USED IN NEWSPAPERS, ON TELEVISION NEWS, ETC.: *Disaster relief personnel will be on hand to provide information and assistance at the relief center.*

on the other hand
used when you are saying something that is different from or opposite to the idea or fact that you have just mentioned: *When aged cheeses such as cheddar are heated, the fat turns to oil. Processed cheeses, on the other hand, melt more evenly.*

out of *someone's* hands
—see **in the HANDs of** *someone*

play (right) into *someone's* hands
to do exactly what someone you are competing against wants you to do, without realizing it: *If we respond with violence, we'll be playing into their hands – they'll have an excuse to fight.*

H

the right hand doesn't know what the left hand is doing
(also **the left hand doesn't know what the right hand is doing**)
used to say that there is not enough communication in an organization so that different parts of it do not work together as they should: *Because the right hand didn't know what the left hand was doing, I was asked to pay for medical treatment when I was really entitled to receive it for free.*

show/tip your hand
to let other people know your plans in a situation where this might give them an advantage, for example when you are competing: *The general always waited for his enemies to show their hand before committing his forces.*

> NOTE▶ If you show your hand in a game of cards, you let other people see which cards you are holding. This gives them the advantage of knowing what you are likely to do next in the game.

sit on your hands
to not get involved in a situation in which you could be useful ♦ OFTEN USED IN BUSINESS AND POLITICS: *People are dying from this disease every day. The drug companies can't just sit on their hands and do nothing.*

take *someone/something* in hand
1 to try to control someone and improve their behavior: *Women were always taking Jim in hand, trying to make him into the man they thought he should be.*
2 to say you are responsible for a situation or problem and deal with it: *When there's a lack of political, business, and civil leadership, sometimes the people – in this case music lovers – have to take things in hand.*

take *someone/something* off *someone's* hands
to remove or look after someone or something so that another person does not have to deal with him, her, or it: *My brother would be happy to take that old motorcycle off your hands.*
someone/something **is off** *someone's* **hands:** *Your kids will be off your hands in a few years, so what will you do when you're not a full-time mom anymore?*

try your hand at *something*
to try doing something that you have never done before in order to find out if you can do it and like it: *More and more actors are trying their hand at directing movies.*

turn your hand to *something*
to start doing something that is different from what you usually do: *Justin was a music teacher who turned his hand to writing while recovering from a car accident.*

wait on *someone* hand and foot
to do everything for another person to make them comfortable, while they do nothing at all: *I don't think Gary realizes how much energy his wife is putting into waiting on him hand and foot.*

wash your hands of *someone/something*
to behave as if you are not responsible for someone or something that is causing problems: *Jim got into trouble so many times that after a while his parents washed their hands of him.*

> NOTE▶ This idiom comes from a story in the Bible. Pilate, the Roman ruler, washed his hands at Jesus' trial (=a process during which it is decided if someone is guilty of a crime) and said he was not responsible for what happened to Jesus.

win hands down
(also **beat** *someone/something* **hands down**)
to win a game, competition, election, etc. completely and easily, or to be the best of all the things or people that are being compared: *If the election had been held that day, Brown would have won hands down.*
hands-down: *For delicious barbecued ribs, the hands-down winner has to be Bubba's Country Grill.*

work hand-in-hand (with)
if two groups work hand in hand, they work closely together in order to achieve something: *Police have realized that they have to work hand-in-hand with local people to make neighborhoods safer to live in.*
—see also **go HAND in hand (with)**

wring *someone's* **hand**
to greet someone or say goodbye to them by holding their hand tightly and shaking it a lot, especially when this is surprising or annoying to the person: *"Nice to meet you, Jack," said David, wringing his hand and blowing cigar smoke into his face.*
—compare **wring your HANDS**

wring *someone's* **hand**

wring your hands
to show or say that you are worried and upset about something, especially without doing anything about it: *There is no point in wringing our hands about unmarried mothers if we don't give young women better reasons to continue their education.*
—compare **wring** *someone's* **HAND**

you/I have to hand it to *someone*
(also **you've/I've got to hand it to** *someone*)
SPOKEN said when someone has done something very well although they have not been completely successful, or when you do not approve of other things they have done: *You have to hand it to Dennis – he played an incredible game under a lot of pressure.*

handcuffs

golden handcuffs
when a company pays a lot of money to an important worker so that they do not leave: *The almost-free tickets the airlines offer to workers are really golden handcuffs because they make it so hard for their employees to quit.*
—see also **a golden HANDSHAKE**

handle

fly off the handle
to suddenly get very angry: *I was trying to*

explain that it was an accident, but he flew off the handle and wouldn't listen.

get a handle on
to understand a situation so that you can deal with it more successfully: *The book gives enough information for even a complete beginner to get a handle on the subject.*

handshake

a golden handshake/parachute
a large amount of money given to someone important when they leave their job: *The manager of "Playboy" got a golden handshake of nearly $18 million in his severance package when he left the company last month.*
—see also **golden HANDCUFFS**

handwriting
⇨**the handwriting on the wall** —see **the WRITING on the wall**

handy
⇨**COME in handy**

hang
⇨**hang a B.A.**
⇨**LET it all hang out**

get the hang of *something*
to gradually find the right way of doing something, or of using a machine or tool, while you do or use it for the first time: *We thought we were getting the hang of the game, so we decided to try the advanced version.*

hang in there!
SPOKEN used to tell someone to keep trying to deal with a difficult situation, and be brave and determined: *I know it's hard, Kristi, but just hang in there.*

hang loose
SPOKEN used to tell someone to remain calm and relaxed in a difficult situation: *We didn't know what was happening – I just told everyone to hang loose and be prepared.*

hang *someone* out to dry
to do nothing to help someone who is in trouble, especially someone who has

H

worked for you and is being blamed for something bad that has happened: *The company assured me of their support, and then they hung me out to dry – that's the only way to describe it.*

hang up your ___

to stop doing a job, especially because you have reached the age when most people stop working ◆ OFTEN USED IN NEWSPAPERS, ON TELEVISION NEWS, ETC.: *John Travolta has hung up his "Saturday Night Fever" gold chain and made his mark as a serious actor. | When Michael Jordan finally hung up his size 16 high-tops, many of his fans said they thought it would never happen.*

—see also **hang up your HAT**

hard

⇒**hard and fast RULEs**
⇒**the hard SELL**

be hard at it

to be very busy doing something: *"Is the meeting still going on?" "I think so – they were still hard at it when I left ten minutes ago."*

be hard put/pressed to do *something*

used to emphasize that someone finds it difficult to do something: *Suddenly every kid wanted in-line skates, and stores were hard pressed to meet the demand.*

be hard to come by

to be difficult to get or find: *Jobs were hard to come by, and most of the available work was part-time or temporary.*

something is hard/difficult to swallow

(also *something* **isn't easy to swallow**)
used to say that something is difficult to believe or accept: *The thought of spending so much on rent is hard to swallow.*

hardball

play hardball (with *someone*)

to behave in a way that shows you are extremely determined to get what you want, especially to win ◆ OFTEN USED IN BUSINESS AND POLITICS: *It is well known that*

Saltzmann plays political hardball, but he is admired for the speed at which he gets bills through Congress.
hardball: *D'Amato was known more for his hardball political tactics than for his high ethical standards.*

harness

in harness

working at your job: *A good agency will help you to get a job, and also prepare you for the first few months in harness.*

harvest

reap the harvest

to get the good or bad results of work that you did or an effort that you made: *Baldwin has reaped the harvest of hard physical training, winning two races in the last month.*

hash

sling hash

INFORMAL to work in a cheap restaurant, serving food: *Harry would probably get a job pumping gas or slinging hash in some little town somewhere.*

haste

haste makes waste

used to say that if you try to do something too quickly, you will have problems: *The band rushed to get their new album into stores, and unfortunately, haste makes waste – the songs are not as good as they could have been with more time.*

hat

⇒**do *something* at the DROP of a hat**

(*someone* wears) the black hat

used about someone who is not liked, or who is blamed by people for what is wrong in a situation: *All our sales were made according to the law. We're not the black hats here.*
(wear) the white hat: *"We're the white hats in this situation," Sapp said. "We're not just buying the company for its assets, and then running away from it with the profits."*

go/come hat in hand

(also **do *something* hat in hand**)
to ask for money or help in a very

respectful way, from someone who is more powerful than you: *I'm not going to appeal to them hat in hand. If they want to help, that's fine.*

hang up your hat
to leave your job, especially permanently at the end of your working life: *Police Chief Ron Johnson hung up his hat today after forty years of service.*
—see also **HANG up your ___**

hang your hat
1 if you hang your hat somewhere, you live or stay there: *She is looking for somewhere to hang her hat, now that her twenty-year marriage has ended.*
2 if you hang your hat on something, you depend on it in order to achieve something or to make a decision: *There must be something in state law we can hang our hat on to prevent the casino from being built here.*

have your ___ hat on
(also **wearing your ___ hat**)
used to say that you behave in a particular way at a particular time, because you are influenced by the job you are doing or the situation you are in at that time: *I concentrated on management activities and only put my sales hat on if one of the reps was really in trouble.*

I take my hat off to *someone*
SPOKEN used to say that you admire someone for what they have done: *I take my hat off to you for staying in political life for so many years without being discouraged.*

if... I'll eat my hat
OLD-FASHIONED a humorous expression used to say that you would be very surprised if something happened or was true: *If that boy gets accepted to college, I'll eat my hat.*

someone is talking through his/her hat
SPOKEN used to say that someone is talking as if they know something when they do not: *He assured me that my complaint would be dealt with, but I think he was talking through his hat.*

keep *something* under your hat
SPOKEN to keep something a secret: *Katie told me she's quitting at the end of the*

month, but keep it under your hat for now.

be old hat
used to emphasize that something is not new or interesting: *The Internet is already old hat to most academic researchers.*

pass the hat (around)
to collect money from a group of people, asking each of them to give some, so that you can buy or do something: *The School Board wouldn't give students the $800 they needed for a trip to a national science contest, but passing the hat at the meeting got them $500.*

pull *something* out of a/the hat
(also **pull a rabbit out of a/the hat**)
to suddenly produce a solution to a problem when no one is expecting it: *If their manager keeps pulling good young players out of the hat, the Rangers will be hard to beat this season.*

throw your hat into the ring
(also **toss your hat into the ring**)
to announce officially that you are going to compete for a job or in an election: *After protesting about the standard of education in local schools, Palmer has now thrown his hat into the ring as a candidate in the next school board election.*

wear more than one hat
to have more than one job, or have more than one skill that you need to do a job: *The 26 researchers at the lab all wear more than one hat. Therefore, the search for the vaccine will be approached by many different methods.*

> NOTE▶ People sometimes show exactly how many things someone does or is interested in by saying "someone wears two/three/many hats": *I could do a better job if I didn't have to wear so many hats.*

hatch

batten down the hatches
to prepare to deal with a difficult situation, especially by spending less money than usual: *We are having to batten down the hatches this year, and that means cutting the entertainment and training budgets.*

NOTE The "hatches" are the openings in the deck (=the outside floor) of a ship which are closed and fastened with pieces of wood or metal called "battens" before a storm.

down the hatch

1 SPOKEN said before you drink alcohol: *"Nick, here's your beer." "Thanks. Down the hatch!"*
2 if you put food or drink down the hatch, you eat or drink it: *The big food companies don't care what kind of junk our kids are shoveling down the hatch.*

hatchet

bury the hatchet

to agree to stop arguing about something and become friends again: *Our friendship is too important to let it end like this. We need to talk this out and bury the hatchet.*

a hatchet job (on)

severe and unfair criticism of someone, especially in a book or newspaper, on television, etc.: *Democrats condemned the biography, calling it a hatchet job.*

be a/the hatchet man

to do the bad things in a company or organization that more powerful people do not want to do themselves, such as making changes that are not popular or giving people bad news ♦ OFTEN USED IN NEWSPAPERS, ON TELEVISION NEWS, ETC.: *The Vice President said that he does not intend to be the Republican hatchet man, but he will attack the Democrats at every point where they are vulnerable.*

hatter

as mad as a hatter

completely crazy: *Her boss seems to be a reasonable man, but I've only met him twice – he may be as mad as a hatter.*

NOTE In the 1800s, people who made hats often went crazy because they used mercury (=a metal that is liquid at room temperature and is dangerous if it touches the body). The idiom, "mad as a hatter," became popular in 1865 when Lewis Carroll used the Mad Hatter as a character in his children's story *"Alice's Adventures in Wonderland"*.

haul

⇨**over the long haul** —see **in the long RUN**

a long haul
(also the long haul)

used about something that is difficult and will take a long time and a lot of effort to do: *You'd better brace yourself because it's going to be a long haul to get the computer system up and running.*

have

⇨**not have much UPSTAIRS**
⇨**have** *something* **(coming) out the WAZOO/kazoo**
⇨**LET** *someone* **have it**

someone **has been had**

SPOKEN used to say that someone has been deceived, especially by being tricked into paying too much money: *They told you this was a genuine Monet painting? It looks like you've been had, my friend. It's just a copy.*

someone **has been had**

someone **has it coming (to him/ her)**

SPOKEN used to say that someone should be expecting something bad that is going to happen because they have done something to deserve it: *Okay, so I beat him up. He had it coming to him, after the way he treated my sister.*

someone **has (got) it in for** *someone*

SPOKEN used to say that someone is angry with someone else and wants to harm them: *Carey and Jill have been robbed four times – I think someone's got it in for them.*

the haves and have-nots

used when you are comparing the rich people and the poor people in a country or society: *We were driving west along the Santa Monica freeway, which divides Los Angeles' haves from its have-nots.*

have had it up to here (with)
(also **have had it (with)**)

SPOKEN used to say that you are very annoyed with someone or something and do not want to deal with them or think about them any more: *I've had it up to here with political polls and surveys – they don't mean anything.* | *I've had it with your whining. Just shut up, will you?*

have (got) it made
(also **have it made in the shade**)

SPOKEN used to say that someone has everything that they need in order to be successful or have a good life: *Boy, Andy – a new car, house, girlfriend, good job… you've got it made, my friend!*

have it out with *someone*

to try to end a disagreement or a difficult situation by talking to the person who you are angry with and telling them why you are angry: *It's not even worth having it out with Tom. He'll just say nothing is wrong, and that will be the end of the discussion.*

have *someone* right/just where you want them

to have an advantage over someone you are dealing with so that you know that you can succeed easily or get exactly what you want ♦ OFTEN USED IN BUSINESS AND POLITICS: *We had the Yankees right where we wanted them, but we still lost in the last two minutes of the game.*

have what it takes

used to say that someone has the natural abilities, intelligence, etc., or that something has the qualities that are needed to be successful: *Paul's been playing really well – he has what it takes to make it in professional football.*

havoc

wreak/play havoc

to cause a lot of trouble or confusion: *If big, heavy holiday desserts are playing havoc with your weight, try this recipe for flourless soufflé.*

hawk

watch *someone* like a hawk

to watch someone very carefully because you think that they may try to do something wrong: *As bar staff, we handled a lot of money, but the manager watched us like a hawk.*

hay

⇨hit the SACK/hay
⇨a ROLL in the hay

make hay (while the sun shines)

to take the opportunity to do something now because you may not be able to do it later: *Let's make hay while the sun shines. If we get those orders in, then maybe we can stop any more layoffs from happening.*

haywire

go haywire

if a machine or process goes haywire, it stops working correctly and does strange and unexpected things: *Whenever a helicopter flies by, my radio goes all haywire.*

head

⇨be out of your head —see **be out of your MIND**

be banging your head against a/ the wall
(also **be beating your head against a/ the wall**)

SPOKEN to be trying hard to achieve something, but be unable to do it, especially because people are not noticing what you say or do not understand you: *I gave up trying to change things at work – it's like banging your head against a brick wall with those people.*

bite *someone's* head off

SPOKEN to answer or speak to someone in a very angry way, especially without a good reason: *Sorry, I was just asking if you had a good day. There's no reason to bite my head off.*

bring *something* to a head

used to say that an action or event makes a situation which has some problems suddenly get much worse so that it is necessary to do something to solve the problem: *The fact that she would be away for six weeks finally brought things to a head, and Paul demanded to know if she was going to marry him.*

come to a head: *The violence between the two gangs came to a head with the deaths of six members in a fire-bomb attack on a house on the South Side.*

build/get up a head of steam

to begin to increase in strength, energy, or determination: *Pippen's a great player, and he can run straight through you even when he's just getting up a head of steam.*

bury your head in the sand
(also **stick, have, put your head in the sand**)

to ignore a problem or danger because you do not want to deal with it: *Our society's attitude on AIDS is to hope that if we stick our heads in the sand, it will go away.*

head-in-the-sand: *French wine makers need to abandon their head-in-the-sand attitude and face up to the competition.*

take your head out of the sand: *I knew that once I pulled my head out of the sand and recognized the abuse, I'd have to do something about it.*

> NOTE▶ Some people believe that ostriches (=very large birds that cannot fly) put their heads in the sand when there is trouble or danger.

butt heads with someone
(also **butt heads over** *something*)

if two people, groups, or organizations butt heads, they argue about a particular subject, problem, etc.: *In their annual budget meeting, Wilson and the board members are again butting heads over money matters.*

someone can do something standing on his/her head

used to emphasize that someone can do something very easily: *Math questions are easy – I can do them standing on my head, but the chemistry will take longer.*

can't make head nor/or tail of something
(also **can't make heads nor/or tails of something**)

used to say that you cannot understand something: *I can't make heads or tails out of these instructions.*

fall/be head over heels (in love)

to feel a romantic love for someone so strongly that you do not care about anything else: *Jake was head over heels in love with Katie – he would have done anything for her.*

from head to toe/foot

used to emphasize that you are talking about all of someone's body: *Tom came home soaked from head to toe.*

head-to-toe: *The head-to-toe renovation for the Albright theater included a new sound system.*

get a big head

to think that you are better than everyone else because you are successful, famous, etc. ♦ OFTEN USED IN THE NEGATIVE: *Despite her new international status, Chang says, "I'm not going to get a big head about it."*

big-headed: *You're getting so big-headed – you get an "A" on one science test, and suddenly you're Albert Einstein!*

get/have a head start

to have an advantage when you start doing something that helps you to be successful: *Matt is going to have a head start learning to read since his big brother is helping now.*

give *someone* **a head start:** *Give your child a head start by sending her to nursery school.*

get/be in over your head

to try to deal with a situation that is too difficult or complicated: *When you are starting your own business, keep it small and simple at first, and don't get in over your head.*

get into someone's head

to understand what someone thinks and feels so that you can communicate well with them or show what they are like in your acting, writing, etc.: *In my opinion, Jackson is not a good actor, because he never lets the audience get into his character's head.*

get it into your head to do something

to suddenly decide to do something, when there does not seem to be a good reason for it: *Don seems to have gotten it into his head that divorcing his wife is the only way to solve their problems.*

get it through/into *someone's* head that

to make someone understand or accept what you are saying, especially when this is difficult ♦ OFTEN USED IN NEGATIVE STATEMENTS AND QUESTIONS: *How can I get it through your head that she's not coming back – ever?*

someone gets it into his/her head that

used to say that someone has an idea that is not true: *I had somehow gotten it into my head that the test was next week, and I was in a total panic.*

give *someone* his/her head

if someone in authority gives someone their head, they allow people with less authority to decide how they want to behave or how they want to deal with a situation: *We thought we'd take a risk, give him his head, and see what happened.*

go/compete head to head (with *someone*)

to compete in a direct and determined way with another person or group ♦ OFTEN USED IN BUSINESS AND SPORTS: *The A's and the Twins are going head to head this weekend, with both teams needing a win.* **head-to-head:** *Phoenix put its Public Works Department in head-to-head competition with private companies for contracts to handle street repairs.*

go over *someone's* head

to avoid getting permission for something from the usual person by asking someone more important: *Kate was so anxious to change her hours of work that she went over her supervisor's head and asked the manager.*
—compare **be/go over your HEAD**

be/go over your head

if something that you hear or read goes over your head, you cannot understand it: *I remember my first day in this job – half*

the words you were all using went straight over my head.
—compare **go over** *someone's* **HEAD**

something goes to your head

1 (also **let** *something* **go to your head**) used to say that someone starts behaving as though they are very important because they have achieved something or have been praised: *"Saul is a great cook." "Don't let him hear you say that – we wouldn't want it to go to his head."*
2 (also **go straight/right to your head**) if alcohol goes to your head, it makes you feel drunk very quickly: *I can't drink liquor. It just goes straight to my head and I feel sick.*

be hanging over your head

if a problem or difficulty is hanging over your head, you keep worrying about it because you know that you will soon have to deal with it: *With this deadline at work hanging over my head, it's hard to relax on the weekends.*

someone has a good head on his/her shoulders

used about someone who you trust to make sensible decisions: *O'Keefe's mother said, "Matt's always had a good head on his shoulders. We've never worried too much about what he was doing."*

someone has his/her head screwed on (right)

used about someone who is sensible and makes good decisions even though people might not expect them to: *Brian may look crazy, but he's got his head screwed on right; you should pay attention to what he says.*

have your head in the clouds

to think so much about things that you would like to happen that you do not notice or understand what is actually happening: *If you think world peace would mean a cut in military spending and lower taxes, you have your head in the clouds.*

have your head up your ass

a rude expression used in order to say that someone is too interested in themselves and their own worries to deal with other situations or understand other people's problems: *Rhonda's manager has his head up his ass so much that he doesn't even know how overworked his employees are.*

be a head case

SLANG to be crazy: *Sue's a head case, man. Why do you want to go out with her?*

someone's **head/mind is buzzing (with** something**)**

to be thinking about lots of interesting ideas all at the same time: *We left the seminar with our minds buzzing with facts and figures.*

heads up!

SPOKEN used to warn someone that something that is falling or being thrown toward them could hit them: *Someone yelled, "Heads up!" and I ducked just in time.*

heads will roll
(also **heads should, must, etc. roll**)

used to say that some people will have to lose their jobs because they are responsible for the problems a company, organization, etc. is having: *If this kind of negligence had happened at City Bank, heads would have rolled.*

keep a cool head

to stay calm and reasonable even though you are in a difficult situation or other people are upset: *Throughout the tournament, I tried to keep a cool head and to concentrate completely on my game.*

keep your head above water

to manage to deal with all your problems, work, debts, etc. when this is difficult and you almost cannot do it: *We need another person to help run this office; right now I'm struggling to keep my head above water.*

keep your head down

to make sure that people do not notice you, for example by doing your work and not causing any problems: *If the boss is in a bad mood, it's better to just keep your head down and stay quiet.*

knock someone's **heads together**
(also **knock heads**)

to force two groups, organizations, or people who do not agree with each other

to reach an agreement ◆ OFTEN USED IN BUSINESS AND POLITICS: *The trial on Monday was Simm's first real test to show he could knock the jury's heads together and make things happen.*

laugh/scream your head off
(also **shout, yell, etc. your head off**)

to laugh, scream, etc. a lot for a long time: *I have never seen a show as funny as that. We laughed our heads off for two hours straight.*

lose your head

to behave in a very unreasonable way when you are in a difficult or worrying situation: *Nobody knows exactly what happened that day. As far as we know, one of the soldiers lost his head and started shooting.*

opposite **keep your head**: *Luckily, the driver kept his head and managed to steer the bus to the side of the road.*

someone **needs his/her head examined**
(also someone **should have his/her head examined**)

SPOKEN said when you think that someone's remarks or actions are wrong or stupid: *Anyone who takes a boat out in storms like this needs his head examined.*

off the top of your head

SPOKEN if you reply, give an opinion, etc. off the top of your head, you do it quickly without thinking about it much: *"How many people had access to this part of the building?" "I can't tell you off the top of my head – I'll have to check."*

be on a head trip

SLANG used to say that someone is feeling too proud because of something that they have achieved: *Gordon's been on a head trip ever since he was promoted to shift manager.*

put/get your heads together

if two people, groups, organizations, etc. put their heads together, they work together in order to solve a problem: *Congress and the President need to put their heads together and work out some kind of compromise.*

put/lay your head on the block
(also **put/lay your head on the chopping block**)
to do or say something, often deliberately, for which you are likely to be blamed or punished or which is likely to make you fail: *He's put his head on the block on several occasions by voting against the chairman.*

> NOTE▶ In the past, criminals who were to be killed as a punishment put their head on a block of wood so that it could be cut off.

put/stick your head in a noose
(also **put/stick your neck in a noose**)
to say or do something that could risk harming you or the image people have of you: *If we're going to charge him, we need to find employees who are willing to put their heads in a noose and speak against him in court.*

put your head in the lion's mouth
to put yourself in a situation which you know is dangerous or difficult: *People's career choices depend on their temperament. Some people think it's fun to put their head in the lion's mouth, while others avoid it at all costs.*

something **rears/raises its (ugly) head**
used to say that a problem or bad situation appears or happens, often after not happening or existing for a while: *Mandela encouraged people to fight against racism, "wherever and whenever it rears its ugly head."*

scratch your head
to be confused because you do not understand something: *Here's a quiz that will leave you scratching your heads.*
head-scratching: *There was a lot of head-scratching and heated discussion about how the database should be used.*

be/stand head and shoulders above (the rest/*something*)
used to emphasize that you think someone or something is much better than everyone or everything else in the same group or of the same type: *Sandra stood out head and shoulders above the rest in the debate competition.*

stand on your head (to do *something*)
(also **do everything but stand on your head (to do *something*)**)
to make a great effort in order to do something: *I wrote, called people, stood on my head, whatever I could do to get people to send contributions.*

turn heads
to make people notice and like you, especially by looking very attractive: *Cher turned heads when she appeared at the ceremony in a see-through black dress.*

turn/stand *something* on its head
1 to show that an idea or argument is wrong and in fact means the opposite of what it first seemed to: *The lawsuit stands truth on its head. The company is suing people for activities that it approved of, encouraged, and profited from.*
2 to do or make something new and unexpected that changes the way people think about a subject: *Jimi Hendrix's album turned the music industry on its head.*

something **turns your head**
if having money, success, etc. turns your head, it makes you think that you are more important than you were before: *I won't lie to you – the money does turn your head, but I hope I'm still the same person I was when I started.*

headlines

grab the headlines
if an event grabs the headlines, everyone knows about it because it is shocking or unusual and it is reported in all the newspapers, news programs, etc.: *A grisly killing spree in a small town near Detroit has grabbed the headlines tonight.*
headline-grabbing: *Stemple has always run his companies at a slower pace, staying away from the headline-grabbing techniques of his colleagues.*

hear

can't hear yourself think
SPOKEN used to emphasize that there is too much noise around you, especially when it is stopping you from thinking clearly: *Could you guys be a little quieter? I'm trying to finish this report and I can barely hear myself think.*

H

I hear ya
(also **I heard that**)

SPOKEN used to tell someone that you agree with what they are saying, or that you understand what they mean: *"I'm tired of living at home – I'd really like to find a place of my own." "I hear ya!"*

heart

⇨**ABSENCE makes the heart grow fonder**

⇨**a CHANGE of heart**

⇨**do** *something* **to your heart's CONTENT**

⇨*someone's* **heart's DESIRE**

be ___ at heart

used to say what someone is really like, even though they may seem to be something else: *I guess I'm just a country girl at heart – I'd do anything to get out of the city.*

a bleeding heart

used about someone who you think feels too much sympathy for poor people, criminals, or other people who do not have many advantages: *You don't have to be a bleeding heart to feel saddened by the imprisonment of young people.*
bleeding-heart: *We are letting bleeding-heart liberals deter us from passing the laws that the country needs.*

break someone's heart

1 if an event or situation breaks someone's heart, it makes them very sad or upset: *It breaks my heart to see our lakes and rivers destroyed by pollution.*
2 to make someone very unhappy by ending a marriage or romantic relationship: *Diana broke Joel's heart when she left him.*
heartbroken: *Meg was heartbroken when her kitten died.*

close/near to someone's heart

if an idea, plan, or place is close to someone's heart, it is important to them, and they care about it: *Homelessness is what Sweeney writes about most because it is the theme that is closest to his heart.*

cross my heart (and hope to die)

SPOKEN used to promise that what you are saying is true: *Please, please tell me... I cross my heart that I won't tell anyone!*

someone doesn't have the heart to do something

used to say that you are unwilling to say or do something that would make someone unhappy or upset: *Dad did the ironing – all of it. Mom didn't have the heart to tell him she doesn't usually iron the socks.*

eat your heart out

SPOKEN said when you think someone else will wish they had or could do what you have or can do: *I shook Tom Cruise's hand, and he gave me his autograph – so eat your heart out.*

> NOTE▶ This idiom is often used as a joke to say that you have more skill at doing something than someone who is famous for doing it very well: *I learned three new chords on the guitar today. Eric Clapton, eat your heart out.*

follow your heart

to let your emotions influence your decision: *I can't tell you whether you should marry Eric or not. You'll just have to follow your heart.*

(straight) from the heart

if something comes from the heart or is spoken from the heart, it is honest and expresses strong feeling: *I haven't prepared a speech – I want to speak from the heart and tell you what this town means to me.*

get to the heart of something

to understand or deal with the most important part of a problem or situation: *Hammer's Project Diversity gets to the heart of the matter by getting minorities directly involved in local government.*

have a big heart

to be very kind, generous, and helpful: *Grandpa just knows how to love people – he has such a big heart!*
big-hearted: *All proceeds from the Pet Parade this weekend will go to those big-hearted folks down at the Humane Society.*

have a change of heart

to begin to feel and think differently about something, especially so that you change a decision that you have made about it: *After saying that they could not set up a hostel for homeless people, the* committee had a change of heart and started looking for a way to fund it.

have a heart!

SPOKEN used to ask someone not to be strict or unkind: *Hopefully one of the managers at work will have a heart and let us work a half day on Christmas Eve.*

have a heart of gold

used about someone who is very kind, especially when they do not seem to be kind: *Connor plays a tough Southern sheriff with a heart of gold.*

have a heart of stone

to be very unkind or not sympathetic: *You would need a heart of stone not to be moved by the pictures of sick children from the war zone.*

someone's **heart is in the right place**

used to say that even though someone does not seem very helpful or kind, they do care about other people and want to be kind and helpful: *She's very strict with the kids in the classroom, but her heart's in the right place.*

in your heart of hearts

if you know or feel something in your heart of hearts, you really know that it is true although you do not want to admit it or believe it: *We all wanted to support Eileen and her dream to be an actress, but in our heart of hearts, we knew it wasn't going to happen.*

lose heart

—see take HEART

my heart bleeds (for *someone*)

SPOKEN used in order to say that you do not feel any sympathy for someone, especially someone who thinks you should: *Steve and Olga can't afford their vacation in the Bahamas this year – poor things, my heart bleeds.*

> NOTE▶ This idiom uses sarcasm, which is a common way of showing that you dislike or disapprove of someone or something by saying something that is the opposite of what you mean. Sarcasm can often be considered fairly impolite, especially in situations where you do not know people very well.

pour out your heart (to *someone*)
(also **open your heart (to** *someone***))**

to tell someone everything that you are thinking or feeling: *He poured out his heart to me that night, saying that he had no hope for the future.*

set your heart on (doing) *something*

to want something, or want to do something, very much: *Jason's really set his heart on going to Stanford – I hope he gets accepted.*

sick at heart

very sad or upset about something: *I felt sick at heart when I saw the expression on his face, and I knew he would never forgive me.*

strike at the heart of *something*

to do something that damages or begins to destroy a basic idea or way of doing things that is very important to a particular society or group: *If the spending cuts are implemented, they will strike at the heart of our education system.*

take heart

to be encouraged and begin to feel more certain that you will succeed: *Take heart, smokers – the people who gain weight after quitting are less likely to smoke again.*
opposite **lose heart:** *After Lutz saw the results from the campaign polls and knew he was last, he lost heart and dropped out of the election.*

take *something* to heart

to be strongly affected by something that someone says to you so that you think seriously about it or are upset by it: *Claire had obviously taken Jacob's warning to heart, and was extremely polite to the visitors.*

the way to *someone's* heart

the best way to please someone or make them like you: *"That dress makes you look fat." "Hasn't anyone told you that flattery is the way to a girl's heart?"*

wear your heart on your sleeve

to show your true feelings openly: *Nichols has a cynical sense of humor and does not wear his heart on his sleeve; he*

H

may in fact be incapable of directing a sentimental movie.

> NOTE▶ This idiom comes from the very old custom of a man wearing something on his sleeve that was given to him by the woman he loved.

win someone's heart

1 to do nice things for someone to make them love you: *Martin knew the only way to win Sara's heart was to prepare a good Italian meal.*
2 if a type of music, book, product, etc. wins your heart, it has qualities that make you like it very much: *Anderson says that it was country music that first won his heart and got him to play guitar at an early age.*

with all your heart

if you feel something with all your heart, you feel it very strongly: *Vicky and James had married young, and it was obvious that she loved him with all her heart.*

young at heart

used about people who enjoy things that younger people enjoy, even though they are no longer very young themselves: *You know what I love about your grandparents? They're still so young at heart. They never say no to any new experience.*
young-at-heart: *Young-at-heart director Steven Spielberg has unveiled plans for his latest blockbuster movie, starring Gene Hackman.*

your heart goes out to someone

used to say that you feel great sympathy for another person: *Our hearts went out to the couple who lost their son in the accident.*

your heart isn't in it

used to say that you do not really want to do what you are doing: *I've told Brenda that her work needs to improve, but she's getting really bored with the job, and it's obvious her heart's not in it anymore.*

your heart skipped/missed a beat

used to say that you were very excited, surprised, or frightened: *My heart skipped a beat when I saw the tall, elegant figure in the doorway.*

your heart was in your mouth

used to say that you felt very nervous or frightened: *My heart was in my mouth as I stepped into the boss' office.*

heartbeat

in a heartbeat

if something happens or is done in a heartbeat, it happens very quickly, or is done quickly without any thought: *If these guys ask you for anything, just give it to them. Don't say a word, because they'll kill you in a heartbeat.*

heartstrings

tug/tear at someone's heartstrings

to make someone feel very sad or feel great sympathy for someone else: *You cannot leave the home where you grew up without some tugging at the heartstrings.*

heat

the heat is on

used to say that a situation is very difficult, especially because people are criticizing you or expecting you to do something: *The heat is on at Apple Computer to make sure its efforts to get into the new market are successful.*
opposite **the heat is off**: *We knew that we couldn't get into the finals, so the heat was off, and we played better.*

> NOTE▶ These idioms were first used by criminals talking about the police, whom they called "the heat." If the police were looking for them, then "the heat was on." When the police were not looking for them, "the heat was off."

if you can't stand the heat, get out of the kitchen

used to tell someone not to complain about the difficulties of their situation, especially when they are responsible for doing something important or dealing with problems: *As a politician, you get a lot of malicious attention from the media. But that's part of the job – if you can't stand the heat, get out of the kitchen.*

in the heat of the moment

if you do or say something in the heat of the moment, you do it or say it without stopping to think about it, because you are excited or angry: *The decision to arrest the boys was made in the heat of the moment, but it was later upheld in a court of law.*

turn up the heat (on *someone*)
to criticize or threaten someone and make them feel that they have to improve the way that they do things, or that they have to do what you want: *Newspaper interest in the subject of pollution has certainly turned up the heat on the water industry.*

heave-ho

give *someone* **the (old) heave-ho**
SPOKEN to end a relationship with someone, or make someone leave their job: *I wouldn't blame her if she got fed up with Danny and gave him the heave-ho.*
get the (old) heave-ho: *If you keep coming to work late, you're going to get the old heave-ho pretty quickly.*

heaven

be in seventh/hog heaven
to be in a situation that makes you extremely happy: *Ever since Paul got involved with that girl from work, he's been in seventh heaven.*

move heaven and earth to do *something*
to work extremely hard to achieve something, using all your energy and doing everything you can to solve problems: *We intend to move heaven and earth to make sure this dance production goes on as planned.*

heavy
⇨**be heavy GOING**

hedge
⇨**hedge your BETs**

heel
⇨**drag your feet/heels FOOT**
bring/call *someone* **to heel**
to make someone obey you or pay attention to you again after they have stopped doing this ◆ OFTEN USED IN NEWSPAPERS, ON TELEVISION NEWS, ETC.: *The aim*

of Proposition 13 was to bring politicians to heel by limiting their ability to impose taxes.*
come to heel: *The President has been unable to get his senior staff members to come to heel on this issue.*

> NOTE▶ When dogs are taught to obey their owners, they are told to "heel," which means they must walk at the heels of their owner.

come (hard/hot) on the heels of *something*
(also **follow (hard/hot) on the heels of** *something***)**
used to say that something happens soon after something else, especially when both things make a situation worse: *The letter bomb addressed to Dawson came on the heels of a series of attacks on civil rights workers.*

cool your heels
to be forced to spend time waiting with nothing to do: *The lawyers went off to discuss things, leaving me to cool my heels in the waiting room.*

dig your heels in
(also **dig in your heels)**
to refuse to change your opinions or plans even though other people want you to: *My boss wanted to abandon the project, but I dug my heels in and asked that the management look at it again.*

down at the heels
(also **down at heel)**
used about someone who is dirty and wears old clothes, or about something that looks old and in a bad condition: *People who come to the rehab center are down at the heels, they smell a little, and they often make middle-class volunteers feel uncomfortable.*
down-at-the-heels: *Miller plays a down-at-the-heels detective in a case that involves a search for a cocktail waitress's missing brother.*

kick up your heels
OLD-FASHIONED to enjoy yourself, especially by going to parties, dancing, etc.: *We really kicked up our heels on that cruise to Mexico.*

H

take to your heels
OLD-FASHIONED to run away from someone: *The men gave up trying to defend themselves and took to their heels.*

heights

the dizzy heights of
(also the dizzying heights of)
used to say how high the level of something is, or how important someone or something is: *After the dizzying heights reached in the 1980s, global defense spending finally began to fall in 1989.*

> NOTE▶ You may hear people use this idiom humorously to talk about a level that is low or a position that is not at all important: *My promotion at work was to the dizzying heights of mailroom manager.*

hell

⇨**hell's BELLS**
⇨*someone* **is hell-bent on (doing)** *something* —see *someone* **is BENT on (doing)** *something*

all hell breaks loose
used to say that a situation suddenly becomes bad, disorganized, or violent: *When one of the band members jumped off the stage, all hell broke loose.*

all hell breaks loose

catch hell
SPOKEN to be blamed or punished for doing something: *If the contractors do something wrong, I'm the one who catches hell.*

come hell or high water
SPOKEN used to emphasize that you are determined to do something in spite of any problems or difficulties: *I'm going to make him sit down and listen to me, come hell or high water.*

do *something* (just) for the hell of it
SPOKEN to do something without having any good reason except that you want to do it: *Come on, let's open a bottle of champagne just for the hell of it.*

give 'em hell
SPOKEN said when you want to encourage or show support for someone before they do something difficult or frightening, or before they begin a competition: *Don't worry, you'll be OK. Just go in there, be confident, and give 'em hell.*

give *someone* hell
SPOKEN to shout at someone because you are angry with them or blame them for something: *"What did you do when Brian told you what he'd done?" "I gave him hell!"*

go through hell (and back)
to experience a situation that is extremely difficult or bad, especially one that continues for a long time: *The first three days after the accident we went through hell, not knowing if our son would live or die.*

hell for leather
SPOKEN very fast or with a lot of energy: *We were driving hell for leather across Texas; trying to make it home for Darlene's wedding.*

hell hath no fury (like a woman scorned)
said when a woman is very angry at someone: *It's best not to mention Sam if you're talking to Josie – hell hath no fury...*

> NOTE▶ You may hear people change the words in this idiom in order to be humorous and to make it fit a particular situation: *David still wasn't speaking to me – hell has no fury like a teenager who doesn't get his way. | Hell hath no fury like an unsuspecting mule about to be saddled with two ten-foot kayaks.*

hell on earth

used about a situation, experience, or place that is very unpleasant: *The theme park sounded like my idea of hell on earth, but the kids were so excited about going.*

hell on wheels

SPOKEN used about someone who is difficult to control or deal with because they do whatever they want without caring what people think: *Their baby, Sean, is like an angel, but Sara, his sister, is hell on wheels.*

something is going to hell in a handbasket

used to say that a system or organization is quickly becoming worse or being destroyed: *Politicians talk about American life with such enthusiasm while the health-care system collapses, and the cities go to hell in a handbasket.*

a living hell

used about a place or situation that is extremely bad, or where people suffer a lot: *If I don't get these invoices in the mail today, my boss is going to make my life a living hell.*

raise hell/Cain

1 SPOKEN to complain a lot about something in an angry or noisy way because you are determined to get what you want: *If we suspend Lawrence, his parents will come down to the school and raise Cain.*
2 to cause trouble by behaving in an irresponsible way, and being noisy or violent: *Raising hell seems to be the main occupation of the kids on our block.*
hellraiser: *Cole once had a reputation as a hellraiser, but says he's stopped drinking and has settled down.*

> NOTE▶ "Raise Cain" is considered more polite than "raise hell."

be shot/blown to hell

SPOKEN if something you have owned, worked on, etc. for a long time is shot to hell, it is completely ruined: *"Thirty-five years shot to hell," Minarich said this morning, as he looked at the wreckage of the house that burned to the ground last night.*

there'll be (all) hell to pay

SPOKEN used to tell someone that if they do something, someone will be very angry with them: *You'd better have the report ready on Tuesday, or there'll be all hell to pay.*

to hell with *someone/something*

SPOKEN used to say that you do not care about someone or something any more: *So that's your philosophy of life – you just say to hell with anyone else's feelings, as long as you get what you want?*

until/till hell freezes over

SPOKEN used to say that something that has been happening will continue to happen: *We're gonna fight till hell freezes over!*

when hell freezes over

SPOKEN used to say that something will never happen: *She'll get to work on time when hell freezes over.*

help

⇨**a fat lot of help** *someone/something* **is** —see **a fat LOT of good it does** *someone*
⇨**SO help me (God)**

hem

hem and haw

to keep pausing before you speak because you do not want to say something unpleasant or upsetting, or to take a long time to make a decision about something: *We knew it must be bad news because Jane kept hemming and hawing and changing the subject.*

herd

ride herd on *someone*

to watch or control the activities of a person or organization ♦ OFTEN USED IN POLITICS: *The bureau also tries to ride herd on the thousands of charities across the nation.*

here

⇨**HAVE had it up to here (with)**
⇨**that's NEITHER here nor there**

get out of here!

SPOKEN used to say that you do not believe

what someone has told you, or that you are very surprised by it: *"Did you know Josie's pregnant?" "Get out of here! They've only been together for six months."*

—see also **no WAY**

> **NOTE▶** In this idiom people usually say "out of" quickly as if it is really one word that sounds like "ouda."

here goes!
SPOKEN said before you start doing something, especially when you are nervous about doing it: *I've never given a presentation before, but Chris says you're all dying to hear about my trip, so here goes.*

I'm out of here!
SLANG said when you are leaving a place, especially when you are happy to be going: *It's five o'clock – I'm out of here!*

> **NOTE▶** In this idiom people usually say "out of" quickly as if it is really one word that sounds like "ouda."

something **is here to stay**
used to say that a new situation, system, idea, etc. has become a normal part of people's lives, will continue, and should be accepted: *Whether we like it or not, stores that provide their customers with one-stop shopping are here to stay.*

hero

hero worship
(also **hero-worship**)
great admiration for someone who you think is very brave, smart, good, etc.: *Much of this hero worship is very naive. You have to remember this man is a mafia boss and a killer.*
hero-worship: *People have said the fans hero-worship me, but I don't like that term.*

the/an unsung hero
someone who is not praised or famous for something that they have done although they deserve to be: *The unsung heroes behind the fund-raising effort were the volunteers who answered telephones 24 hours a day.*

herring

a red herring
used about information or an idea that you think is not important or necessary, and that may have been mentioned deliberately to take people's attention away from the subject they should be considering: *The Navy says there is no safety problem, that the whole thing is a red herring created by the sailors to cause morale problems.*

het up

be/get het up
SPOKEN to be or become anxious, upset, or slightly angry: *The trouble with you is that you get het up over the silliest things.*

hide

have not seen hide nor hair of someone
SPOKEN to have not seen someone for a long time although you expected to see them: *"Do you know where Mike is?" "No, I haven't seen hide nor hair of him all day."*

someone **will have/tan** someone's **hide**
SPOKEN used to say that someone will punish someone else severely: *Dad'll tan your hide if he finds out that you used his tools without asking.*

high

⇨LEAVE *someone* high and dry

from on high
used to say that orders, messages, etc. are from someone in a position of authority: *We have news from on high that McNeely is giving up his post as president.*

high and mighty
(also **Mister, Miss, etc. High and Mighty**)
used about someone who talks or behaves as if they are more important than other people: *Politicians are sitting there high and mighty, passing legislation to protect women, when they know darned well that their policies will never be enforced. | I've been insulted too*

many times – so the next time Mister High and Mighty walks through that door, I'm going to chase him right out!

someone **is high on himself/ herself**
SPOKEN used to say that someone has begun to think that they are better or more important than they really are: *Jack's been high on himself ever since he beat me at tennis.*

hike

take a hike!
SPOKEN an impolite expression, said when you want someone to go away: *Look, I told you I won't help you, so take a hike!*

hill

not amount to a hill of beans
to have very little importance or value: *I feel like I've been working for nothing – it isn't going to amount to a hill of beans after taxes.*

be over the hill
to be too old to do things well: *I love to tease my brother about his age and say he's over the hill, even though he's only forty.*

hilt

(up) to the hilt
as much as possible or in the best way possible: *Government funds are strained to the hilt just taking care of essential services.*

hindsight

hindsight is 20–20
SPOKEN used to say that it is very easy to say what you could have done to avoid a bad situation after it has happened: *The crew members of Flight 400 made a decision based on the information they had at the time. Hindsight is always 20–20, and we know it should have been done differently.*

> NOTE▶ If the doctor tells you your eyesight is 20–20, it means you can see perfectly.

with/in hindsight
(also **with the benefit, wisdom, clarity, etc. of hindsight**)
used to say that when you think about a situation in the past in which you made mistakes, you understand how you could have prevented the mistakes: *With the benefit of hindsight, it is clear that we should have ordered more supplies.*

hip

joined at the hip
a humorous expression used in order to say that two people spend all their time together: *We're not joined at the hip, you know – I can go on a two-week vacation without Bill.*

shoot from the hip
to say what you think in a direct way, or make a decision very quickly, without thinking about it first: *Tony shoots from the hip – most of the time he doesn't even know what he's saying.*
shoot-from-the-hip: *Simon, a shoot-from-the-hip educator, is a good choice for the job.*

history

someone/something **is history**
SPOKEN used to say that someone or something is gone or is no longer important or interesting: *As soon as Ron finds out what you guys have been doing, you're history.*

...(and) the rest is history
used to say that everyone knows the rest of a story that you have been telling: *Sony, Philips, and Polygram got together to announce the launch of the compact disc, and the rest is history.*

hit

⇨hit pay **DIRT**

hit and miss
(also **hit or miss**)
used to say that something is not planned or organized carefully enough to be sure of success: *Fishing for trout this time of year is hit or miss.*
hit-and-miss: *People who buy illegally recorded tapes know that they may get hit-and-miss sound quality, but the music will be real.*

hit it off (with *someone*)

SPOKEN to like someone else as soon as you meet them: *What happened at the interview? Didn't you hit it off with Thompson?*

someone's hit list

1 the list of things or people that a person or organization wants to make changes to, stop using, spend less money on, etc.: *Once you're on Harden's hit list, you're pretty much there for life. He's a little man who holds a big grudge.*
2 a list of people that a political or criminal organization wants to kill or harm: *Aziz has been at the top of the terrorists' hit list for the past two years.*

hit *someone* where it hurts

to say or do the thing that you know will upset or harm someone most: *We intend to find ways to hit drug traffickers were it hurts – in their pockets.*

hitched

get hitched

SPOKEN a humorous expression meaning to get married: *Rhonda and Damon ran off and got hitched without telling anyone.*

Hobson

⇨Hobson's CHOICE

hog

⇨be in hog heaven —see **be in seventh HEAVEN**

go hog wild

SPOKEN to behave in a very excited or very extreme way: *People are going hog-wild buying lottery tickets – it's never been this busy before.*

go the whole hog

to do something in the most complete and thorough way possible: *Greg doesn't mess around when it comes to camping. He goes whole hog: gourmet meals, air mattress, the works.*

live high on/off the hog

used to say that someone has a very nice life because they have a lot of money to spend, often when you disapprove of this: *When I worked for the airline, I was living high on the hog and I didn't care about what the rest of the world was doing.*

hold

hold *someone/something* dear

to feel that someone or something is very important to you: *Worst of all, I've lost the respect of the person I hold most dear.*

put *something* on hold

to delay doing or starting something: *The expansion of San Francisco airport was put on hold when many of the city's inhabitants objected.*

hole

blow a hole in *something*

if something blows a hole in a plan, idea, etc., it makes it much less effective or useful: *Sol paid me back the next day, which blew a hole in my theory that I'd never see the money again.*

burn a hole in your pocket

if money is burning a hole in your pocket, you want to spend it as soon as you can, especially when you are not sure how to spend it: *Those of you who have money burning a hole in your pocket might enjoy a trip to the casino.*

be full of holes

if an idea, plan, etc. is full of holes, it can easily be proved wrong or has many faults: *It was a typical "B" movie – plot full of holes and bad acting – but I loved it.*

someone has holes in his/her head

OLD-FASHIONED used to say that someone is crazy because they have done something to annoy you: *He has holes in his head if he thinks I'll type his thesis for nothing.*

be ___ in the hole
(also **be in the hole by ___**)

to owe a particular amount of money: *We're already in the hole by $160 because one company still hasn't paid us for the work we did.*

need *something* like a hole in the head

SPOKEN used to emphasize that you do not want something because it would cause problems: *I don't want to speak to any more lawyers. I need another lawyer like I need a hole in my head.*
—compare *someone* **needs** *something* **like a FISH needs a bicycle**

pick holes in *something*

to criticize a plan, idea, etc. in a way that is not helpful: *He identified himself as one of the supervisors, and started picking holes in my sales technique.*

holiday

a busman's holiday

OLD-FASHIONED a vacation when you do something that is like your usual work so that it is not a real vacation: *Many people would say that Gilroy police officer Steve Morrow's second job – a professional boxer – is like taking a busman's holiday.*

> NOTE▶ This idiom originally comes from Britain, and the British word for "vacation" is "holiday."

hollow

⇨RING hollow

holy

the holy of holies

a humorous expression used about a place that some people think is very special, or where only a few people are allowed to go: *In a field on a farm in Nebraska is the car freak's answer to the holy of holies – a reproduction of Stonehenge made out of old cars.*

home

⇨bring home the BACON
⇨the CHICKENS (have) come home to roost
⇨NOTHING to write home about
⇨on home turf/GROUND

bring it home (to you)

(also **bring** *something* **home (to you)**)

to make you realize how serious a problem is, or how difficult or dangerous a situation is: *The murder just brings it home to you that kids aren't safe anywhere – even in a small town.*

hit/strike/be close to home

1 if a situation or something someone says hits close to home, you understand it or are embarrassed or upset by it, because it makes you think of something that is similar to your life: *Perhaps some of our comments on sexual harassment hit a little too close to home for the senator.*

2 if something bad is close to home, you are directly affected by it: *The tragedy of the fire hit close to home for me – one of my students lost everything.*

—compare **hit/strike HOME**

hit/strike home

if something you say hits or strikes home, it has the effect on someone that you wanted: *Reich's emotional plea to save the hospital struck home with both doctors and residents.*

—compare **hit/strike/be close to HOME**

home away from home

a place where you feel as comfortable as you do in your own home: *The hotel was built as a home away from home for American servicemen and their families.*

be home free

1 to be able to succeed or get what you want easily because you have an advantage: *When Mom mentions doing the dishes, I just tell her I have homework, and I'm home free.*

2 to have done the most difficult part of something so that the rest will be easy: *If I can just get the introduction written, I'll be home free.*

the home stretch

the last part of a long and difficult process or situation before something is finished or achieved: *Amber is now on the home stretch of a three-year treatment program for leukemia, and all the signs are promising.*

a man's home is his castle

used to say that people should be allowed to do whatever they like in their own homes, without the government or other people telling them what to do: *Social workers are prevented from protecting victims of domestic violence because of the mentality that a man's home is his castle.*

home run

hit a home run

to do something that is very popular or successful: *The president seems to have*

H

hit a home run with his new economic policy.

NOTE▶ In the sport of baseball, a home run is the best hit a player can make.

homework

do your homework
to find out everything you can about a subject or situation before you have to deal with it: *Clearly, Hunter had done his homework and was able to pinpoint the inaccuracies in the budget plan.*

honeymoon

the honeymoon is over
used to say that a person, group, organization, etc. that was very successful and popular at first has begun to have problems: *The fans were packing the stadium at the beginning of the season when the Sharks were winning. But now that the team is having a losing streak, the honeymoon is over.*

a/the honeymoon period: *When you first meet a client, there is always a honeymoon period when everyone seems to like each other and the atmosphere is full of hope.*

honors

do the honors
to pour drinks or serve food at a social occasion: *Bill Gates himself did the honors at the launch party for Microsoft's new operating system.*

hoof

hoof it
SPOKEN to walk or run, especially when it is hard work: *Police these days are too busy driving around in their shiny patrol cars to hoof it on the streets where the crime is.*

NOTE▶ A hoof is the hard part on the foot of animals such as horses, cows, sheep, etc.

on the hoof
if you do an activity on the hoof, you do it while you are moving around or traveling to different places: *My father was an officer in the Air Force, so I received my education on the hoof.*

hook

fall for something/someone hook, line, and sinker
1 (also **buy/swallow** *something* **hook, line, and sinker**) used to say that someone believes a story, joke, etc. although it is not true, especially when you think they are stupid to do this: *"Did the police believe him?" "Yeah, they bought it hook, line, and sinker."*
2 (also **fall hook, line, and sinker in love**) to feel a very strong love for someone, or like something very much: *As soon as he saw the house, Fielding fell for it hook, line, and sinker.*

get your hooks into someone
to get involved in someone's life so that you can control them: *Deborah had gotten her hooks into Phil eight years ago. When he tried to leave, she threatened to kill herself.*

by hook or by crook
used to emphasize that someone is determined to do something even if it is difficult, using whatever methods they can: *Once Annie decides she wants something, she'll get it by hook or by crook.*

let/get someone off the hook
to allow or help someone to get out of a difficult situation, often one in which they were being blamed for something: *Just saying "sorry" won't get you off the hook – I expect you to clear up the mess you made.*

hooky

play hooky
to stay away from school when you should be there, sometimes used humorously to say that someone is not at work when they should be: *Some people admitted playing hooky from school or work in order to get out and enjoy the sunshine.*

hoop

make someone jump/go through (the) hoops
(also **put** *someone* **through (the) hoops**)
to make someone do lots of difficult things, or answer a lot of questions in

order to get something they want, especially when this seems unfair or stupid: *Many companies were eager to do business in the area, even if it meant jumping through hoops to get there.*

> NOTE▶ A hoop is a large ring that some animals can be trained to jump through to perform.

shoot some hoop
(also **shoot hoops**)
to play an informal game of basketball, or practice your basketball skills alone: *Let's go to the gym and shoot some hoop.*

hoot

don't give/care a hoot
(also **don't give/care two hoots**)
SPOKEN used to emphasize that you do not think that something is important, or care about it: *The people of East St. Louis don't give a hoot about who runs the city – they just want things to improve.*

hop

hop/jump to it
used to tell someone to do something immediately ◆ OFTEN USED BY ADULTS SPEAKING TO CHILDREN: *If you finish your homework quickly, you can watch TV tonight, so you'd better hop to it.*

a hop, skip, and a jump (from)
(also **a hop and a skip**)
OLD-FASHIONED used to say that a place is very close: *"You're from Wisconsin? My family lives in Arrawaso." "Well then we're a hop, skip, and a jump apart."*

hope

⇨**not have a CHANCE/hope in hell (of)**
be hoping against hope
to keep hoping that something you want very much will happen, even though you know it is very unlikely: *Officials are hoping against hope that the flood of pesticide that has leaked into the river will disperse before it reaches Lake Shasta.*

pin your hopes on
to think that one particular person, thing, or event will make you happy, successful, etc.: *Rebecca's parents had always*

pinned all their hopes on her younger brother, never believing that she would make a success of her life.

hopper

in the hopper
used to say that a group of things is waiting for a decision to be made about them ◆ OFTEN USED IN POLITICS: *Over 200 amendments to the bill are in the hopper, with more to come.*

horizon

broaden/expand/widen your horizons
to think about or experience new situations, or new ideas, especially so that you learn more about another country or other people's lives: *American schools have various foreign exchange programs designed to expand their students' horizons.*

be on the horizon
to be expected to happen soon: *He's been looking for a job for six months, but there seems to be nothing on the horizon.*

horn

blow your own horn
to praise yourself for your achievements in a way that shows you are too confident about yourself: *Kahn, founder of the 8-year-old company that did so well last quarter, has plenty of reasons to blow his own horn these days.*

lock horns (with *someone*)
to strongly disagree with someone about a particular subject: *Yoko Ono locked horns with John Lennon's first wife over the best way to celebrate what would have been Lennon's fiftieth birthday.*

be on the horns of a dilemma
to not know which of two choices to make because both seem very difficult or unpleasant: *The question of water usage really has the state on the horns of a dilemma: rationing may cause disease, but too much would be wasteful.*

> NOTE▶ This idiom comes from the idea that an angry bull will throw you, whichever horn you try to hold onto.

hornet

⇨stir up a hornet's NEST

mad as a hornet
(also **madder than a hornet**)
OLD-FASHIONED used to say that someone is extremely angry: *She tried to hit one woman and missed her, and then she got madder than a hornet.*

horse

⇨(straight) from the horse's MOUTH
⇨a one-horse RACE

back/pick the wrong horse
(also **bet on the wrong horse**)
to support someone who is not successful, or make a wrong guess about what is going to happen: *We just bet on the wrong horse – the movie we turned down was the one that made big money.*

be beating a dead horse
SPOKEN used to say that someone is wasting time and effort by talking or worrying about something that cannot be successful, or something that people are not interested in any more: *I don't want to be beating a dead horse. I will step aside if the folks out there reach a point where they don't want to hear my music any more.*
a dead horse: *I don't want to waste my breath on this dead horse, but we bike riders are getting really tired of drivers complaining about us.*

change horses (in midstream)
to stop supporting or working with one person or one set of ideas and start supporting or working with another, while you are in the middle of doing something: *Why should we change our plans? If people are happy with the way the city is being developed, it would be foolish to change horses in midstream.*

something **could choke a horse**
used to say that something is very big, or bigger than usual: *Half an hour later, Mike ate a plate of lasagne that could choke a horse.*

a dark horse
someone who is not well known or not expected to win, but who surprises people by doing very well against com-petitors in business, sports, or politics: *Vicario, considered a dark horse contender this year, still defeated her biggest rival.*
dark-horse: *Ryan's dark-horse challenge to the New York governor was his first run for public office.*

don't/never look a gift horse in the mouth
SPOKEN used to say that someone should accept a present, or something that is free, even if it is not exactly what they want: *The shoes my sister gave me were a little too tight, but I never look a gift horse in the mouth.*

> NOTE▶ This idiom comes from the fact that you can tell how healthy a horse is by looking at its teeth. If someone gave you a horse as a gift, it would be foolish to worry about its health.

someone **gets on his/her high horse**
SPOKEN used to say that you think someone is talking or behaving as if they think they are better than everyone else: *My parents drink and smoke, but as soon as I start talking about legalizing drugs, they get on their high horse.*
opposite **get off your high horse:** *I'd like to tell the mayor to get off his high horse and come and talk to the people he grew up with.*

hold your horses
SPOKEN used to tell someone to be patient, or to wait and listen to what someone else is saying: *"All right, all right, hold your horses, I'm coming," grumbled McAllister, as the banging on the door got louder.*

I could eat a horse
SPOKEN said when you are very hungry: *What time's dinner? I could eat a horse tonight!*

a stalking horse
used about a person or thing that someone uses to hide their true plans or intentions, especially a politician who makes a first attempt to achieve some-thing that a more important politician wants: *Gorbechev wanted to establish his independence and not be the stalking horse for Washington any longer.*

strong as a horse
(also **strong as an ox, bull, etc.**)
used to emphasize that someone is very strong or healthy: *Bea's as strong as an ox. She had surgery only a week ago and she's already back at the gym.*

wild horses would/could not drag *someone*
(also **wild horses would/could not make, force, etc.** *someone*)
used to emphasize that you do not want to do something, and will not do it: *Gloria has invited me, but wild horses would not drag me to that wedding.*

you can lead/take a horse to water (but you can't make it drink)
used to say that although you can give someone the opportunity to do something you cannot force them to do it if they do not want to: *Parents should provide their children with a quiet place to do homework, but they should remember that you can take a horse to water but you can't make it drink.*

hot

⇨ **be BIG/hot on** *something*

have/get the hots for *someone*
SPOKEN to be attracted to someone in a sexual way: *Pete has got a great body – I'm not surprised she has the hots for him.*

(all) hot and bothered
1 used to say that someone is behaving in a way that shows how annoyed, worried, or upset they are about something, especially when you think they are reacting too strongly: *Maggie was all hot and bothered because Mitch told her to be quiet and listen to him.*
2 used to say that someone is sexually excited: *I get all hot and bothered when I watch Nicholas dance.*

be hot to trot
used to say that a person or organization is very eager to get involved in an activity or process: *Paramount is so hot to trot with the latest Bond movie that they have offered actors a bonus for starting filming early.*

be too hot to handle
if a movie, news story, etc. is too hot to handle, it is too shocking to be shown to the public: *Greg is refusing to print the story. I think he found it too hot to handle, and he's worried about upsetting his advertisers.*

hotcakes

sell like hotcakes
(also **go like hotcakes**)
if something sells like hotcakes, a lot of people buy it in a short time: *The CD sold like hotcakes, and three weeks later it was the biggest-selling album of all time.*

sell like hotcakes

hour

the eleventh hour
the last possible time you can do something before it is too late: *New evidence proving Richards' innocence was uncovered at the eleventh hour.*
eleventh-hour: *Crews were supposed to start filming last week, until Dreyfuss did an eleventh-hour back-out.*

someone's **finest hour**
the most important time in someone's life, when they do something good and other people admire them: *I have to admit that my first visit with the Bishop was not my finest hour. I choked on my wine and had to leave the room.*

someone's **hour of need**
the time when someone or something needs help, often used humorously when the situation is not too serious: *You can't leave me now in my hour of need. Who's going to make dinner if you go?*

the wee/small hours

the period of night between about 1 o'clock and 4 o'clock: *Dave threw a memorable party which went on into the wee hours.*

house

⇨people who live in GLASS houses (shouldn't throw stones)

bring down the house
(also **bring the house down**)

if someone who is performing brings down the house, the people who are watching applaud (=hit their hands together) and shout their approval for a long time after they finish: *Young brought down the house with his acoustic guitar solo.*

eat *someone* out of house and home

to eat more of someone's food than is considered polite so that you annoy them: *Since Mike's been here he's been eating me out of house and home, and he hasn't even offered to pay.*

a house of cards

used about a plan or organization that is very likely to fail, especially because it is based on an idea that is not true: *The peace agreement could collapse like a house of cards at the first sign of trouble.*

on the house

if drinks or meals are on the house, you do not have to pay for them because the bar or restaurant pays: *What'll you have? The first drink is on the house.*

put/get/set your (own) house in order

to organize your business, money, or personal affairs, so that you are more effective or are not doing anything wrong: *It's time for Congress to realize they must put the nation's fiscal house in order.*

household

a household name

used about someone or something that is very well known: *Preaching crusades on television and radio have helped make Reverend Billy Graham a household name.*

how

and how!

SPOKEN used when you are answering "yes" to a question in order to emphasize your reply: *"Did it rain last night?" "And how! Didn't you hear it?"*

how about that

SPOKEN said when you are slightly surprised at something you have just found out: *"Paula's going on vacation with Tyrone." "Well how about that!"*

how does *something* grab you?

SPOKEN used to ask someone if they like a suggestion that you are making: *Just stand up and say: "Listen, this is my idea, how does it grab you?"*

how ya livin'?
(also **how's it hangin'?**)

SLANG used to ask if someone is well and happy: *Hey, girl, how ya livin'?*

hue

a hue and cry

angry protests by a group of people about something: *Elliot was afraid that an attempt to close the offices would raise a hue and cry.*

huff

in a huff

angry because someone has offended you: *I asked him if he wanted to eat with us, but he walked out in a huff.*

human

someone is only human

used to say that someone can only be expected to do as much or behave as well as you would expect any normal person to do or behave: *We know medication errors have increased. But nurses are only human, and when they're pushed to the limit, mistakes can be made.*

hump

bust your hump

SLANG to try very hard to do something: *I busted my hump writing that history paper, and the teacher hated it.*

be/get over the hump
to deal with the most difficult part of a problem or situation so that the rest is easier: *Once I'd broken his serve, I was over the hump, and the game started to go better for me.*
something **pushes** *someone/something* **over the hump:** *I'll never forget this win. This might be the win that's going to push us over the hump.*

hung up

get/be hung up on *something*
to think or worry about something more than you need to or should: *Don't get hung up on the first sentence or paragraph of your essay; they're always the most difficult.*

hurdle

clear a hurdle
to deal successfully with a problem: *If*

you've passed the accounting exams, you've cleared the first hurdle. None of the others are as hard.

hush

hush money
money that you pay to someone in order to make them keep something secret: *The minister had an affair with a former church secretary, using church funds to pay her hush money afterwards.*

hymn book

be singing from the same hymn book/sheet
used to say that a group of people all have the same opinion when they are asked about a subject: *"It isn't just Doug Wilder saying it," Strauss said. "Stu Eizenstat, a liberal, has been saying it. I've been saying it. I think we're all singing from the same hymn book."*

H

I

I
⇨I'll SAY

ice

break the ice
to say or do something that makes people feel less nervous and more willing to talk when they have just met each other, for example at a party or a meeting: *To break the ice, the dorm leader asked us to tell the group what our favorite home-cooked meal was.*

not cut much ice (with)
(also **cut no/little ice (with))**
if something you say or do does not cut much ice with someone, it does not persuade them or seem impressive to them at all, usually when you were hoping it would: *A degree in computer science will cut little ice with most employers. They want experience in the fast-moving world of technology.*

keep/put *something* **on ice**
to decide to do nothing about a plan or suggestion for a while, or to stop doing something for a while: *We're going to have to put this project on ice until we can raise some more money.*

be (skating/walking) on thin ice
used to say that someone is in a difficult situation, and that they may have serious problems if they are not very careful: *We're skating on thin ice – we may be getting close to a violation of employees' rights. | You're on thin ice, young lady. One more comment, and you'll spend the rest of the evening in your room.*

icing

the icing on the cake
something that makes a good situation or activity even better: *The Royals were ahead 4–2 at the end of the third period, but that last goal was just the icing on the cake.*

> NOTE▶ Icing is a sweet substance made from sugar and milk and put on cakes.

idea
⇨not have the FOGGIEST (idea)

bounce ideas off *someone*
to ask someone what they think about your plans or ideas before you make a decision: *Fred, could I see you for a few minutes? I'd like to bounce a few ideas off you about the Murphey case.*

what's the big idea?
OLD-FASHIONED said when you are annoyed at something someone has done, and you want them to explain it: *What's the big idea, waking me up at five o' clock in the morning?*

ignorance

ignorance is bliss
used to say that if you do not know about a problem, you cannot worry about it: *Ignorance is bliss to young readers of teen magazines, who could be turned off if they learned their TV idols are twice their age.*

ill

ill at ease
feeling nervous and embarrassed, especially in a social situation: *If you ask me, Jones is too ill at ease with public speaking to make a good politician.*

image
⇨blacken *someone's* NAME/image/
   reputation

be the spitting image of *someone*
used to emphasize that someone looks exactly like someone else: *Paul's the spitting image of his father.*
—see also **be a dead RINGER for** *someone*

imagination
⇨leave NOTHING to the imagination

in
⇨*someone* has (got) it in for *someone*
   —see HAVE

be in for it
SPOKEN used to say that someone is going to be in trouble because they have done something that will make someone angry:

Issie's going to be in for it when Dad finds out she's pierced her eyebrow.

the ins and outs of *something*
all the details and facts of a situation or subject, especially a complicated one: *Larkin learned the ins and outs of Wall Street at Merrill Lynch before starting up his own firm.*

inch

give *someone* **an inch (and he/she will take a mile)**
used to say that if you let someone do one small thing that you do not like or want, they will try to do a lot more: *Give a negotiator like Travis an inch, and he's going to take a mile.* | *Don't you give those kids an inch, or they'll end up doing whatever they like.*

(to) within an inch of your life
if you beat someone to within an inch of their life, you hit them hard many times so that they are badly hurt: *I hate those movies where a guy is beat to within an inch of his life, and then he gets up and acts like nothing happened.*

Indian

⇨an Indian SUMMER

influence

under the influence
used to say that someone cannot drive, walk, think, etc. correctly because they have been drinking alcohol ♦ USED ESPECIALLY BY LAWYERS, POLICE ETC.: *Nelson pleaded guilty to driving under the influence.*

ink

be bleeding red ink
used to say that a business is losing a lot of money ♦ OFTEN USED IN NEWSPAPERS, ON TELEVISION NEWS, ETC.: *Many major New York banks are bleeding red ink and firing thousands of employees.*

NOTE▶ Accountants (=people who take care of financial accounts) used to use red ink to show that a company owed money.

insult

(to) add insult to injury
used to say that someone who caused a bad situation has made it worse, or that someone who has upset you is making you feel even worse: *To add insult to injury, the Lions not only lost the game, but they lost to a team who was rated the worst in the whole league!*

interest

pay *someone* **back with interest**
to harm or insult someone even worse than they have harmed or insulted you: *I'm not a violent man, but if someone hurts me, I pay them back with interest.*

iron

⇨work/get/iron out the KINKS

have many/several irons in the fire (also have other irons in the fire)
to be involved in several activities, or to be considering several different opportunities: *Of course the loss of the Sanderson contract was disappointing, but we have other irons in the fire, so we're not too worried.*

pump iron
to do exercises by lifting heavy weights, to make your muscles bigger: *I've been pumping iron and taking vitamins to try to keep in shape.*

strike while the iron is hot
to do something quickly while you have the opportunity and you are likely to succeed: *Ruby could see that her father was almost persuaded, and she hurried to strike while the iron was hot.*

issue

force the issue
to make it necessary for someone to make a decision or take action, instead of allowing the situation to develop naturally: *I'm sorry to force the issue here, but if we want to keep McMillan with this company, we have to act now.*

fudge the issue
to talk about something in a way that is not exact, especially in order to avoid making a decision or dealing with a

difficult situation: *When a grandparent dies, some parents fudge the issue by telling their children that Grandma or Grandpa has gone away.*

take issue with *someone/something*
to disagree with someone about something, and say why you think they are wrong: *Last year, the "Star" published more than 500 letters from readers, often taking issue with our editorial or opinion columns.*

itch

the seven year itch
OLD-FASHIONED a humorous expression used in order to say that after seven years of being married or in a romantic relationship, people stop feeling satisfied with the relationship: *The seven year itch is often caused by partners who are unwilling to communicate with each other.*

itching

be itching to do *something*
to want to do something very much, especially something new that you want to begin doing: *Finally, Amanda got to do what she had been itching to do for two months – get her hands on the controls of an airplane.*

item

be an item
if two people are an item, everyone knows that they are having a romantic relationship: *Eric and Rachel have gotten to be quite an item. Do you think they'll get married anytime soon?*

ivory

in an ivory tower
used about someone who is so involved in their work or ideas that they do not understand ordinary people and their problems: *It's easy for Thompson in his academic ivory tower to be critical – he doesn't realize how much work is involved in helping abused children.*

tickle the ivories
OLD-FASHIONED to play the piano: *In his latest film, Robertson plays a sexy musician who tickles the ivories in a high-class Las Vegas night club.*

J

jack

before you can say Jack Robinson
used to say that something happens very quickly: *The hurricane hit us and was over before we could say Jack Robinson.*

not ___ jack (shit)
(also **not ___ jack diddly**)
SLANG to not do, have, know, etc. anything at all: *We've been studying for over an hour, and I still don't know jack shit! | I hate this job – I'm not earning jack.*

> NOTE▸ The verbs that are most commonly used with this idiom are "do," "have," "know," "mean," "get," and "earn." You may hear people use this expression without "not" to mean the same thing.

be a jack of all trades
(also **a jack of all trades and master of none**)
to be able to do a lot of different jobs, although you may not be very good at any one of them: *KNTV was such a small station that Haulman had to become a jack of all trades, working as a reporter, editor, cameraman and even weatherman.*

jackpot

hit the jackpot
1 to be very successful or to make a lot of money: *"Leaving Las Vegas" had hit the jackpot when it received praise and numerous awards.*
2 to find information that you need to know, or something important that you need: *Lincoln scholars hit the jackpot when they discovered papers relating to a case Lincoln had when he was a young lawyer.*

> NOTE▸ This idiom comes from gambling (= the practice of risking money on card games, horse races, etc.). If someone hits the jackpot when they are gambling, they win lots of money.

Jane
⇨**JOHN/Jane Doe**

jaw

have a jaw
OLD-FASHIONED have a conversation: *The Colonel was sitting at the side of the hall, having a jaw with a wounded soldier.*

someone's **jaw dropped**
used to say that someone is very surprised: *Kevin's jaw dropped when he realized it was Cindy Crawford standing in front of him.*

jaybird

naked as a jaybird
without any clothes on at all: *The party was great, until Ronnie decided to run around the house naked as a jaybird.*

jazz

... and all that jazz
SPOKEN other things of the same kind as the ones you have mentioned: *"What did you talk about?" "Oh, life, love, and all that jazz."*

Jekyll and Hyde

Jekyll and Hyde
used about someone who has two totally different parts to their character, one very good and the other very bad: *Simon was something of a Jekyll and Hyde – he was warm and friendly to neighbors, but verbally abusive to his wife.*
Jekyll-and-Hyde: *Roth is a real Jekyll-and-Hyde character, who one minute says he loves Amanda, and the next that he hates her!*

> NOTE▸ This idiom comes from R.L. Stevenson's book *"The Strange Case of Dr. Jekyll and Mr. Hyde"* in which Dr. Jekyll finds a drug that changes him into a person called Mr. Hyde, who has all of Dr. Jekyll's most evil qualities.

Jell-O

like trying to nail Jell-O to the wall
SPOKEN used to say that something is very difficult or impossible to do: *Getting a straight answer out of Sophie can be like trying to nail Jell-O to the wall.*

> NOTE▶ Jell-O is the trademark name for a soft food made with sweet fruit juice. It would be impossible to nail it to anything.

jelly

turn to jelly
(also **feel like jelly**)
if a part of your body turns to jelly, it feels very weak because you are very nervous, frightened, or tired: *Every time she looked into Jeff's eyes, her legs turned to jelly.*

jet

the jet set
OLD-FASHIONED rich and fashionable people, for example actors or singers, who travel around the world a lot, and who ordinary people like to read about: *Frank's wife hung out with the jet set – shopping in Paris and getting her hair done in Miami.*

jewel

the jewel in the crown (of)
the most successful or impressive thing that a person, country, organization, etc. possesses or has achieved: *Many people view Stanford as the jewel in the crown of California's numerous universities.*

jiffy

in a jiffy
SPOKEN used to say that you will go somewhere, or do something very quickly: *If you can wait, I'll have those numbers for you in a jiffy.*

Jim

⇨it's ___ (Jim), but **NOT** as we know it

job

⇨a **HATCHET** job on
⇨a **SNOW** job

do a job on *someone*
to damage or harm someone or something: *The sun can do quite a job on your skin if you're not careful.*

don't quit your day job
(also **don't give up your day job**)
a humorous expression used in order to say that someone who is trying out a new activity or skill is not very good at it yet: *Just because you sold one painting doesn't mean you should quit your day job.*

fall down on the job
to fail to do the work that you are supposed to do: *Educators are falling down on the job. As a consequence, students' test scores are dropping.*

get a job
SLANG used to say that someone should stop behaving in a stupid way and do something useful: *You stood in line two days to get tickets to a concert? Get a job!*

lie down on the job
(also **be asleep on the job**)
to make no effort to do the work that you are supposed to do: *You're paid to finish the work, not to lie down on the job.*

Joe

Joe Schmoe/Public
a name used to represent all ordinary people and their thoughts, feelings, and situations: *Carson virtually bought his "not guilty" verdict because he was rich enough to hire lawyers who tore up the prosecutors. If he was Joe Schmoe from nowhere, making $20,000 a year, he'd be in jail.*

> NOTE▶ You may also hear people use other names. For example, people often use Joe Blow, Joe Average, or John Q. Public. The last name can also be made specific in order to talk about people who do a particular type of activity or job: *I wouldn't recognize him if I saw him again. He was just a kind of Joe Businessman, you know, wearing a suit and tie, carrying a briefcase.*

John

John/Jane Doe

a name given to someone by the police or a hospital because they do not know the person's name, especially because they have been killed or badly injured. John is the name used for men, and Jane is used for women: *The victim, still identified only as John Doe, was killed by a shotgun blast to the head.*

joint

case the joint

OLD-FASHIONED if someone who intends to steal something cases the joint, they look around the place they are going to steal from to find out about it: *Very few burglars actually case the joint, as you read in the detective stories – most of them just see an opportunity and take it.*

Joneses

keep up with the Joneses

to try to have all the things that your friends and neighbors (=people who live near you) have, and do all the things that they do, so that you do not appear to be less successful than they are: *Just to keep up with the Joneses, Schmidt has been known to buy his children expensive clothes and take his wife on exotic vacations.*

> NOTE▶ Jones is a common family name in English. "The Joneses" is often used to mean the ordinary family.

joys

be full of the joys of spring

to feel happy, full of energy, and pleased with life, especially because it is spring or because you are young: *Debbie's great charm as a singer is that she's still so young and full of the joys of spring.*

judge

sober as a judge

OLD-FASHIONED used about someone who seems completely sober (=shows no signs that they have been drinking alcohol): *Even though I was as sober as a judge, I* still can't remember dancing with you last night.

judgment

sit in judgment (on/over)

to criticize someone's behavior, especially in a severe or unfair way: *Steve, you're a divorced man – I don't think you're qualified to sit in judgment on other people's relationships.*

jugular

go for the jugular

if you go for the jugular when you are criticizing, fighting, or arguing with someone, you attack them in a way that you know will harm them most: *I decided to go straight for the jugular and ask Rita if she had been having an affair.*

> NOTE▶ The jugular is a large vein (=tube that blood flows through) in your neck that goes directly to your heart.

juice

let *someone* stew in his/her own juice
(also **leave** *someone* **to stew in his/her own juice**)

to let someone worry about something, especially something they have done wrong, without doing anything to help them: *I knew Steph would be expecting me to call, but I was so mad, I just left her to stew in her own juice for a while.*

jump

get/have the jump on *someone*

to have an advantage over someone because you started doing something before they did: *Getting the jump on his fellow congressmen, Larkin is expected to call for increases on tobacco and alcohol taxes in tonight's speech.*

keep/stay/be one jump ahead of *someone*

to have an advantage over someone who you are competing or fighting against: *In this age of international business, an MBA student who speaks Japanese is going to be one jump ahead of an MBA student who doesn't.*

J

jungle

concrete jungle

used about an ugly and unpleasant area of buildings in a city: *Why did they have to build more apartments along the river? They're turning it into a regular concrete jungle!*

jury

the jury is still out (on *something*)

SPOKEN used to say that people do not yet know enough about something to decide whether something is good or bad: *"The jury's still out regarding another increase in taxes," said Rogers.*

> NOTE▶ A jury is the group of people who decide if someone is guilty of a crime in a court of law. "The jury is out" means the jury has left the court room to make their decision.

just

it's just as well (that)

used to say that it is lucky that something happened because if it had not happened there would be problems: *It's just as well Kent was sick today – he'd have been unhappy to see the team lose so badly.*

just like that

SPOKEN if something happens "just like that," it happens quickly or easily: *You think I can raise 3,000 dollars, just like that?*

justice

do justice to *someone/something* (also do *someone/something* justice)

to treat or represent someone or something in a way that is fair and shows their best qualities: *Do you think the movie really does justice to Conroy's book? | Denise, you look great! That haircut really does you justice.*

poetic justice

when something bad or something good happens to someone because they deserve it: *Some would say there is poetic justice in this – I neglected my family for my work, and now I have lost my job and my family too.*

rough justice

when people are punished or rewarded in a way that is unfair, especially a way that is not legal: *Rough justice has come to the front door of the clinic as patients have to fight their way in past the protesters.*

K

kazoo

⇨have *something* **(coming) out the WAZOO/kazoo**

keel

(back) on an even keel
living or operating without problems, especially after a time of trouble: *Getting her life on an even keel again after her break-up with Jim had taken Monica a long time.*

keep

⇨keep *someone* **on the STRAIGHT and narrow**

⇨keep your **COOL**

earn your keep
to earn the money that you need to live, or enough to support yourself: *I started earning my keep at 14, working on my family's cattle ranch.*

keep *someone* guessing
to make it difficult for someone to know what you are going to do next: *Kasparov managed to keep his opponent guessing until he made his last move.*

keep *someone* posted
to continue giving someone information about a situation that they are interested in: *One of the police officers said he would keep me posted, but so far, I haven't heard from him.*

you can keep ___
SPOKEN used to say that you do not want or are not interested in something: *She can keep her beautiful friends and wild parties – I prefer the quiet life.*

ken

beyond *someone's* ken
if an experience, situation or person is beyond your ken, you do not know anything about it or understand it: *The intellectual crowd seems to think the new film by Jarmusch is beyond most Americans' ken.*

kettle

another kettle of fish
(also a different kettle of fish)
used to say that a situation is completely different from the one you are talking about: *The old building was dark and depressing to work in. The new site is a different kettle of fish altogether – it's beautiful.*

a fine/pretty kettle of fish
OLD-FASHIONED a situation that causes you problems: *This is a fine kettle of fish! I don't have a date all year, and now I have two on the same night!*

keyed up

be/get keyed up
to be worried, nervous or excited, especially about something that you are going to do, or that is going to happen: *Since winning the last game, the guys have been keyed up and ready to play.*

kibosh

put the/a kibosh on *something*
to prevent a plan from being successful: *At the last minute, the weather put a kibosh on our outdoor wedding plans.*

kick

better than a kick in the teeth
SPOKEN used to say that although something is not as good as what you hoped for, you will not complain because it is better than having nothing: *"I've never won more than ten dollars in the lottery." "Well, that's better than a kick in the teeth, isn't it?"*

get a kick out of (doing) *something*
SPOKEN to think something is funny, or that something is fun to do: *Jackie's a real character – you'll get a kick out of some of the things she says.*
—see also **get a CHARGE out of** *something*

get your kicks from *something*
(also do *something* for kicks)
to do something for excitement, especially something dangerous: *The local kids get their kicks from racing stolen*

cars. | *Police say the killer is doing it for kicks, choosing his victims at random.*

a kick in the pants/butt/ass

SPOKEN when criticism, punishment, or failure shocks someone and makes them start to behave better, try harder, or work harder: *Coach Hanson is just what this team needed – someone who could give the players a good kick in the butt.*

a kick in the teeth
(also **a kick in the guts, stomach, etc.**)

SPOKEN something someone says or does that makes you very disappointed and upset, especially when you do not except or deserve it: *Noel said his dismissal as coach was a kick in the guts.*

kick *someone* upstairs

to give someone a job at a higher level but with less power than before, usually because they are not effective any more: *Our programming executives often get kicked upstairs to jobs with bigger, more confusing titles.*

kick *someone* when he/she is down

to harm someone when they have already been defeated or are already in a bad situation: *Criticizing the paper for kicking him when he was down, Campbell promised to fight back.*

kid

⇒treat *someone* with kid **GLOVES**

like a kid in a candy store

used to say that someone is very excited and happy about something: *The conference was great! I was like a kid in a candy store with the thousands of things there were to do.*

the new kid on the block

the newest person in a company, activity, school, etc., or the newest product of a particular type: *I first heard Shaeffer play a few years ago, when he was the new kid in the Bay Area club scene.* | *There's a new kid on the block that promises great taste – a brown ale from one of Denver's microbreweries.*

kidding

who is *someone* kidding?
(also **who does *someone* think he's/she's kidding?**)

SPOKEN used to say that someone's reasons or excuses for doing something are not believable: *My wife and I decided that moving would be easier than adding onto the kitchen and bedroom. Who did we think we were kidding?*

you're kidding (me)
(also **are you kidding me?**)

1 SPOKEN said when you cannot believe what someone has just said, or think it is unreasonable or stupid: *"I totally forgot about the test today." "The test is today? You're kidding me!"* | *"Did I tell you the hot water heater's broken again?" "You've gotta be kidding me."*
2 SPOKEN used to emphasize that the answer to a question is definitely "no," or that what someone is saying is definitely not true: *"Was he mad that you left?" "No, are you kidding? He didn't care where I went."* | *"Hey, Butcher. Can you close the store tonight?" "Are you kidding me? I've already been here for 10 hours!"*

kill

move/close in for the kill

to try in a determined way to end an argument, fight, or competition by defeating your opponent: *The next time the 49ers got the ball, they went in for the kill.*

killing

make a killing

to make a lot of money in a short time, especially in business: *By the time he was 22, Westgate had made a killing in the stock market.*

kilter

off-kilter

someone or something that is off-kilter looks or behaves in an unusual, unexpected, and usually funny way: *He's a guy with a unique, slightly off-kilter view of life.*

out of kilter

if a system, organization, or process is out of kilter, it is not working well because the different parts of it are not in balance with each other: *The Earth's rotation is thrown slightly out of kilter by winds, ocean currents, earthquakes, and even melting snow.*

kinds

it takes all kinds (to make a world)

SPOKEN used to say that everyone is different, and often used humorously when you think that what someone else is doing, likes, etc. is strange: *Going fishing on your honeymoon isn't my idea of romance, but it takes all kinds.*

king

⇨the king's new clothes —see the emperor's (new) CLOTHES
⇨a king's RANSOM

kinks

work/get/iron out the kinks

to deal with the last small problems in a new product, plan, system, etc. so that it will be successful: *The group hopes they have a chance to work the kinks out of the new production before opening night.*

kiss

kiss and tell

to have a sexual relationship with someone and then tell everyone about it: *"Don't worry, Dr. Soames," Linda said. "I never kiss and tell."*
kiss-and-tell: *This isn't a kiss-and-tell book – it's a story about my life as the wife of an important politician.*

the kiss of death (for)

used to say that something will definitely make someone or something fail: *Why should living together be the kiss of death to couples intending to get married?*

kit

the whole kit and caboodle

all the parts or pieces of something, or all the parts of a situation: *You can't just buy one pan. It comes in a set, so you have to buy the whole kit and caboodle.*

kite

go fly a kite

OLD-FASHIONED used to tell someone in an impolite way to go away because they are annoying you: *He's always shouting about something – I just wanted to tell him to go fly a kite.*

high as a kite

behaving in a confused, excited, or stupid way because you have taken drugs or alcohol: *The truth was, he was high as a kite on Ecstasy and didn't know where he was going.*

knee

⇨a knee-jerk REACTION/response
be the bee's knees

SPOKEN used to say that you think someone or something is very good, attractive, etc.: *I gave my nephew one of those Nintendo games for his birthday, and he just thinks it's the bee's knees.*

bring *something* to its knees
(also **bring** *someone* **to his/her knees**)

1 to have a very bad effect on an organization or group of people so that it is difficult for it to continue its activity: *A combination of bad luck and mismanagement has brought the bank to its knees.*
2 to defeat a country or its leader in a war: *In World War I, people thought that we would bring the enemy to their knees in a few weeks.*

go down on your knees
(also **go down on bended knee**)

to show a lot of emotion when you are asking someone for something because you want it so much: *What should I do – go down on my knees and ask him for a job? | Do you think Mrs. Briggs would let us use the art room if I went down on bended knee?*

knell

to sound/be the death knell

to cause a plan, process, or organization to fail or stop existing: *The construction of Highway 140 sounded the death knell for the railroad.*

K

NOTE▶ A death knell is the sound made by a bell that is rung when someone has died.

knife

go/cut through *something* like a (hot) knife through butter
to cut or pass through something very quickly and easily: *This is an excellent tool that will go through wood like a knife through butter.* | *Near the end of the race, our horse came slicing through the rest like a hot knife through butter, and finished first.*

go/be under the knife
to have a medical operation: *Cochran went to the hospital for a simple stomach ache, and two hours later he was under the knife.*

be on a knife edge
1 to be in a difficult or dangerous situation in which something very bad may very easily happen: *After the assassination, the country was on a knife edge until Mandela managed to appeal to the people and unite them.*
knife-edge: *The rural communities lead a knife-edge existence under the perpetual threat of drought.*
2 to be in a situation in which no one knows which of two different things will happen, or which of two different decisions will be made: *Three weeks before the election, opinion polls showed that the outcome was on a knife edge.*
knife-edge: *The governor will be facing a knife-edge vote in next week's elections.*

twist/turn the knife (in the wound)
to say or do something that makes someone feel even more upset or embarrassed than they feel already: *"Have you heard from your ex-boyfriend lately? He just got engaged." "No, I hadn't heard – thanks for twisting the knife."*

knight

a knight in shining armor
1 a man who helps a woman in a difficult or dangerous situation, or a man who will always help and protect a woman: *You can't spend your life waiting*
for a knight in shining armor – there isn't one, or if there is he'll be impossible to live with.
2 someone brave who will take risks in order to help people: *The rangers made a plea to the governor for a knight in shining armor to help save the parks from destruction.*

knitting

stick to your knitting
to keep doing the thing that you do best, without trying to do other things that you might not do so well: *We stuck to our knitting during the 1980s, and didn't get involved in financial speculation with the result that the firm is stable – no loans, no lawsuits, no stories about us in the papers.*

knock

⇨**knock/whip** *someone/something* **into SHAPE**

don't knock it
used to tell someone not to criticize something or complain about it: *"I have to spend all weekend cooped up at my aunt's house." "Don't knock it – at least the food's free."*

hard knocks
the difficult or unpleasant experiences you have in life that you learn from: *The left-handed pitcher was last year's biggest phenomenon, but since then he's had a year of hard knocks.*

NOTE▶ You may hear people use "the school/university/college of hard knocks" to talk about the difficult life someone has had: *Rawl says his graduation from the college of hard knocks has made him determined that young African Americans will not be denied a higher education because they cannot afford one.*

knock-down, drag-out
(also **knock down, drag out**)
used about an argument, fight, etc. when you want to emphasize that it was an extremely nasty one: *Amazingly, both sides went away feeling happier, after a knock down, drag out trial full of hostility.*

knock 'em dead

SPOKEN to make people admire you by doing something very well, especially when you are performing, or speaking to a large group of people: *Don't be nervous, just go out there and knock 'em dead.*

Knock it off!

SPOKEN used to tell someone to stop doing something, especially because it is annoying you: *Knock it off, you two – I'm sick of your arguing.*

Knock it off!

KNOCK IT OFF! I'M TRYING TO READ!

knock yourself out

1 to work very hard in order to do something, so that you become very tired: *Angie's parents knocked themselves out to give her a really wonderful wedding.*
2 SPOKEN (also **go ahead/on knock yourself out**) used to tell someone who is trying to do something that you think they will not succeed: *If you think you can write it in a day, go ahead, knock yourself out.*

knot

cut/untie the Gordian knot

to deal with a very difficult and complicated situation, especially in a quick, simple way ◆ OFTEN USED IN NEWSPAPERS: *The Secretary-General stated that the Gordian knot had been untied, and the peace talks could begin.*

tie the knot

if two people tie the not, they get married ◆ OFTEN USED IN NEWSPAPERS, ON TELEVISION NEWS, ETC.: *Over 150 couples tied the knot on Valentine's Day in a romantic ceremony on a dance floor in Oklahoma.*

tie yourself in knots

to become worried and confused when you are trying to do, decide, or talk about something difficult or complicated: *I tied myself in knots trying to speak coherently about my dissertation in front of the committee.*

know

⇨**it's ___ (Jim), but NOT as we know it**
⇨**WHAT do you know!**
⇨**WOULDN'T you (just) know it**

someone **didn't know what hit him/her**

SPOKEN used to say that someone was very surprised or shocked: *When her new boyfriend comes here and sees she's got three kids, the poor man won't know what hit him.*

be in the know

to understand more, or have more information about something than most people have: *I've talked to various people in the know, who say that the government is deeply divided on the question of economic policy.*

know *something* **backward and forward**

to know a system, organization, etc. very well, and understand how it works: *Berry knew the record business backward and forward, and he knew how to be successful.*

know *someone/something* **inside (and) out**

to know a person, system, organization, etc. very well and understand how it works: *Trust me – I know these people inside out – they'll love your idea.* | *Staller is definitely the best guy for the job – he knows the department inside and out.*

not know whether you're coming or going

SPOKEN to feel confused, especially

because you have too much to do: *We're going to the theater tomorrow and to a movie Friday – there's so much going on this week, I don't know whether I'm coming or going.*

someone **wouldn't know**
someone/something **if it jumped up and bit them**
(also *someone* **wouldn't know**
someone/something **if they tripped over it**)
used to emphasize that someone does not know anything about a particular subject or person: *You wouldn't know the stuff was cocaine if it jumped up and bit you. | I really liked Kyle when we were in high school, but I wouldn't know him if I tripped over him now.*

knuckles

⇨be given a **RAP** on/over/across the knuckles

IDIOM ACTIVATOR

This special section contains 10 basic "concept words," for example **PROBLEM** (below). Each concept word is divided into groups of idioms that have similar meanings. So, for example, under **PROBLEM** you have a general group called "having problems," a group called "cause problems for yourself," and so on. Looking at these groups of idioms and checking their definitions in the main part of the dictionary can help you to understand how each idiom is different or similar to the others. For example, some idioms in the group may be most frequently used in spoken language or in business and politics. Others may be only used by or about a particular group of people.

PROBLEM

cause problems for yourself
► the CHICKENs (have) come home to roost
► dig your own GRAVE
► be your own worst ENEMY

having problems
► in deep DOO-DOO
► in deep SHIT ⚠
► in/into deep WATER
► in a FIX
► in/into hot WATER
► not be out of the WOODs (yet)
► in a PICKLE
► in a tight SPOT
► be up the CREEK (without a paddle)
► be down for the COUNT

something prevents progress/achievement
► be a DRAG on something
► a/the MONKEY on someone's back
► be a sticking POINT
► be a stumbling BLOCK

something makes life difficult/unhappy
► be the BANE of someone's life/existence
► a THORN in someone's side

cause problems for someone
► stir up a hornet's NEST
► rain on someone's PARADE
► pull the RUG (out) from under someone

in a situation with difficult choices
► between the DEVIL and the deep blue sea
► between SCYLLA and Charybdis
► a CATCH 22 (situation)
► (caught) between a ROCK and a hard place
► Hobson's CHOICE

⚠ Be careful! The idioms marked with this symbol may be considered offensive or impolite by some people. It is better not to use them.

I
D
I
O
M

A
C
T
I
V
A
T
O
R

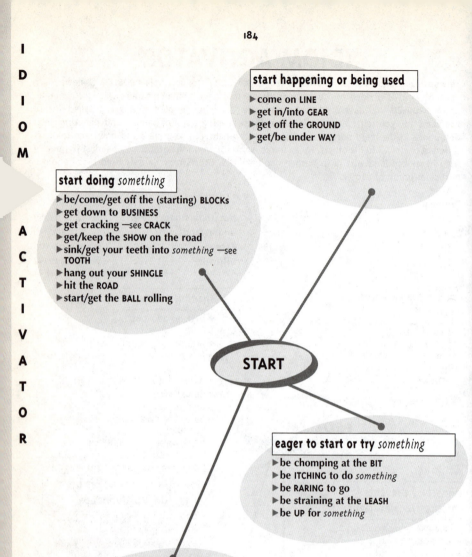

start happening or being used

▶ come on LINE
▶ get in/into GEAR
▶ get off the GROUND
▶ get/be under WAY

start doing *something*

▶ be/come/get off the (starting) BLOCKs
▶ get down to BUSINESS
▶ get cracking —see CRACK
▶ get/keep the SHOW on the road
▶ sink/get your teeth into *something* —see TOOTH
▶ hang out your SHINGLE
▶ hit the ROAD
▶ start/get the BALL rolling

START

eager to start or try *something*

▶ be chomping at the BIT
▶ be ITCHING to do *something*
▶ be RARING to go
▶ be straining at the LEASH
▶ be UP for *something*

start *something* new or try again

▶ a clean SLATE
▶ start with a clean SHEET (of paper)
▶ from SCRATCH
▶ try your HAND at *something*
▶ turn your HAND to *something*

people have the same ideas/opinions/beliefs

▶ BIRDS of a feather (flock together)
▶ great MINDS think alike
▶ be/keep in STEP with
▶ in TUNE with
▶ a meeting of (the) MINDs
▶ be of one MIND
▶ be/get on the same PAGE
▶ be on the same WAVELENGTH
▶ speak the same LANGUAGE
▶ speak with one VOICE

SAME

two people/things look exactly the same

▶ be a CARBON copy
▶ be a dead RINGER for *someone*
▶ like two PEAS in a pod
▶ be the spitting IMAGE of *someone*

two situations/things are the same

▶ same DIFFERENCE
▶ six of one, half a DOZEN of the other

**I
D
I
O
M**

**A
C
T
I
V
A
T
O
R**

two people/things are different

- ▶ be at LOGGERHEADS (with *someone*)
- ▶ be at ODDS with *someone/something*
- ▶ a different ANIMAL
- ▶ never the TWAIN shall meet
- ▶ OIL and water
- ▶ be on a (totally) different WAVELENGTH
- ▶ be POLEs apart
- ▶ not see EYE to eye
- ▶ US and them
- ▶ be WORLDs apart
- ▶ be like NIGHT and day

two situations are different

- ▶ another KETTLE of fish
- ▶ be a far CRY from
- ▶ it's a (whole) new BALL GAME

DIFFERENT

different from other people

- ▶ go/swim against the CURRENT
- ▶ march to (the beat of) a different DRUMMER
- ▶ a rare BIRD
- ▶ stick/stand out like a sore THUMB
- ▶ they broke the MOLD when they made *someone*

a group of different kinds of things/people

- ▶ from all WALKs of life
- ▶ be a mixed BAG
- ▶ THIS, that, and the other (thing)

⚠ **tell** *someone* **to stop doing or saying** *something*
- ►CUT it out!
- ►cut the CRAP/shit!
- ►don't pull that CRAP/shit
- ►get off my CASE!
- ►give it a REST
- ►KNOCK it off!
- ►I'm not (even) gonna GO there
- ►put a SOCK in it!

stop *something* **that is happening**
- ►burst the BUBBLE
- ►put the BRAKES on *something*
- ►pull the PLUG on *something*
- ►stem the TIDE (of)
- ►stop *something* (dead) in its TRACKs

STOP

stop doing *something*
- ►call it a DAY
- ►call it a NIGHT
- ►go cold TURKEY
- ►HANG up your ___
- ►keep/put *something* on ICE
- ►close up SHOP
- ►call it QUITS

stop doing *something* **because it is failing**
- ►cut your LOSSes
- ►give up the GHOST

⚠ Be careful! Most of the idioms in this group are considered offensive or impolite. Check the definitions and examples before using them.

I
D
I
O
M

A
C
T
I
V
A
T
O
R

feeling angry

▶do a slow BURN
▶get/be steamed up —see STEAM
▶have STEAM coming
  out of your ears
▶be/get hot under the COLLAR
▶in high DUDGEON
▶mad as a HORNET

angrily criticize/insult *someone*

▶bite *someone's* HEAD off
▶cut *someone* down to SIZE
▶give *someone* HELL ⚠
▶give *someone* a PIECE of your mind
▶jump down *someone's* THROAT
▶talk TRASH

angry/frustrated

▶FIT to be tied
▶pull/tear your HAIR out

deliberately annoy someone

▶push *someone's* BUTTONs
▶rattle *someone's* CAGE
▶ruffle *someone's* FEATHERs
▶yank *someone's* CHAIN

something makes you angry/annoyed

▶get *someone's* GOAT
▶*something* makes
  my/your BLOOD boil
▶raise *someone's*
  HACKLES

ANGRY

angrily complain about *something*

▶be up in ARMs (about *something*)
▶raise HELL/Cain ⚠

become suddenly very angry

▶blow a FUSE/gasket
▶blow your TOP/stack
▶(almost/nearly) burst a BLOOD VESSEL
▶flip your LID/wig
▶fly off the HANDLE
▶go APE
▶go BALLISTIC/nuclear
▶go BANANAs
▶go through the ROOF/ceiling
▶have a COW
▶have/throw a FIT
▶lose/blow your COOL
▶SEE red
▶GO postal (on someone)

say/do a lot because you are angry

▶let/blow off STEAM
▶vent your SPLEEN

⚠ Be careful! The idioms marked
with this symbol may be considered
offensive or impolite by some
people. It is better not to use them.

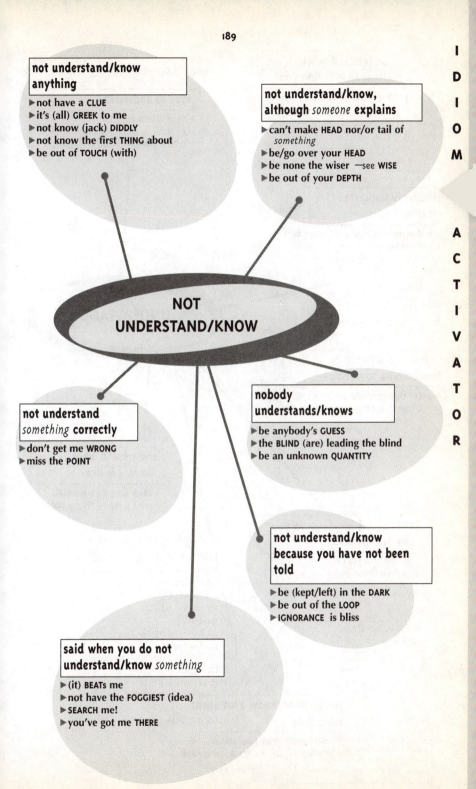

I D I O M

A C T I V A T O R

not understand/know anything

- ▶ not have a CLUE
- ▶ it's (all) GREEK to me
- ▶ not know (jack) DIDDLY
- ▶ not know the first THING about
- ▶ be out of TOUCH (with)

not understand/know, although *someone* **explains**

- ▶ can't make HEAD nor/or tail of *something*
- ▶ be/go over your HEAD
- ▶ be none the wiser —see WISE
- ▶ be out of your DEPTH

NOT UNDERSTAND/KNOW

not understand *something* **correctly**

- ▶ don't get me WRONG
- ▶ miss the POINT

nobody understands/knows

- ▶ be anybody's GUESS
- ▶ the BLIND (are) leading the blind
- ▶ be an unknown QUANTITY

not understand/know because you have not been told

- ▶ be (kept/left) in the DARK
- ▶ be out of the LOOP
- ▶ IGNORANCE is bliss

said when you do not understand/know *something*

- ▶ (it) BEATs me
- ▶ not have the FOGGIEST (idea)
- ▶ SEARCH me!
- ▶ you've got me THERE

IDIOM ACTIVATOR

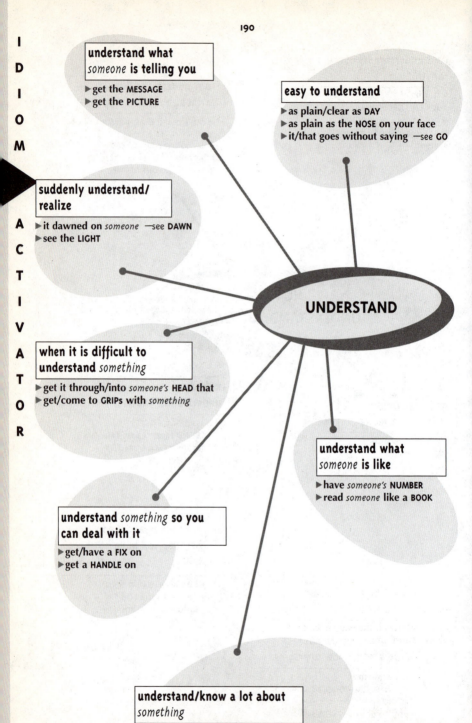

understand what *someone* **is telling you**
- ▶ get the MESSAGE
- ▶ get the PICTURE

easy to understand
- ▶ as plain/clear as DAY
- ▶ as plain as the NOSE on your face
- ▶ it/that goes without saying —see GO

suddenly understand/ realize
- ▶ it dawned on *someone* —see DAWN
- ▶ see the LIGHT

when it is difficult to understand *something*
- ▶ get it through/into *someone's* HEAD that
- ▶ get/come to GRIPs with *something*

UNDERSTAND

understand what *someone* **is like**
- ▶ have *someone's* NUMBER
- ▶ read *someone* like a BOOK

understand *something* **so you can deal with it**
- ▶ get/have a FIX on
- ▶ get a HANDLE on

understand/know a lot about *something*
- ▶ know a THING or two about *something*
- ▶ *someone* wrote the BOOK on *something*

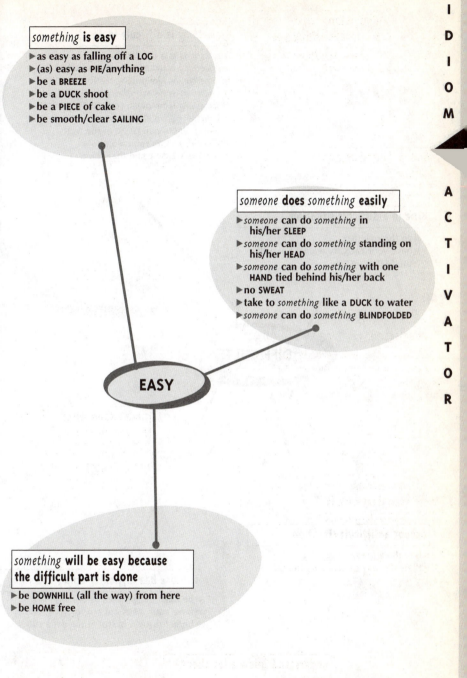

something is easy

► as easy as falling off a LOG
► (as) easy as PIE/anything
► be a BREEZE
► be a DUCK shoot
► be a PIECE of cake
► be smooth/clear SAILING

someone does something easily

► *someone* can do *something* in his/her SLEEP
► *someone* can do *something* standing on his/her HEAD
► *someone* can do *something* with one HAND tied behind his/her back
► no SWEAT
► take to *something* like a DUCK to water
► *someone* can do *something* BLINDFOLDED

EASY

something will be easy because the difficult part is done

► be DOWNHILL (all the way) from here
► be HOME free

I
D
I
O
M

A
C
T
I
V
A
T
O
R

IDIOM

ACTIVATOR

something **is difficult to do**

- ▶ *something* is a tall ORDER
- ▶ *something* is HARD/difficult to swallow
- ▶ *something* is like pulling teeth —see TOOTH
- ▶ *something* is no BED of roses
- ▶ *something* is no mean FEAT
- ▶ *something* is no PICNIC
- ▶ like trying to nail JELL-O to the wall
- ▶ *something* TAKEs some doing
- ▶ that's/it's EASIER said than done

be in a difficult situation

- ▶ go through HELL
- ▶ have your BACK to/against the wall
- ▶ the HEAT is on

DIFFICULT

accept a difficult situation

- ▶ bite the BULLET
- ▶ thats the WAY the cookie crumbles

someone **has difficulty doing** *something*

- ▶ be HARD put/pressed to do *something*
- ▶ have your WORK cut out for you
- ▶ be/get thrown in (to) at the deep END

⚠ Be careful! The idioms marked with this symbol may be considered offensive or impolite by some people. It is better not to use them.

L

labor

a labor of love
something that you do because you like doing it or want to do it although you are not paid for it, and may have to work very hard: *Making her sister's wedding dress was a labor of love.*

ladder

climb (up) the ladder
(also **move, go, etc. up the ladder**)
to become more important and successful in your work by being promoted (=given a job that is more important and better paid): *Moving swiftly up the ladder of corporate responsibility, Sam became the company's youngest ever President.*
—see also **the top/highest RUNG of the ladder**

> NOTE▶ You may hear people use "the ladder" in various ways to mean the series of jobs or achievements by which someone becomes successful: *I started at the bottom of the ladder after college, and progressed steadily upwards over the next twenty years. | The people lowest on the ladder are the most upset about the corporate changes.*

lady

⇨**a ladies' MAN**

it ain't over 'til the fat lady sings
used to say that the final result of a situation or competition cannot be known until it is completely finished because it may change before it is finished: *Sure, we lost today's game, but it ain't over 'til the fat lady sings.*
the fat lady has sung: *"I think the fat lady has sung," said Holland, who believes that the city police chief should resign after today's events.*

ladies who lunch
a humorous expression used about rich women who do not have jobs and spend lots of time shopping and eating in restaurants, especially when you disapprove because you think they do not do anything useful: *Carpaccio, the sedate, gray-walled restaurant for ladies who lunch, now has a sister restaurant for lawyers who party.*

laid

⇨**be laid back —see LAY**

lake

go (and) jump in a lake
an impolite expression used in order to tell someone to go away and stop annoying you: *Can you believe it? I asked Ricky out on a date, and he told me to go jump in a lake!*

lam

on the lam
trying to escape and hide from someone, especially the police: *The man I'm looking for is on the lam from the FBI, and has contacts with the Chicago drug scene.*

lamb

go like a lamb to the slaughter
to accept an unpleasant or dangerous situation without trying to avoid it because you have no choice or do not realize how bad it will be: *Deborah knew before she took the job that it was too much for one person, but went anyway, like a lamb to the slaughter.*

lamppost

between you, me, and the lamppost/fencepost
SPOKEN said before you tell someone something that you do not want them to tell anyone else: *Between you, me, and the lamppost, she's been seeing another guy.*

land

be in the land of the living
to be alive or awake: *It's way too early to be at work! I'm not ready to be in the land of the living yet.*

be in the land of nod
to be asleep ♦ OFTEN USED WHEN TALKING TO CHILDREN: *Daddy's coming home late – you'll be in the land of nod long before he gets home.*

a/the land of milk and honey

used about a place or situation that people want to go to because they think that life there will be good and there will be no problems: *The immigrants did not expect a land of milk and honey, but few of them were prepared for the hardship that awaited them.*

> NOTE▶ This idiom comes from a story in the Bible in which the people of Israel were promised a land full of plenty of food where life would be good. This land is described as "flowing with milk and honey."

land-office

⇨do a land-office BUSINESS

language

speak the same language
(also **speak** *someone's* **language**)
to have the same interests and opinions as someone else: *"Let's quit work early and go have a drink." "Now you're speaking my language."*

lap

drop/dump *something* in *someone's* lap

to give a problem that you have to someone else to deal with: *Lang went on vacation and dumped all this work in my lap to finish for him.*

fall/drop into your lap

if an opportunity or something good falls into your lap, you get it by chance and good luck, without trying to get it: *Jenny invited you to go to Hawaii? You should go – opportunities like that don't often fall into your lap!*

land in your lap

if additional work or something you are responsible for lands in your lap, you have to deal with it although it is not really part of your job: *I was dealing with one of those irritating little problems that always land in your lap at about four o'clock on Friday.*

the last lap

the final part of something that has taken a long time: *Just to warn you – the last lap*

through the mountains is the hardest part of the trip.

live in the lap of luxury

to have a very pleasant life with plenty of money, good food, and beautiful things: *Dave's dream is to win the lottery so he can just sit back and live in the lap of luxury.*

large

⇨BY and large
⇨be living large —see LIVE
⇨WRIT large

at large

1 used to emphasize that you are talking about most of the people in society or in a group: *It's wrong for the community at large to suffer because a few parents cannot control their kids.*
2 if a dangerous person or animal is at large, they have not been caught and may cause harm or damage: *Novak was caught, but his accomplice is still at large.*

lark

⇨happy as a CLAM/lark

last

last but not least

used to emphasize that the last person or thing that you are mentioning is not less important than the others: *I want to thank the people who helped me to write this book: Ellen Jameson my editor, my researcher Chris Wilson, and last but not least, my family who let me spend hours at my computer.*

late

⇨BETTER late than never

lather

be/get in a lather
(also **work yourself into a lather**)
OLD-FASHIONED to become very upset and excited about something, often something that does not seem important or interesting to other people: *Denver fans were in a lather when they first heard that Elway was retiring.*

laugh

have/get the last laugh (on *someone*)

to finally be successful, or receive proof that you are right after being defeated or criticized for being wrong: *Men make jokes about women's driving, but women have the last laugh; they get cheaper car insurance because they have fewer accidents.*

he who laughs last laughs longest/loudest/best

used to say that someone has had a good result from a situation after other people have opposed them or expected them to fail: *I still believe I was fired unfairly, but it doesn't bother me any more – he who laughs last laughs best.*

laundry

air/do your dirty laundry in public

to let other people know embarrassing secrets about yourself, your family, your organization, etc. by discussing them or arguing about them in public: *Where do they find these families who are prepared to go on TV and air all their dirty laundry in public?*

a laundry list of *something*

used to emphasize that there is a large number of something, often problems or unpleasant things: *Daniels came up with a whole laundry list of key problems with the new building proposal.*

laurels

look to your laurels

used to warn someone who is the best at an activity that someone else is becoming very good: *Williams may be issuing a challenge, telling established tennis players to look to their laurels.*

rest/sit on your laurels

to stop trying to achieve anything new, because you are satisfied with what you have achieved already ◆ OFTEN USED IN THE NEGATIVE: *America's favorite car isn't resting on its laurels. The new model is much roomier and the body is much sleeker.*

NOTE▶ In ancient times, leaves from a laurel tree were given to people such as poets and athletes as an honor.

law

someone is a law unto himself/herself

used when you disapprove because someone does what they want to, instead of doing what they are told to do: *Alvin is cute, smart, and rich – but he's a law unto himself and can't be trusted.*

the law of the jungle

a situation in which formal rules or laws are not obeyed, people look after themselves without caring for other people, and the strongest people have all the advantages: *World leaders have the opportunity to create a new world order where the rule of law, not the law of the jungle, governs the conduct of nations.*

lay down the law

to tell people what to do very firmly, especially when this annoys or upsets them: *I'm sorry, Jackie, but I am going to have to lay down the law this time. You have broken the rules too many times.*

Murphy's law

used to say that the worst possible thing always seems to happen at a time when it is most annoying, preventing you from doing what you are trying to do: *"Why is the traffic always worst when you're already half an hour late?" "It's called Murphy's law."*

NOTE▶ Murphy's law is a humorous rule that says: Whatever can go wrong, will go wrong. There are other rules like this that are often called Murphy's Laws, such as: "Nothing is as easy as it looks," and "Everything takes longer than you think it will." Although many people have ideas about who Murphy might be, no one is sure.

take the law into your own hands (also take matters/things into your own hands)

to deal with a problem yourself, often in a violent or unpleasant way, because you do not think that the officials who ought to be dealing with it are doing it correctly: *If justice for Nikki's murder is not done soon, her family is going to take the law into their own hands.*

lay

⇨LEAVE/lay yourself open (to *something*)

be laid back

to be calm and relaxed, with a tendency not to worry about anything: *The interview went really well. Everyone was very laid back and friendly.*
laid-back: *I agree that you're a laid-back guy, but that isn't an excuse for forgetting to pick me up from work!*

lay it on thick

to say something with a lot of false emotion in order to produce a particular effect, such as making someone like you or feel sorry for you: *Rosemary knew that if she laid it on thick, she would get more sympathy from the jury.*

lay *someone* low

1 to make someone become or feel too sick to do the things that they usually do: *Toby sends his apologies, but he's been laid low with bronchitis or something.*
2 to kill or injure someone: *The 26-inch solid aluminum baton can lay a person low without drawing blood.*

the lay of the land

1 the facts about a situation that you need to know before you do something or make a decision: *Before you start working for us, we'd like you to spend a few hours in the office – it'll help you to get the lay of the land.*
2 the appearance and physical features of the land around you: *My job as a forest ranger requires that I really know the lay of the land.*

lay *someone/something* to rest

1 (also **put** *something* **to rest**) to stop people's fear and anxiety about a situation by dealing with it or giving them more information about it: *The appearance of the two leaders at Tuesday's meeting was designed to put to rest any rumors about disagreements between them.*
2 to bury a dead person with a religious ceremony: *The president was laid to rest in Arlington National Cemetery three days after his assassination.*

lead

⇨*something* went down like a lead **BALLOON**

get the lead out

SPOKEN used to tell someone to hurry: *Come on – get the lead out, or you'll be late for school!*

lead *someone* astray

1 to encourage someone to do bad things that they would not normally do: *Eileen was really mad at me – she thought I was leading Margaret astray.*
2 to explain something in a way that makes people have the wrong idea about a situation: *Some of Gorbachev's supporters privately accused him of leading the socialist world astray.*

something will put lead in your pencil

a humorous expression used in order to tell a man that something will increase his ability to have sex: *Come on, have another drink. It'll put lead in your pencil.*

leaf

⇨a FIG leaf

turn over a new leaf

to start behaving better, and intend to do your work well or become a better person: *Andy claims that he's turned over a new leaf, and that he's going to be more helpful with the housework from now on.*

league

be in league with *someone*

an expression meaning to be working with other people to achieve something, used especially when you do not like or approve of them or what they are doing: *Soon after the trial, it was discovered that the managers were in league with the Mafia.*

someone/something is (way) out of *someone's* league

1 if something that someone wants to buy or do is out of their league, they do not have the money or ability to do or buy it: *I know you like the house, but we don't have that kind of money – Beverly Hills is way out of our league.*

2 if someone is out of someone else's league, you think they are too interesting, attractive, etc. to want to have a relationship with that person: *I wasn't trying to be mean, but I said to him, "Joe, this girl's out of your league. Be careful or you'll get hurt."*

be (way) out of your league
to be trying to do something that you do not have the knowledge, intelligence or skill to do, especially when you are working or competing with people who are better than you are: *She's not just incompetent, she's way out of her league.*
—compare **be out of your DEPTH**

leak

take a leak
SLANG to urinate (=get rid of waste liquids from your body) ◆ USED BY MEN: *Can you wait a second? I'm going to go take a leak.*

leap

⇨**LOOK before you leap**

by/in leaps and bounds
if someone or something increases, develops, grows, etc. by leaps and bounds, they do it very quickly: *Darien is progressing by leaps and bounds in his new school.*

take a flying leap
SPOKEN an impolite expression used to tell someone to go away and stop annoying you: *"My husband won't let me wear red." "You ought to tell your husband to take a flying leap."*

lease

give someone/something a new lease on life
1 to make someone happy and active again after they have been tired, unhappy, or sick: *I was hoping that leaving Chicago for a new job would give me a new lease on life.*
have/gain/enjoy, etc. a new lease on life: *Since I stopped drinking I have a new lease on life – I love being with my children and I am able to take care of them.*
2 to change or improve something so that it can continue to exist or be

effective: *The mall development will give the aging department store a new lease on life.*

leash

keep someone on a short/tight leash
to control someone and not allow them to do things that you do not like: *See if you can get Jerry to come out for a drink – his wife keeps him on a pretty short leash nowadays.*

be straining at the leash
to be eager to start doing something: *We were straining at the leash to set up house together, but we couldn't find an apartment we could afford.*

least

to say the least
used to emphasize that something is even worse or more serious than you are saying it is: *When the doctor told me it was cancer, I was terrified, to say the least.*

leave

leave someone/something hanging
1 to fail to tell someone about a decision, plans, etc. so that they have to wait to see what will happen: *Luke didn't tell us his plans. He just left us both hanging.*
2 to do something with the result that plans, problems, etc. cannot be finished or solved: *We have to talk about these problems, Stephen – we can't just leave them hanging.*

leave someone high and dry
to force someone into a difficult situation without any help: *When Gene left the company, we were left high and dry with no technical support.*

leave/lay yourself open (to something)
(also leave/lay yourself wide open (to something))
to behave or operate in a way that makes it likely that something bad will happen to you, especially that you will be blamed or criticized for something: *Any organization that has to handle large sums of money leaves itself wide open to*

corruption.

leave a lot to be desired
(also **leave much, something, everything, etc. to be desired**)
used to say that something is not as good as it should be: *Elaine's cooking often leaves a certain amount to be desired.*

opposite **leave nothing to be desired**: *A relaxing vacation in beautiful Hawaii leaves nothing to be desired.*

leave well enough alone
to not do anything to change a situation because you do not want to make it worse than it was: *If Devon had left well enough alone, he'd probably still have a job.*

something leaves you cold
SPOKEN used to say that something does not interest or excite you at all: *I've never been interested in becoming a lawyer. The idea of working in that kind of competitive world leaves me cold.*

left

⇨be (way) out in left **FIELD**

hang a left/right
SPOKEN used to tell someone to turn right or left, usually when driving a car: *Go out the door and hang a left. You'll see the restaurant across the street.*

left and right
(also **left, right, and center**)
used to emphasize that something is happening a lot or in many places: *New housing developments are being built left, right, and center in Southern California.*

leg

break a leg!
SPOKEN used humorously in order to wish someone good luck, especially before a performance: *"I've never spoken in front of this many people before." "Don't worry, you'll be fine. Break a leg!"*

have a hollow leg
(also **have hollow legs**)
OLD-FASHIONED used humorously to say that someone can eat a lot or drink a lot of alcohol: *He comes home from football and I just can't fill him up. I swear he's got hollow legs.*

have legs
if an idea or plan has legs it is a good one that is likely to succeed: *We need a financial expert to advise us, someone to tell us whether this thing has legs or not.*

not have a leg to stand on
to be unable to win an argument or make people believe you, because you are unable to prove that a complaint, legal charge, or statement you have made is true: *The family had lost close to $100,000. Unfortunately they didn't have a leg to stand on, so I had to advise them not to take the case to court.*

a leg up
an advantage you get in your job, education, etc. because someone gives you to help or money: *The PACE program lets students earn college credit while still in high school, giving them a leg up in their college careers.*

be on his/her/its, etc. last legs
used to say that something is old and no longer strong or working well, or that someone is old, weak, or very tired: *This hair dryer's on its last legs – I have to remember to get a new one.*

---

be on his/her/its, etc. last legs

be pulling *someone's* leg
SPOKEN to tell someone something that is not true, as a joke: *Karin has such a serious face, you can never tell when she's pulling your leg.*

shake a leg

SPOKEN used to tell someone to hurry: *Come on, Cara, shake a leg – it's almost eight o'clock.*

legend

a legend in your own time/lifetime

used to say that someone is very famous during their life: *It was hard to define what was so special about Marilyn Monroe, yet she was a legend in her own lifetime.*

length

go to great lengths to do *something*
(also **go to extraordinary, huge, considerable, etc. lengths to do** *something*)

to be willing to work very hard or do more than you are expected to do in order to achieve something: *It always amazes us that people will go to such extraordinary lengths to avoid paying a $10 parking ticket.*

keep *someone/something* at arm's length
(also **be, remain, operate, etc. at arm's length from** *someone*)

to avoid being closely involved with someone or something ♦ OFTEN USED IN POLITICS AND BUSINESS: *Russian diplomats are attempting to keep reporters at arm's length until the crisis is resolved.*
arm's-length: *Dole called the transaction an arm's-length loan between two acquaintances and insisted there was no conflict of interest.*

leopard

a leopard can't/doesn't change its spots

used to say that people, groups, organizations, etc. cannot easily change their bad qualities: *I don't think a pessimist can turn into an optimist just like that. Can a leopard change its spots?*

lesser

⇨ **the lesser of two EVILs**

let

let (it) fly

to criticize someone angrily, often by shouting at them: *In her autobiography to be published next month, the veteran actress lets fly against Hollywood and the movie industry.*

let *someone* have it

SPOKEN to shout at someone because you are angry at them: *Boy, Maria really let Wayne have it when he forgot her birthday.*

let it all hang out

to relax and do what you like to do, without worrying about what other people think: *The drama coach is trying to get us to loosen up more and let it all hang out. She wants the whole show to be wild and wacky.*

let it rip

to do something with as much energy as you can: *Montana has had so much power in his legs for the last few games – he got out on the field and completely let it rip.*

let it slip (that)
(also **let slip that...**)

to say something that is supposed to be a secret, without meaning to say it: *In the interview, Lindi let it slip that she had a few famous clients who were in serious legal trouble.*

be let off lightly
(also **get off lightly**)

to be punished less severely than you should be for something wrong or illegal that you have done: *Paying a fine instead of going to jail gives criminals the idea they're getting off lightly.*
let *someone* **off lightly:** *The woman columnist at the "Star" argued that the judge had no real understanding of what the girls had suffered and had let their attackers off lightly.*

let *something* slide

1 SPOKEN (also **let** *something* **ride**) to ignore a bad situation or something annoying that someone says, even though you do not like it: *Nancy made such a mean comment about Jill's weight. I was going to say something, but decided to just let it slide.*

L

2 (also **let things slide**) to let standards become worse, without trying to stop it from happening: *Fred had really let things slide at home while Dana was away. He hadn't washed the dishes all week.*

letter

⇨a red-letter **DAY**

follow/obey *something* **to the letter**
(also **carry** *something* **out to the letter**)
to do something exactly in the way that the rules or instructions tell you to do it: *I knew that Adrian would have carried out his grandmother's wishes to the letter.*

the letter of the law
the exact words of a law or agreement, rather than the general meaning: *According to the letter of the law, Davis can refuse to sign the contract if she wishes.*
—compare **the SPIRIT of the law**

level

⇨at **GUT** level

drag/pull *someone* **down to your level**
to influence someone so that they behave or perform as badly as you do and worse than they usually do: *You're not going to let them make a fool of you and drag you down to their level, are you?*

be on the level
to be honest, legal, or true: *She seemed to be on the level, but maybe she was just a good actress. I didn't know her well enough to decide.*

license

a license to print money
used to say that a situation gives someone a big or unfair advantage over other businesses, or a chance to make a lot of money very easily without much work: *People see music publishing as a license to print money, but actually it can be a risky business.*

lick

give *something* **a lick and a promise**
OLD-FASHIONED to do something quickly, without being careful: *I don't have time to clean everything. I'll just give the house a lick and a promise before they come, and that'll have to be good enough.*

licked

have (got) *something* **licked**
SPOKEN to have succeeded in dealing with or solving a difficult problem: *I'm feeling much better now. I think I've finally got this cold licked.*

licking

take a licking
to be beaten badly in a competition: *The Yankees took a licking last night 8–3.*

lid

blow the lid off *something*
to let people know the truth about a situation that had been a secret or that had not been completely understood before: *Maguire wrote an article blowing the lid off the affirmative action program.*

> NOTE▶ You may also hear people use other verbs such as "rip" or "tear" with this idiom: *The book, written by three former body-guards, ripped the lid off Elvis's life.*

flip your lid/wig
SPOKEN to suddenly become very angry: *Andrea just about flipped her lid when she found out that the hotel had lost her reservation.*

keep the/a lid on *something*
to control a situation so that it does not become worse, or so that secret or private information does not become known: *Kline keeps a tight lid on his private life, and rarely speaks to the press!*

lie

give the lie to *something*
to prove that something that many people think is true is not true ♦ OFTEN USED IN

NEWSPAPERS, ON TELEVISION NEWS, ETC.: *The couple posed for photographers at the show's opening, giving the lie to rumors they'd decided to separate.*

lie in wait (for)

1 to hide in a place and wait for someone so that you can attack them: *The four masked men intended to lie in wait for Collins and shoot him.*

2 if something unpleasant or difficult lies in wait for you, it will happen to you: *Shaw will need luck and determination to meet all the challenges lying in wait for him.*

live a lie

to live in a way that makes you feel dishonest and unhappy with yourself because you are behaving as if you believe or feel things that you do not: *It was the guilt of living a lie for 30 years that forced Marjorie into confessing her secret love affair.*

a white lie

a lie that is not very important, often one that you tell because you do not want to upset someone: *After receiving the fourteen picture frames as wedding gifts, we had to start telling little white lies about how much we loved them.*

life

⇨be the **BANE** of *someone's* **life/ existence**

⇨be made (for life) —see **MAKE**

can't/couldn't do *something* to save your life

SPOKEN used to say that someone has never been able to do something: *Kenny cannot give directions to save his life, even if he's got the map right in front of him.*

can't/couldn't for the life of me

SPOKEN used to say that you are having a lot of trouble doing something: *I can't for the life of me get this jar open. Can you do it?*

a charmed life

a life in which someone is always lucky so that even when they are in dangerous or difficult situations, nothing bad happens to them: *I'd been out of school*

less than two days, and I was on the radio. It was the start of what seemed like a charmed life.

do *something* **for dear life**

to hold or hang onto something with all your strength in order to avoid being hurt, or because you are very frightened: *I was sitting in the yard when I saw a cat, hanging on to a branch of the tree for dear life.*

> NOTE▶ This idiom is most frequently used with verbs like "hold on" or "run" because people are usually talking about a dangerous situation when they use it. However, you may hear people use it in a slightly humorous way with other verbs: *I was writing for dear life on the last essay question when they called time.*

get a life!

SPOKEN said when you are annoyed with someone because you think that they are boring or lazy: *You can't just sit around here all day and complain while I do all the work. Get a life!*

it's a dog's life

said when you are complaining about how difficult your life is, often used humorously to show that life is really very good: *It's a dog's life here on vacation – all this sunshine and good food.*

(as) large/big as life

SPOKEN used to emphasize that it is true that someone is with you or near you: *I looked up, and there was Rollins – standing there as large as life. We hadn't seen or heard from him in more than two years.*

larger than life

used about a person, situation, story, etc. which seems more exciting or interesting than ordinary people or situations, with the result that they do not seem to be real: *Army sergeants are often much larger than life – it takes a big personality to bend a squad of twenty young men to your will.*

larger-than-life: *The chef is a larger-than-life character who is genuinely passionate about producing exquisite meals from the very best ingredients.*

life in the fast lane

an exciting way of living that involves dangerous and expensive activities: *Although it might be hard to believe, Bette Midler told us that life in the fast lane wasn't for her.*

life is (just) a bowl of cherries

OLD-FASHIONED used to say that life is pleasant and fun ♦ OFTEN USED IN THE NEGATIVE: *It takes a long time to learn that life isn't a bowl of cherries – it's full of ups and downs.*

the life of the party

used about someone who is funny and entertaining in social situations: *Scott was always the life of the party in college.*

life's too short

SPOKEN said when you do not want to worry, get angry, or work too hard because these things waste time that could be spent doing more pleasant things: *I'm not going to get upset about it. What's the point? Life's too short.*

live/lead the life of Riley

used to say that someone has a very comfortable, easy life without having to work hard or worry about money: *Who knows where Tom is now – maybe in Tangiers, living the life of Riley.*

not on your life!

SPOKEN used to emphasize that your answer to a question is definitely "no": *I'm not going to the hospital – not on your life!*

put/place your life in *someone's* hands

to put yourself in a situation where someone is responsible for what happens to you: *It's scary placing your life in the hands of a doctor you've never even met before.*
someone's **life is in your hands:** *As a teacher you sometimes feel that these children's lives are in your hands.*
—compare **take your life in your (own) hands**

take your life in your (own) hands

to do something that is dangerous or risky: *The roads are so bad in places that if you drive over 40, you're taking your life in your hands.*

—compare **put/place your life in** *someone's* **hands**

light

the bright lights

used about the interesting and exciting events and activities that happen in big cities: *The bright lights of New York are enough to get even the weary traveler to go out exploring.*

bring *something* to light

to do something that makes people understand or hear about new information: *Historical research brings to light many interesting facts about specific causes of events.*
come to light: *New evidence came to light when a surprise witness testified against Matthews.*
—compare **shed (new) light on** *something*

give *someone/something* the green light

(also **give** *someone/something* **a green light**)
to give someone permission to do something that they are planning to do or have asked to do ♦ OFTEN USED IN NEWSPAPERS, ON TELEVISION NEWS, ETC.: *By that time, Congress had given Clinton the green light to begin negotiations.*
get the green light: *The city council finally got the green light to go ahead and start building the access road.*
something **is a green light:** *The lax laws on drugs are a green light for smugglers to bring illegal narcotics into the country.*

someone hides his/her light under a bushel

used to say that someone is afraid to show their abilities and skills to other people: *If I have any criticism of our organization, it's that we've been hiding our light under a bushel for too long.*

in the cold light of day

if you think about a difficult or exciting situation in the cold light of day, you think about it later when you are calm enough to understand the true meaning of it: *In the cold light of day, the arguments all seemed so ridiculous.*

a leading light in/of *something*

used about someone who is important in a particular group: *The album was recorded by many of the leading lights of the Texas music scene.*

the lights are on, but nobody's home
SPOKEN used to say that someone is stupid or slightly crazy: *"Kevin's brother's a little goofy sometimes." "Yeah, the lights are on, but nobody's home."*

the light at the end of the tunnel
hope for the future after a long and difficult period when you have not been hopeful: *I've had a tough time since I started working again, and it's hard to see the light at the end of the tunnel right now.*

the light of *someone's* life
the person someone loves most: *Iris was his only child, the light of his life.*

make light of *something*
to talk or behave as if something that is important or serious is unimportant or funny: *I don't want to make light of a decision like this. I know having a baby changes your life.*

be out like a light
SPOKEN to go to sleep very quickly, and sleep very deeply: *Don was out like a light. He didn't even hear the phone ring!*

punch *someone's* lights out
to hit someone very hard: *One guy offered me only $70 for an original painting. I could've punched his lights out.*

put *someone/something* in a new, good, bad, etc. light
(also **show** *someone/something* **in a new, good, bad, etc. light**)
to make someone or something seem new, good, etc.: *The application form will give the interviewer a picture of you before you arrive, so it is very important that you complete it to show yourself in the best light.*

see *someone/something* in a different, new, bad, etc. light
(also **view** *someone/something* **in a different, new, bad, etc. light**)
to begin to understand someone or something in a different, new, etc. way: *I hope that people who employ me in the future will view my two years of traveling experiences in a positive light.*

see the light
to suddenly understand or believe something, especially something that other people have been trying to persuade you to understand or believe: *Herrera knew if he could just get the public to see the light, he could get a bill legalizing marijuana to the vote.*

something sees the light of day
if information or an object sees the light of day, it is not kept secret or hidden any more, and becomes known or seen: *The recordings and videotapes are expected to see the light of day when the trial begins on Monday.*

shed (new) light on *something*
(also **throw (new) light on** *something*)
to provide new information that makes a difficult subject or problem easier to understand: *Our first witness is likely to shed some light on the events just before Hazelwood's disappearance.*
—compare **bring** *something* **to light**

lightly
⇨be **LET** off lightly

lightning

lightning never strikes twice
used to say that someone is not likely to have the same kind of good or bad luck twice: *On the theory that lightning never strikes twice, I parked my new car in the same area where the old one had been stolen.*

like (greased) lightning
if you move or go somewhere like lightning, you move or go extremely quickly: *Shannon ran like lightning down the field to score the winning goal.*

lightning rod

be a lightning rod for *something*
to be the person who gets all the blame or criticism in a bad situation although you are not the only one responsible for it, or are not responsible for it at all: *During the Gulf War, oil companies like Chevron became lightning rods for the frustration of anti-war protesters even though they do not, as they said, "own or produce oil in the Persian Gulf."*

like

⇨do something like **CRAZY**

if someone **doesn't like it he/she can lump it**
(also **like it or lump it**)
SPOKEN used to say that you do not care whether someone else likes or approves of what you have said or done because you are determined to do or say it: *I told him the truth tonight. If he doesn't like it he can lump it.*

...like anything
SPOKEN used to emphasize that something happens or is done in large quantities for a long time, to a great degree, etc.: *We were eating like anything over the holidays.*

likes

the likes of me, him, her, etc.
used to talk about people like you, or like someone you are talking about: *The play was a little bit too modern for the likes of me.*

lily

gild the lily
to try to improve something that is already good: *My mother persuaded me that wearing all six medals on my uniform was gilding the lily a little.*

limb

go/be out on a limb
to be the only person who takes or has taken a risk, with the result that you are in a weak position: *I'm going to go out on a limb here and suggest we lower our own salaries until the company is making a profit.*

tear/rip someone **limb from limb**
to attack someone in a violent way: *If I find the man who killed my boy, I'll rip him limb from limb.*

limelight

in/into the limelight
in a situation in which you get a lot of public attention because you are famous or have done something important:
Chanel is back in the fashion limelight again with a gorgeous new spring collection.
opposite **out of the limelight**: *Coleman seems to be determined to stay out of the limelight after his love affair with the press went wrong last month.*

> **NOTE**▸ There are many other verbs that can be used with "limelight." For example, you may hear people say "share the limelight," "steal/grab the limelight from someone," "avoid the limelight," etc.: *American car makers don't like the idea of sharing too much of the limelight with Japanese makers at their own North American International Auto Show.* | *In 1953, Vadim introduced Brigitte Bardot at the film festival, where she stole the limelight to such an extent that the stars could only get their pictures taken by posing with her.*

limit

be the (absolute) limit
SPOKEN said when you are very annoyed with a person, often used humorously when you are only a little annoyed: *Preston's the absolute limit! We've tried to compromise, and he keeps rejecting our offers.*

line

⇨the **BATTLE** lines are drawn
⇨be on the **FIRING LINE**
⇨be out of the **FIRING LINE**

all the way down the line
(also **right down the line** or **all along the line**)
at all times during a situation or activity, or including everyone in the situation or activity: *We owe our success to our supporters, who've been very generous all the way down the line.*
—compare **down the LINE/road**

along/on the same lines
(also **along the lines of ___** or **along these/those lines**)
used to say that something is similar to, or done in a similar way to what you are talking about: *This year's conference is going to be run along the same lines as last year's.*

the bottom line is
(also **that is the bottom line**)
used to tell someone what you think the most important part of a situation is, or what the most important thing to consider is: *The bottom line is that kids who have been in trouble once are likely to do it again – we have to find a way of preventing this.*

> **NOTE▶** This idiom comes from business accounts in which the bottom line is the final line that shows how much profit a company has made or how much money was lost.

bring *something* into line (with)
to change a system, process, rule, etc. in order to make it work or fit with another system, process, or set of rules: *Pfeiffer approved the layoffs as a step in bringing the company's costs into line.*

come on line
if a process, machinery, etc. comes on stream it starts to work or be used ♦ OFTEN USED IN BUSINESS: *As new airlines come on line, ticket prices to new destinations will stay reasonable.*

cross the line
(also **step over the line**)
to start behaving in a way that people consider offensive, immoral, dangerous, or extreme although it may be only slightly different from the way you behaved before: *Hayward said the newspaper had crossed the line of decency by reporting on his sex life.*
—see also **there's/it's a fine LINE between**

down the line/road
(also **further down the line/road**)
at a future time: *I'd like to get a college coaching job, but that's still a few years down the line. | Maybe ten years down the road we'll have enough money to move to somewhere warm.*
—compare **all the way down the LINE**

draw the line (at)
to refuse to do something because you disapprove of it or because you think it is unpleasant: *Look, I've eaten a lot of strange things in my life, but I draw the line at blue pork chops.*
—see also **there's/it's a fine LINE between**

drop *someone* a line
to write a short letter to someone: *Be sure and drop me a line when you have a few spare minutes.*

fall into/in line
to behave or happen according to the rules or laws of a company, organization, country, etc.: *A Canadian official said that aid would be cut off if the country did not fall into line with others that were receiving U.N. funds.*
—compare **step out of LINE**

feed *someone* a line
to tell someone something that is not true so that they will do what you want them to do: *Brian feeds all the girls the same line. He'll tell you he's always been too shy to ask girls out.*

get a line on
to get information about someone or something so that you can understand more about them: *She worked for a while as a pharmacist where she got a line on the drugs and poisons that feature in her detective stories.*

in/on the front line
1 used to say that a person or business is involved in, or responsible for all the latest developments in something: *Hoechst's laboratory is on the front line of medical research.*
2 used to say that a person or organization deals with very difficult, unpleasant, and often dangerous problems in their job: *As a cop, you are in the front line every day – you have to be prepared for that.*
front-line: *The crisis center is a front-line service providing vital support to the community.*

lay it on the line
to tell someone the truth about what they have to do in a situation in a very direct, clear, and firm way: *Anderson has laid it on the line to his players – if their performance isn't acceptable, they're out.*

be (way) out of line
1 to behave badly or in a way that is not acceptable in a particular situation: *Did you tell him he was out of line for yelling at Yuri like that?*
step/get out of line: *If you step out of line one more time, Warner, you're off the team. Do you understand?*

2 (also **be out of line with**) if a number, fact, method, etc. is out of line with a group of other similar things, it does not match with or work in the same way as those things: *California's welfare payments, which are among the nation's most generous, seem to be out of line with the state's ability to pay.*
—compare **step out of LINE**

put/lay your job, life, future, etc. on the line
(also **put/lay your neck, reputation, etc. on the line**)
to do something that makes you risk losing something important, such as your job, your life, or the respect other people have for you: *No matter if your business is public or private, you put your reputation on the line when you handle complaint calls.*

read between the lines
to be able to understand the full meaning of something you hear or read, even though you have not been given all the details: *Chrissie assured me that she was happy with Darryl, but reading between the lines I could see that something was bothering her.*

sign on the dotted line
to make a legal promise that you have to keep, usually by signing a piece of paper: *When buying a new home, make sure you have consulted a lawyer before signing on the dotted line.*

step out of line
to do something that you are not allowed to do according to the rules: *Ford was the boss on the movie set. No actor or actress dared step out of line.*
—compare **fall into/in LINE, be (way) out of LINE**

take a hard line
(also **take a tough, firm, strict, etc. line**)
to be determined to make people behave in the way that you want and unwilling to change your opinions at all ♦ OFTEN USED IN BUSINESS AND POLITICS: *Since taking office 18 months ago, Carter has taken a hard line in contract negotiations with teachers.*
hard-line: *The hard-line Communist government denied it was working on nuclear warheads, but refused to allow international inspections.*
opposite **take a soft line:** *So far police have been taking a soft line on the demonstrations. "We're going to do everything we can to help, as long as things stay peaceful," said the Chief of Police.*

take the line/path of least resistance
(also **choose the line/path of least resistance**)
to choose to behave in a way that will cause fewest problems for you, and result in the least opposition from other people: *Don't be afraid to be firm with your children; if you take the line of least resistance, you will actually make things worse.*

there's/it's a fine line between
(also **there's/it's a thin line between**)
used to say that there is only a slight difference between two things or behaviors, one of which is bad: *There's a thin line between making the customer feel welcome and comfortable in the store, and bothering them.*
—see also **cross the LINE, draw the LINE (at)**

> NOTE▶ There are other expressions that use "line" in this way. For example, you may hear people say that someone or something "walks" or "treads the fine line between two things": *I like him, but I always get the feeling he's walking that fine line between arrogance and self-confidence.* You may also hear people talk about "straddling the line" or "blurring the line" when they mean that it is difficult to understand or explain the difference between two things: *Nude dancing straddles the line between entertainment and prostitution, and the debate over its legality has been fierce.*

toe the line
to say or do what someone in authority expects you to, even when you do not agree with them: *Under the Communist regime, newspaper editors had to toe the line or risk being beaten up by the secret police.*

lining
⇨**(every CLOUD has) a silver lining**

link

the weak link (in the chain)

the one person in a group, or part of a system or process that does not work or perform as well as the others, and is likely to make the group, system, etc. fail: *The military big shots decided that Marsden was the weak link in the chain and dismissed him that day.*

lion

⇨in/into the lion's **DEN**
⇨the lion's **SHARE** of *something*
⇨put your **HEAD** in the lion's mouth

throw *someone* to the lions

OLD-FASHIONED to allow someone to be criticized or blamed for something without helping or protecting them: *Jameson knew there'd be trouble, so he threw me to the lions, and denied all knowledge of the situation.*

lip

⇨*someone* is licking his/her lips —see *someone* is licking his/her **CHOP**s

button/zip your lip

used to tell someone not to say something unpleasant, or not to tell a secret ♦ OFTEN USED BY ADULTS SPEAKING TO CHILDREN: *I suggest you button your lip right now, young man!*

something is on everybody's lips
(also *something* is on the lips of)

1 used to say that a lot of people, especially people in a particular group, are talking or thinking about the same subject: *I think the big question on everyone's lips is why or how someone as nasty as Burrows can get appointed as supervisor?*
2 if a word, name, etc. is on your lips, you say it or are about to say it: *The banks were full of anxious customers with one question on their lips: Are we going to lose our life savings?*

my lips are sealed

SPOKEN used to say that you will not tell a secret: *"I bought Steve a new bike for his birthday, but don't tell him." "Don't worry – my lips are sealed!"*

pay lip service to

to say that you like an idea without doing anything to support it: *It's interesting to see you pay lip service to healthy eating and then give a recipe for chocolate cake.*

read my lips

SPOKEN used before a statement in order to emphasize that you want someone to believe or trust you, especially when you are annoyed because they did not believe you when you said it before: *Read my lips, Omid. I do not want to sleep with you.*

liquid

⇨Dutch/liquid **COURAGE**

list

⇨*someone's* **HIT** list
⇨a **LAUNDRY** list of *something*

a/the shopping list
(also *someone's* **shopping list**)

used about the things that someone wants to obtain, or wants someone to do, especially when they are trying to make an agreement with another person or group: *The union intends to present the employers with a shopping list of demands, including more flexible working hours.*

litmus test

a litmus test

used about an event, decision, etc. that clearly shows what someone or something is really like: *Wilkins has an interesting litmus test of corporate ethics. If you would not be happy telling your family about the actions you are taking, he says, then the company would not want you to take that action.*
—compare **ACID test**

live

someone can/could live with *something*

1 used to say that it does not upset someone to deal with or be responsible for an unpleasant situation: *If you publish this, you'll ruin a man's life – can you live with that?*
2 (also I can/could live with *something*)

used humorously to say that you do not care about the bad parts of a situation because there are also very good things about it: *"If you were married to Kim Basinger, you'd have to deal with all those terrible Hollywood people." "I think I could live with that."*

(you) live and learn

SPOKEN said when someone has just made a mistake, or learned something that surprises them: *"I'm sorry. I had no idea that we weren't allowed to play music in the office." "It doesn't matter, live and learn."*

live and let live

used to say that you should not criticize people because they live or do things in a different way from you: *I can't believe they've banned smoking in all public places. Whatever happened to live and let live?*

live it up

to do things that you enjoy, especially things that involve spending a lot of money: *Don't bother looking for the landlord – he's living it up somewhere in Costa Rica.*

someone lives and breathes *something*

used to emphasize that someone loves being involved in a particular activity very much: *My daughter lives and breathes horses.*

He lives and breathes baseball

be living large

SLANG to be having a good time and enjoying life, especially because you have a lot of money: *Since retiring at the age of 41, Dix has been living large.*

livin'

⇨ **HOW ya livin'?**

load

get a load of

SPOKEN used to tell someone to look at someone or something, especially because they are unusual: *Get a load of that guy in the hat!*

be a load off your mind

used to say that you feel happy because you no longer have to worry about something that you have been worrying about for a long time: *It's a huge load off our minds now that we know who the new landlord will be.*

—see also **be a WEIGHT off your shoulders**

take a load off

SPOKEN used to invite someone to sit down when they come to visit you, especially when you know they are tired: *Come in and take a load off. You must be exhausted after all that running around.*

loaf

half a loaf (is better than none)

used to say that the solution to a problem is acceptable, even though it does not do everything that you wanted, because having something is better than having nothing: *Stevens isn't our ideal candidate, but she's better than the Republican. I guess we'll have to settle for half a loaf.*

lock

lock, stock, and barrel

used to emphasize that you mean all or every part or something: *When you left Atlanta, did you take all your stuff and move back home lock, stock, and barrel?*

under lock and key

1 if something is kept under lock and key, it is kept safely in a place that is locked: *The file on Oswald had been kept under lock and key on the sixth floor of the National Archives.*
2 if someone is kept under lock and key, they are in prison, or locked in a place from which they cannot escape: *Even under lock and key, Lecter was more*

dangerous than the maniac he was helping the FBI to track down.

log

as easy as falling off a log
used to say that something is very easy: *Learning Excel is as easy as falling off a log.*
—see also **as easy as PIE**

sleep like a log/baby
to sleep very well: *I always sleep like a baby after my yoga class.*

loggerheads

be at loggerheads (with *someone*)
used to say that two people, groups, etc. disagree very strongly with each other: *At that time, Washington was still at loggerheads with the European Community over farming subsidies.*

loins

gird (up) your loins
a humorous expression meaning to get ready to do something that will be difficult: *It was time to gird up my loins and do battle with thirty over-excited parents, all desperate for their child to be a star.*

long

⇨**in the long RUN**
⇨**SO long!**

the long and the short of it is
(also **that's the long and short of it**)
SPOKEN used to give someone the basic and most important facts about a situation: *The long and short of it is your mother is going into the hospital, and we're not sure how long she'll be there for.*

be long on ___ but short on ___
(also **be short on ___ but long on ___**)
used to say that something or someone has too much of one quality and not enough of another one, usually a more important or necessary one: *Senator Stamp's arguments were dismissed as long on emotion and short on facts.*

> NOTE▶ You may hear people use either the first or second part of this idiom alone.: *The movie's a little long on special effects, but we liked it.* | *Sorry, I'm a little short on patience this evening.*

look

⇨*someone* **(has) NEVER looked back**

give *someone* a dirty look
to look at someone in a way that shows that you are very angry with them or disapprove of them: *My aunt's friends always used to give me dirty looks when I brought my kids over because they knew I wasn't married.*

look before you leap
used to warn someone to think about the results their actions or decisions might have before they do anything: *The best advice my father ever gave me was when he said, "Look before you leap," when I told him I was getting married. Unfortunately, I ignored him.*

look who's talking!
(also **you're a (fine) one to talk** or **you can/can't talk**)
SPOKEN used to tell someone not to criticize another person because they have faults or problems that are similar to the ones they are criticizing someone else for: *"Cathy worries too much about her children." "Look who's talking – you take Robbie to the doctor when he falls over and scratches his knee."* | *"I can't believe Sue isn't done with that report yet." "You can talk – when are you going to finish yours?"*

take a long, hard look at
to think very hard about what is wrong with your behavior or opinions in order to try and solve your problems: *After almost drinking myself to death one night, I decided it was time to take a long, hard look at my life.*

loop

knock/throw *someone* for a loop
SPOKEN to surprise someone so much that they feel confused or not sure of what to do: *Her question threw me for a loop – I didn't think she'd even been paying attention.*

out of the loop

if someone in a group, organization, company, etc. is out of the loop, they do not know about something that is happening in that group, organization, etc. ◆ OFTEN USED IN BUSINESS AND POLITICS: *I've been out of teaching for so long now that I feel a little out of the loop when new teaching methods are discussed.*
opposite **in the loop:** *Matlin's in the loop on all the big decisions, but he's not able to work full time.*

loose

⇨**HANG loose**

on the loose

1 if a dangerous criminal or animal is on the loose, they are free to go anywhere they want, and may harm people: *A coyote was seen on the loose in the Manor Park neighborhood.*
2 used to say that someone whose behavior ought to be or is usually controlled, is free to do whatever they want: *I'm not sure I like the idea of those kids on the loose in New York.*

lord

lord it over *someone*

to behave in a way that shows you think you are better or more powerful than someone else, especially by telling them what to do: *Kitayama's never used his position to lord it over anyone – everyone seems to like him.*

lose

⇨**not lose any SLEEP over** *something*
⇨**lose/blow your COOL**

lose it

1 to lose control of your behavior because you are very angry or very nervous: *When the linesman called that ball out, I thought Agassi was going to lose it.*
2 to stop being good at a job or activity that you used to be good at: *Just when you think MTV is losing it, they bring in a new program that reminds you how good they can be.*
—compare **lose your TOUCH**

loss

⇨ **at a loss for words** —see **be lost for WORDS**

be at a loss (to do *something*)
(also **be at a loss for an explanation, etc.**)

to not know what to do or say in a difficult situation: *We were all at a loss to explain why the students were not in class.*

cut your losses

if a business or person cuts their losses, they stop doing something that is making them lose money in order to prevent the situation from becoming any worse: *The retail chain decided to cut its losses and discontinue its line of fragrances.*

be a dead loss

SPOKEN to be completely useless: *Nineteen out of twenty of the people that came to audition for the part were a dead loss.*

lost

get lost!

SPOKEN an impolite expression used in order to tell someone to go away: *One of those salesmen came to the door, and I told him to get lost.*

lot

⇨*someone* **has a lot to prove** —see *someone* **has** *something* **to PROVE**

a fat lot of good it does *someone*
(also **a fat lot of use** *someone/something* **is** or **a fat lot of help** *someone/something* **is**)

SPOKEN used to emphasize that someone or something is not helpful or useful: *"I'm going to stop paying my rent as a protest." "Fat lot of good that'll do you – he'll throw you out."*
—see also **fat CHANCE**

someone/something **has a lot to answer for**

SPOKEN used to say that someone or something is partly responsible for the way that a person or group of people thinks or behaves, especially when you do not approve of this way of thinking or behaving: *The people who advertise this stuff have a lot to answer for. It's terrible.*

throw in your lot with *someone*
(also **cast your lot with** *someone*)
to join or support someone so that what happens to you depends on what happens to them: *A year and a half ago, I threw my lot in with a million other fat Americans in the diet of the moment.*

love

all's fair in love and war
used to say that rules are not always followed in some situations, especially situations involving competition: *Robinson was willing to do whatever it took to win the game. All's fair in love and war.*

> NOTE▶ People often use another word instead of "war" to make the idiom fit the situation they are talking about or to make a joke: *We were friends, but we'd steal a story from each other whenever we could, claiming all's fair in love and journalism.*

not...for love nor/or money
SPOKEN used to emphasize that you cannot, or will not do something: *I wouldn't eat at that place again for love or money.*

for the love of God/Christ
(also **for the love of Pete/Mike**)
SPOKEN used to emphasize how much you want something to happen, or said when you are very surprised, angry, or frightened: *For the love of God! What happened to you?*

> NOTE▶ Some people think it is offensive to use "God" or "Christ" in this way and therefore say "Pete" or "Mike" instead.

there is no love lost (between)
(also **not much love lost**)
used to say that two people, groups, or organizations dislike each other: *"She didn't even come to see him in the hospital." "Well, there's no love lost between them, is there?"*

lowdown

the lowdown (on *someone/something*)
the most important and useful facts about someone or something, especially ones that can be used in order to gain an advantage: *If you want to get the real lowdown on the Mountain View City Council, take a look at their current economic statement on page five.*

luck

⇒**a hard-luck STORY**
⇒**take POT luck**

beginner's luck
unusually good luck you have when you do something you have never done before: *"I beat you last time." "Beginner's luck – it won't happen again!"*

be down on your luck
to have no money because you have had bad luck for a long time: *Money you donate to the charity will help people who are down on their luck.*
down-on-your-luck: *The paper described Moore as a down-on-her-luck ex-model who lied about her use of drugs.*

the luck of the devil
(also **the luck of the Irish**)
used to say that someone's luck is very good: *It could only have been the luck of the Irish that saved Martin Donnelly in that horrendous crash in the Grand Prix.*

the luck of the draw
used to emphasize that the result of something depends on chance, and cannot be controlled or known before it happens: *My sister passed her driving test before I did – I think it's just the luck of the draw; it depends on what examiner you get, and what kind of mood they're in.*

no such luck
SPOKEN said when you are disappointed because something is not true or did not happen: *I thought that he might offer me something to drink, but no such luck.*

push your luck
(also **be pushing it**)
to risk doing something too much or too often, when it might cause problems, or

to ask someone to do too much, when it might make them angry with you: *"Can we go out for ice cream after we get hamburgers?" "Don't push your luck."*

tough luck

SPOKEN an impolite expression used to say that you do not care about someone's problem: *If he doesn't like what we're having for dinner, then that's his tough luck.*

lull

⇨the CALM/lull before the storm

lump

a lump in your throat

the feeling that you cannot speak because you want to cry: *Every time I watch that scene in Dr. Zhivago, I get a lump in my throat.*

take your lumps

to accept the bad things that happen to you and not let them upset you: *Every word that appears in my column is written by me. If it's good, I want the credit, and if it's bad, I take the lumps.*

lunch

do lunch

SPOKEN to eat lunch together with some-one, especially in order to talk or discuss something: *Well, it was nice seeing you. Give me a call sometime – let's do lunch.*

be out to lunch

SPOKEN used to say that someone is talking or behaving in a confused or slightly crazy way: *The two main characters are both disasters in their own way. Edina is a bitch, and Patsy is permanently out to lunch.*

there is no (such thing as a) free lunch

used to say that you cannot get anything without working for it or paying for it in some way ◆ OFTEN USED IN NEWSPAPERS, ON TELEVISION NEWS, ETC.: *As a country, we must face the fact that there is no free lunch, and that there is a tax bill for every public welfare program.*

lurch

leave *someone* in the lurch

to leave someone without any help or support at a time when you should stay and help them: *Three million jobless Americans were left in the lurch as senators passed a bill cutting federal benefits.*

M

ma'am

wham bam, thank you ma'am

1 SPOKEN a humorous expression used about a situation in which someone, usually a man, has sex with someone who he does not care about, and who he does not see again: *It was just wham bam, thank you ma'am, and he was out the door. I didn't even see him go.*

2 (also **wham bam**) used to say that something happens suddenly, usually without much preparation or warning, and is finished very quickly: *With fruit desserts, you can pretty much throw things together and – wham bam! – you've got something that will warm even the hardest of hearts.*

magic

⇨have the magic TOUCH

make

⇨HAVE (got) it made
⇨make a GO of *something*
⇨WHAT makes *someone* tick

something **can/will make or break** *someone*
(also *something* **is make or break (for** *someone***))**
used to say that someone or something is important enough to make someone or something succeed, or make them fail completely ♦ OFTEN USED IN NEWSPAPERS, ON TELEVISION NEWS, ETC.: *A review by Frank Rich of "The New York Times" can usually make or break a show on Broadway.*
make-or-break: *A make-or-break year could be in store for companies in direct competition with Microsoft Corp.*

be made (for life)

to be so rich that you will never have to work again: *The lucky person who wins the lottery will be made for life!*

make good

1 to become rich and successful after being poor and unknown in your early life: *When she returned to her home town, the local papers were full of stories of "Local Girl Makes Good."*

2 if you make good on a promise, you do what you have promised to do: *Successful companies make good on their promises to be courteous, quick, accurate, and accessible.*

make it big

to become very successful and famous, especially as an actor or musician: *Unlike many tough guys who made it big in movies, Marvin didn't come from a disadvantaged background.*

make it snappy!

SPOKEN a slightly impolite expression used in order to tell someone to do something quickly: *I'll have the breakfast special, and make it snappy.*

be on the make

1 to be trying to have a sexual relationship with someone: *For once, Helen had found a guy who wasn't continually on the make.*

2 to be always trying to get money or advantages for yourself, especially in an unfair or dishonest way: *Paul's always on the make – you can't trust him to do anything except send you his bill.*

they don't make 'em like they used to
(also **they don't make 'em like that anymore**)
SPOKEN used to say that the quality of something is not very good compared to a time in the past: *With the high divorce rate these days, I'd have to say that they don't make marriages like they used to.*

maker

meet your maker

an expression meaning to die, used when you do not want to say this directly: *Thurman's widow would sometimes admit that she was happier since Thurman had gone to meet his maker.*

makings

have the makings of *something*

to have the ability or qualities needed to become a particular kind of person or thing: *Fred wants a kid, but I don't think he has the makings of a good father.*

M

mama

mama's boy
used about a man or boy who allows his mother to protect him too much and is considered weak: *Scott, you're such a mama's boy. Grow up!*

man

⇨**every man has his price** —see everyone has their **PRICE**
⇨**man's best FRIEND**

be as ___ as the next guy/man/woman
(also **do** *something* **as much as the next guy/man/woman**)
used to say that you have as much of a quality as anyone else, or are able to do something as well as anyone else, especially when you are explaining the reason for something you have said: *While Handelman likes a party as much as the next guy, he's staying away from North Beach on New Year's.* | *Remember, your own ideas are just as good as the next person's, and maybe even better.*

big man on campus
a college student who is well-known for being involved in a lot of activities, and who thinks he is very important because of this: *At Brown, Ronnie was a big man on campus, and everyone knew he was near the top of the class.*

every man for himself
used about a situation in which people look after themselves and do not help each other: *We couldn't get out the lifeboats, we just jumped into the water, and after that, it was every man for himself.*

going to see a man about a horse
SPOKEN said when you do not want to tell someone where you are going or why, for example when you need to go to the toilet: *Excuse me a moment – I'm going to see a man about a horse.*

the grand old man of *something*
used about a man who has been involved in an activity or profession for a long time and is greatly respected: *The exhibition evokes thoughts of Monet, the grand old man of Impressionism.*

if you want ...*someone* is your man/woman
(also **if you want ...***someone* **is the man/woman)**
SPOKEN used to say that a particular man is the best person to help someone or do a particular job: *If you want specific details on the new software, McGuire's your man.*

someone is a marked man
used to say that a man is in danger because someone wants to harm or defeat him: *Verkhovensky was a marked man because of the liberal views he held.*

a ladies' man
a man who likes to spend time with women and thinks they enjoy being with him: *Vechey is divorced and sees himself as a real ladies' man.*

man cannot live by bread alone
used to say that people need things for the mind and spirit as well as food, money, and possessions: *Many of John Denver's songs remind us that man cannot live by bread alone.*

a man's gotta do what a man's gotta do
(also **you gotta do what you gotta do**)
SPOKEN a humorous way of saying that you have to do something although you do not want to do it: *I know leaving home won't be easy, but sometimes a man's gotta do what a man's gotta do.*

a man of his word
(also **a woman of her word**)
used about someone who always does what they have promised to do: *I am a woman of my word – I intend to give Tyler his bonus, as we agreed.*

a man of straw
(also **straw man**)
1 an unimportant man who has no power, or someone with a weak character: *My father owns everything – he makes all the decisions. I am just a straw man.*
2 an idea that someone spends too much time arguing about or criticizing, when it is not really very important: *Anytime I try to talk about our relationship, Brad finds a man of straw to talk about instead.*

the man upstairs
OLD-FASHIONED God: *I had just moved away when the rock crashed down exactly where I had been standing. It was a warning from the man upstairs.*

a man/woman after your own heart
a humorous expression used when you like someone because they do the same kinds of thing you do: *My mother-in-law saw me eating chocolate before breakfast and told me I was a woman after her own heart.*

be a man/woman of the world
SPOKEN a humorous expression used about a man or woman who knows a lot about life and is not easily shocked by things, for example sex: *So what happened when you went back to his place, Carrie? You can tell us – we're all women of the world.*

the man/woman on the street
an ordinary man or woman: *What the average man on the street wants to see is a reduction in state taxes.*
man-in-the-street: *Frankenheimer's love of old-fashioned melodrama sometimes works against his man-on-the-street realism, but overall I enjoyed the movie.*

the men in (gray) suits
used when you disapprove of the people who have power in a business or organization, especially when you think that they all have the same ideas, and do not understand ordinary people: *What we don't need is another dull American city run by men in gray suits without an understanding of the past or a vision of the future.*

no more ...than the man in the moon
(also **as much ...as the man in the moon**)
SPOKEN used to emphasize a negative statement: *I assure you, I have as much influence on state taxes as the man in the moon.*

our man in ___
OLD-FASHIONED used about someone who works for you and sends you information from a particular place, especially another country: *Senior career officer Frank Swenson, now our man in Jakarta, is heading for Moscow.*

someone's **right-hand man**
(often someone's **right-hand woman, person, etc.**)
the person who works most closely with someone to help and support them, and is trusted by them ♦ OFTEN USED IN NEWSPAPERS, ON TELEVISION NEWS, ETC.: *Abernathy was Martin Luther King's right-hand man during the civil rights struggle.*

separate the men from the boys
if a difficult situation separates the men from the boys, it shows clearly which people have the ability to do something and which do not: *The eighth round of the tournament is traditionally the one that separates the men from the boys.*

---

separate the men from the boys

to a man
used to emphasize that all the people in a group are doing the same thing or have a particular quality: *The islanders, patriotic to a man, are prepared to fight for their independence.*

you can't keep a good man/woman down
used to say that if someone is determined and good at what they do, they will succeed in spite of difficulties: *Sanchez made two more aces later in the game. You can't keep a good woman down.*

be your own man/woman
used to say that someone does what they

want, without being influenced by other people, or taking orders from them: *The President's wife is very much her own woman, and many think she has increased his popularity with women voters.*

manna

manna from heaven
(also manna in the desert/wilderness)
something very useful or helpful that is received unexpectedly: *Rain, the manna from heaven Midwest farmers hoped for during the drought, has now flooded fields, and damaged crops.*

> NOTE▶ In the Bible, "manna" is bread that came from heaven when the people of Israel had nothing to eat in the desert.

map

Do I have to draw you a map?
SPOKEN said when you are annoyed because you have to spend a lot of time explaining something to someone: *You want me to explain the instructions again? Do I have to draw you a map?*

put someone/something on the map
to make a place, person, or thing famous or well-known ◆ OFTEN USED IN NEWSPAPERS, ON TELEVISION NEWS, ETC.: *The wines made from the grapes we grow here are helping to put Sonoma County on the map.*

wipe something off the map
to destroy a place or a community completely so that it no longer exists: *Experts say that a huge earthquake could wipe parts of California off the map.*

marbles

lose your marbles
SPOKEN to start behaving in a crazy way: *I have no idea why he wants to divorce Christine – he must have lost his marbles.*

pick up your marbles and go home
to leave a discussion or meeting because you are angry ◆ OFTEN USED IN BUSINESS AND POLITICS: *When you enter into a business contract, you have to abide by the rules –*

you can't just pick up your marbles and go home if you disagree.

> NOTE▶ Marbles is a game that children played in the past, using small colored glass balls.

march

steal a march on someone
to get an advantage over someone by doing something before they do it, or before they expect you to do it: *Verisign, a small California firm, appears to have stolen a march on its bigger competitors.*

Marines

tell that to the Marines!
SPOKEN said when you do not believe what someone has said: *So the jokes that men make about women are only made in a spirit of harmless fun? Tell that to the Marines!*

mark

a black mark (against someone)
something that makes people dislike someone or disapprove of them: *The scandals of the past few years have put a black mark on the Democratic Party.*

be close to the mark
if a statement, description, or guess is close to the mark, it is mostly true of almost exact, but not completely: *My job title is Administrative Assistant – office psychologist would be closer to the mark.*
—see note at **hit the MARK**

hit the mark
1 if a statement hits the mark, it is true and exact: *He looked so mad that Jamila knew she had hit the mark.*
2 to be successful in getting the effect that you want: *The film's scenery is spectacular, its soundtrack is great, and most of the acting hits the mark.*
opposite **miss the mark:** *It is easy to write test questions that are perfectly correct with respect to grammar but still miss the mark because the students do not understand them.*

> NOTE▶ A mark is what you aim at when you practice shooting a gun.

leave your mark (on)
to have an important effect on someone or something that lasts for a long time: *Babe Ruth left a permanent mark on baseball history.*

make your mark (in/on)
(also **make a mark in/on**)
to do something new, special, or successful that makes people notice you: *It is very difficult to make a mark in experimental physics these days.*

be (way) off the mark
if a statement, description, or guess is off the mark, it is not correct or true: *The magazine article was way off the mark in many respects, but unfortunately many people have accepted it as the truth.*
opposite **be (right) on the mark:** *Your advice about staying in college was right on the mark.*
—see note at **hit the MARK**

overshoot the mark
to go past the place that you are trying to get to: *After half an hour we realized that we had overshot the mark, and turned back.*
—see note at **hit the MARK**

be quick off the mark
to be good at understanding a situation quickly and doing what needs to be done, especially to gain an advantage: *The Broncos were quick off the mark, and scored a touchdown in the first three minutes.*
opposite **be slow off the mark:** *If you were slow off the mark in taking up the offer of a low interest rate in January, you may have a chance to try again in October.*

NOTE▶ A mark is the place where runners begin a race.

be wide of the mark
used to say that a statement, calculation, or guess is not correct or exact enough: *Predictions of economic growth of 4% per year are probably very wide of the mark.*
—see note at **hit the MARK**

market

corner the market (on)
to gain control of the whole supply of a particular kind of goods, or be the only supplier of a particular service so that people cannot buy it from anyone else: *The mega-farms who can afford to produce at a loss can outlive the family farms and corner the market.*

be in the market (for *something*)
to be interested in buying something, and able to afford it: *The car looks great in the brochure, but I'm not really in the market for a convertible.*

master

be a past master (at *something*)
to be very good at doing something because you have done it a lot: *Frank Langella, the star and driving force of this film, is a past master at playing the evil villain.*

someone **serves two masters**
used to say that someone must live according to two different ideas, or be loyal to two different groups at the same time, especially when this is difficult: *You have the difficult position of serving two masters – the customer who pays you and the supplier who you have to pay.*

mat

go to the mat (for *someone*)
to do everything you can to solve a difficult problem, win an argument, etc., often in order to help someone who is not as powerful as you ♦ OFTEN USED IN BUSINESS AND POLITICS: *Latitia's great to work for. You know she'll go to the mat for you if you're in trouble.*

match

get into a pissing match (with)
SPOKEN a fairly impolite expression meaning to have an argument or competition with someone in order to find out who is best: *I just wanted to have a nice and friendly game of tennis – I didn't want to get into a pissing match with you!*

meet your match
to be defeated or have difficulty in a competition, sport, etc. that you normally win easily because your new opponent is as strong, intelligent, or skillful as you are:

M

Hopkins junior, Casey Jones met his match in high school wrestling Thursday, losing to senior Jerry Hart of Minnetonka.

the whole shooting match
used to emphasize that you are talking about everything in a group of similar things, or everything that is involved in a particular activity: *All you have to do is punch in the program number, and VCR Plus+ will operate the whole shooting match – your video player, TV, and cable box – for you.*
—see also **the whole SHEBANG**

matter

⇨take matters into your own hands
  —see take the LAW into your own hands

as a matter of course
if something is done in a particular way as a matter of course, it is normally done that way: *A large company like yours should supply your customers with this information as a matter of course.*

be no laughing matter
(also **not be a laughing matter**)
used to say that a situation is serious: *The water scared me, and since I didn't know how to swim, it was no laughing matter when Jack pushed me into the deep end.*

McCoy

the real McCoy
used to say that something is real, and not a copy: *When buying art, make sure it is the real McCoy before putting out any money.*
—see also **the genuine ARTICLE**

meal

make a meal (out) of *something*
to spend too much time, effort, or emotion doing something: *We have been rehearsing this scene for three hours now – let's not make a meal out of it.*

a meal ticket
used about a thing or person that someone uses to get the money that they need to live, often in spite of the fact that they do not like or respect that thing or person: *The goal for some desperate women is to find a husband who will be a meal ticket.*

a square meal
a healthy meal that fills your stomach: *You'll feel a whole lot better once you have a good square meal inside you.*

meaning

someone doesn't know the meaning of (the word) ___
used to say that someone has never experienced a particular emotion or situation, or has never learned about a particular idea: *I was attempting to train a group of young people who didn't know the meaning of the word discipline.*

means

by all means
SPOKEN used to give someone permission to do something, or to agree that they should do something: *If you think Ted would be interested in the talk, by all means bring him along.*

by fair means or foul
using any method that is necessary to get or achieve what you want, even unfair, dishonest, or illegal methods: *What made Crighton so difficult to talk to was his insistence on winning every argument, by fair means or foul.*

by no means
(also **not... by any means**)
used to emphasize a negative statement: *Discrimination does exist in this university, and it is by no means a minor problem.* | *Although these books are several years old, they are by no means out of date.*

something is a means to an end
used to say that something is only done or used in order to obtain something else, and is not considered important for any other reason: *For most of my friends, law school was just a means to an end. For me, however, it was an exciting challenge.*

measure

for good measure
if you add something for good measure, you do or use it in addition to what has already been done or used in order to be sure you get the result that you want: *The*

new CD will feature Clapton, with a few guest artists thrown in for good measure.

meat

someone is dead meat
SPOKEN used to say that someone is going to be very angry with someone else: *Touch that TV and you're dead meat!*

the meat and potatoes of something
the most basic and usual parts of a job, profession, or situation: *Crime, parks, and traffic have always been the meat and potatoes of city elections.*
meat-and-potatoes: *Hermann discusses complicated problems in meat-and-potatoes language that we can all understand.*
—compare *someone's* **BREAD** and butter

a meat market
used about a place such as a club that you do not like because most of the people who go there are only interested in having sex with people: *Jen always wants to go dancing at the Starlight – but it's such a meat market! How can she stand it?*

medium

a/the happy medium
a way of doing something that is somewhere between two possible choices, and that satisfies everyone: *When planning a party, you need to find a happy medium between what's going to please you, and what's going to please your guests.*

meet

⇨meet your **MAKER**

meet *someone* halfway
if two people or groups who are trying to make an agreement meet halfway, they each agree to do something the other wants: *If the new highway policy is to succeed, taxpayers will have to meet it halfway.*

meeting

⇨a meeting of (the) **MINDs**

memory

⇨take a **TRIP**/walk/stroll down memory lane

have a memory like an elephant
(also **have the memory of an elephant**)
to be very good at remembering things, especially things that have happened to you: *I doubt if your aunt has forgotten what you said to her. She has a memory like an elephant.*

have a memory like a sieve
SPOKEN to keep forgetting things: *I totally forgot to bring that address for you. I have a memory like a sieve lately.*

men

—see **MAN**

mend

be on the mend
to be getting better after an illness or injury, or after a difficult period: *The flu was terrible, but we're both on the mend now.* | *Mexico's education system appears on the mend after many decades of neglect.*

merrier

⇨the **MORE** the merrier

message

get the message
to understand what someone is telling or asking you, especially after they have told you several times: *Democrats are finally getting the message – voters are concerned about taxes.* | *How many times do I have to tell you "No"? Get the message – I don't want to go out with you!*

messenger

shoot the messenger
to blame or punish the person who tells you that something is wrong instead of the person who is responsible for it: *In organizations that are well known for shooting the messenger, employees learn to avoid their manager in times of trouble or crisis.*

M

method

there's method in *someone's* **madness**

used to say that even though someone is behaving strangely, there is a sensible reason for what they are doing: *If I don't check the books out, then I won't have to pay if I bring them back late. See, there's method in my madness.*

mettle

test your mettle

if a situation, especially a difficult one, tests your mettle, it shows how well you can do something: *The new training exercise will not only teach the new firefighters about the job, it will also test their mettle.*
—see also **SEE what** *someone* **is (really) made of**

prove/show your mettle: *The tiny submarine was designed to go where divers cannot, and it proved its mettle on the first dive.*

Midas

the Midas touch

the ability to earn money very easily ♦ USED ESPECIALLY IN NEWSPAPERS: *Pavarotti, the Italian vocal artist, is a unique performer with the Midas touch.*

> NOTE▶ This idiom comes from the old story of King Midas, who had the ability to turn anything he touched into gold.

middle

(out) in the middle of nowhere

used about a place that you do not like because it is far away from any other towns, houses, people, etc.: *Can you believe it? I was in the middle of nowhere, and my car broke down! I had to walk for miles to find help.*

knock *someone* **into the middle of next week**

SPOKEN to hit someone very hard: *If you ever talk to me like that again, I'll knock you into the middle of next week!*

midnight

burn the midnight oil

to work or study until very late at night: *John has been burning the midnight oil for months, trying to finish this contract.*

might

might makes right

used to say that someone who has power can do whatever they want: *Any country believing that might makes right will be refused foreign aid.*

mile

do *something* **a mile a minute**

used to say that someone or something is doing something very fast: *Debbie came in this morning talking a mile a minute about her trip to Australia – she's so excited.* | *Jill tried to hide behind the door, her heart beating a mile a minute.*

go the/that extra mile

to make a special effort or do more than you have been asked to do in order to achieve something: *We think it's important to go the extra mile, so we offer our customers everything we can possibly think of – like refunds, gifts, and special offers.*

like five, ten, etc. miles of bad road

SPOKEN used to say that something is not enjoyable or not good: *"How was work today?" "Like five miles of bad road."*

be miles off/away

SPOKEN a measurement, guess, or calculation that is completely wrong: *I hate having to guess other people's ages. I'm always miles off and end up insulting someone.*

see/know/tell *something* **a mile away**

used to say that it is very easy to say what someone or something really is, especially if it is supposed to be a secret: *"How did you know it was me? I didn't even say anything." "Yeah, but I'd know your laugh a mile away."*

someone would run a mile

SPOKEN used to say that someone is very unwilling to do something or be involved

M

in a situation: *"So are you and Gary going to have children?" "He'd run a mile if I even suggested getting a dog."*

milk

it's no use crying over spilled milk

SPOKEN used to say that you should not worry about something bad that has already happened: *I was disappointed when Sam didn't call me again, but it's no use crying over spilled milk.*

the milk of human kindness

kindness and sympathy for other people: *How can people wish such terrible things on other people? Whatever happened to the milk of human kindness?*

mill

go through the mill

to have a long, unpleasant and difficult experience: *Souter has been through the mill before when he was being confirmed as a judge in the first district – now he's got to do it again.*
put *someone* **through the mill:** *We should not be putting homeless people through the mill. We should be helping them to rebuild their lives.*

millstone

a millstone around your neck

used about a problem that is stopping you from succeeding or progressing: *This man has been like a millstone around your neck for the last four years – why don't you just get rid of him?*

mince

⇨**not mince your WORDs**

mincemeat

make mincemeat (out) of

to defeat someone easily in an argument, competition, etc.: *Aggressive judges make mincemeat out of unprepared lawyers.*

mind

⇨**give** *someone* **a PIECE of your mind**
⇨*someone's* **HEAD/mind is buzzing (with** *something***)**
⇨**in your mind's EYE**
⇨**be a LOAD off your mind**
⇨**mind/watch your P'S AND Q'S**

blow your mind

SPOKEN if an experience blows your mind, it is so impressive, unusual or shocking that it is difficult to believe: *It blew my mind when I got an "A" on the test without even studying.*
mind-blowing: *These really are mindblowing pictures. I mean, how often do you get to see evidence of an ocean on another planet?*

something **boggles the mind**

used to say that you think an idea, action, or event is so strange or surprising that it is difficult to imagine: *It just boggles my mind to think of how much money the government spends each year on national defense.*
mind-boggling: *"GQ" magazine has made a mind-boggling $150 million this year.*

be bored out of your mind/skull

SPOKEN to be so bored that you feel like you are becoming crazy: *I sat with my brother watching one of his Kung-fu movies, bored out of my mind.*
—see also **be BORED stiff**

> NOTE▶ You may hear people use other words instead of "mind": *Everywhere we looked there were men, bored out of their trees, with nothing to think about but sex.*

cross your mind

if a thought or idea crosses your mind you think about it suddenly, or for a short time: *As we stood there in the freezing cold, about to jump into the ocean, it did cross my mind that we were all crazy. | Even though I hated college, it never crossed my mind that I could quit at any time.*

go out of your mind

to become so confused, worried, frightened, etc. that you feel you are becoming crazy: *I counted the parts twice, but there was still one missing. "I must be going out of my mind," I thought.*
be frightened, worried, etc. out of your mind: *It's late – where have you been? I have been worried out of mind about you!*
—compare **be out of your MIND**

M

great minds think alike

SPOKEN a humorous expression said when someone has the same idea, or says the same thing as you at the same time: *"How did you know I was going to say that?" "Great minds think alike."*

someone **has a mind of his/her own**

used to say that someone or something does what they want to do, instead of doing or thinking what they are told to: *Michelle's father said, "Both my daughters were well-educated and have minds of their own, so I trust them to marry the right man."*

something **has a mind of its own**

used to say that a machine, vehicle, etc. does not do what you want it to do: *My shopping cart had a mind of its own, and refused to go in a straight line, except when I wanted to turn a corner.*

have a closed mind (about)

to be unwilling to change your ideas or opinions on a particular subject: *The President cannot have a closed mind about civil rights issues.*
closed-minded: *I want to be a journalist, but my dad is so closed-minded that he won't even talk to me about it.*
—compare **have/keep an open MIND (about)**

have a good mind to do *something*

SPOKEN said when you are considering doing something because you are angry, especially when you probably will not do it: *I have a good mind to send you home after the way you acted.*

have half a mind to do *something*

SPOKEN used to say that you want to do something, but you will probably not do it because you know it would be stupid, wrong, or might cause you trouble: *Paul's been so moody lately, I've got half a mind to ask him not to come with us.*

have/keep an open mind (about)

to be willing to listen to other people's opinions and change your ideas if you agree: *I'm keeping an open mind until I've heard all the evidence.*
open-minded: *Since I've started traveling overseas, I've become so much more open-minded.*

—compare **have a closed MIND (about)**

have *something* on your mind

to keep thinking about something or worrying about it: *Did you have something specific on your mind that you wanted to talk about?*
be on your mind: *Your dad's health has been on my mind all week. Is he feeling any better ?*

have a one-track mind

to think or talk about only one subject most of the time: *"You just have a one-track mind," Sheila said as he pulled her down and kissed her.*

if/when you put your mind to it

used to say that someone has the ability to achieve something if they decide to make an effort, especially when they do not often do this: *David could do really well in math if he put his mind to it.*

it/*something* slipped your mind

SPOKEN used to say that you temporarily forgot something you were supposed to do: *Haven't I told you that Dawn and Jared are moving? With all the other excitement going on around here, it must have slipped my mind.*

it's all/only in *someone's* mind

used to say that someone is imagining a situation or problem that does not actually exist: *Audrey was tired of going to the doctor and being told that her illness was all in her mind.*

know your own mind

to be very sure of what your opinions are, and what you want to do, and be unlikely to be influenced by anyone else: *Darcy has always been tough and known her own mind, but she's basically a really shy girl.*

lose your mind

to become crazy, or to lose your ability to think clearly: *I'm so bored here that sometimes I think I'm completely losing my mind.*

a meeting of (the) minds

used to say that two people, groups, etc. have similar ideas about a subject, or want the same result, especially when you expect them to disagree ◆ USED

ESPECIALLY ABOUT POLITICS: *Legislative leaders have been asked to hold a meeting of the minds in order to resolve this new financial crisis.*

someone's **mind is in the gutter**
SPOKEN said when you disapprove because someone enjoys thinking or talking about things that shock people, especially sex: *Pat can take any topic and somehow turn the conversation to sex – his mind is really in the gutter.*

mind over matter
used to say that you can do something that seems very difficult, or even impossible, if you really want to: *Marcel says that it's a case of mind over matter, and that anyone could perform the kind of acrobatics that he does.*

nobody in his/her right mind would do *something*
(also **no___in his/her right mind**)
used to say that you think it would be very stupid or unreasonable to do something: *Nobody in their right mind would try to come in and renovate this old building.* | *What man in his right mind would want to go to war?*

be of one mind
(also **be of the same mind**)
used to say that two or more people have the same opinion about a particular situation or want the same things from it: *"We're trying to negotiate the sale of our oldest, continually-operated railroad, and I think we're all of one mind that the service should be maintained," said Philbin.*

be of two minds
to be unable to decide what to do, or what you think about something: *The average citizen is of two minds about health care issues.*

be out of your mind
(also **be out of your head, tree, skull, etc.**)
used to say that someone is crazy, or that their behavior is affected by drugs or alcohol: *Are you out of your mind? You can't drive with that much alcohol in you!*
—compare **go out of your MIND**
—see also **be off your ROCKER**

pay *someone/something* **no mind**
(also **pay no mind to**)
to ignore what is happening or what someone is saying: *Pay him no mind. He's just teasing you.*

read *someone's* **mind**
to know what someone is thinking even though they have not said anything: *What do you want me to say? I can't read your mind, you know.*
mind reader: *Your mother-in-law is not a mind reader – you need to tell her how you feel.*

speak your mind
to say exactly what you think, without feeling embarrassed or shy: *Professor Bell was not afraid to speak his mind, and many students left his lectures in tears.*

mine
be a mine of information (on/about *something*)
used to say that someone knows a lot about a particular subject, or that a book, computer, etc. contains a lot of useful information: *Cancer victims have found the Internet to be a gold mine of information on the disease.*

mint
⇨in mint CONDITION

minute
there's one born every minute
(also **there's a sucker born every minute**)
SPOKEN used to say that someone was stupid to believe or trust something or someone: *You don't even know Ryan, and you let him borrow your car? Well, there's one born every minute!*

up-to-the-minute
including all of the newest information: *Announcers will be providing up-to-the-minute details about the floods.*

misery
put *someone* **out of their misery**
1 to kill an animal or person because they are suffering through sickness or injury: *Doctors often receive requests from terminally ill patients to put them*

out of their misery, but such action would be illegal.
2 to finally explain a situation to someone, or tell them something after you have refused to for some time: *Come on, Rachel, put us out of our misery! Are you guys getting married, or what?*

miss

a miss is as good as a mile
a humorous expression used in order to say that if you have failed, it does not matter whether you failed by a lot or by a little: *The rejection letter said I did very well in the interview, but a miss is as good as a mile if you ask me.*

Mohammed
⇨**Mohammed must go to the MOUNTAIN**

mojo

put/work a mojo on *someone*
(also **put the whammy on** *someone*)
SPOKEN to make someone do something using magic powers, or to be very good at making someone do things so that it seems like you have magic powers: *I swear that woman put a mojo on me. I'd never said things like that to a girl before in my life.*

molasses

slower than molasses (in January)
OLD-FASHIONED used to emphasize that someone does something very slowly: *What's taking you so long? You're slower than molasses in January.*

mold

break the mold
to do something in a way that is new, different, and better than usual: *Hilary Clinton was the first woman to break the mold and change the traditional role of First Lady.*
mold-breaking: *The winners of the Blue Ribbon Education Awards displayed many of the qualities that will be necessary for the mold-breaking schools of the future.*

NOTE▶ A mold is a container that a liquid such as melted metal is poured into so that it will form a particular shape when it becomes solid.

from the same mold (as)
used to say that a person or thing is as good as or very similar to someone or something else of the same type: *Many baseball fans will agree that Puckett and Hrbek were from the same mold.*

they broke the mold when they made *someone*
used to say that you admire someone because there is no one else like them: *"Hannah is crazy! I've never met anyone like her." "Yeah, they broke the mold when they made her."*

moment

something **has its moments**
(also *someone* **has his/her moments**)
used to say that some parts of an experience, an activity or someone's behavior are surprisingly good or enjoyable although most of it is not: *The party really wasn't that great. I mean it did have its moments, but not enough to make me want to stay late.*

the moment of truth
the time when you find out whether something will work well, be successful, etc., especially when you have worked hard for it: *The moment of truth came when I finally put the boat in the water. Would it float?*

Monday
⇨**Monday morning QUARTERBACK**

money
⇨**give** *someone* **a RUN for his/her money**
⇨**HUSH money**

easy money
money that you do not have to work hard to get: *Nineteen-year-old Pascale says modeling is easy money, but it doesn't last long.*

for my money

used before a statement in order to show that it is your own opinion: *For my money, eloping is the way to go if you want to get married without stress.*

get your money's worth

to get something that is worth the price that you paid: *Some publishers feel they haven't been getting their money's worth at the trade show.*

have money to burn

to have so much money that you do not mind what you spend it on: *If you think it's about time for another ski vacation and have some money to burn, Colorado is a great place to go.*

I'm not made of money

(also **You must think I'm made of money** or **Do you think I'm made of money?**)

SPOKEN used to tell someone that something is too expensive, or that you cannot afford it: *Forty-seven dollars just to fix this door? I'm not made of money, you know.*

be in the money

to suddenly get a lot of money, or make a profit, especially if you were not expecting to: *Two Iowa farmers suddenly found themselves in the money when they sold their old tractor at a vintage car auction for $80,000.*

make/lose/spend money hand over fist

to earn, lose, or spend a lot of money in a short time: *Fairfield is making money hand over fist from its new shopping mall.*
hand-over-fist: *Growth in stock trading led to hand-over-fist hiring on Wall Street.*

money doesn't grow on trees

used to tell someone not to waste money, or to take an opportunity to get it: *I can't give you another loan. Money doesn't grow on trees, you know!*
—see also *something* **doesn't grow on TREEs**

money is no object

used to say that someone has the money to pay for what they want, and does not care how much it costs: *If you're retired, and you've done well in business and* money is no object, then a luxury cruise is a great way to pass the time.

money is the root of all evil

used to say that a lot of problems are caused by money or by people trying to get it: *It's easy to see why money is the root of all evil when families start fighting over inheritances.*

money talks

(also **money talks, bullshit walks**)

SPOKEN used to say that you can influence people and make them do what you want if you offer them money: *As a young lawyer, Castino was quick to learn that money talks when you want to get something done quickly.*

> NOTE▶ "Money talks, bullshit walks" is very rude. It is better to use "money talks" unless you are in a situation where you know people very well.

my money's on *someone*

SPOKEN used to say that you think someone will win a competition or sports event, be chosen for a job, etc.: *My money's on Wisconsin to win the Rose Bowl.*

put your money where your mouth is

used to say that someone should take action or spend money in order to make something happen, instead of just saying that they want it to happen: *Motorola puts its money where its mouth is, spending over three-quarters of a billion dollars annually on research and development.*

be right on the money

to have exactly the right idea, or to be doing or saying exactly the right thing: *Your advice was right on the money – I talked to my daughter about staying out late and we have agreed on a midnight curfew.*

the smart money

used about people who know a lot about making money, or about the successful business deals they make ♦ USED ESPECIALLY IN NEWSPAPERS: *People are still guessing what Apple will manufacture next, but the smart money says it will be a new light-weight computer.*

the smart money is on *something*
used to say that the people who know most about a situation think that a particular thing is very likely to happen or produce a profit: *Investors say the smart money this year is on small companies that offer personal services to busy professionals.*

take the money and run
to accept what is offered to you before a situation becomes worse ♦ OFTEN USED IN BUSINESS AND POLITICS: *Shareholders were advised to take the money and run after Carsons announced on Monday that it was having financial difficulties.*

throw good money after bad
used to say that someone should not spend any more money trying to improve a situation because they cannot improve it: *Attempting to strengthen the Civic Center against earthquake damage would be throwing good money after bad, as the structure is already unsound.*

throw money around
to spend a lot of money, especially without caring that you might be wasting it: *In those days the federal government would step in and throw money around like confetti to fuel greater growth.*

throw money at *something*
used when you disapprove because someone is trying to solve a problem by spending a lot of money, instead of thinking about what is really needed: *Critics have accused Arizona of throwing money at its schools' problems without producing any long-term solutions.*

you pays your money and you takes your chances/choice
used to say that it is impossible to say which of two or more choices is the right one: *Some people say that the 1815 settlement prevented wars in Europe, and some say it caused them, so you pays your money and you takes your choice.*

monkey
⇨funny/monkey BUSINESS

make a monkey out of *someone*
SPOKEN to make someone look stupid: *The Warriors made a monkey out of the Knights, winning the game by 21 points.*

a monkey on your back
used about a serious problem that stops you from succeeding at something, especially a feeling that you cannot do it or the knowledge that other people do not expect you to succeed ♦ OFTEN USED ABOUT SPORTS: *The press and the experts had put the monkey on Greg's back that he couldn't win a major tournament.*

monkey see, monkey do
used to say that you disapprove of someone who copies what they see other people doing, without thinking: *It's monkey see, monkey do with these kids. They'll say anything they hear their cartoon heroes saying on TV.*

monkey wrench
throw a monkey wrench into *something*
to do something that will cause problems or spoil a plan or process: *Garcia had threatened to throw a monkey wrench into the summit meeting, by leaking important details to the press.*

monster
the green-eyed monster
sexual jealousy (=a feeling of anger and unhappiness because you think that someone you love is interested in someone else): *After seeing Samantha with another man, I got a touch of the green-eyed monster.*

> NOTE▶ This idiom comes from a line in Shakespeare's play *"Othello."*

month
⇨that TIME of the month

never/not in a month of Sundays
SPOKEN used to say that you think something is very unlikely to happen: *"Do you think we'll get into the finals?" "Never in a month of Sundays."*

moon
⇨promise *someone* the EARTH/moon

ask for the moon
to ask for something that is difficult or impossible to get: *The funeral director's*

bill of $3,000 was a shock – he might as well have asked for the moon.

bark/howl at the moon
to do something that is not effective or wastes time: *If other nations don't adopt similar measures to protect blue sharks, we're just barking at the moon, and the sharks may not survive.*

many moons ago
a humorous expression meaning a very long time ago: *The last time Margaret took a vacation was many moons ago.*

once in a blue moon
used to say that something rarely or almost never happens: *I like skating, but I only get a chance to go once in a blue moon.*

more
⇨**THAT's more like it!**

the more the merrier
SPOKEN used to tell someone that you will be happy if they join you in something you are doing: *Why don't you come camping with us in Telluride? The more the merrier.*

morning
⇨**Monday morning QUARTERBACK**

the morning after the night before
when someone feels sick because they have stayed up late the night before drinking alcohol: *I know I promised to work for you today, Sarah – but it's the morning after the night before – you know how it is.*

morning, noon, and night
used to complain that something is happening all the time: *If you keep eating chocolate morning, noon, and night, you won't be able to fit through the door!*

moth

like a moth to the flame/candle
(also **like moths around a flame/candle**)
used about someone who feels that someone or something is very attractive, and wants to be near them, even though they may cause trouble: *Randall's power and wealth drew women to him like moths to the flame.*

mothballs

put *something* in mothballs
to stop using something, or doing something for a while although you intend to start using or doing it again later: *Most battleships are put in mothballs after a war, but are recalled as soon as another one starts.*

mother
⇨**like mother, like daughter** —see **like FATHER, like son**
⇨**MAMA's boy**

the mother of all ___
used to say that something is the best, worst, biggest, most severe, etc. thing of its kind: *Iniki was the mother of all hurricanes – damaging every building on the island and leaving many people homeless.* | *The Beatles' "White Album" is the mother of all records, if you ask me.*

motions

go through the motions
to do something without trying very hard to succeed or do it well because you have to do it but do not really want to: *You're just going through the motions of being a student! Why don't you quit if you're not going to learn anything?*

mountain

make a mountain out of a molehill
(also **turn molehills into mountains**)
used to say that someone is treating a problem, or treating something they have to do, as if it is very difficult or worse than it actually is: *Look, Dorothy, you're making a mountain out of a molehill. It doesn't matter that I've been chosen to give the lecture this year instead of you.*
—see also **make a funeral CASE out of something**

Mohammed must go to the mountain
used to say that if someone you want to see, especially someone important, will

not or cannot come to you, you have to make an effort to see them, even if this is difficult: *If I wanted to work with Bailey, I realized that Mohammed would have to go to the mountain, so I moved to New York.*

the mountain must come to Mohammed: *The mountain has finally come to Mohammed; the Australian government is asking to meet with representatives of the indigenous people to discuss social problems.*

> NOTE▶ This idiom is from a story in the Islamic religion. The Prophet Mohammed was trying to prove his power, and asked that Mount Safa come to him. When the mountain did not move, he said this showed that God was good because the mountain would have fallen on many people and killed them. He then went to the mountain to thank God for not sending the mountain to him.

move mountains
to achieve something that seems very difficult, or impossible: *Some athletes would move mountains to win a gold medal in the Olympics.*

mouse

as quiet as a mouse
SPOKEN used to say that a person or animal is very quiet: *"Please don't wake the baby." "Don't worry, I'll be as quiet as a mouse."*

mouth

⇨**watch your TONGUE/mouth**
⇨*someone* **will be laughing out of the other SIDE of his/her mouth/face**

down in the mouth
SPOKEN looking very unhappy: *What's wrong, Rita? I've never seen you look so down in the mouth before.*

foam at the mouth
used to say that a group of people is very angry about something ♦ USED ESPECIALLY IN NEWSPAPERS, TELEVISION NEWS, ETC.: *The decision to ax the show had thousands of Star Trek fans foaming at the mouth.*

(straight) from the horse's mouth
used to say that information has come directly from the person who knows the most about a situation: *"Are you sure that Cryer is leaving?" "I heard it straight from the horse's mouth."*

have a big mouth
if someone has a big mouth, they talk a lot and tell other people things that they should not tell: *My father always said I had a big mouth and couldn't keep a secret.*

out of the mouths of babes (and sucklings)
OLD-FASHIONED said when you are surprised, shocked, or amused at something a child has said, often because it shows that they understand more about a situation than you thought they did: *"Did you hear that? Sam just said I was old!" "Well, out of the mouth of babes... He's right!"*

> NOTE▶ This idiom comes from the Bible, where a verse in the *Psalms* says that even small children can speak of the power and goodness of God.

shoot your mouth off
SPOKEN to say something offensive, often because you are angry, without thinking about it: *Ellen's always shooting her mouth off at the boss. She'd better be careful or she's going to lose her job.*

mouthful

what a mouthful!
SPOKEN used to describe a long word or phrase that is difficult to say: *Engelbert Humperdinck – what a mouthful!*

you said a mouthful
SPOKEN used to say that you agree completely with what someone has just said: *"Meredith's father is a little weird, don't you think?" "You said a mouthful."*

move

bust a move
(also bust some moves)
to make an unusual movement while dancing, which is meant to be impressive to other people: *Have you seen Raoul dance? He can bust a move just like John Travolta!*

get a move on
SPOKEN used to tell someone to do something more quickly: *Get a move on, Sally, we're going to be late.*

make the first move
to be the person who tries to start a romantic or sexual relationship when two people who like each other are together: *Despite feminism and the sexual revolution, many women are still embarrassed to make the first move.*

movers

the movers and shakers
the people who are responsible for very important decisions in large organizations, companies, etc., or for new ideas and activities in society ◆ OFTEN USED IN NEWSPAPERS, ON TELEVISION NEWS, ETC.: *Mike Fox was one of the movers and shakers behind the renaming of the McEnery Convention Center.*

mud

as clear as mud
used to say that something is not at all clear or easy to understand: *Your explanation was as clear as mud. Please explain it again, slowly.*

drag *someone* through the mud/dirt
(also **drag** *someone's* **name, reputation, etc. through the mud**)
used when you disapprove because people have harmed someone by saying that they did something wrong: *I hope that the mayor will apologize to the two officers for dragging their good names through the mud.*

here's mud in your eye
OLD-FASHIONED used for wishing someone good luck when you are having a drink together: *I know you're on stage soon, so here's mud in your eye.*

sling/throw mud
to publicly criticize someone or say that they have done wrong, especially so that you can get an advantage over them ◆ USED ESPECIALLY IN POLITICS: *In elections, many candidates sling mud and, now and then, some of them get in trouble with the law for saying too much.*

mudslinging: *Hayze has tried to stay out of the mudslinging and focus on the issues.*

multitude

cover/hide a multitude of sins
used to say that the name that is given to something makes it seem better than it is, or that something can be used to hide the faults in a thing or person: *LaFleur's new fall clothing line is perfect for those people trying to hide a multitude of sins.*

mum

mum's the word
SPOKEN used to tell someone that they must not tell other people about a secret: *Remember, mum's the word – I don't want anyone else to hear about this!*

munchies

have the munchies
SPOKEN to be hungry, especially when you want food that is not healthy: *Lately, I've been getting the munchies all the time – do we have any potato chips?*

NOTE▶ "Munchies" comes from the verb "munch," meaning to chew food noisily.

murder

get away with murder
used when you disapprove because someone is not criticized or punished when they behave in a way that is not acceptable or responsible: *I have to do half Darren's work – Steve lets him get away with murder.*

scream/yell bloody murder
1 to complain very angrily about something: *When Frankie lost the match, he screamed bloody murder that Nick had cheated.*
2 to shout or scream very loudly because you are angry, annoyed or frightened: *Pat grabbed Jack and shoved him into Mrs. Quinn, who screamed bloody murder.*

muscle

flex your muscles/muscle
to do something that shows that you have power, and intend to use it: *It's time for*

M

women to flex their political muscles and insist on equal rights.

music

face the music
to accept responsibility for your actions and give people the chance to criticize you: *Don't you think it's about time you faced the music and told Jack that you are moving out?*

something is (like) music to your ears
used to say that you are very pleased to hear something, or very pleased at an opinion, decision, etc.: *The Republican's promise to cut taxes was like music to the taxpayers' ears.*

mustard

not cut the mustard
to not be good enough for a particular type of activity, especially when competing with other people or things: *He's a great boxer, but his last few performances in the ring just haven't cut the mustard.*

muster

pass muster
to be accepted as good enough for a particular purpose: *Among his stories, only a few pass muster as genuine science fiction.*

M

N

nail

⇨**nail** *someone* **to the WALL**

another nail in *someone's/ something***'s coffin**
(also the final/last nail in the coffin)
used about an event, in a series of bad events, that helps to destroy someone's success, plans, or hopes ◆ OFTEN USED IN NEWSPAPERS, ON TELEVISION NEWS, ETC.: *The Soviet authorities' acceptance of advertising for Western products on state-run radio was yet another nail in the coffin of the Cold War.* | *The final nail in the coffin of plans for a nuclear reactor came when a panel from the Commission advised against it.*

as hard/tough as nails
used about someone who does not seem to feel any emotions, especially fear or sympathy: *Stockton is one of the best players I've ever played against – that guy is as tough as nails.*

hit the nail on the head
to give exactly the right answer to a question or a problem, or to describe something in exactly the right way: *Cal really hit the nail on the head in his column Thursday – I completely agree with him.*

name

⇨**drag** *someone's* **name through the mud** —see **drag** *someone* **through the MUD/dirt**

⇨**a HOUSEHOLD name**

blacken *someone's* **name/image/ reputation**
to say bad things about someone, so that other people have a bad opinion of them: *The papers have used the one bad incident in Bill's life to blacken his name completely.* | *The March disaster, the nation's worst oil spill, blackened the image of the entire industry.*

call *someone* **names**
to say rude or insulting things to someone, usually about their character or appearance: *A gang of boys chased after Becky, calling her names and throwing dirt at her.*
name-calling: *Wayne's condition made him the target of name-calling and violence that ended in murder.*

give *something* **a bad name**
used to say that a failure or something bad has made people have a bad opinion of a situation or activity, group of people, place, etc.: *Players who break the law give the whole sport a bad name.* | *In recent years, salt has gotten a bad name because of its excessive use in the American diet.*

something **has** *someone's* **name on it**
used to say that something is exactly right for someone, or that they will definitely succeed at it: *Somewhere out in the Caribbean is a real paradise with my name on it.*

be ___ in all but name
used to say that something or someone has all the qualities or features of a particular situation or person, even though people do not call them by that name: *The set of values and beliefs taught in public schools is a religion in all but name.*

be ___ in name only/alone
used to say that something or someone has very different features or qualities from the ones that its name makes it seem to be: *The Black Hills are hills in name only – they're actually classified as mountains.*

___ is *someone's* **middle name**
SPOKEN a humorous expression used with a noun in order to show that something is typical of the way a person behaves or typical of their personality: *Determination is my mother's middle name. Nothing will go wrong if she says it won't.*

___ is the name of the game
(also the name of the game is ___)
used to say that something is the most basic and important quality that you need, or the usual thing that you find, in a particular activity ◆ OFTEN USED IN BUSINESS, POLITICS AND SPORTS: *It's good if a player is big, but speed is the name of the game.*

You've got to be quick. | *Remember, in the stock market, the name of the game is to buy low and sell high.*

make a name for yourself (as/in something)

to do something very well so that it makes you famous: *Joan's tried for years to make a name for herself in the business world.*

someone's **name is mud**

used to say that people are angry with someone, or do not like them because they have done something wrong: *If we don't clear all this stuff out of the garage before Dad gets home, our names are going to be mud.*

name names

to tell people the name of the person or people involved in a particular activity, especially when this will embarrass them or cause problems for them ♦ OFTEN USED IN THE NEGATIVE: *"I won't name names, but there are many people in the music industry who are gay. It's not pertinent to the music," said McKagan, "and it's nobody's business."* | *She told me that certain people in the company were not happy with my performance, but she didn't name names.*

you name it (someone's **got it**) (also you name it (someone **has it**))

INFORMAL used to show that there is a large variety of things that could be included in the list of things you are talking about: *People can take classes in wine tasting, massage, investing, dating – you name it.* | *"Does anybody want a drink?" "Sure, what do you have?" "You name it, we have it."*

NOTE▶ You may hear people use other words instead of the second part of this idiom: *I thought I'd seen everything. I'd raised two sons, dealt with drugs, divorce, teenage love – you name it, I'd lived it.* | *Why is the past such a big business today? Vintage pop, vintage Hollywood, vintage beer bottles – you name it, somebody's collecting it.*

napping

⇨be caught napping —see CATCH

nasty

do the nasty

SLANG to have sex: *Do you think John and Leah are doing the nasty?*

native

go native

a humorous expression used to say that someone who has come to visit or live in a foreign country or a new place, behaves, speaks, or dresses the same way as the people who have always lived there: *Unless you're willing to go native on the island, eating in one of the few Western-style restaurants will cost you quite a bit.*

nature

appeal to someone's **better nature**

to try to persuade someone to do what you want by telling them it is a good, kind, etc. thing to do: *Colleen tried another plan, appealing to her sister's better nature.* | *There was no point in appealing to his better nature when he clearly didn't have one.*

let nature take its course (also let time, life, fate, etc. take its course)

to wait for something to develop in the usual or most natural way: *Warren said that instead of trying complicated medical procedures to cure his cancer, he would rather let nature take its course, and die peacefully.* | *Roger decided to let business take its course, and felt no pressure to rush into any new ventures.*

the nature of the beast

the most basic and important feature or quality of the situation, activity, or person you are talking about: *It's difficult to speed up any processes in an organization of this size – that's just the nature of the beast.*

navel

be contemplating your navel (also be gazing/staring at your navel)

to spend too much time thinking about your own problems rather than being concerned with more important things: *Having spent so much time gazing at our national navel, it is now time to raise our heads and consider our position in the world.*

navel-gazing: *We try to work together because it's a good way to eliminate navel-gazing.*

near

⇨**SO near (and) yet so far**

neck

⇨**put/lay your neck on the line** —see **put/lay your job, life, future, etc. on the LINE**

⇨**put/stick your neck in a noose** —see **put/stick your HEAD in a noose**

⇨**be up to your EARs/neck/eyeballs in** *something*

break your neck (doing *something*)
to try very hard to do or get something: *I share your worries about getting this job done, and we're going to break our necks to see that we get it done on time.*

be breathing down *someone's* neck
to pay very close attention to what someone is doing, in a way that makes them feel nervous or annoyed: *I don't need my boss breathing down my neck all day long.*

dead from the neck up
SPOKEN used to say that someone is very stupid: *It's nice to meet someone in this place who isn't dead from the neck up.*

in this/that neck of the woods
(also **in your, his, etc. neck of the woods**)
in a particular area or place: *Most folks in this neck of the woods come from farming families.* | *How are things in your neck of the woods, Pat?*

neck and neck
if two people, teams, groups, etc. are neck and neck in a competition, they have an equal chance of winning: *Greenbaum is running neck and neck with a new candidate, Royce – an old-style Republican from Syracuse.* | *The race was neck and neck until the finish line when Martino stumbled and fell.*

neck-and-neck:
The Tigers and Blue Jays are in a neck-and-neck race for the American League Title.
—see also **be NIP and tuck**

risk your neck
to do something very dangerous in which you could be hurt or killed, or have something else bad happen: *Sharon knew she'd be risking her neck if she stayed in that area any longer.*

stick your neck out
to give your opinion or do something that other people are afraid to do, even though it may cause trouble for you: *I'm not prepared to stick my neck out and make a complaint.*

someone will wring *someone's* neck
SPOKEN used to say that someone is extremely angry with someone else: *If Matt comes here again, I'll wring his neck.*

needle

(like looking for) a needle in a haystack
(also **like trying to find a needle in a haystack**)
used to say that something is very difficult to find: *You're wasting your time trying to find those kids – it'll be like looking for a needle in a haystack.* | *Searching for the receipt in Vivian's files was like trying to find a needle in a haystack.*

neither

that's neither here nor there
SPOKEN used to say that a fact, idea, etc. is not important because it is not related to what you are talking about: *The Kellers have no children, but that's neither here nor there as an indication of a happy marriage.*

nerve

be a bundle of nerves
to be extremely worried or frightened about something: *Investigators could see that Murphy was a bundle of nerves as he sat waiting for news of his wife.*

get on someone's nerves

SPOKEN to annoy someone: *Just quit asking me about my love life, will you? You're starting to get on my nerves.*

touch/hit/strike a raw nerve

to upset someone by mentioning a subject that upsets or embarrasses them: *I know that in talking about suicide, I may have touched a raw nerve.*

nest

feather your nest

to make your house more comfortable by buying things that will make your life easier: *Surveys have shown an increasing trend toward feathering the nest with features such as home offices and exercise equipment.*

leave/fly the nest

if a young adult leaves the nest, they leave their parents' home to become independent: *Our children have recently flown the nest, and we're enjoying some time to ourselves.*

stir up a hornet's nest

to cause a lot of trouble by making a bad situation worse, especially a situation in which people strongly disagree with each other: *Fagan's article has stirred up a hornet's nest of controversy regarding immigration.*

net

slip through the net

used to say that someone who a particular system or organization was supposed to help deal with, or find, has not been helped or noticed: *In our efforts to speed up the licensing process, some dishonest business owners could slip through the net.*

never

⇨never the TWAIN shall meet

someone (has) never looked back

used to say that someone has been happy and successful since they took an opportunity, or something changed in their life or job: *Maria's family left the slums to work in this prosperous town ten years ago and have never looked back.*

news

no news is good news

SPOKEN used to say that it is usually good that you have not received any news from someone because it probably means that nothing bad has happened: *"Have you heard from Tonya recently?" "No, not for a while." "Well, no news is good news, I suppose."*

that's/it's news to me!

SPOKEN said when you are surprised or annoyed because someone has not told you something sooner: *"Marcia says the report has to be ready tomorrow." "That's news to me – I thought she didn't need it until next week."*

niche

carve out a niche (for yourself)

to become successful and respected in your work: *We had to compete with older organizations and carve out a niche for ourselves, but we've done a good job.*

nick

(just) in the nick of time

just before it is too late, or just before something bad happens: *Hackman visited a hospital complaining of chest pain – just in the nick of time to prevent a major heart attack, as it turned out.*

nickel

something is not worth a wooden/plug nickel
(also I wouldn't give a wooden/plug nickel for something)

OLD-FASHIONED used to say that something is not worth anything, or that something you have been told is not true: *You want $500 for your truck? That thing's not worth a wooden nickel!*

> NOTE▶ A nickel is a coin used in the U.S. and Canada worth five cents (1/20th of a dollar). A plug or wooden nickel is a false one.

nickel and dime (someone/something)

to behave in a way that is not generous and that shows you think too much about

unimportant things, especially small amounts of money: *In this era of increased competition, banks are trying to nickel and dime their customers with fees for everything from writing checks to using cash machines.*
nickel-and-dime: *We face big problems that can't be solved with nickel-and-dime solutions.*

night

call it a night
SPOKEN to decide that you have done enough of a job or activity on a particular night, or that you are too tired to continue that night: *OK, let's trying singing it all the way through without stopping, and then we'll call it a night.*
—see also **call it a DAY**

be like night and day
used to say that two things or people are completely different from each other: *The appearance of the two schools is like night and day. It's clear what impact parental involvement can have.*

be like night and day

a night owl
used about someone who has a lot of energy at night, and usually goes to bed very late: *Night owls will soon find out that there aren't a lot of options for entertainment after midnight in this town.*

nines

be dressed to the nines
OLD-FASHIONED to be wearing your best or most formal clothes: *The audience was dressed to the nines, expecting a program of classical ballet.*

nip

be nip and tuck
1 used to say that people or teams are doing equally well in a competition so that it is difficult to know who will win: *The race for the senate seat was nip and tuck until the final votes came in.*
2 SPOKEN used to say that you almost did not finish something or arrive somewhere on time: *It was nip and tuck, but we got to the airport just before our plane took off.*
—see also **NECK and neck**

nitty gritty

get down to the (real) nitty gritty
SPOKEN to start talking about the most basic, important, and practical facts of a subject or activity: *It's time we got down to the real nitty-gritty here: who owns what, and what it's worth.*
nitty-gritty: *Dave has earned his position the hard way – by doing the nitty-gritty jobs that no one else wants.*

no

⇨**be no GO**

no duh
SPOKEN said when you are trying to make someone feel stupid because you already knew about what they have just told you
◆ OFTEN USED BY CHILDREN: *"New York City isn't the capital of New York State." "No duh, I already said that!"*

nobody

⇨**do** *something* **like nobody's BUSINESS**
⇨*someone* **is nobody's FOOL**

no-brainer

be a no-brainer
SPOKEN used about something that is easy to do or does not need much intelligence to understand: *Davis' agent says that the decision to leave the team was a no-brainer. "It would be foolish not to explore other options," he said.*
no-brainer: *The show is typical "Three Stooges" fare. In other words it's total chaos and a lot of no-brainer belly laughs.*

N

nod

get the nod
to get official permission or approval ♦ OFTEN USED IN NEWSPAPERS, ON TELEVISION NEWS, ETC.: *Fleet-Norstar got the nod over its competitor because it was better managed and had the necessary capital.*

noises

make noises about *something*
to talk about something that you want, or intend to do, without saying anything direct or definite ♦ OFTEN USED IN NEWS-PAPERS, ON TELEVISION NEWS, ETC.: *Some large corporations are making noises about moving to areas where the rent is less expensive.*

> NOTE▶ People often put adjectives, such as "encouraging," "hostile," "soothing," etc. in front of "noises" to show that someone feels a particular way about something: *Some car rental companies are making threatening noises about raising their rates by 5 to 7 percent.* | *It's likely that Perot will make presidential noises next year, then stop short of actually announcing his candidacy.*

make (all) the right noises
to say the things that people expect you to say or the things that are considered correct in a particular situation ♦ OFTEN USED IN NEWSPAPERS, ON TELEVISION NEWS, ETC.: *One former director said that Helms made all the right noises about seeing the job as the climax of his government career.*

none

⇨be none the wiser —see WISE

noon

it's high noon (for)
used to say that the results of someone's bad or illegal actions now start to affect them ♦ OFTEN USED IN NEWSPAPERS, TELE-VISION NEWS, ETC.: *It's high noon at the Supreme Court, as both sides prepare for their final day of testimony.*

> NOTE▶ In old Western movies, "high noon" (=12 o'clock in the middle of the day) was the time when men who had been arguing would meet to fight with guns.

nose

as plain as the nose on your face
OLD-FASHIONED used to say that something is very easy to realize, see, or understand: *After a while, the thing Gordon wanted most became as plain as the nose on his face – he wanted a wife.*

brown-nose
an impolite expression meaning to try and make someone in a position of authority like you by being nice to them: *Kiser ought to spend more time working for political change instead of brown-nosing rich and powerful men.*
brown-noser: *This school is full of brown-nosers who'll do whatever it takes to get an "A."*

someone can't see beyond (the end) of his/her nose
used to say that someone is too interested in themselves and their own lives to understand or deal with other situations or other people's problems: *Sometimes the administrators don't seem to see beyond their noses. They forget they're dealing with real human beings.*

cut off your nose to spite your face
to do something because you are angry or in a hurry, even though it will harm you or make a situation worse: *When the national parks were closed to save money, it's like they were cutting off their nose to spite their face. They could have taken in a lot of admission fees over the weekend.*

do *something* with your nose in the air
to behave as if you are better than someone else: *Cramer sat on the beach with his nose in the air and pretended not to notice the rest of us.*

follow your nose
1 to behave in a way that you think is best or right, often in a situation in which

there are no rules: *In search of an answer, I just followed my nose, finding out a lot of interesting information along the way.* **2** to keep going straight ahead: *This weekend's festival won't be hard to find – just get close to the city and follow your nose.*

have/keep your nose to the grindstone

to work very hard for a long time without thinking about anything else: *Cole had a bad reputation when he was younger, but nowadays, he keeps his nose to the grindstone.*

have a nose for *something*

to be naturally good at noticing or finding a particular type of thing: *Though he was trained in science, Maddox has a nose for news in any field.*

hold your nose

to accept that you have to do something that you do not want to do because you feel you do not have a choice ◆ OFTEN USED IN POLITICS: *The average citizen will hold his nose and vote for higher taxes if he thinks he'll gain something.*

keep your nose clean

to avoid getting into trouble and not do anything wrong or illegal: *If you keep your nose clean, Angstrom, you'll have a job for life in the Navy.*

lead *someone* (around) by the nose

to control someone completely so that they do everything you want them to do, especially in a way that makes the person seem stupid: *The organization denies that they lead people around by the nose, telling them what to do in political matters.*

look down your nose (at)

to behave as if someone or something is not good enough for you: *The fashion houses in Paris and New York tend to look down their noses at those who are not graduates of a well-known design school.*

pay through the nose

to pay a lot or too much for something: *Some people are willing to pay through the nose in search of fun and relaxation.*

powder your nose

OLD-FASHIONED used by women to say that they want to go to the bathroom in order to avoid saying this directly, often used humorously: *Vanessa disappeared to powder her nose, and Peter poured more champagne into her glass.*

put *someone's* nose out of joint

to annoy someone by not giving them as much respect as they think they deserve: *Some of the reporters' questions seemed to put Snyder's nose out of joint, and he soon walked out of the room without finishing the press conference.*

be right (there) under *someone's* nose

SPOKEN used to say that something that someone cannot find or understand is really very easy to find or understand: *"Where are my keys?" "Right there, under your nose."*

rub *someone's* nose in it/*something*

to keep reminding someone about something they do not want to think about, especially something that makes them feel ashamed or embarrassed: *There's no need to rub their noses in their championship defeat.*

stick your nose into *something*

to become too involved in, or show too much interest in someone else's private life or affairs so that they become annoyed or angry: *I don't see why my mom needs to keep sticking her nose into my social life – it's my business who I go out with.*

opposite **keep your nose out of** *something*: *I agreed to compromise with him on a couple of things as long as he kept his nose out of my business.*

thumb your nose (at)

to show that you do not respect rules, laws, or people in authority: *Bosses of the water company have been thumbing their noses at the city council for years.*

not

it's ___ (Jim), but not as we know it

SPOKEN a humorous expression used to say that something is strange, unusual, or unexpected: *It's a museum, Jim, but not as*

N

we know it. | "You made a cake?" "Well, it's a cake, Lyn, but not as we know it."

> NOTE▶ This expression comes from the television show *"Star Trek."* When the characters in the program find new creatures during their travels through space, Mr. Spock often says things to Captain Kirk like, *"It's life, Jim, but not as we know it."*

nothing

⇨*someone* **has nothing between the EARs**

⇨*someone* **has nothing to prove** —see *someone* **has something to PROVE**

leave nothing to the imagination
used to show that you disapprove of something that gives too much information relating to sex, especially by showing too many details: *The costume department came up with an outfit for Jeri that leaves almost nothing to the imagination.*

nothing to write home about
used to say that something is not special or interesting: *It's a fairly good restaurant, but nothing to write home about.*

nothing ventured, nothing gained
SPOKEN used to say that you may achieve something if you are willing to take a risk: *Be optimistic and apply for the job – nothing ventured, nothing gained, I always say.*

think nothing of (doing) *something*
to think that something is ordinary and not strange, special, or difficult to do: *Not so many years ago, children would have thought nothing of walking two or three miles to school and back.*

notice

sit up and take notice
to suddenly start paying attention to something that is happening because it surprises or affects you: *Centex's recent success with its "smart homes" will make other builders sit up and take notice.*

now

⇨**(now) THAT's what I call ___**

now you're talking!
SPOKEN used to say that you think someone's suggestion is very good: *"Why don't we stop for a while and have a drink?" "Now you're talking!"*

nuclear

⇨**go BALLISTIC/nuclear**

number

have *someone's* number
to understand what someone is like, so that you are able to deal with them: *"Mom says I have to stay home tonight because I'd just get into trouble with you guys." "Boy, she's got your number!"*

someone's number is up
(also *someone's* **number has come up**)
used to say that someone is about to stop being lucky or successful: *This could be the year that many politicians discover their number's up.*

X number of
(also **X amount of** or **X dollars, people, etc.**)
SPOKEN said when you do not know the exact quantity of what you are talking about: *When planning the project, we budget for X number of working hours, anything extra has to be specially approved.* | *Government accountants now have a system to check whether a program really will cost X dollars if the administration office makes a claim.*

number one

look out for number one
to take care of yourself and not worry about other people: *I'm not here to make sacrifices – it's high time I started looking out for number one.*

nut

go nuts
SPOKEN to behave in a crazy, angry, or excited way: *Stovall told the jury he went nuts after he and his wife separated.*

be nuts about
SPOKEN to like someone or something very much: *You can tell that Mike is totally nuts about Jennie.*

the nuts and bolts of *something*
the practical details of a subject, plan, job, etc.: *The summer classes will focus on the nuts and bolts of reading and math to help students improve their basic skills.* **nuts-and-bolts**: *Instead of nuts-and-bolts advice on parenting, "Family Fun" focuses on activities families can enjoy together.*

a tough/hard/difficult nut to crack
1 someone who is difficult to defeat in an argument, fight, or competition, especially because they are determined and have a strong character: *Farmers have organized a strong defense in this case, which makes them an extremely difficult nut to crack.*
2 a problem or situation that is difficult to deal with: *Minority performers have found movies a tougher nut to crack than music and dance.*

nutshell

(to put it) in a nutshell
(also **that's it in a nutshell**)
SPOKEN said when you are stating the main points of an argument, discussion, etc. in a short, clear way: *"Is that all you're going to say about the problem of noise?" "In a nutshell, yes."* | *To put it in a nutshell, they weren't willing to make any changes.*

N

O

oats

be feeling your oats

SPOKEN to be full of energy and excitement: *Even at 70, Fitzgerald says he still wakes up feeling his oats.*

sow your wild oats

to behave in an irresponsible way and have fun while you are young, especially by having many sexual relationships that are not serious: *Clarence confessed to his new wife that he had sown his wild oats more than once before they were married.*

odd

the odd man/one out

used about someone or something that is different from the rest of the group: *I wasn't at all prepared for my move into the private school, where I was the outsider, the odd man out.*

odds

be at odds with *someone/ something*

1 to disagree with someone: *The young composer was frequently at odds with his family, who wanted him to study law.*
2 if one statement, action, intention, etc. is at odds with another, they are very different when they should be similar: *Government transportation programs are currently at odds with environmental concerns.*

the odds/cards are stacked against *someone*
(also **the deck is stacked against** *someone*)

used to say that it is very unlikely that someone will achieve something because there are too many difficulties that could prevent them from doing this: *Brooks seems confident he can make the climb, even though the odds are stacked against him.* | *All this talk from the government about helping small businesses – where's the help? All the cards are stacked against you.*

stack the odds/deck against *someone*: *The high volume of imported farm goods stacks the deck against even the hardest-working farmer.*

off

⇨COME off it!
⇨on the off CHANCE (that)

be off and running

used to say that an activity, plan, etc. has started happening, or that you are starting to do an activity, plan, etc.: *With the success of Donkey Kong and Pac Man, the first video game boom was off and running.*

offering

a burnt offering

a humorous expression meaning food that has been cooked for too long: *We've had a few disasters in the restaurant, including burnt offerings of various kinds.*

offices

someone's **good offices**

help that you get from someone who has authority or who can influence people: *The company was able to use its good offices to speed up the trade agreement between the two countries.*

oil

⇨burn the MIDNIGHT oil
⇨SNAKE oil

oil and water

used about two things or people that are very different and should not be put together: *From the first day, my manager and I were basically like oil and water.*

oil and water

olive branch

offer/extend an olive branch
(also **hold out an olive branch**)
to show that you want to be more friendly with someone during an argument or fight, by doing something that will please them ♦ OFTEN USED IN NEWSPAPERS, ON TELEVISION NEWS, ETC.: *Senate Democrats are offering an olive branch to Republicans, in the hope of resuming serious negotiations on the issue.*

> NOTE▶   In ancient times, the olive branch was used to represent peace.

omelette

you can't make an omelette without breaking eggs
used to say that you cannot achieve anything without causing some problems: *I believe that you can't make an omelette without breaking eggs, and so you can't hold any public office without making some people angry with you.*

on

⇨be on the **GO**
⇨be on the **MAKE**
⇨be on an **UP**
⇨be on the **UP**
⇨be on the **UP and up**
⇨be **UP** on *something*

be on for *something*
SPOKEN to want to do something or be involved in it: *What about Patrick? Is he on for the football game?*

once

once and for all
1 if you deal with, or decide something once and for all, you finish dealing with it, or make a final decision about it: *This new policy will save money, save lives, and settle the political issue once and for all.*
2 if you say something "once and for all," you say it very firmly and clearly so that you will not have to say it again: *Once and for all, I have never received any money from Valdez.*

once-over

give *someone/something* the once-over
to look at someone or something quickly in order to check what they are like: *Police suggest giving your house the once-over before leaving on a vacation in order to insure that you have locked all the doors and windows.*

one

⇨**CLOCK** *someone* **one**
⇨**GO** one better than
⇨**I OWE** you one
⇨**PUT** one over on *someone*
⇨six of one, half a **DOZEN** of the other
⇨that **BITEs** (the big one)
⇨there's one born every **MINUTE**

be/get one up on *someone*
to do something better than someone you are competing with, or get an advantage over them: *The managers at Supersystems think they can get one up on their competitors, with software that continuously monitors all the functions of a computer system.*

be a great one for (doing) *something*
SPOKEN used to say that someone likes a particular thing or has a particular habit: *Aunt Rita was a great one for quoting the Bible whenever she disapproved of anything.*

not be a great one for (doing) *something*
SPOKEN used to say that someone does not enjoy something, or is not good at something: *My mother was never a great one for housework, and I think I inherited my standards from her.*

have had one too many
(also **have had a few too many**)
to be very drunk: *I always call a taxi when I've had one too many.*

it takes one to know one
SPOKEN used to say that someone can understand someone else's character because they have the same faults themselves: *"You're at the computer*

O

again? You are such a nerd!" "Well, it takes one to know one!"

one and the same
used to emphasize that two things or people are exactly alike: *Unfortunately, sports and business have become one and the same.*

one for the road
SPOKEN a last alcoholic drink before leaving a place: *Come on, Nicholas, it's only 2 a.m. Let's stay and have one for the road.*

the one that got away
used to say that someone did not get the thing that they most wanted: *Warren won five regional titles, but that might never make up for the big one that got away in 1994.*

pull a fast one (on *someone*)
to trick or deceive someone: *Joe realized that his regional manager had been pulling a fast one on him, making the Minneapolis office seem more profitable than it really was.*

—see also **PUT one over on** *someone*

open
⇨**LEAVE/lay yourself open (to** *something***)**

operator

a smooth operator
used about someone who is good at getting what they want by persuading people: *Don McMurphey, smooth operator that he is, soon had the invited audience shouting at each other in a fierce argument.*

order

be in apple pie order
OLD-FASHIONED to be very neat or perfectly arranged: *Myrna's house is always in apple pie order – I don't know how she does it.*

something is a tall order
used to say that something is very difficult to do: *Maintaining healthy working conditions in a stress-filled environment can be a tall order to fill.*

marching orders
the instructions that you have in order to achieve an aim or plan ♦ OFTEN USED IN BUSINESS AND POLITICS: *For now, Adams' marching orders on the defense budget are to stand firm.*

be the order of the day
to be something that most people have or do on a particular occasion: *On a warm Saturday afternoon in May, fishing, swimming, and shopping are the order of the day in this town.*

be out of order
to not be working correctly: *The elevator's out of order – we'll have to climb all those stairs!*

the pecking order
the social system among a group of people or animals, in which each one knows who is more important and less important than themselves: *If you make a mistake in big business, you can quickly lose your place of importance in the pecking order.*

out
⇨**HAVE it out with** *someone*

be out cold
to be unconscious, especially because of being hit: *Kruger threw a real punch and knocked Raft out cold.*

be out of it
SPOKEN to not know or understand what is happening because you are tired, confused, or affected by drugs or alcohol: *After the injection I was completely out of it, so I had no idea what anybody was talking about.*

be (way) out there
SPOKEN used to say that something is very strange or unusual: *Have you seen Cronenberg's new movie? It's way out there.*

over

over and done with
used to emphasize that an unpleasant experience or situation has ended: *I'm tired, and I'd like to get this interview over and done with so I can go home.*

over easy

if eggs are cooked over easy, they are cooked on both sides in a pan of hot oil, so that the yolk (=yellow part in the middle) is still soft: *I don't really like my eggs over easy, only scrambled.*

—see also **sunny SIDE up**

overdrive

go/move into overdrive

to start to be very active, or to work unusually hard or well: *Larry sometimes goes into overdrive, risking his health by missing sleep in order to accomplish everything he wants to do.*

be in overdrive: *City officials are in overdrive trying to contain the damage from the oil spill.*

owe

I owe you one

SPOKEN said when you are thanking someone who has helped you, to tell them you are willing to help them in future: *Thanks for picking me up this late, Jeremy. I owe you one for this.*

you owe me (one)

SPOKEN said when you want to remind someone that you expect them to help you or be nice to you because of something you did for them, or something bad they did to you, often used humorously: *You owe me, kid. I wouldn't have this big belly if it weren't for you!*

owl

⇨**a NIGHT owl**

own

hold your own

to defend yourself or to succeed in a difficult situation: *Stone's new record is sure to hold its own among the alternative rock bands currently dominating the radio.*

ox

⇨**strong as an ox** —see **strong as a HORSE**

P

pace

do *something* **at a snail's pace**
used to emphasize that something is happening or being done extremely slowly, especially when you think it should be faster: *Things seems to be happening at a snail's pace around here.*

put *someone* **through his/her paces**
(also **put** *something* **through its paces**)
to make a person or machine show how well they can do a particular activity or piece of work: *Candidates are put through their paces before a panel of business-men and local politicians.* | *When new cars are tested, professional drivers put them through their paces at different speeds.*

pack

ahead of the pack
having more success than people or organizations you are competing with: *Archer's record puts him three strokes ahead of the pack going into today's PGA final.*

page

be/get on the same page
SPOKEN if two people, groups, etc. who are working together are on the same page, they agree about what they are trying to achieve: *Are we all on the same page here? I don't get the feeling that you understand what I'm trying to say.*

paid

⇨**PUT paid to** *something*

pain

⇨**TEETHING problems/pains**

for your pains
1 used to emphasize that what you get as a result of your actions is not as good as what you deserve: *I went all over town, trying to find this CD that she wanted, and I didn't even get a thank you for my pains.*

2 as a reward for your trouble and effort: *Some dealers began to sell only the riskiest and least promising stock. For their pains, they were paid almost twice as much as the rest.*

growing pains
problems and difficulties that are experienced in a new organization or at the start of a new activity: *We know as a new team we'll have to go through some growing pains, but our goal is to get a good game on the ice every night.*

no pain, no gain
used to say that you do not mind doing something unpleasant because it will have a good result ♦ OFTEN USED ABOUT SPORT OR PHYSICAL EXERCISE: *"We'll have to start at 5:00 a.m. to finish our run on time." "Oh well, no pain, no gain."*

be a pain (in the ass)
SPOKEN a rude expression used about someone who is very annoying, or something that you do not like to do, or that is difficult to do: *Getting people to fill in forms the right way is a pain in the ass – no one wants to do it.*

> NOTE▶ Because these expressions are fairly impolite, it is safer to use "be a pain" (in the neck), or more polite words such as "butt" instead of "ass": *It's not the boy's fault he's a pain in the butt – it's his parents' fault.*

be a pain (in the neck)
SPOKEN used about someone who is very annoying, or something that you do not like to do, or that is difficult to do: *Vacuuming is a pain in the neck, and it never gets things really clean.* | *David, stop being a pain and give Linda her doll back.*

take pains to do *something*
(also **be at pains to do** *something*)
to make a special effort to do something well, or to achieve what you want: *Klausner took great pains to praise every student.* | *Jenkins was at pains to point out that he did not represent any political party.*

paint

⇨**paint** *someone* **into a corner** —see
back *someone* **into a CORNER**

be like watching paint dry
(also **be as exciting, interesting, etc. as watching paint dry**)
used about an activity that you think is extremely boring: *My father loves watching golf on television – for me, it's like watching paint dry.*

pale

beyond the pale
used about people or behavior, ideas, etc. that are too bad or extreme to be acceptable: *At that time, reporting on politicians' drinking problems was considered beyond the pale.*

pall

cast a pall over/on
to spoil an event or occasion by making people feel sad or less confident ◆ OFTEN USED IN NEWSPAPERS, TELEVISION NEWS, ETC.: *The death of five students in a car accident has cast a pall over the university's graduation ceremonies.*

palm

⇨have *someone* **eating out of (the palm of) your HAND**

grease *someone's* palm
to give someone money in a secret or dishonest way in order to persuade them to do something: *I think we'll have to grease a few palms if we want to get our shipment delivered on time.*

have/hold *someone* in the palm of your hand
to influence or control someone so that they pay attention to you or do what you want: *Suzanne held the entire management committee in the palm of her hand and could dictate policy decisions.*

pan

⇨out of the **FRYING PAN (and) into the fire**

Pandora

⇨open (a) Pandora's **BOX**

panties

get your panties in a bunch
SPOKEN to get upset or worry too much about something, especially something that is not important: *It's just two blocks away, man – don't get your panties in a bunch!*

NOTE▶ Because "panties" are women's underwear, some people may think this idiom is slightly impolite.

pants

⇨have **ANTS in your pants**
⇨keep your pants on —see **keep your SHIRT on**

beat the pants off *someone*
(also **ride, act, etc. the pants off** *someone*)
SPOKEN to defeat someone completely and easily in a game or competition, or to be much better than someone in an activity: *The last time we played the Hornets, they beat the pants off us.* | *Don't worry about me – I can ride the pants off any of those Ivy League boys.*

bore/scare the pants off *someone*
(also **charm, shock, etc. the pants off** *someone*)
SPOKEN used to emphasize that someone or something bores, frightens, etc. someone very much: *Be aware of your audience – ask yourself, are they with me, or am I boring the pants off them?*

catch *someone* with his/her pants down
1 to embarrass someone by finding out something about them that they do not want anyone to know: *It's the price of fame in the U.S. – someone will eventually catch you with your pants down and the story will be in every paper.*
2 SPOKEN to make someone feel ashamed or embarrassed by asking them to do something when they are not ready or able to do it: *They caught us with our pants down because we couldn't produce the figures to prove they were wrong.*

someone puts his/her pants on one leg at a time
used to say that someone important or famous is just like anyone else: *Always*

remember that the guy who's hiring you is just another professional who puts his pants on one leg at a time.

smarty pants
(also **smarty-pants**)
used about someone who is annoying because they always say smart things or have the right answer to questions ◆ OFTEN USED BY CHILDREN OR BY ADULTS TALKING TO CHILDREN: *"See, I told you you were wrong!" "Yeah, all right smarty pants."*

someone wears the pants (in the family/house)
used to say that it is someone other than the husband who makes decisions in the family, especially the wife: *Bill liked the idea of a trip, but his wife didn't look too pleased. It's easy to see who wears the pants in that family.*

paper

someone couldn't ___ his/her way out of a (wet) paper bag
used to say that someone is very bad at doing something: *Alvin couldn't teach his way out of a paper bag.*

get your walking papers
(also **be given your walking papers**)
to be dismissed from your job: *When Rick was given his walking papers, Mark was right there, ready to take over his job.*

on paper
used to emphasize that the idea you get about something by looking at written accounts, numbers, etc. may be different from what that thing is really like: *Polly's plan looks good on paper, but do we have the resources for it?*

be a paper tiger
used to say that although a government, army, or organization is supposed to have a lot of power, really it does not have any: *We need funds to enforce the law, otherwise we're going to look like a paper tiger.*

a paper trail
used about documents, letters, etc. that give proof of how something was done, especially when this is used to prove that someone has done something wrong ◆ OFTEN USED IN BUSINESS AND POLITICS:

Police are following a paper trail, checking credit cards and criminal records.

not worth the paper it's written/ printed on
used to say that a document has no value, especially when it is a formal promise or agreement, and you think the person who has made it does not intend to keep it: *Any contract with Zefco isn't worth the paper it's printed on. They never meet their deadlines.*

par

be below/under par
1 (also **not be up to par**) to fail to reach the usual or expected standard of quality: *The band started the evening slightly under par, but gradually improved.*
2 (also **not feel up to par**) to feel slightly sick or weak: *You may not feel up to par for three weeks or more after a case of the flu.*

something is par for the course
used to say that something that happens is exactly what you would expect to happen, especially when it is something bad: *Wet snow, biting winds and freezing temperatures are par for the course in Iowa in February.*

be on a par (with)
to be equal to someone or something else, for example in quality, value, or importance: *If the applicants are all on a par, we give preference to those who applied first.*
put *someone* **on a par with**: *Turkey's population of 58 million puts it on a par with France or Great Britain.*

up to par
at a standard that is as high as expected, or high enough to be acceptable: *Intense competition can be a good thing if it helps to keep a company up to par.*

parachute
⇨**a golden HANDSHAKE/parachute**

parade

be on parade
to go or be placed in front of people in

order to be seen and admired: *Working mothers can find it hard to deal with the idealized images of motherhood on parade in women's magazines.*

rain on *someone's* parade
to spoil someone's important or exciting plans: *Just when Alexandra's about to be made editor, her father-in-law rains on her parade by giving the job to someone else.*

paradise

be living in a fool's paradise
to be happy about your situation when you should not be because you believe that it is good or has no problems, when that is not really true: *At least we're not living in a fool's paradise – we're trying to be realistic about the problems we're going to face with a bad economy.*

pardon

⇨pardon me for living/breathing —see **EXCUSE me for living/breathing!**

part

look the part
to seem to be a typical type of person, especially to seem like exactly the right kind of person to do a job: *He really looks the part of an old professor – tweed jacket, saddle shoes, and even smoking a pipe.*

be part and parcel of *something*
used to emphasize that something is a part of a situation and is closely connected with it: *Children's mastery of reading is part and parcel of their growth as writers and thinkers.*

partner

someone's partner in crime
a humorous expression meaning someone who helps someone else, especially to do something that they should not do: *I want you guys to do some real work today. Bill, where's your partner in crime?*

party

bring *something* to the party
to add something good to a situation or

activity that you are involved in: *As a Harvard M.B.A., the company's new president brought significant business experience to the party.*

party animal
SLANG someone who enjoys going to a lot of parties and drinking a lot of alcohol: *To his parents, John is a nice boy who calls his grandparents regularly, not some party animal.*

a party pooper
someone who spoils other people's fun, especially by refusing to do something that everyone else wants to do: *"Can we go? I need to go to bed." "You're such a party pooper, Lisa, it's only 9:20."*

past

⇨I wouldn't **PUT** it past *someone* (to do *something*)

pasture

new/fresh/greener pastures
a new and different situation, especially a better job: *After five years, most of the people who joined the department with me had left for greener pastures.*

be put out to pasture
to be made to leave your job because you are too old: *Some of the political veterans had been put out to pasture, and they resented it.*

pat

⇨have *something* **DOWN** pat
⇨pat *someone* on the **BACK**
⇨pat yourself on the **BACK**

patch

go through a bad/difficult/rough patch
(also **hit a bad/difficult/rough patch**)
to experience a difficult and unpleasant time when you have many problems: *One of Baker's strengths as a manager has been his ability to calm the team when they hit a rough patch.*

path

⇨lead *someone* down the **GARDEN** path

⇨off the beaten **TRACK**/path
⇨take the **LINE**/path of least
  resistance

pause

give you pause (for thought)

to make you stop and think again,
especially about what you are doing or an
idea that you thought was right: *When we
look more closely at the movies our
children are watching, we see images of
violence that give us pause.*

pavement

pound the pavement

to try very hard to find a job: *With
thousands of men and women pounding
the pavement, some job seekers are
realizing they have to move to another
city.*

pay

⇨hit pay **DIRT**

peace

hold your peace

to say nothing although you may want to
speak: *Paula knew she could answer the
question, but held her peace and let her
husband answer.*

peanuts

if you pay peanuts, you get monkeys

used to say that an employer who pays
low wages will not be able to employ
good workers: *We have no hope of
attracting the best applicants – if you pay
peanuts, you get monkeys.*

pearls

cast pearls before swine

OLD-FASHIONED to show or offer something
special to someone who will not enjoy it
or understand how valuable it is: *Don't
bother explaining the painting to Dwayne
– it would be like casting pearls before
swine.*

peas

like two peas in a pod

used about two people or things that are
exactly like each other: *She and her sister
are like two peas in a pod – I can never
tell which of them is which.*

pedal

put the pedal to the metal

SPOKEN to drive a car very fast: *Let's put the
pedal to the metal and see how fast this
thing can go.*

pedestal

put/place someone on a pedestal

to behave to someone and talk about
them as if they were perfect, instead of
treating them like an ordinary person: *In
the traditional culture, a woman was
either placed on a pedestal or despised –
she was better or worse than men, but
never their equal.*

peg

take someone down a peg (or two)

(also **knock, bring, etc.** someone **down a peg (or two)**)
to make someone realize they are not as
important as they think they are, or as
good at something as they think they are:
*Don's not a bad guy, but he needs to be
taken down a peg or two.*

> NOTE▸ This idiom comes from the time
> when the navy used sailing ships. A ship
> would have to bring its flag down to a
> lower position if a more important ship
> was in the area. The different positions
> for the flag were shown by pegs (=sticks)
> in the ship's mast (=tall pole that held the
> sails).

pegged

have someone/something pegged

to understand someone or something
completely so that you know what they
will do next or what will happen next: *Just
when you think you've got John pegged,
he'll do something to surprise you.*

pen

the pen is mightier than the sword
used to say that you can achieve more through communication than you can with violence: *I've come to believe that the pen is mightier than the sword, so when I give an interview I stress what people can do politically to change things.*

penny

cost a pretty penny
OLD-FASHIONED to cost a lot of money: *These days, original Coke bottles cost a pretty penny.*

pennies from heaven
OLD-FASHIONED money that you do not expect to get: *It wasn't exactly pennies from heaven, but Carlos Rangel spotted a truckload of counterfeit $20 bills that had been dumped in the Miami River.*

pinch pennies
to be careful to spend as little money as possible: *I'll be glad when I don't have to pinch pennies anymore, and I can buy some new clothes.*
penny-pincher: *Here's a penny-pincher's guide to the best Christmas videos.*

people

⇨**people who live in GLASS houses (shouldn't throw stones)**

per

⇨**AS per usual**

perch

knock *someone* off his/her perch
to make someone who is very successful fail, or to become less successful than they are: *Several teams are hoping to knock the reigning state champions off their perch this year.*

petard

be hoist with/by your own petard
(also **be hoist on your own petard** or **be hoisted by/with your own petard**)
to have problems because of something you have done or said that was intended to give you an advantage or cause problems for other people: *It is ironic to see the company, which has fought some celebrated lawsuits to defend its interests, hoist on its own petard in a dispute over copyright.*

> NOTE▶ This idiom comes from a line in Shakespeare's play *"Hamlet."* A "petard" was an early kind of bomb that might explode and kill the soldier who was putting it in position.

Peter

be robbing Peter to pay Paul
to take money from one part of a system or organization that needs it, and use it in another part of the system or organization so that you deal with one difficulty but still have problems ♦ USED ESPECIALLY ABOUT BUSINESS OR POLITICS: *If your monthly credit card bills are over 20 percent of your income, you're probably robbing Peter to pay Paul, and are paying too much in interest charges.*

phoenix

rise like a phoenix from the ashes
to be successful again after seeming to have failed completely: *A party that has been outlawed may go underground, reorganize, and rise like a phoenix from the ashes.*

> NOTE▶ In a very old Greek story, the phoenix is a beautiful bird, the only one of its kind. It lives for a few years, makes a nest, and then sets fire to the nest. It burns itself to ashes (=soft gray powder that remains after something has been burned) and then lives again, rising from the ashes.

phone

hold the phone
SPOKEN used to tell someone to wait a minute: *Hold the phone! I've already paid for those classes – I don't owe anything.*

P

phrase

to coin a phrase
SPOKEN said humorously when you have just said something so familiar and ordinary that it may sound funny, or when you have slightly changed a familiar phrase to make it sound funny: *The county needs to change its attitude and play a more active role in bringing business here. To coin a phrase, government is fiddling while Brown County burns.*

pick

take your pick
SPOKEN used to tell someone to choose what they like best among several possible things: *There are lots of good places to eat – just look at the menus and take your pick.*

pickle

be in a pickle
OLD-FASHIONED to have problems that are difficult to solve: *I'm in a real pickle here. Can you help me figure out my taxes?*

picnic

something is no picnic
SPOKEN used to say that something is difficult and involves a lot of work: *Staying home with the kids is no picnic. There's no rest unless they're taking a nap.*

picture

get the picture
SPOKEN to understand a situation that someone is describing or explaining: *Not only has the movie been remade, but now there are T-shirts, posters – well, you get the picture.*

look at the big picture
to understand the whole of a situation and not just some of the details: *Jerry should look at the big picture before he starts criticizing the team.*
big-picture: *Susie Richardson says she's taken a big-picture view of her problems.*

out of the picture
used to say that someone or something is no longer involved in a situation: *The FBI had dropped out of the picture, and left the investigation to the police.*
opposite **in the picture:** *It would have been much more difficult to arrest Cadwell if his girlfriend hadn't been in the picture.*
—see also **put** *someone* **in the PICTURE**

paint a rosy picture (of *something*)
to describe a situation as better than it really is: *Just before independence, the leaders had painted a rosy picture of the future.*

picture perfect
(also **picture-perfect**)
used to emphasize that a thing, event, etc. looks exactly the way you think it should: *The forecasters are predicting picture perfect weather for New Year's Day.*

pretty as a picture
OLD-FASHIONED used to say that someone is very pretty: *Andrea's mother dressed her in red, and told her she looked pretty as a picture.*

put *someone* in the picture
to give someone information about a situation so that they can understand it ◆ OFTEN USED IN BUSINESS MEETINGS: *John will be joining our meeting today. Sandy, could you take a few minutes and put him in the picture about the project?*
—see also **out of the PICTURE**

pie

⇨**be in apple pie ORDER**
⇨**a PIECE/slice of the pie**

as easy as pie/anything
SPOKEN used to say that something is very easy: *The test should be as easy as pie if you can get enough driving practice.*
—see also **as easy as falling off a LOG**

eat humble pie
to admit that you were wrong about something, especially when you must do this publicly and it is embarrassing: *If Richards wants to rejoin the company, she will have to eat humble pie, and ask them to take her back.*

pie in the sky
used about an idea, plan, etc. that you think will never happen: *Agnos insists*

that the proposal for a new baseball stadium is not just pie in the sky.
pie-in-the-sky: *The city council can't have any more pie-in-the-sky plans without the money to support them.*
—see also **be a PIPE dream**

piece

⇨**tear** *someone/something* **to pieces**
  —see **tear** *someone/something* **to SHREDS**

give *someone* a piece of your mind
to tell someone how angry you are with them and why: *I'm going to give that woman a piece of my mind. She can't just go around picking flowers from people's gardens.*

give someone a piece of your mind

go to pieces
1 to be unable to control your emotions or behavior because something has upset you: *I know that if James breaks up with Tracy, she's going to go to pieces.*
2 SPOKEN used to say that someone's work or skill in an activity has become less good, or that a situation has become worse and more confused: *I leave the store for a week and everything goes to pieces!*

someone is a piece of work
used to say that someone is very unusual, annoying, or not nice: *Laverne, at 62, is truly a piece of work – eight rhinestone cocktail rings the size of golf balls, and earrings to match.*

love *someone* to pieces
SPOKEN to love someone very much: *I love Wanda to pieces, but I don't believe in marriage.*

pick up the pieces (of *something*)
to try to get a relationship or situation back to the state it was in before, after something bad has happened and spoiled it: *Our counselors have special skills to help consumers pick up the pieces when they get into difficulties with their credit cards.*

be a piece of cake
used to say that something is very easy: *After getting our daughter through high school and on to college, raising an 8-year-old seems like a piece of cake.*

a piece/slice of the action
an opportunity to be involved in a business, activity, etc. that is successful and exciting: *Now that the price of stocks is going up, everyone wants a piece of the action.*

a piece/slice of the pie
the part of something, especially an amount of money, that one group of people receive when several groups are each getting a part of it: *In the 1960s, the economy was healthy, and people could afford to be generous and help others get a piece of the pie.*

say your piece
to give your opinion in a very direct way: *Say your piece, Marvin – if you can't say it in front of Mark, I don't want to hear it.*

be thrilled to pieces
SPOKEN very excited and pleased that something has happened: *My grandmother was thrilled to pieces when I told her I was coming to visit.*

someone wants a piece of *someone*
SLANG used to say that someone wants to meet and talk with someone, especially someone famous: *We all want a piece of Jamal. He's become a hero to this city. We don't get many of those.*

pig

⇨**a GUINEA PIG**
⇨**in a pig's EYE!**

buy a pig in a poke
SPOKEN to buy something without looking at it carefully first: *We want to justify the costs of the playground project so nobody is buying a pig in a poke.*

P

happy as a pig in shit

SPOKEN a rude expression used to say that someone is very happy and enjoying what they are doing: *Look at that idiot Lembowsky – just sitting there on his bike, happy as a pig in shit.*

—see also happy as a CLAM

pill

a bitter pill (to swallow)

used about something very unpleasant that you have to accept: *Anna's rejection was a bitter pill to swallow, but he dealt with it well.*

sugar-coat the pill

to do something to make an unpleasant job or situation seem less unpleasant ♦ OFTEN USED IN POLITICS: *To call the armed forces "volunteer" is to sugar-coat the pill. The truth is that it is composed largely of people who are there because it is their only hope of getting an education.*

pillar

⇨a TOWER/pillar of strength

from pillar to post

OLD-FASHIONED from one place or difficult situation to another without achieving much: *As a politician, your private life is not your own, and you're ridiculed from pillar to post.*

pilot

on automatic pilot

doing the things that you usually do, but without thinking about them, especially because you are tired or thinking about something else: *After the argument with Steven, Jean passed the rest of the day on automatic pilot.*

> NOTE▶ When a pilot (=person who flies a plane) puts a plane on automatic pilot, the plane flies by itself, and the pilot can rest or do something else.

pin

you could hear a pin drop

SPOKEN used to say that people are being very quiet, especially because they are listening to someone: *You could have heard a pin drop in that hall while David was telling his story.*

pinch

feel the pinch

to start having difficulties with money, because you are not making as much as you used to make: *I stopped working a few months ago, and now I'm starting to feel the pinch when it comes to paying the bills.*

in a pinch

1 used to say that something can be done or used if necessary, though it would not normally be done or used: *The large back seat seats three adults very comfortably, or four in a pinch.*
2 in a difficult or dangerous situation: *Wilcox wants the team to know they can count on him in a pinch.*

pink

⇨be TICKLED pink

in the pink

OLD-FASHIONED feeling very healthy: *Moderate humidity and plenty of fresh air will help keep your plants in the pink.*

pipe

be a pipe dream

used to say that an idea or plan is impossible and will never happen: *Of course every school should have a full, up-to-date library, but for most schools this remains a pipe dream.*

—see also PIE in the sky

put that in your pipe and smoke it

used to tell someone that they must accept what you say although they may not like it: *Tell Roger I'm running my own business now – he can put that in his pipe and smoke it!*

pipeline

something is in the pipeline

used to say that a plan, idea, or event is being developed or prepared and will happen or be completed soon: *A spokesperson for the company said that a new drug to help AIDS patients is in the pipeline, and may be available in the next two years.*

piper

he who pays the piper calls the tune

used to say that the person who is paying for something is likely to be, or should be, able to decide what that thing will be like: *The government must make certain that taxpayers are getting a good service for their money – in the end, he who pays the piper must call the tune.*

> NOTE▶ You may hear people change the words of this idiom slightly: *It seemed that unions were being asked to pay the piper when they were not even allowed to call the tune.*

pay the piper

to suffer the results of something bad or wrong that you have done: *The condition of nuclear weapons plants is terrible – it's time to pay the piper and clean up the mess of 40 years.*

piss

> NOTE▶ Some people may think that idioms using the word "piss" are offensive.

⇨go piss up a **ROPE!**

full of piss and vinegar

SPOKEN full of energy and excitement: *We went out into the warm New Orleans night, full of piss and vinegar, ready for an evening of fun.*

piss and moan

SPOKEN an impolite expression meaning to complain a lot in a way that is very annoying: *Colleen will probably piss and moan that she doesn't have enough room for all her stuff in the new house.*

> NOTE▶ Because some people think "piss" is offensive, it may be better to use "whine" instead of "piss and moan": *Why don't you stop whining and ask for a raise?*

pisser

that's/it's a (real) pisser!
(also **what a pisser!**)
SLANG an impolite expression used to say

that a situation is bad, annoying, or disappointing: *What a pisser! I was really looking forward to seeing you on Monday.*

> NOTE▶ "That's/it's a bummer" means the same as this idiom and is not offensive.

pit

⇨**pit your WITS against** *someone*

something **is the pits**

SPOKEN used to say that something is extremely bad: *It's really the pits when Steph has to work nights.*

pitch

⇨**be at (a) FEVER pitch**

pit stop

make a pit stop

SPOKEN to stop when driving on a long trip, for food, gas, etc.: *I have to use the bathroom – can we make a pit stop here?*

> NOTE▶ This idiom comes from the sport of car racing. Drivers make a pit stop to put more gas in their car, check the engine, etc.

pity

more's the pity

OLD-FASHIONED used when describing a situation to say that you wish it was not true: *Most candidates are judged on how they look on television rather than on real presidential potential. More's the pity.*

place

all over the place

1 used to emphasize that there is a lot of something in many places: *Lockwood is a new company, but their products and supplies are already all over the place.*
2 used to say that something is not neatly arranged or well organized, or that someone is not behaving in a sensible and organized way: *Your paper is all over the place. You need to sit down and make a list of the main points you want to make.*

P

something **falls into place**

1 if things in your life or situation fall into place, they start to happen in the way that you want: *I finally got a job interview, so if things keep falling into place, I'll be working soon.*

2 if something you have been trying to understand falls into place, you finally understand it: *I didn't know why Jane was acting so weird, until I found out she thought I was gay. Then everything fell into place.*

be going places

used to say that you think a person or group is likely to be successful because they are very good at what they do: *I heard them for the first time on Friday, and I can tell you this band's going places.*

be in the right place at the right time

to be given an interesting or useful opportunity, especially because of chance or luck: *Officer Leong denied that he had been exceptionally brave in arresting the armed robbers, saying, "I just happened to be in the right place at the right time."*

know your place

to behave in a way that shows you know which people are more important than you are: *"When I was a teacher," said Mrs. Wheelan, "students knew their place. They were more respectful."*

P

a place in the sun

a situation in which you will be happy and have everything you need: *After years of wandering, Jason has found a place in the sun and settled down.*

put *someone* **in his/her place**

to show someone that they are not as important as they think they are: *She asked me to get them all coffee – well, that put me in my place.*

take second place (to)

to become or be considered less important than someone or something else: *Concern over a nuclear holocaust has begun to take second place to worries about pollution.*

plan

⇨**GAME plan**

plank

walk the plank/gangplank

if someone in a position of authority walks the plank, he or she leaves their job because of something illegal or bad that has happened in their organization, company, etc. ◆ OFTEN USED IN NEWSPAPERS, TELEVISION NEWS, ETC.: *Lieutenant Governor Murphy was forced to walk the plank and drop out of the race for governor after a public disagreement with Governor Hawkins.*

plate

have a lot on your plate
(also **have (more than) enough on your plate**)

SPOKEN to have a lot of work to do or a lot of problems to deal with: *I know Gail has a lot on her plate these days, but I hope she can type up this report for me.*

platter

hand *something* **to** *someone* **on a (silver) platter**

to make it very easy for someone to get something or succeed at something: *I hope you're not expecting the perfect job to be handed to you on a silver platter.*

play

something **is child's play**

used to say that something is very easy to do or deal with, especially when people think it is difficult: *A cheap lock is child's play for a thief, so it's worth investing in a good deadlock for your front door.*

play dirty

to behave in a way that is not fair, especially in order to gain an advantage for yourself ◆ OFTEN USED IN BUSINESS, POLITICS, AND SPORTS: *Rooney wanted the top job, and he was willing to play dirty in order to get it.*

play hard to get

1 to try to make it difficult for someone to have a romantic relationship with you:

Bridget was polite but cool to him, obviously playing hard to get.
2 to delay accepting a job, financial offer, etc. that you really want in order to make the person who is offering it more eager for you to take it: *Some shareholders played hard to get, until the offer to buy was too good to resist.*

play it cool

SPOKEN to behave in a calm way, even though you may be very excited, worried, etc.: *She had a powerful urge to slap Tim's face, but decided to play it cool for a while.*

play it safe

to not do anything that involves risks: *All her life Jackie had played it safe and done what others expected her to do.*

a play on words

an interesting or amusing way of using words or phrases so that they can have two very different meanings: *The union's slogan, "Part-time America Won't Work," is more than a clever play on words. It summarizes the fears of American workers today.*

play with yourself

SLANG to touch or rub your own sexual organs for pleasure: *I bet Scott's up in his room, playing with himself again.*

be (all) played out

used to say that someone has no more energy, or that people have no new ideas about a subject: *Discussion of the impeachment hearings has been all played out as far as I'm concerned.*

playing field

a level playing field

a situation in which different people, companies, countries, etc. can all compete fairly because no one has any special advantages: *We have to create a level playing field on which all individuals have the opportunity to participate in the economy, regardless of their race or gender.*

please

⇨**PRETTY please (with sugar on top)**

plot

the plot thickens

a humorous way of saying that a situation is more complicated, strange, or interesting than it seemed at first: *"But that wasn't all that happened!" "Aha, the plot thickens! Well, you'll have to tell me more later."*

plug

pull the plug on *something*

to prevent a plan or business from being able to continue, usually by deciding not to give it any more money ◆ OFTEN USED IN BUSINESS AND POLITICS: *Redevelopment officials, desperate for more housing, are not likely to pull the plug on the condominium project.*

plunge

take the plunge

to finally decide to do something difficult or risky, especially after thinking or worrying about it for a long time: *David finally decided to take the plunge and sell his business so he could travel around the world.*

pocket

dig/dip into your pocket
(also put/stick your hand into your pocket)

to pay for something expensive with your own money: *Havers dipped his hand into his own pocket when he heard how one of his plumbers had charged a single mother $300 for a simple repair.*

be in *someone's* pocket

to be controlled by someone because they give you money or support ◆ OFTEN USED IN POLITICS AND BUSINESS: *A large number of senators are in the pocket of the tobacco industry, claim activists.*

line your (own) pockets

to make a lot of money and keep it for yourself when it should be paid out to other people in the organization, company, etc.: *As a lawyer, Sniffen uses other people's misfortunes to line his own pockets.*

out of pocket
if you pay for something out of pocket, you pay for it yourself instead of getting the money from someone else, such as your employer: *Because of this accident, we have to pay $250 out of pocket because the insurance won't pay for counseling.*
out-of-pocket: *The company claims that the out-of-pocket cost of developing the new drug was $128 million.*

pocketbook

vote with your pocketbook
to make a decision based on which choice will cost you the least money ◆ USED ESPECIALLY IN NEWSPAPERS, ON TELE-VISION NEWS, IN POLITICS, ETC.: *Shareholders are listening to the protesters' ideas, but they're probably going to vote with their pocketbooks.*

> NOTE▶ "Pocketbook" is an old-fashioned word for a purse (=a bag that you carry your money in).

point

⇒be a sore SPOT/point
⇒get BROWNIE points

belabor the point
to discuss or explain something again and again, or in too much detail so that people who are listening become annoyed: *Since you have already stated in your letter that you know something is wrong with you, I won't belabor the point. However, I feel strongly that you should get some help from a counselor.*

be beside the point
to not be directly connected with the main subject or problem that you are talking about: *The art festival attracted huge crowds. Most of the art wasn't very good, but that's beside the point.*

the boiling point
when people are very angry, and it seems that they might do something violent or lose control of their tempers: *The situation was clearly reaching boiling point when officials announced their decision to ignore the cease-fire.*

a jumping-off point
a place that you start from when you are going somewhere, or an idea that you start with when you are thinking or writing about something: *The group uses traditional Japanese drumming as a jumping-off point, but their performances have become steadily more original and modern.*

miss the point
to not understand the main idea of what someone is saying, or the main idea of a situation: *This kid said his dad had bought him every card ever printed, and I told him, "I think you're missing the point of baseball cards. You're supposed to buy a few, trade them with your friends, and build up a collection slowly."*

the point of no return
the time during a process or activity when it becomes impossible to stop it or change the way it happens or works: *Uncontrolled use of water is depleting supplies to the point of no return.*

score points off *someone*
to make someone seem unintelligent or wrong, or make yourself seem better than they are, especially by saying something smart: *The meeting was useful because people didn't try to score points off each other – each suggestion was welcomed, not criticized.*
point-scoring: *The important thing now is not point-scoring but negotiating.*

score points with *someone*
to do something that makes other people approve of or like you: *The airline was one of the first to score points with passengers by banning smoking on all domestic flights.*

a sticking point
a problem that stops you from making an agreement or arrangement because people cannot agree about it: *The sticking point, of course, is price. Montrose insists his company is worth $200 million.*

not to put too fine a point on it
(also **without putting too fine a point on it**)
used to show that you are about to say something very direct, especially something that is unpleasant but true, or a criticism of someone or something: *"The constitutional argument, not to put too fine a point on it, is almost certainly wrong," said Prof. Carter.*

poison

what's your poison?
(also **name your poison**)
OLD-FASHIONED a humorous way of asking someone which alcoholic drink they would like: *Let me get you a drink. What's your poison?*

pole

be poles apart
used to emphasize that two people, ideas, etc. are very different from each other: *We're hoping for a compromise, but the parties are poles apart, especially on the issue of health care.*

someone **wouldn't touch** *something/someone* **with a ten-foot pole**
used to say that someone does not like, trust, or approve of something or someone and does not want to become involved with it, him, etc.: *I wouldn't touch Nick's offer with a ten-foot pole – I've never trusted him with money.*

pool

⇨a big fish in a little/small pool —see a big **FISH** in a little/small pond

pooper

⇨a **PARTY** pooper

Pope

Is the Pope a Catholic?
(also **Is the Pope Catholic?**)
used as an answer to a question in order to say that the answer is clear and definitely "yes": *"Are you sure about that?" "Is the Pope a Catholic? Of course I'm sure."*

NOTE▶ There are many other questions people use in the same way as this one. Some other common ones are: *Does a bear shit in the woods?* (impolite), *Is the Earth round?*, *Is a frog's ass watertight?* (impolite). Be careful, though. This way of using questions as answers may seem rude unless you know someone very well.

porcelain

⇨drive the porcelain **BUS**
⇨pray to the porcelain **GOD**

port

any port in a storm
SPOKEN used to say that you will take any help or solution that is available when you are having trouble, even if it is from a person, organization, etc. that you do not like: *I wasn't in love with Martha. I was just looking for any port in a storm after my divorce.*

possum

play possum
SPOKEN to pretend to be asleep or dead so that someone will not hurt or annoy you: *Townsley testified that after he was shot, he played possum until he thought the gunman had left.*

NOTE▶ "Possum" is another word for opossum, a North American animal that protects itself from its enemies in this way.

postal

⇨**GO** postal (on *someone*)

pot

⇨(the pot of gold at) the **END** of the rainbow

go to pot
to become worse or fail: *A lot of people think the legal system in this country has gone to pot.*

not have a pot to piss in
an impolite expression meaning to be very poor: *If Ken doesn't get a job soon, he's not going to have a pot to piss in.*

NOTE▶ "Not have two cents to rub together" is a more polite way of saying this.

the/a melting pot
used about a place where people from many different countries come to live

together and form one society, or about an activity that is influenced by many different styles or ideas: *We lived in Manhattan when it was a melting pot for immigrants from all over Europe.* | *The island's music scene is a melting pot of cultures and ideas, instruments and influences.*

the pot calling the kettle black

used to say that you should not criticize someone for something because you have done the same thing or have the same fault: *You think I don't take criticism? That's the pot calling the kettle black!*

shit or get off the pot

a rude expression used in order to tell someone to do what they say they will, when they have been talking about doing it for too long: *Ron's pretty bad at making decisions, so sometimes you just have to tell him to shit or get off the pot.*

> NOTE▶ "Fish or cut bait" is a more polite way of saying this.

take pot luck

to take whatever is available, without being able to make a choice or choose something when you do not know which of the available things is the best: *If you want to go to a movie, we could take pot luck and hope there's something good on in town.*

> NOTE▶ This idiom comes from the time when an unexpected guest would share whatever food a family had cooking in the pot. A pot luck supper or dinner is an occasion to which each person brings one type of food and everyone shares. You do not know exactly what you might eat until you arrive.

a watched pot (never boils)

OLD-FASHIONED used to say that if you are not patient and want something to happen too much, it seems to take a long time, or does not happen at all: *Instead of waiting for Pete to call, why don't you call him or write a letter? You know what they say about watched pots never boiling.*

potato

drop *someone/something* like a hot potato

to suddenly stop being involved with someone or dealing with a problem, usually because it is embarrassing to you
◆ OFTEN USED IN BUSINESS AND POLITICS: *After you lose, the lobbying firms will drop you like a hot potato because they don't need your vote anymore.*

a hot potato

used about a subject that a lot of people are talking or arguing about, but that no one wants to deal with or be responsible for because it upsets or offends people
◆ OFTEN USED IN POLITICS: *Cost-benefit analysis is a basic management tool in private enterprise, but it remains a political hot potato in Washington.*

small potatoes

used about something or someone that is not very big or important compared with other things or people of the same kind: *Claudia's travel business was very small potatoes compared to Luigi's commercial empire.*

pound

⇨pound the PAVEMENT

have/take/want your pound of flesh
(also **demand, extract, claim, etc. your pound of flesh**)

to say that someone must give you what they owe you, or do something that they ought to do for you even though it will make them suffer a lot: *The banks always seem quite happy to take their pound of flesh from customers, even good customers who are only overdrawn by a small amount.*

> NOTE▶ This idiom comes from Shakespeare's play, "*The Merchant of Venice*," in which Shylock demands a pound of flesh from Antonio if he cannot pay the money he owes.

powder

⇨powder your NOSE

keep your powder dry
to wait calmly until you see how a situation develops before deciding what to do: *Both sides are keeping their powder dry until the interest-rate situation stabilizes.*

take a powder
OLD-FASHIONED to leave a place quickly, especially to avoid getting into trouble: *I think Gardiner decided to take a powder when he realized the police would be looking for him.*

powder keg

a powder keg
used about a very dangerous situation, in which something could go wrong at any time: *A lot of pharmacies are sitting on a powder keg because they have millions of dollars worth of drugs in vaults with very little security.*

power

more power to you
SPOKEN used to say that you approve of what someone is going to do, and wish them luck: *If Esther wants to spend her life helping kids with drug problems, then more power to her.*

the powers that be
the people who have positions of authority in an organization and who make important decisions that affect your life: *The powers that be in City Hall have finally agreed that more money needs to be spent on public transportation.*

practice

practice makes perfect
used to say that if you do an activity regularly or work at a skill regularly, you will become very good at it: *If practice makes perfect, then John should be an expert in getting a divorce.*

practice what you preach
to behave in the way that you tell others to behave: *Dr. Ulene tries to practice what he preaches, jogging regularly and eating a low-fat diet.*

praise

damn someone with faint praise
to say something about someone that sounds fairly nice, but shows that you do not really have a high opinion of them: *Smith damned him with faint praise, saying only that he'd played a fine game.*

sing someone's praises
to say how good someone or something is in an excited way: *Mrs. Clark was singing your praises yesterday. She thinks you're one of the best students in the class.*

prayer

not have a prayer (of doing something)
used to say that someone has no chance of achieving what they want to: *We don't have a prayer of managing our expenses better unless we plan our employment strategy better.*

presence

grace someone with your presence
SPOKEN used to show that you are annoyed with someone who has arrived at an event, meeting, etc. because they do not usually come to this kind of event when they should: *Ah, Kevin. How nice of you to grace the department with your presence today.*

NOTE▶ In the past if someone important "graced you with their presence," it meant that you felt very grateful that they were there. This idiom uses sarcasm, which is a common way of showing that you dislike or disapprove of something or someone by saying something that is the opposite of what you mean.

press

⇨be HARD put/pressed to do *something*

(a) bad press
used to say that someone or something has been criticized a lot by newspapers, politicians, etc.: *Despite its recent bad press, a golden suntan is not all bad, provided you are careful and build it up slowly, without getting sunburn.*
opposite **(a) good press:** *Democracy did*

not always have the good press it enjoys today – in ancient Rome, it was seen as ultimate chaos.

a full-court press

when you work hard with other people to get something done or to influence someone: *On the last day of the trial the defense put on a full-court press in order to convince the jury.*

> NOTE▶ This idiom comes from the game of basketball, when all the players work together to try to score points quickly.

be hot off the press

used about a book, piece of writing, etc. that has just been printed and is now available: *The 450-page report was delivered to City Hall hot off the press.*

be hot off the press

pretty

pretty please (with sugar on top)

SPOKEN used when you are asking for something that you want very much, and someone is not willing to give it to you ◆ USED ESPECIALLY BY CHILDREN: *"Mom, can we have some ice cream?" "No, you'll spoil your dinner." "Oh, pretty please?"*

price

at a price

used to say that in order to get what you want, you may have to pay a lot of money, or accept something bad: *Even in the middle of December, fresh strawberries are available in some stores – but at a price.*

—see also what PRICE ___?

at any price

used to say that someone is determined to get something, whatever it costs, or whatever problems or danger they must deal with to get it: *Alan and Laurel wanted a child so much that they were willing to adopt at any price.*

everyone has their price
(also **every man has his price**)

used to say that it is possible to make someone do what you want, even something bad or illegal, if you offer them enough money or give them something they want very much: *"You can't get access to the safe – there are twelve security guards patrolling the building." "Everyone has their price, my friend."*

pay the price (for)
(also **pay a terrible, heavy, high, etc. price (for)**)

used to say that someone is now suffering because of a mistake they or someone else made before: *We've paid a heavy price for our mistakes this season. I just hope the team does better next year.*

what price ___?

1 used to say that a change or development that is generally considered to be good also has some very bad results ◆ OFTEN USED IN NEWSPAPERS, ON TELEVISION NEWS, ETC.: *Towns throughout the world all look the same now, with their fast-food restaurants and gas stations. What price progress?*

2 used to say that something good is being threatened, destroyed, or treated as if it was worthless ◆ OFTEN USED IN NEWS-PAPERS, ON TELEVISION NEWS, ETC.: *What price justice, if a serial killer is allowed to go free because of a slight hitch in the legal system?*

pride

(take) pride of place

to be the most important thing in a group, or to be considered the best or most important of several things, people, or ideas: *Before the 1950s, U.S. art had never taken pride of place in the international art arena.*

give *something* **pride of place:** *A single large houseplant, given pride of place against a plain background, can be a dramatic addition to any room.*

swallow your pride

to do something although it will embarrass you, for example, to admit that you were wrong or need help: *Just swallow your pride and tell them you need help with the computer.*

prisoners

someone **takes no prisoners**
used to say that someone is determined to succeed, will not let anyone stop them, and will not be stopped by feelings of kindness or politeness: *Kevin Ward will be taking no prisoners against Rochester in the game on Sunday.*

problem

⇨have an **ATTITUDE** (problem)
⇨**TEETHING** problems/pains
⇨a thorny **QUESTION**/problem

production

make a production (out) of *something*
to make something that you have to do seem more complicated or difficult than is necessary: *Neither of us made a big production of splitting up. Hakeem just moved out of the apartment.*

profile

keep/maintain a low profile
to try not to do anything that will make people notice you or pay too much attention to you, especially when this is difficult because you are famous or important: *Diplomats were instructed to keep a low profile, and not to take sides in the conflict.*
low-profile: *The Secretary of State is planning a low-profile visit to Moscow next month.*

program

get with the program
SPOKEN used to tell someone to start giving you their attention, or to start doing what they are supposed to do: *Some guys may think they're on the team already. But those guys better get with the program – there may be changes between now and the start of spring training.*

proof

the proof is in the pudding
(also **the proof of the pudding (is in the eating)**)
used to say that you only find out if an idea or plan is good by seeing what the results of trying it are: *I'm not sure if I trust the stock market, but I guess the proof is in the pudding since the people using it are making money.*

prophet

a prophet of doom
used about someone who believes that bad things will happen in the future, and often says so: *I don't agree with the prophets of doom who say the Vikings will never qualify for the Super Bowl again.*

proud

⇨**DO** *someone* **proud**

prove

someone **has** *something* **to prove**
(also *someone* **has a lot to prove**)
used to say that someone has to try especially hard because people do not expect them to do well: *I was happy with the team's performance on Saturday, but they've still got a lot to prove.*
opposite *someone* **has nothing to prove:** *I have nothing to prove by fighting Lewis again – I know I can beat him.*

p's and q's

mind/watch your p's and q's
to be very careful about what you do or say in order not to offend anyone or behave in an unsuitable way: *You have to mind your p's and q's here – Lieutenant Denholm is a very important man.*

public

go public
1 to tell everyone about something that was private or a secret: *Elton John decided to go public about being gay after a close friend died of AIDS.*
2 to make the stock (=the equal parts into which the total value of a company is divided) of a private company available

for people to buy for the first time: *Once Netscape went public, the value of its shares skyrocketed.*

in the public eye
1 if someone is in the public eye, many people know about them and are interested in the things that they do: *Government officials are in the public eye, and they should behave themselves.*
2 if a subject, activity, or problem is in the public eye, many people know about it and have opinions about it because of reports in newspapers, on television, etc.: *Our aim is to keep environmental issues in the public eye.*

opposite **out of the public eye**: *The university found him an embarrassment, and did their best to keep him out of the public eye.*

pull
⇨pull a fast **ONE** (on *someone*)

pump
⇨pump **IRON**
⇨pump up the **VOLUME**

get/be pumped up about
something
to become very excited about or interested in doing something: *The team was really pumped up for the state championship, but we lost the first game.*

prime the pump
to provide money or take action at the start of an activity in order to make it easier for it to be successful later ♦ OFTEN USED ABOUT FINANCIAL ACTIVITIES: *Small businesses should get tax advantages to prime the pump and encourage them to start growing.*

punch

beat *someone* to the punch
to do or get something before someone else does, when you are competing against them: *The Columbia astronauts say that their satellite will be able to relay the information first, and they expect to beat the Hubble telescope to the punch.*

pack a punch/wallop
to be very effective or powerful ♦ OFTEN USED IN NEWSPAPERS, ON TELEVISION NEWS,

ETC.: *Black Star packs more punch than regular beers, yet tastes lighter, so it's easy to drink quite a few.*

pleased as punch
very pleased: *NASA engineers said they were "as pleased as punch" with the pictures sent back by the space probe.*

not pull any punches
to say or write exactly what you think, even if it offends or shocks people: *The documentary pulls no punches in showing the gross negligence and complacency of the airline that allowed the crash to happen.*

roll with the punches
to accept criticism or problems without being upset, and not let them stop you from doing what you have decided to do: *After the stock market crash, many of the nation's stronger industries rolled with the punches and absorbed the shock.*

punching bag

use *someone* as a punching bag
1 to publicly criticize a person or organization and blame them for everything that is bad about a situation: *We will not let the health department be used as a punching bag for ACT UP or any other AIDS group.*
2 to hit someone a lot: *If you don't stay away from Stefan's wife, he's likely to be back here to use you as a punching bag.*

purposes

at cross purposes
used to say that two people or groups are having difficulty in talking or working together because they have different ideas about a situation or are trying to do different things: *Merging the three agencies will ensure that we're co-operating instead of working at cross purposes.*

purse

hold/control the purse strings
to control the money in a family, business, etc.: *Since the late '80s, a growing number of women control the purse strings in marriages.*

tighten/loosen the purse strings: *NASA's prediction that it could meet its schedule* *could help loosen the purse strings at the White House.*

make a silk purse out of a sow's ear
(also **make/turn a sow's ear into a silk purse**)
to completely change something from being bad to being good ♦ OFTEN USED IN THE NEGATIVE: *In an ultimate case of making a silk purse out of a sow's ear, a garbage dump on the Palo Alto bayshore has been transformed into a park.*

push

⇨push your **LUCK**

when/if push comes to shove
1 when a situation becomes very difficult, or when you finally need to take action: *The behavior of the markets shows that when push comes to shove, there is no safer currency in the world than the U.S. dollar.*
2 used when you are saying what you think is the basic and most important truth about a situation: *They may be our friends, Patrice, but when push comes to shove, they're still thieves.*
—see also **when/if it comes to the CRUNCH**

put

⇨be/get **ONE** up on *someone*
⇨be **HARD** put/pressed to do *something*
⇨put *something* on **HOLD**

I wouldn't put it past *someone* (to do *something*)
SPOKEN used to say that you think it is likely that someone has done or will do something: *"Do you still think Norman might attack you?" "I wouldn't put it past him."*

put one over on *someone*
to trick or deceive someone, especially in order to get something for yourself: *Jason really put one over on you last night. You totally believed Eva was his sister.*
—see also **pull a fast ONE (on** *someone***)**

put paid to *something*
to make it impossible for something to happen or continue: *Yugoslavia's various ethnic groups had lived side by side for decades. But the war has put paid to all that.*

you're putting me on
SPOKEN used to tell someone that you think they are trying to make you believe something that is not true, especially as a joke: *"This receiver lets us listen to messages from outer space." "You guys are just putting me on."*

putty

be putty in *someone's* **hands**
to be very easily controlled or influenced by another person: *Wyler was a great director, but he believed in bullying actors until they were putty in his hands.*

> NOTE▶ Putty is a soft substance that becomes hard when it dries, and is used, for example, to hold glass in window frames. When it is soft, you can make it into different shapes with your hands.

P

Q

quantity

be an unknown quantity
used to say that no one knows what someone or something is like, or what effect they will have on your situation: *Our new personnel director is a bit of an unknown quantity, and he is the last place I'd go for help with a problem.*

quarter

at close quarters
at or from a very short distance away: *The trip gave us an opportunity to see several kinds of rare water birds at close quarters.*

give/ask no quarter
WRITTEN to show no pity or expect no pity when you are in a fight or competing with other people: *In the second half of the game, the defense gave no quarter, and the result led to a victory for the Bears.*

quarterback

Monday-morning quarterback
SPOKEN someone who annoys you because they give advice about how something should have been done, after it has happened: *Carr worked hard to produce the best that he could. It's easy for people to be Monday-morning quarterbacks and criticize it, but that's unfair.*

> NOTE▶ In football, the quarterback is the player who tells the other players what to do in the game. Many football games are played on weekends, so Monday morning would be too late to give advice about the game.

question

⇨the 64,000 DOLLAR question

something begs the question
used about a statement, discussion, or situation that makes you want to ask more important questions, ideas, etc. because they have not been mentioned or dealt with: *The whole affair begs the question why reporters were allowed into the junior high school in the first place.*

good question!
SPOKEN said when you do not know the answer to someone's question: *"So, why do they keep looking at houses if they can't afford to move?" "Good question!"*

be out of the question
used to say that something will not be possible, or is not allowed: *Would another small loan be out of the question?*

pop the question
to ask someone to marry you: *I never expected Chris to pop the question so quickly. After all, we've only known each other for two months!*

a thorny question/problem
(also a thorny issue, subject, topic, etc.)
a problem that is difficult to deal with because people disagree and have strong feelings about it: *The court is considering the thorny question of an adopted child's right to know its natural parents.*

quick

cut someone to the quick
to make someone feel very upset or offended by saying or doing something: *Diana's rude remarks about dinner cut Mom to the quick.*

quit

have a ___ that (just) won't quit
SLANG used to talk about a beautiful feature that someone has: *Have you seen the new kid yet? He has muscles that just won't quit!*

quits

call it quits
to stop doing something after you have been doing it for a long time: *It has been nearly five years since Johnny Carson told America he was calling it quits.*

quote

quote, unquote
SPOKEN used before a word or phrase when you want people to understand that it is someone else's phrase or opinion, and that you do not agree with it: *I don't want to discuss his quote, unquote apology. If that's the best he can do, then forget it.*

R

R

___ R Us

a humorous expression used in order to say that a person or group has a particular style, quality, or skill: *Backstage at the Metallica concert there is a certain Boys R Us attitude. These guys are tough.*

> **NOTE▶** This idiom comes from the name of a very large group of toy stores called "Toys R Us" (trademark), which is famous for having a large variety of toys.

race

⇨the RAT race

a one-horse race

used about a game, competition, election, etc. in which one person is much better than the others and will definitely win: *Hamer's recent arrest will turn the election into a one-horse race for Castino.*

a race against time

used about a situation in which something important must be done or completed quickly: *In the movie, two young police officers find themselves in a frantic race against time to disarm the explosives.*

rack

go to rack and ruin

if a place, building, organization, etc. goes to rack and ruin, it gradually gets into a very bad condition because it is not being taken care of: *Over the years, they've let the company go to rack and ruin.*

rag

on the rag
(also **O.T.R.**)

SLANG a very impolite expression used about a woman who is having her period (=the time each month when blood passes from a woman's body), especially when she is behaving in an unreasonable way: *What's her problem – is she on the rag or something?*

(from) rags to riches

used about someone's progress to success, when they were poor at first and have become very rich: *It is part of the American legend that any immigrant family can go from rags to riches.*
rags-to-riches: *His life is a rags-to-riches story that is as dramatic as a Hollywood movie.*

rage

be all the rage

used to say that something is very popular and fashionable: *A few years ago, flavored coffee was all the rage. Now, it's gourmet tea.*

rail

go off the rails
(also **run off the rails**)

if a system, organization, or process goes off the rails, it starts to have problems and does not work or develop as it should ◆ OFTEN USED IN NEWSPAPERS, ON TELEVISION NEWS, ETC.: *His statement indicated that a plan to resolve the state's disputes had gone off the rails just 18 hours after it had been accepted.*

(as) thin as a rail

very thin: *Has Linda been sick recently? She's as thin as a rail!*

rain

⇨rain on *someone's* PARADE

someone doesn't know enough to come in out of the rain

used about someone who is not sensible about avoiding trouble or taking care of himself or herself: *Tom Cruise's girlfriend, played by the unfortunate Laura Joyce, is a woman who doesn't know enough to come in out of the rain.*

rain or shine

used to emphasize that something always happens whether the weather is good or bad: *My aunt had a red hat which she wore to work every day, rain or shine.*

take a rain check (on *something*)

SPOKEN used to tell someone that you cannot do something with them now, but you would like to do it at another time: *"We're going out for dinner after work.*

*Want to come?" "Sorry, I can't tonight –
but I'll take a rain check."*

> NOTE▶ In the U.S., a rain check is a ticket
> that you get at a store because something
> you want to buy at a special lower price is
> temporarily not available. You can use the
> ticket to buy it at the lower price when it
> is available again.

when it rains it pours
SPOKEN said when several things of a
similar kind have happened to you all at
once, especially when you are annoyed
or surprised by this: *I can't believe that I
hadn't even looked at a man in two years,
and now I have three dates. When it rains
it pours.*

rainbows

be chasing rainbows
to be trying to get or achieve something
difficult or impossible: *I'm still chasing
rainbows. In a couple of years, if I still
haven't managed to get into professional
football, I'll come back home and coach.*

raking

someone is raking it in
SPOKEN used to say that someone is
making a lot of money, especially without
working very hard: *I saw Randy driving
around in his new Porsche. That guy must
be raking it in.*

ranch

don't bet the ranch on *someone/
something*
(also **I wouldn't bet the ranch on**
someone/something)
SPOKEN used to say that you cannot be sure
that something is true or will happen: *I
still think I can win the election, so don't
bet the ranch on Bigelow.*

rank

break ranks
to fail to support the group or organization that you are in, by doing or saying
something different from what you have
all agreed to do or say ◆ OFTEN USED IN
NEWSPAPERS, ON TELEVISION NEWS, ETC.: *One
major oil company broke ranks with the*
*rest of the industry and supported the
tough new anti-pollution laws.*

close ranks
to unite more closely in a group by
supporting each other and not admitting
any disagreement ◆ OFTEN USED IN NEWS-
PAPERS, ON TELEVISION NEWS, ETC.: *Even
though Republicans appear to be closing
ranks behind their controversial leader,
the picture could change within the next
week.*

pull rank (on *someone*)
to use your position of authority unfairly
in order to gain an advantage or to make
someone do something for you: *Joe was
determined to show he could still handle
danger. That's why he pulled rank on
Stewart and took the assignment.*

the rank and file
the ordinary people in an organization
who do not have power and authority:
*Meara's appointment has proven to be
popular among members of the union's
rank and file.*
rank-and-file: *Rank-and-file party members
meet at the convention to nominate
candidates for President and Vice President.*

swell the ranks of
to make a group of people larger by
joining it or making people join it: *Factory
closures and layoffs have swollen the
ranks of the city's unemployed.*

ransom

a king's ransom
a very large amount of money: *If we were
offered a king's ransom, we might
consider moving to Medford, but it's
definitely our last choice.*

rap

get a bum rap
to be punished too severely for
something, or to be unfairly criticized for
something: *Wallberg thinks the band gets
a bum rap. "They work hard and always
have," he said.*

be given a rap on/over/across the
knuckles
(also **have/get your knuckles rapped**)
to be criticized, but not severely, for
something that you have done wrong

◆ OFTEN USED IN NEWSPAPERS, ON TELEVISION NEWS, ETC.: *In the past, companies involved in illegal dealings have gotten away with a rap on the knuckles.*

take the rap (for)
to be blamed or punished for a mistake or crime, especially for something that you did not do: *We can prove that Greenburger was set up to take the rap for the murder of Radin.*

raring

be raring to go
(also **be raring to do** *something*)
to be very eager to begin doing something: *September is the best time to start a new project, when everyone's back from their vacations and raring to go.*

raspberry

blow a raspberry
to make an impolite noise by putting out your tongue and blowing: *The other team's fans responded to the touchdown by booing and blowing raspberries.*
—see also **a BRONX cheer**

rat

go down like a rat sandwich
(also **be as popular, welcome, etc. as a rat sandwich**)
used to say that someone or something is very unpopular: *Now the rest of the U.S. will find out why the governor of Alabama has gone down like a rat sandwich in the South.*

> NOTE▶ You may hear people use other expressions that make a comparison with something disgusting, for example "like a turd in a swimming pool": *If he told his favorite joke, I imagine it went down like a turd in a swimming pool.*

the rat race
used about a situation, especially people's daily work, that you think is difficult and unpleasant because people are always competing with each other and trying hard to get advantages for themselves: *On Monday morning, it's back to the rat race.*

smell a rat
to begin to think that someone is trying to

deceive you, or that something about a situation is wrong: *Nelson was unsure about the plan. "What if they see us beforehand and smell a rat?" he asked.*
—see also *something* **SMELLs fishy**

raw

in the raw
1 used to say that something is in its most basic, natural, or typical state, especially when this is unpleasant: *In the towns and settlements of the Gold Rush, Jack London saw and recorded human nature in the raw.*
2 (also **in the buff**) wearing no clothes: *Moonstone is one of the few places along the New England coast where nudists are allowed to sunbathe in the raw.*

ray

catch/bag some rays
SLANG if you catch some rays, your skin becomes brown or pink from sitting in the sun: *I'm not just sitting around bagging rays, you know – I'm working hard.*

a ray of sunshine
used about someone or something that makes you feel happier and makes your situation seem better: *Winter may not be everyone's favorite time of year, but fresh citrus fruits can bring a ray of sunshine into your day.*

razor

⇨**be on a razor's/razor EDGE**

reaction

⇨*someone's* **GUT reaction**

a knee-jerk reaction/response
used about an opinion or idea that someone has given too quickly, without thinking carefully first: *Some environmentalists tend to have a knee-jerk reaction to any type of development.*

> NOTE▶ You can use "knee-jerk" with other nouns that show types of reactions: *The union leaders' knee-jerk rejection of a 30 percent wage increase is not going to help their members.* | *People are still disturbed by AIDS, but there's less knee-jerk fear than five years ago.*

R

read

read too much into *something*
to think that a situation, action, etc. has more meaning or importance than it really has: *I wouldn't try to read too much into Greg's comment. I'm sure he didn't mean anything by it.*

ready

be ready to roll
to be ready to start doing something, or ready to start operating or being used: *Everybody was packed and ready to roll by 5:00.*

real

⇨**GET real!**

someone/something **is for real**
SPOKEN used to say that something is true, or that someone is or does exactly what they say, even though it is difficult to believe ♦ OFTEN USED IN QUESTIONS AND NEGATIVES: *After Duke finished his speech, I looked at my friends. "Is this guy for real?" they asked.*

reap

you reap what you sow
(also **as you sow, so shall you reap**)
used to say that anything good that you do will finally bring you a good result, or that anything bad will bring a bad result: *You reap what you sow, and Jerry may eventually regret his behavior in Friday's game.*

rear

bring up the rear
1 to be at the back of a line of people who are moving, or to be the last in a race: *We watched as the runners went past, with one woman with an injured knee bringing up the rear.*
2 to be the last person in a group to do something, or to be less successful than other people in a group: *The best salaries go to musicians in symphonies and opera. Musical theater brings up the rear.*

rearguard

fight a rearguard action
to make a determined effort to prevent something from happening, even though you think it is too late to succeed: *Malloy, his wife and daughters have been fighting a rearguard action to prevent their home from being destroyed by developers.*

reason

for reasons best known to himself/herself
used to emphasize that you do not understand what someone's reasons for doing something are: *I wanted to travel in Europe this summer, but my parents, for reasons best known to themselves, were totally opposed to the idea.*

it stands to reason
used to emphasize that what you are saying is sensible and should be easy to understand: *It stands to reason that you'll be more enthusiastic about studying English if you know it's going to help you in your career.*

recipe

be a recipe for ___
used to say that you think a plan or situation will definitely have a particular result, especially a bad one: *If we rely on commercial organizations to provide all our health care, then surely that is a recipe for disaster. | Trying to get the development approved by the whole community is always a recipe for long meetings and endless delay.*

record

a broken record
used about someone who keeps saying the same thing again and again: *I know it's getting to be a broken record, because I say it each spring, but this year will be La Russa's toughest challenge.*

(just) for the record
1 SPOKEN used to say that you want to make something clear, or to be sure that it has been recorded correctly ♦ USED ESPECIALLY IN OFFICIAL MEETINGS: *For the record, my salary has never been $16*

million, as was reported in Monday's business section.
2 used when you are giving information that you think may interest people, though it is not the main thing you are talking about: *Just for the record, field mustard is not a native plant. It was introduced from Europe.*

off the record
if someone in authority or a politician says something off the record, he or she is not making an official statement, and does not want newspapers, television news, etc. to tell people exactly what was said: *State Department officials, speaking off the record, say that they cannot yet be certain that the change of policy will be successful.*
off-the-record: *At an off-the-record meeting with reporters, the police chief outlined his concerns about terrorist activity.*

on the record
1 if someone in authority or a politician says something on the record, he or she is saying it officially and wants newspapers, television news, etc. to tell people what was said: *The President gave all officials who had been at the meeting permission to discuss it with the press, on the record.*
2 if something that has been said at a meeting, in a court of law, etc. is on the record, it has been included in the official record of the meeting: *The court has put it on record that you intend to have Mr. Bigelow testify to the jury. Is that correct?*

set/put the record straight
to tell people the true facts about a situation when you think that they have a wrong idea about it: *The Historical Society is helping to set the record straight on the history of local Native American tribes.*
—see also **SET** *someone* **straight**

red
⇨a **red-letter DAY**
⇨**SEE red**

be in the red
to have no money in your bank account: *The plant continued operating in the red, until the board of directors finally shut it down.*
—compare **be in the BLACK**

redhanded
⇨**CATCH** *someone* **redhanded**

rein
give *someone/something* **(a) free rein**
(also **allow** *someone/something* **(a) free rein)**
1 to give someone the freedom to do what they want, especially to allow someone who works for you, to decide how they will do their job: *Daley gave his police force free rein to crack down on Vietnam War protesters.*
2 (also **give free rein to** *something*) to let your feelings or ideas be fully expressed, without trying to control or limit them: *Children would prefer to give free rein to their tendency to be dirty and messy.*

keep a tight rein on *someone/ something*
(also **keep** *someone/something* **on a tight rein)**
to control someone or something very strictly: *It is impossible to be competitive in business today without keeping a tight rein on costs.*

take (up) the reins
(also **take over the reins)**
to take control of a country or organization: *Giordano had to cut short her vacation in order to take up the reins of the Texas bank.*

> NOTE▶ "Reins" are long narrow bands of leather that are fastened around a horse's head to control it. The expression "the reins" can be used in various ways to mean control over a country or organization: *Analysts agree that the President is holding the reins at a time of real change in society.* | *Stevens had no intention of letting Personnel, or anyone else, take the reins out of his hands.*

remain
who will/shall remain nameless
SPOKEN said when you want to say that someone has done something wrong, but you do not want to mention their name: *A certain person, who will remain nameless, forgot to turn the coffee maker off last night.*

R

reputation

⇨**blacken** *someone's*
NAME/image/reputation

response

⇨**a knee-jerk REACTION/response**

rest

⇨**LAY** *someone/something* **to rest**

no rest for the weary/wicked
used humorously to say that, even though
you are tired, you have to keep working:
*Just as Shirley sat down, there was a
knock at the door. "No rest for the weary,"
she thought.*

retreat

beat a (hasty) retreat
to leave a place quickly, especially
because you are afraid or embarrassed:
*Finding themselves surrounded by large
men with kitchen knives, the health
inspectors beat a hasty retreat.*

beat a (hasty) retreat

rhyme

without rhyme or reason
(also **there is no rhyme or reason (to/
for** *something***)**)
used to emphasize that you cannot think
of a reason why someone did something
or why something happened: *Results
seemed to vary between regions, with no
rhyme or reason.*

ribs

stick to your ribs
if a food sticks to your ribs, it continues to
give you energy for a long time after you
eat it so that you do not feel hungry for a
long time: *We recommend that you have
a hearty breakfast, something that will
really stick to your ribs, before starting
any of the exercises.*

rich

that's rich (coming from *someone*)
SPOKEN used to say that you are surprised
by what someone has said and think it is
unreasonable, especially when they are
criticizing another person for doing
something that they do themselves: *"I
can't believe how some people waste
money." "That's rich! You spend more
than anybody I know."*

riddles

talk/speak in riddles
to say things in a way that is not clear so
that people cannot easily understand
them: *At a time when the city needs firm
guidance, the mayor seems determined to
talk in riddles.*

ride

⇨**let** *something* **ride** —see **LET**
something **slide**

get a free ride
1 to have the advantages of a situation
which other people are paying for, or in
which other people are doing most of the
work ♦ OFTEN USED IN NEWSPAPERS, ON TELE-
VISION NEWS, ETC.: *Why should other
countries with small defense budgets get
a free ride, thanks to America's military
presence all over the world?*
give *someone* **a free ride:** *The proposed tax
changes will give the rich a free ride, while
the poor pay the penalty.*
2 to be allowed to do what you want,
without being criticized by your
opponents ♦ OFTEN USED IN NEWSPAPERS, ON
TELEVISION NEWS, ETC.: *Cable TV companies
have been getting a free ride for too long.
It's time they were subject to stricter
regulations.*

R

go/be/come along for the ride

SPOKEN to go somewhere with other people or do what they are doing just for enjoyment, not because you need to do it or are seriously interested in it: *I went over to Kevin's, and he and Jo were going out for something to eat, so I just went along for the ride.*

be riding high

to be very confident and successful: *The President, riding high on his foreign policy successes, is attempting to use some of that popularity to boost his domestic agenda.*

a rough/bumpy ride

a time when there are a lot of difficulties and problems, or when there is a lot of opposition and criticism ◆ OFTEN USED IN NEWSPAPERS, ON TELEVISION NEWS, ETC.: *Investors face a bumpy ride as the stock market continues to react to political developments.*

opposite **a smooth ride:** *If you and Curt ever do get married, it won't be a smooth ride.*

take *someone* for a ride

SPOKEN to trick or deceive someone, especially in order to get money from them: *Before paying for a package tour, read all the paperwork carefully to make sure you're not being taken for a ride.*

right

⇨hang a **LEFT/right**
⇨be on the right **TRACK**

ring

⇨run **CIRCLEs/rings around** *someone*

go/reach/grab for the brass ring
(also **get the brass ring**)

to try to achieve or get something that is the best of its kind: *At the time I was searching for that brass ring, saying "I'm as good as him, why am I not on the national news?"*

ring hollow
(also **have a hollow ring**)

if a statement, promise, etc. rings hollow, you do not feel that it is true or sincere: *Politicians' talk about rising living standards must ring hollow to people in areas devastated by failed industries.*

ring true

if a statement, description, etc. rings true, it gives the effect of being completely true, and you believe it at once: *Crosby's live act consists mainly of stories and anecdotes that ring true with everyone.*

ringer

be a dead ringer for *someone*

used to say that someone looks exactly like another person: *Have you ever met her brother? He's a dead ringer for Nicolas Cage.*

—see also **be the spitting IMAGE of** *someone*

riot

⇨**RUN riot**

someone/something **is a riot**

SPOKEN used to say that someone or something is very funny: *There was always a party somewhere, and Sam Fermoyle was a riot when he'd had a few drinks.*

read (*someone*) the riot act

to give someone a strong warning that they must stop causing trouble or doing something that you do not like: *Ask your doctor to read your husband the riot act when he comes in for his next blood pressure check.*

> NOTE▶ In nineteenth-century Britain, reading the Riot Act to a crowd of people was an official warning that they were causing trouble and must separate and leave. If they did not do this, they were breaking the law.

rip

⇨**LET it rip**

rise

get a rise out of *someone*

to make someone show that they are annoyed or embarrassed, by making jokes or insulting them: *We could usually get a rise out of Mr. James by pretending that we thought Bob Dylan was a better poet than Dylan Thomas.*

rise and shine

SPOKEN used to tell someone to wake up

R

and get out of bed: *Rise and shine, honey. It's time for school.*

river

sell someone down the river

to do something that harms someone or a group of people that trusted you in order to get an advantage for yourself: *Bert is heartless. He'd sell his own mother down the river.*

> NOTE▶ In the U.S. before 1865 slaves (=black workers who were owned by their employer) could be sold to other employers who often made them work harder and treated them worse. The idea of the river probably comes from the fact that the slaves would be sent to their new place by boat on the river.

road

⇨down the LINE/road
⇨ONE for the road

hit the road

SPOKEN to begin a trip: *Well, it's getting late. We'd better hit the road.*

the road to hell is paved with good intentions

OLD-FASHIONED used to say that it is no good intending to do something if you do not actually do it: *I thought I could work at night, then do other things during the day. But the road to hell is paved with good intentions, and the business soon went under.*

take the high road

to do or say what is morally right, especially in a situation in which other people are not doing this: *Turner has urged advertising companies to take the high road in TV shows they sponsor.*
opposite **take the low road:** *The Senate has taken the low road on civil rights, but that is no reason for the House to do the same.*

rock

⇨hit/reach rock BOTTOM

(caught) between a rock and a hard place

a difficult situation in which any choice that you make will have bad results: *In deciding whether to use plastic or glass bottles, the supermarkets are between a rock and a hard place, with environmental concerns on one side and customer preference on the other.*
—see also **between the DEVIL and the deep blue sea**

get your rocks off

1 SLANG to get sexual satisfaction, especially by masturbating (=touching your own sexual organs): *I bet Shawn spends all his time getting his rocks off in his room.*
2 a fairly impolite expression meaning to get a feeling of satisfaction and excitement: *Actors love new experience – they get their rocks off on that.*

have rocks in your head

SPOKEN an impolite expression used to say that someone is stupid: *"I asked Diane to marry me, but she said no." "Well, at least you don't both have rocks in your heads."*

on the rocks

1 an alcoholic drink on the rocks has ice in it: *Hatton ordered two vodkas on the rocks and carried them over to where Louise was sitting.*
2 if a marriage or business is on the rocks it is not working well and will soon fail: *I got the impression that their marriage was on the rocks and that they were staying together for the sake of the children.*

(as) solid as a rock

1 used about a group, person, or organization that you can trust because they are strong and not likely to change: *In California, support for the Democrats was as solid as a rock.*
2 strong and firm and not likely to break: *You can stand on this chair – it's as solid as a rock.*
rock-solid: *The Republicans enjoy rock-solid political support across all five southern states.*

(as) steady as a rock

1 not moving and not likely to move or fall: *He stood behind the trees, steady as a rock, waiting for the deer.*
2 used about someone who has a strong character and is calm and determined:

My grandfather was a respected man in his community, steady as a rock and, like a rock, incapable of change.
rock-steady: *I admired his rock-steady determination, even though it frustrated me.*

rocker

be off your rocker
to be slightly crazy: *Finally, there's someone here who's not completely off his rocker.*
—see also **be out of your MIND**

rocket

something isn't rocket science
used to say that something is not very difficult and complicated: *Although making a good shoe isn't rocket science, it is difficult to automate the production line efficiently.*

someone isn't a rocket scientist
(also *someone* **is no rocket scientist**)
SPOKEN used to say that someone is not a very intelligent person: *"Is Danny a good student?" "Let's just say he's no rocket scientist."*

rod

rule *someone* with a rod of iron
(also **run** *something* **with a rod of iron**)
to control an organization or group of people so strictly that they are too frightened to disobey you: *Ferdi's mother was a tough old woman who had run her family with a rod of iron after her husband had died.*
—compare **rule/control** *someone* **with an iron FIST**

roll

be on a roll
used to say that a person, team, or business is being very successful and keeps achieving what it wants ♦ USED ESPECIALLY IN NEWSPAPERS, MAGAZINES, ETC.: *The Rockets are on a roll, with eight straight wins.*

a roll in the hay
the act of having sex: *Nicole realized that she wanted more out of the relationship than a quick roll in the hay.*

rolling

be rolling in it
SPOKEN to have a lot of money: *"How could Nicki afford a car like that?" "Are you kidding? Her dad's rolling in it."*

Rome

fiddle while Rome burns
used when you disapprove because someone is spending too much time or attention on unimportant matters instead of trying to solve bigger and more important problems: *This is fiddling while Rome burns. We're spending hours arguing about small details when in fact the cost of the whole operation is too high.*

NOTE▶ According to an old story, while the city of Rome burned in 64 B.C., the emperor (=ruler) Nero played a violin and watched the flames.

Rome wasn't built in a day
used to tell someone to be patient because what they want to happen will take a long time: *It took a long time to train for the marathon, but Rome wasn't built in a day, and if you want to get good at something, you have to stick to it.*

when in Rome (do as the Romans do)
used to say that it is best to behave in the same way as the people around you in a situation, even if you would not normally do so: *I didn't normally drink alcohol, but I didn't want to refuse their hospitality. When in Rome, I thought, and took a small sip.*

roof

go through the roof/ceiling
1 used to say that something has suddenly become much more expensive, or that the amount of something, especially a financial activity, has suddenly increased a lot: *Running your air conditioner around the clock can cause your electricity bill to go through the roof.*
2 SPOKEN (also **hit the roof/ceiling**) to suddenly become very angry: *Alison'll go through the roof when she sees what you've done to her dress.*

R

raise/lift the roof
if a group of people raise the roof, they make a lot of noise, by singing, shouting, etc.: *CeCe Winans and Shirley Caesar raised the roof with their medley of gospel songs.*

rooftops

shout *something* from the rooftops
(also **yell, scream, etc.** *something* **from the rooftops**)
to try to make people listen to what you are saying, or tell everyone about something: *The American people have finally said at the polls what they have been screaming from the rooftops for two years – that they care about the economy and they want a President who listens.*

room

⇨**a/some breathing SPACE/room**

a smoke-filled room
used about a meeting where a business or political decision is made secretly by a small group of people: *Our spies from the Democrats' smoke-filled rooms say that Jackson won't run for election next year.*

roost

rule the roost
to have complete control over a situation, or be the most important thing in it: *There was no question about who ruled the roost in our house.*

root

⇨**the GRASS roots**

put down roots
1 to begin living in a place and decide that you are going to live there for a long time: *Weil plans to travel frequently, rather than put down roots in the city.*
2 if an organization, system, or plan puts down roots, it is accepted and becomes successful: *Japanese steel manufacturers are beginning to put down roots in America's industrial heartland.*

root and branch
1 used about a change that affects every part of an organization or system: *In order to cut costs significantly, we will have to make some root and branch cuts in spending.*
2 if you oppose or destroy something root and branch, you oppose or destroy it totally: *We want to get rid of racism, root and branch.*

take root
if an idea or system takes root, it becomes accepted or established: *Ms. Bhutto claimed that all she wanted was to see democracy take root in Pakistan after more than 40 years of military rule.*

rope

give *someone* enough rope (and they'll hang themselves)
(also **give** *someone* **a lot of rope**)
used to say that it is easy to get rid of someone whom you do not like or trust. Just let them do or say anything they want, and they will probably make a mistake and be forced to leave: *That Forbes woman causes too much trouble. One of these days they'll give her just enough rope to hang herself with.*

go piss up a rope!
SLANG an impolite expression used to tell someone to stop annoying you: *I do my best to take care of my kids, and if that's not good enough for you, go piss up a rope.*

know/learn the ropes
to know or learn how to do a particular job, or how to deal with a particular situation: *It takes time to learn the ropes – you can't expect to do everything right away.*

> NOTE▶ This idiom comes from the time when sailors (=men who work on ships) had to know how to deal with the ropes on ships.

on the ropes
if a person, organization, system, etc. is on the ropes, it is unsuccessful and about to fail: *Two mediocre movies put Stallone's career back on the ropes, prompting him to return to the role that made him a star, in Rocky II.*
—see also **on the ROCKs**

show/teach someone the ropes
to quickly show someone how to do a particular job, or how to deal with a particular situation: *When the Johnsons bought a computer, I went over to set it up and show them the ropes.*

rose
⇨*something* **is no BED of roses**
⇨**see** *something* **through rose-colored GLASSES**

come out smelling like roses
to get an advantage from a situation, when you ought to be blamed, criticized, or harmed by it: *These tax cuts do nothing to help the poor, and the only people who come out smelling like roses are the very wealthy.*

everything's/it's coming up roses
used to say that someone is being successful, or that something is happening exactly as it is supposed to, and there are no problems: *It is time for politicians to realize the threat posed by industrial pollution instead of pretending that everything's coming up roses.*

rough
rough and ready
1 very simple and basic, or made, or done very quickly without much preparation: *These checks are just a rough and ready way to get the basic information.*

2 used about someone who is not very polite or good at dealing with people: *Chaney got his first movie roles playing rough and ready characters in low-budget westerns.*

take the rough with the smooth
to be willing to accept the unpleasant parts of a situation as well as the pleasant parts: *I knew that I needed the press as much as they needed me, so I always treated journalists with respect and was happy to take the rough with the smooth.*

roughshod
ride/run roughshod over
to completely ignore the feelings, opinions, or rights of other people: *Some officials say the governor is willing to ride roughshod over industry for his own personal gain.*

route
go down the ___ route
to follow a particular course of action: *We were offered a chance to go down the Hollywood route, but I wanted to retain creative input in my films.* | *We may have to stop all recruitment, but I don't want to go down that route unless it's really necessary.*

row
⇨**be on SKID row**

have a tough/hard row to hoe
to be in a situation that is very difficult to deal with: *Until education in dance and drama gets the full support of the school system, we'll have a hard row to hoe.*

rub
rub it in
SPOKEN to remind someone of a mistake they have made, something embarrassing that they have done, or of a situation where you have an advantage over them
♦ OFTEN USED IN THE NEGATIVE: *"I've won two more games than you." "I know. You don't have to rub it in."*

there's/here's the rub
(also **therein lies the rub**)
used to say that you think something

R

which has just been said shows the problem that makes a situation difficult: *Network computers need really fast connections. Here's the rub: the people who would benefit most from cheap Internet computers would need the most expensive networks to make them work well.*

> **NOTE▶** This idiom is from a line in Shakespeare's play, *"Hamlet."* You may hear people use "the rub" in other expressions that show what is difficult or bad about the situation: *Pepsi-cola was willing to donate $15,000 for the parks. The rub was that the playgrounds must be called "Pepsi" parks and they must erect a sign to that effect.*

rubber

burn rubber

to start driving your car so fast that the wheels make a loud noise and leave black marks on the surface of the road: *Gary hit the brakes and threw the car into reverse, burning rubber.*

where the rubber meets the road

a situation in which you use an idea rather than just thinking about it, especially one in which you find out whether the idea is practical or not: *We want to empower our employees and put the decision-making closer to where the rubber meets the road.*

> **NOTE▶** This idiom comes from an American commercial for car tires, which uses "rubber" to mean "tire" and tries to sell the tires by showing that they work very well in real situations on the road.

Rube Goldberg

Rube Goldberg

used about a system, machine, etc. that does something ordinary in a way that is very complicated and not at all practical: *He'd invented a Rube Goldberg device that used a system of ropes and pulleys to fill a kettle.*

rug

someone **lies like a rug**
(also **you lie like a big dog (on a rug))**
SLANG an impolite expression used to say that someone is not telling the truth, often used humorously: *You lie like a rug, Justin – I never said that!*

pull the rug (out) from under
someone

to suddenly stop supporting someone, or take away something that they depend on for success in a plan: *The Seminoles, playing their first conference game, proceeded to pull the rug out from under fifth-ranked North Carolina.*

> **NOTE▶** You may hear people use other verbs instead of "pull," to show how suddenly and completely this is done: *These people have kids to feed and house payments to make, and now they're having the rug swept from under them by the system they work for.*

sweep something **under the rug/**
carpet

to ignore a problem in your organization or group, especially something wrong that someone has done, and try to stop people from finding out about it: *Use of excessive force by officers has been allowed or swept under the carpet in the past.*

rule

the golden rule

the most important rule or principle to remember when you are doing something: *Now the goal is to follow the golden rule of customer service, treating people the way you want to be treated.*

hard and fast rules

rules that are exact, definite, and strict
◆ OFTEN USED IN THE NEGATIVE: *Obviously in car insurance we can't lay down hard and fast rules that apply to every car.*

a rule of thumb

a piece of advice or general rule which is usually true, or gives you a good enough idea of how to do something: *As a rule of thumb, if a turkey weighs less than 12lbs., allow about three-quarters of a pound per serving.*

R

NOTE▶ In past times, brewers (=people who make beer) used to test the temperature of beer with their thumb to see if it was ready.

work to rule
if a group of employed people work to rule, they protest by only doing exactly what their job contract says, and refusing to do anything more: *Teachers have responded by picketing before and after classes, and by working to rule.*
work-to-rule: *If the education board doesn't agree to negotiations, we will institute a work-to-rule policy.*

rumor
rumor has it (that)
used before a statement to say that you have heard that it is true but are not sure that it is: *Rumor has it that the legendary Trocadero on 4th Street is going to be torn down.*

run
⇨**have a RUN-IN with** *someone*

give *someone* a run for his/her money
to do very well in a sport or activity, even though the person or team you are competing with is much better than you, and will probably win or be the best ◆ OFTEN USED IN NEWSPAPERS, ON TELEVISION NEWS, ETC.: *Reinach said, "I couldn't believe it – this was my first time at*

give *someone* a run for his/her money

Wimbledon and suddenly I was winning the first set and giving Martina a run for her money."

go on a ___ run
SPOKEN to go to buy something, especially alcohol or food, that you want to drink or eat immediately: *"Is that the last can?" "Yeah, I'm just going on a beer run. Do we need anything else?"* | *Don't start the next video yet. I need to go on a cigarette run.*

in the long run
(also **over the long haul**)
used to talk about the effects that a change, process, or decision will have a long time in the future: *Artificial turf is unpopular with players because of the damage to joints that it does over the long haul.*

in the short run
used to talk about the immediate effects that a change, process, or decision will have: *I'm going to offer a program that will create half a million jobs in the short run.*

run amok
1 to suddenly start behaving violently or in a way that is not controlled: *The place looked as though an army of drunken students had run amok with spray paint.*
2 used to say that something is happening in a way that is extreme or crazy: *Kubrick's 1968 film heightened people's anxieties about technology run amok in the future.*

run/go deep
if a feeling or belief runs deep, it has a very strong affect on a person, organization, etc. for a long time: *Feelings about the death of a parent are bound to go deep, and a person's immediate reac-tion may not reveal how they really feel.*

run *someone/something* ragged
to make someone very tired by giving them too much work or too many problems: *The cold temperatures ran utility services and plumbers ragged, with burst water pipes all over the city.*

run riot
1 if a feeling, idea, or person runs riot, they are totally free and cannot be controlled: *Shannon had let her*

R

imagination run riot on the costume designs for the play's 21st-century warlords, serfs, and robots.
2 if a plant or a disease runs riot, it grows or increases too quickly and successfully: *Tropical foliage ran riot over most of the yards in the neighborhood.*

run with it
to do as much as you can to develop an idea, or use an opportunity to achieve as much as you can: *While clinical psychologists dismissed the theory, a few authors picked it up and ran with it, producing several bestselling books.*

run-around

give *someone* the run-around
to avoid giving someone a definite answer, especially when they are asking you to do something: *I sent a fax because I was just given the run-around when I called them.*

get the run-around: *I told Mike this morning I was tired of getting the run-around and wanted answers to my questions.*

runes

read the runes
to examine a situation and understand it because of your special experience and skill: *Those who are skilled in reading the runes predict that the rebels will make an offer of peace talks.*

> **NOTE▶** This idiom is used more often in written than in spoken English.

rung

the top/highest rung of the ladder
the highest level or position in a system or organization, especially a very important job: *Although he did not reach the top*

rung of the ladder as a musician, Mann had a distinguished career.
—see also **climb (up) the LADDER**

> **NOTE▶** You may also hear people talk about other rungs of the ladder between the lowest and the highest: *Why should women technicians be relegated to the lower rungs of the ladder?* | *That was a really important album that helped push the group up a few more rungs on the ladder.*

run-in

have a run-in with *someone*
to have an argument or disagreement with someone, especially someone in an official position: *Prior to his arrest for Booker's murder, Williams had had plenty of run-ins with the law.*

running

be in the running (for *something*)
to have a good chance of getting a job, prize, etc.: *Rivlin was still in the running for the position of vice chairman.*

rush

get the bum's rush
(also **be given the bum's rush**)
to be forced to leave a place where you are not wanted: *When Rossi found out I was a reporter, I was immediately given the bum's rush.*

rut

get (stuck) in a rut
(also **be (stuck) in a rut**)
to feel bored because you seem to be living or working in a situation that never changes: *We're always looking for better ways to market our products, not to get stuck in a rut.*

S

saber

saber-rattling
if a country is involved in saber-rattling, it threatens to use military force or go to war, although it may not be seriously intending to do this: *There had been some saber-rattling in the first week of the confrontation, but it was quiet for weeks after that.*

rattle your saber: *The two countries are once again rattling their sabers over a century-old border dispute.*

sack

hit the sack/hay
SPOKEN to go to bed and sleep: *It's late – I'm going to hit the sack.*

hop/jump in the sack
SPOKEN used to say that someone has sex without thinking seriously about who they have it with: *You know he'll hop in the sack with anybody who's willing.*

sackcloth

wear/don sackcloth (and ashes)
to behave in a way that shows everyone that you are very sorry for something you have done, often used humorously: *I don't believe that anybody has to wear sackcloth and ashes forever after being convicted of a crime.*

> NOTE▶ This idiom comes from a very old Hebrew custom of wearing sackcloth (=rough cloth) and ashes (=gray powder that is left after you burn something) for some religious ceremonies.

safe
⇨BETTER safe than sorry

said
⇨you said it! —see SAY

that's/it's easier said than done
SPOKEN used to say that it would be difficult to do what someone has suggested: *"Just find someone new to go out with and you'll forget all about Chris." "Good advice, but that's easier said than done."*

sailing

be smooth/clear sailing
if work or an activity is plain, smooth, etc. sailing, it is easy to do or achieve: *Now that we've finished installing all the electricity and plumbing, building the rest of the house should be smooth sailing.*

sails

trim your sails (to *something*)
to change your behavior, especially to spend less money, in order to deal with a difficult situation ◆ OFTEN USED IN BUSINESS AND POLITICS: *Cohen is very flexible. He will trim his sails to suit the administration.*

salad

someone's **salad days**
the time when someone was young and did not have much experience of life: *Her later music is very different from the precise, classically-based works of her salad days.*

salt

no ___ worth his/her salt would do *something*
(also **any ___ worth his/her salt would do** *something*)
used to say that someone who is good at their job would do a particular thing: *Any farmer worth his salt would have killed that old cow long ago.*

> NOTE▶ In ancient Rome, soldiers were paid in salt instead of money.

rub salt in/into someone's **wounds**
(also **rub salt in/into the wound**)
to do something that makes someone feel even more embarrassed or upset about their situation than they already do: *The Museum of Western Art was officially shut down and, to rub salt into the wound, the building was turned into a meat storage facility.*

S

NOTE▶ Sailors (=men who work on ships) were punished in the past by being beaten with a rope. Salt was put on their wounds because people thought it would help them get better but, of course, it just made them hurt more.

the salt of the earth
used about a person or group of people you admire because they are good, honest, ordinary people: *He grew up on a farm, working out in the fields all the time. His family is the salt of the earth.*
salt-of-the-earth: *We like our politicians to be salt-of-the-earth types.*

same

⇨**ONE and the same**

same old, same old
SPOKEN used to say that everything is the same as usual: *"Hi, Sean. How's it going?" "Oh, you know – same old, same old."*

sand

be built on sand
if a relationship, organization, etc. is built on sand, it is likely to fail or end because the ideas or rules it is based on are not good or moral: *I'm not surprised about the divorce – the whole marriage was built on sand.*

the shifting sands of *something*
used about a situation that keeps changing so that it is difficult to deal with: *Policy makers have a hard time keeping up with the shifting sands of public opinion.*

sandwich

⇨**go down like a RAT sandwich**

one sandwich short of a picnic
(also **a few/couple sandwiches short of a picnic**)
SPOKEN a humorous expression used about someone who is very stupid or slightly crazy: *Come on, let's face it – nobody trusts the guy because he's at least one sandwich short of a picnic.*

sardines

be packed like sardines
(also **be crammed, squeezed, etc. like sardines**)
if a group of people or things is packed like sardines, they are pushed together in a small space: *I can't believe people commute to work everyday in those subways. They are packed like sardines.*

sauce

(what's) sauce for the goose (is sauce for the gander)
(also **(what's) good for the goose (is good for the gander)**)
OLD-FASHIONED used to say that if one person is treated in a particular way, then you should treat other people in the same situation in the same way: *American businesses have become more profitable by expanding across the globe, but U.S. wages have not risen that much. What has been sauce for the goose has not been sauce for the gander.*

NOTE▶ This idiom sounds less old-fashioned if it is shortened or if people's names are used instead of "goose" and "gander": *You have to think about what the children need. What's sauce for us isn't sauce for them.*

save

save it
SPOKEN an impolite expression used to tell someone to stop talking because you do not want to hear their opinion or because their opinion cannot change the situation: *Save it, Len – Dennis will never agree to a plan like that.*
—see also **don't waste your BREATH**

say

⇨**to say the LEAST**
⇨**WHAT do you say we...**
⇨**WHEN all is said and done**

as they say
used to show that what you are saying is a famous phrase or idiom that everyone knows: *When he was 17, Olajuwon*

picked up a basketball for the first time. The rest, as they say, is history.

don't say I never give you anything
SPOKEN a humorous expression said when you give someone something that is silly, unusual, etc.: *"A pen shaped like a banana?" "Merry Christmas. Don't say I never gave you anything."*

I'll say!
SPOKEN used to emphasize that you agree with what someone has just said: *"That's a pretty big house." "I'll say!"*

you can say that again
SPOKEN used to emphasize that you agree with what someone has just said, especially if they are criticizing or complaining about something: *"Deb's gained a lot of weight recently." "You can say that again."*

you said it!
1 SPOKEN (also **you said it; I didn't!**) used to tell someone that something unpleasant or upsetting they have just said is true when you do not want to say it directly: *"I'm sure Allen's motives are political." "You said it – I didn't!"*
2 SPOKEN used to say that you agree with someone and understand how they feel: *"Let's go home." "You said it – I'm tired!"*

scare
⇨**scare** *someone* **out of their WITs**

scene
⇨**set the STAGE/scene (for)**

be done behind the scenes
(also **happen behind the scenes**)
to be done or happen privately or secretly while other things are happening in public: *Senators are still negotiating behind the scenes and should come to an agreement soon.*
behind-the-scenes: *The book provides a behind-the-scenes look at the filming of Spielberg's latest epic.*

scent
throw/put *someone* off the scent
to prevent someone from finding out information that you do not want them to

know, by telling lies or trying to make them think of something else: *He needed to throw Graham off the scent, so he tried to change the subject to give himself time to think.*

scheme
in the (grand) scheme of things
used to show that something is not very important or bad when you compare it to larger problems or events in your job, life, etc.: *It may seem like a lot, but in the grand scheme of things, a loss of $5,000 isn't going to hurt the company that much.*

school
be from the old school
someone who is from the old school has old-fashioned qualities or beliefs: *Chilton has repaired hundreds of baseball gloves. "I'm from the old school," he says. "I believe a glove should last a lifetime."*

science
⇨*something* **isn't ROCKET science**
blind *someone* with science
to tell someone something in a complicated way, using lots of technical words that are difficult for ordinary people to understand: *Instead of blinding us with science and all these charts and figures, why don't you show us what you mean?*

scientist
⇨*someone* **isn't a rocket scientist** —see *something* **isn't ROCKET science**

scoop

get the scoop (on *someone/ something*)
SPOKEN to find out important, exciting, or secret information about someone or something, especially information about someone's personal life: *"Did you get the scoop on the new neighbors yet?"*
what's the scoop (on *someone/something*)?: *So what's the scoop on Allie? Is she going to ask him out?*

score

know the score
to know all the facts of a situation, especially when you know which ones are most important or useful: *As a four-term senator from California, Cranston knows the score on political fundraising.*

settle an old score
to do something to harm or upset someone because they have harmed or upset you in the past: *The report said that many of the former employees who were interviewed were only interested in settling an old score.*

scratch

from scratch
if you start, make, or do something from scratch, you start or make something completely new rather than using, changing, or adding to something that already exists: *Mason started his company from scratch with one computer in his spare bedroom. | If I'd had more time, I would have made the cake from scratch instead of using a mix.*

scream

be a scream
used to say that someone or something is very funny: *Spiegel is a scream as the incompetent dog catcher who never manages to catch a single mutt.*

screw

have a screw loose
SPOKEN to behave in a strange way, or to be slightly crazy: *Fernando might have a screw or two loose, but he'd never hurt anyone.*

put the screws on *someone*
to force someone to do what you want by threatening them or making things difficult for them: *We need to put the screws on convenience stores or anyone who sells cigarettes to kids.*

tighten/turn the screws on
to make a person, group, organization, etc. do what you want them to do, especially when you are trying to stop them from doing something wrong or illegal: *The anti-terrorism law aims to tighten the screws on groups operating on U.S. territory.*

scruff

take/grab *something* by the scruff of the neck
to take determined action in order to deal with a difficult problem or reorganize a system: *Congress seems to be dominated be political action groups. I'd like to take it by the scruff of the neck and shake it up a little.*

scum

the scum of the earth
the worst people you can imagine: *He's really the scum of the earth. He lies all the time and just uses other people for their money.*

Scylla

between Scylla and Charybdis
in a situation in which there are two possible choices or actions both of which are equally bad: *The manager was polite, trying to guide the conversation between Scylla and Charybdis to keep it from descending into argument.*

sea

be at sea
to be confused or not know what to do in a particular situation: *In any class, it soon becomes apparent that some children are at sea.*

a sea change
a definite and important change in a situation or in people's opinions: *Any*

efforts to revive the manufacturing sector will require a sea change away from values of the 1980s which drove young people away from industry.

seams

be bursting at the seams
(also **be bulging, popping, creaking, etc. at the seams**)
to be so full of people or things that there is hardly any room for someone or something else to fit in: *There are not enough teachers, so classrooms are bursting at the seams with students.*

come/fall apart at the seams
1 if a plan, organization, etc. comes or falls apart at the seams, so many things are going wrong with it that it is very likely to fail: *The company came apart at the seams when Johnson left.*
2 if someone comes apart at the seams, they become very upset or nervous and have trouble controlling their emotions: *Whenever anyone told Kris, "This is an important game," she just fell apart at the seams and couldn't concentrate.*

search

search me
SPOKEN said when you do not know the answer to a question: *"Do you know where the scissors are?" "Search me."*

season

open season on ___
a time when many people are criticizing, attacking, or trying to make damaging changes to something or someone ♦ OFTEN USED IN NEWSPAPERS, ON TELEVISION NEWS, ETC.: *With all of Trump's financial problems, it's become open season on the tycoon.*

NOTE▶ Open season is the time each year when it is legal to kill particular animals or fish.

seat

⇨be (sitting) in the CATBIRD seat
back seat driver
someone who likes to give the driver of a car advice about how to drive or which way to go, especially when the driver does not want or need advice: *Okay, everybody – quiet! I've had enough of back seat drivers for one day.*

fly by the seat of your pants
to use your natural ability and intelligence to do something when you have not been able to learn, develop, or find out the correct way to do it: *Singleton, obviously flying by the seat of his pants, manages to produce an entertaining movie.*
seat-of-the-pants: *Levi Strauss' innovative use of computers stands out in an industry infamous for its instinctual, seat-of-the-pants approach to business.*

be in the driver's seat
to control everything that happens in an organization, situation, or relationship: *Giving parents a choice in where their kids go to school puts them in the driver's seat in education.*

in/on the hot seat
in a situation, job, etc. in which you have to make important decisions or answer difficult questions: *Dan and Gail are the ones in the hot seat – I'm going to let them make a decision, and I'll support them.*

take a back seat (to)
1 to let someone else make important decisions or be responsible for doing something: *De Beauvoir argued that women had taken a back seat to men and occupied a secondary position in society.*
2 if one thing takes a back seat to something else, people give less attention to the first thing because they think the second is more important or interesting: *Does Newton's murder take a back seat now that the police have a new one to think about?*

second

finish a close second
(also **come in a close second**)
to almost be as good as someone or something else, or to almost beat them in a competition, game, etc.: *Eggs come closest to providing the ideal protein pattern, milk comes in a close second, and meats follow.*

security

a security blanket

used about something that makes you feel safer or more confident although it may not really be very effective or useful: *I knew I couldn't hold down a full-time job and have my own business. So I gave up my security blanket and followed my dream.*

see

⇨ **see how the other HALF lives**

⇨ *someone* **wouldn't be caught/seen dead** —see **CATCH**

see red

to suddenly become very angry because of something that someone has said to you: *Farmers saw red when they found out their fields were being proposed as future nature reserves.*

see what *someone* is (really) made of

(also **find out what** *someone* **is (really) made of**)

to find out how strong, determined, or skillful someone is by watching them behave or perform in a difficult situation: *It's been a shock to lose so many games. We'll find out what we're made of in the next few weeks.*

show *someone* **what you're (really) made of:** *Go on, Terry – show these big-city coaches what you're made of.*

seed

go to seed

1 if a building or place goes to seed, it begins to look old and ugly because no one takes care of it: *The central bus station was hardly used and had gone to seed.*

2 if a person goes to seed, their body, clothes, hair, etc. look as if they do not take care of them: *Webber had once been a high-powered lawyer, but had since gone to seed.*

> **NOTE▶** This idiom comes from plants that should be picked before the seeds form, for example so that the young leaves can be eaten.

the seed corn (of *something*)

the people, materials, etc. that you take care of now because they will be useful in the future: *Research and development shouldn't be cut from the budget. It's the seed corn for our company's future technology.*

seeds

sow/plant the seeds (of *something*)

to start a process that will have a particular result: *Cutting off foreign aid to these developing countries is just sowing the seeds of disaster.*

sell

the hard sell

when you try to persuade someone to buy something or do something by talking a lot, arguing, and putting a lot of pressure on them: *Neil's been doing the hard sell on this biography, telling people there's stuff in it that no one has even guessed at before.*

hard-sell: *Despite a hard-sell marketing campaign, the college's enrollment has declined in recent years.*

sell *someone/something* short

to not give someone or something the praise, attention, or treatment that they deserve: *From the way she'd described herself, I pictured her as ugly and overweight. She's obviously been selling herself short.*

send *someone* **packing**

send

send *someone* **packing**
to make someone leave their job, a place, or a relationship: *The city's vote sent the current mayor packing after Jordan won the election easily.*

senses

come to your senses
to realize that what you are doing is not reasonable, and start behaving in a reasonable way: *Ryan started out as a comedian, but after two difficult years in depressing nightclubs, he came to his senses and went back to college.*
bring *someone* **(back) to his/her senses:** *Mom turned around and hit Dad one day, and I think it finally brought him to his senses.*

take leave of your senses
OLD-FASHIONED to start to behave in an unreasonable or stupid way: *Have you taken leave of your senses? You can't order the boss around like that!*

serve

(it) serves *someone* **right**
SPOKEN used to say that you think someone deserves a bad thing that has happened to them, especially because they have caused it: *"Tom and Linda missed their flight yesterday." "Well, it serves them right. They never get anywhere on time."*

service

⇨**pay LIP service to**

set

⇨**the JET set**
⇨**set the WORLD on fire**

set *someone* **straight**
to tell someone the right or best way to do something when they are doing it wrong, or tell them the truth about something when they believe something that is untrue: *Like my mother always said: women always know right from wrong. Ask us – we'll set you straight!*
—see also **set/put the RECORD straight**

sex

the fair sex
an old-fashioned expression meaning women that is often used humorously: *As a bachelor, you'll never find me lacking in my admiration for the fair sex.*

shade

⇨**have it made in the shade** —see **HAVE (got) it made**

put *someone/something* **in the shade**
(also **leave** *someone/something* **in the shade)**
to be so good or impressive that other things or people seem less impressive in comparison: *Ginny, elegantly dressed as usual, put the other women at the dinner in the shade.*

shades of ___
used to say that a situation, an event, or someone's behavior reminds you of something similar that happened or was done before: *Many banks are in trouble, the stock market is overvalued, people are losing their jobs – there are shades of the crash of 1929. | Smiley's novel is about an Iowa farmer who divides his land among his three daughters. Shades of "King Lear."*

shadow

beyond/without a shadow of (a) doubt
definitely and without any doubt at all: *We proved it was suicide, beyond a shadow of doubt.*

cast a shadow over *something*
if troubles or problems cast a shadow over a good or happy situation, they make it seem less good or more difficult to enjoy: *The border attack threatened to cast a shadow over the summit meeting.*

someone **is a shadow of his/her former self**
(also *something* **is a shadow of its former self/glory)**
used to say that someone or something is less strong, healthy, powerful or important than in the past: *San Diego has lost 50,000 jobs and its real-estate industry is a shadow of its former booming self.*

S

be scared/afraid of your own shadow

used about someone who is extremely shy or nervous: *We couldn't even get him to introduce himself at the meeting; he was so scared of his own shadow.*

shaft

get the shaft
(also **get shafted**)

INFORMAL to be treated unfairly: *I work, and I pay taxes, and I sent my kids to fight in a war. So why are people like me still getting shafted by the government?*

shake

do *something* **in two shakes (of a lamb's tail)**

OLD-FASHIONED used to say that you will do something very soon: *"Mom, come on, let's go." "I'm coming. I'll be there in two shakes of a lamb's tail."*

get a fair shake
(also **be given a fair shake**)

to be treated fairly: *Clark feels that the media hasn't given him a fair shake since he started this campaign.*
want/expect/deserve, etc. a fair shake: *We don't want any sympathy from the jury. We want a fair shake.*

no great shakes

used to say that you think someone is not very good at what they do, or something is not very good, useful, important, etc.: *Howie was no great shakes as a pianist, but he really enjoyed playing.*

shame

put *someone/something* **to shame**

to be so much better than someone or something else so that it makes the other thing seem bad or ordinary: *The discussions that these 14- and 15-year-olds have in their English literature classes would put many undergraduate college classes to shame.*

shape

get/be bent out of shape

SPOKEN to be very angry or upset: *People can get really bent out of shape if their wedding videos don't look just like a real movie.*

knock/whip *someone/something* **into shape**

to make a determined effort to teach a person who is not experienced to do something well, or to improve something that is not very good: *Mr. Sanders said he was determined to whip failing students into shape, or else kick them out of school.*

the shape of things to come

used about a situation, event, etc. that shows how things will be in the future: *The country's response to these important questions will determine the shape of things to come on its borders.*

shape up (or ship out)

used to say that someone should start behaving in a particular way, or leave: *Inefficient companies will be forced to shape up or ship out in this competitive atmosphere.*

share

the lion's share of *something*

used about the biggest part of something, especially money, food, or work, that is taken or done by one person: *Fitcher wrote the lion's share of the script, in addition to playing a leading role.*

shave

⇨ **a close shave** —see **a close CALL**

shebang

the whole shebang
(also **the whole enchilada**)

used to emphasize that you are talking about everything in a group of similar things, or everything that is involved in a particular activity: *You know that big volleyball tournament that was on ESPN? Her sister was the director for the whole shebang.*
—see also **the whole BALL of wax, the whole shooting MATCH, the (whole) WORKS**

sheep

the black sheep of the family

used about someone who is considered embarrassing by other members of their family or group because they are less successful or more immoral than the rest:

I never met Doug's parents – judging by what he told me, I think he was the black sheep of the family.

sheet

⇨**be singing from the same HYMN BOOK/sheet**

as white as a sheet/ghost
very pale because you are afraid, sick, etc.: *What's wrong? You're as white as a sheet.*

start with a clean sheet (of paper)
to be given a chance to do something in a new way, or without being blamed for your former mistakes: *The company has solved its problems, and the new president can start with a clean sheet.*

be three sheets to the wind
OLD-FASHIONED to be drunk: *Halfway through the reception, the bride's father was three sheets to the wind and dancing with everybody.*

shell

come out of your shell
to become less shy and more confident: *Ken always comes out of his shell when he's had a few drinks.*
bring someone out of his/her shell: *When we started talking about politics, it seemed to bring Brenda out of her shell.*

shell game

be a shell game
a plan or way of doing things that tricks people by changing things so that they seem good or better when they are not
♦ OFTEN USED IN NEWSPAPERS, ON TELEVISION NEWS, ETC.: *It's a shell game. Planners are playing with the money, shifting it on the books from one year to another.*

> NOTE▶ A shell game is a game in which someone has to guess which of three shells a small ball is hidden under after the person in control of the game has moved the shells around very quickly. The person in control of the game can usually move the shells so skillfully that the player is tricked.

shelves

be flying off the shelves
if a product is flying off the shelves, it is very popular and a lot of people are buying it: *Jerseys bearing the teams' new logos have been flying off the shelves at sporting goods stores.*

shine

take the shine off *something*
to spoil a pleasant or successful occasion by making it seem less good or special: *Tiredness and depression are likely to take the shine off your first days at home with your new baby.*

---

take the shine off *something*

take a shine to
to decide that you like someone as soon as you first meet or see them, especially if you cannot explain why: *Ben didn't seem too interested in Dinah, but he took a real shine to Annie and asked for her phone number.*

shingle

hang out your shingle
to start your own business, especially as a doctor or a lawyer: *His plan is to hang up his shingle in Brooklyn and specialize in helping immigrants from Africa.*

ship

⇨**SHAPE up (or ship out)**

jump/abandon ship

to leave an organization, a political party, etc. because you think it will fail: *Many executives have jumped ship after their bonuses for last year were not as big as in previous years.*

leave/desert/abandon a sinking ship

used to say that people are leaving a company, organization, etc. because they know that it is in trouble: *I don't want people to think I am deserting a sinking ship, but I think it is better for the team if I make a clean break.*

> NOTE▶ You may also hear people call a company, organization, etc. that is in trouble "a sinking ship," or say that the people leaving it are "rats leaving a sinking ship": *Two of the president's chief aides have resigned – possibly the first rats to leave the sinking ship.*

run a tight ship

to manage a company or organization very effectively by having strict rules: *Remember, I'm the boss, and I run a tight ship in this department, young man.*

ships that pass in the night

OLD-FASHIONED used about two people who meet by chance for a short time, and are attracted to each other: *I didn't think it would last with Stan – we were more like ships that pass in the night.*

when your ship comes in

used to say what you will do when you become rich, usually used humorously: *Our house still needs a lot of work, which we can't afford now – but one day, when our ship comes in, we'll get it done.*

> NOTE▶ This idiom comes from a time when business people and the wives of sailors (=men who work on ships) waited for ships to return so that they could be paid for their goods that were sold abroad, or use the money their husbands brought home.

shirt

⇨a HAIR shirt

keep your shirt on

(also **keep your pants on**)

SPOKEN used to tell someone to be calm and patient, and not get angry or upset: *"Hurry up, Jess, or we'll be late." "Keep your shirt on – we have plenty of time."*

lose your shirt

to lose a lot of money, especially because of making a bad decision in business: *Profits aren't good, but I'll be happy if I can just stay in business for the next few years without losing my shirt.*

take/have the shirt off someone's back

used when you disapprove because someone has taken or wants to take all of someone else's money: *Prices are rising so quickly, they're taking the shirt right off our backs.*

someone would give you the shirt off his/her back

used to say that someone is very generous and helpful: *Malcolm is the kind of guy who'd give you the shirt off his back.*

shit

> NOTE▶ Some people find the word "shit" offensive. It is better not to use it.

⇨shit a BRICK
⇨cut the CRAP/shit
⇨don't pull that CRAP/shit
⇨someone is full of CRAP/shit
⇨not ___ JACK (shit)
⇨shit or get off the POT

get your shit together

SPOKEN to organize yourself so that you have a better chance of doing what you want or being successful: *This week I'm going to get my shit together and actually make up a portfolio of all my best paintings.*

> NOTE▶ This expression is considered offensive by some people. "Get your act together" means the same thing, but is not offensive.

not give a shit

SPOKEN a rude expression used to say that you do not care about something: *We wasted a lot of time trying to recruit young people who basically didn't give a shit about politics.* | *"You can't park here – it's for disabled people." "Who gives a shit?"*

give *someone* **shit**

SPOKEN to talk to someone in a way that is offensive, for example by lying to them, criticizing them, or insulting them: *I'm an experienced news cameraman, and if reporters give me shit, I can very easily make them look stupid.* | *"I was at Carla's last night, Dad." "Don't give me that shit. I called her mother, and she said you were both out."*

be in deep shit

SPOKEN to be in a very difficult situation, or to be in trouble because people are angry with you: *Somebody saw Brad hit the other car, and they called the cops. He's in pretty deep shit with his folks right now.*

not know shit (from shinola)

SPOKEN a rude expression meaning someone does not know anything at all: *Carl doesn't know shit from shinola, and I'm not going to waste my time trying to explain everything to him.*

> NOTE▶ "Shinola" (trademark) is a type of shoe polish (=a liquid for cleaning your shoes).

no shit!

1 SPOKEN said to emphasize that you agree completely with someone and understand how they feel: *"It was really windy this morning!" "Yeah, no shit! I thought the house was going to blow down."*
2 SPOKEN said when you are very surprised at what someone has just said: *"I saw Rick today. He got a job as a record producer." "No shit! I never thought he'd do anything worthwhile."*
3 SPOKEN (also **no shit Sherlock!**) a rude expression said when you think that someone is being stupid because they have just said something that you knew already: *"You have to heat the oven first." "No shit! I have baked cookies before, you know."*

be on *someone*'s shit list

SPOKEN if you are on someone's shit list, they are very angry with you at that time: *It seems like I'm on everybody's shit list these days. Can't I do anything right?*

same shit, different day
(also **SSDD**)

SLANG a rude expression used to say that everything is the same as usual: *"What's happening, Joe?" "Nothing much – you know, same shit, different day."*

> NOTE▶ "Same old, same old" means the same as this idiom, but is not offensive.

shit happens

SPOKEN used to say that bad things often happen and that there is nothing anyone can do about it: *It took me a long time to get used to the idea that I didn't have a job anymore, but now I just think, you know, shit happens.*

the shit hits the fan

SPOKEN used to say that a situation suddenly becomes very difficult, or that people become angry or upset, especially because they have found out about something: *The shit's going to hit the fan when Dad finds out where I was last night.*

> NOTE▶ You can use other words instead of "shit" in order to be more polite: *You know how it is, one thing goes wrong, and then another, and then everything hits the fan.* | *Five weeks have passed since the news about Thurson's decision hit the fan.*

shoot the shit

SLANG an impolite expression meaning to talk in an informal and friendly way about lots of different things, usually about things that are not very important: *"Sorry to interrupt." "No, no, you're not interrupting – we were just shooting the shit."*

> NOTE▶ "Shoot the breeze" means the same as this idiom, but it is more polite.

S

someone thinks his/her shit doesn't stink

SPOKEN a rude way of saying that someone thinks they are better than other people: *There goes that Nancy Murphy. She's so fancy, she thinks her shit doesn't stink.*

tough shit

SPOKEN a rude way of telling someone that you do not care what they think, or do not have any sympathy with their problems: *I'm going to park my car here no matter what. If they don't like it, that's tough shit.*

shithouse

> NOTE▸ Some people find the word "shithouse" offensive. It is better not to use it.

built like a brick shithouse

a rude expression used about someone who is big, has a wide body, and looks very strong: *Doug's not much taller than me, but he's built like a brick shithouse.*

shiver

give you the shivers

to make you feel afraid, or anxious and upset: *I don't like being alone in the building at night – it gives me the shivers.*

send a shiver up/down your spine

to make you feel afraid, or give you a feeling of excitement that includes fear or anxiety: *The words "income tax return" are always enough to send a shiver down my spine.*
—see also send a CHILL down your spine

shoe

fill *someone's* shoes
(also **step into** *someone's* **shoes**)

to do the job that someone else used to do: *The new mayor, Susan Hammer, had to prove that she could fill her predecessor's shoes.*

if the shoe fits (wear it)

SPOKEN used to tell someone that you think a criticism of them is true or fair: *"So you're saying I'm a pig?" "Hey, if the shoe fits, wear it."*

be in *someone's* shoes

1 used to say how you would feel or what you would do if you were in someone else's situation: *"Kate can't decide whether to quit her job or not." "Well, if I were in her shoes, I would wait and see what other jobs were available before I quit."*
2 (also **walk/stand in** *someone's* **shoes**) to know from experience what someone else's situation is like: *I decided to work with troubled teenagers because I have walked in their shoes, and I understand their problems.*

put yourself in *someone's* shoes

to try to understand what someone else's situation is like: *If Jennifer put herself in our shoes once in a while, she might understand the problems we're having.*

the shoe is on the other foot

used to say that someone who caused problems for other people in the past is now in a similar situation to the people they caused problems for: *Carstens justified the policy by saying their rivals would take similar action if the shoe were on the other foot.*

wait for the other shoe to drop

to wait for the next part of an unpleasant process to happen: *After our research funding was cut, it didn't take long for the other shoe to drop. Budget cuts have been announced for all universities.*

shoestring

on a shoestring
(also **on a shoestring budget**)

if you live, manage a business, etc. on a shoestring, you do it with very little money to spend: *For the five years after Matt was born, we were living on a shoestring.*

shoo-in

be a shoo-in

used to say that someone is very likely to win an election or competition, or be chosen for a job ♦ OFTEN USED IN NEWSPAPERS, ON TELEVISION NEWS, ETC.: *Marcus was a shoo-in to succeed Jacobson as team manager.*

shoot

⇨be a DUCK shoot

shop

⇨a/the shopping LIST

close up shop

to close a store or business, or stop an activity, either permanently or for a short time: *Congress is about to close up shop for the Fourth of July holiday.*

set up shop

to start a business or activity: *Foreign banks have been setting up shop on U.S. soil in increasing numbers over the last few years.*

talk shop

to talk about your work with someone else who is involved in it, especially when you could be relaxing and talking about things that interest other people: *Let's not talk shop tonight. I'd rather forget about work until tomorrow.*

short

⇨BRING someone up short
⇨be caught short —see CATCH
⇨FALL short (of something)
⇨in the short RUN
⇨be LONG on ___ but short on ___
⇨SELL someone/something short

short and sweet

SPOKEN used about something, such as a meeting or a speech, that is shorter than you expected, especially when you are pleased or surprised by this: *We have one other item of business before lunch, and I'll try to keep it short and sweet because we have all worked hard this morning.*

shorts

eat my shorts

SLANG an impolite expression used to tell someone to stop annoying you or to go away: *"What's wrong, Jeff? Are you embarrassed?" "Eat my shorts!"*

shot

a big shot

used about an important or powerful person, especially one who behaves as if they are very important: *Levin's grandfather was a big shot in the art world who knew everybody.*
big-shot: *The Ryans hired a couple of big-shot lawyers to represent them in court.*

(not) by a long shot

used to emphasize that a negative statement is true: *I don't enjoy making a recording as much as I enjoy playing to an audience – not by a long shot.*

call the shots/tune

to make the decisions in a situation and tell other people what to do: *Local leaders have been given more power to make rules and call the shots in health care.*

give someone a shot (at)

to let someone try to do something, especially something that is difficult: *She's a young actress, but directors decided to give her a shot at the lead role.*

give something a shot

SPOKEN to attempt to do or achieve something, especially something that is difficult: *Scuba diving wasn't really an interest of hers, but at least she gave it a shot.*

give something your best shot

to try to achieve something with as much effort as you can, even though you know how difficult it is: *Even if you don't get the job, at least you'll know you gave it your best shot.*

something is a cheap shot

used about a remark or joke about someone which you think is not fair or reasonable: *I have heard the news story, and I regard it as just another media cheap shot about the Vice President.*
take a cheap shot at someone: *Instead of intelligent jokes, Martin has to resort to taking cheap shots at short people and minorities.*

like a shot

SPOKEN used to emphasize that someone goes somewhere or does something very quickly and eagerly: *If a burglar sets off your alarm system, he'll be out of there like a shot.*
—compare **... like a BAT out of hell**

S

be a long shot

1 used to say that a plan is worth trying, even though you think it is not likely to succeed: *We could put an ad in the paper, asking for volunteers. It's a long shot, but it might work.*
2 if someone is a long shot, they are not likely to be chosen for a job, or win an election, competition, etc. ♦ OFTEN USED IN NEWSPAPERS, ON TELEVISION NEWS, ETC.: *Turner, a former Democrat, is considered a long shot to win next Tuesday's mayoral election.*
long-shot: *Fipke began his long-shot search for diamonds in Canada's Yukon territory.*

a parting shot

a final remark that someone makes, especially as they leave a place, that warns or criticizes the person they are talking to: *Michael remarked, "It's good to be free," which could be interpreted as a parting shot at his former employers.*

a shot across the/*someone's* bow

(also **a warning shot (across** *someone's* **bows)** or **a shot across the/***someone's* **bows)**
something that you do or say to warn someone that you oppose what they are doing and will try to make them stop it ♦ OFTEN USED IN NEWSPAPERS, ON TELEVISION NEWS, ETC.: *All industrial companies that pollute the environment should regard the new law as a shot across the bows.*

> NOTE▶ The bow is the front part of a ship. This idiom comes from a fighting ship firing toward another ship to warn it that it may attack.

a shot in the dark

an attempt to guess something without having all the facts, or an attempt to do something when you think it will be difficult to succeed: *Making the movie with so little money was a gamble – a total shot in the dark. I never thought it would work out so well.*

shoulder

⇨be a **WEIGHT** off your shoulders

someone is looking over his/her shoulder

used to say that someone is very worried or being very careful because they expect that something dangerous or bad may happen to them: *Many employees are looking over their shoulder, wondering if they will be the next to lose their job.*

someone is looking over your shoulder

used to say that someone is checking and judging what you are doing because they do not trust you to do it well: *Even if I get this promotion, I'll still have my old boss looking over my shoulder.*

rub shoulders with *someone*

(also **rub elbows with** *someone*)
to meet and spend time with people who are different from you, especially people who are important or famous: *We had a chance to rub elbows with state senators at the Capitol Bar.*

a shoulder to cry on

used about someone whom you can tell about your problems and ask for sympathy and advice: *The organization provides support and a valuable shoulder to cry on for families who have lost a parent.*
cry on *someone's* **shoulder:** *People liked Dick and thought he was a reliable and hard worker, but nobody went to cry on his shoulder or tell him their secrets.*

shoulder to shoulder

1 if people are standing shoulder to shoulder, they are close together: *All the students were standing shoulder to shoulder at the graduation ceremony.*
2 used to say that people are working together in an attempt to achieve something or defend something: *We remembered the days when we had fought shoulder to shoulder against the invaders.*

show

get/keep the show on the road

to start an activity that you have planned, or to manage to continue it in spite of difficulties: *Maybe I should give David a call and get this show on the road – we'll have to meet him in town if we want to eat before the movie.*

steal the show

to get more attention than anyone else, especially in a situation where other people are supposed to be more important than you: *Raymond has been performing since he was eight, when he stole the show at a talent contest in New Orleans.*

showers

be sent to the showers

if a baseball player is sent to the showers, he is ordered to stop playing in the game because he is playing badly or has broken the rules: *Carney was sent to the showers and replaced by Romero.*

shreds

tear *someone/something* to shreds

(also **rip** *someone/something* **to shreds**)
1 (also **tear** *someone/something* **to pieces**) to criticize someone's character and ideas, or something that they have written or said in a very unkind and severe way: *My theory was torn to shreds by someone who had worked out the actual cost of the plan.*
2 to destroy something completely: *The soles of our hiking boots had been ripped to shreds on the jagged rocks.*

shrift

get short shrift

(also **be given short shrift**)
to receive very little attention, or sympathy: *Complex issues such as educational policy tend to get short shrift on the TV news.*
give something short shrift: *The judge gave short shrift to an argument based on the defendant's right to freedom of speech.*

shuffle

get/be lost in the shuffle

to receive very little attention because people have too many other things to do or to think about: *With all the things we have to worry about, safety kind of gets lost in the shuffle.*

side

⇨err on the side of **CAUTION**
⇨**FIGHT** shy of doing *something*
⇨play both **ENDs/sides** against the middle

the flip side

used to introduce a different way of considering a situation, especially when you begin to talk about its bad effects after describing its good ones: *The flip side of the farmers' success story is, of course, the destruction of wildlife by pesticides.*

get on the wrong side of *someone*

to annoy someone or make them angry, especially someone who can cause serious problems for you: *If you get on the wrong side of Sarah Forbes, you might as well start looking for another job right away.*

have *something* on your side

used to say that something is an advantage to you and will help you to achieve what you want: *Barnes did not have much experience in politics, but he had youth and enthusiasm on his side.*
something is on your side: *It will be a hard struggle, but justice is on our side.*

keep/stay on the right side of *someone*

to be careful not to annoy someone because you want them to help you and not to cause problems for you: *Kendra tried to stay on the right side of her landlord so that he wouldn't raise the rent.*

look on the bright side

to see the good points of a situation that is bad in other ways: *I know you'll miss the money. Still, look on the bright side – you always said you wanted to retire early.*

be on the side of the angels

used to say that someone is doing what is good or morally right: *"We're not the ones polluting the environment," insisted Mr. Whelan, "we're on the side of the angels."*

be on the wrong side of 40, 50, etc.

used to say that someone is older than a particular age: *He's wrinkly and on the wrong side of 60, but tough guy Clint still looks right for those leading roles.*

S

the other side of the coin

used to introduce a different or opposite part of a situation, problem, idea, etc.: *It's sometimes a little lonely working at home – but on the other side of the coin, I can make my own hours and wear whatever I want.*

split your sides

OLD-FASHIONED to laugh a lot, and very loudly: *A few days ago I was going through the yearbook and found some pictures of you that made me split my sides laughing.*

side-splitting: *Rich told us a joke with a side-splitting punchline.*

> NOTE▶ This idiom is often used sarcastically when you do not think something is funny at all (see note about sarcasm at "my HEART bleeds (for you): *"They liked that joke when I told it down at the bar." "I'm sure they were splitting their sides."*

be/stay on the safe side

to make the safest choice in order to avoid any possible problems or difficulties: *The village water is probably okay, but to be on the safe side, drink bottled water.*

sunny side up

eggs that are cooked sunny side up are cooked in hot oil without being turned over so that the yolk (=yellow part in the middle) stays soft: *"How would you like your eggs?" "Sunny side up, with bacon and wheat toast on the side."*

—see also **OVER easy**

two sides of the same coin

used to say that two problems or situations are so closely related that they are really just two parts of the same thing: *It is becoming apparent that political unrest and religious fundamentalism are two sides of the same coin.*

someone will be laughing out of the other side of his/her mouth/face

OLD-FASHIONED used to say that someone may be happy or confident now, but that they will be unhappy later because of what they are doing now: *Reggie thought his idea was great, but he's laughing out of the other side of his mouth now.*

the wrong/other side of the tracks

used about a poor part of a town or of society: *My dad had a difficult childhood growing up on the wrong side of the tracks.*

sidelines

be/sit/stand on the sidelines
(also **stay, remain, wait, etc. on the sidelines** or **watch from the sidelines**)
to avoid being fully involved in an argument, fight, or activity that you are interested in or should be involved in: *Many investors remained on the sidelines, waiting for an upsurge in the market's activity.*

> NOTE▶ There are other expressions that use "the sidelines" in this way. For example, you can "cheer from the sidelines," or "be pushed to the sidelines," or "come in from the sidelines": *We are not just cheering from the sidelines, we are going to get in there with money and help.* | *While education standards have improved overall, children with special needs have been pushed to the sidelines.*

sideswipe

take a sideswipe at

to make a remark or a joke that criticizes someone or something while you are talking about something different: *Smith took a sideswipe at the rest of the committee by begging for more young members with new ideas.*

sidewalk

sidewalk superintendent

someone who annoys people by watching them work and giving advice about how to do it, even when they do not know anything about it: *Joggers and part-time sidewalk superintendents watched as work crews tore up a three-block stretch of State Street.*

sight

have *someone/something* in your sights

to decide that you can win or achieve something, or defeat someone in a sport, competition, etc., and that you will try to do it: *The team had the championship in their sights as they started game one of the play-offs.*

> NOTE▶ This idiom and "set your sights on something" come from shooting. You look along the sights on the top of a gun when you are aiming it at something.

lose sight of *something*
to forget to think about the reason why you are doing something or forget something important that you should consider while you are doing it: *We can never lose sight of the reason why we became teachers – we're here to help the children.*

out of sight, out of mind
SPOKEN used to say that when you do not see someone or something you do not think or care about them: *As soon as I'm gone, Todd will forget all about me. It's out of sight, out of mind with him.*

not a pretty sight
SPOKEN used humorously to say that something or someone is not nice to look at: *Sheila was not a pretty sight after her 15-hour bus ride through the desert.*

set your sights on *something*
to decide that you want something and will make a determined effort to achieve it: *Logan had set his sights on becoming a lawyer, seeing this as a way of helping disadvantaged people.*
set your sights high/low: *Our aim is to encourage young people to set their sights a little higher, by making them aware of training opportunities.*

be a sight
OLD-FASHIONED used to say that a place looks very messy and bad, or that someone looks messy, strange, or funny: *Rhonda was really a sight that night – her lipstick was smudged across her face.*

be a sight for sore eyes
used to say that someone or something is very pleasant or attractive to look at: *Well, this sure is a sight for sore eyes! It's good to see you again, Tracy.*

sign
⇨see DOLLAR signs

a sign of the times
used about a thing or situation that you think is typical of the present state of society, especially one that shows how bad it has become: *It's a depressing sign of the times that people don't even know who their next-door neighbors are.*

signed, sealed, and delivered (also **signed and sealed**)
used to say that an agreement has been made or an arrangement has been completed, and the things that have been decided are now certain and will not be changed: *Everything is signed, sealed, and delivered; the two companies have merged, and Maddox is their chairman.*

signals
⇨SMOKE signals

silk
⇨make a silk PURSE out of a sow's ear

silver
⇨hand something to *someone* on a (silver) PLATTER

sin

as ugly as sin
very ugly: *My wife loves those dogs, but I think they're ugly as sin.*

sink

sink or swim
used about a situation in which someone must succeed by their own efforts without help from anyone else: *Playing singles tennis is tough. It's either sink or swim, and I guess I've been sinking a lot lately.*
sink-or-swim: *Most teacher trainees get sink-or-swim training, instead of close supervision.*

sit

sit down and do *something*
to try to solve a problem or deal with something you have to do by giving it all of your attention: *It's time we sat down and organized our finances.*

S

sit tight

to avoid taking any action, or to stay in one place until the situation changes and you have an opportunity to do, what you want: *They decided to sit tight until interest in the case had died down, and then head for Florida.*

be sitting pretty

used to say that someone is in a good situation with many advantages: *Garner was sitting pretty in the opinion polls two months before the election.*

six

⇒six of one, half a **DOZEN** of the other

be at sixes and sevens

OLD-FASHIONED used to say that a situation is disorganized and confused, or that a group of people do not agree: *Getting ready for the wedding, we were all at sixes and sevens, getting in each other's way.*

size

cut *someone* down to size

to criticize or insult someone in order to make them feel that they are not as successful or important as they thought they were: *I think too many journalists are attracted by the chance to cut everyone else down to size and make themselves feel better.*

that's about the size of it

SPOKEN used to tell someone that you think their opinion of a situation is correct: *"So we're going to have to pay for the rest of the work ourselves?" "That's about the size of it."*

try *something* (on) for size

to try something and see if it is suitable for you, or to consider an idea and decide what you think about it: *Try this fact on for size: Of the top 100 economies in the world, 47 are corporations.*

skeleton

a skeleton in the closet

an embarrassing secret about something that happened to you in the past: *We needed someone new to come in and take charge, someone without any skeletons in their closet.*

skid

be on skid row

to have a very bad quality of life because you have no home and no job and drink too much alcohol or take too many drugs: *Even if Josh loses a few thousand dollars, he won't end up on skid row.*

NOTE▶ "Skid row" is a name given to the part of a city in the U.S. where there are a lot of homeless people, especially people who are always drunk, using drugs, etc.

be on the skids

to be in a bad situation that is getting worse, and be likely to fail ♦ OFTEN USED IN BUSINESS: *By the end of that month, I was beginning to realize that my business was on the skids.*

hit the skids: *The problems the industry finds itself in today started about 14 months ago, when the car and truck sales began hitting the skids.*

put the skids on

to make it likely or certain that a plan, business, or organization will fail ♦ OFTEN USED IN BUSINESS: *The recession temporarily put the skids on his plans for a new business, but in 1996 he opened the first store in the chain.*

skies

—see **SKY**

skin

do *something* by the skin of your teeth

used to say that you just managed to do something, and almost failed to do it: *Kim got an "F" in history, and she only passed math by the skin of her teeth.*

get under your skin

1 to annoy you: *We should let Josh work with someone else – I think Andy's beginning to get under his skin.*

2 to attract you or make you feel interested, especially for reasons that you do not understand: *My two-year-old niece was making me crazy for the first few days, but after a week she managed to get under my skin.*

give/slip me some skin

SLANG said when you hit someone's hand with your hand to show that you are happy about something or happy to see them ◆ OFTEN USED BY YOUNG MEN: *What's happening, man? Give me some skin!*
—see also **give me FIVE**

have thick skin

used to say that you do not get upset if people criticize you or do not like you: *Actors and actresses have to have thick skin to survive all the rejection they get.*
thick-skinned: *Be careful what you say about my cooking – I'm not thick-skinned, you know.*

it's no skin off my/our nose
(also **it's no skin off my/our back**)

SPOKEN used to say that you do not care about something that has happened, or do not care what someone thinks or does because it does not affect you: *It's no skin off our nose if Sharon is late – we'll just go without her.*

jump out of your skin

to be so frightened or shocked by something that you make a sudden movement: *Don't sneak up on me like that! I almost jumped out of my skin there.*

make your skin crawl

used to say that someone or something makes you feel afraid or uncomfortable because you do not like them: *I can't stand spiders. They really make my skin crawl.*

save your/someone's skin

to do something in order to save yourself or someone else from danger or from being in trouble: *Hugo realized that the only way to save his skin was to make a deal with the police.*

skin *someone* alive

SPOKEN to be very angry with someone, or punish them severely: *I'm late again, and I know my mother will skin me alive this time.*

skinny

get/give the skinny on

OLD-FASHIONED to get or give the most important and useful information about something: *Look at our sales brochure to get the skinny on our new herbal teas.*

skip

skip it

SPOKEN used to tell someone that you do not want to continue talking about something: *"I saw you out with Phil last night." "Just skip it, okay? That's none of your business."*

skull

⇨**be bored out of your MIND/skull**
⇨**be out of your skull** —see **be out of your MIND**

skunk

drunk as a skunk

SPOKEN a humorous expression meaning very drunk: *Remember last New Year's Eve? Greg arrived at the party already drunk as a skunk.*

sky

⇨**BLOW** *something* **sky-high**

praise *someone/something* to the skies

OLD-FASHIONED to praise someone or something very much: *He had never said a kind word to her before, yet now he was praising her to the skies.*

the sky's the limit

used to say that there are no limits to what someone can do, achieve, or earn, or to the amount of money that may be spent on something: *The sky appears to be the limit as far as chief executives' salaries are concerned.*

slack

cut *someone* (some) slack
(also **cut** *someone* **(a little) slack**)

SPOKEN to make it easier for someone to do something, or criticize them less because of their special situation: *Come on, cut me some slack. I only owe you fifty bucks. You'll get it back next week, I promise.*

pick/take up the slack

to do or provide something that is needed

S

in a situation or organization when someone or something else has stopped doing or providing it ♦ OFTEN USED ABOUT FINANCE AND BUSINESS: *The Bulls are really missing Anderson, but their coach is hoping Scott and Rodriguez will pick up the slack.*

slam

be a slam dunk
SLANG used about something that is very easy to do, or that is very successful ♦ OFTEN USED IN BUSINESS AND POLITICS: *The Bay Area's latest Nobel Prize is a $1–million slam dunk for Steven Chu and two of his scientific colleagues.*
slam-dunk: *The president's chief science adviser has criticized those who advocate "slam-dunk solutions" to the problem of global warming.*

slap

be (like) a slap in the face
used to say that a decision or action is very disappointing or insulting to a group of people, and does not show respect for their feelings or opinions: *For generations now, the attention and praise given to General Custer has been like a slap in the face to Native Americans.*

a slap on the wrist
used about a punishment or criticism that you do not think has been serious or severe enough: *Many of the software giant's competitors considered the fine imposed by the federal government a mere slap on the wrist.*
be/get slapped on the wrist: *The ex-governor was slapped on the wrist for his use of military planes for personal travel.*
wrist-slapping: *The days of wrist-slapping for violations of safety laws are over.*

slate

a clean slate
the chance to succeed in a new situation or activity without problems or mistakes from the past preventing you: *One way of dealing with the oil spill would be to dig up the beaches completely and provide a clean slate for natural populations to rebuild.*

NOTE► A slate is a small smooth board that children used to write on in school in the past. When they had finished one piece of work, they would rub the writing off and start again.

wipe the slate clean
to agree to forget about mistakes, arguments, or crimes that happened in the past: *We're calling a meeting for this afternoon to resolve all minor disputes, and wipe the slate clean for the new year.*

sleep

someone can do something in his/her sleep
used to say that someone can do something very easily, especially because they have done it many times before: *Don't worry, I've driven to the Bronx so many times I could do it in my sleep.*

not lose any sleep over something
used to say that you are not very worried about a problem or situation: *The Mayor, who is facing five charges of possessing cocaine, said, "I won't lose any sleep over these allegations. Justice is done in the courts, not in the newspapers."*

sleep on it
to delay making a decision until the next day so that you have more time to think about it: *There's no need to sign anything today. Why don't you go home and sleep on it?*

sleeve

have/keep something up your sleeve
(also have an ace/card/trick up your sleeve)
to have a secret plan, advantage, or argument that you can use to be successful in a situation if other plans fail: *Explaining the plan, Ross paused; he had an ace up his sleeve, but he wasn't sure whether to tell them yet.*

NOTE► This idiom comes from card games in which someone could cheat by hiding a card in his sleeve (=the part of a shirt, coat, etc. that covers your arm) until he needed it.

someone **is laughing up his/her sleeve**
used to say that someone is secretly laughing at you, especially because they know something about a situation that you do not: *By celebrating the crass and commercial, Warhol was laughing up his sleeve at the art world.*

roll up your sleeves
used to say that you are getting ready to work hard at something: *The Mustangs' manager, Jeff Connors, admitted that he was disappointed, but said, "It is now time for us to roll up our sleeves and fight to win our next game."*

slice
⇨any WAY you slice it
⇨a PIECE/slice of the action
⇨a PIECE/slice of the pie

slicker
⇨a CITY slicker

slide
⇨LET something slide

slip
⇨LET it slip (that)
a Freudian slip
something you say that is different from what you intended to say, and shows your hidden emotions or thoughts, especially about sex: *"As soon as you're finished with your coffee, I want you in bed," he said. "Oh, how about that for a Freudian slip?"*

> NOTE▶ This phrase comes from Sigmund Freud's ideas about the way the human mind works.

a slip of the tongue
used about something that you have said by mistake when you did not mean to say it, especially if it is something you should not have said: *"Eight thousand? I thought you said it would cost six thousand." "Oops, that was just a slip of the tongue. It will cost six thousand dollars."*

slope
be on a/the slippery slope
(also **go, head, slide, etc. down a/the slippery slope**)
used to say that what someone is doing will begin a bad process that will get worse and more difficult to control as it continues: *Jerry has started going to Vegas every weekend. I'm worried he's heading down a slippery slope toward a gambling addiction.*

slouch
someone **is no slouch (at *something*)**
used to say that someone is very good at something, works hard at something, or has a particular quality: *Sarah is an excellent student. And she's no slouch at sports, either.*

slow
⇨do a slow BURN

slum
slum it
to spend time in worse conditions than the ones you are used to, often used humorously: *Businessmen are having to slum it in economy class seats because of widespread company cutbacks.*

sly
do *something* on the sly
to do something secretly: *Although my mother had forbidden it, Anita and I continued to meet on the sly, on the way home from school.*

smart
⇨don't get CUTE/smart with me

smell
something **smells fishy**
(also *something* **seems, sounds, etc. fishy**)
used to say that you do not believe a story or think that a situation is what it seems to be, and that you think something wrong or illegal is happening: *Something was starting to smell fishy – whenever we got*

S

raided by the police, Rob was nowhere to be found.

smell *something* **fishy:** Tenants first smelled something fishy when their landlord disappeared and didn't leave a forwarding address.

—see also **smell a RAT**

smile

⇨wipe the **GRIN**/smile off *someone's* face

smoke

blow smoke (up *someone's* ass)

to try to deceive someone: *You could tell from what they were saying that these guys weren't just blowing smoke. They were deadly serious.*

> NOTE▶ It is better to say just "blow smoke" because many people think using the word "ass" is offensive.

go up in smoke/flames

1 to be completely destroyed by fire: *By the time I got there, the fire had gone right through the office; I watched while a whole year's work went up in smoke.*
2 if someone's efforts, plans, or hopes go up in smoke, they fail completely and the situation has changed: *Their hopes of a win went up in flames when the Rangers scored twice in the last quarter.*

smoke and mirrors

a way of deceiving someone by taking their attention away from what is important ♦ OFTEN USED IN POLITICS: *It's hard to figure out what's behind the political smoke and mirrors.*

smoke signals

used about things that a company, government, etc. says or does that show someone what they are thinking or planning when they are not stating this directly: *We were still hoping that the Stenning Group would make a bid to buy our company, although the smoke signals from them read simply "message received".*

where there's smoke, there's fire

(also **there's no smoke without fire**)
used to say that if people are saying something bad or shocking about some-one, then it is probably partly true: *No one is exactly sure if the rumors of sexual misconduct are true, but where there's smoke, there's usually fire.*

snail

⇨do *something* at a snail's **PACE**

snake

a snake in the grass

used about someone who pretends to be your friend, but does something to harm you: *I should have known Richards was a snake in the grass – he was only after our money.*

snake oil

used about something that someone is trying to sell you or trying to make you believe when it does not work or is not true: *A lot of the software out there is pure snake oil, but consumers are fooled by glossy packaging.*

> NOTE▶ People sometimes call someone who sells products that do not work or tells lies a "snake oil salesman": *Some "time consultants," though some are merely snake-oil salesmen, can provide genuinely useful tips to help you use your time more efficiently.*

snap

snap out of it

SPOKEN to quickly stop yourself from feeling sad or upset: *Oh, snap out of it – you're not a little girl anymore, and you can't get what you want by screaming.*

snappy

⇨**MAKE it snappy!**

sneeze

something **is nothing to sneeze/ sniff at**

(also *something* **is not to be sneezed/ sniffed at**)
used to say that something is impressive or important, especially if it does not seem so at first: *Where the state tax officials are concerned, an error of $10 is nothing to sniff at.*

sniff

⇨*something* **is nothing to sniff at** —see *something* **is nothing to SNEEZE at**

snit

be in a snit
used to say that someone is annoyed about something when you think they are being unreasonable: *"What's wrong with Lucy?" "She's in a snit about something again."*

snooze

you snooze, you lose
SPOKEN used to emphasize that if you decide not to do something, you do not get the advantages from it: *Tickets bought in advance can be up to 20 percent cheaper. Remember, you snooze, you lose.*

snow

as pure/clean as the driven snow
used to say that someone has never done anything wrong or illegal, or that they have not had any sexual experiences: *She has a reputation for being pure as the driven snow, but I could tell you some stories that would surprise you.*

a snow job
SPOKEN lies and tricks that someone uses to try to make people believe something that is untrue: *Marian must have done a huge snow job to get him to run an errand like that for her.*

snowball

⇨**not have a snowball's chance in hell** —see **not have a CHANCE/hope in hell (of)**

snuff

be up to snuff
to be good enough, or as good as usual ◆ OFTEN USED IN THE NEGATIVE: *Cooper's performance on Broadway wasn't quite up to snuff.*

so

so and so
(also **so-and-so**)
1 used to mean a particular person, when you do not give their name: *She'd point someone out and say "That's so-and-so," but I never remembered their names.*
2 used about someone who is bad or not dependable: *That Jack Davis sure is one mean old so-and-so.*

so far, so good
SPOKEN used to say that everything has been happening successfully until now, especially when you think that you may soon have problems: *I held my breath and climbed onto the saddle. So far, so good – then I realized I didn't know how to steer a horse.*

so help me (God)
SPOKEN used to emphasize that you really mean what you are saying or promising ◆ OFTEN USED IN MOVIES, BOOKS, ETC.: *You kids had better behave, or, so help me, I'll give you all a beating you'll never forget.*

so long!
OLD-FASHIONED used to say goodbye: *Well, thanks for letting us stay. So long, Cliff!*

so near (and) yet so far
OLD-FASHIONED used to say that although someone almost achieved what they wanted, in the end they failed: *Everywhere we went in the park, we ran into other families. All that wilderness and isolation was so near, yet so far.*

so there!
SPOKEN said when you want to make someone feel bad, or to stop them arguing with you ◆ USED ESPECIALLY BY CHILDREN OR BY ADULTS SPEAKING LIKE CHILDREN: *I don't earn much money, but my job's more important than yours, so there!*

so what?
SPOKEN an impolite expression used to say that you think something that has just been mentioned is unimportant, often when you are annoyed because someone is criticizing you for doing something: *"You were on the phone for an hour!" "Yeah, so what?"*

soapbox

get on your/a soapbox

to express strong opinions about something for a long time, and try to persuade other people that you are right: *A lot of celebrities get up on their soapbox and talk about their most recent movies, and they don't talk about what people are really interested in – their private lives.*

NOTE▶ This idiom comes from a time when people made informal speeches standing on strong wooden boxes that were used for transporting soap.

society

⇨a mutual **ADMIRATION** society

sock

knock *someone's* **socks off**
(also **blow** *someone's* **socks off**)

to seem surprising or impressive to someone: *Inside the magazine, we have a recipe for a Thai fish sauce that will knock your socks off.*
knock-your-socks-off: *This citrus orange is a knock-your-socks-off color, but not everyone would dare to wear it.*

knock *someone's* **socks off**

pull your socks up

SPOKEN used to tell someone to improve their work: *Customers have been complaining about you, Barbara, so unless you pull your socks up I'm going to have to find a new salesperson.*

put a sock in it!
(also **put a cork in it!**)

SPOKEN used angrily to tell someone to stop talking, making a noise, or complaining about something: *"Mom, Tina keeps saying I smell!" "If you two don't put a sock in it, I'm going to stop the car."*

sock it to *someone*!

1 SPOKEN (also **sock it to 'em**) used to encourage someone either to hit or defeat someone, or to make yourself seem impressive to a group of people: *You have a wonderful voice, Candice, now get on that stage and sock it to 'em!*
2 to take strong action against someone, or to do something that surprises or seems impressive to them: *Cities are socking it to travelers, either through car rental taxes or hotel taxes.*

sold

be sold on *something*

to like something very much, for example an idea, a plan, or something you might buy or choose ♦ OFTEN USED IN THE NEGATIVE: *Look, just forget it – I can see you're not exactly sold on the idea.*

something

⇨someone **has** *something* **to PROVE**

someone **is up to** *something*
(also *someone* **is up to no good**)

SPOKEN used to say that you think someone is doing something that they should not be doing: *Do you think the kids are up to something upstairs? They're very quiet.*
—compare **not be UP to** *something*

make *something* **of yourself**

to get a good job and be successful, especially so that your family can be proud of you: *People like my uncle Charlie outraged my dad's belief that it was a man's duty to make something of himself by being successful in business.*

son

son of a bitch!
(also **son of a gun!**)

1 SPOKEN a very rude expression used in order to insult someone, usually a man: *I can't believe that son of a bitch dared to come over here.*

2 SPOKEN said when you are surprised about something: *They chose Burrows instead of you? Son of a bitch!*

> NOTE▶ "Son of a gun" is much more polite than "son of a bitch," but some people think it sounds old-fashioned.

song

make a song and dance about *something*
used to say that someone is complaining or talking a lot about a situation or problem, and making it seem more important, complicated, or difficult than it is: *Woods was making some huge song and dance about being a citizen of the world.*

sorrows

drown your sorrows
to drink a lot of alcohol to try to forget about a problem: *Travis put his coat on and went down to the Roadhouse to drown his sorrows in a glass of beer.*

sorts

be/feel out of sorts
to feel sick or upset: *People who stay up too late drinking on Saturday night don't need expert advice on why they feel out of sorts on Sunday.*

soul

bare your soul
to tell someone your most private feelings and thoughts: *Connie was so depressed about her breakup that she went to a bar and bared her soul to a complete stranger.*

sell your soul (to)
to be willing to do anything in order to get or achieve something, even if you think it is immoral: *Hannah knew that she would have willingly sold her soul for a single kiss from him.*

be the soul of ____
OLD-FASHIONED used to say that someone has a lot of a good quality: *Gina's mother, always the soul of propriety, was horrified when her daughter moved in with Hank.* |

Don't worry, I'll be the soul of discretion – your secret is safe with me.

sound

⇨to sound/be the death KNELL

be wired (for sound)
if someone is wired for sound, they are wearing electronic equipment to secretly record or broadcast their conversations with other people: *Gibson allegedly offered the officer, who was wired for sound, half an ounce of cocaine.*

sour

go/turn sour
if a relationship, an arrangement, or a situation goes sour, it stops working well and begins to fail: *Negotiations had been making some progress, but talks suddenly turned sour on Tuesday when a car bomb exploded, killing three people.*

south

go south
used to say that something fails or does not work correctly: *California's citrus crop went south when a hard freeze killed more than 60% of the navel oranges.*

sow

⇨you REAP what you sow

space

a/some breathing space/room
a short time when you can stop doing something difficult or tiring so that you can think about the situation you are in: *The extra month gives us some breathing space to look for potential investors, to try and avoid bankruptcy.*

watch this space
used to tell people to expect more interesting news about the person, company, team, etc. that you are talking about ◆ USED ESPECIALLY IN NEWSPAPERS, ON TELEVISION NEWS, ETC.: *Casey's leather and gemstone coats are already being worn by a number of famous names. This designer is hot, so watch this space.*

S

spade

call a spade a spade
used to say that someone is not afraid or embarrassed to speak about things directly and honestly, even if this is impolite or unpleasant: *Adam could be outspoken at times, but he always called a spade a spade, and people learned to respect him for that.*

in spades
used to emphasize that something is happening or being done to a great degree or in a great amount: *Recently, Eric had been low on good spirits and laughter, but now he had them in spades.*

sparks

sparks fly
used to say that an argument, performance, or sports game is very exciting and full of strong emotions ♦ OFTEN USED IN NEWSPAPERS, ON TELEVISION NEWS, ETC.: *The Pope's decision to publicly support the death penalty sent sparks flying in Rome.*

speak

speak for yourself!
SPOKEN used to tell someone that you do not have the same opinion as they do, or that you have not had the same experience they have had: *"Oh, everybody gets involved in a little crime, does a few drugs in college, things like that." "Speak for yourself! I never did any of that stuff."*

speed

up to speed
1 if a company or organization gets or comes up to speed, it starts to work as well as it can after having worked badly or slowly: *If work on the space station is stopped, it will take NASA at least five years to get up to speed on a new project.*
2 if someone is up to speed, they understand as much about a situation, process, subject, etc. as the people who understand it best: *Dave here can bring you up to speed on the Lamberton project.*

spell

fall/be/come under *someone's* spell
to become so attracted to a person or organization that they can make you do whatever they want you to do: *Tyminski appealed to young Polish voters who were not under the spell of the Solidarity movement.*

spenders

(the) last of the big spenders
SPOKEN a humorous expression used in order to laugh at someone because they are always worried about money and always trying not to spend too much: *Watch out – here comes the last of the big spenders. Maybe he'll actually buy something today.*

spick

spick and span
extremely clean and neat: *Your room needs to be spick and span before you go out and play today.*

spin

take a spin in *something*
(also **take** *something* **for a spin**)
SPOKEN to go for a short drive or ride in a car: *Mike let me take his Porsche for a spin yesterday. What a car!*

spirit

if/when the spirit moves you
(also **whenever, anytime, etc. the spirit moves you**)
used to say that someone does something whenever they want to do it, rather than worrying about when they should do it, or caring what people think: *Norbert gambled, drank too much, and anytime the spirit moved him, would take off and not come back for maybe a month.*

the spirit is willing but the flesh is weak
used to say that you want to do something, but you are too tired or weak to do it, especially used as an excuse: *"How's the diet going?" "Not too well. The spirit is willing but the flesh is weak."*

the spirit of the law
the intended or general meaning of the law, rather than the exact words: *Immigration lawyers claim the department is ignoring the spirit of the law, and not allowing people into the country for its own political reasons.*
—compare **the LETTER of the law**

that's the spirit!
SPOKEN said when you want to encourage someone to keep trying, even though the situation is difficult: *"Well, I don't care what Mike thinks. I'll go without him." "That's the spirit, Heather!"*

spit

spit and polish
thorough cleaning and polishing ◆ USED ESPECIALLY ABOUT THE ARMY, ETC.: *Troops were putting on the spit and polish for the Vice President's visit.*

splash

make a splash
to do something that makes a lot of people notice you: *Terrell made a big splash when he announced plans to build a 120-room motel on the edge of town.*

spleen

vent your spleen
to say or write all the things that have been making you angry for a long time: *In an unexpected outburst, Roberts vented her spleen in the Post, saying most of the articles written about her were total garbage.*

spoken

be spoken for
1 used to say that someone is married or has a serious relationship with someone else: *"That guy over by the window is cute." "That's Jerry. He's already spoken for, though."*
2 used to say that something is not available because someone else wants it: *Businessmen who support the museum may have a gallery, lecture hall, or garden named after them (the parking lot is not spoken for).*

spoon

someone was born with a silver spoon in his/her mouth
used about someone whom you disapprove of because they have a lot of advantages because their parents are rich and important: *I don't know how she affords all that stuff. I guess from what Dad says, she was born with a silver spoon in her mouth.*

spot

a blind spot
when someone always ignores part of a subject that is hard to understand or deal with, or ignores a bad quality that someone has, even though they know the subject, person, etc. very well: *Mom has a huge blind spot where Noah is concerned – everything he does is wonderful.*

do something on the spot
to do something immediately, often without thinking about it very carefully: *The car looked OK, so he bought it on the spot.*
—compare **be on the SPOT, put** *someone* **on the SPOT**

have a soft spot for someone
to like and care about someone or something very much: *I think Mrs. Adams has a soft spot for you, Tom.*

hit the spot
if something, especially a type of food or drink, hits the spot, it is exactly what you wanted or needed at a particular time: *A cold beer would really hit the spot right now.*

a hot spot
1 a place that is very popular for a particular type of entertainment: *The Talking Heads regularly played at legendary hot spots such as CBGB's in New York.*
2 a place where war, trouble, or fighting is likely to happen: *Dr. Ryding will soon be off again to another of the world's hot spots, helping the casualties of war.*

in a tight spot
in a difficult or dangerous situation: *I can pay off what I borrowed, but if they want the interest too, I'll be in a very tight spot.*

S

be on the spot

to be in the place where something is happening: *A good journalist has a flair for being on the spot when important events happen.*

on-the-spot: *CNN provided on-the-spot news coverage throughout the crisis.*

—compare **do** *something* **on the SPOT, put** *someone* **on the SPOT**

put *someone* on the spot

to put someone in a difficult situation by asking them questions which they cannot answer or which are embarrassing to answer: *Jamie really put me on the spot when he asked whether I had a date for the winter ball.*

—compare **do** *something* **on the SPOT, be on the SPOT**

be rooted to the spot

to be so shocked, surprised, or frightened that you cannot move: *People were literally running for their lives, but I was rooted to the spot.*

be a sore spot/point

a subject that is likely to make someone upset or angry if you talk about it: *The issue of human rights had been a sore spot in diplomatic relations between the two countries for years.*

spotlight

in/under the spotlight

suddenly getting a lot of attention from newspapers, television, etc.: *The department is under the spotlight once again, following news of an investigation into possible tax evasion.*

opposite **out of the spotlight:** *Baker preferred to keep her children out of the spotlight, even as her own career skyrocketed.*

put/turn/focus the spotlight on: *The Persian Gulf Crisis put the spotlight on America's dependence on oil imports.*

spread

spread yourself too thin

to try to do too many things at the same time so that you are unable to do any of them well: *I'm worried that Jim's going to end up spreading himself too thin with all these plans of his.*

spring

there is a spring in *someone's* step

OLD-FASHIONED used to say that someone seems happy and full of energy: *We all noticed the change in her right away – there was a real spring in her step.*

spur

do *something* on the spur of the moment

to do something quickly without thinking about it before you do it: *I decided, on the spur of the moment, to go up to Seattle to talk to Don about my job offer.*

spur-of-the-moment: *We didn't plan the trip at all. It was a spur-of-the-moment decision.*

square

⇨**a square MEAL**

be back to/at square one

to be in exactly the same situation that you started from, even though you seemed to be making progress for a while: *The fire destroyed all our files related to the research project, so now we're back to square one.*

squeeze

someone's main squeeze

OLD-FASHIONED someone's boyfriend or girlfriend: *Show us how you would dance a slow dance with your main squeeze.*

put the squeeze on

1 to try to force someone to do something they do not want to do by making them feel that they have no other choices: *Increased competition in the international marketplace is putting the squeeze on North American producers.*

2 to try to stop prices, costs, etc. from getting too high: *A tight control on the money supply put the squeeze on inflation.*

stab

take/make a stab at doing *something*

to try to do something, especially when you have not prepared for it in any way: *When my mother saw I had some*

S

creativity, she encouraged me to take a stab at writing.

take a stab in the dark
to make a guess, without any information to help you: *Just take a stab in the dark. How many countries are there in the world?*

stack
⇨blow your **TOP/stack**

stag

go stag
OLD-FASHIONED if a man goes stag to a party, event, etc., he goes without a woman: *I was going to ask Amy to Jim's party, but then I decided I'd just go stag.*

stage

set the stage/scene (for)
to do something that makes it possible or easier for events to happen or for plans to work: *The stage was being set for vast political and social changes in East Asia.*

stakes

pull up stakes (and...)
to leave your home to go and live in another place: *Many workers who are asked to pull up stakes have their costs paid by the company.*

stamp

put your stamp on *something*
to have an effect on something that people will recognize is from you: *"Coach Cole is putting his stamp on the team," Daner said. "Players are walking around with their heads held high."*

stand
⇨stand *someone* in good **STEAD**

a one-night stand
1 an occasion when two people have sex, but do not intend to see each other again: *Sure, I've had a few one-night stands, but with Jill it's really different.*
2 a person someone has sex with once but does not intend to see again: *In spite of all the passing lovers and casual one-night stands, I was always essentially alone.*

stand firm
(also **stand pat**)
to refuse to change your opinion or decision about something: *Analysts say that when the stock market has problems, big investors are more likely to stand pat, while small investors sell.*

standard

the standard bearer of *something*
someone who acts as the leader of a group of people who have the same aims or interests: *Pastor Tokes appears to be the standard bearer of a younger, more radical generation of clergymen.*

> NOTE▶ A "standard" is the flag of an army put on a pole, and the person who carries it into a battle is the "standard bearer."

stand up

stand up and be counted
to say something or make your opinion clear, even if this is dangerous or might cause problems for you: *As individual citizens, we have to stand up and be counted and let the people in Washington know what we think.*

stars

have stars in your eyes
to be very hopeful that you will become famous in the future, especially in movies, sports, etc.: *Bremer arrived in Hollywood as an 18-year-old with stars in her eyes, but quickly realized it's not that easy to make it big.*
starry-eyed: *How does a starry-eyed kid get a chance to play ball with the big-time boys?*

reach/shoot for the stars
to believe that you can achieve something even though it is difficult: *"We want to shoot for the stars," Green said before the game. "We think we can do better."*

thank my/our/your lucky stars
SPOKEN used to say that you are grateful for something or feel very fortunate, especially because you have avoided an unpleasant or dangerous situation: *Alice thanked her lucky stars that her husband arrived home before the blizzard started.*

S

start

⇨for STARTERs
⇨get/have a HEAD start

get/be off to a flying start
to be very successful when you are starting to do something: *Our vacation got off to a flying start when we were offered a free place to stay on the first night*
give *someone/something* **a flying start:** *The programs developed by the Open Society Institute gave governments a flying start in their turnover to a democratic system.*

starter

for starters
(also **for a start**)
SPOKEN used to emphasize the first and most important of several reasons or things you want to mention: *"Why don't we open our own restaurant?" "Well, for starters, we couldn't get a bank loan."*

state

state of the art
(also **state-of-the-art**)
used about equipment, methods, buildings, etc. that use the most modern and recently developed ideas, systems, or materials: *The 3-D movie will take you into a new dimension, using state of the art computer graphics.*

the state of play
what is happening now, in a process that has not finished yet, or in a situation that is still developing: *What's the current state of play in the Middle East?*

stay

stay put
SPOKEN to remain in one place and not move: *The roads are pretty bad. Just stay put until we can get to you.*

stead

stand *someone* in good stead
if something you learn stands you in good stead, it is very useful to you later: *Learn to overcome your shyness; it will stand you in good stead for the rest of your life.*

steam

get/be steamed up
to become excited and angry or worried: *Most of the men weren't bothered by the ad, but the women were all steamed up about it.*

go full steam ahead (with)
to do something with a lot of energy: *We've decided to go full steam ahead with our plans to move.*

NOTE▶ Some of the "steam" idioms come from the time when ships operated by steam power. If a ship traveled full steam ahead, it was going as fast as it could. A ship could also travel under its own steam, or be pulled by smaller boats, for example through a narrow place.

have steam coming out of your ears
to be very angry: *By this time, Matthew was jumping up and down with steam coming out of his ears.*

let/blow off steam
to get rid of your anger or excitement by doing something noisy or active: *We'll stop at the next exit to let the kids run around and let off some steam.*

pick/build up steam
if a plan, idea, etc. picks up steam, it gradually becomes more important, and more people become interested in it: *Interest in recycling has slowly picked up steam over the last decade.*
—see also **run out of STEAM**

NOTE▶ We get this idiom and several others from the time when train engines operated by steam power. An engine would build up steam when its fire was made hotter at the beginning of its trip. It could also run out of steam if the fire became low, or it did not have enough water, and would have to let off steam if the pressure of steam became too high.

run out of steam
to begin to lose energy, or to become slower or weaker: *I started to run out of steam before I was halfway around the track.*
—see also **pick/build up STEAM**

S

under your own steam
if you go somewhere under your own steam, you get there alone, without anyone else's help: *"Do you need a ride?" "No, we can get there under our own steam."*

steer

get a bum steer
to be given the wrong information by someone, often deliberately: *Bill got a bum steer from some insurance salesman and bought the wrong policy.*
give *someone* **a bum steer:** *Whoever gave you this tax information gave you a bum steer – it's all wrong.*

stem
⇨**stem the TIDE (of)**

from stem to stern
from one end of a ship or boat to the other: *Huge surges of Pacific water now rocked the boat from stem to stern.*

step

be/keep in step (with)
1 if people or their ideas are in step, they agree with each other or are very similar: *The President felt compelled to keep in step with public opinion.*
2 if two processes are in step or happen in step, they agree with each other so that they can work well together: *Computerization means that payroll and personnel data are always in step.*

be/keep/stay one step ahead (of)
to have an advantage in a situation because you are better prepared for what is going to happen, or know more than other people: *Our network of consultants around the world helps us to stay one step ahead of the competition.*

be out of step (with)
if people or their ideas are out of step, they do not agree with each other or are different: *The existing law on drugs is considered to be out of step with what is actually happening in the community.*

a step in the right direction
an action that brings you nearer to what you want to achieve: *Gloria hasn't started her diet yet, but she's started exercising,* and that's definitely a step in the right direction.

step on it!
SPOKEN used to tell someone to hurry: *If you don't step on it, we're going to miss the plane.*

take steps to do *something*
to do the things that are necessary in order to achieve something ◆ OFTEN USED IN NEWSPAPERS, ON TELEVISION NEWS, ETC.: *So far the UN hasn't taken any steps to end the war or help the people of this country.*

watch your step
1 to be careful about what you say or do so that you do not cause problems for yourself: *Late again, Carly? You'd better watch your step or you'll lose your job.*
2 SPOKEN used to warn someone to be careful when they are walking, or they might hurt themselves: *Watch your step. That railing is a little loose.*

stew
⇨**let** *someone* **stew in his/her own JUICE**

be in a stew
to be very upset, confused, or excited about something: *When I walked into the office on Wednesday, everyone was all in a stew about Laura's resignation.*

stick
⇨**get the short END of the stick**

someone's been beat/hit with an ugly stick
SLANG an impolite expression used about someone who you think is very ugly: *"What does she look like?" "Well, let me put it this way – like she's been hit with an ugly stick."*

a/the big stick
used about a method of making someone do what you want by threatening to use your power ◆ OFTEN USED IN POLITICS: *Like Teddy Roosevelt, Parker believed that you should speak softly and carry a big stick.*

have a stick up your butt/ass/ behind, etc.
SLANG to behave or walk in a way that does not seem natural, and that makes

S

people think you cannot relax or have fun: *For the first two minutes on stage, I acted like a fool with a stick up my ass and pudding for brains.*

more ___ than you can shake a stick at
SPOKEN used to emphasize that you are talking about a lot of something: *Time-Life Music has produced more compilation albums than you can shake a stick at.*

stick-in-the-mud
(also **stick in the mud**)
used about someone who is behaving in a way that is boring or a little old-fashioned: *"No, I don't think I'll come along." "Come on, Al, don't be such an old stick-in-the-mud."*
stick-in-the-mud: *This company is never going to grow if the executives continue this stick-in-the-mud management style.*

stick-in-the-mud

sting
take the sting out of *something*
to make an unpleasant situation, statement or action less upsetting and easier to accept: *"Mom, you know you're not exactly the world's best driver," said Jo, smiling to take the sting out of her words.*

stink
make a stink/fuss
to complain loudly when you are annoyed about something: *Unless parents start making a stink about all the sex on*

TV, the networks will just keep showing that filth.*

stir
cause/create a stir
to make everyone very excited by doing or saying something shocking or unusual: *The new dress designs by fashion students are causing quite a stir on the runways.*

stitch
have/keep *someone* in stitches
SPOKEN to make someone laugh so much that they cannot stop: *I made such a mess of cooking Pauline's dinner; I had her in stitches.*

a stitch in time (saves nine)
used to say that if you spend a little time or effort dealing with a problem when it first appears, you will probably stop it turning into a very big problem that is more difficult to deal with: *We are determined to continue our armed surveillance of the area; a stitch in time may save a lot of lives.*

stomach
find *something* difficult/hard to stomach
(also **can't stomach** *something*)
to be unable or unwilling to accept an action, situation or attitude because you think it is unpleasant or wrong: *For those who can't stomach the thought of staying in a chain motel, there is the option of renting a condo or even a houseboat.*

not have the stomach for *something*
1 to have no desire to do something because you think it is unpleasant or dangerous: *I don't know how anyone has the stomach to work in a slaughterhouse.*
2 OLD-FASHIONED to have no desire to eat or drink something: *Adam realized he had no stomach for the greasy lamb chops he had ordered.*

turn your stomach
to make you feel angry, upset or as though you are about to vomit (=bring food up from your stomach through your mouth): *The smell that met us as we opened the door was about enough to turn our stomachs.*

stone

⇨(just) a stone's **THROW** away

leave no stone unturned

used to say that you will try every method and do everything possible in order to achieve something: *The principal spoke to the whole school, and said he would leave no stone unturned to find the person responsible for the graffiti.*

a rolling stone

used about someone who never stays in the same job, relationship, house, etc. for very long, and avoids being responsible: *We needed to find a place to live. A mother with five kids doesn't want to become a rolling stone.*

> NOTE▶ This idiom comes from a very old expression, "a rolling stone gathers no moss," which is rarely used now, but means that if you continue to move from place to place, you do not have to have any responsibility.

be set in stone
(also **be carved, cast, written, etc. in stone**)

used to say that a plan, decision, idea, etc. is completely fixed, and no part of it can be changed ♦ USUALLY USED IN THE NEGATIVE: *When it comes to what kind of beer goes with what food, there are no rules set in stone. Let your own taste guide you.*

stops

pull out all the stops

to do everything you can in order to achieve something: *Laurie's family pulled out all the stops for her wedding, and even hired a horse-drawn carriage to bring her to the church.*

> NOTE▶ This idiom comes from the organ, a large musical instrument in which the sound is made by air passing through pipes. The stops control the flow of air, and if you pull out all the stops, the organ makes as loud a sound as it can.

store

mind the store

to give attention to a problem and do something to solve it: *Everybody assumes somebody else is minding the store, but in the end nobody's really paying any attention to environmental problems.*

set (great) store by *something*

to think that something is important or valuable: *Patrick loves to travel, and thinks this is why he has never set much store by material possessions.*

storm

take *something* by storm

to be extremely successful or popular in a particular place, group, or organization: *Woods took the golf world by storm when he won the Masters' tournament in Augusta.*

weather the storm
(also **ride (out) the storm**)

to experience a difficult situation without being too badly affected by it ♦ OFTEN USED IN BUSINESS AND POLITICS: *Investors who are willing to ride out the current storm in the stock market could see big returns over the next few years.*

story

⇨a shaggy **DOG** story

a hard-luck story

a story that you tell someone in order to make them feel sorry for you: *She had her own hard-luck story: two marriages, two troubled kids, and a drinking problem.*

to make/cut a long story short

SPOKEN used before a statement to tell people that because the story you are telling them is long and complicated, you are only going to give them the most important facts: *"Why did you break up with your previous girlfriend?" "Well, to make a long story short, her parents didn't like me and they wouldn't let us get married."*

stove

slave over a hot stove

a humorous expression meaning to spend a lot of time cooking for someone: *There's*

no way my mom is going to slave over a hot stove on her vacation – she would rather just spend the money and eat out all the time.

straight

⇨**GIVE it to me straight**
⇨**SET** *someone* **straight**

get *something* **straight**

SPOKEN said when you want to be sure that everyone understands the truth about a situation: *Can you go through the procedure again, just to make sure we've got it straight?*

keep *someone* **on the straight and narrow**

to make someone live in an honest or moral way, especially if they have not always done this: *Davies said that it was the support of his wife, Jeanine, that helped him kick his cocaine addiction, and kept him on the straight and narrow.*
opposite **stray/slip from the straight and narrow:** *Believe me, he's not the first politician to stray from the straight and narrow.*

straits

be in dire straits

to be in a very serious and difficult situation, especially because you do not have enough money ◆ USED ESPECIALLY IN NEWSPAPERS, MAGAZINES, ETC.: *The losses in the overseas securities market put the company in dire straits.*

stranger

⇨**stranger THINGs have happened**

someone **is no stranger to** *something*

used to say that someone has often experienced a particular situation, and so will not have any trouble dealing with it again ◆ OFTEN USED IN NEWSPAPERS: *Taylor, who is a well-known music journalist, is no stranger to broadcasting either, having worked for CBS.*

straw

draw the short straw

to have to do something that no one else

wanted to do, especially because you were chosen by chance: *Bethany drew the short straw, so she will give the first talk.*

be grasping/clutching at straws

to try hard to find a solution or something to make you hopeful, even when you know it is unlikely that any exist: *The doctors admit they're grasping at straws with this new treatment.*

the last/final straw

used about the problem that makes you so angry, or makes things so difficult, that you finally decide to change or leave the situation that you are in: *When Mandy didn't bother to come home for Christmas dinner, that was the last straw.*
—compare **be the STRAW that breaks the camel's back**

be the straw that breaks the camel's back

used about the last in a series of problems, that makes someone unable to deal with a situation: *Chavez had often experienced racism, but this insulting treatment was the straw that broke the camel's back.*
—compare **the last/final STRAW**

streak

talk a blue streak

to talk a lot, very quickly, and without stopping: *Once Jolisa gets going, she'll talk a blue streak, and you won't be able to stop her.*

street

___ is a two-way street

used to say that the opinions and feelings of both sets of people involved are important in a process or activity: *Learning is a two-way street for students and teachers at Lincoln High. "You have to accept that these kids are extremely bright," said math teacher Art Hoffman.*

strength

give me strength!

SPOKEN said when you are annoyed about something: *"I'll only go with you if you'll let me drive." "Give me strength!"*

stretch

⇨the HOME stretch

not by any stretch of the imagination

used to emphasize that something cannot be considered or described in a particular way: *Now the Palace Hotel was many things, but it was not, by any stretch of the imagination, a palace.*

stride

do *something* without breaking stride

to continue doing something easily and calmly, even though things happen that could interrupt you or surprise you: *Stern maintains the art of pacing a radio show, cutting from one outrageous comment to the next joke without breaking stride.*

hit (your) stride

to start speaking or doing something better or more confidently after you have been doing it for a time: *After four or five shaky episodes, Fox's new teen sitcom has hit its stride.*

put *someone* off their stride

to make someone pause in what they are saying or doing, or stop them from doing it so well by surprising, annoying, or interrupting them: *Mrs. Grower tried to interrupt, but the principal refused to be put off his stride.*

take *something* in stride

to react to a change or difficult situation in a calm and organized way, without being too upset by it: *I used to be able to take things in stride, but lately every little thing seems like a major disaster.*

strike

strike it rich

to suddenly become very rich or very successful: *We stayed in Vegas for five days, hoping to strike it rich, but had to be content with a couple of free cocktails.*

two/three/several strikes against *someone/something*

two or more things that make it extremely difficult or impossible for someone or something to be successful: *These girls*

have at least three strikes against them – they're poor, they have only one parent, and they can't afford to go to college.

> NOTE▶ In the game of baseball, a player who has three strikes is out (=loses the chance to try to hit the ball).

string

⇨hold/control the PURSE strings
⇨be tied to *someone's* APRON STRINGS

have/keep *someone* on a string

used when you disapprove because someone can control another person, and make them do what they want: *Don't you realize Sonya's keeping you on a string just in case she can't find anyone else?*

pull (some) strings

to secretly use your influence with important people in order to get what you want or to help someone else: *Jack knows somebody who might be able to pull a few strings and get our names onto the guest list.*
string-pulling: *Joseph knew that his son would never get into art school without some serious string-pulling.*

pull the strings
(also **pull *someone's* strings**)

to control what another person or an organization does, without having a right or any official power to do this: *Many people today feel that they have lost control of their lives, and become puppets with someone else pulling their strings.*

> NOTE▶ This idiom comes from a puppet (=a model of a person or animal with strings attached to parts of its body). The person who pulls the strings controls the movement of the puppet.

with no strings attached

used to say that an agreement or arrangement has no bad or unexpected parts so that someone can get or do what they want without having to give or do anything they do not want to: *Ray offered her a free trip to the Bahamas, with no strings attached.*

stripes

earn your stripes
to do something that shows that you deserve your job, position, or rank: *She earned her stripes the hard way – she started at the bottom of a little company and turned it into a giant corporation.*

stroke

at a/one stroke
if something is done at a stroke, it happens suddenly because of one action or event: *Two thousand jobs will be created at a stroke by the building of the new car plant.*

different strokes for different folks
SPOKEN used to say that people are different, and you should not treat them the same, or expect them to behave in the same way: *Your way of dealing with your kids worked for you – it takes different strokes for different folks.*

paint *something* in broad strokes
(also **draw, sketch, etc.** *something* **in broad strokes**)
to describe something in a general way, not giving a lot of details: *The movie only paints Dillinger's character in broad strokes, so we never really understand what makes him do the horrendous things he does.*

stroll

⇒take a **TRIP**/walk/stroll down memory lane

strong

⇒**COME** on strong

struck

be struck dumb
OLD-FASHIONED to be so shocked that you cannot speak: *On arriving, he was struck dumb with horror and amazement at the destruction of the place.*

stuck up

stuck up
(also **stuck-up**)
used about someone who thinks they are better or more important than other people, and is unfriendly to them: *He had a reputation for being stuck up – always impressed by his own good looks and money.*

stuff

don't sweat the small stuff
used to tell someone not to worry or become upset about unimportant things or small problems: *My mother's advice when we got married was, "don't sweat the small stuff."*

the hard stuff
strong alcoholic drinks: *Ken enjoyed a beer or two, but he knew he had to avoid the hard stuff.*

someone is made of sterner stuff
used to say that someone has a stronger character than other people: *"Won't you be afraid, waiting here in the dark?" "Not at all – I'm made of sterner stuff than that."*

strut your stuff
to do something that you do well, usually in a way that shows you are proud of yourself: *The competition gives kids with good minds a chance to strut their stuff.*

style

cramp *someone's* style
to limit someone's freedom or make them feel uncomfortable, especially by being with them when they do not want you: *If you want to be alone with Julie, just let me know – I don't want to cramp your style.*

subject

drop the subject
to stop talking about something because someone does not want to talk about it any more, especially because it is upsetting or annoying someone: *Lisa looked furious when I asked about Ray, so I dropped the subject and told her about my day.*

sublime

from the sublime to the ridiculous
used to say that a silly thing or event is following an important or serious one: *One of the elements of humor is surprise, going from the sublime to the ridiculous.*

such

such as it is/was
FORMAL said just after you mention something to show that it is not very good: *The play makes its point, such as it is, in about eight minutes, and then continues for another two and a half hours.*

sucker

⇨there's a sucker born every minute —see **there's one born every MINUTE**

be a sucker for *something*
used to say that you like someone or something a lot, especially someone or something that other people do not like, or that you are a little ashamed of: *Why, she wondered, was she such a sucker for broken-hearted men?*

sugar

⇨sugar-coat the **PILL**

a sugar daddy
1 a rich older man who gives a young person presents and money in return for their company, and often for sex: *"Here's my sugar daddy," Eve said, putting her arm around a gray-haired man who must have been at least sixty.*
2 someone who is rich and willing to give a person, group, or organization the money that they need: *When a wealthy businessman took over the team, they thought they had acquired a sugar daddy with endless resources.*

suit

follow suit
to do the same thing that someone else has just done: *When the nation's fourth-largest bank lowered interest rates, other major commercial banks were expected to follow suit.*

NOTE▶ A "suit" is one of four types of playing cards. Your "strong/long suit" is the one you have most of in your hand (=group of cards you are holding). In some games you have to "follow suit" (play the same type of card as the last player).

___ is *someone's* strong/long suit
used to say that someone is good at a particular thing or knows a lot about it
♦ USUALLY USED IN THE NEGATIVE: *Making polite conversation has never been Tom's strong suit.*

summer

an Indian summer
1 a period of time in the fall when the weather is warm and sunny: *An Indian summer leads to extra-ripe grapes with a higher sugar content.*
2 a happy or successful period of time near the end of your working life, or when you are old: *Seventies bands seem to be enjoying an Indian summer of popularity.*

sun

think the sun shines out of *someone's* backside/behind/ass (also think the sun shines out of *someone*)
SPOKEN to admire someone so much that you think everything they do is good: *Marie really likes him – she thinks the sun shines out of his backside.*

Sunday

Sunday driver
someone who annoys other people by driving too slowly: *"Did you have a good trip?" "This afternoon was okay, but there were a lot of Sunday drivers out this morning."*

superintendent

⇨**SIDEWALK** superintendent

sure

⇨sure **THING!**

surface

scratch the surface (of *something*)

to deal with only a very small part of an important subject: *We like to think we know a lot about schizophrenia, but actually we've only scratched the surface.*

suspicion

have a sneaking suspicion

to think that something may be true, without having any definite information: *Fran thinks the director is leaving, and I have a sneaking suspicion she may be right.*

swallow

⇨*something* is **HARD/difficult** to swallow

swallow *something* whole

to believe or accept something completely without asking any questions: *He's always turning up late with some fantastic excuse, expecting me to swallow it whole!*

swear

swear up and down (that) (also **swear blind (that)**)

OLD-FASHIONED used to emphasize that someone says they are telling the truth: *Tyler swore up and down that he hadn't taken the money.*

sweat

⇨don't sweat the small **STUFF**
⇨sweat **BLOOD**

break out into a cold sweat (about *something*) (also **break into a sweat (about *something*)**)

to become nervous or frightened about something: *I break out in a cold sweat just thinking about asking the bank for a loan.*

from/by the sweat of your brow

by your hard work or effort: *You have never had to earn a single cent from the sweat of your brow.*

no sweat

SPOKEN used to say that you can do something easily: *"Are you sure you can carry that bag?" "Sure, no sweat."*

> **NOTE**▸ "No problem" means the same as this idiom, and is used more frequently.

sweat it out

to wait or be patient until something bad or frightening ends: *I sat there in the lawyer's office, sweating it out, looking the facts in the face, and trying to anticipate the worst that could happen.*

sweep

a clean sweep

1 a victory for one party or group in all parts of a race, competition or election, for example by winning the first three places in a race: *The poll also indicated a clean sweep for the Democrats in elections for lieutenant governor and attorney general.*

2 a complete change in a country or organization, made by getting rid of a lot of people or things: *The whole political structure should be brought down and destroyed – a clean sweep, that's what they need.*

sweetness

someone/something is all sweetness and light

OLD-FASHIONED used to say that someone or something is very nice and friendly, especially when you think that they are not really like this: *She storms out of the office all mad, but I know she'll be all sweetness and light with her friends.*

swim

be in the swim of things

OLD-FASHIONED to know what is happening in a particular area of activity that is fashionable or popular, and be involved in it: *"It's good to be back in the swim of things," said Jack Miller upon his return to work following open-heart surgery.*

swimmingly

⇨**GO swimmingly**

swing

get into the swing (of *something*)
to start doing something well and enjoying it: *It won't take long for Susan to get back into the swing of things after she has the baby.*

in full swing
if an event or process is in full swing, it has been going on for some time and a lot is happening: *The party was in full swing on the floor below.*

swing it
SPOKEN to find a way to deal with a difficult problem, often by doing something that is not usually allowed: *Work visas are very difficult to get. Unless your friend has a family connection in this country, I'm not sure that you'll be able to swing it.*

swipe

take a swipe at *someone*
to publicly criticize someone or something, especially in a speech, a piece of writing, etc. that is mostly about something else ♦ USED ESPECIALLY IN NEWS-PAPERS: *In its more realistic scenes, the movie takes a swipe at homelessness in 1990s America.*

swoop

in/at one fell swoop
if you do a lot of things in one fell swoop, you do them at the same time, with one decision, action, etc.: *Someone had pressed the wrong key and deleted all the files in one fell swoop.*

> NOTE▶ This idiom comes from a line in Shakespeare's play "*Macbeth*."

sword

cross swords (with)
to argue with someone: *It isn't the first time he and Dan have crossed swords over his teaching methods.*

be a double-edged sword
used to say that a plan, achievement, etc. that someone hopes will bring them success could also harm them ♦ USED ESPECIALLY IN NEWSPAPERS: *For women, the sexual liberation of the Sixties was a double-edged sword.*

the/a sword of Damocles
something bad that may affect your situation at any time, and make it much worse: *Since my illness was diagnosed, I have lived with the sword of Damocles hanging over my head.*

system

(it's) all systems go
used to say that a plan or process is ready to start: *Once we get gas in the car, it'll be all systems go for our road trip.*

beat the system
to find ways to achieve what you want, even though society's rules or powerful organizations do not allow it or approve of it: *Dave thought he could beat the system by borrowing money from different sources, but he just got deeper and deeper into debt.*

buck the system
to not be at all affected by society's rules and powerful organizations, and do the opposite of what they allow or approve of: *As an abused husband, it is very hard to fight for custody of your children, and buck the entire court system and its traditions.*

get *someone/something* out of your system
1 (also **get it out of your system**) to do something such as talking, writing, or using a lot of energy that helps you to stop feeling angry, unhappy, etc.: *I had such a bad day at the office – I went for a swim to get it out of my system.*
2 to stop wanting to do something, or wanting to be with someone after a romantic relationship has finished: *All my friends keep telling me that the only way I'm going to get him out of my system is to meet somebody else.*

S

T

tab

keep tabs on *someone* or *something*
to watch someone or something carefully so that you know where they are, what they are doing, or what is happening: *The company has decided to keep tabs on the number of phone calls employees make.*

pick up the tab (for)
to pay for something, especially when you are not responsible for paying: *Port officials argue that the city should have picked up the tab for fixing the environmental damage.*

run up a tab (of)
if you run up a tab at a bar, store, etc., you agree to pay for everything at a later time: *At one conference, officials ran up a bar tab of $12,700 – paid for by the office.*

table

bring *something* to the table
to suggest something to be considered or discussed in a formal meeting ◆ OFTEN USED IN BUSINESS OR POLITICS: *It's a question of the person's credentials and what kinds of ideas they're actually bringing to the table that will determine who we choose.*

drink *someone* under the table
to drink a lot more alcohol than someone else can, without getting drunk: *Brenda was willing to bet that she could drink any of the guys under the table.*

get/go/come, etc. back to the table
if a country, political organization, etc. gets back to the table, they return to discussions that they were having with another country or organization in order to try to reach an agreement: *We'll have to go back to the table with an open mind and overcome our differences.*
get/bring/force, etc. *someone* back to the table: *Sandoval hopes to bring people to the table to discuss important health issues.*

on the table
if an offer, idea, etc. is on the table, someone has suggested it so that it can be considered and discussed: *The President said the option of lifting the U.N. arms embargo was still on the table.*

put *something* on the table
if one group in a formal discussion or meeting puts something on the table, they tell the other group what they are offering, or what they want to talk about ◆ OFTEN USED IN BUSINESS AND POLITICS: *We put a very fair bid on the table, and we are not prepared to go any higher.*

turn the tables (on *someone*)
to suddenly gain an advantage over someone who is in a stronger position than you, especially in a fight, game, or competition: *Police say that two clerks at a convenience store turned the tables on a potential robber, firing five shots at him, and forcing him to flee empty-handed.*
the tables are/have turned: *Now the tables are turned somewhat, and men have begun complaining of discrimination at work.*

under the table
if you buy, sell, or do something under the table, you do it secretly because it is dishonest or illegal: *Taber is officially unemployed, but he does a few jobs for friends who pay him under the table.*
under-the-table: *I don't like to see young people involved in under-the-table deals.*
—compare **under the COUNTER**

tack

change tack
(also **try a different tack**)
1 to try a different way of dealing with a problem or situation because what you tried before was not successful: *In December, AT&T decided to change tack and began offering its online service for free as an attempt to gain market share.*
2 to start to talk about something different that is not connected with what you were talking about before: *I decided to try a different tack – she might be interested in sports.*
a change of tack: *If Nick was surprised by her sudden change of tack, he didn't show it.*

get down to brass tacks
SPOKEN to start talking about things that are important, when you meet someone to discuss a plan, situation, etc.: *Why don't*

we order some lunch and then get down to brass tacks?
—see also **get down to BUSINESS**

tail

be chasing your (own) tail
to spend a lot of time and energy trying to do something, without any success: *Nobody knows who's in charge around here, so nothing ever gets done on time. It's like chasing your own tail.*

be on *someone's* tail
1 (also **be on the tail of** *someone*) to be chasing or following someone very closely: *Now even the national news organizations were on his tail.*
2 SPOKEN if a car is on your tail, it is annoying you because it is following your car too closely: *We drove across a mile-long bridge with a huge truck on our tail the whole time.*

the tail (is) wagging the dog
used to say that a small or unimportant part is controlling or affecting the whole of a situation or process: *In its efforts to boost CD sales, the music industry has tried to make records obsolete, rather than letting the marketplace do it. It's a classic case of the tail wagging the dog.*

turn tail
to leave a difficult situation because you cannot deal with it: *At the first sign of danger, Robb turned tail and left the scene.*

with your tail between your legs
if you go somewhere with your tail between your legs, you are embarrassed or unhappy because you have failed at something or have been defeated: *Last night, Jerry came in with his tail between his legs and asked if he could stay with us because Cindy had thrown him out.*

> NOTE▶ When a dog is afraid or unhappy, it puts its tail between its legs.

tailspin

go into a tailspin
if a system, organization, etc. goes into a tailspin, it suddenly stops being effective and begins to fail: *After the election, the nation's economy went into a tailspin.*

take

⇒**HAVE what it takes**
⇒**take a long, hard LOOK at**

do a double take
to look at or think about something again just after you see it for the first time because it surprises you: *I walked by him and did a double take because he really did look just like Chris Kakoulis.*

be on the take
if someone with power or authority is on the take, they are willing to do something wrong if they are given money: *Nick thought that the referees were on the take, which is why we lost both our games.*

take *someone/something* for granted
1 (also **take it for granted that**) to be sure that something is true or will happen, especially when you should not be: *It's very easy to take good health for granted, but we need health insurance just in case a serious problem develops.* | *When I was younger I took it for granted that I'd be able to play ball all the time. Now, I'm lucky if I manage one or two hours a week.*
2 to expect someone to always be there when you need them, and never be grateful or show them any special attention: *Never take your children for granted. All too soon they'll be moving out and starting families of their own.*

take *something* hard
SPOKEN to become sad because of something that happens or that someone does: *Jake took his brother's death very hard. They'd always been close.*

take it easy
1 (also **take things easy**) to relax and not do very much: *Why don't you sit down and take it easy for a while?*
2 SPOKEN used to tell someone to stop being angry or worrying and relax: *Hey, take it easy! Nobody's saying it was your fault.*
3 SPOKEN said when you are leaving someone: *"Bye, see you next week." "Yeah, take it easy."*

take it from me
SPOKEN used to emphasize that someone

T

can believe what you are saying because you know about the subject you are talking about: *Take it from me – you don't want to make Phil mad. I've seen how violent he can get.*

take it or leave it

1 SPOKEN used to say that someone can accept an offer or refuse it, but there can be no discussion about it: *I'll give you $1,500 for the car. That's my final offer – take it or leave it.*

2 used to say that someone does not have a strong opinion about something, and does not like or dislike it very much: *Some people find smoking addictive, and some can either take it or leave it, but the majority of people do not smoke at all.*

not take *something* lying down

used to say that you will not accept being treated badly, and you are getting angry and will take action: *When we heard about the layoffs, we weren't about to take it lying down and started organizing the workforce.*

be taken with/by

to like or be attracted by someone or something: *I was especially taken with an emerald and diamond necklace in the display window. | We were so taken by the local residents' kindness and simplicity that we stayed longer that we had planned.*

something takes some doing

used to say that something is difficult and needs a lot of effort, skill, or determination: *"How are you going to get that thing down from the ceiling?" "I don't know yet, but it's going to take some doing."*

you can't take *someone* anywhere

SPOKEN a humorous expression said when someone who is with you is behaving in a way that embarrasses or annoys you: *Look at you. You've got chocolate all over you – I can't take you anywhere!*

tale

live to tell the tale

used to say that someone is still alive after a dangerous experience, and often used humorously when the experience is not really dangerous: *Will really doesn't like*

his real name. Nobody calls him *"Willard" and lives to tell the tale.*

an old wives' tale

used about a piece of advice, for example about health problems, that people believed in former times, but that most people now think is not true: *Some people say if the sky turns red in the evening, it won't rain the next day, but I think that's an old wives' tale.*

tell tales

OLD-FASHIONED to tell someone in authority something that is untrue, or that is a secret, in order to cause problems for someone else: *She's been telling tales behind my back! Well, whatever she told you, it's a lie.*

tells a/the tale

used to say that something you see, especially something you read or someone's behavior, makes the truth about a situation clear: *Experts have long claimed that students' math skills lagged behind their grade levels; periodic state tests told the tale.*

talk

⇒**NOW you're talking!**

⇒**you can/can't talk** —see **LOOK** who's **talking!**

⇒**you're a (fine) one to talk** —see **LOOK** who's **talking!**

I'm/we're talking ___

SPOKEN used to emphasize how much money something costs or how much someone has: *It's going to cost a fortune. You're talking $100 for labor alone.*

someone is all talk (and no action)

used to say that someone is always talking about what they have done, or what they are going to do, but never actually does anything: *It's still usually a case of all talk and no action when teenage boys discuss sex in the playground.*

talk about ___

SPOKEN used to emphasize how much of a quality a person or thing has, or how true a statement is: *Wow, talk about timing – somebody was just pulling out of a parking space in front of the door when we got there.*

talk dirty
to talk in a sexual way to someone in order to make them feel sexually excited: *Oh, I like it when you talk dirty.*

be the talk of the town
used to say that everyone is talking about someone or something because they are very interested, shocked, excited, etc. ♦ OFTEN USED IN NEWSPAPERS, MAGAZINES, ETC.: *The battle over the stadium development is currently the talk of the town.*

talk tough
to try to frighten or seem impressive to people by telling them what you want or what you will do if they disobey you: *Buchanan talks tough, but her readers know she's just a softie at heart.*

walk your talk
to do what you say you will or what you tell other people to do: *You can't just tell your kids to be polite and respectful, you have to walk your talk.*

tangent

go off on a tangent
(also **fly off on a tangent**)
to suddenly start thinking or talking about a completely different subject: *Better editing would have helped prevent the author from going off on so many tangents.*

tank

built like a tank
used about someone who has a broad chest, shoulders, etc. and looks very strong: *It isn't easy to make a perfectly tailored suit for a man who is built like a tank.*

NOTE▶ You can change this idiom by using other large, solid objects instead of "tank": *The team had signed a new player who was built like a one-ton truck.*

tap

on tap
1 available and ready to be used when you need it: *When starting your own business, you should have at least six months' income on tap for your own safety.*
2 if an event or an activity is on tap, it is going to happen ♦ USED IN NEWSPAPERS: *Scary story readings and costume contests are some of the events on tap for Halloween.*

tape

red tape
official rules or processes that seem unnecessary and prevent things from being done quickly and easily: *There is a considerable amount of red tape and legal expense involved in setting up a corporation.*

NOTE▶ Government officials used to tie their papers together with red tape (=a long thin piece of material like string).

tar

⇨**tar** *someone* **with the same BRUSH**

task

take *someone* to task
to tell someone that you disapprove of something that they have done: *Reich took U.S. retailers to task for purchasing goods which had been produced by what he called slave labor.*

taste

an acquired taste
used about something that people only begin to like after they have tried it a few times: *I love acid-house music, but I suppose it's an acquired taste.*

get a taste/dose of your own medicine
to be treated badly in the same way that you have treated someone else: *Dave got a taste of his own medicine when his neighbors decided to throw their trash on his lawn.*
give *someone* **a taste/dose of their own medicine:** *After years of being humiliated by my husband's affairs, I decided to give him a dose of his own medicine.*

leave a bad taste in your mouth
if something unpleasant that happens to you, or that you learn about, leaves a bad

taste in your mouth, you remember it for some time and feel angry or upset: *As an accountant, I have to say that the article on illegal accounting practices left a very bad taste in my mouth.*

there's no accounting for taste

SPOKEN used to say that you do not understand why someone likes someone or something that you do not like: *"I don't know what Mel sees in that woman." "They seem happy together. There's no accounting for taste, I guess."*

there's no accounting for taste

tea

not (do *something*) for all the tea in China

used to emphasize that you do not want to do something, and no reward would be big enough to make you do it: *Parvis won't stop here – not for all the tea in China.*

tears

⇨be bored to tears —see be BORED stiff
⇨shed CROCODILE tears

not shed tears (over)

to feel glad that someone or something is gone or has stopped because you did not like or approve of it: *Nobody would shed tears if the rebels were stopped tomorrow and their leaders locked away forever.*

tee/T

... to a T/tee

1 used to emphasize that something is done exactly right, or is exactly what is wanted: *The role of 1950s wife and mother seemed to suit her to a tee.*

2 used to emphasize that something shows exactly what someone is like: *Fred Wilson fits that description to a T.*

> NOTE▶ In this idiom, "T" or "tee" comes from a tool called a T-square, which is used to make sure that the corners of something are cut to exactly the right angle.

teeth

—see TOOTH

teething

teething problems/pains

used about the small problems that a company, product, system, etc. has at the beginning: *The C–17s showed few of the teething problems that most new airplanes suffer.*

telephone

talk on the big white telephone

SLANG to vomit (=bring food up from your stomach through your mouth) into the toilet: *"Bob?" "I just heard him talking on the big white telephone in the bathroom."*

tell

I/I'll tell you what...

1 SPOKEN (also **tell you what**) used to introduce a suggestion: *Tell you what – why don't you write down the weekends you're free, and I'll try to organize something.*

2 used to emphasize that you really mean what you are saying: *I tell you what, I'm not looking forward to standing up in court tomorrow and telling my side of the story.*

tell *someone* flat out

to tell someone in a direct and impolite way, with no discussion, that you will not do what they have asked you: *I told them flat out that I wasn't going to help them.*

tell it like it is

SPOKEN to say exactly what you think or what is true, without hiding anything that might upset or offend people: *Penn is not willing to compromise his beliefs and always tells it like it is when the subject of human rights comes up.*

T

tell-it-like-it-is: *"The company might be first in the state, but it's only 47th when the whole country is considered,"* says Vargas, in his typical tell-it-like-it-is management style.

...tell me about it
SPOKEN used to tell someone that you have experienced the situation they are telling you about, or that you have the same feelings that they do: *"What a rotten day!" "Yeah, tell me about it!"*

tell me another (one)
OLD-FASHIONED used when you do not believe what someone has told you: *"Did you know Bill's getting a new Mercedes?" "Tell me another one."*

tell *someone* where to go
SPOKEN to speak to someone angrily because what they have just said is insulting or unfair: *Caferelli asked me to work late again, but I told him where to go.*

that would be telling
SPOKEN said when you cannot tell someone something because it is a secret: *"I know who did it." "Who?" "Ah, but that would be telling."*

there's no telling
used to say that it is impossible to guess what will happen or what is true: *There's no telling when the flood waters will recede enough for people to move back into their homes.*

you're telling me!
SPOKEN used to emphasize that you already know and agree with what someone has said: *"He's such a pain to live with!" "You're telling me!"*

tempest

a tempest in a teapot
used to say that someone is treating a problem as if it is worse or more difficult than it actually is: *The vast majority of residents have dismissed the controversy as a tempest in a teapot. "Most people don't even care what happens," said one.*

ten

ten to one
INFORMAL used to emphasize that something is very likely: *Ten to one the Jays won't win the pennant this year.*

tenterhooks

be on tenterhooks
to be nervous and excited because you are waiting for something to happen: *Carl was on tenterhooks, waiting for his supervisor's decision about the new job.*

> NOTE▷ Tenterhooks are used to stretch cloth tightly when it has just been woven.

term

come to terms with *something*
to accept a situation that is difficult for you to accept: *It will take us a long time to come to terms with the loss of our daughter.*

in no uncertain terms
if you tell someone something in no uncertain terms, you tell them it in a clear, firm and usually angry way: *Students have to be told in no uncertain terms that drug use will not be tolerated on school grounds.*

territory

something comes/goes with the territory
used to say that something, especially a problem, is a usual part of a particular job, situation, etc. that people should expect: *Since I became mayor, people have been more interested in my private life, but I guess that goes with the territory.*

test

⇨the ACID test
⇨a LITMUS TEST

put *something* to the test
to test or find out how good something is, or how true a statement or idea is: *This new equipment will really be put to the test on our next expedition to the Himlayas.*

something will stand the test of time
used to say that something is so good that people will continue to like it, use it, believe it, etc. even after a long time: *Bacharach's melodies are true classics that are sure to stand the test of time.*

T

thanks

no thanks to *someone/something*

SPOKEN used to say that someone did not help you to do something, or tried to prevent you from doing it: *Well, I finally finished the book – no thanks to you and your interruptions.*

that

⇨ **JUST like that**
⇨ **that makes TWO of us**

that does it!

SPOKEN said when you are annoyed or angry about a situation, and something happens that makes you refuse to deal with it any more: *"That does it!" said Rex. "You can fix this stupid machine on your own."*

that does it!

THEN YOU COULD TRY...

THAT DOES IT! NEXT TIME, FIX IT YOURSELF!

that's *someone* all over

SPOKEN used to say that a particular way of behaving is typical of someone: *"He's blaming me, and it was his fault!" "Yeah, that's Adams all over."*

—see also **THAT's** *someone* **for you**

that's all she wrote

SPOKEN used to say that you cannot stop what happens next in a situation, especially when it is bad: *Although cilantro grows here, it's not worth the effort to plant it. Once you harvest it, that's all she wrote. It doesn't grow back again next year.*

that's *someone* for you

SPOKEN used to say that a particular way of behaving is typical of a particular group of people or a particular person: *I suppose I shouldn't have expected them to clean up after themselves. That's teenagers for you.*

—see also **THAT's** *someone* **all over**

that's more like it!

SPOKEN said when you are satisfied with an improvement that has been made: *"Well, I finally got the car to start." "That's more like it!"*

...(and) that's that

1 SPOKEN used to emphasize that nothing will persuade you to do what you have refused to do: *I'm not typing your homework assignment for you, and that's that!*

2 used to emphasize that something is finished or cannot be changed: *They don't have a student council – the principal makes the decisions, and that's that.*

(now) that's what I call ___

SPOKEN used when you want to emphasize that you think something is very good, attractive, interesting, etc.: *Mmm, that smells good. Now that's what I call home cooking.*

that's what you think

SPOKEN used to tell someone that you know that what they have just said is wrong: *"David would never cheat on me." "That's what you think. I saw him coming out of Cindy's house Sunday morning."*

> **NOTE▶** When you say this idiom, the stress is put on the word "you."

that's where *someone/something* comes in
(also that's where *someone/something* comes into it)

SPOKEN used when you are describing a situation, to explain why someone or something is important or necessary in that situation: *You can take a four-wheel-drive vehicle almost anywhere in the area, at least until you run out of gas. That was where the vodka came into it. Each bottle given to a border guard translates into 5 gallons of gas.*

that's where we came in
(also **...which is where we came in**)
SPOKEN used to say that you are talking about the same subject that you began a conversation, explanation, or story with: *So the demand goes up, and companies produce more goods, until the market is overloaded, and that's where we came in. It's a cycle that can't be broken.*

then

then again
SPOKEN used to say that although something is true, something else is also true and should also be considered: *I don't really like this top anymore. But then again, if I wore it under a jacket, it might still look nice.*

there

⇨**BEEN there, done that (seen the movie, bought the T-shirt)**
⇨**be getting there** —see **GET**
⇨**HANG in there!**
⇨*someone* **is not ALL there**
⇨**SO there!**
⇨**there's no telling** —see **TELL**

be there for *someone*
SPOKEN to be ready to help someone or be kind to them when they have problems: *Jeff is great. He's always there for me, ready to talk.*

there you go/are
1 said when you give someone something: *"Who ordered the potato skins?" "I did." "Okay, there you go."*
2 SPOKEN used to tell someone that they should have expected what has just happened, or that you thought it would happen: *"Bob, do you know where those new people next door are from?" "Uh, Texas, I think." "There you go, Marge – I knew they were from the South."*

you've got me there
SPOKEN used to say that you do not know the answer to a question: *"Do you know how to start this thing?" "Let me see – no, you've got me there."*

they

⇨**they don't MAKE 'em like they used to**

thick

⇨**LAY it on thick**

be as thick as thieves
OLD-FASHIONED used to say that two people or groups are very friendly and share a lot of secrets, especially when you are annoyed by this or disapprove of it: *Those two have been as thick as thieves lately – I wonder what they're planning.*

do *something* **through thick and thin**
to keep doing something in spite of difficulties or problems: *Alda's new movie is about couples who remain friends through thick and thin.*

be in the thick of *something*
(also **be in the thick of it**)
to be involved in the busiest, most active, most dangerous, etc. part of a situation: *Smith was in the thick of the action during the first half of the game, scoring several goals.*

thick and fast
used to say that things are happening or coming in large amounts or numbers: *Rumors were flying thick and fast that there would be layoffs in the next months.*

thing

⇨**be just the TICKET/thing**
⇨**take things into your own hands** — see **take the LAW into your own hands**

all good things (must) come to an end
used to say that you have to accept it when something pleasant ends: *The Cardinals had won five straight championships, but this time only finished in fourth place. "We were hoping for more, but all good things must come to an end," said captain Danny Fisher.*

all (other) things being equal
used to say that unless something that you do not know about changes the situation, you think a particular thing will happen or be decided: *All other things being equal, the larger your sample group, the more accurate your survey results will be.*

T

be all things to all people

1 to please or be useful to all types of people when this is not possible: *Giant retailers which try to be all things to all people are being overtaken by specialist stores that appeal to a small market.*
2 used to say that different groups of people can each get a different advantage from something such as a situation or product: *Multimedia has become all things to all people because it has such a wide variety of applications.*

> NOTE▶ This idiom comes from *I Corinthians* in the Bible.

do the/that ___ thing

SLANG used to say that you do a particular thing, including all of the different activities involved in it: *Do you want to do that downtown shopping thing for a while? I have some stuff I need to get. I I'll let you do the plumber thing. I'm going to take the dog for a walk.*

do the wild thing

SLANG to have sex: *Do you wanna do the wild thing, honey?*

do your own thing

SPOKEN to do what you want to do, without following rules or copying other people: *I'm my own man and I do my own thing – I don't need anybody.*

do your thing

SPOKEN to do something that you like doing, are good at doing, or have been planning to do: *It's great that the band is still together, and still doing their thing after all these years.*

first things first

SPOKEN used to say that you have to deal with the most important parts of a plan or situation before you can start thinking about the less important parts: *First things first – where is everybody going to sit?*

for one thing

SPOKEN used to give a reason for what you are saying when there are other reasons, but it is an important one: *Well, for one thing, I don't have enough money to go with you, and anyway, I can't take time off work.*

have a good thing going

SPOKEN to be in a situation in which you will earn a lot of money, gain a lot of advantages, etc.: *How stupid can you be? You thought you had a good thing going and that nobody would notice that you were stealing their jewelry?*

have a thing about

SPOKEN to like or dislike someone or something so much that it is unusual or unreasonable: *The magazine's designers seem to have a thing about animal-print fabrics. I Like Jessica, I had a thing about public displays of emotion – I didn't want to watch other people kissing.*

How are things (going)?
(also How's things?)

1 SPOKEN used to ask someone how they are, what they have been doing, etc. when you have not seen them for some time: *Hi, Tina. How are things going at college?*
2 SPOKEN used to ask someone about their situation or something they are doing: *How are things down there? Do you need more paper?*

it's (just) one of those things

SPOKEN said when you are disappointed or annoyed by something that has happened that you could not prevent or change: *We couldn't meet the deadline because too many people were away – it's just one of those things.*

not know the first thing about

SPOKEN used to say that someone does not know anything about something or someone: *Why did you ask Jerry? He doesn't know the first thing about fixing cars.*

know a thing or two about *something*

used to say that someone has a lot of knowledge gained from experience of something: *Reed, who knows a thing or two about poetry, will be reading from his new book next Wednesday.*

make things lively for *someone*

OLD-FASHIONED to make a situation more difficult for someone, especially because you are angry with them or do not like them: *We managed to make a few raids across the river and make things lively for the enemy for a month or two.*

of all things
SPOKEN used to emphasize that you are surprised at what someone has chosen or what has happened: *In 1996, Calvin left the army to become, of all things, a gourmet chef.*

one thing led to another
used to say that you are not giving the details about how a situation developed, because it is a common situation that everyone understands: *We started kissing, and one thing led to another, and I didn't leave until the next afternoon.*

be onto a good thing
SPOKEN to have found a situation that is helpful for you, especially a way of getting money: *Alger knew he was onto a good thing with his stories about a brave orphan who is finally successful.*

stranger things have happened
SPOKEN used to say that you should not be sure that an idea is completely stupid or impossible, even if it seems unlikely to succeed or happen: *The Twins are ahead 5–0, but they could still lose the game. Stranger things have happened.*

sure thing!
SPOKEN used to answer "yes" in a friendly way to a question: *"Julia, could you hand me that spoon?" "Sure thing."*

the thing is...
SPOKEN used to introduce an explanation, especially about a problem that stops you from doing something: *Normally I'd say "yes," but the thing is, I already promised Kari I'd take her home.*

things go from bad to worse
used to say that a situation that is already bad is getting even worse: *After Ted got sick, things just went from bad to worse.*

things that go bump in the night
a humorous expression meaning things that frighten you, especially at night, because you cannot explain them: *Check out the things that go bump in the night, if you dare, in the Haunted House at the Saratoga Festival Park.*

what with one thing and another
SPOKEN used to say that there are several reasons why something happened, especially when you are explaining why you have not done something: *You know how it is – what with one thing and another, we haven't been able to get over to see you.*

think
⇨ COME **to think of/about it**

someone **has another think coming**
SPOKEN used to say that what someone is thinking is completely wrong, or that what they are expecting will not happen: *If he thinks I'm going to start serving him breakfast in bed, he's got another think coming!*

> NOTE▶ Although "think" is the original word used in this idiom, you might also hear people say "*someone* has got another thing coming": *If they are stupid enough to think we won't fight back, they've got another thing coming!*

think out loud
to say what you are thinking, as a way of planning what to do or making suggestions: *"Maybe we should report it to the principal," Maria said. "I'm just thinking out loud here. I don't know what other option we have."*

not think straight
SPOKEN to be unable to think correctly, because you are tired, nervous, confused, etc.: *The kids have been so noisy today, I just can't think straight.*

think twice (about)
to think carefully before doing something, or to be unlikely to do it because you know that the result may be bad: *You can't make your home completely secure, but good locks and lighting will make a burglar think twice.*

not think twice
used to say that someone does not worry or think carefully about something, because they think it is usual and normal, or because it is something that they want to do: *Some students wouldn't think twice about skipping class.*

someone **thinks he's/she's it**
SPOKEN used to say that someone thinks they are very important or special when they are not: *"Look at that guy in his red Ferrari." "Yeah, he really thinks he's it."*

T

wishful thinking
when you believe or hope that something unlikely is going to happen or is true because it is what you want: *After such a long period of manufacturing decline, to hope for a recovery might seem like wishful thinking.*

this
⇨**GET this!**

this and that
SPOKEN used to mean various different things when it is not important to say what they are, or you do not want to: *Grandpa just helps out a little around the store, you know, this and that.*

this, that, and the other (thing)
SPOKEN used to emphasize that you are talking about several things of different kinds when it is not important to say what they are: *Every magazine you read tells you shouldn't have too much fat, too much milk, too much of this, that and the other thing.*

Thomas

a doubting Thomas
used about someone who does not believe that something is true, or says that it has not been proved to them: *At least now all the doubting Thomases of the world will realize the possibilities of cloning.*

NOTE▶ Thomas was the follower of Jesus Christ who did not believe that Jesus had been seen alive again after his death.

thorn

a thorn in *someone's* side
used about someone or something that keeps causing problems or annoying a person or organization: *Klein, the Herald's political reporter, has been a thorn in the side of state legislators for over a decade.*

thought

have second thoughts (about)
to change your mind about something you have decided to do: *Did you ever* have any second thoughts about joining the army?

on second thought
SPOKEN used to say that you have changed your mind: *I'll have a baked potato. No, on second thought, make that a salad instead.*

perish the thought!
used humorously to say that you disapprove of something or do not want it to happen ◆ USED ESPECIALLY IN NEWSPAPERS AND MAGAZINES: *Producers do not want Geraldo Rivera to change his abrasive interview style, perish the thought, but they would like him to concentrate on less controversial topics.*

thousand

be batting a thousand
to be extremely successful: *We've gotten every contract we've bid for this year, so we're batting a thousand right now.*

NOTE▶ In the game of baseball, if you bat a thousand you are successful every time you try to hit the ball. This happens very rarely.

thread

be hanging by a thread
1 if someone's life is hanging by a thread, they are very likely to die: *For six months after he was born, our son's life hung by a thread.*
2 to be in a difficult situation that is very likely to end or fail ◆ OFTEN USED IN NEWSPAPERS AND MAGAZINES: *The last thing Sikorsky wants is another bad result. His job is hanging by a thread already.*

throat

be at each other's throats
if two countries, groups, people, etc. are at each other's throats, they fight or argue all the time ◆ OFTEN USED IN NEWSPAPERS, MAGAZINES, ETC.: *We cannot deal with tomorrow's problems if we are at each other's throats over economic and trade issues.*

T

grab *someone/something* **by the throat**

(also **take, seize, etc.** *someone/ something* **by the throat**)

1 if a performance, book or idea grabs someone by the throat, it makes them feel very interested, excited, frightened, etc. ◆ USED ESPECIALLY IN NEWSPAPERS, MAGAZINES, ETC.: *The latest Brady Coyne novel grabs you by the throat with the opening scene and doesn't let go until the end.*

2 to make a successful attempt to control or deal with something, using a lot of energy ◆ USED ESPECIALLY IN NEWSPAPERS, MAGAZINES, ETC.: *The 49ers had this game by the throat, allowing the Rams just one field goal.*

have *something* **shoved/rammed down your throat**

(also **have** *something* **forced, thrust, pushed, etc. down your throat**)

used to say that someone is trying to force you to accept a plan or idea that they think is very good although you do not agree: *I like vinyl records, and I don't want the latest technology shoved down my throat.*

shove/ram *something* **down** *someone's* **throat**: *Why do some people act like they have to ram their morals down everybody else's throats?*

someone **is cutting/slitting his/her own throat**

used to say that what someone is doing will cause them a lot of trouble in the future, even though they hope it will bring them an advantage: *If you wait much longer to buy a car, you're just cutting your own throat. Somebody else will come along and get all the good bargains.*
—see also **shoot yourself in the FOOT**

jump down *someone's* **throat**

SPOKEN to angrily criticize someone as soon as they say something, usually when you think this is unfair: *Fifty thousand fans, 50 players and two coaches were ready to jump down Nelson's throat if he made a bad call.*

something **sticks in *someone's* throat/craw**

1 if an idea or situation sticks in your throat, you dislike it, and it is very difficult for you to accept: *What really sticks in my throat is the way that people with*

problems get help, but ordinary, hard-working people have to struggle.

2 if something that you are trying to say sticks in your throat, you are unable to say it, especially because of a strong emotion: *Thelma tried to call for help, but the words just stuck in her throat.*

throes

be in the throes of (doing) *something*

to be dealing with a situation, process, or activity that is bad and difficult: *Couples in the throes of divorce and custody battles will often use every method they can to harm each other.*

throttle

at full throttle

(also **full-throttle**)

used to say that a person or group is working hard with a lot of energy, especially in order to achieve something: *Los Altos Police Chief Ron Jones is retiring, and the search for his successor is at full throttle.*

through

through and through

1 used to emphasize that someone is definitely and completely a particular type of person: *Carter is a country girl through and through.*

2 completely or in every part: *Politicians are wasting their time trying to improve a system that is rotten through and through.*

throw

⇨**throw in the TOWEL**

(just) a stone's throw away

used to say that something is very close: *Calderon's tidy home is just a stone's throw from the proposed development site.*

throwback

a throwback to (a time when)

(also **a throwback to the 50s, 60s, 70s, etc.**)

used to say that something is unusual now, but very similar to something that happened or existed in the past: *Fox's new movie is a throwback to the romantic* comedies of the 30s and 40s. | The coach said that Norton was exceptional – a throwback to the old days when football players never left the field during the game.

thumb

be all thumbs

used to say that you are unable to do things neatly and carefully with your hands: Nick is all thumbs when it comes to fixing anything around the house.

give something/someone the thumbs up

1 if a person or organization in authority gives a plan or suggestion the thumbs up, they say that they approve of it and will allow it to happen ◆ OFTEN USED IN NEWSPAPERS, ON TELEVISION NEWS, ETC.: Heather gave us the thumbs up, so we can start work on the project as soon as we like.
2 to say that you approve of something or like it, especially when you are telling other people whether to use it or not ◆ OFTEN USED IN NEWSPAPERS, ON TELEVISION NEWS, ETC.: Surprisingly, kids gave our new Healthy Eating menu a big thumbs up.
get the thumbs up: Plans for the new football stadium got the thumbs up from officials and fans today. Building will begin in April.
opposite give something/someone **the thumbs down:** The mayor was given the thumbs down by some residents in this crime-plagued city.

have a green thumb

to be good at taking care of plants so that they grow well: Craig never has much luck with plants. He just doesn't have much of a green thumb.

stick/stand out like a sore thumb

used to say that someone or something is very easy to notice, or looks wrong or strange because they are so different from everyone or everything around them: Look at that purple house – it sticks out like a sore thumb as soon as you come around the corner.

twiddle your thumbs

to do nothing, either because you have nothing to do, or because you are waiting for something to happen: Don't just sit around twiddling your thumbs – there's plenty of filing to do.

under someone's **thumb**

used to say that someone is completely controlled by a person or organization: Sarah's got you totally under her thumb – you do everything she tells you.

thunder

steal someone's **thunder**

to get all the praise and attention that someone else was expecting by doing something better than them, or doing it before them: The Republican-led Congress believes that Clinton stole their momentum, stole their ideas, stole their thunder.

tick

⇨WHAT makes someone tick

ticket

⇨DREAM ticket

be just the ticket/thing

used to say that something is exactly what is needed in a particular situation ◆ USED ESPECIALLY IN ADVERTISEMENTS: This new jazz compilation album is just the ticket for young lovers, old lovers, and jazz swingers everywhere.

be a ticket to something

used to say that what someone is doing will have a particular result: We're starting to realize that an MBA degree isn't necessarily an instant ticket to success.

tickled

be tickled pink
(also **be tickled to death**)

to be very pleased that something has happened ◆ USED ESPECIALLY IN NEWSPAPERS, MAGAZINES, ETC.: Pauline's mother was tickled pink that her daughter was finally getting married.

tide

stem the tide (of)
(also **stem the flow, swell, etc. (of)**)

to stop a situation that is affecting the whole of an area, country, etc., or something that is being done by a lot of people ◆ USED ESPECIALLY IN BUSINESS AND POLITICS: The White House is very

T

concerned at the flood of illegal immigrants and intends to stem the tide with tighter controls.

swim/go against the tide
(also **row, stand, etc. against the tide**)
to have opinions or ideas on a particular subject that are the opposite of most people's at the time: *In the late 1980s, Albania swam against the tide of democratic reforms in eastern Europe.*
opposite **swim/drift/float with the tide**: *Andy was not the kind of man to swim with the tide just because it was convenient.*

> **NOTE**▶ You may hear people use "tide" in other phrases related to this. For example, you can say that "the tide is flowing *someone's* way" or "the tide is running against *someone*": *With the tide of scientific opinion running against them, Stone's theories are losing influence.* People also talk about "the tide of *something*" in many different phrases: *The factories are now empty, left behind by the tide of progress.*

the tide is turning
used to say that people's opinions are changing so that they no longer approve of someone or something: *The legal tide appears to be turning away from city-wide rent control policies.*
something **turns the tide**: *Beasley's spectacular touchdown pass helped turn the tide in West Virginia's favor in the second quarter of the game.*

tie
tie one on
SPOKEN to get drunk: *Hey, let's go out and tie one on after work.*

tied
⇨**FIT to be tied**

tiger
⇨**be a PAPER tiger**

tightrope
walk a tightrope
used to say that someone is in a situation where they must be very careful about what they say or do, especially because they may easily offend either one of two groups who oppose each other: *With fighting likely to erupt at any minute, U.N. troops are walking a tightrope between the rebel forces and the government army.*

tilt
(at) full tilt
1 if something or someone moves at full tilt, they move as fast as they can: *Danni hadn't been looking where she was going, and ran full tilt into a tall stranger.*
2 used to emphasize that something is happening or being done with a lot of energy and force: *Textile mills were running full tilt a year ago, but are now at only 80% of capacity.*
full-tilt: *People are throwing bottles – it's a full-tilt riot here.*

time
⇨**(just) in the NICK of time**
⇨**over the COURSE of time**

ahead of his/her/its time
used to say that someone or something uses very modern ideas or methods, which are not used by most other people until later: *LaLanne was way ahead of his time in his emphasis on a low-fat diet.*

all in good time
SPOKEN used to tell someone to be patient because what they want will happen or be dealt with later: *"When will you let us know?" "All in good time. We have to see some other people first."*

at the best of times
used to say that something that is usually bad, wrong, difficult, etc. is even worse now: *Running an airline is an expensive business at the best of times; during a recession, it can be a way of using up money very quickly.*

bide your time
to wait patiently for the right moment to do something, or until something happens: *I'd advise you to bide your time and see what turns up in the way of a job.*

big time
SPOKEN used to emphasize that something happens in an extreme way, or that something is serious: *You messed up big time, Doug.*

big-time: *Boothe had been telling big-time lies and finally got fired.*
—compare **the big TIME**

the big time

when someone has reached the highest level of their job and become famous, especially in the entertainment business, sports, or politics: *We've spent years traveling around the state, playing in half-empty bars, but we're ready for the big time now.*
hit/make the big time: *Snell hit the big time when he became a writer and producer for a radio station in San Francisco.*
—compare **big TIME**

do *something* in your own good time

SPOKEN used to say that you will do something when you are ready to do it, and not when other people want you to do it: *Knowing Bobby, he'll tell us his plans in his own good time.*

do *something* in your own time

1 to work or study outside the hours you are paid to work, or outside the time that you spend in school: *An individual who writes a computer program will own the copyright to it if he wrote it in his own time, using his own equipment.*
2 to do something without hurrying, taking all the time that you need: *Take a few days to think it over and let us know in your own time when you make a decision.*

do time

to spend time in prison: *He'd done some time in Joliet when he was younger.*

be/fall behind the times

to not use modern ideas or methods which are already being used by other people: *The government's systems of collecting and analyzing data have fallen behind the times. | People in rural areas tend to be way behind the times on issues like women's rights.*

fall on hard times
(also **hit hard times**)

used to say that a person, or company is no longer as rich and successful as they used to be: *America's auto industry had fallen on hard times in the mid-1980s.*

for old times' sake

used to say that someone is doing some-thing because it reminds them of happy times in the past ♦ OFTEN USED IN REQUESTS: *One day, just for old times' sake, I paid a visit to Winston Street, where Donald and I had grown up.*

for the time being

for a short time from the present, but not permanently: *Greta can stay with us for the time being, until she finds a place of her own.*

from time to time

sometimes, but not regularly or very often: *It's a good idea to clean out your kitchen cupboards from time to time.*

from/since time immemorial

since a very long time ago: *Since time immemorial, people have turned to music to celebrate life.*

give *someone* a hard time

to criticize someone a lot, or cause problems for them: *My parents have been giving me a hard time about finding a job.*

not give *someone* the time of day

used to say that you refuse to talk to someone because you do not like or respect them: *He's my son-in-law, but I wouldn't give him the time of day if I could help it.*

have all the time in the world

to have as much time as you want or need to do something: *When we retire, we'll have all the time in the world to spend together.*

have no time for

used to say that you dislike someone or something and do not think they are good, useful, or helpful: *My father had no time for priests, and was always ready to tell them so.*

have the time of your life

to enjoy yourself a lot: *I really am having the time of my life – this is the best vacation I've ever had.*

have time on your hands

to be bored because you have a lot of time and do not know what to do in it: *If you find that you have too much time on your hands when you retire, take up a new interest.*

in no time (at all)
(also **in next to no time**)
used to say that something happens very quickly or soon, especially when this is surprising: *If you follow the doctor's instructions, you'll be back on your feet in no time.*

it's about time
1 SPOKEN used to say that you think something should happen soon or should already have happened: *I think it's about time we went home.*
2 SPOKEN said when something happens that you think should have happened earlier: *"Nick and Jane are getting married." "It's about time! They've been going out together forever."*

it's high time (that)
used to say that something must be done and should have been done already: *It's high time that something was done about the state of our roads.*

kill time
to do something that is not very useful or interesting so that you do not feel bored while you are waiting for something to happen: *I occasionally dropped into the library to kill time between classes.*

——————
kill time

be living on borrowed time
1 used to say that someone is likely to lose their job, or that an organization, company, etc. is not likely to exist for much longer: *Gyms like these have been living on borrowed time ever since the aerobics craze of the 1980s ended.*
2 used to say that someone is at risk of dying, especially because they have a serious illness: *Peter knew that he was living on borrowed time, and he wanted to spend time with his son and daughter.*

long time no see
SPOKEN said when you meet someone who you have not seen for a long time: *Chuck, long time no see! How's it going?*

make up for lost time
to try to get as much experience of an activity as you can because you did not have or use an opportunity to do this before: *Her parents had been very strict with her, and now, in her first year at college, Sarah was making up for lost time.*

many a time
OLD-FASHIONED often: *I've said to my son many a time, "The trouble with the world today is everybody wants too much money."*

many's the time
OLD-FASHIONED used at the beginning of a sentence to say that something often used to happen: *Many's the time I admired that old car when I was a young man.*

be marking time
to spend time not doing very much or not achieving anything, especially because you are waiting to see how a situation develops, or waiting for something to happen: *Many law school graduates found themselves working in bars or driving taxis, just marking time while sending out dozens of job applications.*

NOTE▶ When soldiers mark time, they move their legs as if they were marching, but stay in the same place.

move with the times
to change your methods, opinions, behavior, etc. in order to stay modern
♦ OFTEN USED IN NEWSPAPERS, MAGAZINES, ETC.: *You've got to move with the times –*

a web site can attract lots of new clients to your business.

(there's) no time like the present

SPOKEN used to say that there is an opportunity to do something now, and no good reason to wait: *The kids are at their grandma's, so there's no time like the present to put a little romance back into our marriage.*

(there's) no time to lose

used to say that you must do something quickly because there is not much time: *David knew he had to get her to the hospital. There was no time to lose.*

once upon a time...

1 used at the beginning of traditional children's stories: *Once upon a time there were three bears who lived in a house in the woods.*

2 used to say that something was true or existed in the past, but not anymore: *Once upon a time, used cars were bought only by people who were short of cash. But all that has changed.*

pass the time of day (with *someone*)

to say "hello" to someone and have a short conversation with them about unimportant things: *I never really talked with Roger much, except just to pass the time of day.*

play for time

to try to delay something so that you have more time to prepare for it or to decide what to do: *Bonar played for time, introducing minor reforms to solve the country's most immediate problems.*

show *someone* a good time

to take someone to a lot of social events and other types of entertainment so that they enjoy themselves: *Craig took me to dinner, bought me flowers, and walked with me on the beach. He really knows how to show a girl a good time!*

that time of the month

SPOKEN an expression meaning the time each month when blood passes from a woman's body, sometimes used in a rude way when you think a woman is behaving in an unreasonable way: *"I'd rather not go swimming," she whispered.*

"It's that time of the month." | I don't know what's wrong with her. Must be that time of the month.

there's a first time for everything

SPOKEN used humorously to say that although something has never happened before, that does not mean that it can never happen: *"Maybe Jamal will pay for my ticket tonight." "Well, there's a first time for everything, I suppose."*

the third time is a/the charm

SPOKEN said when you have tried but failed to do something twice and hope to be successful the third time, or after you have been successful the third time ♦ OFTEN USED ABOUT SPORTS: *In the NBA championships this year, the Houston Rockets are hoping the third time's a charm.*

time and tide wait for no man

used to say that you must make decisions and take opportunities when you can, or it will be too late: *You'll have to give them your answer soon, or they might offer the job to someone else. Time and tide wait for no man, you know.*

time flies

SPOKEN used to say that a period of time seems to pass very quickly: *The fair lasted all day, but the time just flew; we were having such a good time.*

time is on your side

(also **have time on your side**)

used to say that you have plenty of time to do something, or that the passing of time will bring you an advantage: *If you start investing early on in life, time is on your side – you'll have the chance to make mistakes and learn from them.*

the time is ripe (for)

used to say that conditions are right for someone to do something or for something to happen: *The time is ripe for educational reform in our city's schools.*

(only) time will tell

used to say that it will become clear at some time in the future whether or not something is true, right, successful, etc.: *Only time will tell if Morgan is the right man for the job.*

tip

something is on the tip of your tongue
SPOKEN if a word, especially a name, is on the tip of your tongue you cannot remember it right away although you think you will soon: *Wait a minute – her name is on the tip of my tongue. Something like Terri, Tori – that's it! It was Toni.*

(just) the tip of the iceberg
used to say that something is a small sign of a problem that is much larger: *"This is just the tip of the iceberg," said Sergeant Schmidt.   "We expect to make more arrests in the next few weeks."*

tire

a spare tire
used humorously about the fat around someone's waist: *Honey, you're getting a serious spare tire there. Too much beer, maybe?*

tit

tit for tat
(also **tit-for-tat**)
used about something that a group does in order to harm a group which harmed them: *A series of tit-for-tat nighttime arson attacks began around the segregated city.*

titty

tough titty
(also **tough titties**)
SPOKEN an impolite expression used to tell someone that they must accept or agree to something even though they do not like it: *I'm turning the television off, so tough titty.*

tizzy

in a tizzy
to be so excited or worried about a situation that you do not think clearly or behave reasonably: *The celebrity rapper's visit to Madonna's home sent photographers into a tizzy last weekend.*

today

here today, gone tomorrow
used to say that you cannot be certain that something will continue to exist or happen: *There's no job security nowadays – you can be here today and gone tomorrow.*

toe

⇨**toe the LINE**

go/stand toe-to-toe (with someone)
if two people, groups, teams, etc. go toe-to-toe with each other, they try very hard to beat each other in a fight, competition, or argument ♦ USED ESPECIALLY IN NEWSPAPERS, MAGAZINES, ETC.: *The Utes and the Spartans went toe-to-toe in a thrilling game that went into overtime.*
toe-to-toe: *The conflict, which began as a small uprising, has grown into a toe-to-toe battle between thousands of soldiers.*

go toes up
SPOKEN a humorous expression meaning to die: *You know Riggs, he won't retire till he goes toes up.*

keep you on your toes
SPOKEN to make you keep noticing what is happening, and stop you from relaxing, because you do not know what is going to happen next: *Gumbel not only works hard himself, he keeps everyone around him on their toes too.*
be/stay on your toes: *You've got to stay on your toes in this job – every second counts.*

make your toes curl
to give you an uncomfortable feeling of dislike or embarrassment: *The thought of spending an evening alone with Jess makes my toes curl.*

put/stick/dip your toe in the water
to start slowly doing an activity that you have not done before in order to see if it works or if people approve of it ♦ OFTEN USED IN BUSINESS: *Everyone's afraid to be the first utility in 12 years to stick a toe in the water and build a nuclear plant.*

step on someone's toes
to offend or annoy someone, especially by criticizing their work, or doing work that they think they are responsible for: *I*

don't want to step on anybody's toes, but I'm going to have to rewrite this report.

together
⇨GET it together

token
by the same token
used to connect what you are going to say with what you have just said because they are based on the same idea: *Some women blame themselves if their children don't do well in school. By the same token, a child's accomplishments can be so important that the mother pushes him too hard to succeed.*

toll
take its toll (on *something*)
(also **take a heavy toll (on** *something***)**)
if a difficult situation or harmful event takes its toll on a person or organization, it causes problems that gradually make them weaker: *Assaults have taken their toll on hospital employees, with several off duty because of injuries suffered on the job.*

Tom
every Tom, Dick, and Harry
(also **any Tom, Dick, or Harry**)
an expression meaning everyone, used especially when you disapprove because there is no limit on who can do a particular activity: *We don't hand out these licenses to every Tom, Dick, and Harry.*

NOTE▶ You may hear people change the third name in this idiom, for example to show that it includes women: *This is a luxury vehicle that you won't see just any Tom, Dick, or Harriet driving.*

tomorrow
do *something* like there's no tomorrow
used to say that people are doing something a lot, or too much: *After her divorce, Sheila started spending money like there was no tomorrow.*
—see also **do** *something* **like it's going out of FASHION/style**

tomorrow is another day
used to say that you should not feel too upset, worried, etc. about a bad situation because it might improve in the future: *If you don't hear from him today, don't worry. Tomorrow is another day.*

ton
come down on *someone* like a ton of bricks
to punish someone severely, or tell them angrily that they have done something wrong: *I made the mistake of criticizing her son, and she came down on me like a ton of bricks.*

hit *someone* like a ton of bricks
if an idea hits you like a ton of bricks, it suddenly comes into your head in a way that surprises you: *As I was falling asleep one night, it suddenly hit me like a ton of bricks – why not apply those management principles to your personal life too?*

tongue
bite your tongue
to stop yourself from saying something you were just about to say, especially because it would be impolite, etc.: *Angie was going on and on about how they can't pay back their loans, but I just had to bite my tongue.*
—compare **hold your TONGUE**

give *someone* a tongue-lashing
to talk to someone very angrily and for a long time about something they have done wrong: *Fabrese was rarely moved to anger, but on this occasion he gave Harrison an hour-long tongue-lashing.*

guard your tongue
OLD-FASHIONED used to tell someone to be careful of what they say so that they do not tell a secret: *He was angry with himself for telling her about the money; in the future, he must guard his tongue or risk losing everything.*

hold your tongue
OLD-FASHIONED to stop yourself from speaking, even though you want to say something, sometimes used to tell someone not to speak: *Pat wanted to ask who Jen's new boyfriend was, but she decided it was best to hold her tongue.*
—compare **bite your TONGUE**

loosen someone's tongue

to make someone say something that they would not normally say: *Three-quarters of a bottle of wine had loosened her tongue, and she found herself telling Ricky her life story.*

set/start tongues wagging

used to say that a shocking event or situation is making everyone think and talk about what has happened: *Thurmond set a few tongues wagging when he married a woman 23 years younger than himself.*

a sharp tongue

when someone always talks to other people in a bad or unkind way: *Lula had a sharp tongue and could be very strict with her children.*

someone speaks/talks with (a) forked tongue

used to say that someone is not speaking the truth about what they believe or intend to do ◆ USED IN POLITICS: *The Washington Post accused the President of talking with forked tongue.*

(with) tongue in cheek

used to say that you are doing or saying something as a joke, and do not really mean it: *Wesley claims that his remarks were made tongue in cheek, and did not think people would take them seriously.*
tongue-in-cheek: *The program is a tongue-in-cheek look at recent events in Washington.*

> NOTE▶ Pushing out your cheek with your tongue while someone was talking was used in former times as a sign to another person that you thought the speaker was not telling the truth.

watch your tongue/mouth

SPOKEN used to tell someone to stop talking about something, or to stop being so rude: *If you don't learn to watch your tongue, you're going to end up in trouble one of these days.*

tool

someone is not the sharpest tool in the box

used to say that someone is not very intelligent, especially compared to other people: *She's not the sharpest tool in the box, but she's great with people.*

tooth

⇨ an EYE for an eye (a tooth for a tooth)

⇨ would give his/her EYE TEETH to do *something*

be armed to the teeth

to possess a lot of weapons: *Both sides are armed to the teeth, and the chances of peace appear remote.*

cut your teeth on *something*

if a young person cuts his or her teeth on a particular piece or type of work, that is the first work that they do, from which they learn to do their job: *We were hoping to employ new writers who needed the chance to cut their teeth on something challenging.*

> NOTE▶ We say that a baby is "cutting its teeth" when teeth begin to appear in his/her mouth for the first time.

fight tooth and nail

to try very hard to achieve something, especially when someone is trying to prevent you: *Richards fought tooth and nail to preserve the independence of a company whose roots go back to Philadelphia in the 1890s.*

gnash your teeth
(also **wail, cry, weep, etc. and gnash your teeth**)

to be very angry and upset, sometimes used humorously: *We were suggesting environmental taxes fifteen years ago; it makes us gnash our teeth that we don't get the credit for that now that everyone wants them.*
teeth-gnashing: *After all the demonstrations and teeth-gnashing surrounding the abortion issue, surprisingly little legislation has been passed.*

grit your teeth

to be determined to continue doing something, even though you find it very difficult: *You just have to grit your teeth and remind yourself that it doesn't matter what other people say.*

have a sweet tooth

to like sweet foods: *Those with a sweet tooth will love Delight low-fat vanilla and chocolate ice cream.*

something is like pulling teeth

used to say that something is very difficult to do: *Sometimes it's so easy to win ball games, and sometimes it's like pulling teeth.*

—see also **be like getting BLOOD out of a stone**

someone lies through his/her teeth

used to emphasize that someone is saying something that is completely untrue, without being embarrassed or ashamed: *The police say that we attacked them, but they're lying through their teeth.*

long in the tooth

used to say that someone or something is old, or too old: *I'm getting a little long in the tooth to go out drinking every weekend.*

set your teeth on edge

1 if something that you hear, taste, or smell sets your teeth on edge, it gives you an uncomfortable feeling because it is very unpleasant: *Deep voices or loud machines can set a sensitive child's teeth on edge.*
2 used to say that a situation or someone's behavior is unpleasant and gives you an uncomfortable feeling: *He never looked at me, and spoke with an insincere politeness that set my teeth on edge.*

show your teeth

to let someone see your anger or strength in order to warn them not to start an argument or fight: *The region has started to show its teeth, with major implications for security in the area.*

sink/get your teeth into *something*

to begin working hard at something that interests you and uses all your ability: *After several years away from the spotlight, Moore finally has a role she can sink her teeth into.*

top

⇨**not have a lot (going on) up top**
—see **not have much UPSTAIRS**

⇨**on top of the WORLD**

blow your top/stack

to get so angry about something that you lose control of what you are saying or doing: *One day on set, I got so angry with John Huston that I just blew my stack and started hitting him.*
—compare **lose/blow your COOL**
—see also **blow a FUSE/gasket**

come out on top

to win or succeed at something you were trying to do: *In today's hectic business world, only the toughest will come out on top.*

go over the top

to do something in a way that is too extreme: *The trouble with Tom is, he can't have fun without going over the top.*
be over the top: *I don't think a $4.5 million transfer fee is over the top for Young – he's a very good player.*

on top of *something*

1 in addition to other problems, so that a situation becomes even worse: *It was the lack of privacy on top of everything else that made me decide to leave the army.*
2 if you are on top of a problem, you are dealing with it and think you will soon be able to solve it: *The work was extremely dull, but at least I was on top of it and could do it well.*

push/put *someone* over the top

to make someone more successful than other people, especially in a game or competition: *Coach Fields has one last attempt to push the team over the top.*

to top it all (off)

SPOKEN used before a statement to say that something is the last in a series of annoying, unpleasant, or funny events: *Betty fell downstairs and broke her ankle, and then to top it all off, got the flu.*

the top of the heap/pile

used about the highest, most powerful, or richest positions in society, a company, an organization, etc.: *Within twelve years, June had been promoted to the top of the heap in the marketing department.*
opposite **the bottom of the heap/pile:** *O'Neill said he was concerned that most politicians did little to improve the lives of those at the bottom of the heap.*

torch

carry a torch for *someone*
to feel love for someone or something when you cannot have a relationship or you are far away: *Brosnan plays a scientist still carrying a torch for his sweetie who was killed two years before.*

carry the torch
to publicly support an idea, group, etc., either by your words or actions ♦ OFTEN USED ABOUT POLITICS: *He has come to Washington carrying the torch for resumption of western aid to his country.*

pass the torch
(also **hand on the torch**)
to give someone else the knowledge, skills, etc. that you have so that they can continue your work, support your ideas etc.: *On Saturday, four Colts greats came onto the field before the game to pass the torch to a new Baltimore football team.*

> NOTE▶ The "torch" in the idioms "carry the torch" and "pass the torch" was the flame that was carried by several runners, one after another, to a place where games would be held, in ancient Greece. This was an important religious ceremony, and something like it is done before the Olympic Games.

touch

⇨the **MIDAS** touch

the/a common touch
if a famous or powerful person has the common touch, they understand what ordinary people like, want, or need: *Amory possesses a warmth and common touch which makes him popular with rural voters.*

have the magic touch
used to say that someone is very good at an activity, or is always successful: *Carlo had the magic touch; he could make anything grow.*

something is touch and go
used about a dangerous or risky situation, when you cannot be sure what is going to happen, and do not know if you will get the result that you want: *After the thunderstorm last weekend, our*

electricity has been touch and go at best.
touch-and-go: *Even after a touch-and-go recovery following his accident, Dawson refuses to wear a motorcycle helmet.*

be/keep/stay in touch (with)
1 to continue to write to, speak to, or spend time with someone that you know: *Cellular phones have made it easier for people to stay in touch.*
get in touch (with *someone***):** *Police say that the car was last seen in Hunter's Point, and want anyone who has seen it since to get in touch with them.*
2 to have all the information about a subject, or know what people are thinking or feeling: *Dr. Garcia still reads a lot to stay in touch with technological developments.*
get in touch (with *something***):** *The ads said that meditation will help you get in touch with "universal life energy."*
—compare **be out of TOUCH (with)**

lose touch (with)
1 to stop communicating with someone you know, especially gradually, for example because you live far away from each other or no longer have the same interests: *I've lost touch with a lot of my friends from high school.*
2 to stop understanding or caring about a situation, someone's feelings, or a particular set of skills or ideas: *A number of national polls suggest we may be losing touch with our ethical standards.*
—see also **be out of TOUCH (with)**

be out of touch (with)
1 to no longer understand or care about a situation, someone's feelings, or set of ideas: *A lot of politicians are really out of touch with average Americans' concerns.*
2 to not be communicating with someone: *Communication was difficult, and we knew we would be out of touch for at least six weeks, until we reached Khartoum.*
—compare **be/keep/stay in TOUCH (with)**
—see also **lose TOUCH (with)**

the/a personal touch
(also **the/a human touch**)
1 if a system, organization, situation, etc. has a human touch, it has a quality that makes people feel comfortable and cared for: *Paintings and flowers add a personal touch to the doctor's waiting room.*

T

2 used to say that something is being done by a person rather than a machine: *More complex deals will still need the human touch, but soon the majority of simple trades will be done automatically by computer.*

put the finishing touches on
to do the last few things that complete something or make it perfect: *Adding candles and a nice bottle of wine can put the finishing touches on any romantic dinner.*

a soft/easy touch
used to say that it is easy to make someone believe you or do what you want, or that it is easy to get money from them: *Ask Mom if she'll give you $5 – she's usually a soft touch.*

tough
⇨tough **TITTY**
⇨when the **GOING** gets tough

towel
throw in the towel
to stop trying to achieve something because it has been too difficult: *Tucker says it's too early to throw in the towel. "We're still refining our operations," he said.*

tower
⇨in an **IVORY** tower
a tower/pillar of strength
used about someone who is always there to give you help, sympathy, and support, especially when you are in trouble: *Ever since I was a child, my mother has been a tower of strength to everyone who knows her.*

town
go to town
SPOKEN used to say that someone is doing something in an excited way, often spending a lot of money: *Have you seen the dinner Kirstin has prepared? She really went to town!*

a one-horse town
used about a town that you think is small

and boring: *I grew up in a one-horse town and couldn't wait to leave.*

paint the town red
to go out to bars, clubs, etc. to enjoy yourself at night: *We're gonna go down to New York and paint the town red.*

track
⇨be hot on the **TRAIL/**track of
cover your tracks
to hide something, usually wrong or illegal, that you have done so that no one finds out: *The renters replaced carpeting, rerouted electricity and repainted the apartment in order to cover their tracks.*

have the inside track
to have an advantage that makes you the most likely person to be chosen for a job, win a competition, etc. ♦ USED IN NEWS-PAPERS, MAGAZINES, ETC.: *He knew that other candidates were more experienced, but felt that he had the inside track because of his background.*

keep track of
to know what is happening to someone or something, and always have information about them: *Keep track of daily spending to ensure that your budget is staying on target.*

lose track of
1 to not know what is happening to someone or something: *When he was out of the office so much, Phil lost track of some key projects.*
2 to forget what time it is, what you are talking about, etc., because you are thinking of other things: *Our discussions were always so lively and spirited that it was easy to lose track of the time.*

make tracks (for)
to leave a place, especially quickly, and go somewhere else: *Rushton was making tracks for New York when the message came for him to go to Venice.*

off the beaten track/path
in a place that is quiet and far from a lot of people: *The area they take people to is off the beaten path, where tourists don't usually go.*

be on the fast track (to/for *something*)

1 to be likely to be successful soon, especially to be very good at your job and likely to be promoted (=given a more important job) quickly: *Rivers should be on the fast track to a head coaching job.*
2 to be likely to be dealt with quickly: *A biography of the Iraqi leader has been put on the fast track for publication.*
fast-track: *Monday, the city agreed to a fast-track plan to hire 45 new police officers.*

be on the right track

1 used to say that someone or something is behaving or working in a way that is likely to have the good result that is wanted: *The American economy is on the right track, and we'd like to keep it that way.*
2 used to say that someone's answer to a question or problem is probably right or almost right: *If we're on the right track and Dora did take the money, shouldn't we tell the police?*
opposite **be on the wrong track:** *Three out of four voters say the country is on the wrong track.*

stop *something* (dead) in its tracks
(also **stop** *someone* **(dead) in his/her tracks**)

to stop a process or activity from continuing or developing, or to make someone stop what they are saying or doing: *In the past, researchers thought anti-viral drugs would be enough to stop the AIDS epidemic in its tracks.*

stop (dead) in your tracks
(also **be stopped in your tracks**)

to stop suddenly because something has surprised or frightened you or made you angry: *The doctor stopped in his tracks with a look of amazement on his face.*

trail

blaze trails
(also **blaze a trail**)

to be the first person, organization, etc. to do something new and different, which encourages other people to do it also: *Dottie West blazed a trail for female country music singers.*
trail-blazing: *The group's trailblazing new album features an exciting mix of exotic musical textures.*

be hot on the trail/track of
(also **be hot on** *someone's* **trail/track**)

to be close to finding someone you are trying to catch, find, or talk to, or something you want to get: *According to reports, police are hot on the trail of the thief, who stole several cars in the past month.*

trap

⇨shut your FACE/trap

fall into the trap (of)

to make a common mistake when doing an activity or starting a process: *A key to Graham's success was staying true to his country boy instincts, without falling into the trap of city sophistication.*

keep your trap shut

SPOKEN an impolite way of telling someone not to talk or not to tell someone a secret: *If you'd kept your trap shut, we wouldn't be in this mess!*

trash

one man's trash is another man's treasure

used to say that something which one person thinks is useless may be very valuable to someone else: *I don't know why he keeps that old car in the back yard – still, one man's trash is another man's treasure, I suppose.*

stop (dead) in your tracks

T

talk trash

SLANG to say critical or unkind things to someone, often in a joking way: *When opposing teams talk trash on the basketball court, the Warriors take it personally.*

treasure

⇨one man's TRASH is another man's treasure

treatment

give *someone* **the silent treatment**
to refuse to speak to someone, especially because you are angry with them: *Jack gave Marcia the silent treatment during the ride home and didn't talk to her for the rest of the evening.*

tree

⇨be out of your tree —see be out of your MIND

something **doesn't grow on trees**
SPOKEN used to emphasize that something is very difficult to obtain, and you should consider it to be valuable: *Jobs like that don't exactly grow on trees, you know; particularly when you're over fifty.*
—see also MONEY doesn't grow on trees

someone **is barking up the wrong tree**
used to say that someone has the wrong idea about a situation, or about how to get a particular result: *Ferrell insists he had nothing to do with the bombing, and said that federal agents are barking up the wrong tree.*

trial

⇨a trial BALLOON

trick

⇨someone's BAG of tricks
⇨have a trick up your sleeve —see have/keep *something* up your SLEEVE

do the trick
used to say that something solves a problem or provides what is needed to get a good result: *The soup's almost ready – one more sprinkle of salt should do the trick.*

someone **doesn't miss a trick**
used to say that someone always knows exactly what is happening and can get advantages from every situation: *When it came to cutting costs on exports, Roy didn't miss a trick.*

how's tricks?
SPOKEN used to greet someone in a friendly way: *Hi, Jamie. How's tricks?*

someone **is up to his/her old tricks**
used to show that you disapprove because someone is behaving badly in a way that they have done before: *Pete's up to his old tricks again – he's taken another two-hour lunch break.*

it's/that's the oldest trick in the book
used to say that someone who has been cheated or deceived should have realized what was happening: *Politicians always promise tax cuts in order to win votes – it's the oldest trick in the book.*

tricks of the trade
clever methods that are used, especially in a particular job, and are learned by experience: *Being a master reporter isn't just knowing the tricks of the trade – you also have to have some skill.*

use/try every trick in the book
to use every smart method that you know in order to achieve what you want: *Victoria used every trick in the book to get Patsy into trouble with her boss.*

trim

in fighting trim/form
used about someone who is in very good condition: *Despite his long spell away from the game, Harris was in fighting trim Monday.*

trip

⇨be on a HEAD trip

an ego trip
when you do something because it makes you feel more important, but do not really care about it: *Critics called Sullivan's proposals a wasteful ego trip.*

take a trip/walk/stroll down memory lane

to spend some time remembering your past: *Take a trip down memory lane at the reunion of the Class of '68 at the Plaza Hotel on August 14th.*

trooper

swear like a trooper

to swear a lot: *Samantha swore like a trooper when she found out I dented her new car.*

trophy

trophy wife

a young beautiful woman who a rich successful man marries after he has left his first wife: *Jason isn't the first executive to dump an inconvenient family in favor of a trophy wife.*

trouble

⇨**trouble with a capital T** —see ___ with a **CAPITAL** ___

go to a lot of trouble

to use a lot of time and effort in order to do something correctly: *Your mother went to a lot of trouble to make this meal. Now eat it.*

something spells trouble/disaster

(also *something* **spells doom, problems, bad news, etc.**)

if a situation or action spells trouble, danger, etc. it makes you expect trouble, danger, etc.: *An economic slowdown in Europe could spell trouble for the United States.*

trust

not trust *someone* as far as you could throw him/her

(also **not trust** *someone* **farther than you could throw him/her**)

SPOKEN used to emphasize that you would not trust someone at all: *You'll have to watch Dave with the money – I wouldn't trust him any farther than I could throw him.*

truth

⇨**take/accept** *something* **as the gospel truth** —see **take/accept** *something* **as GOSPEL**

to tell you the truth

SPOKEN used when giving your personal opinion or admitting something: *To tell you the truth, I haven't gotten a good night's sleep since the heat wave started.*

tub

a tub of lard

SPOKEN an impolite expression used about someone who is short and very fat ♦ OFTEN USED BY CHILDREN: *I don't want that tub of lard on my team!*

tug

a tug of war

(also **a tug-of-war**)

used about a situation in which two people or groups are trying very hard to get or keep the same thing, or to get the most power or influence: *Two couples are going to court in a bitter tug of war over a 12–year-old girl.*

tune

⇨**call the SHOTs/tune**

⇨**march to a different tune** —see **march to (the beat of) a different DRUMMER**

someone (has) changed his/her tune

used to say that someone is expressing a very different opinion from the one they were expressing before, especially when you are surprised or annoyed by this: *Schools that had refused to admit students with special needs quickly changed their tune when government grants became available.*

dance to *someone's* tune

OLD-FASHIONED to behave in the way that someone who is more powerful than you wants you to: *Our nation is not willing to dance to the tune of others, without being able to express our views freely.*

in tune with

understanding of, in agreement with, or suitable for the people, situation or events you are involved with: *Some builders are*

T

striving to build homes that are more in tune with the needs of young single people.

sing a different tune

to completely change the opinions you have expressed before: *Corporations have been singing a different tune than they were five months ago. They're showing an interest in workers' well-being.*

to the tune of

used to emphasize a large number or amount: *The waves from the recent hurricane destroyed property all along the coast to the tune of $100 million.*

tunnel

someone has tunnel vision

used to say that someone only thinks about one part of a situation, instead of considering all of its parts: *Too often, company executives develop a tunnel vision, and focus only on cutting expenses.*

> NOTE▶ Tunnel vision is a medical condition in which someone can only see things that are straight ahead.

turf

⇨on home turf/GROUND

turkey

go cold turkey

to stop taking a strong drug that you are addicted to (=that you feel you must have) all at once, without trying to make it easier by taking other drugs or reducing the amounts you take little by little: *Sara's battles with emphysema convinced her to give up cigarettes cold turkey.*

talk turkey

SPOKEN to talk seriously about what is important in a situation ♦ OFTEN USED IN BUSINESS AND POLITICS: *Polls show that candidates who are willing to talk turkey with the public have much higher ratings.*

turn

⇨go/turn SOUR

at every turn

used to emphasize that something keeps happening, especially that someone keeps being stopped from doing what they want to do: *Our efforts to establish an alternative school were challenged at every turn by the administration.*

do someone a good turn

to do something that helps another person: *Although Carter's nightclub has met with opposition, he is convinced that he is doing the town a good turn.*

one good turn deserves another

OLD-FASHIONED used to say that if someone does something nice for you, you should do something nice to thank them: *If you help me mow the lawn, I'll help you wash the car – one good turn deserves another.*

speak out of turn

to say something that is unsuitable or wrong at a particular time or in a particular situation: *If Sandy made a suggestion, Luke would give her an irritated look, as if she had spoken out of turn.*

take a turn for the better/worse

to suddenly get much better or worse: *Sandy's health took a turn for the worse while she was on vacation in Florida, and she had to be rushed to the hospital.*

turn around and say/do something

SPOKEN to do or say the opposite of what someone expected, or the opposite of what you have been doing or saying: *Sometimes Derek can remember the tiniest details, then he'll turn around and forget his own birthdate.*

turn something inside out

1 (also turn *something* upside down) to change something completely: *The fire turned our lives inside out. We lost everything that was of value to us.*
2 (also turn *something* upside down) if you turn a place inside out, you search every part of it, especially so that it is messy or damaged: *The police turned the apartment inside out, but found nothing.*
3 to examine something thoroughly, often trying to look at it in a completely different way: *"I like taking common ideas and turning them inside out," says Jeuneman.*

twain

never the twain shall meet
used to say that two things are so different that they can never exist together: *Sometimes when I have a huge fight with Chris, I think men are men, and women are women, and never the twain shall meet.*

twinkling

in the twinkling of an eye
used to say that something happened very quickly: *The score went from 0–0 to 8–0 in the twinkling of an eye.*

two
⇨be of two MINDs

it takes two to tango
used to say that if a problem, situation, or argument involves two people, they are both equally responsible for it: *If you are caught fighting, you are never innocent – remember, it takes two to tango.*

put two and two together
to guess the meaning of something you have heard or seen: *I put two and two together, and told the police; they found Eva that night.*

> **NOTE▶** You can also say that someone has "put two and two together to make five," meaning that they have guessed wrongly about something, but this expression is much less frequent: *In my opinion, the police are expert at putting two and two together to make five.*

that makes two of us
SPOKEN used to tell someone that you agree with them or understand how they feel: *"I'd like to work in Hawaii." "Yeah, that makes two of us."*

two-step

the Aztec two-step
SPOKEN when you need to go to the toilet very often because you are sick, especially when you are on vacation in a hot country: *Karl had a bad case of the Aztec two-step and stayed in the hotel.*

T

U

underground

go underground
to start doing something secretly or hide in a secret place: *In late October, I went underground to avoid being taken to jail.*

unglued
⇨COME unglued

up
⇨HAVE had it up to here (with)
⇨*someone* is up to SOMETHING

it's/that's up to you
SPOKEN used to tell someone that they should make a decision themselves, and need not ask you for advice: *"I don't know which weekend we should have the party." "It's totally up to you, Jed."*

be on an up
SPOKEN to feel happy, especially after you have been unhappy: *Kevin's on a definite up right now – do you think it will last?*

be on the up
used to say that something is increasing, improving, or becoming more successful: *With interest rates on the up, the mood on the financial markets has turned to fear.*

be on the up and up
used to say that someone's actions are honest and legal: *Remember that an absence of complaints does not necessarily mean that a company is on the up and up.*

be up against it
to have to deal with a difficult situation: *I am so up against it financially, I'm living from week to week.*

be up and about
to be healthy enough to walk around and have a normal life after being sick or injured: *Yolanda should be up and about again within a week.*

be up and down
1 SPOKEN to sometimes feel well and happy, and sometimes feel sick and un-happy: *How are you? I hear you've been up and down lately.*
2 SPOKEN used to say that you are sometimes successful and sometimes unsuccessful: *Our team has been up and down, but I hope we do better tomorrow.*

be up and running
used to say that a new system, organization, machine, etc. is working well: *We should have the phone system up and running within a couple of days.*

be up for *something*
SLANG to want to do or try something: *We're going for a drink after work – are you up for it?*

be up on *something*
SPOKEN to know a lot about a particular subject: *That kid's really up on his Roman history, isn't he?*

ups and downs
the mixture of good and bad experiences that happen in any situation or relationship: *Mick and Jerry had plenty of ups and downs in their 15 years together.*

not be up to *something*
to not have the energy, interest, or ability to do a particular activity: *You've never done any serious hiking before, so you may not be up to this.*
—compare *someone* is up to SOMETHING

up yours!
TABOO a very impolite expression used in order to insult someone when they have said or done something that annoys you: *As I walked away, I heard him mutter, "Up yours, too."*

up-front

be up-front (about *something*)
(also **be up front** or **be upfront**)
to be honest and direct about the way you feel: *I've always been fairly up-front about how I approach things, and this project is no different.*

upstairs
⇨KICK *someone* upstairs

not have much upstairs
(also **not have a lot (going on) up top**)
SPOKEN a slightly impolite way of saying

that someone is somewhat stupid: *Don't even consider Sam. He doesn't have a lot going on upstairs.*

uptake

be quick on the uptake
to be good at understanding a situation quickly and doing what needs to be done, especially in order to gain an advantage: *You have to be quick on the uptake to get a letter published in a newspaper – readers' letters come in by fax and e-mail, and are printed the next day.*
opposite **be slow on the uptake:** *If you were slow on the uptake in taking up the offer of a low interest rate in January, you may have a chance to try again in October.*

us

us and them
used about a situation in which two groups feel that they are very different, and behave like enemies when they should be working together: *Do you feel there's a sort of us and them attitude between the arts and the business world?*

use

⇨**a fat lot of use** *someone/something* **is** —see **a fat LOT of good it does** *someone*

usual

⇨**AS per usual**

U-turn

make/do a U-turn
used about a complete change of ideas, plans, etc. ♦ OFTEN USED IN NEWSPAPERS, ON TELEVISION NEWS, ETC.: *The President has endured criticism of his policy U-turns as well as his personal life.*

> NOTE▶ If a car makes or does a U-turn, it turns around completely in the road and drives back the way that it was coming from. This idiom is almost always used about politicians or political parties who do the opposite of what they have promised to do.

U

V

vacuum

in a vacuum
existing completely separately from other things, and having no relationship to them ♦ OFTEN USED IN THE NEGATIVE: *The committee will not be making decisions in a vacuum; it will call witnesses and examine documents.*

vale

the vale of tears
LITERARY the difficulties in life: *In this vale of tears, we must take what we're sent.*

variety

variety is the spice of life
used to say that doing many different things is what makes life interesting: *Variety is the spice of life, and there's plenty of it on the menu at Brando's Grill.*

vengeance

with a vengeance
used to emphasize that something is being done much more than is expected or normal: *Nicky began drinking with a vengeance when his band started becoming popular.*

verge

on the verge of (doing) *something*
used to say that someone is going to, or is likely to do or experience something very soon: *I was just on the verge of calling Jim to break up with him when he came to the door.* | *Problems with her career left Zola on the verge of a nervous breakdown.*

victim

⇨a FASHION victim

victory

a Pyrrhic victory
used about a situation in which you are successful, but you suffer so much that it was not worth winning: *Capistran won the right to stay in the U.S., but it was a Pyrrhic victory because his English isn't good enough to revive his journalistic career.*

> NOTE▶ Pyrrhus was a king in the third century B.C. He defeated the Romans, but he lost a lot of soldiers while fighting.

view

a bird's-eye view (of *something*)
1 a view of a place from a position high above it: *From our apartment on the 14th floor, we had a bird's-eye view of the parade.*
2 a general description of a subject or situation: *The book offers a bird's-eye view of championship tennis.*

do *something* with a view to (doing) *something*
to do something for a particular purpose: *People with learning difficulties should be encouraged to live outside the family home, with a view to eventual independence.*

take a dim view of *something/someone*
used to say that someone does not approve of something, or does not think it is a good idea: *Elizabeth's family took a dim view of her decision to go into show business.*

a worm's-eye view (of *something*)
an idea of what is happening, as it is seen from a low position in an organization or situation: *Individual parents gave a worm's-eye view of the situation as they saw it.*

vine

wither/die on the vine
if a plan, idea, etc. withers on the vine, it fails before it has a chance to develop, especially because no one is interested in it: *Gingrich would let Medicare wither on the vine through reduced funding.*

vinegar
⇨full of PISS and vinegar

violet

a shrinking violet
used about someone who is very shy and easily frightened: *Kelly's definitely no shrinking violet – she'll tell you what's on her mind.*

virtue

by virtue of
if something happens by virtue of something else, it happens because of it: *Buckley knows that by virtue of her position, many women see her as a role model.*

make a virtue of necessity
to get an advantage out of something that you have to do or cannot change: *Because of Mama's failing health, they had made a virtue of necessity by moving to the city, closer to their children.*

vision

⇨*someone* **has TUNNEL vision**

have visions of (doing) *something*
to think or imagine that something is likely to happen, especially when it is not really very likely: *Ten-year-old Phil has recently taken up tennis and has visions of becoming a second Pete Sampras.*

vocabulary

__ is not in *someone's* **vocabulary**
used to say that someone does not like, agree with, or believe in a particular idea: *The words "vacation" and "time off" are not in my personal vocabulary.* | *"Guilt"*

is definitely not in Moore's vocabulary when she talks about the failure of her business.

voice

give voice to
to express your feelings or opinions: *Cipriani was, in effect, giving voice to a growing nationalist movement in the West Indies.*

speak with one voice
if a group of people speak with one voice, they all express the same opinion ♦ USED ESPECIALLY IN POLITICS: *The Democratic and Republican leadership spoke with one voice in support of the peace agreement.*

a voice (crying) in the wilderness
used about someone who has an idea or gives a warning that most people do not agree with or pay any attention to: *I remember Dr. King as a voice in the wilderness, crying out for equality and justice.*

volume

pump up the volume
(also **pump it up**)
SLANG to play music more loudly, or make more noise: *Sonics fans pumped up the volume before the tip-off, trying to make the other team nervous.*

speak volumes (about)
to express something very clearly, without using words: *The shocked looks on the Northridge players' faces spoke volumes.*

V

W

wad

blow your wad
(also **blow the whole wad**)
to spend all of your money: *We prefer to go to an inexpensive restaurant two or three times a week rather than blow the whole wad on one fancy meal.*

wagon

circle the wagons
(also **draw/pull your wagons into a circle**)
if a group of people circle the wagons, they work together in order to prevent something that may harm them ♦ USED ESPECIALLY IN BUSINESS AND POLITICS: *The tobacco companies are pulling their wagons into a circle now that the practice of smoking appears to be under threat.*

> NOTE▶ During the time that Americans and Europeans were moving into the Western parts of America, they defended themselves when attacked by making a circle with their wagons (=vehicles pulled by horses) to protect them as they fired their guns.

fix someone's wagon
(also **fix someone's little red wagon**)
OLD-FASHIONED to cause someone to get into trouble or fail at something because you do not like them or they have done something similar to you: *So Dan thinks he can take advantage of me like that, huh? Well, I'll fix his little red wagon.*

go/be on the wagon
to decide not to drink any alcohol, often because you have been drinking too much: *Sometimes I would go on the wagon for a few days, just to prove to myself that I could do it.*
opposite **fall off the wagon**: *It was at Rick's bachelor party that I really fell off the wagon.*

hitch your wagon to someone
(also **hitch your wagon to a star**)
to try to become more successful by forming an association with someone or something that is already successful: *The company is hitching its wagon very closely to Microsoft's star.*

wait

⇨**LIE in wait (for)**

wait and see
SPOKEN said when you are telling someone to be patient because they will find out about something later: *"What are you going to get me for my birthday?" "You'll just have to wait and see."*

wake

(leave/bring something) in its wake
if an event leaves a bad situation in its wake, the bad situation comes after the event or is caused by it: *A tornado ripped through Madison County Tuesday, leaving $40 million worth of destruction in its wake.*

in the wake of
if something happens in the wake of another event, it happens after it, and often as a result of it: *Counselors are available for students who want to talk about their fears in the wake of the fire.*

walk

⇨*someone* **is a walking ENCYCLOPEDIA**
⇨**take a TRIP/walk/stroll down memory lane**
⇨**walk your TALK**

from all walks of life

from all walks of life
(also **from every walk of life**)
used to emphasize that people come from many different types of job, family background, etc.: *The organization has over 3,000 members throughout the country, from all walks of life.*

walk all over *someone*
to treat someone without any respect: *Don't be too soft on him, or he'll end up walking all over you.*

wall

be bouncing off the walls
SPOKEN to be very nervous or excited, and full of energy: *I'd been working late, and I didn't want to go home and be bouncing off the walls, so I stopped for a drink.*

be climbing the walls
SPOKEN to be impatient, annoyed, and full of extra energy because you are bored or want something to happen that has not happened: *It rained all day, and by five o'clock, the kids were climbing the walls.*

drive *someone* up the wall
SPOKEN to annoy someone a lot: *I can't get the last crossword clue, and it's driving me up the wall!*

go to the wall
1 if a person or company goes to the wall, they fail, usually because they have no more money: *Many small investors went to the wall when the stock market crashed.*
2 to be so sure that what you believe in is right that you are ready to suffer because you support it: *I know Coach Thompson would go to the wall for his players, and they do their best to please him.*

hit a brick wall
(also **run/come up against a brick wall**)
to be in a situation where something is preventing you from doing or achieving what you want: *We can give you some tips on tracing your family tree, and what to do when you run up against a brick wall.*

hit the wall
to reach the point in a process where it is difficult to achieve any more or go any

further: *Everyone talks about hitting a wall at the 24-mile mark when you run the marathon, and that's just what happened to me.*

like talking to a (brick) wall
used to say that you are annoyed because someone refuses to listen to your advice, explanation, etc.: *Talking to Daniel is like talking to a brick wall.*

nail *someone* to the wall
(also **nail *someone's* ass to the wall**)
to catch or punish someone because they have done something wrong, or because you are very angry with them ♦ USED ESPECIALLY IN NEWSPAPERS: *The Commissioner was eagerly awaiting the slightest slip on Donaldson's part, so that he could jump in and nail his ass to the wall.*

off the wall
used about someone or something that is very strange or unusual: *Jessica's new furniture designs are completely off the wall.*
off-the-wall: *The Canadian comedy troupe specializes in off-the-wall characters in everyday situations.*

walls have ears
OLD-FASHIONED used to warn people to be careful what they say because other people could be listening: *"What are you going to do?" "They say walls have ears – I'd better whisper."*

wallop
⇨**pack a PUNCH/wallop**

wand

you can't wave a magic wand
used to say that you cannot do something difficult or impossible that people want you to do: *We've had a terrible season, but I can't just wave a magic wand and change what has already happened.*

wane

on the wane
becoming smaller, weaker, or less important: *Figures show that the outbreak of dysentery is on the wane, with only nine cases reported last month.*

W

want

⇨**HAVE** *someone* **right/just where you want them**

war

⇨**a TUG of war**

wage war on

to be fighting someone or trying to destroy or deal with something: *Johnson won the 1964 Presidential election by promising to wage war on domestic poverty and racism.*

a war/battle of nerves

when two people, organizations, or countries are trying to defeat each other by using threats, warnings, etc. but no violence: *Mother and daughter stared at each other, and Kate realized it was now a battle of nerves between them.*
—see also **a BATTLE of wits**

a war of words

used about a very angry or serious argument between two people or groups who strongly disagree about something ◆ USED ESPECIALLY IN NEWSPAPERS: *The war of words between the U.S. and Canada over acid rain reached new heights last week.*

warm

you're getting warm

SPOKEN used to tell someone that they have almost guessed the truth about something which they are trying to find out from you: *"What's in the box? Is it a CD player?" "No, but you're getting warm. It is something electric."*

warpath

be on the warpath

used to say that someone is very angry about something, or that they are very determined to change a situation: *Look out – Mom's on the warpath about our messy rooms again.*

warrant

⇨*someone* **is signing his/her own DEATH warrant**

warts

warts and all

including all the bad parts as well as the good parts of something: *I liked Stone's movie, warts and all, but some people might find it too violent.*

warts-and-all: *Getz, one of the greats of jazz, is the subject of a new warts-and-all biography.*

> NOTE▶ A wart is a small hard raised spot on your skin. This idiom comes from the 17th-century British politician, Oliver Cromwell, who told a painter to paint a picture of him and include his warts and anything else that made him look ugly.

wash

something **doesn't/won't wash (with** *someone***)**

used to say that what someone is saying is hard to believe: *I thought of telling the policeman that it wasn't my car, but didn't really think it would wash with him.*

it'll all come out in the wash

SPOKEN used to say that a problem is not very serious and will soon be solved: *"Who's going to arrange the next meeting? I can't do it." "Never mind, it'll all come out in the wash."*

washed up

be washed up

used to say that a person or organization has failed and will never be successful again: *They said I was all washed up – my career was over.*

waste

lay waste to *something*

to completely destroy something: *Non-native animals, such as dogs and rats, have laid waste to much of the native Caribbean fauna.*

waste not want not

OLD-FASHIONED used to tell people not to waste food, clothes, etc.: *Eat the rest of your vegetables – waste not want not.*

watch

⇨watch your STEP

on someone's watch

if something happens on someone's watch, it happens during the time they have power and are responsible for making rules, laws, etc. ♦ OFTEN USED IN BUSINESS AND POLITICS: *The financial losses that occurred on Reigle's watch are higher than anything we've known.*

water

blow *something* out of the water

to destroy a business or organization, or show that an idea or plan is not true or will not work: *Motown blew its competitors out of the water in the late 1960s.*

be dead in the water

used to say that a business or plan has failed completely or has no chance of succeeding ♦ OFTEN USED IN NEWSPAPERS AND MAGAZINES: *We have to work with big names such as Sony and IBM; if we don't, we're dead in the water.*

not hold water

used to say that a plan, argument or idea is not true or does not work: *Environmentalists say the power company's argument simply doesn't hold water.*

in/into deep water

in a situation in which you have problems doing or achieving something, especially because you do not know enough about it: *Psychologists can get into deep water trying to explain everything in terms of early life experiences.*

in/into hot water

in trouble with people in authority because of something you have said or done ♦ OFTEN USED IN NEWSPAPERS AND MAGAZINES: *This is not the first time that Durenberger has been in hot water with the Senate Ethics Committee.*

something is like water off a duck's back

used to say that advice, warnings, rude remarks, etc. have no effect on someone: *Of course there are rules, but it's all just like water off a duck's back with these kids.*

it's/that's (all) water under the bridge

used to say that it is better not to think about something in the past because it is over now: *Bo Diddley is still upset at how badly he was paid by record companies. He told us before: "Sure it's all water under the bridge, but my kids suffered because of that water."*

a lot of water has gone/passed/ flowed under the bridge since

used to say that a lot of time has passed, or that a situation has changed a lot since a particular event: *A lot of water has flowed under the bridge since we won the trophy; it will be interesting to see what has been happening to the members of the team.*

muddy the waters

to make a situation confusing and hard to understand, especially if it was originally not confusing: *Most of us are bewildered by computer jargon, and there is also a huge choice of monitors to muddy the waters when you are buying a new machine.*

still waters run deep

used to say that someone who you think is very boring or calm may surprise you with hidden emotions and qualities: *Mark looks calm, but still waters run deep, and he can be a lot of fun once you get to know him.*

test the water/waters

to find out what reaction people have to a plan or idea before you begin to use it ♦ OFTEN USED IN BUSINESS AND POLITICS: *In his speech, the mayor was clearly testing the water to gauge reactions to his proposal.*

be treading water

used to say that a business or person is not developing and becoming more successful: *Now, after six years of treading water in my relationship and in my job, I no longer see customers as individual people.*

> NOTE▶ Treading water is a way of swimming in which you stay in one place.

waterworks

turn on the waterworks

OLD-FASHIONED to start crying, especially deliberately, in order to make someone do what you want: *Don't turn on the waterworks – I guarantee you it won't work on me.*

—compare shed **CROCODILE tears**

wavelength

be on the same wavelength

(also **be on** *someone's* **wavelength**)

used to say that someone has similar ideas and opinions to another person and that they understand each other very well: *I really like working with Leah – we're usually on the same wavelength where our jobs are concerned.*

opposite **be on a (totally) different wavelength**: *I just couldn't talk to some of those people last night; I felt like I was on a totally different wavelength.*

waves

make waves

1 to cause problems or upset people by refusing to accept what is happening and trying to change things: *Gates said that he had not spoken out against his employers' treatment of black workers because he didn't want to make any waves.*

2 to seem impressive to people by doing something very well or in a new way

♦ OFTEN USED IN NEWSPAPERS AND MAGAZINES: *Japanese dancers Eiko and Koma are making waves with their slow-motion studies in movement.*

way

⇨**all the way down the LINE**

⇨*someone* **couldn't ___ his/her way out of a (wet) PAPER bag**

⇨**be in the FAMILY way**

⇨**___ is a two-way STREET**

⇨**see/know which way the WIND is blowing**

⇨**the way to** *someone's* **HEART**

⇨**where there's a WILL there's a way**

any way you slice it

(also **whichever way you slice it**)

used to say that a statement is true whichever way you think about it: *Saturday's game was a classic, any way you slice it.*

be behind/with *someone* all the way

to support someone completely in what they are doing, and help them as much as you can: *Lieutenant Roache is doing a great job on the Stuart case, and we're behind him all the way.*

by the way

SPOKEN used before or after you say something that is not directly connected to what you are talking about, for example something that you meant to say earlier: *"I saw a good show on TV last night." "Oh, really? By the way, did you pick up my stuff from the cleaners?"*

> NOTE▶ In an e-mail message, this phrase is often shortened to "btw."

something **could swing either way**

used to say that you cannot tell in advance which of two results an action, game, election, etc. will have: *The game could have swung either way in the last twenty minutes.*

every which way

1 in all directions at the same time: *I heard a crash and looked up – glass was flying every which way.*

2 using every possible method: *The statue has been burned, spray-painted, and vandalized every which way since they put it up in the park.*

get/be under way

if an event, plan, or development gets under way, it starts to happen or people start working on it: *Though the new water treatment plant is well under way, the district is still encouraging residents to conserve water.*

go all the way

1 SLANG to have sex, rather than just kissing or touching: *We didn't go all the way on our first date.*

2 to be completely successful in what you are doing, or to do it in the most complete or extreme way possible: *I think that Fernandez will go all the way and win the tournament.*

go back a long way
(also **go way back**)
1 if two people or groups go back a long way, they have known each other or been working together for a very long time: *Sam and I go way back. We sat next to each other in first grade and got into trouble.*
2 if an idea or activity goes back a long way, it has existed, or been happening for a long time: *Rap music comes from roots that go way back in American and African culture.*

go out of your way to do *something*
to make an additional effort to do something that you do not have to do or are not expected to do: *Mattie went out of her way to make us feel welcome at the party.*

go the way of
to fail or become worse in the same way that someone or something else has done: *He used to have standards. Now he seems to have gone the way of all writers, forgetting everything else in the hope of a Hollywood screenplay.*

go your own way
1 to behave or do something in the way that you want to, even though this may not be what other people expect or want you to do: *I'm not interested in having a family. I just want to live my own life and go my own way.*
2 if a country, area, or part of an organization goes its own way, it becomes independent and manages its own affairs: *Southern Europe continued to go its own way, preserving its Latin roots.*

something goes/cuts both ways
used to say that an idea, decision, or change has both good and bad results, or that it has two different or opposite effects: *Freedom of speech goes both ways – if you want to be able to say whatever you want, you have to listen to people who disagree with you.*

be going *someone's* way
to happen in the way that someone wants or hopes ◆ OFTEN USED IN THE NEGATIVE: *We've been putting in a lot of effort, but things don't seem to be going our way.*

have come a long way
used to say that someone or something has improved or changed a lot: *The Eagles have come a long way since their disastrous first game of the season.*

have a long way to go
used to say that a person or organization will have to work hard and improve a lot before they succeed at something: *We still have a long way to go before we achieve the equality that Martin Luther King fought for.*

not have much in the way of
SPOKEN used to say that there is not enough of something, especially when you are disappointed or annoyed by this: *They don't have much in the way of facilities – there's not even a tennis court.*
What do you have in the way of ...?: *What do you have in the way of desserts?*

have a way with
1 to be good at dealing with people and making them like you: *Jorge had a way with the older people at the center – he treated them with respect and made sure they had fun.*
2 to be good at something, especially language or mathematics: *McCourt has a lovely way with words in his memoir of his impoverished childhood.*

have your wicked way with *someone*
a humorous expression meaning to have sex with someone, usually a woman, who is very good, pure, and not experienced: *Do you think I invited you here just so that I could have my wicked way with you?*

be in a bad way
SPOKEN to be sick, very upset, or in a bad situation: *Jake couldn't leave Kathy. She was in such a bad way, feeling so depressed.*

in a big way
a lot, to a great degree, or in the most complete way: *Bookstores are moving onto the Internet in a big way.*

in more ways than one
used to emphasize that something happens or is true in many ways or for many reasons: *Wearing black leather can be hot in more ways than one.*

W

not know which way to turn

SPOKEN to be confused and unable to make a decision about what to do: *Kids today have so many choices about which career to choose, they don't know which way to turn.*

be laughing all the way to the bank

used to say that someone is very happy because they are making a lot of money quickly or easily: *The movie's been criticized for being too violent, but the studio isn't quite so upset. They're laughing all the way to the bank after a record first week.*

> NOTE▶ You may hear people use other words instead of "laughing" and "bank" in this idiom to make it fit a particular situation more exactly: *Record label bosses are singing all the way to the bank following their artists' success.* | *Without any real opposition for the South Carolina Senate seat, the Republicans should be laughing all the way to the ballot box.*

learn *something* the hard way
(also **discover, find**, etc. *something* **the hard way**)

to learn something by making mistakes or having an unpleasant experience: *I learned the hard way that there is no escaping your problems and that alcohol and drugs only make it more difficult to face them.*

look the other way

to ignore an activity or behavior that is illegal or not allowed, especially if you should try to prevent it: *Customs officials were paid up to $75,000 to look the other way as drugs were brought into the country.*

make way for

1 to be replaced by someone or something else: *An entire block of Victorian houses will be torn down to make way for a shopping center.*
2 to make space for someone or something by moving or being moved: *Miss Welland made way for him by pushing back her chair.*

mend/change your ways

to improve your behavior and stop doing something bad which you have been doing for a long time: *Tyson said at the time, "I've learned my lesson, and changed my ways – I just hope my fans can forgive me."*

no two ways about it

SPOKEN used to emphasize that something is true: *No two ways about it, that was the hardest test I've ever taken.*

no way

1 SPOKEN (also **no way José**) said when you want to emphasize that you will not agree to something or that something is not true: *"Can I have a bite of your pizza?" "No way José – get your own."*

> NOTE▶ In this idiom, "José" is pronounced Ho-zay, with the stress on the second syllable.

2 SPOKEN said when you do not believe someone, or are very surprised at what they have just said: *"The cat hissed at me and tried to scratch me." "No way, this little one?"*
—see also **get out of HERE**

a parting of the ways

used about a situation in which two people or groups who have been living or working closely together decide to live or work separately: *Barnoe refused to say whether Scheer had been fired, calling it "an amicable parting of the ways."*

pave/smooth the way for

if one action or event paves the way for another, it makes it easier for it to happen by preparing the situation: *The translation of Aristotle's writings into modern European languages helped pave the way for the rise of universities.*

rub *someone* the wrong way

to annoy someone by what you say or do: *Barb is always complaining about how much water I use – it obviously rubs her the wrong way.*

see your way clear to

SPOKEN to agree or decide to do something that may be difficult, especially giving someone money: *If you could see your way clear to helping the Sacred Heart Community Center, then please give us a call.*

be set in your ways
used to say that you always do things in the same way and do not like doing them differently: *Employers used to believe that younger employees would be less set in their ways and more flexible, but a recent survey challenges this view.*

someone swings both ways
used to say that someone is sexually attracted to both men and women: *"Is he gay?" "Well, I think he swings both ways."*

take the easy way out
to choose the easiest solution to a problem that is not the best because it does not deal with it fully: *Congress has taken the easy way out by sending the difficult decisions to the states.*

take *something* the wrong way
SPOKEN to be offended by something someone has said or done because you have not fully or correctly understood what they were trying to do or say: *My comments on the players were meant to be useful, not critical – I'm sorry people took them the wrong way.*

that's the way the cookie crumbles
SPOKEN used to say that you must accept things the way they are, even though you may not like it: *You're going to lose a few games every season. That's just the way the cookie crumbles.*

that's (just) the way it goes
SPOKEN used when something bad happens to say that you cannot change the situation: *I agree it's not fair, but that's just the way it goes.*

there are ways and means (of doing *something*)
used to say that there are effective ways of achieving something, without saying exactly what they are, sometimes because they are secret or illegal: *The company has ways and means of finding out what the competition is up to.*

there's more than one way to skin a cat
used to say that there is more than one way of achieving something: *Just as there's more than one way to skin a cat, there's more than one way to develop new technologies.*

way to go!
1 SPOKEN said when someone does something very well, or when you are happy for them because something good has happened: *Are you done? Way to go. It looks great!*
2 SPOKEN used humorously when someone has done something stupid: *Way to go, Carly. Now there are papers all over the floor.*

wise in the ways of ___
used to say that someone understands all about how to deal with a situation, or how a particular person or organization is likely to behave: *Andrew, aged seven, is wise in the ways of street survival – don't get noticed and you won't get hurt.*

you can't have it both ways
SPOKEN used to say that someone should choose one way of doing things and accept the results, instead of wanting advantages from both of two possible decisions or actions: *You can't have it both ways – you can't have huge development and still have the same lifestyle as the past.*

wayside

fall/go by the wayside
used to say that someone has failed to achieve what was expected, or that something has failed because it is no longer being given any attention: *The training program is very tough, and more than half of the trainees have fallen by the wayside before the end of the first year.*

wazoo

have *something* (coming) out the wazoo/kazoo
(also **have** *something* **up the wazoo**, **have** *something* **up the ying yang**)
SLANG a humorous expression used to say that you have a very large amount of something: *We have had snow up the wazoo this year.*

W

wear

be/look none the worse for wear
used to say that someone or something looks fairly good, even though they have been in a situation that could have hurt or damaged them, or made them tired or sick: *The cat was a little shocked, with bruised ears and a broken claw, but otherwise, none the worse for wear.*

be/look the worse for wear
used to say that something looks old and in bad condition, or that someone looks tired and sick: *Here I was, returning from a major conference, plainly the worse for wear. Somehow, I managed to find the office.*

wear thin
used to say that something that was amusing or pleasant at first is not enjoyable anymore because it has continued for too long: *Germano's childlike voice begins to wear thin after a few songs.*

weather

⇨weather the **STORM**

keep a weather eye on
OLD-FASHIONED to keep your attention on a situation so that you will notice any changes that may cause problems for you: *The government is keeping a weather eye on inflation.*

be under the weather
SPOKEN to be sick, but not seriously sick: *Donna's not coming along today – she's a little under the weather.*

web

a tangled web
used about a situation which is very complicated, especially because lots of different people or organizations want different things from it: *Set in San Diego, the play examines the tangled web woven by people who conceal certain truths from others.*

wedding

hear wedding bells
used to say that you think that two people will get married: *"He makes me laugh,*

and I feel really comfortable with him." "Ooh, do I hear wedding bells?"

wedge

drive a wedge between
to cause anger or disagreement between two people or groups that stops them from being friendly or working together: *Arguments about the new space station continue to drive a wedge between the scientific community and NASA.*

weight

carry/feel the weight of the world on your shoulders
used to say that someone feels very worried and unhappy because of their problems or the things they have to do, especially when they think they are even greater than they really are: *No wonder Sam has high blood pressure. He always carries the weight of the world on his shoulders.*

carry weight
if an idea, statement, or opinion carries weight, it has a lot of influence over the way people think: *Negative political ads don't carry as much weight as they did seven or eight years ago.*

(a) dead weight
used about someone or something that does not add any advantage to a company, organization, etc. and instead prevents it from making progress ♦ OFTEN USED IN BUSINESS AND POLITICS: *The federal deficit is a major dead weight on our economy.*

pull your weight
to work as hard to achieve something as other people who are working with you: *There have been complaints that some of the newest members of the team have not been pulling their weight.*

throw your weight around
used to say that someone is using their power or authority in a way that is not fair or reasonable, often in order to show people how powerful they are: *The lawyers portrayed Roentgren as a judge blinded by his power and trying to throw his weight around the legal system to help his friends.*

throw your weight behind
someone/something
to show that you strongly support an idea, person, organization, etc. ◆ OFTEN USED IN NEWSPAPERS, ON TELEVISION NEWS, ETC.: *Jesse Jackson threw his weight behind his old opponent, standing beside him at a rally in Tennessee.*

be a weight off your shoulders
used to say that you feel happy because you no longer have to worry about something that you have been worrying about for a long time: *I'm really relieved the trial is over – it's a huge weight off my shoulders.*
—see also **be a LOAD off your mind**

worth his/her weight in gold
used to say that someone or something is extremely good, helpful, or useful: *Any secretary who can read my notes is worth her weight in gold.*

welcome

overstay/wear out your welcome
to stay in a place that you are visiting or working for too long, so that the people who always live or work there become annoyed: *Be careful not to ask too many favors. You may wear out your welcome.*

well
⇨**it's JUST as well (that)**

wet

be all wet
OLD-FASHIONED to be completely wrong: *It's a nice story, but it's not true. Whoever told you is all wet.*

whack

out of whack
SPOKEN if a system or process is out of whack, it is not working correctly: *Ever since I fell down the stairs, my back has been completely out of whack.*

take a whack at *something*
SPOKEN to try to do something: *I used to be pretty good at this game – let me take a whack at it.*

whale

have a whale of a time
OLD-FASHIONED to enjoy a social event or activity very much, for example a party, vacation, sports event, etc.: *Somebody walked past, saw these kids having a whale of a time, and wondered what was going on.*

wham
⇨**wham bam thank you MA'AM**

whammy
⇨**put the whammy on** *someone* —see **put/work a MOJO on** *someone*

a double whammy
when someone is not lucky because two bad or difficult things that they cannot control happen at the same time ◆ OFTEN USED IN NEWSPAPERS, ON TELEVISION NEWS, ETC.: *The small farming community has been hit with the double whammy of a winter freeze and summer flooding.*

> NOTE▶ You may hear people use "triple whammy" or "quadruple whammy" if three or four bad things happen: *The effects of war, recession, and drought have been a triple whammy for tourism in the area.*

what
⇨**SO what?**

...and/or what have you
SPOKEN said at the end of a series of things in order to show that there are other things of the same kind that you are not mentioning: *We'll have to use a brush to get all the mud off the wheels and the fenders and grille and what have you.*

for what it's worth
SPOKEN used before a statement in order to say that your opinion may not be very interesting or important: *For what it's worth, I never thought his poetry was very good.*

> NOTE▶ In e-mail messages, this phrase is sometimes shortened to "fwiw."

W

W

know what's what
(also **remember, understand, etc. what's what**)

SPOKEN in order to say that someone knows, remembers, understands, etc. a complicated situation or subject: *It's a pleasure to read this brisk account written by a veteran journalist who knows what's what.*

...or what?

1 SPOKEN used to emphasize your opinion, usually a criticism of someone or something: *I'm thinking, is she stupid or what? She gives up a career in the fashion industry to become an accountant.*
2 SPOKEN used to show someone that you are annoyed because they are taking too long to do something they have agreed to do: *Are we going shopping or what?*

what do you know!

SPOKEN said when you are surprised and happy about something you have just heard or seen: *"See, there's a Holiday Inn we can stay at about a mile from his house." "Well, what do you know. That's lucky."*

what do you say we...

SPOKEN used to suggest something such as a solution to a problem: *Chris, you've had this box of cereal for three months now. What do you say we throw it out?*

what gives?

OLD-FASHIONED used to ask what is happening, especially when you feel that something should have happened but has not: *So, Wilson, what gives? When are you going to tell us what's going on here?*

what goes around comes around

used to say that if you are nice and do good things, then good things will happen to you later, and if you are bad, then bad things will happen to you: *Things weren't good for the girls' team for a while – but they've worked hard, and what goes around comes around. They're finally getting the respect they deserve.*

what got into *someone*?

SPOKEN used to show that you are surprised because someone is behaving very differently from the way they usually behave: *What got into you? I mean, what makes you think you can say things like that?*

what makes *someone* tick

used about the thoughts, desires, opinions, etc. that make someone behave in the way that they do: *My father was always interested in psychology, in what makes people tick.*

what's cooking?

OLD-FASHIONED used to ask what someone is doing or planning: *Hey everybody – you look busy, what's cooking?*

what's eating him/her?

SPOKEN used to ask why someone seems annoyed, upset, etc.: *"Leave me alone." "What's eating you? I just asked how you were doing."*

what's it worth (to *someone*)

used to ask what someone will give you or do for you if you do what they want
♦ OFTEN USED IN BOOKS AND TELEVISION SHOWS ABOUT CRIME: *"So can you help me?" "I might be able to. What's it worth to you?"* | *Find out what it's worth to Halpin to have the tapes destroyed.*

what's up?

1 SPOKEN (also **what's up with** *someone/ something*?) used to ask why someone seems upset or angry or is behaving strangely, or why something is not working correctly: *What's up with the CD player? I can't make it work.*
2 SLANG (also **what's happening?**) used to greet someone: *"Hey, man, what's up?" "Not much."*

what's with *someone/something*?

SPOKEN used to ask someone the reason for something unusual, or to ask why someone is behaving strangely: *What's with the microphone? Are you recording us?*

NOTE▶ It sounds rude and very direct to say "what's with you?".

whatever

whatever turns you on

SPOKEN said when you do not like something that someone else likes or does in order to say that they have the right to like it or do it: *I just can't stand country music, but whatever turns you on, I guess.*

whatnot

... and whatnot
SPOKEN said at the end of a list of things when you do not want to give the names of all of the rest of the things: *I'm going to go through all Dad's letters and bills and whatnot, and see if I can make any sense of what he's left behind.*

wheat

sort (out) the wheat from the chaff
(also **separate/sift the wheat from the chaff**)
to choose the good or useful things or people from a large group, and get rid of the rest: *ninety-nine percent of calls to the police are likely to be worthless, but experienced detectives can quickly sort the wheat from the chaff.*

wheel

⇨a big **CHEESE/wheel**

keep the wheels turning
(also **start, set, get, etc. the wheels turning**)
to do whatever is necessary to make a process or plan work or continue to work well ♦ OFTEN USED IN BUSINESS AND POLITICS: *A manager's job is to keep the wheels turning, not by solving the routine questions, but by tackling the tough ones.*

reinvent the wheel
to work on something that you think is new and different, but that already exists, or has already been done by someone else: *We didn't want to waste marketing resources by reinventing the wheel if we didn't have to.*

set the wheels in motion
to do what is necessary to make a plan or process begin: *Why did the police wait so long before setting the wheels in motion to track down the killer?*

spin your wheels
to be in a situation in which there is very little or no progress: *If you don't know how to find the right information, you can spend a lot of time just spinning your wheels.*

the squeaky wheel (gets the grease)
used to say that the person who complains the most is the one who gets what they want: *Pinot was the squeaky wheel in the department who got the money for developing his programs.*

the third/fifth wheel
someone who is with a group of people, even though the group does not want him/her or they do not feel comfortable with him/her: *It was nice of Becky and Matt to let me go with them, but I felt like the third wheel all night.*

wheel and deal
to do a lot of skillful things that are sometimes slightly dishonest in order to get what you want in business or politics: *No one in baseball can wheel and deal the way Rosen can.*
wheeling and dealing: *You wouldn't believe the wheeling and dealing that's going on to get the movie started.*
wheeler-dealer: *Seymour is a former real estate wheeler-dealer from Anaheim.*

the wheels are turning
SPOKEN used to say that someone is thinking about something, especially when it is difficult to understand or very complicated: *At first he didn't believe what we'd said, and then you could almost hear the wheels turning when he realized it was true.*

wheels within wheels
SPOKEN used to say that a situation is complicated because many different people or events are influencing each other: *The music industry, with its inside deals and wheels within wheels, is enough to confuse the toughest business minds.*

when

⇨when the **GOING gets tough**

when all is said and done
used after an explanation or story to give your opinion about it, or to give the most important facts about it: *He had his problems like everyone else, but when all is said and done, he was a great man who did a lot for this community.*

W

where

⇨ **THAT's where** *someone/something* **comes in**

⇨ **THAT's where we came in**

where does *someone* get off (doing *something*)

SPOKEN said when you are angry because someone has said or done something unfair or insulting: *Where does she get off calling me lazy? I've been working like a dog all week.*

where *someone* is coming from

SPOKEN why someone behaves or thinks the way they do: *It was great having Paul on guitar – he understands where we're coming from musically.*

where it's at

SPOKEN used about a place or activity that is very popular, exciting, and fashionable: *Hey, dudes – come on over to my place. This is where it's at!*

while

⇨ **do** *something* **while the GOING's good**

be worth your while

SPOKEN used to say that the money, time, or effort you use to do something will give you results that you will be happy with or gain an advantage from: *Dardis assured Bernstein that it would be worth his while to fly down to Miami again, and that new witnesses were willing to talk.*

—compare **WHAT's it worth (to** *someone***)**

> NOTE▶ People, especially in movies and books, sometimes say that someone will "make it worth *someone's* while" when they offer someone money, support, etc. if the person agrees to do something dishonest: *"I'm assuming you'll make it worth my while if I say I'll help you," she said quietly.*

whip

crack the whip

to make someone you have control over work very hard ◆ OFTEN USED IN BUSINESS: *He has been urging Winter to crack the whip, arguing that the company needs a good shake-up in order to survive.*

I WANT THESE DONE BEFORE YOU LEAVE!

whirl

give *something* a whirl

SPOKEN to try something that you are not sure you are going to like or be able to do: *"You sure you know how to get there?" "Yeah, pretty sure. I'll give it a whirl."*

whisker

be/come within a whisker of (doing) *something*

used to say that someone very nearly did or experienced something ◆ OFTEN USED IN NEWSPAPERS, ON TELEVISION NEWS, ETC.: *Sullivan came within a whisker of winning Brown's Senate seat in 1986.*

do *something* by a whisker

used to say that someone was just barely able to do something, or to emphasize that they almost succeeded: *McMurphey escaped bankruptcy by a whisker as his debts soared to $8.9 million.*

whistle

blow the whistle (on)

to tell someone, especially someone in authority, about something that is wrong or illegal because you think it should be stopped: *The former oil-rig worker was dismissed after blowing the whistle on safety violations made by his drilling company.*

whistleblower: *Several whistleblowers have complained in recent months that the Forest Service favors commercial interests over environmental ones.*

(as) clean as a whistle

1 used to say that someone has not done

anything wrong or illegal: *I've never taken any drugs, ever. I'm as clean as a whistle; they can test me any time.*
2 used to say that something is very clean: *The place was as clean as a whistle. No burger wrappers, papers, cups or plastic forks lying around.*

wet your whistle
OLD-FASHIONED to have a drink, especially an alcoholic one: *Let's stop and wet our whistles before the game.*

who

a/the who's who of __
the most important or famous people in a particular group or organization: *The production credits read like a who's who of contemporary rock musicians.* | *Over the past 45 years, Carter has worked with the who's who of the theater.*

whoop

whoop it up
SPOKEN to have a lot of fun with a group of friends, often when you are celebrating something: *I found an old photo from '85 of me and my friends whooping it up in Greece.*

whoopee

make whoopee
OLD-FASHIONED to have sex: *It's a horrible thing to realize that you've been making beds and meals for someone who is secretly making whoopee with another woman.*

whys

the whys and wherefores (of something)
the reasons or explanations for something: *Most of the news conference was devoted to the whys and wherefores, details, and logistics.*

wide

be wide open
if a competition or race is wide open, any of the people competing could win it: *The producers say it's wide open as to who of the many young actors on Broadway will play the part of Ricky.*

widow

a football widow
(also a tennis, basketball, etc. widow)
used about a woman whose husband spends most of his time playing or watching a particular sport: *I've resigned myself to being a football widow from September to January, but it means I've got time for myself.*

wig

⇨ **flip your LID/wig**

wiggle

get a wiggle on!
SPOKEN said when you want someone to do something more quickly ♦ OFTEN USED WHEN SPEAKING TO CHILDREN: *All right, get a wiggle on. It's already 8:30.*

wildfire

spread like wildfire
if news spreads like wildfire, a lot of people find out about it very quickly: *Some people started screaming, and then the panic spread like wildfire through the plane.*

will

where there's a will there's a way
used to say that if you really want to do something, you will find a way to do it: *If her welfare payments were cut, Castro said she would survive by cutting out things for her kids. "Where there's a will, there's a way, and I'd make it work," she said.*

willies

give someone the willies
SPOKEN to make someone feel nervous or frightened: *Barney said some guy died here, but don't tell the kids – it'll just give them the willies.*

wind

break wind
a polite expression for when someone lets gas escape from their body, making a bad smell and usually a noise: *A man standing in front of us broke wind right in the middle of the speech and got very embarrassed.*

W

get wind of *something*
to find out about something that other people wanted to be secret or private, especially accidentally or not officially: *When neighbors got wind of the development plans, they formed a committee to protest.*

get your/a second wind
(also **catch/find your second wind**)
to find the energy or strength to continue to do something or to develop further, after a period of being weak or tired: *Dad started back down the hill, leaving the rest of us to get our second wind.*

something is (blowing) in the wind
used to say that a plan or idea is likely to happen or be used, but it is not definite yet: *We didn't know exactly what was going on, but by the end of May, we knew that there were some changes blowing in the wind.*

leave *someone* twisting/swinging in the wind
(also **let** *someone* **twist/swing in the wind**)
to not help someone who is having serious problems, especially because you can gain an advantage from their problems ◆ OFTEN USED IN BUSINESS AND POLITICS: *There was no indication that the U.S. or Germany would cut interest rates, which left countries with weaker economies twisting in the wind.*

run/go like the wind
to move very quickly: *The colt ran like the wind, its hooves stirring up clouds of dust.*

sail close to the wind
to take a risk by doing or saying something that is almost dishonest or illegal, and that may cause problems for you: *Ramon left quite a mess behind him when he disappeared. He'd been sailing close to the wind for years, although not even his closest friends knew.*

be scattered to the (four) winds
to be broken up and lost, or spread over a wide area: *The building's old bricks had crumbled to dust and were scattered to the winds.*

see/know which way the wind is blowing
(also **see/know which way the wind blows**)
to find out what most people think about something, or what is likely to happen next in a situation, before you decide what to do: *Kimball is passionate about politics, and unconventional in that he doesn't need to know which way the wind blows before he states his opinion.*

be spitting/pissing in the wind
SPOKEN to waste time and effort trying to do something that is impossible: *All these changes they're talking about making in the company structure – they're just spitting in the wind.*
—compare **whistling in the WIND**

> NOTE▶ It is much more polite to say "spitting in the wind" than to say "pissing in the wind."

take the wind out of *someone's* sails
to make someone feel much less confident about what they are doing or saying: *A 42 percent drop in the stock's price has taken the wind out of shareholders' sails.*

whistling in the wind
when someone makes a promise, demand, or statement that has no effect or produces no useful results ◆ USED ESPECIALLY IN NEWSPAPERS: *When their parents stop lying and whistling in the wind, the girls will stop being so difficult and will learn to behave.*
—compare **be spitting/pissing in the WIND**

windmills

be tilting at windmills
1 used to say that someone wastes time on ideas that are not practical or important: *Critics of the proposal bluntly likened it to tilting at windmills.*
2 to try to solve a problem or start work on a plan that seems impossible to achieve: *Devens says he knows something about tilting at windmills. He started Alaska's only accredited community college in 1979 with a budget of $118,000 and no teachers.*

window

something goes out (of) the window
used to say that a promise, rule, way of doing things, etc. is ignored or forgotten completely in a particular situation: *All my good intentions to stick to my diet went out the window when I saw the fantastic meal he'd made.*

a window of opportunity
a limited period of time which is the only time you can do something or the best time to do something ◆ USED ESPECIALLY IN BUSINESS: *We agree there's a window of opportunity here to move the negotiations forward, and we don't want to lose it.*

wine

wine and dine *someone*
to try to seem impressive to someone by making or buying them good meals ◆ USED ESPECIALLY IN NEWSPAPERS, MAGAZINES, ETC.: *The 53-year-old Rolling Stone wined and dined the millionaire model at his French mansion as the media tried to catch a glimpse.*

wine, women, and song
OLD-FASHIONED an enjoyable life of drinking, dancing, and having fun: *Goldeen was accused of using city funds for wine, women and song.*

wing

clip *someone's* wings
to limit someone's freedom, power, or ability to work effectively: *Mama always said she wanted a strong man, but then whenever they showed signs of independence, she'd clip their wings real fast.*

do *something* on a wing and a prayer
to do something hoping that you will succeed, even though you do not have the money, knowledge, or help you really need in order to do it well: *The city is operating on a wing and a prayer at this point. A lot of essential repairs have not been made.*

be (standing/waiting) in the wings
1 to be waiting for an opportunity to do something, especially to take another person's job: *The team has two young quarterbacks waiting in the wings if Martez decides to retire.*
2 if a plan, idea, or change is waiting in the wings, it will soon be used or happen: *There is a feeling in the market these days that another wave of Japanese investment is in the wings.*

spread your wings
to do something new that is more exciting or difficult than anything you have ever done before: *The classroom buzzed with discussion. "Here the students have a chance to spread their wings," explained Mr. Anzalone.*

take *someone* under your wing
to help and protect someone, especially someone who is younger or less experienced than you are: *The boy had had little formal education until Edward took him under his wing.*

try your wings
to try to do something that you have never done before to see whether you will be successful: *You remember what it was like being young and eager to try your wings.*

be under the wing of
to be controlled or operated by a particular person or organization: *Roth ran for the Senate in 1980 under the wing of the National Congressional Club.*

wing it
SPOKEN to do something without planning or preparing for it, or without paying too much attention to details or rules: *Have you thought out some responses to likely interview questions, or do you intend to wing it?*

wink

forty winks
OLD-FASHIONED a very short period of sleep: *There's enough time for you to catch forty winks before dinner.*

(as) quick as a wink
OLD-FASHIONED very quickly: *Patrice shot*

W

out of the door, quick as a wink, before anyone could stop her.

not sleep a wink
(also not get a wink of sleep)
to not be able to sleep at all: *I feel terrible. I didn't sleep a wink last night.*

a wink's as good as a nod (to a blind man)
OLD-FASHIONED used humorously in order to say that something has been understood even though it has not been said directly, especially when it concerns something illegal: *Don't say any more, Barry – a wink's as good as a nod. I know what to do.*

wire

something comes/goes/gets (right) down to the wire
SPOKEN used to say that the time when a plan, activity, job, etc. is supposed to end is very close: *The negotiations went right down to the wire, but we reached an agreement just before the deadline.*
down-to-the-wire: *The 49ers won a down-to-the-wire 14–10 victory over Phoenix yesterday.*

get in under the wire
to do something at the last possible moment before it is too late: *Carter was allowed to participate at the Pan American games, getting in under the wire after a long argument with the authorities.*

have/get your wires crossed
if two people get their wires crossed, each of them is confused by what the other one says or does, and they make mistakes: *We must have gotten our wires crossed. The meeting is Thursday night, not Tuesday.*

someone is a live wire
used to say that someone is very cheerful and funny and has a lot of energy: *Devine's a smart man, a real live wire, who always knows what's going on.*

wisdom

⇨**with the wisdom of hindsight** —see with/in **HINDSIGHT**

wise

get/be wise to *someone/ something*
SPOKEN to realize that someone is doing something that is not honest: *She used to meet him secretly, until her parents got wise to what was going on.*

be none the wiser
(also not be any the wiser)
used to say that you still do not understand or know about something, especially when something has happened that could have made you understand or realize it: *I opened up the back of the TV set, but when I looked inside, I was none the wiser as to what was wrong.*

wish

I/you wish!
SPOKEN used to say that you do not think something is true, even though you or someone else might wish that it was: *"You look as if you've lost some weight." "I wish!"* | *"Do you think I look like Michelle Pfeiffer?" "You wish!"*

your wish is my command!
SPOKEN a humorous expression used to say that you are ready to do anything someone asks you to do: *Where would you like me to take you this evening? Your wish is my command.*

> NOTE▶ "Your wish is my command" is what a genie (=a spirit who lives in a bottle and does magic) is supposed to say to the person who owns him.

wit

⇨**at your wits' END**

gather/collect your wits
to try hard to control yourself and think clearly and calmly: *When he knocked on the door, I tried to collect my wits and find the right paperwork.*

have/keep your wits about you
to be ready to think clearly and calmly in a difficult situation so that no one can gain an advantage over you: *You had to have your wits about you when you played poker with my father and Uncle Charlie.*

pit your wits against *someone*

to use all your intelligence to try and beat someone or something in a competition or difficult situation: *The one-player option lets you pit your wits against the computer.*

scare *someone* out of their wits
(also **scare the wits out of** *someone* or **scare** *someone* **witless**)

to make someone feel very frightened: *What did you do that for? You scared me out of my wits!*

to wit

FORMAL used to give more detailed information about something that has just been mentioned: *All the data confirm what we know instinctively, to wit: a caring two-parent family is more likely to raise happy kids than a single-parent family.*

with

be with it

1 SPOKEN to be able to think clearly and understand things well: *I'm sorry, I don't know what's the matter with me – I'm just not with it this morning.*

2 SPOKEN to wear fashionable clothes and know about new ideas: *At the time, I thought I was really with it because I had a pair of silver leather platform boots.*

witless

⇨scare *someone* **witless** —see **scare** *someone* **out of their WITS**

wives

⇨an old wives' **TALE**

woe

woe betide *someone*

OLD-FASHIONED used to warn someone that they will have problems if they do something, often used humorously: *It's surprising how many old laws are still in force. For example, woe betide any man who kisses his wife in public on a Sunday in a small town in New Hampshire.*

wolf

the big bad wolf

used about someone who makes people feel frightened or threatened: *At the conference the main theme was "international co-operation," although huge international corporations are still seen as big bad wolves.*

cry wolf

to keep asking for help when you do not need it, or saying that there is a problem or danger when there is not so that when you do need help or there is a problem, no one believes you: *"There've been a lot of businesses crying wolf," said Phillip Vincent, an economist with First Interstate Bank. "It makes you wonder what the situation really is."*

> **NOTE▶** This idiom comes from an old story about a boy who was looking after sheep and, as a joke, called out that a wolf (=animal like a large dog) was coming. His friends ran to help him, but when a wolf really came, they thought his cry for help was another joke, and they did not come.

keep the wolf from the door

to earn enough money to buy the basic things that you need to live, but no more: *I'm working part-time in a coffee shop, just to keep the wolf from the door, that's all.*
—compare keep **BODY** and soul together

a lone wolf

used about someone who prefers to spend time alone and has few friends: *Connors was one of the greatest players in U.S. history but a lone wolf.*

throw *someone* to the wolves

to let someone be attacked or criticized, or let them get into a difficult situation in order to gain an advantage for yourself, especially when they have done nothing wrong: *Officer Merrit has been cleared of any guilt, but the Attorney General is willing to throw him to the wolves, simply in order to gain popularity with certain groups of voters.*

be a wolf in sheep's clothing

used about someone who seems to be nice and friendly, but is not, or something that seems to be good, but is not: *"This* bill is a wolf in sheep's clothing," she said. "Many have attempted to mislead Congress by calling it a pro-family, pro-woman bill. It is anything but that."

woman

⇒ **be as ___ as the next guy/ MAN/woman**

⇒ **if you want...** someone **is your MAN/woman**

⇒ **a MAN/woman after your own heart**

⇒ **the MAN/woman in the street**

⇒ **be a MAN/woman of the world**

⇒ someone's **right-hand woman** —see someone's **right-hand MAN**

⇒ **a woman of her word** —see **a MAN of his word**

⇒ **you can't keep a good MAN/woman down**

⇒ **be your own MAN/woman**

make an honest woman (out) of someone
SPOKEN a humorous expression meaning to marry a woman who you have been having a romantic relationship with for a long time: No doubt the whole neighborhood has been waiting for me to make an honest woman out of you.

wonder

do wonders (for)
(also **work wonders for**)
to have a good effect on something or be very effective at solving a problem: Working outside all day does wonders for your health.

no/small/little wonder
(also **it's no/small/little wonder**)
SPOKEN used to say that you are not surprised by something: No wonder you're tired if you walked all that way. | When doctors have to work such long hours – sometimes 16 to 18 hour shifts – it's little wonder that mistakes are made.

a one-hit wonder
used about a singer, musical group, etc. that has only one successful song and then is never very successful again, or about the song that was successful: Carey's second release proved that she wasn't a one-hit wonder, but a major star.

wonders will never cease
(also **will wonders never cease?**)
SPOKEN said when you are very surprised and pleased about something: Frank jogs three mornings a week now. Will wonders never cease?

wood

dead wood
used about the people or things in an organization that are no longer useful or needed ♦ OFTEN USED IN BUSINESS: Fivaz was hired to clear out the dead wood from the police force.

knock on wood
SPOKEN said after you have just said that things are going well for you, when you want your good luck to continue: I haven't had the flu this year, knock on wood.

not be out of the woods (yet)
used to say that there will probably be more problems before a situation improves: Gladys is feeling much better, but she isn't out of the woods yet.

woodwork

crawl/come out of the woodwork
used about people who suddenly arrive or appear in large numbers when you have not seen them before or do not often see them: Whenever a major player is injured, so-called "experts" start coming out of the woodwork to discuss the situation.

wool

dyed-in-the-wool
used about someone who has strong beliefs or feelings that are very unlikely to change: Maybe dyed-in-the-wool traditional types do not believe in alternative medicines because they think good medicine has to hurt to work.

pull the wool over someone's eyes
to deceive someone by not telling them the truth, or by hiding some information from them: Todd is pulling the wool over your eyes, and you're making it easier for him because you want to believe what he's saying.

word

⇨a **PLAY** on words

be as good as your word
to do exactly what you have promised to do: *Jill said she'd be here at 8:00 sharp, and she turned out to be as good as her word.*

not breathe/say a word
SPOKEN to not tell anyone anything at all about something because it is very important that no one knows about it: *I can't believe Mark knew about this all along, and he never said a word.*

by word of mouth
if you get information or news by word of mouth, you hear about it from other people, instead of reading it, seeing an advertisement, etc.: *Scott's business has grown by word of mouth, and now much of his work comes from private commissions.*
word-of-mouth: *A personal, word-of-mouth recommendation is probably the best method of advertising.*

(be forced to) eat your words
to publicly admit that what you said was wrong: *The show is fantastic, and all those critics who doubt us will be eating their words on our first night on Broadway.*

famous last words
SPOKEN said when someone has said too confidently that they can do something or that something will happen: *"Don't worry, I'll be perfectly OK on my own." Famous last words, she thought, as she stepped out into the dark street.*

from the word go
from the beginning: *The marriage was a disaster from the word go although I didn't realize this until it was all over.*

the F-word
(also **the B-word, the M-word, etc.**)
used to talk about rude words, or about a subject you do not want to mention, by using only the first letter of the word. The "F" represents the word "fuck" which is considered very rude by many people: *Any student who uses the F-word in class will be sent to the principal's office.* | *My dog doesn't like baths. We can't even use the B-word around her, or she runs and hides.*

not get a word in edgewise
to not get a chance to speak because someone else is talking too much: *Anytime I talk to Sonny, I have trouble even getting a word in edgewise.*

give *someone* **your word (that)**
to promise someone very seriously that you will do something: *Oh God, Ray, I have to tell somebody, but you have to give me your word you won't tell anyone else.*

hang on *someone's* **every word**
(also **hang on** *someone's* **words**)
to listen very carefully to everything someone says: *The minister was surrounded by a group of admirers who hung on his every word.*

someone **has the last word**
1 (also *someone* **has the final word**) used to say that a particular person has the power to make important decisions, or to change decisions made by other people in lower positions ♦ OFTEN USED IN BUSINESS AND POLITICS: *The Supreme Court always has the final word in such matters.*
2 to be the person who makes the final point in a discussion or argument, especially when this makes you feel you have won: *You always have to have the last word, don't you?*

have a word (with *someone*)
SPOKEN to talk to someone, usually privately, especially because you want to get advice or help from them, or give them advice: *I'll see if I can have a quick word with Frances before the meeting.*

have words (with *someone*)

have words (with *someone*)

(also **exchange words with** *someone*) to argue with or speak angrily to someone: *At the end of the game Edwards exchanged words with the referee, but it doesn't seem to have developed into anything.*

in a word ___

used to give a simple answer or explanation using one word that says everything you want to say: *The show was fantastic, full of color and life – in a word, sensational. | I didn't like the doctor who visited. His bedside manner was, in a word, frightening.*

in so many words

used to say that someone says what they mean very clearly and directly, sometimes in a way that upsets or offends people: *Cara doesn't like me, and she made it clear in so many words.*

—compare **not in so many WORDs**

not in so many words

used to say that someone means something, but that they do not say clearly or directly: *"Did you tell him you wanted to break up?" "Not in so many words, but I think he knew."*

—compare **in so many WORDs**

something is a dirty word (with *someone*)

used to say that someone does not like or approve of a particular activity or quality: *In politics, "liberal" has become a dirty word.*

___ isn't the word for it

SPOKEN used to emphasize that a particular word is not strong enough to describe something, especially an emotion: *"I don't know how we won this game. It was pure luck." "Luck isn't the word for it." | "That's good news." "Good isn't the word for it. It's great news."*

keep your word

to do exactly what you promised to do: *We have kept our word since the last election – taxes have not risen.*

be the last word in ___

used to emphasize that something is the best, most modern, etc. thing of its type: *I had thought my clothes were the last word in modesty, but my host suggested that I cover myself a little more. | Gurung recalls his days as a graduate student, when the IBM 650 was the last word in computer wizardry.*

be lost for words

(also **at a loss for words**)

unable to say anything because you feel so surprised, shocked, unhappy, etc.: *Momentarily at a loss for words, she could only stare at the man who had opened the door.*

mark my word(s)

SPOKEN used to tell someone that they should pay attention to what you are saying: *We haven't heard the last of him, you mark my words.*

not mince (your) words

SPOKEN to say exactly what you think or feel, even though this may offend people: *The warnings on cigarette packs do not mince words: "Smoking causes lung cancer and heart disease."*

(upon) my word

OLD-FASHIONED said when something unusual or surprising happens: *Upon my word, young lady, you were very brave to jump into the river like that!*

put in a (good) word for *someone*

to say good things about someone to a person in a position of authority, especially in order to help them get a job or so that they avoid being punished: *If you're still interested in the sales job, I can put in a good word for you.*

put words in(to) *someone's* mouth

to say that someone said something that they did not actually say, or suggest that they are going to say something that they do not intend to say: *I did not say you were lazy! Don't you dare put words into my mouth!*

(just) say the word

SPOKEN used to tell someone that they only have to ask and you will do what they want: *Hey, if you want any help with dinner, just say the word.*

take *someone* at his/her word

to choose to believe what someone says, even though it is possible that they do not mean what they are saying: *Because Darla had a good relationship with the* department managers, they were willing to take her at her word.

take my word for it
SPOKEN used to say that someone should believe that what you say is true: *Life can be good, Marie. Take my word for it.*

word for word
1 if you repeat or copy something word for word, you express it in exactly the same words as before: *Tikhon knows the passage by heart and can recite it word for word.*
word-for-word: *She gave a word-for-word account of the conversation she had overheard.*
2 if you translate a piece of writing word for word, you translate the meaning of each single word instead of translating the meaning of a whole phrase or sentence: *It is inadequate and sometimes completely misleading to translate the text word for word.*
word-for-word: *A word-for-word translation will never give the full meaning and flavor of an article.*

the word is (that)
(also **word has it (that)**)
used to say that you have heard that a particular thing has happened or is true: *The word is that KGO is not renewing Ward's contract, and his show could be finished by October.* | *Word has it that the prisoner will be released early tomorrow.*

someone's word is law
used to say that everyone always obeys a particular person, even when this does not seem reasonable: *Coleman was a strict disciplinarian whose word was law with the players.*

words fail me
SPOKEN used to say that you do not know how to describe what you are feeling, because you are so surprised, angry, etc.: *Emily, you are the most... well, words fail me.*

you took the words (right) out of my mouth
SPOKEN said when someone describes something in exactly the way you were going to: *"My God, how can she wear that in public?" "You took the words right out of my mouth."*

work W

(it's) all in a day's work
SPOKEN used to say that someone can do something easily or well, even though it may be difficult or unpleasant, because it is part of the activities they do every day: *Describing paintings, discussing the problem of drugs, surfing the net – it's all in a day's work for today's grade school teachers.*

all work and no play (makes Jack a dull boy)
SPOKEN used to say that it is not good for you to work too hard; you need to relax too: *Don't wear yourself out. All work and no play, you know.*

> **NOTE** This is a very old phrase, and the last part of it is rarely used anymore, except when people change the words slightly to make it fit a particular situation or make it funny: *We know that all work and no play makes the birth rate decline, but we were surprised at how low the numbers had gone.*

do *someone's* dirty work
to do the unpleasant or dishonest things that someone else does not want to do: *The dictator can no longer count on the army and the police to do his dirty work for him.*

have your work cut out for you
used to say that someone will have to work very hard in order to achieve something: *Dani has her work cut out for her keeping those kids amused.*

in the works
used to say that something is being planned or developed ◆ OFTEN USED IN BUSINESS: *There are seven homeless shelters in the county with three more in the works.*

make short/light work of *something*
to finish something such as a job or a meal quickly and easily: *He enrolled in the School of Arts after making very short work of the entrance exam.*

nice work if you can get it
SPOKEN said when you think someone's job is very good, easy, or enjoyable, and

you wish you had a similar job: *Clooney said his first task on set was to kiss Michelle Pfeiffer – nice work if you can get it!*

be working it
SLANG used about someone in a social situation, at a party, etc. who is talking and behaving in a confident way, especially so that they are sexually attractive: *We were up on one of those platforms dancing, and we were working it.*
work it: *Hey girl, you look great! Work it.*

the (whole) works
SPOKEN used to emphasize that you are talking about everything in a group of similar things, or everything that is involved in a particular activity: *They had everything at the party – a clown, face painting, games, the works.*
—see also **the whole SHEBANG**

worker

someone is a fast worker
used about someone who can get what they want very quickly, especially when starting a sexual relationship: *She's a fast worker – she's only been here a week, and she's trying to chase after Paul.*

world

⇨**live/be in a DREAM world**

(have/get) the best of both worlds
used to say that by combining two situations, ways of doing things, etc., you are getting all their advantages, and none of their disadvantages: *Now I have the best of both worlds. I can keep up my career and still spend time with my daughter.*
opposite **the worst of both worlds:** *This legislation discourages tobacco companies from building factories here, yet allows them to continue advertising, giving us the worst of both worlds.*

a brave new world
used about a new period that is starting after great changes have happened, especially when most people think the changes are good but you do not: *Welcome to the brave new world of*

college football, where new conferences and new TV deals are quickly changing a sport that has long prided itself on tradition and stability.

NOTE▶ This phrase comes from a line in Shakespeare's play "*The Tempest.*" It was also used by Aldous Huxley as the title of a book about a time in the future when everything is controlled using science, and people can make no choices for themselves.

do *someone* a world of good
SPOKEN to make someone feel much better than they do now: *The award did a world of good for my confidence. It helps to be recognized like that.*

for all the world like
(also **for all the world as if**)
used to emphasize that something looks or seems exactly like something else: *They rode off on their motorcycles looking for all the world like the evil bikers from Mad Max.*

not (do *something*) for the world
OLD-FASHIONED used to emphasize that you would never do something: *I couldn't leave my family for the world.*

have the ___ world at your feet
to be greatly admired by a particular group of people, and be given many opportunities because you are very good at doing a job, sport, etc.: *When Schmitt graduated from college in 1979, he had the corporate world at his feet, with more than 30 job offers to choose from.*

have the world at your feet
used to say that someone is very successful and popular and can get everything that they want from life: *The ten-year-old pianist and wonderchild could have the world at his feet, but he's not interested in fame.*

in a world of your own
not noticing what is happening around you because you are thinking about your own feelings, problems, interests, etc.: *When they're playing on the computer, they're in a world of their own.*

someone is dead to the world
used to say that someone is so deeply

asleep that they cannot be woken and do not react to anything: *"When did Shannon call?" "At about 10:00 – you were still dead to the world."*

someone **is not long for this world**
used to say that you do not think someone will live for very much longer: *I don't think Aunt Tillie is long for this world.*

mean/be the world to *someone*
used to say that someone or something is extremely important to someone: *This job means the world to her – she'll be devastated if she doesn't get it.*

move/come up in the world
used to say that a person or place is more successful, or has more money than they used to: *Sandy was ambitious and bright and wanted to move up in the world.*
opposite **come/go down in the world:** *The Jarvis family had clearly come down in the world since their grandfather built the mansion.*

the ___s of this world
used to show that a group of people are all similar in some way, by using one person's name to represent the whole group: *We all have to deal with the Frederick Smiths of this world – try not to let him upset you.*

on top of the world
extremely happy: *When we won the regional title, we were on top of the world.*

out of this world
used to emphasize that something is very good, large, impressive, etc.: *The demand for Star Trek souvenirs has been out of this world. Our first shipment sold out immediately.*

set the world on fire
to be new, exciting, and surprising, and receive a lot of attention ♦ OFTEN USED IN THE NEGATIVE: *Tony's a nice enough kid, but he'll never set the world on fire.*

(it's a) small world
SPOKEN said when you are surprised because you have met someone you know whom it was very unlikely that you would meet, or when you have found out that someone is connected to you in a way that you did not expect: *It's such a small world! At a party in Seattle I met a friend of a friend, who taught English in Singapore with one of my friends from high school.*

think the world of *someone*
to admire, respect, or like someone very much: *She was one of our best employees. The customers thought the world of her.*

watch the world go by
to sit somewhere pleasant and do nothing except watch people living their lives around you: *Most of the bars have terraces where you can sip a glass of beer and watch the world go by.*

what is the world coming to?
SPOKEN used to say that you are surprised and shocked at a situation or action that you do not approve of: *Three dollars for a grapefruit? What is the world coming to?*

what/why in the world...?
(also **how, where, who, etc. in the world...?**)
SPOKEN used to emphasize that you are very surprised by something because it does not seem sensible or normal: *What in the world did you do to your hair? | Why in the world would you want to name a dessert "blood orange"? It sounds disgusting!*

the world is your oyster
used to say that someone has lots of chances to do exciting or new things because they are young, rich, successful, etc.: *My father used to tell me that with a good education, the world would be my oyster.*

> NOTE▶ This idiom comes from a line in Shakespeare's play *"The Merry Wives of Windsor."*

a world of difference
a big difference: *There's a world of difference between being a great musician and being a great teacher of music.*

(*someone*** thinks) the world revolves around him/her**
SPOKEN used to say that someone thinks that they are more important than anyone else, and that everyone should pay attention to them: *I'm so glad I don't work with*

W

Jake – he thinks the world revolves around him and his stupid TV show.
(*someone* **thinks**) **the world revolves around** *something*: *To me, the world revolves around family, church, school, and community.*

be worlds apart
(also **be a world apart**)
to be very different: *College Station, a town of 50,000, is worlds apart from the intense atmosphere of Washington.*

worm

⇨a worm's-eye **VIEW** (of *something*)

someone must have had worms for breakfast
SPOKEN used to say that someone cannot sit still: *What's the matter with you this morning?   Did you have worms for breakfast?*
—see also **have ANTS in your pants**

the worm turns
used to say that someone who is usually very quiet or does not complain when they are treated badly, suddenly starts to behave differently and fight against the way they are being treated: *Michael used to bully the other boys, especially Patrick, but I don't think he ever expected the worm to turn.*

worse

⇨be/look none the worse for **WEAR**
⇨be/look the worse for **WEAR**

if worse comes to worst
used before a statement in order to suggest that there is a solution to your problems, even if the problems develop in the worst possible way: *If worse comes to worst and we lose the house, we can always move in with Annie's parents.*

worst

⇨the worst of both worlds —see
   (have/get) the best of both **WORLDs**

worth

⇨do *something* for **ALL** you are worth
⇨for **WHAT** it's worth
⇨**WHAT's** it worth (to *someone*)

wouldn't

wouldn't you (just) know it
1 SPOKEN said when you are slightly annoyed because something unexpected has happened, especially something that causes problems for you: *The drive into the mountains was beautiful, but wouldn't you just know it, it started raining as soon as we got out of the car.*
2 SPOKEN said when someone says something that you agree with, although you did not want to be the person to say it: *"He listens to music like 'Jane's Addiction' and all that stuff." "Wouldn't you know it!"*

wounds

⇨rub **SALT** in/into *someone's* **wounds**

lick your wounds
to think about and get used to a situation or event that has publicly embarrassed or disappointed you a lot ♦ OFTEN USED IN NEWSPAPERS, ON TELEVISION NEWS, ETC.: *Gold dealers are licking their wounds after the sharpest single-day drop in the price of gold in recent memory.*

wraps

keep *something* under wraps
to keep something secret from the public ♦ OFTEN USED IN BUSINESS AND POLITICS: *The report is being kept tightly under wraps to avoid controversy.*
be under wraps: *The guest list is still under wraps, but there will be plenty of celebrities on hand.*

take the wraps off *something*
to tell people about a new plan, product, etc. for the first time ♦ OFTEN USED IN BUSINESS AND POLITICS: *Renault is set to take the wraps off what it claims is the first eco-friendly car.*

wreck

be a nervous wreck
used about someone who is extremely nervous or anxious: *Davis was always a nervous wreck before she went on stage.*

be a nervous wreck

wringer

go through the wringer
to have a long, unpleasant and difficult experience so that you feel sick or physically and mentally tired: *Jodie only played for fifteen minutes, but she felt like she'd been through the wringer.*
be put through the wringer: *Because of the publicity in celebrity divorce cases, it is often the children of the couple who are put through the wringer.*

writ

writ large
FORMAL used to emphasize that something is in its most extreme or noticeable form: *The United Nations is an example of democracy writ large.*

write
⇨**THAT's all she wrote**

writing

the writing on the wall
(also **the handwriting on the wall**)
something that makes people realize that a situation is going to become difficult or unpleasant: *The rejection of Seascape's latest building proposal by the planning commission is the handwriting on the wall.*

> NOTE▶ This idiom comes from a story in the book of *Daniel* in the Bible, in which the King of Babylon sees a hand writing on the wall. The writing says that an enemy will kill him and take his power.

wrong
⇨**DO** *someone* **wrong**

don't get me wrong
SPOKEN used before you give an opinion in order to emphasize exactly what it is so that people do not think that you are trying to say something else: *Don't get me wrong – I like Jackson's music; it's just that this isn't my favorite album.*

two wrongs don't make a right
used to say that just because someone has done something harmful or unfair to you, this does not mean that you should do the same type of thing to them: *Going to war is not the answer. Two wrongs don't make a right, and we should try to solve this through diplomacy.*

you can't go wrong (with)
SPOKEN used to say it is best to do or use something because no one will be upset, offended, or annoyed by it: *I'll just get her a gift certificate from a CD store. You can't go wrong with that.*

W

Y

yadda

yadda yadda (yadda)
(also **yada yada (yada)**)
SPOKEN used to show that what someone is saying is very boring, especially because you have heard it many times before: *I began to give my daughter "the lecture" – the one about her being the older one, responsible for setting a good example... yadda, yadda, yadda.*

yard

⇨**not in my back yard** —see **not in my BACKYARD**

the whole nine yards
used to emphasize that you are talking about everything in a group of similar things, or everything that is involved in a particular activity: *I remember our high school prom. We had long dresses, white gloves, limousines – the whole nine yards.*

yarn

spin a yarn
to tell a long story, or give a long, and often untrue, explanation or excuse for something: *Jerry and Dave never failed to disagree, and they could both spin a delightful yarn about topics as obscure as 19th-century vice-presidential candidates.*

years

not/never in a million years
SPOKEN used to say that you are very unlikely to do something: *"Can you imagine Jerry going to an art gallery?" "No way, not in a million years."*

something **puts years on** *someone*
(also *something* **puts ten, fifteen, etc. years on** *someone*)
SPOKEN used to say that something, often a bad experience, makes someone look older: *It puts ten years on you when you wear your hair that way.*
opposite **take years off** *someone*: *She's lost a little weight, and it's taken years off her.*

yes

yes and no
SPOKEN used to show that there is not one clear answer to a question: *"Are you happy with your new job?" "Well, yes and no."*

yesterday

I wasn't born yesterday!
(also **do you think I was born yesterday?**)
SPOKEN said when you are angry because someone is treating you as if you were stupid, especially when you think they are trying to trick you: *Do you think I'm going to believe that? I wasn't born yesterday, you know!*

yet

yet again
used to emphasize that something that has happened many times before is happening again, especially if it is something bad or unpleasant: *Yet again, the Twins have failed to hold on to an early-game lead. This time, they lost to the Yankees 5–3.*

ying yang

⇨**have** *something* **up the ying yang** —
see **have** *something* **(coming) out the WAZOO/ kazoo**

yonder

the wild/wide blue yonder
OLD-FASHIONED the sky: *Sleek fighter planes roared off into the wild blue yonder, leaving white trails behind them.*

you

⇨**BETTER you than me**
⇨**it's/that's UP to you**
⇨**you can KEEP** *something*
⇨**you can SAY that again**
⇨**you can't TAKE** *someone* **anywhere**
⇨**you said it SAY**
⇨**you'd BETTER believe** *something*
⇨**you've got me THERE**

yours

⇨**UP yours!**

Z

zone

a ___-free zone

SPOKEN a humorous expression used in order to say that a particular activity does not happen in a particular place, especially because it is not allowed: *Mayor Brown has considered closing Market Street to cars, making the area an automobile-free zone.* | *We couldn't find a decent place to have a cup of coffee.*

The whole town was like a caffeine-free zone.

> NOTE▶ This idiom comes from expressions such as "military-free zone," "nuclear-free zone," and "weapons-free zone," which are often used in agreements between governments or political organizations.

Z's

catch some Z's

SLANG to sleep: *"You look tired." "Yeah, I'm going home to catch some Z's."*

Exercises

Exercise 1

Match the idiom with its meaning.

1 After ten years of dating, Sarah and Mike finally decided to *tie the knot*. ....
2 Although everyone trusted her, Angie was *in cahoots with* Joe to gain control of the company. ....
3 Isabel was able *to turn the tables* on her captor when she found his gun. ....
4 Anton *was a shoo-in* to win the election because he was popular with women and minority voters. ....
5 Because of her liberal beliefs, Mia *was* often *at odds with* her very conservative father. ....
6 The students *were up in arms* when the chancellor closed the university. ....

a to work secretly with someone, especially to do something dishonest
b to get married
c to disagree with someone
d to protest something you are angry about
e to be very likely to win an election, competition, or be chosen for a job
f to suddenly gain an advantage over someone who is in a stronger position

Exercise 2

Complete each item with the correct idiom

a smart aleck   **b** shrinking violet   **c** red flag   **d** Achilles' heel   **e** cold fish
f dark horse

1 When the restaurant manager noticed that pages were missing from the accounting records, it was an immediate ....
2 Dana's mother knew that she was a .... , so she did not try to defend her when the school principal called.
3 Juliet was considered a .... for the award, but she won it by a solid majority.
4 Although popular with many voters, Ladd's .... was his connection to organized crime.
5 I used to think of my cousin Marvin as a .... , but he has helped me on a number of occasions.
6 Although he's an aggressive athlete on the field, off the field, Damon is a ....

Exercise 3

Animal idioms: Choose the correct animal to complete the idiom.

  a horse **b** monkey **c** mouse **d** dog **e** cat **f** bird

1 Although people consider him a talented filmmaker, his last production is *a* .... *on his back* because it lost more money than any other movie in history.
2 "I can't eat this! It's awful! It could *choke a* .... !" exclaimed Brett.
3 It was a pleasure meeting your aunt. She is an interesting person, *a rare*......... indeed.
4 Many of the President's critics considered his appearance at a children's hospital a .... *-and-pony-show*, organized to impress the voters.
5 Rick had to be *as quiet as a* .... when he left, otherwise he would wake his children.
6 After winning the election, Wilson promised not to become *a fat* .... like so many of the other representatives in Washington.

Exercise 4

Food idioms: Choose the correct food to complete the idioms.

  a carrot **b** apple **c** cucumber **d** fruit **e** salad **f** nut

1 Although the woman's son was trapped under the car, she was *cool as a* .... when she called for help.
2 Despite having a high income, Shari's attitude toward money has not changed since her .... *days*. She still saves as much as she can.
3 The coach used both *the* .... *and the stick* to get his team to train harder.
4 The abandoned mine became *forbidden* .... as soon as the authorities warned the children to stay away from it.
5 At first, Roz was a *tough* .... *to crack*, but she has been a loyal friend for years.
6 The teacher knew that the new student was *a bad* .... as soon as other students began to imitate his disruptive behavior.

Exercise 5

Circle the meaning of each idiom.

1 Clint's solution will help us *in the short run*, but we'll have the same problem again in five years.
  a many years from now
  b in the immediate future
2 Ada often bought things she didn't really like in her effort to *keep up with the Joneses.*
  a appear as successful as her neighbors
  b distinguish herself from others

3 Teaching the most advanced class always *kept the professors on their toes*.
   a made the professors more alert
   b made the professors uncomfortable

4 Meg can stay up all night and *be none the worse for wear* the next day.
   a look tired and sick
   b look fairly good

5 Plans for buying new police cars were *put on the back burner* when the fire destroyed the town's hospital.
   a delayed
   b moved forward

6 Everyone likes Fischer, but *the jury is still out* on his ability to manage the department.
   a people don't agree
   b people don't know enough to decide

Exercise 6

Match the comments and the responses.

1 I'm upset. I really thought we would win the match. ....
2 Have you seen her dress? It's awful! ....
3 Sylvia doesn't like any of the ideas for the party. ....
4 My dad bought me a car! ....
5 What did you think about the chemistry seminar? ....
6 Tara followed me around campus all day. ....

a There's no accounting for taste.
b I was bored out of my mind.
c Tomorrow is another day.
d She's a wet blanket.
e She's got it bad for you.
f Wonders will never cease.

Exercise 7

Color idioms: Choose the correct color to complete the idioms.
   a blue   **b** black   **c** red   **d** white   **e** green   **f** pink

1 To avoid misunderstandings, the head of our department won't agree to anything unless it is *in black and* ....
2 Joan was *tickled* .... that her coworkers had organized a surprise party for her.
3 Other school districts are .... *with envy* because of our new library.
4 *Out of the* .... , Lisa's husband came home from work and asked for a divorce.
5 When his assistant criticized his report, Eric *saw* ....
6 After years of working hard, the Lees were finally *in the* ....

Exercise 8

Are the idioms used correctly? Write C for *correct* or I for *incorrect*.

1 Trent *put a damper on the evening* by bringing the host's old girlfriend to the party. ....
2 Kendra has been the receptionist for such a long time that she's become *part of the furniture*. ....
3 Jim's jokes are always funny and polite. Everyone thinks he is *beyond the pale*.
   ....
4 When his professor gave him a low grade on his paper, Alan *rolled with the punches* and dropped the class. ....
5 The team *felt out of sorts* because they finished the project two days early. ....
6 When the lawyer didn't follow the proper procedures, the judge *came down on her like a ton of bricks*. ....

Exercise 9

Success and failure: Write S if the idiom refers to *success* or F if it refers to *failure*.

1 The Russians made *a clean sweep* of the figure skating championships when they finished first, second, and third. ....
2 Yuko *has a way with animals*, so she is planning to become a vet. ....
3 After Lily's throat surgery, her singing career was *washed-up*. ....
4 The new advertising campaign has worked *like a charm* by increasing the company's profits more than 75%. ....
5 When interest rates were raised, the US housing market *went into a tailspin* because it was too expensive to buy a home. ....
6 The gymnast's career *hit the skids* when his trainer died. ....

Exercise 10

Number idioms: Choose the correct number to complete the idioms.

a ten **b** five **c** six **d** two **e** eight **f** forty

1 Some directors won't hire that actor as a romantic lead because they think she is on the wrong side of ....
2 .... to one he doesn't pass his final exam.
3 I'm hurrying! I'll be ready in .... shakes!
4 I don't mind if we walk or take the bus. It's really .... of one, half dozen of the other to me.
5 The coach told us to take .... before beginning the last hour of practice.
6 The Congressman found himself behind the .... ball when the newspapers published an article about his recent stock purchases.

Exercise 11

Match the beginnings and ends of the sentences.

1 My college roommate was a *walking encyclopedia* who ....
2 The reporter started to fall asleep during the press conference because he ....
3 George was unable to manage his team effectively because he ....
4 Debbie had the *best of both worlds* as a child because her family ....
5 Rod and Beth disliked seeing other tourists during their vacation, so they ....
6 Greta was the *ace in the hole* because she ....

a ...was *bored stiff.*
b ...had a home in the country and an apartment in the city.
c ...could answer anything immediately.
d ...was unwilling *to look at the big picture.*
e ...traveled *off the beaten track.*
f ...could both illustrate and design the books.

Exercise 12

Complete the paragraph using each idiom once. You may have to change the verb forms.

a not lift a finger **b** as thick as thieves **c** roll up his sleeves **d** the third wheel
e bad blood **f** go up in smoke

Although there's (1)..................... between Tim and Pablo now, they used to be best friends. They used to do everything together, and people often remarked that they were (2)..................... , sometimes making others feel like (3)..................... . However, their friendship (4)..................... when they had to do a science project together. Pablo (5)..................... and made an effort to do his best. However, despite his promises to help, Tim would (6)..................... . Since then, Pablo has refused to speak to Tim.

Exercise 13

Courage and fear: Write C if the idiom refers to *courage* or F if it refers to *fear*.

1 Although the doctors didn't think he would ever walk again, Li knew it was just *mind over matter*, and within a year, he could run. ....
2 I had wanted to see the movie, but it really *gave me the shivers*. ....
3 Relief workers often *risk their necks* to get aid to the people who need it most. ....
4 Ted *was a bundle of nerves* until his daughter telephoned from the airport. ....
5 Carly's *heart was in her mouth* when she stepped onto the stage for the first time. ....
6 Angelo decided to become a paramedic because he had always wanted *to put his head in the lion's mouth*. ....

Exercise 14

Parts of the body: Choose the correct body part to complete the idioms.

a arm **b** leg **c** foot **d** eye **e** ear **f** hand

1 Jake has had his .... on that sports car for months.
2 Ken's mother put her .... down and demanded that he help around the house.
3 I sent the new employee to Jenny because she'll hold her .... until she learns the procedures.
4 Sheila was furious when she discovered that she hadn't won the lottery, but that her husband had only been pulling her ....
5 Lorena didn't want to go bowling, but after her friends twisted her ...., she went.
6 Ivan is a nice person, but last time I saw him, he bent my .... for an hour talking about his new apartment.

Exercise 15

Complete each idiom with the correct form of the verb.

1 In an effort to .... steam, Tyler went to the gym. (blow off)
2 The media .... dirt on all the Senators as soon as the Vice President's scandalous affairs became public knowledge. (dig up)
3 I have to .... the kinks before I apply for a patent. (work out)
4 David must .... his ways if he expects to live until thirty-five. (change)
5 Minoru .... in his father's footsteps and became a journalist. (follow)
6 As head of the department, Melanie .... on the firing line when two professors suddenly left. (is)

Exercise 16

Choose the correct idiom.

1 If our manager leaves, it will be difficult to find someone to ....
   a fill her shoes **b** be in her shoes
2 Michelle thought that Charles was a great movie director, but when he asked her to perform nude, she thought he ....
   a had crossed the line
   b had drawn the line
3 Martin was very good at .... , but he was usually not able to manage a team or complete his plans.
   a keeping the wheels turning
   b setting the wheels in the motion

4 Everyone knew that Ryan .... for the job because he was the only candidate who knew all the members of the hiring committee.

  a had the inside track

  b was on the fast track

5 The man's wallet was stolen when he .... and left his pocket open.

  a lowered his guard **b** was on his guard

6 Carlos had many problems of his own to think about, so he .... while his friend complained.

  a lent an ear **b** listened with half an ear

Exercise 17

Unscramble the words to make idioms. You may need to change the verb forms.

1 When Alison found another woman's sweater in her boyfriend's car, she
.... (off the handle fly)

2 The apartment .... once they started renting it to university students. (seed go to)

3 Charlie was caught in a terrible avalanche, but he
.... (tale the to live tell)

4 Bruce's wife .... of his decision to leave his well-paying job. (view dim a take of)

5 Emilio .... when he wears a tuxedo. (like dollars a look million)

6 After the earthquake, all the doctors in the city
.... (put be on alert red)

Exercise 18

Circle the idiom that is most different in meaning from the other two. The key word is underlined.

1 **a** bring down the <u>house</u> **b** knock your <u>socks</u> off **c** fan the <u>flames</u>

2 **a** the <u>time</u> is ripe **b** get in under the <u>wire</u> **c** the eleventh <u>hour</u>

3 **a** different <u>strokes</u> for different folks

  b there's more than one <u>way</u> to skin a cat **c** it takes all <u>kinds</u>

4 **a** go under the <u>knife</u> **b** crack the <u>whip</u>

  c <u>run</u> somebody ragged

5 **a** roll with the <u>punches</u> **b** take something on the <u>chin</u> **c** foam at the <u>mouth</u>

6 **a** send a <u>chill</u> down your spine **b** be a <u>scream</u>

  c scare someone out of their wits

Exercise 19

Find the idiom. Use the key word to find an idiom that can replace the words in italics. You may have to change the forms of some of the words.

1 Don't *continue asking for favors*, or I'll stop collecting your mail when you go away. (luck)

....

2 My brother can *always criticize* my plans, but he can never offer any suggestions. (holes)

....

3 Amy *made a bad situation worse* when she refused to follow the policies that she didn't like. (nest)

....

4 Margaret was very friendly and helpful to everyone. *She would give you anything.* (shirt)

....

5 Elena *always knows exactly what is happening*, so do all your work before you leave. (trick)

....

6 I have an old stereo that is *not being used*. If you want it, you can have it. (dust)

....

Exercise 20

Some idioms have more than one meaning. Look up the idioms and write the number of the correct meaning. If you can't find an idiom, use a different key word.

1 Derrick is a great friend, but he often annoys me because he only sees things *in black and white*. ....

2 Julie was happy when she had her baby because it was difficult being pregnant during the *dog days*. ....

3 The coach told Pam that she was *out of line* for missing practice. ....

4 I never deposit my money at an automated teller machine. I prefer giving my money to *a warm body*. ....

5 Let's *put this issue to bed* so that we can leave before midnight. ....

6 The Senator *made good* on his offer to support the farmers in Washington. ....

The Longman Defining Vocabulary

Words used in the definitions in this dictionary

All the definitions in this dictionary have been written using the words on this list.

The Defining Vocabulary has been carefully chosen after a thorough study of all the well-known frequency lists of English words. Furthermore, only the most common and "central" meanings of the words on the list have actually been used in definitions. We have also used a special computer program that checks every entry to ensure that words from outside the Defining Vocabulary do not appear in definitions.

Word class restrictions

For some words in the list, a word class label such as *n* or *adj* is shown. This means that this particular word is used in definitions only in the word class shown. So **age**, for example, is used only as a noun and not as a verb. But if no word class is shown for a word, it can be used in any of its most common word classes: **answer**, for example, is used in definitions both as a noun and as a verb.

Compound words

Definitions occasionally include compound words formed from words in the Defining Vocabulary, but this is only done if the meaning is completely clear. For example, the word **businessman** (formed from **business** and **man**) is used in some definitions.

Prefixes and suffixes

The main list is followed by a list of common prefixes and suffixes. These can be added to words in the main list to form derived words, provided the meaning is completely clear. For example, the word **walking** (formed by adding **-ing** to **walk**) is used in some definitions.

Phrasal verbs

Phrasal verbs formed by combining words in the Defining Vocabulary (for example, **put up with something**) are NOT used in definitions in the dictionary, except in a very small number of cases where the phrasal verb is extremely common and there is no common equivalent. So, for example, **give something up** (as in give up smoking) and **take off** (as in the plane **took off**) are occasionally used.

Proper nouns

The Defining Vocabulary does not include the names of actual places, nationalities, religions, and so on, which are occasionally mentioned in definitions.

A

a
abbreviation
ability
able
about
above *adv*, *prep*
abroad
absence
absent *adj*
accept
acceptable
accident
according (to)
account *n*
achieve

acid
across
act
action
active
activity
actor, actress
actual
add
addition
address
adjective
admiration
admire
admit
adult

advanced
advantage
adventure
adverb
advertise
advertisement
advice
advise
affair
affect
afford
afraid
after *adv*, *conj*, *prep*
afternoon
afterward
again

against
age *n*
ago
agree
agreement
ahead
aim
air *n*
aircraft
airport
alcohol
alive
all *adv*, *determiner*,
predeterminer, *pron*
allow
almost
alone
along
alphabet
already
also
although
always
among
amount *n*
amuse
amusement
amusing
an
ancient
and
anger *n*
angle
angry
animal
announce
announcement
annoy
another
answer
anxiety
anxious
any
anymore
anyone
anything
anywhere
apart
apartment
appear
appearance
apple
appropriate
approval
approve

area
argue
argument
arm
army
around
arrange
arrangement
arrival
arrive
art
article
artificial
artist
as
ash
ashamed
ask
asleep
association
at
atom
attach
attack
attempt
attend
attention
attitude
attract
attractive
authority
available
average *adj*, *n*
avoid
awake
away
awkward

B

baby
back *adj*, *adv*, *n*
background
backward(s) *adv*
bad
bag *n*
bake
balance
ball
band *n*
bank *n*
bar *n*
barely
base *n*, *v*
baseball
basic

basket
basketball
bath
bathtub
battle *n*
be
beach
beak
beam *n*
bean
bear
beard
beat
beautiful
beauty
because
become
bed
beer
before
begin
beginning
behave
behavior
behind *adv*, *prep*
belief
believe
bell
belong
below *adv*, *prep*
belt *n*
bend
beneath
berry
beside(s)
best *adj*, *adv*, *n*
better *adj*, *adv*
between
beyond *adv*, *prep*
bicycle *n*
big
bill *n*
bird
birth
bite
bitter
black
blade
blame
bleed
blind
block
blood
blow
blue

board
boat
body
boil
bomb
bone
book *n*
boot *n*
border
bored
boring
born
borrow
both
bottle
bottom *n*
bowl *n*
box *n*
boy
brain
branch
brave
bread
break *v*
breakfast
breast
breath
breathe
breed
brick
bridge *n*
bright
bring
broad *adj*
broadcast
brother
brown *adj, n*
brush
bucket
build *v*
building
bullet
bunch *n*
burn
burst
bury
bus *n*
bush
business
busy
but *conj*
butter *n*
button *n*
buy *v*
by

C

cake
calculate
call
calm
camera
camp
can *n, v*
candy
cap *n*
capital
car
card
care
careful
careless
carriage
carry
case *n*
castle
cat
catch *v*
cattle
cause
ceiling
celebrate
cell
cent
center *n*
centimeter
central
century
ceremony
certain
chain
chair
chance
change
character
charge
chase *v*
cheap
cheat *v*
check
cheek
cheerful
cheese
chemical
chemistry
chest
chicken
chief
child, children
chin
chocolate

choice
choose
church
cigarette
circle *n*
circular
citizen
city
claim
class
clay
clean
clear
clerk
clever
cliff
climb *v*
clock
close
cloth
clothes, clothing
cloud
club
coal
coast *n*
coat
coffee
coin
cold
collar
collect *v*
college
color
comb
combination
combine *v*
come
comfort
comfortable
command
committee
common
communicate
communication
company
compare
comparison
compete
competition
competitor
complain
complaint
complete
compound *n*
computer

concern *v*
concerning
concert
condition *n*
confidence
confident
confuse
connect
connection
conscious
consider
consist
container
continue
continuous
contract *n*
control
convenient
conversation
cook
cookie
cool
copy
corn
corner *n*
correct *adj*
cost
cotton
cough
could
council
country
courage
course
court
cover
cow
crack
crash
crazy
cream
creature
crime
criminal
criticism
criticize
crop *n*
cross *n, v*
crowd *n*
cruel
crush *v*
cry
cup
cupboard
cure

curl
current *n*
curtain
curve
customer
cut

D

daily *adj, adv*
damage
dance
danger
dangerous
dark
date *n*
daughter
day
dead
deal *n*
deal with
death
debt
decay
deceit
deceive
decide
decision
decorate
decoration
decrease
deep
defeat
defense
defend
definite
degree
delay
deliberate
delicate
deliver
demand
department
depend
dependent
depth
describe
description
desert
deserve
design
desirable
desire
desk
destroy
destruction

detail *n*
determination
determined
develop
dictionary
die *v*
difference
different
difficult
difficulty
dig
dinner
dip *v*
direct
direction
dirt
dirty
disappoint
discover
discovery
discuss
discussion
disease
dish
dismiss
distance *n*
distant
divide *v*
do
doctor
document
dog
dollar
door
double *adj, v*
doubt
down *adv, prep*
draw *v*
drawer
dream
dress
drink
drive
drop
drug
drum *n*
drunk *past participle, adj*
dry
duck *n*
dull
during
dust *n*
duty

E

each
eager
ear
early
earn
earth
east
eastern
easy
eat
economic
edge
educate
educated
education
effect
effective
effort
egg
eight
eighth
either
elbow
elect
election
electric
electricity
electronic
else
embarrass
emotion
emphasize
employ
employer
employment
empty
enclose
encourage
end
enemy
energy
engine
engineer
enjoy
enjoyable
enjoyment
enough
enter
entertain
entertainment
entrance
envelope
environment
equal

equipment
escape
especially
establish
even *adj, adv*
evening
event
ever
every
everyone
everything
everywhere
evil
exact
examination
examine
example
excellent
except *conj, prep*
exchange
excite
excited
exciting
excuse
exercise
exist
existence
expect
expensive
experience
explain
explanation
explode
explosion
explosive
express *v*
expression
extreme
eye
eyelid

F

face
fact
factory
fail
failure
faint *adj, v*
fair *adj*
fairly
faith
faithful
fall
false
familiar

family
famous
far
farm
farmer
farther
farthest
fashion
fashionable
fast *adj, adv*
fasten
fat
father
fault *n*
favorable
favorite
fear
feather
feature
feed *v*
feel *v*
feeling(s)
female
fence
fever
few
field *n*
fierce
fifth
fight
figure *n*
fill *v*
film
final *adj*
finally
financial
find *v*
find out
fine *adj*
finger
finish
fire
firm *adj, n*
first *adv, determiner*
fish
fit *adj, v*
five
fix
flag
flame
flash
flat
flesh
flight
float

flood
floor
flour
flow
flower
fly
fold
follow
food
foot *n*
football
for *prep*
forbid
force
foreign
forest
forever
forget
forgive
fork
form
formal
former
fortunate
forward(s) *adv*
four(th)
frame *n*
free
freedom
freeze
frequent *adj*
fresh
friend
friendly
frighten
frightening
from
front *adj, n*
fruit
full
fun
funeral
funny
fur
furniture
further
future

G

gain
gallon
game
garage
garden
gas

gasoline
gate
gather
general
generally
generous
gentle
get
gift
girl
give
glad
glass
glue
go
goat
god, God
gold
good
goodbye
goods
govern
government
graceful
grade
gradual
grain
gram
grammar
grand *adj*
grandfather
grandmother
grandparent
grass
grateful
grave *n*
gray *adj, n*
great
green
greet
greeting
ground
group *n*
grow
growth
guard *v*
guess *v*
guest
guide
guilty
gun

H

habit
hair

half
hall
hammer *n*
hand *n*
handle
hang
happen
happy
hard
hardly
harm
harmful
hat
hate *v*
hatred
have
he
head *n*
health
healthy
hear
heart
heat
heaven
heavy
heel
height
hello
help
helpful
her(s)
here
herself
hide *v*
high
high school
hill
him
himself
his
historical
history
hit *v*
hold
hole
holiday
hollow *adj*
holy
home *adv, n*
honest
honor *n*
hook *n*
hope
hopeful
horn

horse *n*
hospital
host
hot
hotel
hour
house *n*
how
human
humorous
humor
hundred(th)
hungry
hunt *v*
hurry
hurt
husband

I

ice *n*
idea
if
ignore
ill
illegal
illness
image
imaginary
imagination
imagine
immediate
immediately
importance
important
impressive
improve
improvement
in *adv, prep*
inch
include
including
income
increase
independent
indoor(s)
industrial
industry
infect
infection
infectious
influence
inform
information
injure
injury

ink
inner
insect
inside
instead
institution
instruction
instrument
insult *v*
insurance
insure
intelligence
intelligent
intend
intention
interest
interesting
international
interrupt
into
introduce
introduction
invent
invitation
invite
involve
inward(s)
iron *adj, n*
island
it
its
itself

J

jaw
jewel
jewelry
job
join
joint
joke
judge
judgment
juice
jump
just *adv*
justice

K

keep *v*
key *n*
kick
kill
kilogram
kilometer

kind
king
kiss
kitchen
knee
kneel
knife
knock
knot
know *v*
knowledge

L

lack
lady
lake
lamb
lamp
land
language
last *adv, determiner*
late
lately
laugh
laughter
law
lawyer
lay
layer *n*
lazy
lead *v*
leaf
lean
learn
least
leather
leave
left
leg
legal
lend
length
less
lesson
let
let go of
let out
letter
level *adj, n*
library
lid
lie
lie down
life
lift

light
like *prep, v*
likely
limit
line *n*
lion
lip
liquid
list *n*
listen
literature
liter
little
live *v*
load
loaf *n*
local
lock
lonely
long
look
look for
loose
lose
loss
lot
loud
love
low *adj*
lower *v*
loyal
loyalty
luck
lucky
lung

M
machine
machinery
magazine
magic
mail
main
make
make into
make up
male
man
manage
manager
manner
many
map
march
mark *n*

market *n*
marriage
married
marry
match
material
mathematics
matter
may
me
meal
mean *v*
meaning
means
measure
meat
medical
medicine
meet
meeting
melt
member
memory
mental
mention *v*
mess
message
messy
metal
method
meter
middle *adj, n*
might *v*
mile
military *adj*
milk
million(th)
mind
mine *n, pron*
mineral
minister
minute *n*
mirror
miss
mist
mistake
mix *v*
mixture
model *n*
modern
moment
money
monkey
month
monthly

moon
moral *adj*
more
morning
most
mother
motor
mountain
mouse
mouth
move *v*
movement
much
mud
multiply
murder
muscle
music
musician
must
my
mysterious
mystery

N
nail
name
narrow
nasty
nation
national
natural
nature
navy
near *adj, adv, prep*
nearly
neat
necessary
neck
need
needle
negative
neither
nerve
nervous
nest
net
network
never
new
news
newspaper
next
nice
night

nine
ninth
no *adv, determiner*
noise
none
nonsense
no one
nor
normal
north
northern
nose
not
note
nothing
notice
noun
now
nowhere
number *n*
nurse
nut

O

obey
object *n*
obtain
occasion
ocean
o'clock
odd
of
off *adv, prep*
offense
offend
offensive *adj*
offer
office
officer
official
often
oil *n*
old
old-fashioned
on *adv, prep*
once
one
onion
only
onto
open *adj, v*
operate
operation
opinion
opponent

opportunity
oppose
as opposed to
opposite
opposition
or
orange
order
ordinary
organ
organize
organization
origin
original
other
ought
our(s)
out *adj, adv*
outdoor(s)
outer
outside
over *adv, prep*
owe
own *determiner*
owner
oxygen

P

pack *v*
package
page *n*
pain
painful
paint
painting
pair *n*
pale
pan
pants
paper
parallel
parent
park
part *n*
particular
partly
partner
party *n*
pass *v*
passage
passenger
past
path
patience
patient *adj*

pattern *n*
pause
pay
payment
peace
peaceful
pen
pencil
people
pepper
per
perfect *adj*
perform
performance
perhaps
period
permanent
permission
person
personal
persuade
pet *n*
photograph
phrase
physical
piano
pick *v*
pick up
picture *n*
piece *n*
pig
pile *n*
pilot *n*
pin
pink
pipe *n*
pity
place
plain *adj, n*
plan
plane
plant
plastic
plate
play
pleasant
please
pleased
pleasure
plenty
plural
pocket
poem
poet
poetry

point
pointed
poison
poisonous
pole
police
polish
polite
political
politician
politics
pool *n*
poor
popular
population
port
position *n*
positive
possess
possession
possible
possibility
possibly
post
pot *n*
potato
pound *n*
pour
powder *n*
power *n*
powerful
practical
practice
praise
pray
prayer
prefer
preparation
prepare
present *adj, n*
preserve
president
press *v*
pressure *n*
pretend
pretty *adj*
prevent
previous
previously
price *n*
priest
prince
principle
print
prison

prisoner
private *adj*
prize *n*
probably
problem
process *n*
produce *v*
product
production
profession
profit *n*
program
progress *n*
promise
pronounce
pronunciation
proof
property
proposal
protect
protection
protective
protest
proud
prove
provide
public
publicly
pull
pump
punish
punishment
pure
purple
purpose
push
put

Q

quality
quantity
quarrel
quarter *n*
queen
question
quick
quiet *adj, n*

R

rabbit
race
radio
railroad
rain
raise *v*

range *n*
rank *n*
rapid
rare
rat
rate *n*
rather
raw
reach
react
reaction
read *v*
ready
real
realize
really
reason
reasonable
receive
recent
recently
recognize
record *n, v*
red
reduce
reduction
refusal
refuse *v*
regard *v*
regular
related
relative
relation
relationship
relax
religion
religious
remain
remark *n*
remember
remind
remove
rent
repair
repeat *v*
reply
report
represent
representative *n*
request *n*
respect
responsible
rest
restaurant
restrict

result
return
reward
rice
rich
rid
ride
right
ring
ripe
rise
risk
river
road
rob
rock *n*
roll *v*
romantic *adj*
roof
room
root
rope
rose
rough
round *adj*
row
royal
rub
rubber
rude
ruin
rule
ruler
run
rush *v*

S

sad
safe *adj*
safety
sail
salary
sale
salt
same
sand *n*
satisfaction
satisfactory
satisfy
save
say *v*
scale *n*
scatter
scene
school

science
scientific
scientist
scissors
screen
screw
sea
search
season *n*
seat
second *adv, determiner, n*
secrecy
secret
secretary
see
seed
seem
seize
sell
send
sensation
sense
sensible
sensitive
sentence
separate
serious
seriously
servant
serve
service
set
settle
seven(th)
several
severe
sew
sex
sexual
shade
shadow
shake
shame *n*
shape
share
sharp
she
sheep
sheet
shelf
shell *n*
shelter
shine *v*
shiny
ship *n*

shirt
shock
shoe
shoot
shop
shore
short
shot
should
shoulder
shout
show
shut
shy
sick
sickness
side
sideways
sight *n*
sign
signal
silence *n*
silent
silk
silly
silver
similar
similarity
simple
since
sincere
sing
single
singular
sink *v*
sister
sit
situation
six(th)
size *n*
skill
skillful
skin
skirt
sky
slave
sleep
slide *v*
slight
slip *v*
slippery
slope
slow
small
smart

smell
smile
smoke
smooth
snake
snow
so
soap
social
society
sock
soft
soil
soldier
solid
solution
solve
some *determiner, pron*
somehow
someone
something
sometimes
somewhere
son
song
soon
sore *adj*
sorrow
sorry
sort *n*
soul
sound *n, v*
soup
sour
south
southern
space *n*
spade
speak
special *adj*
specific
speech
speed *n*
spell *v*
spend
spin *v*
spirit
in spite of
split
spoil
spoon
sport(s)
spot *n*
spread *v*
spring

square
stage *n*
stair
stamp
stand *v*
standard
star *n*
start
state
statement
station
stay
steady
steal
steam
steel
steep
stem
step
stick
sticky
stiff
still
sting
stitch
stomach
stone
stop
store
storm *n*
story
straight
strange
stranger
stream *n*
street
strength
stretch
strict
strike *v*
string *n*
strong
structure *n*
struggle
student
study
stupid
style *n*
subject *n*
substance
subtract
succeed
success
successful
such

suck
sudden
suffer
sugar
suggest
suit
suitable
suitcase
sum
summer
sun
supper
supply
support
suppose
sure
surface
surprise
surround
swallow *v*
swear
sweep
sweet
swell
swim
swing
sword
sympathetic
sympathy
system

T

table
tail
take
take care of
talk
tall
taste
tax
taxi
tea
teach
team
tear
technical
telephone
television
tell
temper
temperature
temporary
ten(th)
tend
tendency

tennis
tense
tent
terrible
terror
test
than
thank
that
the
theater
their(s)
them
then
there
therefore
these
they
thick
thief
thin
thing
think
third
this
thorough
those
though
thought
thousand(th)
thread
threat
threaten
three
throat
through
throw
thumb
ticket
tie
tiger
tight
time *n*
tire *v*
tired
tiring
title
to
tobacco
today
toe
together
toilet
tomorrow
tongue

tonight
too
tool
tooth
top *adj*, *n*
total *adj*, *n*
touch
tour
tourist
toward
tower
town
toy
track
trade *n*
tradition
traditional
traffic
train
training
translate
transparent
trap
travel
treat *v*
treatment
tree
tribe
trick
trip *n*
tropical
trouble
truck
true
trunk
trust
truth
try *v*
tube
tune *n*
turn
twice
twist
two
type *n*
typical

U

ugly
uncle
under *prep*
understand
underwear
undo
uniform *n*

union
unit
unite
universal
universe
university
unless
until
up
upper
upright
upset *v*, *adj*
upside down
upstairs
urgent
us
use
useful
useless
usual

V

vacation
valley
valuable
value *n*
variety
various
vegetable
vehicle
verb
very
victory
view *n*
violence
violent
visit
voice
vote
vowel

W

wages
waist
wait *v*
wake
walk
wall
wander
want
war
warm
warmth
warn
warning

wash
waste
watch
water
wave
way
we
weak
wealth
weapon
wear
weather
weave
wedding
week
weekly
weigh
weight
welcome
well
west
western *adj*
wet
what
whatever
wheat
wheel
when
whenever
where
whether
which
whichever
while *conj*
whip
whisper
whistle
white
who
whole
whose
why
wide
width
wife
wild *adj, adv*
will
willing
win *v*
wind *n, v*
window
wine
wing
winter
wire

wisdom
wise
wish
with
within *prep*
without *prep*
witness *n*
woman
wood
wooden
wool
word *n*
work
world
worm
worry
worse
worst
worth
would
wound
wrap *v*
wrist
write
wrong *adj, adv, n*

Y

yard
year
yearly
yellow
yesterday
yet
you
young
your(s)
yourself

Z

zero

Prefixes and suffixes that can be used with words in the Defining Vocabulary

-able
-al
-an
-ance
-ar
-ate
-ation
dis-
-ed
-en
-ence
-er
-ery
-ess
-ful
-ible
-ic
-ical
im-
in-
-ing
-ion
ir-
-ish
-ist
-ity
-ive
-ization
-ize
-less
-like
-ly
-ment
mid-
mis-
-ness
non-
-or
-ous
re-
-ry
self-
-ship
-th
un-
-ward(s)
-work
-y

Answer Key

Exercise 1:   1b   2a   3f   4e   5c   6d

Exercise 2:   1c   2a   3f   4d   5e   6b

Exercise 3:   1b   2a   3f   4d   5c   6e

Exercise 4:   1c   2e   3a   4d   5f   6b

Exercise 5:   1b   2a   3a   4b   5a   6b

Exercise 6:   1c   2a   3d   4f   5b   6e

Exercise 7:   1d   2f   3e   4a   5c   6b

Exercise 8:   1C   2C   3I   4I   5I   6C

Exercise 9:   1S   2S   3F   4S   5F   6F

Exercise 10:   1f   2a   3d   4c   5b   6e

Exercise 11:   1c   2a   3d   4b   5e   6f

Exercise 12:   1e   2b   3d   4f (*went* up in smoke)   5c (*rolled* up his sleeves)   6a

Exercise 13:   1C   2F   3C   4F   5F   6C

Exercise 14:   1d   2c   3f   4b   5a   6e

Exercise 15:   1 blow off   2 dug up   3 work out   4 change   5 followed   6 was

Exercise 16:   1a   2a   3b   4a   5a   6b

Exercise 17:   1 flew off the handle   2 went to seed   3 lived to tell the tale
4 took a dim view   5 looks like a million dollars   6 were put on red alert

Exercise 18:   1c   2a   3b   4a   5c   6b

Exercise 19:   1 Don't push your luck, or I'll stop collecting your mail when you go away.
2 My brother can always pick holes in my plans, but he can never offer any suggestions.
3 Amy stirred up a hornet's nest when she refused to follow the policies that she didn't like.
4 Margaret was very friendly and helpful to everyone. She would give you the shirt off her back.
5 Elena doesn't miss a trick, so do all your work before you leave.
6 I have an old stereo that is gathering dust. If you want it, you can have it.

Exercise 20:   1 (2)   2 (2)   3 (1)   4 (2)   5 (1)   6 (2)